GUIDE TO JAPANESE REFERENCE BOOKS

GUIDE TO

Japanese

REFERENCE BOOKS

日本の参考図書

Chicago, 1966

AMERICAN LIBRARY ASSOCIATION

Copyright © 1966 by the American Library Association
Manufactured in the United States of America
Library of Congress catalog card number 66-23396

FOREWORD

We who have lived so long with Winchell's **Guide to Reference Books** are well aware that we could not live without it. We have been reminded by its modest compiler that because of general availability and space considerations, emphasis was necessarily placed on reference books in English and to some extent, European titles. Even these titles have increased in number and their mastery and use in reference service are made possible through Miss Winchell's **Guide.**

American librarians cannot live by the publications of the Western world alone, however, though these may be the bread of our daily work. We need to know the encyclopedias, bibliographies and indexes, biographical dictionaries and directories, yearbooks and statistics which are currently available in other languages.

That we now have such a guide to basic Japanese reference books is due to the indefatigable energy of a group of Japanese library specialists, who not only prepared the original work and its revision, but have here provided English annotations of its titles for the benefit of those of us who do not read Japanese. Such an act of generosity should make us deeply humble.

To some Doubting Thomas who may ask, "What use is such a guide to me if I can't read Japanese?" our reply is, "Read the annotations and see how much you can learn."

September, 1965

Frances Neel Cheney
Associate Director
Peabody Library School

PREFACE

Early in 1960 a group of interested Japanese librarians, feeling the lack of a suitable guide to their reference materials, met to consider how to meet the need. They offered to select and annotate reference materials which might be useful to the general public. Fortunately, the significance and value of this undertaking made a favorable impression on the Rockefeller Foundation, which agreed to help in financing it. This led to the formal establishment, in March, 1961, of the Compilation Committee in the Library of the International House of Japan.

With the Committee bearing the major responsibility and with unstinted cooperation and assistance from more than one hundred persons in various fields, the work was completed in fifteen months. The first edition met with a very good public response. Meanwhile, however, new reference books in nearly every field continued to be published. Moreover, omissions and deficiencies in the first edition came to our attention. A revised edition was then proposed. At the same time, at the suggestion of scholars in the United States, arrangements were made for an English translation. Work on the second Japanese edition and the translation progressed simultaneously. The translation generally follows the revised Japanese text, with some modifications made in the interest of non-Japanese users. Although it is by no means perfect, we shall be gratified if this English edition proves useful to reference librarians and to men and women of scholarly interests.

We are again indebted to the Rockefeller Foundation for this revision and translation, and to the Asia Foundation for help in the preparatory stages. Publication of the English edition has been made possible by the generosity of the American Library Association and that of the Japanese edition by the generosity of the Japan Library Association. As in the case of the first edition, the work has received valuable support from the members of the Compilation Committee, the National Diet Library and other institutions and libraries. Many specialists in the various fields of art and science unselfishly spent hours on the translation. Others who participated in this work include Mr. Don Brown, who rewrote the English translation word by word and edited annotations; Mrs. Frances Cheney, who reviewed the entire work; Miss Yuki Monji, who advised on entries; and Mrs. Pauline Love and Mrs. Dorothy Nyren, who supervised publication. Without the collaboration of these organizations and individuals, publication of this guide would not have materialized, and I hereby extend my grateful acknowledgement to all of them.

July, 1965

Shigeharu Matsumoto
Chairman, the Board of Directors
International House of Japan

INTRODUCTION

The first Japanese edition was published in 1962 by the Compilation Committee made up of the following nine members:

Fujikawa, Masanobu; Japan Library School, Keio University

Fukuda, Naomi; International House Library

Kitajima, Takehiko; Library Science, Gakugei Daigaku

Kobayashi, Yutaka; Japan Information Center for Science and Technology

Kono, Tokuyoshi; Japan Telephone and Telegraph Co.

Mori, Hiroshi; Juntendo Daigaku Library

Oda, Yasumasa; National Diet Library

Shono, Arata; National Diet Library

Tsuda, Yoshinari; Medical School Library, Keio University

The revision was based on the first edition, done in consultation with specialist librarians and reviewed by scholars in their respective fields. The International House Library was entrusted with both the compilation of the Japanese editions and the translation into English. Hiroshi Mori was in charge of the technical editing of the Japanese manuscript.

The editors profited by using a large number of bibliographies and catalogues. They found, however, that listings in them were not always accurate or consistent, and therefore great pains had to be taken to check them with the original sources. Locating a book was a difficult task, and it was necessary to make use of many libraries other than the National Diet Library. This led to the discovery that many of them had relatively few reference books. One of the chief reasons for this lack was the absence of a convenient guide to such materials.

Despite careful review and indefatigable assistance from a large number of persons from all over the country in the selection of materials, there is a certain lack of uniformity in the selection of reference books in print. Some fields have a great number of reference tools, many of them almost identical, while others have only a few or none at all. This lack of balance cannot but be reflected in the selection and arrangement of materials.

The first edition was an attempt to provide a starting point toward, and the second edition was intended to be a revision into, a basic guide. For the above reasons for limitations placed on the guide, the editors must be content if their labors have provided some useful information to strengthen the reference collections of various libraries.

In preparing this new edition, the listings in the first edition were scrutinized closely and compared with more recent publications. As a result, many titles have been deleted when superseded by new books, deprived of their value due to obsolescence, or judged too specific in nature. New and revised editions have replaced earlier editions.

In this revision and translation, I wish to express my deep gratitude to many persons who so generously and tirelessly gave us their sincere collaboration throughout the making of the guide: to Mr. Hiroshi Mori whose conscientious work was most instrumental in successful completion of the second Japanese edition; and to the International House Library staff, especially Yukio Fujino who checked all the entries, and Hatsuko Hirayama who kept a smooth flow of manuscripts among the authors, translators and reviewers in Japan and to the editors in the United States.

July, 1965

Naomi Fukuda, Librarian
International House of Japan

EXPLANATORY NOTES

1. Scope

This guide is restricted in principle to books and periodicals published up to September, 1964, materials which in their entirety are useful as references. Parts of publications, regardless of their intrinsic value, have been excluded. Individual volumes or separately printed supplements of collected works and series that may be used independently as reference works are, however, included.

Works have been selected when they are considered helpful to the general user and valuable in building a basic collection of a library. Highly specialized and very simple works have been excluded.

In general old and out-of-print books have been excluded since they are difficult to obtain and likely to be of limited value. Some of them have been included, however, because better works do not exist.

In fields where adequate reference works are scarce, some titles are listed which are useful as substitutes for reference works.

2. Arrangement

There are four major divisions, General works, Humanities, Social Sciences, and Science and Technology, each subdivided as shown in the table of contents. Within each class, materials are arranged roughly as follows: bibliographies, dictionaries, manuals, chronologies, biographical dictionaries and directories, illustrated books and miscellaneous tables, yearbooks, statistics and primary materials. There is, however, considerable variation because of differences in class characteristics and quantities of materials. Each entry has a code number to facilitate cross referencing and indexing.

3. Entries

As the primary purpose of an entry is to show clearly what a work is about and how it may be used, minute analysis of content and the history of different editions have been omitted, unless needed for some obvious reasons. For serial publications, the initial years and numbers of issues as of 1964 have been investigated and noted whenever possible. The publication date given for a book is that of the copy examined and is not necessarily that of the first edition or most recent impression. As a rule, new-style characters (*tōyō kanji*) have been used in preference to those of the classic style. When a work has more than two authors or editors, a single representative name is given, followed by "et al." Editors and compilers are not distinguished from authors. When the author and editor are identical, and when the publisher or his name is given in the title, repetition is avoided. Translated titles are in parentheses, but English and other Western language titles given on title pages along with Japanese titles are entered after the Japanese titles without parenthesis.

4. Annotations

The editors have endeavored to indicate the contents of the publications as objectively as possible to help general users and acquisition officers to determine whether the books in hand will serve their purposes or not. Critical reviewing has been deliberately avoided though in some cases comparisons with earlier editions or similar works have been made and limitations pointed out. Furthermore, occasionally works are listed without annotations.

5. Cross references and indexes

Cross references have been suggested in the notes, in the introductions to classes, and elsewhere. Occasionally, supplementary titles are given in non-analytical form. Reference to a useful title in another section has been indicated in the following manner: → **N18**. For effective use of the Guide, readers are advised to consult the table of contents and the index.

TABLE OF CONTENTS

❀ This table of contents lists only a few of the subdivisions of some sections. To locate specific subjects see index.

SOCIAL SCIENCES

SCIENCE · TECHNOLOGY

GENERAL WORKS

Section
A

❧ General bibliographies dealing with many subjects, reference books on newspapers, periodicals, libraries, books, and publishing, and encyclopedias are included. Subject bibliographies are listed with their subjects; yearbooks of a general character, directories of learned societies, and institutions are listed in the section on social sciences.   → **J39-J48, P31-P34.**

Bibliography of bibliographies

Kokuritsu Kokkai Toshokan   A1
国立国会図書館
Sekai no shoshi tenjikai...世界 の 書誌 展示会 目録 と 解説 (World bibliography exhibit. Catalogue and commentary) 1957. 72p.

Lists 493 important bibliographies of bibliographies published in various countries, bibliographies compiled by UNESCO, and modern Japanese bibliographies in various fields. Only materials in book form are included with annotations. There is an introductory review of the development of bibliographies in Asia, Japan and the West.

Amano, Keitarō   天野 敬太郎   A2
Honpō shoshi no shoshi 本邦書誌 の 書誌 (Bibliography of Japanese bibliographies) Osaka, Mamiya Shōten, 1933. 370p.

Lists bibliographies published between the appearance of Kūkai's *Goshōrai mokuroku* in 1277 and the end of 1932. Not annotated. Arranges 200 pre-1868 items chronologically, and those after 1868 by Nippon Decimal Classification. Subject and author indexes. Supplemented under "Books

and articles on bibliography" in *Shuppan nenkan* (Publishers' yearbook) from 1935 to 1943 and since 1945 in *Toshokan zasshi*, Library journal, and *Nihon kosho tsūshin* (Japan old book news). Revised edition will be published in 1965 in 2v.

Keiō Gijuku Daigaku Toshokan   A3
慶応義塾大学図書館
Nihon koshomoku tenkansho kaidai 日 本 古 書 目 展 観 書 解題 (Annotated bibliography of old Japanese book lists, displayed in the Keiō University Library) 1956. 60p.

Gives a history of bibliographies from Nara period (8th century) to 1868 by listing items selected from the collections of Shigemoto Kōda, Haruki Kurokawa, and Mayori Kurokawa, which have been acquired by Keiō University Library, each with detailed annotation, especially items since the 1600s.

Sugiura, Kyūen   杉 浦 丘 園   A4
Edo jidai no shomoku 江 戸 時 代 之 書 目 (Bibliographies of the Edo period, 1600 - 1867) Kyoto, Unsensō, 1929. 102p.

Lists and annotates booksellers' lists, bibliographies, and catalogues of collections compiled from 1600 to 1868. Appendix contains book lists, catalogues of rare books, and library catalogues compiled in 1870s.

Saitō, Shōzō   斉 藤 昌 三   A5
Shomotsushi tenbō 書物誌展望 (Survey of journals on books) Yagi Shoten, 1955. 252p.

Annotated bibliography of 130 periodicals related to books published from 1887 to 1945, with appendix listing articles on books in the periodicals: *Aisho shumi, Shomotsu no shumi, Shomotsu tenbō, Nihon kosho tsūshin,* and *Shosō*.

1

Monbushō Daigaku Gakujutsukyoku   **A6**
文 部 省 大 学 学 術 局
Nihon ni okeru niji kankōbutsu no genjō
日 本 に お け る 二 次 刊 行 物 の 現 状 (Present
state of Japan's secondary publications) 1961.
82p.   (Gakujutsu geppō, v.13, no.9-10, Jan.,
1961)

Lists and annotates index journals, indexes appearing in periodicals, yearbooks, and monographs
on social sciences; abstract journals, and scientific
and technological abstracting services which appear
in card or periodical form; pre- and postwar bibliographies covering works in all fields published
in Japan; and postwar union catalogues. Discusses
Japanese secondary bibliographical publications
in Western languages and annotates foreign publications to which Japan contributes.

National bibliographies

✿ Comprehensive list of publications of a
country, usually published periodically and
cumulated.   In Japan the so-called national
bibliography started with **A9** in 1948 and publications prior to 1948 must be covered by trade
catalogues.   For books before 1868, **A8** is the
most comprehensive list, though it includes a few
lost books.   Such deficiencies may be covered by
printed catalogues of large libraries of long
standing and special collections **(B9-B14);**
various bibliographies **(A1-A6)** should also be
consulted.   The following titles are useful as
supplementary catalogues.

**Edo jidai shorin shuppan shoseki mokuroku
shūsei** (Collection of catalogues of trade books,
1600-1867) ed. by Keiō Gijuku Daigaku Fuzoku
Kenkyūjo Shidō Bunko.   Inoue Shobō,   1962-64.
4v.   **A7**
Photo reprint of 15 trade catalogues. Index in v.4.

Kyōho igo Osaka shuppan shoseki mokuroku
(Catalogue of books published in Osaka after
1724) ed. by Osaka Tosho Shuppangyō Kumiai.
Osaka, Seibundō, 1964. 436p. **A7a**
Reprint of 1936 ed. Registered list of books ap-
plied for publication, 2d month, 1724-12th month, 1873.

Kyōho igo Edo shuppan shomoku (Catalogue
of books published in Edo after 1727) ed. by
Hideo Higuchi and Haruhiko Asakura.   Toyohashi, Mikan Kokubun Shiryō Kankōkai, 1962.
521p.   (Mikan kokubun shiryō, supp. 1)   **A7b**

Registered list of books applied for publication,
3d month, 1727 - 3d month, 1815.   List of maps of
Edo appended.

Meiji bunka shiryō sōsho (Meiji civilization
documents series) v.7, Bibliography.   Kazama
Shobō,   1963.   596p.   **A7c**
Contains 6 catalogues published in Meiji period.

Meiji bunken mokuroku (Bibliography on Meiji
period) by Yoshio Takechi.   Nihon Hyōronsha,
1932.   316p.   **A7d**
Classified catalogue of books, 1868-90.

Iwanami Shoten 岩 波 書 店   **A8**
Kokusho sōmokuroku 国 書 総 目 録 (General
catalogue of Japanese books) 1963- .   2v.
In progress.

Most comprehensive list of existing books written,
edited, or translated by Japanese to 1867; to be
completed in 8v., including about 500,000 titles
checked against holdings of 426 libraries in Japan.
Arranged by title in Japanese syllabic order, with
correct reading of title, number of volumes, alternate titles, subjects, author, date of completion,
manuscript or printed, availability in collected
works, and location.   Books known by alternate
or abridged titles are also entered under those titles.   Includes some important lost titles but excludes documents, with the exception of a few concerning the lives of common people in modern times,
maps, pictures, etc.

A9
Zen Nihon shuppanbutsu sōmokuroku   全 日 本
出 版 物 総 目 録 Japanese national bibliography. 1948- .   Comp. by Kokuritsu Kokkai
Toshokan.   1951- .   16v.   Annual.

Nos. 1 and 2 cover from April, 1948 through Dec.,
1949.   Became an annual with no.3, listing new
publications acquired by National Diet Library during the previous year.   Corrects omissions to make
the bibliography as complete as possible.   Divided
into government and non-government sections, subdivided into monographs, periodicals, and others,
including Braille, discs (to 1956), and motion pictures (to 1956).   The latest edition (1961) issued
in 1964.   An annual cumulation of the following:

Nōhon shūhō (Current acquisitions weekly)
no.1- .   Comp. by Kokuritsu Kokkai Toshokan.
June, 1955- .   Weekly.   **A9a.**
Has a most comprehensive coverage.   Published
since Sept., 1948, appearing with varying frequency
until it became a weekly.   Divided into government and

non-government sections, the former arranged by institutions and the latter classified by NDC. Used as a copyright register and a checklist for ordering printed cards. List of periodicals published as an annual supplement, **B40**.

A10

Shuppan nenkan 出 版 年 鑑 (Publishers' yearbook) 1950- . Comp. by Shuppan Nyūsusha. 1951- . 15v.

Classified list of new trade books, reprints, and periodicals published during the year. Gives publishing trends, statistics, and directories. Indexed each year from 1952 edition on. Only comprehensive source for finding books of the year; serves as a national bibliography until **A9** is published. This is an annual cumulation of the following:

Shuppan nyūsu (Publishers' news) no.1- . Comp. by Shuppan Nyūsusha. Nov., 1946- . 3 times a month. **A10a.**

Classified list of new trade books, giving authors, titles, sizes, pages, prices, publishers, and NDC numbers. Discusses publishing trends, foreign news, forthcoming books, and topical bibliographies. The last issue of each month contains an index of articles on books and libraries. Has been in publication since 1941 under different titles.

❦ Following titles cover the years prior to **A9** and **A10**.

A11

Tokyo Shosekishō Kumiai tosho sōmokuroku 東京書籍商組合図書総目録 (Tokyo Publishers' Association's catalogue of books) Tokyo Shosekishō Kumiai, 1893-1940. 9v.

The most comprehensive lists of prewar books; v.1 (1893) lists 9,867 titles arranged by publishers with index in Japanese (i-ro-ha) order and classified index. v.2 (same year as v.1) lists 10,844 titles; v.3 (1906), 18,844 titles; v.4 (1911), 20,908 titles; v.5 (1918), 19,806 titles; and v.6 (1923), 22,506 titles. The 1929 edition excludes out-of-print titles which were lost in the 1923 earthquake and lists 16,617 titles indexed according to Japanese syllabic order by authors and subjects. The last, v.9, lists 38,000 titles.

Kyōdō Shuppansha 協同出版社 **A12** Gendai tosho sōgō mokuroku 現代図書総合目録 (Union catalogue of current books) 1944. Nihon Shuppan Haikyū, 1944. 1416p.

A13

Shuppan nenkan 出版年鑑 (Publishers' yearbook) 1926-1928. Kokusai Shichō Kenkyūkai, 1926-28. 3v.

Classified lists with newspaper and periodical titles, survey articles, laws, and regulations.

A14

Shuppan nenkan 出 版 年 鑑 (Publisher's yearbook) 1929-1940. Tokyo Shosekishō Kumiai, 1929-40. 12v.

List of books selected from publications presented to the Ministry of Interior for censorship. The last edition (covering 1939) lists about 28,000 books and 920 government publications.

A15

Shuppan nenkan 出 版 年 鑑 (Publishers' yearbook) 1930-1941. Tokyodō, 1930-41. 12v.

The forerunner of **A10**. Based on the monthly *Tokyodō geppō*, gives classified lists of books, publishing and reading trends, library activities, statistics, obituaries, and bibliography of books. Includes lists of books not for sale and government publications.

A16

Shoseki nenkan 書籍年鑑 (Yearbook of books) 1942. Kyōdō Shuppansha, 1942. 1426p.

A17

Nihon shuppan nenkan 日 本 出 版 年 鑑 (Japan publishers' yearbook) 1943-48. Kyōdō Shuppansha, 1943-48. 3v.

❦ There is no record for 1948-49 comparable to **A10**.

A18

Nihon sōgō tosho mokuroku 日本総合図書目録 (General catalogue of Japanese books) 1958- . Comp. by Nihon Shoseki Shuppan Kyōkai, 1958- . 37v. Annual.

Lists books in print in separate volumes on natural and applied sciences, humanities, social sciences, literature, art, language, dictionaries, juvenile books, and books of summaries for students. Arranged by Nippon Decimal Classification. Each title designated as either popular or scholarly.

A19

Shomeibetsu choshabetsu Nihon shoseki mokuroku 書名別・著者別日本書籍目録 (Title and author catalogue of Japanese books)

July-Sept., 1963- . Nihon Shuppan Hanbai, 1963- . Quarterly.

Trade list of books. Annual cumulation.

Newspapers

✿ General catalogues, directories, yearbooks, and indexes of newspapers and periodicals are listed below. Catalogues of holdings of individual libraries and union catalogues are listed under **B37-B42.**

Ueda, Jūrō 上田十郎 **A20**
Shinbun kankei tosho mokuroku 新聞関係図書目録 (Catalogue of books on newspapers) Morioka, Iwate Nippōsha Rōdō Kumiai, 1954. 41p.

Chronological list from 1872 to 1954. → **A9, A10, B39.** For transitional period to modern Japan from 1850s to 1880s, the following titles are useful:

Tokyo shinbun zasshi benran (Manual of Tokyo newspapers and periodicals) Hōki Shooku, 1882. 20p. **A20a.**

Shinbun zasshi meisai benran (Detailed manual of newspapers and periodicals) Kaishin Shooku, 1888. 83p. **A20b.**

Dai Nihon shinbun zasshi benran (Manual of Japanese newspapers and periodicals) Hōki Shooku, 1891. 48p. **A20c.**

A21
Shinbun sōran 新聞総覧 (Directory of newspapers) 1907-43. Nihon Denpō Tsūshinsha, 1907-43. 35v. Annual.

Contents include publishers' history, contemporary situation, staff, frequency, and format. Arranged by prefectures. Also includes relevant articles, statistics, and organizations. The forerunner is *Dai Nihon shinbunshi seikan* (Directory of Japanese newspapers) ed. by Asajirō Umezawa. 1894. 102p.

Nihon Shinbun Kyōkai 日本新聞協会 **A22**
Chihō betsu Nihon shinbunshi 地方別日本新聞史 (History of Japan's newspapers) 1956. 538p.

Arranged by prefectures, describes briefly the establishment and progress of newspapers published in Japan from 1860 to 1956. Title and personal name indexes. A useful manual.

A23
Nihon shinbun nenkan 日本新聞年鑑 (Yearbook of Japanese newspapers) 1924-41. Comp. by Shinbun Kenkyūjo. 1924-40. 17v.

Contains annual survey and directory of companies, with history, staff, and subscription rate; arranged by prefectures. Appendix lists news agencies and advertising agencies. Published in 1921 as *Nihon kisha nenkan* (Yearbook of Japanese newspaper men).

A24
Nihon shinbun nenkan 日本新聞年鑑 Japanese newspaper annual. 1947- . Comp. by Nihon Shinbun Kyōkai. Dentsū, 1947- . 18v.

Records main events of newspaper world. Lists for each company, including broadcasting companies, date of establishment, history, motto, circulation, frequency, subscription fee, advertising rates, wire services subscribed to related business, and executive staff. Contains agreements, laws, and rules of the Newspaper Association. Appendix surveys non-member newspaper companies and news agencies, main newspapers abroad, and Japanese language newspapers abroad; contains a directory of reporters. Index. War-time events are included in the 1947 first edition, succeeding **A21.**

A25
The Japanese press. 1949- . Comp. by Nihon Shinbun Kyōkai. 1949- . 16v. Annual.

Written in English, contains trends of the year, directory, and relevant laws and regulations.

Periodicals

Shuppan Nyūsusha 出版ニュース社 **A26**
Nihon zasshi sōran 日本雑誌総覧 (Directory of Japanese magazines) 1963. 398p.

Lists 7,380 current magazines, including general magazines; scholarly journals of universities, academic societies, and organizations; private magazines; public relations magazines; and company bulletins. Introduction contains brief history of magazines in Japan. Directory of publishers and title index. → **J6.**

Kokuritsu Kokkai Toshokan **A27**
国立国会図書館
Nihon gakujutsu zasshi mokuroku 日本学術雑誌目録 Directory of Japanese learned periodicals. 1957. Raiburarī Byūro, 1957-58. 3v.

Lists 3,132 titles published in 1957 by universities, research institutes, academic associations, and publishers. Arranged by romanized Japanese, followed. by Japanese orthography and English translations. Gives address, year of establishment, frequency, size, language, availability of abstracts in foreign languages, price, and changes of title, if any. Science sections superseded by *Directory of Japanese scientific periodicals*, 1962. Natural sciences, medical sciences, and industry. 1962. 229p.

Monbushō Daigaku Gakujutsukyoku **A28**
文部省大学学術局
Bibliographical list of Japanese learned journals: humanities and social sciences. 1958. 114p.

Lists about 1,600 titles with editor, publisher, and address; gives information about contents, indexes, reviews. Too many abbreviated notes make it difficult to use. Also published are:
Bibliographical list of Japanese learned journals; natural and applied sciences. No.2 and supp. 1962-64. 2v.

Shiritsu Daigaku Toshokan Kyōkai **A29**
私立大学図書館協会
Shiritsu daigaku shuppan chikuji kankōbutsu mokuroku 私立大学出版逐次刊行物目録 (Catalogue of periodical publications of private Japanese universities) 1958. 172p.

Lists and identifies current journals (in Japanese and European languages), yearbooks, and library bulletins alphabetically by names of universities. Does not include non-official journals by students or professors, university bulletins, or newspapers.

Nihon Keieisha Dantai Renmei **A30**
日本経営者団体連盟
Zenkoku shanaihō meikan 全国社内報名鑑 (List of news bulletins of Japanese companies) 1963. 984, 42p.

Lists 1,955 representative Japanese company bulletins published for employees. Separate title indexes for newspapers and magazines.

A31
Zasshi nenkan 雑誌年鑑 (Yearbook of periodicals) 1939-42. Comp. by Kyōdō Shuppansha. 1939-42. 4v.

Lists journals and yearbooks of Japan, the former colonies, and major foreign countries. Brief summary of events of the year, list of organizations and staffs appended.

INDEXES

Kobe Shiritsu Toshokan 神戸市立図書館 **A32**

Sengo kokunai jūyō nyūsu sakuin 戦後国内重要ニュース索引 (Index of important domestic postwar events) Aug., 1945-60. Akashi Shuppan, 1960-61. 2v.

Lists and identifies important events in Japan with dates and source references. Covers mainly political, economic, and social problems. Arranged by subject. Appendix contains chronology, list of changes in laws, and subject index to chronological tables found in other books.

Kokuritsu Kokkai Toshokan **A33**
国立国会図書館
Zasshi kiji sakuin 雑誌記事索引 Japanese periodicals index.

Jinbun kagaku hen (Humanities and social sciences) v.1, no.1, Sept., 1948- . Monthly. (Quarterly from v.6 to v.15, no.1)

A selective index to articles considered important by the compilers. About 1,000 periodicals in the National Diet Library are indexed. Arranged by catch words, but from v.16, no.7, July, 1963, became a classified index under broad subject classes with subdivisions. Author index and list of periodicals.

Shizen kagaku hen (Natural sciences) v.1, no.1, Jan., 1950- . Monthly.

Covers about 1,000 periodicals, though with changes in content and frequency. Became a monthly with v.11, no.3, July, 1960. Similar to *Humanities* in arrangement, but without index. The English edition, *Japanese periodicals index: Natural sciences*, Aug., 1960 - June, 1964, was an adaptation of the Japanese volume.

A34
Bibliography of the humanistic studies and social relations. No.1 (1952)- . Comp. by Monbushō Jinbun Kagaku Ōbun Mokuroku Henshū Iinkai. Gakujutsu Bunken Fukyūkai, 1955- . 9v. Annual.

Yearly index of articles, essays, lectures, collected works, and monographs.

Rikkyō Daigaku Toshokan **A35**
立教大学図書館
Jinbun kagaku bunken mokuroku annai 人文科学文献目録案内 (Guide to bibliography of humanistic studies) 1960. 49p.

Rearranges section in **A33** on humanities from Sept., 1948 to Mar., 1959 according to Nippon Decimal Classification. List of periodicals appended.

Nihon Gakujutsu Kaigi 日本学術会議 **A36**
Bunkakei bunken mokuroku 文科系文献目録
(Bibliography of literature, philosophy and history) 1952- . 17v. In progress.

Former title: *Bungaku tetsugaku shigaku bunken mokuroku.*

Includes monographic works, pamphlets, periodical and newspaper articles published since 1945, grouped in series of specific subjects. Each volume contains classified list and indexes, though criteria for selection of items differs in each issue. Published series follow:

I. **Nihon bungaku hen** (Japanese literature) and supp. 1945-50. 1952-55. 2v. **G49.**

II, XII. **Seiyō bungaku gogaku hen** (Western literature and languages) and supp. 1945-59. 1954-61. 2v. **G15.**

III. **Tōyō bungaku gogaku hen** (Oriental literature and languages) and supp. 1945-56. 1954-58. 2v. **G29.**

IV. **Shūkyō kankei gakujutsu hen** (Religion) 1945-54. 1955. 151p. **D38.**

V. **Nihon minzokugaku hen** (Japanese folklore) 1945-54. 1955. 138p. **N56.**

VI. **Kokugogaku hen** (Japanese language) 1945-55. 1957. 281p. **F132.**

VII. **Kyōikugaku hen** (Pedagogy) 1945-57. 1958. 317p. **P3.**

VIII. **Nihon kodaishi hen** (Ancient history of Japan) 1946-57. 1959. 122p. **H151.**

IX. **Seiyō kotengaku hen** (Western classics) 1868-1957. 1960. 189p.

X. **Chūgoku tetsugaku shisō hen** (Chinese philosophy) 1945-59. 1960. 293p. **D14.**

XI. **Bigaku hen** (Aesthetics) 1945-59. 1961. 148p. **E1.**

XIII. **Bunka jinruigaku hen** (Cultural anthropology) 1945-61. 1962. 95p. **N57.**

XIV. **Nihon kindaishi, denki hen** (Modern history of Japan and biography) 1935-61. 1963. 65p. **H15.**

XV. **Nihonjin no seikaku kenkyū hen** (Personality studies on Japanese people) 1945-61. 1963. 177p. Includes some prewar items.

✿ Indexes of specific periodicals are listed in the following articles. See also **A6.**

"Nihon kaku zasshi sōmokuji sakuin ichiran" (List of general indexes of Japanese periodicals) comp. by Keitarō Amano. *Toshokankai,* v.9, no.1 Aug., 1957. **A37.**

"Hōbun zasshi sōmokuji sakuin ichiran" (List of general indexes of magazines in Japanese language) *Hikone Ronsō,* no.42 May, 1958. **A37a.**

Zasshi no riyō to sakuin (Uses of periodicals and indexes) by Kunimi Suyama. Shun'yōdō, 1954. 85p. (Toshokan kōza: seiri hen, 8) **A37b.**

Zasshi ronbun sakuin, shōroku shosai kankōbutsu chōsa (Survey of index and abstract journals) Kenkyū Renmei, 1943. **A37c.**

Government documents

✿ Bibliographies of social sciences, especially on statistics, **J12-J23,** include many government publications.

Kokuritsu Kokkai Toshokan **A38**
国立国会図書館
Kanchō kankōbutsu tenjikai 官庁刊行物展示会 (Exhibition of government publications) Catalogues and annotations. 1958. 75p.

Lists 1,448 titles, including about 50 representative titles published by post-1868 Meiji government, catalogues of government publications with brief annotations, and representative postwar publications. Includes periodicals and semi-governmental publications.

Kokuritsu Kokkai Toshokan **A39**
国立国会図書館
Kanchō kankōbutsu sōgō mokuroku 官庁刊行物総合目録 (Union catalogue of government publications) 1952-60. 8v.

Lists monographs and periodicals published by central government. Arranged by NDC with library locations. v.1 covers from Sept., 1945 through 1950. Became an annual from v.3, 1953 and ceased publication with v.8, 1958, superseded by **A9.** Index of publishing government agencies.

Kokuritsu Kokkai Toshokan **A40**
国立国会図書館
Kankōchō chikuji kankōbutsu ichiran 官公庁逐次刊行物一覧 (Directory of periodic government publications) 1960. 104p.

Lists periodicals as of Dec., 1959. Gives title, subtitle, frequency, availability, and type of readers.

Kokuritsu Kokkai Toshokan **A41**
国立国会図書館
Ōbun ni yoru kanchō kankōbutsu ichiran 欧文

による官庁刊行物一覧 List of Japanese government publications in European languages. 1959. 91p.

Includes publications of the Diet, Supreme Court, public corporations, and Bank of Japan from 1945 to 1958. Lists and identifies publications in English, in both English and Japanese texts, and in Japanese with English title or resumé. List of SCAP publications, 1946-1952, appended.

A42

Kanchō kankō tosho geppō 官庁刊行図書月報(Monthly bulletin of government publications) 1939-43. Comp. by Naikaku Insatsukyoku.

Continued from the quarterly *Kanchō kankō tosho mokuroku*, Dec. 1927-37. Classified by government ministries and by subjects.

A43

Seifu kankōbutsu geppō 政府刊行物月報 (Monthly bulletin of government publications) v.1, no.1- . Comp. by Seifu Kankōbutsu Fukyū Kyōgikai. Seifu Kankōbutsu Sābisu Sentā, 1957-

No.1 lists publications for 1956. Became a monthly since no.2 listing monographs and regular and irregular publications by ministries, giving compiling agencies, titles, contents, frequencies, prices, dates of publication, and publishers. From Apr., 1961 on, includes reviews of important domestic and foreign government documents.

Collected works

❧ Catalogues and indexes of series and collected works are listed below.

Kawashima, Gosaburō 川島五三郎 **and A44 Yagi, Toshio** 八木敏夫
Zenshū sōsho sōran 全集叢書総覧 (Directory of complete and collected works) 1868-1955. 3d rev. ed. Yagi Shoten, 1956. 244, 64p.

Arranged by title, with volume, publisher, year of first publication, and price. Despite some errors in inclusion due to ambiguous definitions of collections by the publishers, this is a convenient directory. Contents of main works are analyzed in the appended list.

Shuppan Nyūsusha 出版ニュース社 **A45**
Zenshū sōgō mokuroku 全集総合目録 (General list of collected works) Postwar continuations. 1962. 157p.

Classified list of collected works, complete works,

general series, and lecture series as of Sept., 1962. Title index.

Kotensō 古典荘 **A46**
Meiji Taishō Shōwa zenshū sōsho kanbetsu shomei kakaku jiten 明治大正昭和全集叢書巻別書名価格事典 (Directory of titles and prices of works contained in collections of Meiji, Taishō and Shōwa) Gifu, Taishū Shobō, 1950. 165p.

Lists titles contained in collections published from 1868 to 1949.

Kawashima, Gosaburō 川島五三郎 **A47**
Sōsho zenshū shomoku 叢書全集書目 (List of collected works) Tokyo Koshosekishō Kumiai, 1931-36. 5v.

Gives titles contained in collected works from 1868 to 1930, covering politics and law, economics, history, archaeology, geography, religion, philosophy, and education.

Hirose, Toshi 広瀬敏 **A48**
Nihon sōsho sakuin 日本叢書索引 (Index of Japanese collected works) Rev. and enl. ed. Kazama Shobō, 1957. 93, 9, 761p.

Lists classical works from *Kojiki* and *Nihon shoki* to pre-1868 works contained in collections. Arranged by title with locations in the collected works, published up to 1956. Supplementary work to this revised edition follows:

Nihon sōsho 247shu shomei sakuin (Index of titles contained in 247 Japanese collected works) by Genryō Yajima. Sendai, Tōhoku Daigaku, 1958. 122p. Mimeo. **A48a.**

Watanabe, Shigeru 渡辺茂 **A49**
Sōgō shiryō sakuin 綜合史料索引 (General index of historical documents) Rev. and enl. ed. Komiyama Shoten, 1959. 606p. Mimeo.

Lists, with occasional abstracts, 652 collections (1868-1957) of Japanese historical documents. Consists of title index of collections and index of documents, with location in the collections. To be used with **A48.**

Yajima, Genryō 矢島玄亮 **A50**
Bunka kyōikukei kinen ronbunshū 66shu ronbun sōmoku 文科教育系記念論文集六十六種論文総目 (List of 66 humanistic and educational commemorative essays) Sendai, Tōhoku Daigaku Kyōiku Kyōyō Gakubu Toshokan, 1957. 124p. Mimeo.

Index of commemorative articles from 1912 to 1955.

Yajima, Genryō 矢島玄亮 **A51**
Sōsho kōza zenshū ronshū 502shu bunrui sakuin 双書講座全集論集 502 種分類索引 (Classified index of 502 collected works, lectures, complete works, and collections of essays) Nihon Bunken Gakkai, 1958. 270p. Mimeo.

Index of titles on humanistic and educational studies contained in collections from 1868 to 1956.

✤ General catalogues or annotated catalogues of titles in large serial set follows: See also **G81**.

Kokusho kankōkai shuppan mokuroku: Nihon kokoku shoshi (Catalogue of books published by Japanese History Books Publishing Society: history of old printed books of Japan) Kokusho Kankōkai, 1909. 115, 194, 22p. **A52.**

Kaitei Shiseki shūran sōmoku kaidai...(Annotated list of contents and index of titles in rev. *Shiseki shūran*, collection of history books) Reprint ed. Kondō Shuppanbu, 1932. 98, 17p. **A52a.**

Shintei zōho Kojitsu sōsho sakuin (Index of rev. and enl. *Kojitsu sōsho*, series on ancient customs) Meiji Tosho, 1957. 497, 43p. (Shintei zōho Kojitsu sōsho, v.38) **A52b.**

Shinkō Gunsho ruijū (Classified collection of miscellaneous books, newly collated) v.23 and v.24. Naigai Shoseki, 1936. 2v. **A52c.**

Gunsho ruijū seizoku bunrui sōmokuroku (Classified catalogue of main and supplementary sets of *Gunsho ruijū*) and chronology. Zoku Gunsho Ruijū Kanseikai, 1959. 410p. **A52d.**

Gunsho kaidai (Annotated catalogue of books in *Gunsho ruijū*) Zoku Gunsho Ruijū Kanseikai, 1960- . 26v. In progress. **A52e.**

Nihon Shiryō Kenkyūkai **A53**
日本資料研究会
Nihon nenkanrui sōmokuroku 日本年鑑類総目録 (General catalogue of Japanese year-books) Seiwadō, 1964. 236p.

Classified list of 2,800 current titles. Dates of first publication are noted where confirmed. List of publishers, title index.

Regional bibliographies

A54

Oyama jinbun kagakushi nenpyō 小山人文科学史年表 (Oyama chronology of humanities and sciences) Seikatsu Hyakka Kankōkai, 1955. 470p.

Chronological list of important writings, with titles and authors and indication of whether they have been translated into Japanese: it extends from primitive writings to 1935. Entries from 1400 A.D. are in separate columns for the humanities, art and literature and the natural sciences (including technology), with another column showing political events. Index of personal names with birth and death dates.

Nis-So Hon'yaku Shuppan Konwakai **A55**
日ソ翻訳出版懇話会
Sobieto kankei tosho sōmokuroku ソビエト関係図書総目録 (Catalogue of books on Soviet Russia) 1958-63. 2v.

Lists postwar Japanese translations of Soviet books (1945-1962) and books concerning Soviet Russia, text books on Russian language, Soviet translations of Japanese books, and prewar Japanese translations of Soviet literature. List of main Soviet publishers. Author index.

Nihon Daigaku, Kokusai Kenkyūjo **A56**
日本大学国際研究所
Afurika bunken sōran アフリカ文献総覧 (Bibliographical survey of Africa) 1959. 107p. (Kokusai Kenkyūjo kenkyū hōkoku, 5)

Lists about 2,500 foreign and 350 Japanese titles, including periodicals and articles.

Tenri Toshokan 天理図書館 **A57**
Africana; catalogue of books relating to Africa in the Tenri Central Library. Tenri, 1960-64. 2v. (Tenri Central Library series, 24, 27)

Lists about 5,000 foreign books relating to Africa, including the Tojō library of 3,000 titles with many rare 18th century books collected before 1940 by Takesada Tokugawa, former director of Naval Engineering Institute. Author and title indexes.

Monbushō Daigaku Gakujutsukyoku **A58**
文部省大学学術局
Ajia chiiki sōgō kenkyū bunken mokuroku アジア地域綜合研究文献目録 (Bibliography of Asian studies) Nihon Gakujutsu Shinkōkai, 1959-63. 5v.

Union list of books in Western, Russian, and

Chinese languages on socio-economic studies of Asia in about 20 research libraries, including University of Tokyo, Hitotsubashi University, Tōyō Bunko, University of Kyoto and others. Covers 1960-62. List of periodicals appended. Author index.

Centre for East Asian Cultural Studies **A59**
A survey of Japanese bibliographies concerning Asian studies. 1963. 200, 17p.

Classified list from end of the 19th century to 1962, arranged by Japanese romanized titles with English translations. Supplemented as follows:

Bibliography of bibliographies of East Asian studies in Japan. Tōyō Bunko, 1964. 190, 16p. (Bibliography, no.3) **A59a.**

Lists about 830 titles dealing with East Asia, Inner Asia, and Southeast Asia.

Tōhō Gakkai 東方学会 **A60**
Books and articles on Oriental subjects published in Japan. v.1 (1954)- . 1955- . 9v. Annual.

Lists and annotates in English books and articles published during the previous year on countries and areas, including only foreign relations studies for Japan. Entries are by romanized name, with characters of Japanese authors, followed by titles in English and in Japanese.

Tōyō Bunko 東洋文庫 **A61**
A classified catalogue of books in European languages in the Tōyō Bunko, 1917-1936. 1944-51. 2v.

v.1, General reference works. - Asia, East Asia and the Pacific. v.2, Author index.

Ajia Keizai Kenkyūjo **A62**
アジア経済研究所
Tōnan Ajia kankei shiryō sōgō mokuroku 東南アジア関係資料総合目録 Union catalogue of documentary materials on Southeast Asia. 1964. 5v.

Lists foreign books primarily in the social sciences in 32 major libraries of Japan as of Dec., 1961, arranged by country of origin. Index in v.5.

Taiheiyō Kyōkai 太平洋協会 **A63**
Nan'yō bunken mokuroku 南洋文献目録 (Bibliography of Southeast Asian studies) Chūō Kōronsha, 1941. 173p.

Lists Japanese books and articles as of Mar. 1941, concerning Indonesia, Indo-China, Thailand, Malaya, Borneo, and the Philippines; based on holdings in 7 libraries, including Mitsubishi Economic Research Institute.

Nihon Takushoku Kyōkai 日本拓殖協会 **A64**
Nanpō bunken mokuroku 南方文献目録 (Bibliography of studies of areas bordering the southern Pacific) Enl. ed. Daidō Shoin, 1944. 322p.

Lists Japanese books and articles concerning Southeast Asia, Australia, New Guinea, and Hawaii.

Nanpōshi Kenkyūkai 南方史研究会 **A65**
Ōbun Indo bunken sōgō mokuroku 欧文インド文献綜合目録 Union catalogue of books and pamphlets in Western languages on India. 1959. 374p. Mimeo.

Covers social sciences and humanities, listing, by author, 5,457 titles in 21 research libraries, including those of the universities of Tokyo, Kyoto, Kyūshu, and Hitotsubashi, and those of Tenri, Tōyō Bunko, etc.

Tōyō Bunko 東洋文庫 **A66**
A classified catalogue of books. Section XII: India, in the Tōyō Bunko acquired during the years 1917-1959. 1950-52. 2v.

Author index in v.2.

Kanbara, Tatsu 神原達 **A67**
Nepāru bunken mokuroku ネパール文献目録 (Bibliography of Nepal) Hōbundō, 1960. 121p.

Lists foreign books.

Kawabe, Toshio 河部利夫 **et al.** **A68**
Bibliography of Thai studies. Tokyo Gaikokugo Daigaku, Kaigai Jijō Kenkyūjo, 1957. 75p. Mimeo.

Classified catalogue of European books on Thailand.

Nihon Oriento Gakkai **A69**
日本オリエント学会
Isuramu kankei bunken mokuroku イスラーム関係文献目録 (Bibliography of Islamic studies) No.1. 1959. 47, 17p.

Lists about 1,200 Japanese works, including translations and periodical articles, classified by subjects. English table of contents; index of authors and translators.

Kotake, Fumio 小竹文夫 **A70**
Kin hyakunenrai Chūgokubun bunken genzai shomoku 近百年来中国文文献現在書目 (Catalogue of Chinese publications of the last century in Japanese libraries) Tōhō Gakkai, 1957. 838p. Mimeo.

Union catalogue of Chinese books and periodicals (1851-1954) in the National Diet Library, Tokyo

University: Dept. of Chinese Literature and Philosophy and Institute for Oriental Culture, and Oriental Library. Arranged by title in Japanese syllabary, each with author, number of volumes, date of publication, and location. Appendix contains catalogue of books in the possession of the committee of Modern Chinese Studies and catalogue of Kamiyama collection in Tokyo University, Dept. of Chinese Literature and Philosophy.

Kindai Chūgoku Kenkyū Iinkai　**A71**
近代中国研究委員会
Kindai Chūgoku kankei bunken mokuroku ihen 近代中国関係文献目録彙編 (Bibliography of bibliographies on modern China) 1960. 44p.

Ishikawa, Tadao　石川忠雄　**A72**
... Gendai Chūgoku kankei shuyō zasshi ronbun mokuroku　現代中国関係主要雑誌論文目録 (Catalogue of important postwar Japanese articles on contemporary China) Keiō Gijuku Daigaku, Hōgaku Kenkyūkai, 1956. 100p.

Covers politics, economics, law, social affairs, culture, etc. from Jan., 1946, to July, 1955.

Kokuritsu Kokkai Toshokan　**A73**
国立国会図書館
Chūgoku Chōsen tosho sokuhō　中国朝鮮図書速報 (Acquistition list of Chinese and Korean publications) 1956- . Irregular. Mimeo.

Includes books and periodicals with volume numbers. No. 40 published in Nov., 1964.

Chōsen Kindai Shiryō Kenkyūkai　**A74**
朝鮮近代史料研究会
Chōsen kankei bunken shiryō sōmokuroku 朝鮮関係文献資料総目録 (Catalogue of books and documents on Korea) Chigasaki, Chōsen Shiryō Kenkyūkai, 1961. 180p. Mimeo.

Classified list of 4,333 items in possession of Yūhō Kyōkai and Chūō Nikkan Kyōkai (Central Korea-Japan Association). Includes valuable original documents of Government-General of Korea during Japanese administration.

Nit-Chō Kyōkai　日朝協会　**A75**
... Chōsen ni kansuru tosho mokuroku 日本で出版された朝鮮に関する図書目録 (Catalogue of Japanese books on Korea) 1945-1960. 1960. 38p. Mimeo.

Sakurai, Yoshiyuki　桜井義之　**A76**
Meiji nenkan Chōsen kenkyū bunkenshi 明治年間朝鮮研究文献誌　(Bibliography of

Korean studies, 1868-1912) Seoul, Shomotsu Dōkōkai, 1941. 421p.

Lists and annotates monographic works, reports and maps. Title and author indexes.

Hara, Sanshichi　原三七　**A77**
... Chōsen kankei bunken mokuroku 今西博士蒐集朝鮮関係文献目録 Catalogue of the Korean materials collected by the Late prof. Dr. R. Imanishi. Shoseki Bunbutsu Ryūtsūkai, 1961. 374, 84, 5p. Mimeo.

Divided into Chinese and Korean, Japanese, and European sections. Title index.

Iwamura, Shinobu　岩村忍　**and**　**A78**
Fujieda, Akira　藤枝晃
Mōko kenkyū bunken mokuroku　豪古研究文献目録 (Bibliography of Mongol studies) 1900-1950. Kyoto, Jinbun Gakkai, 1953. 46p. (Tōyōshi kenkyū bunken ruimoku, supp. 1)

Lists Japanese books and articles.

Poppe, Nicholas　et al.　**A79**
Catalogue of the Manchu-Mongol section of the Tōyō Bunko. Tōyō Bunko, 1964. 387p.

Classified list of books in Manchu and Mongolian. Gives titles in original language with English and Chinese translations. Indexes by original title as well as Chinese and Japanese.

Yuan, T'ung-li　袁同礼　**and**　**A80**
Watanabe, Hiroshi　渡辺宏
Shinkyō kenkyū bunken mokuroku　新彊研究文献目録 Classified bibliography of Japanese books and articles concerning Sinkiang, 1886-1962. 1962. 92p. (Shinkyō kenkyū sōkan, no.2)

Lists 1,166 titles. Author index.

Taiwan Aishokai　台湾愛書会　**A81**
Taiwan bunken tenkan mokuroku　台湾文献展観目録 (Catalogue of the exhibition of books on Taiwan) Taipei, 1934. 51p.

Lists, with annotations when necessary, about 420 titles of books on Taiwan in Japanese, Chinese, and European languages.

Higa, Shunchō　比嘉春潮　**A82**
Ryūkyū bunken mokuroku　琉球文献目録 Bibliography of the Ryūkyūs. Naha, Ryūkyū Daigaku, 1962. 120, 118p.

Classified list of about 2,200 Japanese books and articles related to the Ryūkyūs located in 31 major libraries in Japan; University of California, Berkeley; and University of Hawaii.

Kokuritsu Kokkai Toshokan Shibu Ueno To- **A83**
shokan 国立国会図書館支部上野図書館
Ryūkyū bunken mokuroku kō 琉球文献目録
稿 (Bibliography on the Ryūkyūs. Preliminary ed.) 1952. 57p.

Books in the former Ueno Library, now in National
Diet Library.

Ryūkyū Seifu Rippōin Toshoshitsu **A84**
琉球政府立法院図書室
Sengo Okinawa no bunken kaidai 戦後沖縄の
文献解題 (Annotated bibliography on postwar
Okinawa) Naha, Ryūkyū Seifu Rippōin Jimukyoku, 1961. 160p.

Covers 950 postwar and 250 prewar titles in the
Legislature Library. Title index.

WESTERN BOOKS ON JAPAN

Kokuritsu Kokkai Toshokan **A85**
国立国会図書館
Gaikokujin no Nihon kenkyū 外国人の日本
研究 「資料展示会」 An annotated catalogue
of the Exhibition of materials on the study of
Japan by foreigners. 1954. 58p.

Pt.1 lists past and present representative books
and bibliographies of Japanese studies by foreigners.
Pt.2 surveys the activities of organizations in 14
European and American countries studying Japan.

Kokuritsu Kokkai Toshokan **A86**
国立国会図書館
Nihon kankei Ōbun tosho mokuroku 日本関係
欧文図書目録 Catalogue of materials on
Japan in Western languages in the National Diet
Library. (Preliminary ed.) 1963. 306, 74p.
Mimeo.

Lists about 2,300 books, classified under bibliography, humanities, social sciences, and natural
sciences. Subject and author indexes.

Tōyō Bunko 東洋文庫 **A87**
A classified catalogue of books on the section
XVII. Japan, in the Tōyō Bunko, acquired dur-
ing the years 1917-1956. 1957-59. 2v.

Author index in v.2.

Tōyōgaku Infōmeishon Sentā **A88**
東洋学インフオメイション・センター
A selected list of books on Japan in Western
languages (1945-1960) Tōyō Bunko, 1964. 74p.
(Studies on Asia abroad, 1)

Supplement to *A selected list of books and arti-*

cles on Japan, comp. by Hugh Borton and others.
Harvard-Yenching Institute, 1954. 272p.

Kokusai Bunka Shinkōkai **A89**
国際文化振興会
K.B.S. bibliography of standard reference books
for Japanese studies with descriptive notes.
1959- . 10v. In progress.

v.1, Generalia; v.2, Geography and travel; v.3,
History and biography, pt.1; v.4, Religion; v.5, A,
History of thought, pt. 1; v.6, A, Language; v.6, B,
Literature, pt. 1; v.7, A, Arts and crafts; v.7, B,
Theatre, dance and music; v.8, Manners, customs,
and folklore.

Nichi Futsu Kaikan 日仏会館 **A90**
Bibliographie de l'orientalisme japonais, 1955-
1956. 1958-62. 2v.

Yabuki, Katsuji 矢吹勝二 **A91**
Japan bibliographic annual. Hokuseidō, 1956-
57. 2v.

Annotated bibliographies

Heibonsha 平凡社 **A92**
Sekai meicho daijiten 世界名著大事典
(Encyclopedia of the world's great books) 1960-
62. 8v.

Reviews classics under titles in Japanese translations arranged in Japanese syllabary with original
foreign titles. v.6 lists representative encyclopedias, language dictionaries, complete works,
and collected works; v.7 consists of indexes of
titles, authors, and subjects; and v.8 contains a
bio-bibliography of about 6,800 authors.

Katsura, Gojurō 桂五十郎 **A93**
Kanseki kaidai 漢籍解題 (Annotated dictionary of Chinese classics) Meiji Shoin, 1905.
980p.

The best and only one published in Japan. Contains about 1,500 titles indispensable for Chinese
classical studies, arranged chronologically under
13 sections such as classics, history, Confucianism,
literature, politics, etc., each with subdivisions.
Explains each title, giving author, format, history,
annotation, and references. Indexes of titles, title
variations and authors.

Nagasawa, Kikuya 長沢規矩也 **A94**
Shina shoseki kaidai 支那書籍解題 (Annotated dictionary of Chinese classcs) Bibliographies. Bunkyūdō, 1940. 391, 23p.

Lists catalogues of Chinese classics easily accessible in Japan. Gives titles, number of volumes, editors or authors, introduction or postscript, and brief explanation.

Nagasawa, Kikuya 長沢規矩也 **A95**
Shinagaku nyūmonsho ryakkai 支那学入門書略解 (Guide to Sinology) New ed., rev. Ryūbun Shokyoku, 1945. 154p.

Lists and annotates basic books on Sinological studies under classes: general, dictionaries, bibliographies, classics, schools of philosophy, history, geography, literature, essays, and language.

Chōsen Sōtokufu 朝鮮総督府 **A96**
Chōsen tosho kaidai 朝鮮図書解題 (Annotated dictionary of Korean books) Seoul, 1919. 708p.

Lists and annotates briefly the Korean books of the former Government-General of Korea. Grouped under classics, history, Confucianism, and collected works. Short biographical list of authors and editors included.

Maema, Kyōsaku 前間恭作 **A97**
Kosen sappu 古鮮冊譜 (List of old Korean books) Tōyō Bunko, 1944-57. 3v. (Tōyō Bunko sōkan, 11)

Most authoritative annotated list of Korean books, arranged by title in Japanese syllabary with brief biographical notes on authors.

Samura, Hachirō 佐村八郎 **A98**
Kokusho kaidai 国書解題 (Annotated dictionary of Japanese books) Rev. and enl. ed. Rikugōkan, 1926. 2v.

Lists and annotates about 25,000 Japanese books from ancient times to 1867. Covers all subjects, from religion, law, politics, history, geography, sports, and games, to natural and applied sciences. Includes biographies of authors in annotations. Author, subject, and Chinese character indexes. Appendix, compiled by Tomosaburō Hamano, contains catalogue of collected works.

Okano, Takeo 岡野他家夫 **A99**
Kindai Nihon meicho kaidai 近代日本名著解題 (Annotated list of great books of modern Japan) Ariake Shobō, 1962. 391, 36p.

Includes Japanese works, translated books, periodicals, and collected works which influenced modernization of Japan (1850-70s). Small number of titles, but each title is explained in detail in relation to the general condition of the period. Author and title indexes.

Hatano, Ken'ichi 波多野賢一 **and** **A100**
Yayoshi, Mitsunaga 弥吉光長
Kenkyū chōsa sankō bunken sōran 研究調査参考文献総覧 (Directory of reference books for scholarly research) Asahi Shobō, 1934. 13, 26, 877p.

Lists about 10,000 Japanese reference books published before 1932, including articles, with brief annotations for important titles. Classified by form, e.g. bibliographies, dictionaries, indexes, yearbooks, etc. Contains list of foreign bibliographies and an article on use of reference books. Dated, should be used with care. The first attempt to compile a guide to reference books follow:

Naigai sankō tosho no chishiki (Foreign and Japanese reference books) by Kei Tanaka and Miyahiko Mōri. Toshokan Jigyō Kenkyūkai, 1930. 5, 19, 325p. **A100a.**

Yayoshi, Mitsunaga 弥吉光長 **A101**
Sankō tosho no kaidai 参考図書の解題 (Annotated guide to reference books) Risōsha, 1955. 259p. (Toshokan jitsumu sōsho, 8)

Lists about 4,000 reference books including some foreign titles as of 1952. Arranged by NDC and usually annotated. Author, title, and subject indexes.

Book selection

A102
Sentei tosho sōmokuroku 選定図書総目録 (General catalogue of books recommended by Japan Library Association) 1950- . Comp. by Nihon Toshokan Kyōkai. 1950- . 15v. Annual.

Lists books recommended during the year for selection by libraries and readers; cumulated from weekly, *Sentei tosho sokuhō* (Bulletin of recommended books) and other reviews. Author, title, and subject indexes.

A103
Gakkō toshokan kihon tosho mokuroku 学校図書館基本図書目録 (Catalogue of basic books for school libraries) 1963. ed. Comp. by Zenkoku Gakkō Toshokan Kyōgikai. 1963. 396p.

Revised annually to include new selections from previous years. Arranged for use by elementary, junior high, and senior high school libraries. Lists of publishers, book dealers and library equipment makers appended. Index classified by types of schools.

LIBRARIES, BOOKS AND PUBLISHING

LIBRARIES

DIRECTORIES

Ajia Keizai Kenkyūjo　　　　　**B1**
アジア経済研究所
Ajia shokoku shiryō chōsa　　アジア諸国資料
調査 Documentary materials in Asian countries.
1960.　332p.　(Chōsa kenkyū hōkoku sōsho, 6)
　Describes publication and distribution of books,
libraries, and documentation centers in India, Pakis-
tan, Ceylon, and Southeast Asian countries, surveyed in 1958, arranged by countries.　Subject and
proper name indexes, tables.

Nihon Gakujutsu Kaigi　日本学術会議　**B2**
Nihon toshokan sōran　日本図書館総覧　(Directory of Japanese libraries)　Shizen Kagaku-
sho Kyōkai, 1954.　582, 23p.
　Lists 2,019 public, universities and colleges (except junior colleges), and research institute libraries, location, staff, size, and special features of each
collection, as of Sept., 1953.　Arranged by type of
library under prefectures.　Index.

　　　　　　　　　　　　　　　　　B3
Nihon no toshokan　日本の図書館　Statistics on libraries in Japan.　1953- .　Comp.
by Nihon Toshokan Kyōkai.　1954-56, 1960,
1962- .　7v.　Annual.
　Former title: *Nihon no kōkyō toshokan* (Public libraries in Japan). 1952.
　Statistical survey of public, university and college
libraries, listing size of staff, size of collection,
budget, etc.　Special libraries not included.

Senmon Toshokan Kyōgikai　　　　**B4**
専門図書館協議会
Chōsa kikan toshokan sōran　調査機関図書
館総覧 Directory of research libraries.
1956.　375p.
　Lists about 1,000 specialized academic libraries,
including research institutes, university, and company libraries.　Brief notes on history, features of the
collection, and accessibility as of 1955.　Indexed by
name of institution, location, subject, and periodical
publications.

Shiritsu Daigaku Toshokan Kyōkai　　**B5**
私立大学図書館協会
Shiritsu daigaku toshokan sōran　私立大学図
書館総覧 (Directory of private university
libraries)　1961.　2v.
　Libraries of 4 universities and 63 colleges are
described in tabular form as to administration, budget, buildings, collections and circulation,　courses
on librarianship, general organization and condition.
v.2, supplement, contains floor plans of 43 libraries.

Kokuritsu Kokkai Toshokan　　　　**B6**
国立国会図書館
Zenkoku tokushu korekushon yōran　全国特殊
コレクション要覧　(Directory of special
collections in Japan)　1957.　130p.
　Lists names of special collections arranged
alphabetically by romanized names of collectors
under prefectures.　Includes rare books, documents,
and specialized and memorial collections.　Gives
subject, number of collected items, donor's name
and biography, accessibility, and printed catalogue
for each collection.　Indexes of names of special
collections and of subjects.

Iwasaru, Toshio　岩猿敏生　**et al.**　**B7**
Nihon bunko meguri 日本文庫めぐり (Visit-

ing special collections in Japan) Shuppan Nyūsusha, 1964. 246, 8p. (Dokushojin series)

Surveys of about 100 important special collections; gives subjects covered, significance, history, accessibility, and printed catalogue for each collection. Index.

Nihon Toshokan Kyōkai   B8
日本 図 書 館 協 会

Toshokan shokuin meibo   図 書 館 職 員 名 簿 (Library staff directory) 1960. 188p.

Lists public, university and college libraries in Japan with notes on location, days closed and names of staff members.

Library catalogues

✤ Catalogues of large libraries and special collections are useful in supplementing lack in national bibliographies. Listed here are printed catalogues of National Diet Library, union catalogues and catalogues of Chinese classics and rare books.

Teikoku Toshokan wa-kan tosho shomei moku-roku   B9
帝 国 図 書 館 和 漢 図 書 書 名 目 録
(Title catalogue of Japanese and Chinese books in the Imperial Library) Teikoku Toshokan, 1899-1944. 10v.

Pt.1, published in 1899, is a catalogue as of 1893, except that books held prior to 1888 and listed in pt.1 of *Tokyo Toshokan zōkasho mokuroku* are omitted; pt.2, pub. 1903, lists additions 1894-99; pt.3, pub. 1913, additions 1900-11; pt.4, in 3v., pub. 1936-37, additions 1912-26; pt.5, in 4v., pub. 1942-44, additions 1927-35; pt.6, in 2v., pub. 1962, additions 1936-40.

Basic catalogues for classified and subject catalogues of the former national library now in the National Diet Library. They list books deposited in the Ministry of Home Affairs since 1875 (date of the copyright law) and comprise a kind of national bibliography from 1893 to 1940. Title entries in old Japanese orthography, arranged in syllabic order with name of author, date of publication, series notes, number of volumes, and call number.

Kokuritsu Kokkai Toshokan shibu Ueno Toshokan wa-kanjo shomei mokuroku: Kosho no bu   B10
国 立 国 会 図 書 館 支 部 上 野 図 書 館 和 漢 書 書 名 目 録   古 書 之 部 (Catalogue of Japanese and Chinese books in the Ueno branch of the National Diet Library. Old books) 1952-59. 2v.

Teikoku Toshokan Kokuritsu Toshokan wa-kan tosho bunrui mokuroku   B11
帝 国 図 書 館 · 国 立 図 書 館 和 漢 図 書 分 類 目 録 (Classified catalogue of Japanese and Chinese books added to Imperial Library and the succeeding National Library) Jan. 1941-Mar. 1949. Kokuritsu Kokkai Toshokan, 1964. 1144p.

A continuation of **B9**, pt.6, listing 32,890 acquisitions excluding old books, classified by Nippon Decimal Classification. Subject index.

Kokuritsu Kokkai Toshokan zōsho mokuroku   B12
国 立 国 会 図 書 館 蔵 書 目 録 (National Diet Library catalogue) 1948-1958. Kokuritsu Kokkai Toshokan, 1960- . 3v. In progress.

Classified catalogue of about 500,000 volumes listed in *Shūsho tsūhō* (Acquisition list) from 1948 to 1958. Published to date are: v.1, General works, philosophy and religion, history, and geography; v.2, Social sciences; v.3, Science, technology, and industry. Contains a large number of prewar publications processed during the period. Student reference and juvenile books not included. Author and subject indexes.

Kokuritsu Kokkai Toshokan zōsho mokuroku: wa-kanjo no bu   B13
国 立 国 会 図 書 館 蔵 書 目 録 和 漢 書 の 部 (National Diet Library catalogue. Japanese and Chinese books) 1957- . Kokuritsu Kokkai Toshokan, 1958- . 5v. Annual.

Formerly entitled *Shūsho tsūhō* (Acquisition list), issued first as a monthly beginning in Nov. 1948, then at greater intervals until with the 1955 ed. pub. in 1957 it became an annual under the title *Zōsho mokuroku* (Library catalogue). Contents classified by Nippon Decimal classification. Title index.

Kokuritsu Kokkai Toshokan zōsho mokuroku: yōsho hen   B14
国 立 国 会 図 書 館 蔵 書 目 録 洋 書 編 (National Diet Library catalogue. Foreign books) Part I, 1948-1958. Kokuritsu Kokkai Toshokan, 1963. 1374p.

Catalogue of 22,959 books in western languages from April 1948 to Dec. 1958. Generalia, philosophy, religion, and social sciences.

Union catalogues

✤ Lists of union catalogues are discussed

in **A6** and "Sengo hensan kankō no sōgō mokuroku ni tsuite" (Postwar union catalogues; introduction and criticism) by Hidemasa Nishizawa, in *Toshokan zasshi* (Library journal), v.54, no.6, June, 1960.

B15

Kokuritsu Kokkai Toshokan gyōsei shihō shibu toshokan tosho sōgō mokuroku 国立国会図書館行政司法支部図書館図書総合目録 (Union catalogue of books in the executive and judicial branch libraries of the National Diet Library) 1952-1958. Kokuritsu Kokkai Toshokan, 1954-60. 7v.

Lists annual acquisitions (except government publications) in two sections, Japanese-Chinese and Western language books, classified by Nippon Decimal Classification, with author and title indexes. Since 1959 Western language books are listed in **B16**; publication discontinued. Branch libraries: Cabinet Library, Statistical Bureau, Defense Agency, etc., publish their own catalogues. See **B24, A38.**

B16

Shinshū yōsho sōgō mokuroku 新収洋書総合目録 Union catalogue of foreign books. 1954- . Comp. by Kokuritsu Kokkai Toshokan. 1958- . 7v. Annual from 1959.

The first 3v. (from A to R), published in 1958, list monographs acquired 1940-54, and cover 15 universities, two public (Hibiya and Osaka) libraries, and National Diet Library. Became an annual with 1959 edition. 1962 edition, published in 1964, covers 49 libraries in Japan.

Chinese classics and Rare books

✻ Listed below are only selected catalogues. See **B6, B7** for detailed information.

Tōyōgaku Infōmeishon Sentā **B17**
東洋学インフォメーション・センター
Nihon ni okeru kanseki no shūshū 日本に於ける漢籍の蒐集 Collection of Chinese books in Japan; a catalogue of catalogues of Chinese books in public and private collections. Tōyō Bunko, 1961. 202, 10p. (Studies on Asia in Japan, 2)

Lists catalogues and bibliographies published since 1601. Index of owners.

B18
Dai Tōkyū Kinen Bunko shomoku 大東急記念文庫書目 (Catalogue of Dai Tōkyū Memorial Library) Dai Tōkyū Kinen Bunko, 1955. 563, 52p.

Dai Tōkyū Kinen Bunko kichōsho kaidai (Annotated catalogue of rare books in Dai Tōkyū Memorial Library) by Kikuya Nagasawa and Kazuma Kawase. Dai Tōkyū Kinen Bunko, 1956. 2v. **B18a.**

B19
Kanazawa Bunko kosho mokuroku 金沢文庫古書目録 (Catalogue of old books in Kanazawa Library) Kanazawa Bunko, 1939. 554p.

Kunaishō Zushoryō 宮内省図書寮 **B20**
Teikoku Wa-Kan tosho mokuroku 帝国和漢図書目録 (Catalogue of Japanese and Chinese books) 1916-26. 2v.

Kunaishō Zushoryō 宮内省図書寮 **B21**
Zushoryō kanseki zenpon shomoku 図書寮漢籍善本書目 (Catalogue of Chinese classics in Zushoryō) 1930. 122p.

B22
Kyoto Daigaku Bungakubu shozō kanseki mokuroku 京都大学文学部所蔵漢籍目録 (Catalogue of Chinese classics in the Faculty of Letters, Kyoto University) Kyoto, Ibundō, 1959. 316, 111, 52p.

B23
Kyoto Daigaku Jinbun Kagaku Kenkyūjo kanseki bunrui mokuroku 京都大学人文科学研究所漢籍分類目録 (Classified catalogue of Chinese classics in the Institute of Humanistic Studies, Kyoto University) Kyoto, Jinbun Kagaku Kenkyū Kyōkai, 1963- . 1v. In progress.

B24
Naikaku Bunko kokusho bunrui mokuroku 内閣文庫国書分類目録 (Classified catalogue of Japanese books in Cabinet Library) Naikaku Bunko, 1961-62. 3v.

B25
Naikaku Bunko kanseki bunrui mokuroku 内閣文庫漢籍分類目録 (Classified catalogue of Chinese classics in Cabinet Library) Naikaku Bunko, 1956. 598, 125p.

B26

Hōsa Bunko tosho mokuroku
蓬左文庫図書目録 (Catalogue of books in Hōsa Library) Nagoya, Kyōiku Iinkai, 1956-60. 2v.

B27

Seikadō Bunko tosho bunrui mokuroku 静嘉堂文庫図書分類目録 (Classified catalogue of books in Seikadō Library) Seikadō Bunko, 1929-39. 2v.

Seikadō Bunko tosho bunrui mokuroku 静嘉堂文庫図書分類目録 (Classified catalogue of books in Seikadō Library) Supplement. Kokuritsu Kokkai Toshokan, 1956. 142p. **B27a.**

B28

Seikadō Bunko kanseki bunrui mokuroku 静嘉堂文庫漢籍分類目録 (Classified catalogue of Chinese classics in Seikadō Library, and catalogue of Korean books) Seikadō Bunko, 1930-1951. 2v.

B29

Sonkeikaku Bunko kokusho bunrui mokuroku 尊経閣文庫国書分類目録 (Classified catalogue of Japanese books in Sonkeikaku Library) Sonkeikaku Bunko, 1939. 795, 176p.

B30

Sonkeikaku Bunko kanseki bunrui mokuroku 尊経閣文庫漢籍分類目録 (Classified catalogue of Chinese classics in Sonkeikaku Library) Sonkeikaku Bunko, 1934-35. 2v.

B31

Tenri Toshokan kisho mokuroku 天理図書館稀書目録 (Catalogue of rare books in Tenri Library) Japanese and Chinese books. Tenri, Tenri Toshokan, 1940-60. 3v. (Tenri Toshokan sōsho, 12, 15 and 25)

B32

Tōhō Bunka Kenkyūjo kanseki bunrui mokuroku 東方文化研究所漢籍分類目録 (Classified catalogue of Chinese classics in the Institute of Oriental Studies) Kyoto, Kyoto Inshokan, 1945. 2v.

Tōyō Bunko 東洋文庫 **B33**
Iwasaki Bunko Wa-Kanjo mokuroku 岩崎文庫和漢書目録 (Catalogue of Japanese and Chinese books in Iwasaki Library) 1934. 484, 82p.

B34

Tōyō Bunko Chōsenbon bunrui mokuroku 東洋文庫朝鮮本分類目録 (Classified catalogue of Korean books in Oriental Library) and catalogue of Annan books. Tōyō Bunko, 1939. 101, 15p.

B35

Tōyō Bunko kanseki sōsho bunrui mokuroku 東洋文庫漢籍叢書分類目録 (Classified catalogue of collected Chinese classics in Oriental Library) Tōyō Bunko, 1945. 795, 12p.

Yoshizawa, Yoshinori 吉沢義則 **B36**
Nihon kokan shomoku 日本古刊書目 (Catalogue of old Japanese books) Teito Shuppansha, 1933. 456p.

Lists books published from 8th century to 1595, divided into Nara, Heian, Kamakura, and Muromachi periods, giving title, number of volumes, and name of owner for each entry. Lists titles having no date separately in Japanese syllabic order. Chronological tables appended. Index.

Newspapers and Periodicals

Kokuritsu Kokkai Toshokan **B37**
国立国会図書館
Zenkoku kōkyō toshokan chikuji kankōbutsu sōgō mokuroku 全国公共図書館逐次刊行物総合目録 (Union catalogue of periodicals in public libraries of Japan) v.1- . 1963- . 2v. In progress.

In print as of Dec., 1961 are v.1, Kyoto-Osaka area, and v.2, Tōkai and Hokuriku area; to be completed by 1966. Classified under government publications, newspapers, magazines and scholarly journals, yearbooks and statistics, directories and catalogues.

B38

Teikoku Toshokan zasshi shinbun mokuroku 帝国図書館雑誌新聞目録 (Catalogue of periodicals and newspapers in the former Imperial Library) Teikoku Toshokan, 1937. 157p.

Catalogue of magazines and newspapers from 1860s to 1935, in National Diet Library. May be used with **B39**. Supplementary catalogue covering 1936-1948 was published by National Diet Library.

Tokyo Teikoku Daigaku Hōgakubu   **B39**
東京帝国大学法学部

Tōtenkō 東天紅   Naigai Tsūshinsha, 1930-41. 3v.

Lists about 3/4 of some 6,000 titles of newspapers and periodicals in Meiji Shinbun Zasshi Bunko in Tokyo University. Arranged by title in Japanese syllabic order; gives place of publication, publisher, frequency, subject, and number of issues in the Library. Appendix of v.1 contains chronological table (1868-70) of first date of publication and lists of *Nishikie shinbun* (Newspapers in colored prints), special supplementary numbers, and books about newspapers and magazines. Appendix of v.2 is a classified list and chronological tables (1868-1912) of v.3 is by prefecture.

Chikuji kankōbutsu mokuroku 逐次刊行物   **B40**
目録 (Catalogue of periodical publications) 1955-56 - . Kokuritsu Kokkai Toshokan, 1957- . 6v. Annual.

Cumulative list of newspapers, magazines, and bulletins acquired during the year by National Diet Library, and listed in **A9a**. Divided into government, with central and local subdivisions, and non-government, subdivided by forms. Coverage is more comprehensive than **A9**.

Kindai Chūgoku Kenkyū Iinkai   **B41**
近代中国研究委員会

Chūgokubun shinbun zasshi sōgō mokuroku 中国文新聞雑誌総合目録 (Union catalogue of Chinese newspapers and periodicals) Ed. by Chūzō Ichiko. 1959. 171p.

Covers holdings as of 1957 of 23 libraries, including Oriental Library, National Diet Library, China Institute, Tenri Library, and major university libraries. Arranged by phonetic reading of Chinese characters, giving title, frequency, place of publication, publisher, location, and missing numbers. Supplement follows:

Tōyō Bunko shinshū Chūgokubun shinbun zasshi mokuroku (Catalogue of new Chinese newspapers and periodicals in Tōyō Bunko) Jan., 1958 - Nov., 1961. Tōyō Bunko, 1961. 27p. Mimeo. **B41a.**

Monbushō Daigaku Gakujutsukyoku   **B42**
文部省大学学術局

Gakujutsu zasshi sōgō mokuroku 学術雑誌 綜合目録 (Union list of scholarly journals) Nihon Gakujutsu Shinkōkai, 1957-62. 7v.

Arranged alphabetically by title. Lists numbers in the library with their locations.

"Humanistic studies" in Japanese, as of 1957. (Includes psychology, geology) Includes libraries of 48 universities and institutes. In European languages, as of 1955. Supp. 1, as of 1958. Includes libraries of 61 universities and institutes.

"Natural sciences" in Japanese, as of 1957. Includes libraries of 61 universities and institutes. In European languages, as of 1955. Supp.1, as of 1958; supp. 2, as of 1960. Includes libraries of 107 universities and institutes.

LIBRARY SCIENCE

BIBLIOGRAPHY

Monbushō Daigaku Gakujutsukyoku   **B43**
文部省大学学術局

Gakujutsu tosho sōgō mokuroku: Toshokangaku 学術図書総合目録 図書館学 (Union catalogue of scholarly books: Library science in European languages) Nihon Gakujutsu Shinkōkai, 1958. 260p.

Lists 6,180 titles in 110 university libraries, as of 1956. Arranged alphabetically by authors, with title, publication date, and location. No index.

INDEXES

B44

Toshokan kenkyū 圕研究 (Bulletin of the League of Young Librarians) v.16 and general index. Comp. by Fujio Mamiya. Osaka, Seinen Toshokan'in Renmei, 1943. 138,178p.

Contains general index of articles, including translations, in the entire 16v., 1928-43; title indexes of illustrations, tables, book reviews, advertisements, and meetings; list of authors, with brief biographies; and list of members of the League. Translated articles are indexed by original title. Chinese names are listed by Japanese readings, with cross references from Chinese readings. Reprint edition published in 1955.

Nihon Toshokan Kyōkai   **B45**
日本図書館協会

Toshokan zasshi sōsakuin 図書館雑誌総 索引 (General index of *Toshokan zasshi-The Library journal*) 1907-1960. 1964. 237p.

General index of major articles from no.1 to 1960. List of subscribing libraries appended.

DICTIONARIES

Mamiya, Fujio 間宮不二雄   **B46**
Ō-Chū-Wa taiyaku toshokan daijiten 欧中和 対訳図書館大辞典 (Comprehensive library dictionary in European, Chinese and Japanese languages) Rev. and enl. ed. Japan Raiburarī Byūrō, 1952. 645p.

Annotated list of terms related to libraries, books, printing, and binding in European, Chinese and Japanese languages. Illustrated when necessary. Explanation of "four corner system" for identifying Chinese characters, glossary of bibliographical terms in Chinese classics, and list of Western names in Chinese characters appended. Index.

Uemura, Chōzaburō 植村長三郎   **B47**
Tosho toshokan jiten 図書・図書館事典 (Dictionary of books and libraries) Buntokusha, 1951. 571, 28p.

Lists and explains subjects related to libraries, books, manuscripts, printing, and binding. Western language index.

Monbushō 文部省   **B48**
Gakujutsu yōgoshū : Toshokangaku hen 学術用語集図書館学編 Japanese scientific terms: Library science. Dai Nihon Tosho, 1958. 307p.

Nakamura, Hatsuo 中村初雄   **B49**
Jitsumu hikkei toshokan yōgo jiten 実務必携図書館用語辞典 (Practical dictionary of essential library terms) Dōgakusha, 1951. 120p.

Gives brief explanations to mainly English terms.

Amano, Keitarō 天野敬太郎   **B50**
Taiyaku shoseki yōgo jiten 対訳書籍用語辞典 Dictionnaire à l'usage de la librairie ancienne. Yūshōdō Shoten, 1962. 201p.

Re-issue by the International Association of Old Bookstores (1956) of the dictionary compiled by M. Hertzberger with Japanese terms added by Keitarō Amano. A glossary containing 1,225 terms in French, English, German, Swedish, Danish, Italian, Spanish, Dutch and Japanese. Arranged alphabetically by French term. Japanese index.

Nihon Toshokan Kyōkai, Bunken Jōhō **B51**
Katsudō Iinkai 日本図書館協会文献情報活動委員会
Dokyumenteishon yōgoshū ドキュメンテーション用語集 (Glossary of documentation) 1963. 118p.

Terms selected from about 20 western books on documentation, translated into Japanese with definitions.

Collison, Robert L.   **B52**
Kokusai kikan dantai no bunken jōhō katsudō 国際機関・団体の文献情報活動 Bibliographical services throughout the world, 1950-59. Tr. by Kunio Saitō. Nihon Yunesuko Kokunai Iinkai, 1963. 97p.

Lists 83 international organizations including United Nations, describing dates of establishemnt, objectives and bibliographical activities.

HANDBOOKS

Nihon Toshokan Kyōkai   **B53**
日本図書館協会
Toshokan handobukku 図書館ハンドブック JLA librarians' handbook. Rev. and enl. ed. 1960. 875p.

Systematically describes administration, management, practical work. Survey article on libraries of the world and chronological tables (Japanese and foreign) appended. Index.

Nihon Toshokan Kyōkai   **B54**
日本図書館協会
Jidō toshokan handobukku 児童図書館ハンドブック (Handbook of children's libraries) 1963. 179p.

Deals with children's library in general, services for children, collecting and organizing books, facilities and administrative problems. Appendix contains chronological table of children's libraries covering 1879-1945 for Japan and 1797-1941 for foreign countries and list of references. Index.

BOOKS AND PUBLISHING

✱ Bibliographic matters of publishing are covered in this section. For publishing trends of the year see **A10** and for printing see **E78-E83.**

DICTIONARIES

Emori, Kenji 江守賢治   **B55**
Hon no shōjiten 本の小事典 (Little dictionary of books) Meiji Tosho, 1955. 401p.

Lists and explains terms by subjects: books, paper, printing, binding, history of the book, handling of books, libraries, and related topics. Readable, with many illustrations and subheadings. Appendix contains annotated list of reference books, microfilm materials, prices of books, publishing prizes, organizations, statistics, laws and regulations. Index.

Uehara, Michio 植原路郎 **B56**
Jitsuyō hon no jiten 実用本の辞典 (Practical dictionary of books) Shuppan Nyūsusha, 1964. 254p.

Briefly explains terms of book making, printing, binding, editing, materials. Lists of quotations about books and reference works appended. Index.

Copyright

Ito, Nobuo 伊藤信男 **B57**
Sōgō kindai chosakuken bunkashi nenpyō 綜合近代著作権文化史年表 (Chronological study of copyright law in modern times) Nihon Chosakuken Kyōkai, 1960. 181p.

Section on bibliographical survey lists, according to articles of the law, relevant judgements and studies. Section on chronology lists amendments and cases since 1868.

Banned books

Saitō, Shōzō 斉藤昌三 **B58**
Gendai hikka bunken dainenpyō 現代筆禍 文献大年表 (Chronological list of prohibited publications in modern Japan) Suikodō Shoten, 1932. 432p.

Lists titles of banned books and articles from 1868 to 1926, giving reasons for prohibition, author, place of publication, and publisher. Title index with locations in journals. Pre-1868 banned books are discussed in the preface.

Naimushō Keihokyoku 内務省警保局 **B59**
Kinshi tankōbon mokuroku 禁止単行本目録 (Catalogue of banned books) 1888-1934. 1935. 256p. (Shuppan keisatsu shiryō)

Monbushō Kyōgakukyoku **B60**
文部省教学局
Monbushō suisen narabini Kyōgakukyoku senshō

tosho shisō kankei hakkin tosho ichiran 文部省推薦並教学局選奨図書思想関 係発禁図書一覧 (List of books recommended by Ministry of Education and list of banned books related to ideologies) 1942. 192p.

Monbushō Shakai Kyōikukyoku **B61**
文部省社会教育局
Rengōkokugun Sōshireibu kara bosshū o meizerareta senden'yō kankōbutsu sōmokuroku 連合国軍総司令部から没収を命ぜら れた宣伝用刊行物総目録 (Allied Forces GHQ censorship list of prohibited propaganda materials) 1949. 418p.

Lists about 7,700 books on nationalism and militarism published before and during the War and confiscated by GHQ in accordance with a memorandum of March 17, 1946.

Collectors' seals

Mimura, Seizaburō 三村清三郎 **B62**
Zōsho inpu 蔵書印譜 (Collectors' seals) Bunkōdō Shoten, 1932. 2v. (Japanese style binding)

Lists seals and biographies of collectors by name of collector. Texts of seals appended.

Maruyama, Sueo 丸山季夫 **et al.** **B63**
Zōshomei inpu 蔵書名印譜 (Collectors' seals) Hakuundō, 1952-55. 4v.

Facsimilies of seals, primarily pre-1868 with a few post-1868, not found in **B62**. Gives brief biographies of collectors and index of texts of seals.

Ono, Noriaki 小野則秋 **B64**
Nihon no zōshoin 日本の蔵書印 (Seals of Japanese collectors) Kyoto, Geibunsha, 1954. 231p.

Discusses aspects of collectors' seals with illustrations of seals. Gives index by collector's name to text of seal and index by text to name. Covers more post-1868 collectors than **B62** and **B63**.

ENCYCLOPEDIAS

❧ Encyclopedias, dictionaries of origins of things, and indexes having comprehensive coverage of subjects are included in this section.

GENERAL

Heibonsha 平 凡 社   **C1**
Sekai daihyakka jiten 世 界 大 百 科 事 典 (World encyclopedia) 1955-63. 33v.

Standard encyclopedia containing about 70,000 signed articles by specialists; Tatsuo Hayashi, chairman of the Editorial Committee. Chronological table of world history, comprehensive list of Japanese cities, towns and villages in v.31; indexes of proper nouns and abbreviations, illustrations and difficult names in v.32; supplementary articles covering 1958-63 in v.33. A new edition, completely revised and enlarged, incorporating supplemented items as well as latest developments and statistical figures in about 82,000 entries in 24v. (5v. in print as of 1965) has been in progress since 1964.

Tamagawa Daigaku Shuppanbu   **C2**
玉 川 大 学 出 版 部
Tamagawa hyakka daijiten 玉 川 百 科 大 辞 典 (Tamagawa encyclopedia) Seibundō Shinkōsha, 1959-63. 31v.

Each volume is devoted to one subject such as mathematics, physics, chemistry, literature and the arts, politics and economics, etc. Provides systematic explanations for students. Index in each volume with general index of 180,000 terms in v.31.

Shōwa Shuppan Kenkyūjo   **C3**
昭 和 出 版 研 究 所
Nihon hyakka daijiten 日 本 百 科 大 事 典 (Encyclopedia of Japan) Shōgakkan, 1962-64. 13v.

Its 50,000 entries are briefly explained and lack balance in treatment.

Heibonsha 平 凡 社   **C4**
Daihyakka jiten 大 百 科 事 典 (Encyclopedia) 1930-52. 32v.

A representative prewar encyclopedia and a useful comprehensive survey of things Japanese, supplementing **C1**. Index in v.28. Reprinted in 1951-53, 15v. in abridged size.

Heibonsha 平 凡 社   **C5**
Kokumin hyakka jiten 国 民 百 科 事 典 (Popular encyclopedia) 1961-62. 8v.

Its 18,000 entries are simply explained, intended for home rather than Library use.

Heibonsha 平 凡 社   **C6**
Shōhyakka jiten 小 百 科 事 典 (Little encyclopedia) 1955. 1307, 18p.

Handy, with about 40,000 entries and 3,000 illustrations. Concise explanations.

RUISHO

❧ Encyclopedic compilations of quotation and extracts, selected from classics and classified by subject, with critical explanations and reference to sources. Invaluable for historical research.

Jingū Shichō 神 宮 司 庁   **C7**
Koji ruien 古 事 類 苑 (Historical encyclopedia of Japan) Reprint ed. Hyōgensha, 1927-30. 51v.

A collection of primary source materials touching all phases of pre-modern Japanese life, institutions, literature, society, industry, astronomy, geology, customs, etc. Useful manual for initial stages of historical research. Each subject has an introduction, résumé, marginal headings, sources and quotations, selected from books published before 1868. v.51 contains a table of contents for the entire set and a general index in Japanese syllabic order. In view of the large number of old books and documents discovered since publication, this encyclopedia necessarily has deficiencies; nevertheless, it remains extremely valuable. First edition, pub. 1896-1914. 60v. reduced size edition, pub. by Naigai Shoseki, 1931-36.

Mozume, Takami 物集高見 **C8**
Kōbunko 広文庫 (Comprehensive library of literature) Kōbunko Kankōkai, 1916. 20v.

Classified selection of texts from about 10,000 Japanese, Chinese and Buddhist books listed in **C13**, arranged in dictionary form by subject (astronomy, geography, biography, tools and utensils) with greater emphasis on literary and cultural matters than **C7**.

Shibata, Shōkyoku 柴田宵曲 **C9**
Zuihitsu jiten 随筆辞典 (Dictionary of subjects treated in Japanese miscellanies) Tokyodō, 1960-61. 5v.

v.1, Clothing, food, housing; v.2, Arts and amusements; v.3, Customs and folklore; v.4, Strange tales; v.5, Annotated bibliography. While **C14** lists only titles without texts, this dictionary includes selected texts for each subject. Useful for locating sources for study of society and culture of the Edo period, 1600-1867.

ORIGINS OF THINGS

✤ A kind of encyclopedia explaining origins of Japanese social life and customs. Sources are not usually cited.

Ishii, Kendō 石井研堂 **C10**
Meiji jibutsu kigen 明治事物起源 (Origin of civilization in the Meiji period, 1868-1912) Rev. and enl. ed. Shun'yōdō, 1944. 2v.

First ed. 1907. Lists and annotates about 3,000 topics under 21 subject groupings dealing with social, cultural and scientific aspects of post-1868 Japanese civilization. Some source citations. Table of contents in each volume should be used to supplement brief index in v.2.

Hioki, Shōichi 日置昌一 **C11**
Hanashi no daijiten 話の大事典 (Dictionary of beginnings) Banrikaku, 1950-51. 4v.

Dictionary explaining origins of food, drink, manners and customs, performing arts, laws and other things in Japan with many illustrations and quotations from prose and poetry. No sources given.

Hioki, Shōichi 日置昌一 **C12**
Monoshiri jiten ものしり事典 (Book of knowledge) Kawade Shobō, 1952-54. 10v.

Similar to **C11**, but with more entries, explains origins of Japanese words, manners, customs, performing arts, cultural and political matters.

SUBJECT INDEXES

Mozume, Takami 物集高見 **C13**
Gunsho sakuin 群書索引 (Subject index to Japanese classics) Kōbunko Kankōkai, 1916-17. 3v.

An index to **C8**, listing about 50,000 items covering all subjects with citation to sources, arranged in Japanese syllabic order. Volume numbers cited in this index refer to the editions in the author's possession and may not be applicable to other editions.

Ōta, Tamesaburō 太田為三郎 **C14**
Nihon zuihitsu sakuin 日本随筆索引 (Index of Japanese miscellanies) Reprint ed. Iwanami Shoten, 1963. 2v.

Subject index to about 500 books containing important essays and miscellaneous writings of 1600-1867 period. Serves as a guide to sources when studying society, customs, and culture of premodern times. Arranged in Japanese syllabic order with sources. Supplementary works follow:

Nihon zuihitsu 74shu sakuin (Index of 74 books of Japanese miscellanies) by Genryō Yajima. Sendai, 1957. 157p. Mimeo. **C14a.**

Shin zuihitsu sakuin (New index of miscellanies) containing 258 books of essays from 1868 to 1956. By Genryō Yajima. Sendai, 1957. 166p. Mimeo. **C14b.**

Mikan zuihitsu 68shu sakuin (Index of 68 unpublished miscellanies) by Genryō Yajima. Sendai, Tōhoku Daigaku Fuzoku Toshokan, 1964. 185p. (Sankō shiryō, 61) **C14c.**

Kyoto Daigaku, Tōyōshi Kenkyūkai **C15**
京都大学東洋史研究会
Chūgoku zuihitsu sakuin 中国随筆索引 (Index of Chinese miscellanies) Nihon Gakujutsu Shinkōkai, 1954. 1018p.

Index to tables of contents of about 160 Chinese collections of essays, stories, studies, ancient matters, and strange tales from the 7th to 20th century. Contains valuable source materials. Arranged in Japanese syllabic order. Entries covering several subjects are listed again under each subject with sources.

Saeki, Tomi 佐伯富 **C16**
Chūgoku zuihitsu zatcho sakuin 中国随筆雑著索引 (Index of Chinese essays and miscellanies) Kyoto, Kyoto Daigaku Tōyōshi Kenkyūkai, 1960. 1144p.

Continuation of **C15**, indexing tables of contents of 46 collections not listed in **C15**. Arranged by title and major subjects in the texts in Japanese syllabic order; easier to use than **C15**.

DICTIONARIES

Kokuritsu Kokkai Toshokan **C17**
国立国会図書館
Nihon no jisho tenjikai 日本の辞書展示会 (Exhibition of Japanese dictionaries) Catalogue and explanation. 1955. 38p.

Divided into pre- and post-1868 periods, annotates 299 representative encyclopedias, dictionaries of Chinese characters Japanese and foreign languages, and subject dictionaries from ancient times to 1954. Explains development and historical significance of dictionaries in Japan.

Shuppan Nyūsusha 出版ニュース社 **C18**
Jiten jiten sōgō mokuroku 辞典事典総合目録 List of dictionaries and encyclopedias. 1961. 247p.

Lists pre- and postwar Japanese encyclopedias, dictionaries of languages and of specialized subjects. Short list of representative foreign dictionaries appended. Directory of publishers and title index.

Monbushō 文部省 **C19**
Gakujutsu yōgoshu 学術用語集 Japanese scientific terms. 1954-64. 12v.

Compiled by the Ministry of Education with the assistance of learned societies and organizations to standardize usage of scientific terms. Each volume consists of two sections: Japanese-English with entries in romanized Japanese followed by Japanese orthography and English equivalents; and English-Japanese, also with romanized form. Published volumes follow:

Butsurigaku hen (Physics) Dai Nihon Tosho, 1954. 221p. **Q48.**

Denki kōgaku hen (Electrical engineering) Denki Gakkai, 1957. 685p. **R220.**

Doboku kōgaku hen (Civil engineering) Doboku Gakkai, 1954. 395p. **R43.**

Dōbutsugaku hen (Zoology) Dai Nihon Tosho, 1954. 128p. **S66.** Section 3, Names of important divisions of animal kingdom and larval names.

Kagaku hen (Chemistry) Rev. ed. Nankōdō, 1964. 457p. **Q60.**

Kenchikugaku hen (Architecture) Nihon Kenchiku Gakkai, 1955. 360p. **R79.**

Kikai kōgaku hen (Mechanical engineering) Nihon Kikai Gakkai, 1955. 564p. **R124.**

Saikō yakingaku hen (Mining and metallurgy) Nihon Kōgyōkai, 1954. 263p. **R267.**

Senpaku kōgaku hen (Naval architecture and marine engineering) Zōsen Kyōkai, 1955. 526, 4p. **R197.**

Shokubutsugaku hen (Botany) Dai Nihon Tosho, 1956. 155p. **S25.** Section 3, Standard Japanese family names corresponding to Latin names.

Sūgaku hen (Mathematics) Dai Nihon Tosho, 1954. 146p. **Q29.** Section 3, Statistical terms: Japanese-English and English-Japanese.

Toshokangaku hen (Library science) Dai Nihon Tosho, 1958. 307p. **B48.** Section 3, List of abbreviations and terms relating to books and paper.

PHILOSOPHY AND RELIGION

❦ Also included are ethics and mythology. As reference books on philosophy are relatively few, use must be made of introductory works, histories of philosophy on specific schools or special regions. References on ancient philosophy often are found in books on religion or mythology.

PHILOSOPHY

BIBLIOGRAPHY

Kuno, Osamu 久野収　　　　　　　**D1**
Tetsugaku no meicho 哲学の名著　(Great books of philosophy) Mainichi Shinbunsha, 1959。 352, 23p. (Mainichi Library)

　Historical survey of ancient, medieval and especially modern European philosophy, briefly summarizing the lives and works of representative philosophers. Glossary of terms. Author index. Reprinted in Mainichi Echo books, 1964.

Shunjūsha 春秋社　　　　　　　　**D2**
Tetsugaku meicho kaidai 哲学名著解題 (Bibliographical introduction to great works of philosophy) 1956. 397p.

　Gives notes on the lives and major works of 104 Occidental and Oriental philosophers from ancient to modern times. Detailed table of contents.

Shimomura, Toratarō 下村寅太郎 **and**　**D3**
Danno, Yasutarō 淡野安太郎
Tetsugaku kenkyū nyūmon 哲学研究入門 (Introduction to research in philosophy) Koishikawa Shobō, 1949. 555, 43, 44p.

　Includes useful bibliographical notes in outlining the history of Occidental and Oriental philosophies

and their schools. Chronology from ancient times to 1949 and chart of schools appended. Name and subject indexes.

DICTIONARIES

　　　　　　　　　　　　　　　　　D4
Gendai tetsugaku jiten 現代哲学辞典　(Cyclopedia of contemporary philosophy) Iwasaki Shoten, 1951. 551p.

　Summarizes world trends, including those in Japan, and discusses major works. Japanese and foreign references. Subject and name indexes.

Heibonsha 平凡社　　　　　　　　**D5**
Tetsugaku jiten 哲学事典 (Dictionary of philosophy) 1954. 1294, 94p.

　Explains or identifies 7,000 terms, topics and persons, including some from related disciplines, each with references. Gives works under authors. Maps showing places of philosophical interest in China, India, Greece and the rest of Europe appended. Japanese and foreign-language indexes.

　　　　　　　　　　　　　　　　　D6
Iwanami tetsugaku shōjiten 岩波哲学小辞典 (Iwanami's concise dictionary of philosophy) Ed. by Kichinosuke Itō. Rev. and enl. ed. Iwanami Shoten, 1958. 1394p.

　Useful for succinct information, with cross references, on topics and persons, arranged alphabetically, with Japanese headings romanized, giving, where appropriate, English, French and German equivalents. Name and subject indexes in English, French and German.

Miki, Kiyoshi 三木清　　　　　　**D7**
Gendai tetsugaku jiten 現代哲学辞典

(Dictionary of contemporary philosophy) Nihon Hyōronsha, 1949. 620p.

Terms explained under inclusive topics with subdivisions. Source references. Name and subject indexes. Reprint of 1936 ed.

Akademiia Nauk SSSR. Institut Filosofii   **D8**

Tetsugaku jiten 哲学辞典 (Dictionary of philosophy) Tr. by Sobieto Kenkyūsha Kyōkai. Iwasaki Shoten, 1956. 614p.

Translation of Masao Nonaka's *Kratkii filosofskii slovar'*, 4th ed., 1954, with about 600 entries based on Marxism and Leninism emphasizing the relationship between theory and practice. Includes such subjects as chemistry, physics and biology, and covers Asian and African philosophies. Index.

Takashima, Zen'ya 高島善哉 et al.   **D9**

Sekai shisō jiten 世界思想辞典 (Dictionary of world thought) Kawade Shobō, 1950. 796p.

Explains the roles and summarizes the works of representative philosophers. Indexes of names, titles and schools of thought.

Shisō no Kagaku Kenkyūkai 思想の 科学研究会   **D10**

Tetsugaku ronri yōgo jiten 哲学・論理用語 辞典 (Dictionary of terms in philosophy and logic) Kyoto, San'ichi Shobō, 1959. 312, 18, 21p.

Limited in number of entries but gives examples of usage for most terms in modern logic. List of 100 important philosophical books and genealogy of schools of philosophy appended. Concise and useful.

CHRONOLOGY

Hayami, Keiji 速水敬二   **D11**

Tetsugaku nenpyō 哲学年表 (Chronological table of philosophy) Iwanami Shoten, 1950. 311p.

Gives on facing pages events in philosophy, with lives of philosophers and their works, and Occidental and Oriental cultural events. Dates according to both Japanese and Western calendars. Genealogical chart of schools of philosophy appended. General index and index of philosophers.

Kindai Nihon Shisōshi Kenkyūkai 近代 日本思想史研究会   **D12**

Kindai Nihon shisōshi nenpyō 近代日本思 想史年表 (Chronology of history of modern Japanese thought) Aoki Shoten, 1957. 197p. (Kindai Nihon shisōshi, 4)

Three columns tabulate books and articles, cultural, and social events from 1868 to 1945. Includes references for all volumes of the *Kindai Nihon shisōshi*. Index.

Yamada, Munemutsu 山田宗睦   **D13**

Gendai shisōshi nenpyō 現代思想史年表 (Chronology of modern thought) Kyoto, San'ichi Shobō, 1961. 284p. (Nihon gendaishi nenpyō)

Gives 1868-1959 events and explanatory notes on facing pages. Includes bibliographical references.

Oriental philosophy

→ A93, A94, G32

Nihon Gakujutsu Kaigi 日本学術会議   **D14**

Bungaku tetsugaku shigaku bunken mokuroku. X: Chūgoku tetsugaku shisō hen 文学・哲 学・史学文献目録 X: 中国哲学・思 想編 (Bibliography of literature, philosophy and history. X: Chinese philosophy) 1960. 293p.

Classified list of Japanese monographs and periodical articles, 1945-59, on philosophy, religion, education and culture. Includes some early Japanese and Korean studies on China. Indexes of periodicals and authors.

Chūgoku Shisō Shūkyōshi Kenkyūkai 中国思想宗教史研究会   **D15**

Chūgoku shisō shūkyō bunka kankei ronbun mokuroku 中国思想・宗教・文化関係論 文目録 (List of articles on Chinese philosophy, religion and civilization) 1960. 331p.

Classified list of Japanese periodical articles and essays in collected works from 1868 to 1957. Author index.

Morimoto, Kakuzō 森本角蔵   **D16**

Gokyō sakuin 五経索引 (Index to the Five Chinese Classics) Meguro Shoten, 1935-44. 3v.

Lists terms in "Book of changes", "Book of history", "Book of odes", "Spring and autumn annals", and "Book of rites" in Japanese syllabic order, each with source, frequency of appearance in texts, usage examples with locations. Lists of words arranged by characters with reference sources appended.

Morimoto, Kakuzō 森本角蔵   **D17**

Shisho sakuin 四書索引 (Index to the Four Books) Fumaidō, 1952. 1906p.

Covers "The great learning", "The mean", "Analects" and "Mencius" in the manner of **D16**.

Hayashi, Taisuke 林泰輔 **D18**
Rongo nenpu 論語年譜 (Chronological records of the Analects) Ōkura Shoten, 1916. 2v.

Lists in four columns events in the history of the work and its influence, critiques, manuscripts, and editions, with introductory essay on the life of Confucius, compilation of the "Analects" and its influence. Facsimiles of stone inscriptions and pages of old printed books and handwritten copies appended. Indexes of titles, names and quotations.

Tokyo Daigaku Bungakubu **D19**
東京大学文学部
Sō Gen gakuan jinmei sakuin 宋元学案人名索引 (Index of names in Handbook of Sung-Yüan studies) Seki Shoin, 1935. 143p.

Gives names of persons, places and schools of philosophy in Huong Tsung-i's 100v. *Sung Yüan hsueh an*, 1875, a history of Confucian thought in the Sung and Yüan periods (1000-1368).

Shibunkai 斯文会 **D20**
Nihon jugaku nenpyō 日本儒学年表 (Chronological table of Japanese Confucianism) 1922. 449p.

Lists developments from 200 to 1922, including studies in Sinology, with sources. No index.

Ogawa, Kandō 小川貫道 **D21**
Kangakusha denki oyobi chojutsu shūran 漢学者伝記及著述集覧 (Survey of lives and works of Japanese Sinologists) Seki Shoin, 1935. 781p.

Covers 1,256 scholars from 1619 to 1934.

Seki, Giichirō 関儀一郎 **and** **D22**
Seki, Yoshinao 関義直
Kinsei kangakusha denki chosaku daijiten 近世漢学者伝記著作大事典 (Bio-bibliographical dictionary of modern Japanese Sinologists) Ida Shoten, 1943. 717p.

Entries on about 3,000 Sinologists from 1619 to 1940, with genealogical charts of schools of Confucian studies appended.

Ueno, Kenchi 上野賢知 **D23**
Nihon Saden kenkyū chojutsu nenpyō … 日本左伝研究著述年表 (Chronology and classified catalogue of Japanese studies on the Tso commentary) Tōyō Bunka Kenkyūjo, 1957. 131p.

(Tōyō Bunka kenkyū kiyo, no.1)

Lists chronologically and also by subjects works from 702 to 1957 on Tso Ch'iu-ming's commentary on the "Spring and autumn annals" of Confucius. Author and title indexes.

Japanese classic scholars

Ōkawa, Shigeo 大川茂雄 **and** **D24**
Minami, Shigeki 南茂樹
Kokugakusha denki shūsei 国学者伝記集成 (Biographical dictionary of scholars of Japanese classics) Kunimoto Shuppansha, 1934. 2v.

Gives personal histories, publications, etc., with sources, of about 610 Shintoists, historians, literary critics and linguists arranged by the years of their deaths, from 1596 to 1903. Chronological table of scholars appended. Indexes of names and alternative names.

Nihon Bungaku Shiryō Kenkyūkai **D25**
日本文学資料研究会
Kokugakusha denki shūsei 国学者伝記集成 (Biographical dictionary of scholars of Japanese classics) Supplement. Kunimoto Shuppansha, 1935. 629, 47p.

Adds to those in **D24** scholars who died from 1903 to 1934, including Sinologists and poets who wrote on the classics. Indexes cover names in **D24**.

PSYCHOLOGY

→ **P16, P17**

Kokuritsu Kokkai Toshokan Shibu Ueno Toshokan **D26** 国立国会図書館支部上野図書館
Hōbun shinrigaku bunken mokuroku kō 邦文心理学文献目録稿 (Tentative bibliography of Japanese works on psychology) 1953. 144p.

Classified list of about 2,850 monographs published from 1868 to Mar., 1952, compiled mainly from catalogues of the former Imperial Library, now incorporated into the National Diet Library. Author index.

Heibonsha 平凡社 **D27**
Shinrigaku jiten 心理学事典 (Dictionary of psychology) 1957. 683, 31p.

Explains in detail about 600 subjects, each with subdivisions in which important terms are in boldface, limited strictly to psychology. Notes on persons, symbols, statistical formulas and list of testing methods appended. Indexes of terms in Japanese and European languages.

Ōtsuki, Kenji 大槻憲二 **D28**
Seishin bunsekigaku jiten 精神分析学辞典
(Dictionary of psychoanalysis) Ikubunsha,
1961. 442p.

Entries in Japanese followed by European-language
equivalents, with biographical notes on foreign
psychologists. Chronological table of development
of psychoanalysis appended. European name and
subject indexes.

Suzuki, Kiyoshi 鈴木清 **et al.** **D29**
Rinshō shinri jiten 臨床心理事典 (Dictionary of clinical psychology) Iwasaki Shoten,
1957. 532p.

Divided into introduction and sections on infancy,
childhood, adolescence, young adulthood, maturity
and old age, each with subdivisions. Emphasis
is on psychiatry. Notes on equipment and facilities
and list of testing methods appended. Subject index.

Hatano, Kanji 波多野完治 **and** **D30**
Yoda, Arata 依田新
Jidō shinrigaku handobukku 児童心理学ハ
ンドブック (Handbook of child psychology)
Kaneko Shobō, 1959. 951p.

Carmichael, L.: Manual of child psychology, 1946,
adapted for Japanese use. Explained in simple
terms in 11 chapters by 32 specialists. History of
Japanese child psychology appended. Author index.

ETHICS

❧ Also consult reference books on philosophy.

Furukawa, Tetsushi 古川哲史 **et al.** **D31**
Rinrigaku meicho hyakusen 倫理学名著百選
(One hundred great books on ethics) Kawade
Shobō, 1955. 267p. (Gendai dōtoku kōza, 7)

Limited to books published since 1868, including
some on philosophy and Buddhism, divided into
Occidental, Indian, Chinese and Japanese, with
comments by specialists.

Kaneko, Takezō 金子武蔵 **D32**
Rinrigaku jiten 倫理学事典 (Dictionary of
ethics) Kōbundō, 1957. 409, 159p.

Introductory summary of contemporary studies
of the history of ethical thought in the Occident
and the Orient, scholarship in ethics and moral
education, with many subheadings. Lists of References. Subject and name indexes.

Ōshima, Yasumasa 大島康正 **D33**
Shin rinri jiten 新倫理辞典 (New dictionary
of ethics) Sōbunsha, 1961. 472p.

Covers ethical thought throughout the world since
ancient times, contemporary ethical and moral issues
and representative philosophers, with a list of references for each entry. Subject and name indexes.

Maxims and proverbs

→ F171 - F178

Haga, Yaichi 芳賀矢一 **et al.** **D34**
Kakugen daijiten 格言大辞典 (Comprehensive dictionary of proverbs) Bunshōkaku, 1920.
797p.

In Japanese, Chinese and European sections,
subdivided by subjects, with emphasis on proverbs
and sayings from classical literature. Subject
index.

Maruyama, Rinpei 丸山林平 **D35**
Sekai kakugen jiten 世界格言辞典 (Dictionary of world proverbs) Jitsugyō no Nipponsha,
1954. 481p.

Explains about 5,000 proverbs and sayings under
19 subject headings, with sources and foreign equivalents where possible.

Ono, Shinobu 小野忍 **et al.** **D36**
Sekai no kotowaza jiten 世界のことわざ
辞典 (Dictionary of the world's proverbs) Fuku-
inkan Shoten, 1964. 537p.

A compilation of Japanese, Chinese, English,
American, German, French, Italian, Spanish and
other proverbs and quotations from the Bible, Shakespeare's plays, etc., with notes on their meanings
and sources. Those in European languages other
than English have English translations.

RELIGION

BIBLIOGRAPHY

Moriya, Kankyō 守屋貫教 **D37**
Shūkyō tetsugaku meicho kaisetsu 宗教哲学
名著解説 (Great books of religion and philosophy, annotated) Mikasa Shobō, 1940. 323p.

Detailed discussion of 24 major books from the
time of Plato to 19th century. Bibliography.

Nihon Gakujutsu Kaigi 日本学術会議 **D38**
Bungaku tetsugaku shigaku bunken mokuroku.
IV: Shūkyō kankei gakujutsu hen 文学・哲学
史学文献目録 Ⅳ： 宗教関係学術編
(Bibliography of literature, philosophy and his-

tory. IV: Religion) 1955. 151p.

Classified list of about 6,000 books and articles in Japanese published from Aug., 1945 to June, 1954. Author and periodical title indexes.

Ōkurayama Bunka Kagaku Toshokan   **D39**
大倉山文化科学図書館
Tosho mokuroku: shūkyō bumon 図書目録 宗教部門 (Catalogue of Ōkurayama Library of Humanities and Sciences: religious section) Yokohama, Ōkurayama Bunka Kagaku Kenkyūjo, 1955. 298p.

Lists by author 15,000 books classified by the Nippon Decimal system, divided into those in Japanese or Chinese and those in English. Content notes for collected works and series.

DICTIONARIES

  D40
Sekai shūkyō jiten 世界宗教辞典 (Dictionary of the world's religions) Osaka, Sōgensha, 1953. 689p.

Explains in some detail about 2,000 terms on religion, folk belief and the history and philosophy of religion, with emphasis on ancient and contemporary Japanese religions. Chronology of religions appended. Index.

  D41
Nihon shūkyō jiten 日本宗教辞典 (Dictionary of Japanese religions) Tokyo Sōgensha, 1956. 694p.

Rituals and terms of all religions in Japan under about 4,000 entries.

  D42
Shūkyō jiten 宗教辞典 (Dictionary of religions) Hori Shoten, 1951. 338p.

About 2,300 entries on Shintō, Buddhism, Christianity, Islam, Hinduism, Confucianism, Taoism, Judaism, etc., science of religion, theology, mythology, etc.

DIRECTORY

Kokusai Shūkyō Kenkyūjo   **D43**
国際宗教研究所
Nihon no shoshūkyō 日本の諸宗教 Japan's religions. 1957-59. 6v.

v.1, Directory of the Sectarian Shrine Federation and principal Shintō shrines; v.2, Christian churches and denominations in Japan; v.3, Directory of Buddhist denominations; v.4, New religions; v.5-6, University courses on religions.

YEARBOOKS

  D44
Shūkyō nenkan 宗教年鑑 (Yearbook of religions) 1954- . Comp. by Monbusho Chosakyoku. 1955, 1957- . 9v.

Former titles: Shūkyō nenpō, 1950; Shūkyō yōran, 1951; Shūkyō benran, 1952, 1953.

Gives general trends, developments in individual religions, a directory of religious bodies and statistics.

STATISTICS

Monbushō Chōsakyoku 文部省調査局   **D45**
Sekai no shūkyō jijō 世界の宗教事情 (World religious conditions) 1958. 100p.

Includes many statistics from various sources.

SOURCE MATERIALS

Date, Mitsuyoshi 伊達光美   **D46**
Nihon shūkyō seido shiryō ruijū kō 日本宗教制度史料類聚考 (Collection of historical materials on Japanese religious institutions) Ganshōdō, 1930. 758p.

With emphasis on Buddhism, annotates materials arranged chronologically from 552 to 1912 and gives laws and regulations, excluding anti-Christian edicts, from 1573 to 1912. No index.

Mythology

❧ See also works dealing with ancient and medieval literature and folklore.

Kōzu, Harushige 高津春繁   **D47**
Girisha Rōma shinwa jiten ギリシア・ローマ神話辞典 (Dictionary of Greek and Roman mythology) Iwanami Shoten, 1960. 380p.

Briefly identifies gods and heroes, places, festivals, some literary works, etc., with entries in Japanese syllabary followed by Greek, Latin, English, German and French spellings.

Asakura, Haruhiko 朝倉治彦 **et al.**   **D48**
Shinwa densetsu jiten 神話伝説辞典 (Dictionary of myths and legends) Tokyodō, 1963. 514p.

Summarizes and gives sources and references for myths, legends, ancient tales, songs, folk beliefs. Identifies persons around whom legends have grown. Illustrated. Classified table of contents with 1,200 entries and index of 3,230 terms.

Shintō

BIBLIOGRAPHY

✿ Articles are often found in periodicals on Japanese thought, literature, history and folklore. Indexes of general nature, **A33** and others on related subjects should be consulted.

Katō, Genchi 加藤玄智　　　　　　　　**D49**
Shintō shoseki mokuroku　神道書籍目録　A bibliography of Shintō;　a collection of Shintō literature from the oldest times to 1868, arranged in chronological order.　Meiji Seitoku Kinen Gakkai, 1938.　646p.

Standard index, classified, with indication of important titles and some annotations. Title and author index. Location of manuscripts given.

Katō, Genchi 加藤玄智　　　　　　　　**D50**
Meiji Taishō Shōwa Shintō shoseki mokuroku 明治大正昭和神道書籍目録　　A bibliography of Shintō; a collection of Shintō literature from Meiji 1 (1868) till Shōwa 15 (1940). Meiji Jingū Shamusho, 1953.　707p.

Continues **D49**, listing books by titles in sections on general matters, national polity, sacred books of Shintō, shrines, rituals and worship, the question of shrines and religion, propagation of Shintō principles, and sectarian Shinto. Some entries have romanized titles and brief comments. Name, title indexes.

Saeki, Ariyoshi 佐伯有義　　　　　　　**D51**
Shintō bunrui sōmokuroku 神道分類総目録 (Classified general catalogue of Shintō) Shun'yō-dō Shoten, 1937.　868p.

Lists Japanese books and monographs to 1912 in sections on general aspects, sacred books and classics, national polity, shrines, rituals, regulations for rituals and worship, personages, biographies, literature, chivalry, and popular ethics and belief in Shintō divination. Selected list of works in foreign languages appended. Index of major works.

Okada, Yoneo 岡田米夫　　　　　　　　**D52**
Shintō bunken gaisetsu 神道文献概説 (Introduction to Shintō literature) Jinja Honchō, 1951.　222p.

Explains approaches to Shintō studies with classified list of books to 1868.　Annotated.

Kokugakuin Daigaku Toshokan　　　　**D53**
国学院大学図書館
Shintō shoseki kaisetsu mokuroku 神道書籍 解説目録 Bibliography of Shintō in Kokugakuin University Library.　1960-64.　2v.

Limited to pre-1868 books, including many not in **D49**, from the Shintō section of the collection of three generations of the Kurokawa family of Japanese classic scholars and two other collections. Romanized title and name indexes.

Kokugakuin Daigaku, Nihon Bunka　　**D54**
Kenkyūjo 国学院大学日本文化研究所
Shintō ronbun sōmokuroku 神道論文総目録 (General list of articles on Shintō) Meiji Jingū Shamusho, 1963.　755p.

Classified list of articles in 370 Japanese magazines from 1868 to 1962. Author, subject indexes. With **D50** gives coverage of most Shintō studies since 1868.

Katō, Genchi 加藤玄智 **et al.**　　　　**D55**
A bibliography of Shintō in Western languages, from the oldest times till 1952.　Meiji Jingū Shamusho, 1953.　58, 7p.

Lists 1,138 books and articles. Appendix: 80 books and articles, published between 1941-52.

DICTIONARIES

Heibonsha 平凡社　　　　　　　　　　**D56**
Shintō daijiten　神道大辞典 (Comprehensive Shintō dictionary)　1937-40.　3v.

Defines terms concerning all aspects of Shintō and identifies priests, scholars and shrines. Lists prewar shrines with national and local government support and gives details of national shrine buildings. Illustrated. For folklore and sociological aspects of Shintō, see **N62**, **N64**, **N65**.

Yamakawa, Uichi 山川鵜市　　　　　　**D57**
Jingi jiten　神祇辞典 (Shintō dictionary) Heibonsha, 1924.　828p.

Wide in range.　Analytical index.

Ogura, Kōji 小倉鏗爾　　　　　　　　　**D58**
Kokutai jingi jiten　国体神祇辞典 (Dictionary of national polity and Shintō) Kinseisha, 1940.　1781p.

Quotes scholarly opinions, many of them reflecting prewar ideas, in explaining important terms relating to the national polity, the "Imperial way", the

Japanese spirit, Shintō rituals, etc. Lists national and prefectural shrines with their deities.

Uda, Toshihiko 菟田俊彦   **D59**
Norito jiten 祝詞辞典 (Dictionary of *norito* ⌐Shintō ritual prayers⌐) Meibunsha, 1963. 16, 590p.

Divided into sections on rhetorical terms, including pillow words and pivot-words, with textual uses identified by *Kokka taikan* **G96** numbers; synonyms, giving Japanese and Chinese words of the same meanings, with examples in *norito*; meanings of special terms, with usage examples; deities, with their qualities, the festivals in which they are honored, pronunciations and reference sources; the texts of 38 classical *norito*, and miscellaneous matters, including guidance on how to compose and recite *norito*.

HANDBOOKS

Ichikawa, Toyohei 市川豊平   **D60**
Jinja jitsumu teiyō 神社実務提要 (Summary of shrine administration) Rev. and enl. ed. Jinja Shinpōsha, 1964. 263p.

Explains article by article laws and regulations governing shrines beloging to the Association of Shintō Shrines, with forms of documents for establishment, dissolution, amalgamation, etc.

Jinja Honchō 神社本庁   **D61**
Saishin Jinja Honchō kitei ruishū 最新神社本庁規程類集 (Up-to-date compilation of regulations of the Association of Shintō Shrines) 1962- . Jinja Shinpōsha, 1962- . Loose-leaf.

Covers personnel, apparel, etc.

Jingi Gakkai 神祇学会   **D62**
Jingi ni kansuru seido sahō jiten 神祇に関する制度・作法事典 (Dictionary of ceremonial matters of institutions connected with Shintō) Rev. ed. Kōbundō, 1943. 674p.

Covers prewar rituals, offerings, apparel, procedures, mourning, ancestral deities, buildings, etc. Index.

CHRONOLOGY

Uemura, Tamenori 上村為典   **D63**
Jingishi nenpyō 神祇史年表 (Chronology of Shintō history) Kobe, Hyōgo-ken Shinshokukai, 1941-44. 2v.

Covers from 660 B.C. to 1942, with a list of references for each entry and, from 1868, titles of books, with their authors, published in each year. Appended are a tabular history of shrines, genealogies, bibliography, etc.

ENSHRINED DEITIES

Satō, Saburō 佐藤三郎   **D64**
Shinsen shosaishinmei sōran 新撰諸祭神名総覧 (Comprehensive dictionary of the many enshrined deities, newly compiled) Meibunsha, 1935. 584p.

Identifies and gives the significance and associations of each Shintō deity, with etymologies and origins explained. Introductory material on the meaning of the term (*kami*) for the objects of Shintō worship and the kinds, genealogies, titles, rankings, of deities. No index. More comprehensive than Zenzō Yabe's *Shosaishinmei jiten* (Dictionary of the many enshrined deities), 1931.

Suginomori, Yoshitsugu 椙杜吉次   **D65**
Dai Nihon shinmei jisho 大日本神名辞書 (Dictionary of Japanese deities) Rev. and enl. ed. Ganshōdō, 1926. 354p.

Identifies, with quotation of references, deities enshrined with and without official ranking, those mentioned in ancient books but not enshrined and personages accorded reverence, with genealogies of deities and Imperial families. Expanded from 1912, supplement to **D69**.

SHRINES

Jinja Honchō 神社本庁   **D66**
Jinja meikan 神社名鑑   (Shrine dictionary) 1962. 959p.

Lists about 6,000 shrines, arranged by prefectures, each with a photograph and information as of 1961, including its location, prewar ranking, enshrined deity, festivals, size and type of main building, land holdings, attached shrines, treasures, names of priests, number of adherents, origin, history, etc. Some entries need verification by **D67** or **D68**.

Nihon Denpō Tsūshinsha   **D67**
日本電報通信社
Jinja taikan 神社大観 (Comprehensive survey of shrines) 1940. 872p.

Gives for each of about 5,000 shrines, arranged by prefectures and rankings, as of 1938, illustration, location, deity, observances, origin, history, special rituals and any national treasures. Guide to sectarian Shintō and charts appended. Index of shrine names.

Hinode Shinbunsha 日出新聞社   **D68**
Nihon shaji taikan 日本社寺大観 (Comprehensive survey of Japanese shrines and temples) Kyoto, 1933. 2v.

More detailed than **D66** and **D67** in historical

descriptions of about 2,000 shrines, with other information as of 1933. Illustrated. Indexes. See **D128** for temples.

D69

Fu-ken-gō sha Meiji jinja shiryō 府県郷社
明治神社誌料 (Source materials on shrines supported by local governments in the Meiji period) Meiji Jinja Shiryō Hensanjo, 1912. 3v.

Based on the officially required records kept by each shrine, gives the origins, histories, land holdings, buildings, national treasures, rankings, enshrined deities, festival dates, numbers of adherents, of about 580 shrines supported by prefectural and metropolitan governments and 3,450 supported by village and other local governments as of 1919, arranged by prefectures. For information about the deities of these shrines, see **D65.**

Nihon Denpō Tsūshinsha **D70**
日本電報通信社
Jinja kozushū 神社古図集 (Collection of old shrine pictures) 1942. 123p. 130 plates.

Contains pictures and plans of temples built before 1615, with explanations by specialists and introduction by Naokazu Miyaji.

BIOGRAPHIES

Nishida, Jūichi 西田重一 **D71**
Shintō jinmei jiten 神道人名辞典 (Dictionary of Shintō personages) Jinja Shinpōsha, 1955. 379p.

Identifies more than 3,000 priests, scholars, patriots, officials and others associated with Shintō from ancient times.

CONCORDANCES

Ōkura Seishin Bunka Kenkyūjo **D72**
大倉精神文化研究所
Shinten sakuin 神典索引 (Index of Shintō sacred books) Reprint ed. Yokohama, 1937. 396p.

Indexes names of deities, persons and places, objects and subjects in *Shinten* (Shintō sacred books), a collection in modern Japanese of the texts of the *Kojiki, Nihon shoki, Kogo shūi, Senmyō, Nakatomi no yogoto,* and extracts from other classics published in 1936 by the Ōkura Institute for Spiritual Culture.

Jingū Kōgakkan 神宮皇学館 **D73**
Rikkokushi jingi sakuin 六国史神祇索引 (Index of Shintō in the six national histories)

Uji Yamada, 1933. 539p.

Covers all Shintō references in the *Nihon shoki* and the five succeeding officially compiled national histories to 888, keyed to their texts in the two old editions (1897, 1915) of *Kokushi taikei* (Collection of Japanese historical materials), published by Keizai Zasshisha.

Buddhism

BIBLIOGRAPHY

Ono, Genmyō 小野玄妙 **D74**
Bussho kaisetsu daijiten 仏書解説大辞典 (Encyclopedic commentary on Buddhist books) Daitō Shuppansha, 1933-36. 12v.

Lists by titles some 65,500 sutras, works in series, old manuscripts and printed books, including some that have been lost, and modern books and articles published by Oct. 31, 1932, in Japanese, Chinese and European languages, each with full bibliographical information, and location.

Ōmura, Seigai 大村西崖 **and** **D75**
Nakano, Gishō 中野義照
Nihon Daizōkyō bussho kaidai 日本大蔵経
仏書解題 (Bibliographical introduction to materials in the Japanese Tripitaka) Zōkyō Shoin, 1922. 2v.

Added Japanese works not in **D81.** Lists and annotates 753 writings.

D76

Shōwa shinsan kokuyaku Daizōkyō 昭和新
纂国訳大蔵経 (Japanese translation from the Tripitaka newly edited in the Shōwa era) Commentary section: v.2, Commentary on Buddhist scriptures. Tōhō Shoin, 1930. 16,580p.

Shigeta, Kanjirō 重田勘次郎 **D77**
Kaisetsu Dai Nihon kōtei Daizōkyō 解説
大日本校訂大蔵経 (Commentary on the Japanese revised edition of the Tripitaka) Shukusatsu Daizōkyō Kankōkai, 1937. (2615p.) 12 plates.

Summarizes each of the 1,916 writings with index, notes on illustrations and biographical sketches of those who worked on the edition, known as *Shukusatsu zōkyō* (Abridged Tripitaka), popularly called Tokyo edition.

Takakusu, Junjirō 高楠順次郎 **and** **D78**
Ono, Genmyō 小野玄妙
Shōwa hōbō sōmokuroku 昭和法宝総目録

(Shōwa complete catalogue of Buddhist canons) Daizō Shuppan, 1929-34. 3v. (Taishō shinshū Daizōkyō, supp.)

Gives detailed tables of contents of 77 Japanese, Chinese and Korean editions of the Tripitaka and other compilations, listing 3,360 writings.

D79

Taishō shinshū Daizōkyō sōmokuroku 大正 新修大蔵経総目録 (Complete catalogue of the Taishō new compilation of the Tripitaka) Ed. by Junjirō Takakusu. Daizō Shuppan, 1932. 487p.

Lists, in the order of their appearance, the 3,053 writings in the comprehensive and authoritative 100v. Taishō Tripitaka, 1924-34 (being reprinted), consisting of Chinese Tripitaka and Chinese and Japanese works. Title index.

D80

Dai Nihon kōtei Daizōkyō mokuroku 大日本 校訂大蔵経目録 (Catalogue of the Japanese revised edition of the Tripitaka) Kyoto, Zōkyō Shoin, 1905. 2v.

Lists 1,621 writings based on the Korean edition of the Chinese Tripitaka, with Japanese reading marks. The edition is known as *Manji zōkyō* (Swastika Tripitaka), popularly called Kyoto edition.

D81

Dai Nihon zoku Zōkyō mokuroku 大日本続蔵 経目録 (Catalogue of supplement to the Japanese revised edition of the Tripitaka) Kyoto, Zōkyō Shoin, 1912. 34,57 leaves.

Added Chinese Buddhist works not in **D80**. Lists 1,659 writings.

Bussho Kankōkai 仏書刊行会 **D82** Dai Nihon Bukkyō zensho sōmokuroku 大日本 仏教全書総目録 (Complete catalogue of comprehensive collection of Japanese writings on Buddhism) Dai Nihon Bukkyō Zensho Hakkō-jo, 1922. 206p.

Key to texts in 160v. compilation of pre-1600 Japanese basic works on doctrines, rituals, temple histories and lives of important Buddhists. Indispensable for research on Japanese Buddhism.

D83

Kokuyaku Issaikyō sōsakuin 国訳一切経 総索引 (Index of the Tripitaka in Japanese translation) Daitō Shuppansha, 1936. 660p.

Indexes the Indian portion of the Chinese Tripitaka with Chinese characters rearranged in Japanese reading order.

Mizuno, Kōgen 水野弘元 **D84** Nanden Daizōkyō sōsakuin 南伝大蔵経 総索引 (Complete index of the Tripitaka according to the southern tradition) Nihon Gakujutsu Shinkōkai, 1960-61. 3v.

Indexes the 70v. Japanese translation of the Buddhist scriptures in Pali used in Ceylon and Southeast Asia, published 1935-41, with separate index of Pali equivalents of the Japanese entries.

Chibetto Daizōkyō Kenkyūkai **D85** 西蔵大蔵経研究会 Chibetto Daizōkyō eiin Pekin-ban sōmokuroku 西蔵大蔵経影印北京版総目録 (Complete catalogue of the Peking facsimile edition of the Tibetan Tripitaka) Kyoto, Ōtani Daigaku Toshokan, 1961. 4v.

Includes writings not in the Chinese Tripitaka. Tibetan index in v.4.

Tōhoku Daigaku Hōbungakubu **D86** 東北大学法文学部 Chibetto Daizōkyō sōmokuroku 西蔵大蔵経 総目録 (Complete catalogue of the Tibetan Tripitaka) Sendai, 1934. 2v.

Ōtani Daigaku Toshokan **D87** 大谷大学図書館 Chibetto Daizōkyō Kanjuru kandō mokuroku 西蔵大蔵経甘殊爾勘同目録 (Collated catalogue of the Bkah-hgyur of the Tibetan Tripitaka) Kyoto, 1930. 477p.

Based on the Peking edition in Ōtani University Library, notes divergences from other editions.

Ryūkoku Daigaku Toshokan **D88** 竜谷大学図書館 Bukkyōgaku kankei zasshi ronbun bunrui mokuroku 仏教学関係雑誌論文分類目録 (Classified catalogue of periodical articles concerning Buddhism) Kyoto, 1931-61. 2v.

v.1 lists some 15,000 periodical articles from 1868 to 1930 with list of periodicals cited, author and subject indexes. v.2 adds 27,000 articles pub. 1931-55. Limited to Japanese periodicals.

Butten Kenkyūkai **D89** 仏典研究会 Bukkyō ronbun sōmokuroku 仏教論文総目録 (General catalogue of articles on Buddhism) Ushio Shobō, 1931. 648,8,81p.

Similar to **D88** but lists only about 12,600 articles, classified by subject. Subject index.

Meiji Bukkyōshi Hensanjo　　**D90**
明治仏教史編纂所
Meiji nenkan Bukkyō kankei shinbun zasshi
mokuroku 明治年間仏教関係新聞雑誌
目録 (List of ⌐Japanese⌐ newspapers and
magazines concerned with Buddhism during the
Meiji period, 1868-1912) 1934. 48, 13p.

Gives publishers, editors, any sect affiliations,
objectives, foundation dates and any title changes
of over 760 publications concerned with Buddhism
in general, sects and religion in general with a
Buddhist emphasis.

Bandō, Shojun 坂東性純 **et al.**　　**D91**
A bibliography on Japanese Buddhism. Cultural
Interchange Institute for Buddhists, 1958. 13,
180p.

Lists pre-1958 works in European languages,
including some by Japanese.

Hanayama, Shinshō 花山信勝　　**D92**
Bibliography on Buddhism. Ed. by the Commemoration Committee for Prof. Shinshō Hanayama's Sixty-first Birthday. Hokuseidō, 1961.
13, 869p.

Lists by author about 5,000 books and 10,000
articles in European languages. Subject index.

Individual sects

Furukawa, Eishun 古川英俊 **and**　　**D93**
Nakamura, Kōjun 中村孝順
Nihon Tendai shūten mokuroku 日本天台宗
典目録 (Catalogue of Japanese Tendai sect
canonical works) Sakamoto-mura (Shiga Pref.),
Hieizan Senshūin, 1941. 43, 22, 260p.

Shibuya, Ryōtai 渋谷亮泰　　**D94**
Shōwa genzon Tendai shoseki sōgo mokuroku
昭和現存天台書籍総合目録 (General
catalogue of Tendai books extant in the Shōwa
period) Meibunsha, 1943. 2v.

Okada, Keishō 岡田契昌 **et al.**　　**D95**
Mikkyō shoseki mokuroku 密教書籍目録
(Catalogue of books on esoteric Buddhism)
Shingi Shingonshū Buzanha Shūmusho, 1929.
203, 42p.

Lists holdings especially on Shingon sect, in
Taishō University Library.

Chizan Gakkai 智山学会　　**D96**
Chizan gakushō chojutsu mokuroku 智山学匠
著述目録 (Bibliography of works of scholars

of the Chizan school, Shingon sect) 1935.
134, 21p.

Lists by authors and locates copies. Title index.

Komazawa Daigaku Toshokan　　**D97**
駒沢大学図書館
Shinsan Zenseki mokuroku 新纂禅籍目録
(Newly compiled bibliography of Zen books)
Rev. and enl. ed. 1962. 612, 62p.

Divided into two sections, pre-1868 and from
1868 to 1961, with brief annotations and location
of copies. List of books in Western languages
appended. Author and title indexes.

Koyama, Entai 小山円泰　　**D98**
Kōso ibunroku kaidai 高祖遺文録解題
(Annotations of the List of writings of Saint
Nichiren, 1222-1282) Minobu (Yamanashi Pref.),
Sozan Gakuin Shuppanbu, 1911. 182p.

Moriya, Kankyō 守屋貫教　　**D99**
Meiji igo Nichiren shugi chojutsu mokuroku
明治以後日蓮主義著述目録 (Bibliogra-
phy of post-1868 works on Nichiren teachings)
Risshō Daigaku, 1933. 176, 17p.

Nichirenshū Daigaku 日蓮宗大学　　**D100**
Nichirenshū shūgaku shōjo mokuroku 日蓮宗
宗学章疏目録 (Bibliography of scholarly
commentaries on teachings of the Nichiren sect)
Suharaya Shoten, 1918. 461p.

DICTIONARIES

Mochizuki, Shinkō 望月信享　　**D101**
Bukkyō daijiten 仏教大辞典 (Encyclopedic
dictionary of Buddhism) Rev. and enl. by Zen-
ryū Tsukamoto. Kyoto, Sekai Seiten Kankō
Kyōkai, 1954-63. 10v.

Standard work covering terms, writings, rites,
sects, temples, personages and all other aspects
of Buddhism, with many quotations from Buddhist
literature, illustrations, references, maps, genealogical charts and detailed Buddhist chronology
to 1954. This latest expansion of the original 1909-
31 edition retains the addenda of the 1932-36 edition
and has a supplement, v.9-10, of 1,800 new entries,
including matters related to Hinduism and biographies of Western and Indian scholars. Indexed in
Chinese and Japanese, Tibetan, Sanskrit, and Pali.
See **D117**.

Ryūkoku Daigaku 竜谷大学　　**D102**
Bukkyō daijii 仏教大辞彙 (Comprehensive

Buddhist lexicon) Reprint ed. Fuzanbō, 1935-40. 6v.

Similar in scope to **D101**, with somewhat simpler language and emphasis on interpretations of the Shin and Jōdo sects. Quotations from sources and illustrations.

Oda, Tokunō 織田得能 **D103**
Bukkyō daijiten 仏教大辞典 (Cyclopedia of Buddhism) Rev., reduced-size ed. Daizō Shuppan, 1954. 1784, 20, 110p.

Indispensable in study of Japanese literature because of richness in citations from literary classics. Index. Also useful in explaining Buddhist terms in literature are the next two dictionaries:

Kokubungaku 12shu butsugo kaishaku (Explanations of Buddhist terms in 12 Japanese literary works) Kōyūkan, 1901. 533, 4p. **D103a.**

Bukkyō jirin (Glossary on Buddhism) by Nobumasa Fujii. Meiji Shoin, 1912. 916, 64, 102p. **D103b.**

Ui, Hakuju 宇井伯寿 **D104**
Bukkyō jiten 仏教辞典 (Dictionary of Buddhism) Reprint ed. Tōsei Shuppansha, 1953. 1148p.

Notable for large number of entries and simplicity of explanations. Gives for sutras and other writings their volume and page numbers in standard collections.

Taya, Raishun 多屋頼俊 **et al.** **D105**
Bukkyōgaku jiten 仏教学辞典 (Dictionary of Buddhist studies) Kyoto, Hōzōkan, 1955. 465, 12, 58p.

Emphasizes doctrinal matters, which it explains in simple terms. Arranged under broad topics with analytical index.

Ishida, Mizumaro 石田瑞麿 **et al.** **D106**
Shin Bukkyō jiten 新仏教辞典 (New dictionary of Buddhism) Seishin Shobō, 1962. 555, 46, 22p.

Covers wide range with 3,700 entries and 3,500 cross references. List of sects, chronology and maps appended. Indexed by Chinese characters and romanized words.

Individual sects

D107
Mikkyō daijiten 密教大辞典 (Encyclopedic dictionary of esoteric Buddhism) Kyoto, Mikkyō Daijiten Kankōkai, 1931-33. 3v.

Explains the doctrines, rituals, etc. of esoteric Buddhism, and gives biographies of important personages.

Tomita, Kōjun 富田斅純 **D108**
Himitsu jirin 秘密辞林 (Esoteric Buddhism dictionary) Kaji Sekai Shisha, 1911. 1134p.

Covers the terminology, ceremonies, and biographies of the secret aspects of the Shingon sect.

Bukkyō Senmon Gakkō 仏教専門学校 **D109**
Jōdoshū jiten 浄土宗辞典 (Dictionary of the Jōdo sect) Daitō Shuppansha, 1943. 751p.

Hōzōkan 法蔵館 **D110**
Shinshū jiten 真宗辞典 (Dictionary of the Shin sect) Kyoto, 1954. 820p.

Okamura, Shūsatsu 岡村周薩 **D111**
Shinshū daijiten 真宗大辞典 (Comprehensive dictionary of the Shin sect) Reprint ed. Rokuyaon, 1963. 3v.

Covers doctrines, history, rituals, legends, biographies, and temples.

Yamada, Kōdō 山田孝道 **D112**
Zenshū jiten 禅宗辞典 (Dictionary of the Zen sect) Reprint ed. Kōyūkan, 1928. 1145p.

Explains terms and practices and gives information about temples, writings and personages, with emphasis on the Sōtō branch.

Jinbo, Nyoten 神保如天 **and** **D113**
Andō, Bun'ei 安藤文英
Zengaku jiten 禅学辞典 (Dictionary of Zen studies) Shōbō Genzō Chūkai Zensho Kankōkai, 1958. 68, 13, 1558p.

About 20,000 entries. Index of characters by strokes.

Nakagawa, Jūan 中川渋庵 **D114**
Zengo jii 禅語字彙 (Zen glossary) 2d ed., rev. by Fukuzan Imai. Morie Shoten, 1956. 711, 134p.

Nakamura, Matae 中村又衛 **D115**
Gendaigoyaku Hokke jiten 現代語訳法華辞典 (Dictionary of the modern Japanese translation of the Lotus sutra) 4th ed. Shinjinsha, 1962. 1088p.

Nichiren sect.

Shishiō Bunko 師子王文庫 **D116**
Honge shōten daijirin 本化聖典大辞林 (Dic-

tionary of Buddhist scriptures of Nichiren sect)
6th ed.   1929.   3v.

Explains about 16,000 terms in the Lotus sutra
in 16 categories.

CHRONOLOGY

Mochizuki, Shinko　望月信享　　　　**D117**
Bukkyō dainenpyō 仏教大年表 (Comprehensive chronological tables of Buddhism) 4th
ed., rev. and enl. Kyoto, Sekai Seiten Kankō
Kyōkai, 1956. 458,176p. (Bukkyō daijiten,
v.6)

Lists events in all fields of Buddhism, each
with references, from Buddha's birth to 1954 in
parallel columns for Japan, China, and India and
other countries. Tables of sects and lists of head
temples and priests appended.   Indexes.

Hashikawa, Tadashi　橋川正　　　　**D118**
Shinsen Nihon Bukkyō nenpyō 新撰日本仏
教年表 (Newly compiled chronology of Japanese Buddhism) Naigai Shuppan, 1927. 464,69p.

Extends from 522 to 1927 in columns on persons,
giving birth and death dates and achievements; on
temples and sects, with foundation dates and memo-
rable events; on writings, with compilation and
publication dates, and on such miscellaneous matters as inscriptions, art and laws. Tables of chief
temples of each sect, etc. appended. Name index.

Individual sects

Shibuya, Jigai　渋谷慈鎧　　　　**D119**
Nihon Tendaishū nenpyō 日本天台宗年表
(Chronology of the Japanese Tendai sect) Kyoto,
1938.   472p.

Lists names of head priests of Tendai temples
from 767 A.D. to 1936.

Shingonshū Buzanha Jimukyoku　　　**D120**
真言宗豊山派事務局
Shingonshū nenpyō 真言宗年表 (Chronology
of the Shingon sect) 1931. 836p.

Detailed chronology from the birth of Kōbō Daishi
(774-835) to 1931.

Fujimoto, Ryōtai　藤本了泰　　　　**D121**
Jōdoshū dainenpyō 浄土宗大年表 (Compre-
hensive chronology of the Jōdo sect) Daitō
Shuppansha, 1941. 917,49p.

Lists main events from the birth of Hōnen (1133-
1212) to 1940.

Mori, Daikyō　森大狂　　　　**D122**
Nihon Zenshū nenpyō 日本禅宗年表 (Chronology of the Japanese Zen sect) Ryuginsha,
1934.   408p.

From 1141 (birth date of Yōsai, founder of the
Japanese Rinzai sect) to 1933.

Shiraishi, Kogetsu　白石虎月　　　　**D123**
Zenshū hennenshi 禅宗編年史 (Chronologi-
cal history of the Zen sect) Yawatahama (Ehime
Pref.), Kannondō, 1937-43.   2v.

Covers China and Japan from 379 A.D. to 1387.
Sources cited for each entry.

Risshō Daigaku, Nichirenshū Shiryō　　**D124**
Hensankai 立正大学日蓮宗史料編纂会
Nichirenshū nenpyō 日蓮宗年表 (Chronology
of the Nichiren sect) 1941. 8,290,96p.

From the birth of Saint Nichiren in 1222 to 1940.

Tomiya, Nisshin　富谷日震　　　　**D125**
Nisshū nenpyō 日宗年表 (Chronology of the
Nichiren sect) Kyoto, Heirakuji Shoten, 1935.
349p.

Events of Nichiren Buddhism, listed with reference to Buddhism in general and main events of
Japanese history. Lists names of principal Nichiren
temples.

Yamada, Nisshin　山田日真　　　　**D126**
Nisshū ryūge nenpyō 日宗竜華年表 (Chronology of the Nichiren sect) Kyoto, Myōkenji,
1952.   184,64p.

Limited to Myōkenji branch.

TEMPLES

Hori, Yoshizō　堀由蔵　　　　**D127**
Dai Nihon jiin sōran 大日本寺院総覧
(Survey of Buddhist temples in Japan) Meiji
Shuppansha, 1916. 2760p.

Gives detailed historical and other data for about
71,000 temples and other structures in existence
in 1916, classified by geographical areas. Many
illustrations.

Hinode Shinbunsha　日出新聞社　　　**D128**
Nihon shaji taikan: Jiin hen 日本社寺大観
寺院編 (Comprehensive survey of Japanese
shrines and temples) Kyoto, 1933.   22,926,
182p.

Gives sect affiliations, histories, buildings, treasures, main festivals, etc. of major temples, with introductory history of Japanese Buddhist temples by Yūshō Kamuroji.

Itō, Yoshisaburō 伊藤由三郎 **D129**
Zenkoku jiin meikan 全国寺院名鑑 (Nationwide temple directory) Osaka, Zenkoku Jiin Meikan Hakkōjo, 1930. 1648p.

Lists under prefectures, giving the affiliation, address and head priest of each temple. Headquarters, Tokyo branch offices and chief temples of sects appended.

BIOGRAPHIES

Washio, Junkei 鷲尾順敬 **D130**
Nihon bukka jinmei jisho 日本仏家人名辞書 (A biographical dictionary of Japanese Buddhists) 2d ed., rev. and enl. Kōyūkan, 1911. 1267p.

Broadest work of its kind, it sketches the lives of about 6,000 priests, monks, nuns, sculptors and artists from the introduction of Buddhism to 1868, arranged by their religious names. References and many portraits. Tables and indexes. List for more recent Buddhist leaders follows:

Gendai Bukkyōka jinmei jiten (Biographical dictionary of contemporary Buddhists) 1917. 662, 12p. **D130a.**

Matsuda, Fumio 松田文雄 **D131**
Keitoku dentōroku Zensōmei sakuin 景徳伝灯録禅僧名索引 (Index to names of Zen monks in *Ching-tê ch'uan-teng-lu*) Komazawa Daigaku Toshokan, 1957. 66p. Mimeo.

Lists names of about 1,700 Zen monks of India and China whose biographies are in *Ching-tê ch'uan-teng-lu* (Ching-tê edition of the biographical record) compiled by Tao-yüan in 1004.

Ōkubo, Dōshu 大久保道舟 **D132**
Sōtōshū daikeifu 曹洞宗大系譜 (Comprehensive genealogical table of the Sōtō sect) Bukkyōsha, 1934. 339, 138p.

Lists 23,500 Sōtō Zen priests in China and Japan from Bodhi Dharma to 1932, with emphasis on Japan since 1200.

ATLASES

Ōshio, Dokusan 大塩毒山 **D133**
Indo Bukkyōshi chizu narabini sakuin 印度仏教史地図並索引 (Historical atlas of

Indian Buddhism and index) Daiyūkaku, 1938. 2v.

Ōshio, Dokusan 大塩毒山 **D134**
Shina Bukkyōshi chizu narabini sakuin 支那仏教史地図並索引 (Historical atlas of Chinese Buddhism and index) Daiyūkaku, 1938. 2v.

SCULPTURES OF BUDDHA

❧ Iconography included under arts, see **E45-E47.**

CONCORDANCES

→ **D83, D84**

D135
Taishō shinshū Daizōkyō sakuin: Agonbu, mokurokubu, Hokkebu 大正新修大蔵経索引 阿含部 目録部 法華部 (Index to Taishō new compilation of the Tripitaka: Agomas section, catalogue section, Lotus sutra section) Tokyo, Taishō Issaikyō Kankōkai, 1940-47. 3v.

Kawakami, Kozan 川上弧山 **D136**
Yōbun shōroku Daizōkyō sakuin 要文抄録大蔵経索引 (Index of key words in the Tripitaka, with excerpts) Kyoto, Daizōkyō Sakuin Kankōkai, 1927-28. 3v.

Lists words and quotes passages in which they are used, each with identification. Indexes, commentaries, etc. appended. Based on the Ōbaku adition Tripitaka, 1669-81.

Ōshima, Chūtarō 大島仲太郎 **D137**
Myōhō Rengekyō sakuin 妙法蓮華経索引 (Index of the Lotus sutra) Kyoto, Heirakuji Shoten, 1941. 148, 10p.

Nakamura, Hajime 中村元 **D138**
Bukkyōgo hōyaku jiten 仏教語邦訳辞典 (Dictionary of Buddhist terms translated into Japanese) Tokyo Daigaku Kyōzai Kumiai, 1947. 23, 499p.

Alphabetical list of technical terms related to Buddhism found in Japanese classics and poems, with translation into colloquial Japanese; sources cited.

Katō, Shūkō 加藤宗厚 **D139**
Shōbō genzō yōgo sakuin 正法眼蔵要語索引 (Concordance of the *Shōbō genzō*) Risōsha, 1962-63. 2v.

Lists some 15,000 words in *Shōbō genzō* (Eye of the righteous law), major work of Dōgen (1200-53), giving the textual context of each and its page in the Iwanami Bunko edition. Index of hard-to-read words and table collating the Iwanami Bunko paging with that in the reduced-size Honzan edition appended.

❧ The following three are similar concordances of works of Nichiren, 1222-1282.

Asai, Yōrin 浅井要麟 **D140**
Shōwa shinshū Nichiren Shōnin ibun zenshū 昭和新修日連聖人遺文全集 (Shōwa new compilation of the complete works of Saint Nichiren) Supp. Index. Reprint ed. Kyoto, Heiraku-ji Shoten, 1956. 700p.

Risshō Daigaku, Nichiren Kyōgaku Kenkyūjo 立正大学日蓮教学研究所 **D141**
Shōwa teihon Nichiren Shōnin zenshū 昭和定本日蓮聖人全集 (Shōwa authorized version of the complete works of Saint Nichiren) v.4, General index. Minobu (Yamanashi Pref.), 1959. 298,48,35p.

Satomi Nihon Bunkagaku Kenkyūjo 里見日本文化学研究所 **D142**
Nichiren Shōnin ibun sakuin 日蓮聖人遺文索引 (Index to writings of Saint Nichiren) Kyoto, Satomi Seishin Bunka Kenkyūjo, 1932. 505p.

SANSKRIT STUDIES

Maruyama, Tatsuon 丸山達音 **D143**
Darani jiten 陀羅尼辞典 (Dharani dictionary) Rev. ed. Morie Sashichi, 1898. 2,3,149 leaves.
Introduction to terms in the Dharani in the Siddham script.

Kawakatsu, Masatarō 川勝政太郎 **D144**
Bonji kōwa 梵字講話 (Lectures on Sanskrit) 2d ed. Kyoto, Kawahara Shobō, 1946. 134p.
Not a study of Sanskrit in the modern sense, but an introduction to the Siddham script.

❧ For Sanskrit and Pali language dictionaries, see **F124, F125**.

Christianity

BIBLIOGRAPHY

Kirisutokyō Shigakkai 基督教史学会 **D145**
Nihon Kirisutokyōshi kankei Wa-kanjo mokuroku 日本基督教史関係和漢書目録 Bibliotheca christiana japonica; catalogue of books and manuscripts relating to the early Christian mission in Japan, 1590-1890. Bunkōdō Shoten, 1954. 129p.
Lists about 1,700 monographs (Chinese books limited to those which influenced Japanese Christianity) from the first introduction in 1550 to 1890, classified by Catholic, Orthodox, Protestant, and related history. Gives location of titles in libraries. Bibliographical study included in the preface.

Ebisawa, Arimichi 海老沢有道 **D146**
Christianity in Japan; a bibliography of Japanese and Chinese sources. International Christian University, 1960. In progress.
Pt.1 covers 1543-1858. Lists 3,648 items with some notes and locations of MSS.

Yoshida, Tora 吉田寅 **D147**
Tōyō kirisutokyōshi kenkyū ronbun mokuroku kō 東洋基督教史研究論文目録稿 (Preliminary bibliography on Oriental history of Christianity) Ajiashi Kenkyūkai, 1955. 16p. Mimeo.
Covers Nestorianism, pre-18th century Catholicism, and modern Christianity. Lists articles chronologically by date of publication.

Aoyama Gakuin Daigaku Majima Kinen Toshokan 青山学院大学間島記念図書館 **D148**
Meijiki Kirisutokyō kankei tosho mokuroku 明治期基督教関係図書目録 (Catalogue of books on Christianity in the Meiji period) 1954. 119p. Mimeo.
A special collection of 2,064 books, in the Aoyama Gakuin University Library.

Nihon Shingakkō 日本神学校 **D149**
Kirisutokyō bunken karimokuroku 基督教文献仮目録 (Preliminary bibliography on Christianity, 1838-1897) 1932. 126p.

Ebisawa, Arimichi 海老沢有道 **D150**
Kirishitan tenseki sōkō 切支丹典籍叢考

(Studies on early Christian books in Japan) Takubundō, 1943.   261p.

Surveys Japanese books first printed by the Portuguese Jesuits and other early Christian literature, with discussion of their cultural and religious significance.   Bibliography.   Title and name index.

Ebisawa, Arimichi 海老沢有道 **and** **D151**
Sukeno, Kentarō　助野健太郎
Kirishitanshi bunken kaidai キリシタン史 文献解題 (Annotated bibliography on history of early Christianity in Japan) Yokohama, Kirisutokyō Shigakkai, 1955. 50p. (Kirishitan kenkyū series, 2)

Lists Japanese and foreign books, including Japanese translations, classified as source materials, histories, biographies and other forms.

Doi, Tadao 土居忠雄　　　　　**D152**
Kirishitan bunken kō 吉利支丹文献考 (Bibliographical studies on early Christianity in Japan) Sanseidō, 1963.   15,426p.

Collection of 17 articles on historical materials, with many references to relevant literature. Indexes of titles, subjects, sources of quotations, and terms in European languages.

Kokuritsu Kokkai Toshokan　　　**D153**
　国立国会図書館
Nichi-Ō bunka kōshō bunken mokuroku 日欧 文化交渉文献目録 (Bibliography on cultural relations between Japan and Europe) Katorikku Bunka Kyōkai, 1949.   86p.

Classified catalogue of 589 books and manuscripts on St. Francis Xavier, early Christianity in Japan and related subjects, including bibliographies and catalogues, from the Oriental Library, Sophia University Library and other collections exhibited in commemoration of the 400th anniversary of Xavier's arrival in Japan.   Locates copies.   Author index.

DICTIONARIES

Jōchi Daigaku 上智大学　　　　**D154**
Katorikku daijiten カトリック大辞典 (Encyclopedia of Catholicism) Fuzanbō, 1952-60.   5v.

Explains in detail history, doctrines, dogmas, organization, literature, etc. of Catholicism, including that in Japan, with references for each entry and supplemental references in v.5. Indexes of names and subjects in European languages, Japanese and Chinese names, Mohammedanism, canons and decrees.   First published in 1940 in cooperation with Herder publishing house of Germany.

Kobayashi, Yoshio 小林珍雄　　　**D155**
Kirisutokyō hyakka jiten キリスト教百科 事典 (Encyclopedia of Christianity) Enderle Shoten, 1960.   1914p.

Concisely explains terms, including those in **D158**, liturgical matters and objects, etc. and identifies persons associated with early and present-day Christianity in Japan.   Many illustrations.

Nihon Kirisutokyō Kyōgikai　　　**D156**
　日本基督教協議会
Kirisutokyō daijiten キリスト教大事典 (Cyclopedia of Christianity) Kyōbunkan, 1963. 11, 1204, 242p.

Scholarly coverage from the Protestant viewpoint of about 10,000 terms, persons, places and writings, with references. Chronology of Christianity to 1963, illustrations and maps appended.   Indexes of names and subjects in European languages.

Takagi, Jintarō 高木壬太郎　　　**D157**
Kirisutokyō daijiten 基督教大辞典 (Comprehensive dictionary of Christianity)   Enl. ed. Keiseisha Shoten, 1951.   1542p.

About 3,000 entries on denominations, doctrines, dogmas, terms, liturgy, writings, persons and places. Chronology of church history from 81 A.D. to 1910 appended.   Classified index and index of European terms.

Kobayashi, Yoshio 小林珍雄　　　**D158**
Kirisutokyō yōgo jiten キリスト教用語辞典 (Glossary of Christianity) Tokyodo, 1960.   464p.

Lists basic terms in their original languages, giving Japanese equivalents, and then rearranges in syllabic order the Japanese terms relating to theology, dogma, the church calendar, canons, etc., with explanations.   Illustrations.   Church organization chart, chronology of church history and Japanese-Chinese glossary of Catholic terms appended.

YEARBOOKS

D159
Kirisutokyō nenkan 基督教年鑑 (Yearbook of Christianity) 1948- .   Comp. by Kirisuto Shinbunsha.   1948- .   9v.   Biennial.

Surveys trends in Japan and gives statistics and directories.

D160
Nihon Kirisuto Kyōdan nenkan 日本基督教団 年鑑 (Yearbook of United Church in Japan)

1943- . Comp. by Nihon Kirisuto Kyōdan. 1943, 1948- . 18v.

Includes directories of churches, missions and committee members of the United Church and statistics of each church district.

BIBLE

Bibliography

Nihon Shin'yaku Gakkai 日本新約学会 **D161**
Nihon ni okeru Shin'yaku bunken 日本における新約文献 (Japanese New Testament studies) Tokyo Shingaku Daigaku, 1961. 36, 17p. Mimeo.

Lists books, including translations, in two sections, from 1868 to 1944 and from 1945 to 1960, with supplementary list of 1946-60 articles in 15 periodicals.

Yamaya, Seigo 山谷省吾 **D162**
Shin'yaku Seisho kaidai 新約聖書解題 (Bibliographical studies of the New Testament) Shinkyō Shuppansha, 1948. 341p.

Surveys Japanese literature on selected topics in books of the New Testament. Subject index.

Dictionaries

Nichiyō Sekaisha 日曜世界社 **D163**
Seisho daijiten 聖書大辞典 (Comprehensive dictionary of the Bible) Enl. ed. Shinkyō Shuppansha, 1961. 1423, 78p.

Explains about 4,500 Bible terms, with maps and illustrations. Appended are comparative tables of the Four Gospels and chronology of the Old and New Testaments. Has useful bibliographical introduction and survey of Bible studies. Indexes of Japanese and English terms and key words of chapter headings and paragraphs.

Aiura, Tadao 相浦忠雄 **et al.** **D164**
Seisho jiten 聖書事典 (Dictionary of the Bible) Nihon Kirisuto Kyōdan, 1961. 1032p.

Briefly explains about 4,000 terms, with introductory survey of Bible philosophy, history and archaeology, the Apocrypha and pseudepigrapha. Illustrations.

Tokiwa, Takaoki 常葉隆興 **et al.** **D165**
Seisho jiten 聖書辞典 (Dictionary of the Bible) Inochi no Kotobasha, 1961. 825, 29, 41p.

Explains briefly subjects and terms. Chronological table, list of names of persons and maps appended. Index.

Shinkyō Shuppansha 新教出版社 **D166**
Seisho shinjiten 聖書新辞典 (New dictionary of the Bible) 1957. 681p.

Explains about 2,700 terms. Appended are an introduction to the Bible, chronology, comparative tables and maps.

Handbook

Halley, Henry Hampton **D167**
Seisho handobukku 聖書ハンドブック (Bible handbook) Tr. and ed. by Shinkyō Shuppansha. Sendai, Seisho Tosho Kankōkai, 1953. 742p.

Translation of *Pocket Bible handbook*, 19th ed., 1952, giving simple outline of the Bible, in which recent archaeological finds are cited, to which have been added a history of Protestantism in Japan and list of Japanese translations of the Bible. Index.

Concordances

Nihon Kirisutokyō Kyōgikai **D168**
日本基督教協議会
Seisho goku daijiten 聖書語句大辞典 (Comprehensive dictionary of Biblical terms) Kyōbunkan, 1959. 1641p.

Lists in Japanese syllabic order about 200,000 words and phrases in the 1955 New Testament and 1958 Old Testament editions published by the Nihon Seisho Kyōkai, with equivalents in original languages. Index of Hebrew and Armenian terms in Old Testament and index of Greek terms in New Testament, both with Japanese equivalents.

Shinkyō Shuppansha 新教出版社 **D169**
Konkorudansu コンコルダンス (Concordance) 1957. 524p.

Indexes literary and colloquial Japanese translations of the Old and New Testaments, with separate section on persons, places and weights and measures.

Yūki, Chōji 結城長治 **D170**
Kōgo Shin'yaku Seisho goku sakuin 口語新約聖書語句索引 (Concordance of New Testament in colloquial translation) Budō no Ki Shoen, 1958. 728p.

Kurosaki, Kōkichi 黒崎幸吉 **D171**
Shin'yaku Seisho goku sakuin 新約聖書語句索引 : 和一希 (Concordance of New Testament) Japanese-Greek. Kobe, Eien no Seimeisha, 1953. 1063p.

Kurosaki, Kōkichi 黒 崎 幸 吉. **D172**
Shin'yaku Seisho goku sakuin 新 約 聖 書 語 句
索 引 ： 希 一 和 (Concordance of New Testament) Greek-Japanese. Kobe, Seisenkai, 1955.
892p.

Tsukamoto, Toraji 塚 本 虎 二 **D173**
Fukuinsho idō ichiran 福 音 書 異 同 一 覧
(Summary of differences in the Gospels) Itō
Setsu Shobō, 1954.   392p.

39

FINE ARTS

❧ Covers fine arts in general, sculpture, painting, music, drama and such applied arts as physical culture, photography and printing. Related materials will be found in history, literature and other subject fields. Listing of illustrated publications is limited to those which are general or comprehensive.

GENERAL WORKS

BIBLIOGRAPHY

Nihon Gakujutsu Kaigi 日本学術会議 **E1**
Bunkakei bunken mokuroku. XI: Bigaku hen
文化系文献目録 XI: 美学編 (Bibliography of literature, philosophy and history. XI: Aesthetics) 1961. 148p.

Classified listing of 1945-59 Japanese books and articles on aesthetics, literature, music, art, motion pictures and drama.

DICTIONARIES

Kawade Shobō 河出書房 **E2**
Sekai bijutsu daijiten 世界美術大辞典
(Comprehensive dictionary of world art) 1954-56. 4v.

About 4,000 entries cover subjects, terms, artists and works, with many illustrations and references. Detailed accounts under nations and periods, with subdivisions. Chronology from 3200 B.C. to 1955. Name and subject indexes.

Kurata, Saburō 倉田三郎 **et al.** **E3**
Zōkei kyōiku daijiten 造形教育大辞典
(Comprehensive dictionary of formative arts education) Fumaidō, 1954-57. 6v.

About 20,000 entries on art and handicraft education simply explained. List of national treasures and chronology of world art history appended. General index, foreign-language index and index of difficult characters.

Takiguchi, Shuzō 滝口修造 **et al.** **E4**
Gendai bijutsu jiten 現代美術事典 (Contemporary art dictionary) Hakuyōsha, 1952. 440p.

Illustrated survey of painting, sculpture, industrial arts, architecture, stage settings, commercial arts, photography, design and costume, with chronological table and bibliography appended. General index and indexes of persons, technical terms and illustrations.

Takeuchi, Toshio 竹内敏雄 **E5**
Bigaku jiten 美学事典 (Dictionary of aesthetics) Kōbundō, 1961. 518p.

Divided into sections on general aesthetics, history of art theories, aesthetic systems, science of the fine arts, musicology, science of literature, theater, cinema and art education. Subject and name indexes.

CHRONOLOGY

→ E2, v.4

Zōkei Kyōiku Kenkyūkai **E6**
造形教育研究会
Sekai bijutsu nenpyō 世界美術年表 (World art chronology) Fumaidō, 1956. 236p.

Gives important events by years from 20,000 B.C. to 1956 in parallel columns for Japan and, in lesser detail, the rest of the world, with those of unknown dates listed at the end of each century. General index.

Nakamura, Ryōhei 中村亮平 **E7**
Taishō Sekai bijutsu nenpyō 対照世界美術年表 (Comparative chronology of world art) Unsōdō, 1938. 410p.

Lists artists and art critics, their achievements, works of art, buildings, etc. from 4500 B.C. to 1937. Bibliography of art chronologies appended. Index of names and subjects.

COLLECTIONS

Heibonsha 平凡社 **E8**
Sekai bijutsu zenshū 世界美術全集 (Collection of world art) 1953-55. 29v.

Color and monochrome photographs show representative works from ancient times to the present arranged by periods and countries, in volumes averaging about 200 pages, each with text on periods, schools of art, concepts and a bibliography. General index. There is a 30v. popular edition in which the bibliographies are cumulated in a separate volume.

Kadokawa Shoten 角川書店 **E9**
Sekai bijutsu zenshū 世界美術全集 (Collection of world art) 1960- . 32v. In progress.

To be completed in 40v. v.1-11, Japan; v.12-17, China; v.18, Korea; v.19, India; v.20-22, the Orient; v.23, Folk arts; v.24, America; v.25-37, Europe; v.38, Postwar world art; v.39, World art manual; Supp. vol., Postwar Japanese art. Color and monochrome illustrations with brief explanations.

Zayūhō Kankōkai 座右宝刊行会 **E10**
Gendai Sekai bijutsu zenshū 現代世界美術全集 (Collection of modern world art) Kawade Shobō, 1953. 12v.

Color and black-and-white gravure plates of representative works, with lives of artists and lists of references.

Kōdansha 講談社 **E11**
Sekai bijutsu taikei 世界美術大系 (World art collection) 1961- . 26v. In progress.

Each volume devoted to a region or nation, including Africa and Indonesia, except for v.1, on primitive art, and v.24, on contemporary art. To be completed in 29v., with illustrated dictionary of art history, regional and historical art maps and sections on architecture and design.

Occident

Imaizumi, Atsuo 今泉篤男 **and** **E12**
Yamada, Chisaburō 山田智三郎
Seiyō bijutsu jiten 西洋美術辞典 (Diction-

ary of Western art) Tokyodō, 1954. 782p.

Explains some 3,800 topics in popular terms. Lists of names of colors, including English and French terms; galleries and museums; monographs and periodicals specializing in art history; and an outline history of Western architecutre, sculpture and painting, etc. appended. Indexes of names and technical terms and subjects.

Uchida, Iwao 内田巌 **et al.** **E13**
Kindai bijutsu jiten 近代美術事典 (Dictionary of modern art) Hakuyōsha, 1950. 282p.

Emphasis is on 19th century European painting, sculpture and architecture, with introductory outline history, 1748-1947 chronology and genealogies of schools of art. Persons, technical terms and schools indexed.

Orient

Bijutsu Kenkyūjo 美術研究所 **E14**
Tōyō bijutsu bunken mokuroku 東洋美術文献目録 (Bibliography of Oriental art) Literature on old art published in periodicals. Zayūhō Kankōkai, 1941-54. 4v.

Classifies articles on pre-1868 Oriental art, extending as far as Central Asia and Iran, in more than 500 Japanese periodicals from 1868 to 1935. Supplemented by two volumes (Title page title: Tōyō kobijutsu bunken mokuroku) bringing the coverage from 1936 to 1950. There is a separate list of periodicals cited in the main volume with library locations as of 1935.

Noma, Seiroku 野間清六 **and** **E15**
Tani, Shin'ichi 谷信一
Bijutsu kantei jiten 美術鑑定事典 (Art appraisal dictionary) Tokyodō, 1963. 406p.

Illustrated guide to judgment of paintings, prints, sculpture, calligraphy, lacquer ware, swords, ceramics and other Oriental art works. Artists' seals, rankings of artists, genealogies of schools, etc. appended. Indexes of names, illustrations and seals.

JAPAN

BIBLIOGRAPHY

❋ For current bibliographical information, **A7-A36** are useful; see also **E34** and the following:

Bijutsu nenkan (Fine arts yearbook), annual supplement of the magazine *Bijutsu techō* (Fine arts notebook), published by Bijutsu Techōsha. **E16**.

INDEX

Kokka sakuin 国華索引 (Kokka index) No. **E17**
1-753. Kokkasha, 1956. 424p.

Classified index of illustrations, articles and notes in 753 issues, 1889-1954, of the authoritative magazine *Kokka*, devoted to Japanese painting, sculpture, architecture, crafts and calligraphy.

DICTIONARIES

Noma, Seiroku 野間清六 **and** **E18**
Tani, Shin'ichi 谷信一
Nihon bijutsu jiten 日本美術辞典 (Dictionary of Japanese art) Rev. ed. Tokyodō, 1958. 726p.

About 5,500 entries, with 630 plates, Outline of Japanese and related Oriental art and art history appended. Indexes of persons, terms and subjects, schools, and era names.

Ikeda, Tsunetarō 池田常太郎 **E19**
Nihon shoga kottō daijiten 日本書画骨董大辞典 (Cyclopedia of calligraphy, painting and curios) 7th ed. enl. Seikōkan, 1935. 1697, 364p.

Gives biographical sketches of calligraphers and artists arranged by pseudonyms. Curios are arranged by kinds. Includes some Chinese art objects. Chronology from early times to 1935. Indexed by characters.

HANDBOOK

Okudaira, Hideo 奥平英雄 **E20**
Nihon bijutsu benran 日本美術便覧 (Handbook of Japanese art) Bijutsu Shuppansha, 1952. 355p.

Sections on painting, calligraphy, sculpture, crafts and architecture give outline histories, lists of artists arranged chronologically by schools and explanations of terms. Directory of shrines, temples, castles and other old structures, genealogies of artists, chronology, etc. appended. Index.

CHRONOLOGY

Kobayashi, Takeshi 小林剛 **and** **E21**
Fujita, Tsuneyo 藤田経世
Nihon bijutsushi nenpyō 日本美術史年表 (Chronology of Japanese art history) Sōgensha, 1952. 316, 72p. (Sōgen sensho, 228)

Records some 3,000 art works and events from 1

A.D. to 1952, with parallel notes on developments in politics, culture and foreign arts. Detailed indexes.

Minamoto, Toyomune 源豊宗 **E22**
Nihon bijutsushi nenpyō 日本美術史年表 (Chronology of Japanese art history) Kyoto, Hoshino Shoten, 1940. 290p.

Parallel columns list art objects, artists, and art and historical events from 160 B.C. to 1939. Genealogies, table of death dates of poet monks of the five Zen temples, etc. appended. Index includes owners of art objects. Companion volumes are the same author's *Nihon bijutsushi* (History of Japanese art), 1930, and *Nihon bijutsushi zuroku* (Illustrated history of Japanese art), 1932, the latter translated into English in 1935.

BIOGRAPHIES

E23
Bijutsujin Nenkan 美術人年鑑 (Artists' yearbook) 1951- . Comp. by Nihon Bijutsu Shinkōkai. Bijutsu Hyōronsha, 1950, 1958- . 6v.

Gives works, awards, memberships in organizations and brief biographies under names of painters, sculptors, industrial artists and calligraphers. Directories of museums, organizations, schools, art critics and art dealers appended. Index.

E24
Bijutsuka meikan 美術家名鑑 (Artists' who's who) 1956- . Comp. by Tōru Shimizu. Bijutsu Kurabu, 1956- . 9v. Annual.

Former title: *Gendai bijutsuka meikan.* 1917-55.

Gives organization memberships, awards, brief biographies and works, with prices, of contemporary painters, sculptors, industrial artists and calligraphers. List of deceased artists, genealogies of schools and chronology appended. Classified index of names.

Shimizu, Tōru 清水澄 **E25**
Koshoga jinmei jiten 古書画人名辞典 (Biographical dictionary of old calligraphers and painters) Bijutsu Kurabu, 1954. 399p.

Gives the real names, birthplaces, brief personal records, chief works and death dates of calligraphers and artists from the 7th century to the 19th, listed by their commonly known names. List of different persons of the same name, glossary of technical terms, etc. appended.

Kobayashi, Tsutomu 小林勉 **E26**
Kokon Nihon shoga meika zenden 古今日本書画名家全伝 (Biographies of old and new

masters of Japanese calligraphy and painting) Nishōdō, 1931. 401, 343p.

Describes in detail the lives and works of some 3,600 from the 8th century to the present, with history of calligraphy in China and Japan. Genealogies and signatures and seals appended.

COLLECTIONS

Tokyo Kokuritsu Hakubutsukan　　**E27**
東京国立博物館
Nihon bijutsu zenshū　日本美術全集　Pageant of Japanese art.　Tōto Bunka Kōeki Kabushiki Kaisha, 1953.　6v.
v.1-2, Paintings; v.3, Sculpture; v.4, Ceramics and metalwork; v.5, Textile and lacquer; v.6, Architecture and gardens.　Mainly black and white illustrations, a few in color, with brief explanations at end of each volume.

Tanaka, Ichimatsu　田中一松　**E28**
Nihon bijutsu taikei　日本美術大系　(Outline of Japanese art)　Kōdansha, 1959-61.　11v.
Shows and comments on representative works in architecture, sculpture, painting (3v.), ceramics, lacquer ware, textiles and dyeing, and metalwork from ancient times to 1912, with separate volume on recent art.　v.11 gives a general survey, chronology and indexes of objects by artists and owners.

Tazawa, Yutaka　田沢坦　**and**　**E29**
Ōoka, Minoru　大岡実
Zusetsu Nihon bijutsushi　図説日本美術史　(Illustrated history of Japanese art)　Iwanami Shoten, 1957.　2v.
Text, with supplementary illustrations (v.1), keyed to 293 pages of small plates arranged chronologically from ancient times to 1868 (v.2), with locations indicated.　Special section on Buddhist art.

Imaizumi, Atsuo　今泉篤男　**et al.**　**E30**
Kindai Nihon bijutsu zenshū　近代日本美術全集　(Modern Japanese art collection)　Tōto Bunka Kōeki Kabushiki Kaisha, 1953-55.　6v.
Covers the period from 1868 to date.　Mainly black and white illustrations, a few in color, with brief explanations at end of each volume.

Zayūhō Kankōkai　座右宝刊行会　**E31**
Gendai Nihon bijutsu zenshū　現代日本美術全集　(Contemporary Japanese art collection)　Kadokawa Shoten, 1955-56.　10v.
Color and black-and-white reproductions of representative works of leading post-1868 painters, with comments and brief biographies.

Tanaka, Toyotarō　田中豊太郎　**E32**
Mingei zukan　民芸図鑑　(Pictorial book of folk art)　Hōbunkan, 1960-63.　3v.
Shows and explains objects made to 1900 in various parts of Japan and selected pieces from the Japan Folk Art Museum.　Many illustrations in color.

YEARBOOKS

E33
Bijutsu nenkan　美術年鑑　(Art yearbook) 1957- .　Comp. by Bijutsu Shuppansha.　1957- .　8v.
Surveys events and trends in Western-style painting, Japanese painting, sculpture, architecture, design, crafts and photography, with reproductions of outstanding works, reports on art circles abroad, list of major exhibitions, obituaries and directories of organizations and artists.

E34
Nihon bijutsu nenkan　日本美術年鑑　(Japan art yearbook) 1936- .　Comp. by Tokyo Kokuritsu Bunkazai Kenkyūjo Bijutsubu.　1936-49, 1952- .　22v.
Shows important works of the previous year in painting, sculpture, crafts and architecture, chronicles exhibits and other events and lists obituaries, bibliography, laws and regulations relating to art and directories of institutions, organizations, artists and others in art circles.

Cultural properties

Monbushō　文部省　**E35**
Nihon kokuhō zenshū　日本国宝全集　(Complete collection of Japanese national treasures)　Nihon Kokuhō Zenshū Kankōkai, 1924-39.　84v.
Photographs of 1,860 paintings, sculptures, buildings and other works designated by the Government as national treasures before 1939, with detailed descriptions.

Bunkazai Hogo Iinkai　　**E36**
文化財保護委員会
Maizō bunkazai yōran　埋蔵文化財要覧　(Handbook of buried cultural properties)　Yoshikawa Kōbunkan, 1957- .　3v.　In progress.
Lists excavations by prefectures, discoveries of sites and state-owned properties, with photographs, descriptions and references.

Bunkazai Hogo Iinkai　　**E37**
文化財保護委員会
Shitei bunkazai sōgō mokuroku　指定文化財

総合目録 (Union catalogue of registered cultural properties) Ōkurashō Insatsukyoku, 1958. 3v.

Lists works of fine and applied arts, structures, monuments, ethnographic materials and skills registered as of 1958 under the Law for Protection of Cultural Properties, classified by prefectures, with registration dates, names of owners and other information. Standards for national treasures and important cultural properties appended. Classified indexes. Supplemented by serial publications: *Kokuhō mokuroku* (Catalogue of national treasures), 1951- . 17v.; *Jūyō bunkazai mokuroku* (Catalogue of important cultural properties), 1951- . 22v.; and *Kinenbutsu mukei bunkazai minzoku shiryō mokuroku* (Catalogue of monuments, ethnographic materials and skills), 1959- . 6v. Former title: Kinenbutsu mokuroku.

Bunkazai Hogo Iinkai   **E38**
文 化 財 保 護 委 員 会

Shinshitei jūyō bunkazai zusetsu 新指定重要 文 化 財 図 説 (Newly designated important cultural properties, illustrated) 1955- . 5v. In progress.

Shows and describes works registered since 1951.

Bunkazai Hogo Iinkai   **E39**
文 化 財 保 護 委 員 会

Kokuhō zuroku 国 宝 図 録 (Illustrated catalogue of national treasures) Bunkazai Kyōkai, 1952-61. 7v.

Shows and comments on paintings, sculptures, calligraphic and historical documents, craft works and buildings registered from 1951 to 1955 under the Cultural Properties Protection Law. There is an abridged English edition, titled *National treasures of Japan, 1952-62.* 6v.

Bunkazai Hogo Iinkai   **E40**
文 化 財 保 護 委 員 会

Kokuhō jiten 国 宝 事 典 (Cyclopedia of national treasures) Kyoto, Benridō, 1961. 495, 12p.

Photographs and descriptions of 735 paintings and other objects and 196 buildings registered as of Dec. 1, 1960, with dimensions, locations and other information. The text is based on **E39**. Supplement adds registrations to Mar., 1961. Glossary, chronological table of production dates, catalogue classifying objects by areas and owners, and location map appended. Indexes of terms, owners, artists and names of treasures.

SCULPTURE

Sawayanagi, Daigorō   沢 柳 大 五 郎   **E41**
Zusetsu Seiyō Chōkoku nenpyō 図 説 西 洋 彫 刻 年 表 (Illustrated chronology of Western sculpture) Seibundō Shinkōsha, 1959. 390p.

Compilation of small photographs arranged chronologically by schools with names, dates, materials, sizes, locations and background information. Table of Egyptian dynasties, lists of sculptors classified by countries and maps appended. Indexes of sculptors, shrines and sanctuaries.

Kuno, Takeshi   久 野 健   **E42**
Nihon no chōkoku 日 本 の 彫 刻 (Japanese sculpture) Yoshikawa Kōbunkan, 1959. 166p.

Photographs show about 200 representative works from the end of the 6th century to the present, with outline history of Japanese sculpture and section on regional aspects of sculpture. Chronology to 1956, illustrations of special features of Buddhist statues and notes on the techniques of making them appended. Glossary index of technical terms.

Ueno, Naoteru   上 野 直 昭 **and**   **E43**
Sakamoto, Manshichi   坂 本 万 七
Nihon chōkoku zuroku 日 本 彫 刻 図 録 (Japanese sculpture, illustrated) Asahi Shinbunsha, 1957. 70, 95p. 144 plates.

Chronological arrangement of photographs of excavated clay figures to the 7th century and Buddhist images to the 12th century, with text explaining the characteristics and techniques of each period.

Buddhist statues

Sawa, Takaaki   佐 和 隆 研   **E44**
Butsuzō zuten 仏 像 図 典 (Iconography of Buddhist images) Yoshikawa Kōbunkan, 1962. 294p.

Useful in study and appreciation of Buddhist art, assembling illustrations of images in Japan, including line drawings in Keijū's 11th century *Zuzōshō* (Selection of drawings of images), classified under Buddha, Goddess of Mercy, saints, messengers, other divinities and high priests, each with explanation of its name and symbolism. Iconographic manual of images registered as national treasures and important cultural properties appended. There is an abridged version, without iconographic explanations but including guide to old temples and list of Sanskrit titles of Buddha as follows:

Butsuzō annai (Guide to Buddhist images), ed. by Takaaki Sawa. Yoshikawa Kōbunkan, 1963. 2, 6, 319p. **E44a.**

Iwanami Shoten 岩波書店 **E45**
Butsuzō ikonogurafii 仏像イコノグラフィー
(Buddhist images: iconography) 1951. 64p.
(Iwanami shashin bunko)

Guide to appreciation, with examples and brief
explanations of the religious significance of images
of Buddha, under Nyorai, Bosatsu, Myōō and Ten.

Kimura, Shōshū 木村小舟 **E46**
Nihon butsuzō zusetsu 日本仏像図説 (Illustrated Japanese Buddhist images) newly compiled. Nihon Butsuzō Zusetsu Kankōkai, 1952.
443p.

Groups important images in eight categories, with
simple question-and-answer explanations. Catalogue of images in the Osaka-Kyoto region designated national treasures by 1927 appended.

E47
Shōwa shinsan kokuyaku Daizōkyō 昭和新纂
国訳大蔵経 (Japanese translation from the
Tripitaka newly edited in the Showa era) Commentary section: v.1, Buddhist images iconography. Tōhō Shoin, 1930. 265p.

Explains religious significances of images with
illustrations.

PAINTING

Occident

E48
Kindai kaiga jiten 近代絵画事典 (Dictionary
of modern painting) Tr. by Jun Ehara and others.
Kinokuniya Shoten, 1960. 339p.

Translation of F. Hazan's *Dictionnaire de la pein-
ture moderne*, 1954, with some 240 entries on painters, schools and other matters concerned primarily
with the École de Paris from the Impressionist
period to World War II. Color plates. Index of persons and subjects.

Miwa, Fukumatsu 三輪福松 **E49**
Zusetsu Seiyō kaiga nenpyō 図説西洋絵画
年表 (Pictorial chronology of Western painting) Seibundō Shinkōsha, 1958. 360p.

About 2,000 photographs of paintings from ancient
times to the present arranged chronologically. List
of 129 significant Western paintings in Japan, table
of Egyptian dynasties, comparative chronology of
ancient Oriental art, genealogies of major painters,
art maps, etc. appended. Index of painters, with
birth and death dates.

China

Harada, Bizan 原田尾山 **E50**
Shina gagakusho kaidai 支那画学書解題
(Annotated bibliography of Chinese books on
painting) Bunkyūdō, 1938. 475p.

Lists chronologically and comments on about
300 titles collected by the author, with brief biographies of their authors. Classified table of contents; author and title index.

Harada, Bizan 原田尾山 **E51**
Nihon genzai Shina meiga mokuroku 日本現在
支那名画目録 (Catalogue of famous Chi-
nese pictures in Japan) Bunkyūdō, 1938. 462p.

Arranged chronologically, each with name of artist, title, material, style, size, signature, any in-
scription, owner, transmission, biography of the
artist, etc. Index of artists.

Japan

Dictionaries

Saitō, Ryūzō 斉藤隆三 **E52**
Gadai jiten 画題辞典 (Dictionary of painting
subjects) Rev. and enl. ed. Hakubunkan, 1925.
441p.

Lists subjects common to many Oriental pictures
from ancient times, with their meanings, sources
and examples of famous paintings in which they
are used. Subject index arranged by character
strokes.

Sawada, Akira 沢田章 **E53**
Nihon gaka jiten 日本画家辞典 (Dictionary
of Japanese painters) Kigensha, 1927. 2v.

v.1 is a biographical dictionary of professional
and famous amateur artists who died before Oct.,
1927, arranged by their brush names giving their
careers, styles, pseudonyms, etc., with references.
v.2 reproduces seals and signatures of major artists.
Examples of forged seals appended. Index of names
other than real names.

Oki, Takuji 緒木卓爾 **E54**
Gendai Nihon gaka jiten 現代日本画家辞典
(Dictionary of contemporary Japanese painters)
Nihon Bijutsu Shinpōsha, 1956. 259p.

Gives personal histories, achievements, affiliations and other information provided by the artists
themselves, including many who are little known.
Index of professional names.

Chronology

Wada, Mankichi 和田万吉 **E55**
Nihon kindai gaka zaisei nenpyō 日本近代
画家在世年表 (Chronological listing of
modern Japanese painters) Maruzen, 1915.
484p.

Shows active periods and contemporaneity of
artists more than 20 years old from 1559 to 1913,
arranged yearly by date of birth. Index of brush
names with birth and death dates.

PICTURE SCROLLS

Okudaira, Hideo 奥平英雄 **E56**
Emaki 絵巻 (Picture scrolls) Bijutsu Shuppansha, 1957. 289p.

Comprehensive survey of the history, subjects,
styles and painters of classical scroll paintings,
with catalogue of extant scrolls, biographical sketches of painters, illustrations, references, etc. Indexes
of artists, scroll titles and subjects. Later illustrations in books are treated in the following:

Ehon no kenkyū (Studies of illustrated books) by
Katsunosuke Nakata. Bijutsu Shuppansha, 1950.
285p. **E56a.**

UKIYOE

Harigaya, Shōkichi 針ヶ谷鐘吉 and **E57**
Suzuki, Jūzō 鈴木重三
Ukiyoe bunken mokuroku 浮世絵文献目録
(Bibliography of ukiyoe literature) Mitō Shooku,
1962. 104p.

Lists in chronological order Japanese works published from 1877 to 1962, including albums of reproductions and books on related subjects.

Inoue, Kazuo 井上和雄 **E58**
Ukiyoeshi den 浮世絵師伝 (Biographies
of ukiyoe artists) Watanabe Hangaten, 1931.
266p.

Gives dates, schools and careers of more than
900 artists from early 17th century arranged by their
professional names. Many illustrations of signatures and seals.

Shimizu, Tōru 清水澄 **E59**
Ukiyoe jinmei jiten 浮世絵人名辞典 (Biographical dictionary of ukiyoe artists) Directory
of contemporary print artists. Bijutsu Kurabu,
1954. 160p.

Gives short biographies and lists representative
works, with market prices, of major artists of the
past, including those known for paintings rather
than prints, but only addresses and affiliations of
contemporary artists. Short history of ukiyoe by
Muneshige Narasaki, table of schools, genealogies,
list of contemporary print publishers, etc. appended.
Index.

Urushiyama, Tendō 漆山天童 **E60**
Shinsen ukiyoe nenpyō 新撰浮世絵年表
(Newly compiled ukiyoe chronology) Keikō Sho-
in, 1934. 244p.

Extends from early 17th century to the 1860s.

Zayūhō Kankōkai 座右宝刊行会 **E61**
Ukiyoe zenshū 浮世絵全集 (Ukiyoe collection) Kawade Shobō Shinsha, 1957-58. 6v.

Color and black-and-white plates of early prints
and prints of beautiful women (2v.), flowers and
birds, actors and landscapes, with descriptive and
historical notes. Appended in supp. volume are
a survey by Shizuya Fujikake, charts of schools,
brief biographies of artists, chronology, glossary,
comparative tables of styles and sizes of prints
and bibliography. Index.

Kōdansha 講談社 **E62**
Nihon hanga bijutsu zenshū 日本版画美術
全集 (Complete collection of Japanese block-
prints) 1960-62. 8v.

Chronoligical arrangement of plates from early
times to present, with emphasis on prints from the
17th to 19th centuries. Supp. v., titled *Nihon hanga
benran* (Handbook of Japanese prints) is useful guide
for research and appreciation, giving explanations
of kinds of prints, styles and tools, glossary, biographical sketches of artists, list and genealogies
of engravers and printers, chronology and bibliography, including Western works.

COLOR NAMES

Uemura, Rokurō 上村六郎 and **E63**
Yamazaki, Katsuhiro 山崎勝弘
Nihon shikimei taikan 日本色名大鑑
(General survey of Japanese color names) Rev.
ed. Kyoto, Kōbunsha, 1950. 83 plates.

Defines and gives the etymologies of names from
ancient times. Helpful in determining colors mentioned in classical literature and giving classical
names to modern colors. Index.

Nihon Shikisai Kenkyūjo **E64**
日本色彩研究所
Shikimei daijiten 色名大辞典 (Comprehen-

sive dictionary of color names) Tokyo Sōgen-sha, 1954. 2v.

v.1 gives two hundred samples of colors and shades, each with its Japanese, English and French names. v.2 defines color names and related terms, with appended bibliography of pre-1868 Japanese and Chinese literature on colors, tables of English, French and German color names, lists of similar color names, etc.

Nihon Shikisai Kenkyūjo   **E65**
日本色彩研究所
Shin shikimei chō 新色名帖 (New color-name book) 1954. 200 sheets.

Based on the Nippon Shikisaisha's *Iro no hyōjun* (Color standards), 1931, it shows 277 colors of practical use divided into pure and impure.

DESIGN

Yamaguchi, Masaki 山口正城 **et al.**   **E66**
Dezain shōjiten デザイン小辞典 (Little dictionary of design) Enl. ed. Dabiddosha, 1962. 266p.

Emphasizes industrial design of the present century and includes related fine arts, architectural and engineering terms and persons. Index of foreign words.

Sen'i Ishō Sōsaku Kyōkai   **E67**
繊維意匠創作協会
Sekai moyō zukan 世界模様図鑑 (Illustrated world dictionary of design) Kawade Shobō Shinsha, 1954-55. 3v.

v.1 shows and explains traditional designs and styles of various Western countries with emphasis on architectural ornamentation and folkcraft patterns; v.2, those of Japan; and v.3, those developed in modern times. Also covers color tones. Chronological charts of designs in the West, the East, Japan, Korea and China. Each volume indexed.

CALLIGRAPHY

DICTIONARY

Nigensha 二玄社   **E68**
Shodō jiten 書道辞典 (Calligraphy dictionary) Rev. ed. 1956. 136p. (Shodō kōza, 8)

Identifies persons, mostly of the past, and explains terms related to Chinese and Japanese calligraphy.

DIRECTORY

Satō, Yūgō 佐藤祐豪   **E69**
Gendai shosakka seinenbetsu meikan 現代書作家生年別名鑑 (Directory of modern calligraphers and associates listed by birth dates) Ōkura Shobō, 1958. 154p.

Includes seal makers, black-ink artists, composers of Chinese poems and critics, with parallel columns giving achievements of individual calligraphers and others. Chronology from 1868 to 1958, genealogies, addresses and lists of associations, newspapers and magazines concerned with calligraphy and prominent retailers of writing materials appended.

STYLES OF WRITING

Fujiwara, Sosui 藤原楚水   **E70**
Shodō rikutai daijiten 書道六体大字典 (Comprehensive dictionary of the six styles of calligraphy) Sanseidō, 1961. 1459p.

Reproduces characters written in the six styles by famous calligraphers of all periods taken from documents, monuments, seals and other sources. Lists of sources appended.

Hōshokai 法書会   **E71**
Gotai jirui 五体字類 (Five styles of characters) 17th ed., rev. and enl. Seitō Shobō, 1960. 615p.

Gives 46,675 characters, 4,478 in printed, semi-cursive, cursive and two ornamental styles and the others in one or more styles, with sources indicated.

Endō, Yūshi 円道祐之   **E72**
Genji sokkai sōsho daijiten 原字速解草書大字典 (Comprehensive dictionary for quick identification of cursive-style Chinese characters) Ōkura Shoten, 1935. 992p.

Arranged by the ways in which their strokes are written, characters by noted calligraphers since the Han period are accompanied by their printed forms, readings and names of writers. Indexes of characters by strokes, pronunciations and names of calligraphers.

Haruna, Yoshishige 春名好重   **E73**
Kohitsu jiten 古筆辞典 (Cyclopedia of old Japanese writing) Taitō Shodōin Shuppanbu, 1943. 206p.

Describes writing styles of the past, mainly from the 8th century to the 13th, and lists important calligraphers by their death dates. Index of calligraphers.

SOURCE MATERIALS

Heibonsha 平凡社   **E74**
Shodō zenshū 書道全集 (Complete calligraphy collection) 1954-63. 25v.

Covers Chinese calligraphy to 1909 in 14v. and Japanese calligraphy to 1925 in 11v., with introductory outline, plates, notes, chronology and biographical sketches in each volume.

Kawade Shobō 河出書房   **E75**
Teihon shodō zenshū 定本書道全集 (Standard calligraphy collection) 1954-57. 19v.

Gives examples, with transliterations and notes, of Chinese calligraphy to 1909 and of Japanese to the present, brief biographies of calligraphers and reproductions of seals.

PHOTOGRAPHY

Kikuchi, Shin'ichi 菊池真一 **et al.**   **E76**
Kagaku shashin benran 科学写真便覧 (Scientific photography manual) New ed., rev. Maruzen, 1959-64. 3v.

v.1 covers history, theory, traditional and new techniques and equipment; v.2, chemicals and their use; and v.3, such special fields as infra-red and high speed photography. Reference list. Subject index in each volume.

    E77
Shashin gijutsu benran 写真技術便覧 (Handbook of photography techniques) Koronasha, 1956. 783p.

Covers basic matters of techniques, including micrographic and medical and industrial X-ray photography. List of manufactures.

PRINTING

Insatsu Jihōsha 印刷時報社   **E78**
Insatsu hyakka jiten 印刷百科辞典 (Printing encyclopedia) Osaka, 1959. 491p.

Detailed explanation of printing under chapters with many samples of printing styles and papers.

Nihon Insatsu Gakkai 日本印刷学会 **E79**
Insatsu jiten 印刷事典 (Printing dictionary) 1963. 477, 50, 55p.

Defines 4,629 terms, with emphasis on those related to Japanese printing. Illustrations, reference list and glossary of English terms. English index.

Kobori, Shōzō 小堀正三   **E80**
Gendai insatsu gijutsu sōran 現代印刷技術総覧 (Survey of contemporary printing art) Nihon Insatsu Shinbunsha, 1962. 895p.

Explains relief, lithographic and gravure printing, binding and printing equipment. Glossary appended.

    E81
Monbushō kankōbutsu seisaku benran 文部省刊行物制作便覧 (Production manual for Ministry of Education publications) Kyōiku Shuppansha, 1952. 670p.

Sets standards and gives guidance in planning, designing, choice of paper and type, editing, printing and binding. Subject index.

Insatsu Gakkai 印刷学会   **E82**
Insatsu yūzā gaido 印刷ユーザガイド (Users' guide to printing) 1960. 248p.

Covers printing, choice of papers and binding, with many samples, tables, cost estimates, directory of specialized printers, etc. Index.

    E83
Nihon insatsu nenkan 日本印刷年鑑 (Japan printing yearbook) 1957- . Nihon Insatsu Shinbunsha, 1957- . 8v.

Surveys developments, with statistics, charts and tables. Gives standards, requirements for the licensing of printers and lists of members of the Federation of Japanese Printers' Union, schools and training institutes and related organizations and of books and articles. Directory of printers and persons in related businesses (519p.) issued as supplement to 1957 edition.

CERAMICS

Ono, Ken'ichirō 小野賢一郎 **et al.**   **E84**
Tōki daijiten 陶器大辞典 (Ceramics encyclopedia) Hōunsha, 1949. 6v.

Worldwide in coverage but emphasizes Japanese and other Oriental ceramics, with many illustrations. Includes catalogue of Japanese national treasures and other important pieces, giving names, owners, locations, etc. Chronology of Japanese, Korean and Chinese ceramics. General index.

Katō, Tōkurō 加藤唐九郎   **E85**
Tōki jiten 陶器辞典 (Ceramics dictionary) 2d ed., rev. and enl. Shima Shobō, 1961. 1120p.

Abridgement of **E84** concentrating on history and appreciation of Japanese ceramics but including some Korean and Chinese and a few European topics, with many illustrations. References. Indexes of subjects, persons and inscriptions.

Yūzankaku 雄山閣 **E86**
Tōki yōgo jiten 陶器用語辞典 (Dictionary of ceramic terms) 1960. 256p.

Defines about 7,000 terms, many with illustrations.

Zayūhō Kankōkai 座右宝刊行会 **E87**
Sekai tōji zenshū 世界陶磁全集 Collection of world's ceramics. Kawade Shobō Shinsha, 1955-58. 16v.

Photographs, some in color, divided into Japanese (6v.), including volume on tea utensils, Chinese (5v.), Korean (2v.), Western (1v.) and contemporary (1v.), with introductory text, explanations, diagrams, chronology, references, list of kilns and English table of contents in each volume. Directory of contemporary Japanese ceramic artists and general index (v.16).

Heibonsha 平凡社 **E88**
Tōki zenshū 陶器全集 (Ceramic collection) 1957-62. 30v.

Photographic survey by periods, kilns and artists of Japanese, Chinese and Korean ceramics to early modern times, with texts by specialists, chronologies and genealogies.

SWORDS

Gōroku, Teiji 郷六貞治 **E89**
Nihontō bunrui mokuroku 日本刀分類目録 (Classified catalogue of Japanese swords) Shun'yōdō, 1944. 138p.

Classifies by periods, schools and swordsmiths about 1,600 swords registered as of Mar., 1944, as national treasures or important craft objects, with measurements, names and addresses of owners, etc. Index of owners.

Shimizu, Tōru 清水澄 **E90**
Tōken banzuke 刀剣番付 (Graded list of swords) Rev. ed. Bijutsu Kurabu, 1958. 2v.

Explains styles and schools and gives inscriptions, places where they were forged, dates, brief histories, evaluations and market prices of old swords, from 701 to 1595, and new swords, to 1911, with graded list of famous swords appended. Index in each volume.

Fujishiro, Yoshio 藤代義雄 **E91**
Nihon tōkō jiten 日本刀工辞典 (Dictionary of Japanese swordsmiths) Fujishiro Shōten, 1937-38. 2v.

Lists by professional names makers of old swords, from 958 to 1595, and new swords, to 1926, with their family names, provinces, specialties, rankings, careers, teachers and followers, styles and techniques, and inscriptions. Illustrations of patterns on blade surfaces.

Iimura, Yoshiaki 飯村嘉章 **E92**
Tōken yōran 刀剣要覧 (Sword handbook) Tōken Bijutsu Kōgeisha, 1958. 325p.

Illustrated guide to understanding and appreciation, with lists of sword prices and swordsmiths appended.

MUSIC

BIBLIOGRAPHY

Ogawa, Takashi 小川昂 **E93**
Honpō yōgaku kankei tosho mokuroku 本邦洋楽関係図書目録 (Bibliography of Western music in Japan) Ongaku no Tomosha, 1957. 425p.

Classified list of books published in Japan from 1868 to 1956, excluding scores, practice manuals and textbooks. Author index.

Kokuritsu Kokkai Toshokan **E94**
国立国会図書館
Ongaku bunka shiryō tenrankai mokuroku 音楽文化資料展覧会目録 (Catalogue of exhibition of musicology materials) 1950. 202, 23p.

Classifies by periods and comments on 817 scores, books, bibliographies and instruments, including some of foreign origin which have influenced Japanese music. Kunio Yanagita's classification plan for folk songs and Kashō Machida's developmental charts of Japanese music and narrative samisen music (jōruri) appended.

DICTIONARIES

Heibonsha 平凡社 **E95**
Ongaku jiten 音楽事典 (Music dictionary) Rev. ed. 1959-60. 5v.

Covers Western, Japanese and other Oriental music, with emphasis on history. References. Lists of music organizations appended. Name and subject index. First edition, 12v., 1949-57.

Horiuchi, Keizō 堀内敬三 **et al.** **E96**
Ongaku jiten 音楽辞典 (Music dictionary) Rev. ed. Ongaku no Tomosha, 1960. 2v.

v.1 defines terms, explains instruments and types

of music, and gives national music histories, with illustrations; v.2 identifies composers, with list of compositions except for the Japanese, and performers. Indexes of foreign-language terms and foreign musicians.

Koizumi, Hiroshi 小泉洽 **E97**
Ongaku jiten 音楽辞典 (Music dictionary) Tokyodō, 1958. 755p.

Gives Japanese equivalents and definitions of Latin, English, French, Italian and German terms related to techniques, theories, instruments and musical history. Illustrations.

Shimofusa, Kan'ichi 下総皖一 and **E98** Chikamori, Kazushige 近森一重
Gakugo jiten 楽語辞典 (Dictionary of musical terms) Rev. and enl. ed. Ongaku no Tomosha, 1953. 257, 16p.

Classified entries, with emphasis on terms used in courses approved by the Ministry of Education. Indexes.

Shimazaki, Akatarō 島崎赤太郎 **E99**
Shōkai gakugo jiten 詳解楽語辞典 (Detailed dictionary of musical terms) Kyōeki Shoten, 1952. 484p.

Gives Japanese equivalents and explanations of Western terms. Abbreviations, signs and chronology appended.

BIOGRAPHIES

Togashi, Yasushi 富樫康 **E100**
Nihon no sakkyokuka 日本の作曲家 (Japanese composers) Ongaku no Tomosha, 1956. 307p.

Brief biographical sketches of 63 contemporaries, with outline of Western music in Japan, survey of trends in composition and lists of compositions and composers.

Fujita, Fuji 藤田不二 **E101**
Ensōka daijiten 演奏家大事典 (Comprehensive dictionary of musical artists) Ongaku no Tomosha, 1954. 481p.

Identifies European and American concert instrumentalists, singers, conductors, ensembles and choral groups, with many photographs.

Watanabe, Mamoru 渡辺護 **E102**
Gendai ensōka jiten 現代演奏家事典 (Dictionary of contemporary musical artists) Shūdōsha, 1956. 519p.

Classified listing, with brief biographies or his-

tories, outstanding performances and recordings, of European and American pianists, violinists, organists, string quartets, conductors, orchestras, opera companies, singers and choral groups. Indexes.

CHRONOLOGY

Irino, Yoshirō 入野義郎 and **E103** Shibata, Minao 柴田南雄
Ongakushi nenpyō 音楽史年表 (Chronology of music history) Sōgensha, 1954. 530p.

Lists musicians, works, events and related matters of Europe and America from 1 A.D. to 1950, divided into four periods, each with outline history. Index.

YEARBOOK

E104
Ongaku nenkan 音楽年鑑 (Music yearbook) 1947- . Ongaku no Tomosha, 1946- . 19v.

Surveys Japanese and Western events and trends, lists organizations and gives regulations governing use of musical works.

ILLUSTRATIONS

Sakka, Keisei 属啓成 **E105**
Shinpen ongaku rekishi zukan 新編音楽歴史図鑑 (Pictorial history of music, new edition) Ongaku no Tomosha, 1957. 294p.

Photographs of musicians, concert halls, instruments, etc. and other illustrations, with brief explanations, show developments from ancient times.

Sugawara, Meirō 菅原明朗 **E106**
Gakki zukan 楽器図鑑 (Illustrated book of musical instruments) Ongaku no Tomosha, 1950. 407p. 32 plates.

Explains principles, structures, use, history, etc. in sections on present-day string, wind and percussion instruments. Tables of pitch and tone range and Japanese and foreign names of instruments appended.

WORKS

NHK Kōkyō Gakudan ＮＨＫ交響楽団 **E107**
N-kyō meikyoku jiten Ｎ響名曲事典 (Dictionary of famous music in the NHK Symphony Orchestra repertoire) Heibonsha, 1958-59. 6v.

Describes symphonies, concertos, operas and other works performed and a few not yet performed, arranged chronologically by birth dates of composers, including Japanese (v.6). History of performances and annotated list of recordings appended.

Sakka, Keisei 属啓成 **E108**
Meikyoku no jiten 名曲の事典 (Dictionary
of famous music) Ongaku no Tomosha, 1954.
358p.
Chronological arrangement of representative Western works, with biographical sketches and characteristics of composers. Table of contents lists composers with their birth and death dates and with list
of works.

Nippon Hōsō Kyōkai 日本放送協会 **E109**
Shin gaikoku gakkyoku no yobikata 新・外
国楽曲の呼び方(New index of foreign musical compositions) Nippon Hōsō Shuppan Kyōkai; 1962. 477p.
Arranged by composers, with titles in original
spellings, followed by Japanese translations. Title
and author indexes.

Chosakuken Shiryō Kenkyū Kyōkai **E110**
著作権資料研究協会
Ongaku sakuhin benran 音楽作品便覧 (Handbook of musical works) 1960. 2v.
Lists about 17,000 popular songs, including foreign
and children's songs, with first lines, authors and
composers, and contemporary Japanese instrumental
works.

Ongaku no Tomosha 音楽之友社 **E111**
Meikyoku kaisetsu zenshū 名曲解説全集
(Collection of explanations of great music) 1959-
64. 18v.
Interprets frequently heard classical and contemporary works, giving for each its history, performance
time and an excerpt from the score, divided into
types of compositions and arranged by birth dates
of composers. Useful for appreciation. General
index.

Horiuchi, Keizō 堀内敬三 **et al.** **E112**
Sekai dai ongaku zenshū 世界大音楽全集
(Collection of world's great music) Ongaku no
Tomosha, 1956-62. 122v.
Gives scores of instrumental works in 75v. and
vocal works in 45v. Index volume for each group.

Light music

Nippon Hōsō Kyōkai 日本放送協会 **E113**
Keiongaku benran 軽音楽便覧 (Handbook of
light music) Nippon Hōsō Shuppan Kyōkai,
1961. 419p.
Alphabetical listing of foreign songs popular in
Japan to 1957, with type of music, Japanese title,
author and composer, publisher, copyright date,

any reviews, etc. for each. Index of Japanese titles
followed by original titles.

Kōno, Ryūji 河野隆次 **E114**
Jazu no jiten ジャズの事典 (Jazz dictionary) Osaka, Sōgensha, 1957. 513, 90p.
Gives biographies of singers, lyric writers and
composers and explains terms and instruments. Bibliography. Indexes of persons and compositions.

Records

Ongaku no Tomosha 音楽之友社 **E115**
Sakkyokukabetsu yōgaku rekōdo sōmokuroku
作曲家別洋楽レコード総目録 (General
catalogue of recordings of Western music arranged by composers) 1958- . Semiannual.
Lists Japanese pressings of recordings by Western performers of Western music and a few of Japanese compositions made abroad.

Japanese music

Hōsō Bunka Kenkyūjo **E116**
放送文化研究所
Tōyō gagaku goi 当用雅楽語彙(Current court
music, *gagaku*, glossary) Nippon Hōsō Kyōkai,
1954. 160p.
Explains songs, the words of which are given in
full, instrumental numbers, dances, instruments,
costumes and accessories.

Ogawa, Morinaka 小川守中 **E117**
Kabu hinmoku 歌舞品目 (List of singing and
dancing things) Nihon Koten Zenshū Kankōkai,
1930. 2v. (Nihon koten zenshū, 3d series)
Classifies and explains compositions, instruments,
costumes, etc. used in court music, *gagaku*, with
references. Reprint of the 1823 edition.

E118
Gidayū nenpyō 義太夫年表 (Chronology of
gidayū ballads) Osaka, Gidayū Nenpyō Kankōkai, 1956. 851p.
Records 1868-1912 performances, divided into
those in the puppet theater and those elsewhere,
giving programs, stage settings and comments.

Tokyo Ongaku Gakkō 東京音楽学校 **E119**
Kinsei hōgaku nenpyō 近世邦楽年表 (Chro-
nology of modern, 1600-1867, Japanese music)
Rikugōkan, 1912-27. 3v.

v.1 records theatrical narrative songs, *jōruri*, of three representative schools from 1716; v.2, Edo-style *nagauta* from 1704; and v.3, puppet-theater narrative songs, *gidayū*, from 1677; with brief synopses, biographies of composers, performers, actors and playwrights.

Saitō, Gesshin 斉藤月岑   **E120**
Seikyoku ruisan 声曲類纂 (Classified compilation of materials on vocal music) Rev. by Tokutarō Fujita. Iwanami Shoten, 1941. 489p. (Iwanami bunko)

Annotated and revised reprint of the original 1847 edition, giving biographies of composers, writers and performers of popular songs, with emphasis on theatrical narrative songs, *jōruri*, from the 17th century to the 19th, information on performances, references, etc. Illustrations. Index.

FOLK MUSIC

Kodera, Yūkichi 小寺融吉   **E121**
Kyōdo min'yō buyō jiten 郷土民謡舞踊辞典 (Dictionary of native folk songs and dances) Rev. enl. ed. Fuzanbō, 1941. 489, 64p.

Gives locales, origins, forms, etc., excluding Okinawan and Ainu, and explains terms. Index by prefectures and classified subject index.

DANCING

Opera and Ballet

Ōtaguro, Motoo 大田黒元雄   **E122**
Kageki daijiten 歌劇大事典 (Comprehensive opera dictionary) Ongaku no Tomosha, 1962. 807p.

Factual coverage of works, terms, composers, librettists, companies, conductors, orchestras, singers, etc., with entry headings in original languages. Japanese index.

Akiyama, Tatsuhide 秋山竜英   **E123**
Opera barē jiten オペラ・バレー事典 (Opera and ballet dictionary) Sōgeisha, 1961. 331p.

Covers foreign and Japanese titles, persons and terms. Photographs.

Japanese dancing

Nihon Buyō Kyōkai 日本舞踊協会   **E124**
Nihon buyō sōran 日本舞踊総覧 (Japanese

dance survey) Nihon Shūhōsha, 1952. 443p.

Summarizes history, comments on music, sets, stage properties and costumes. Gives directory of dancers by schools and lists of Japanese dancers of Western dances, musicians, others related to dancing and institutions. Bibliography. Photographs.

Asakawa, Gyokuto 浅川玉兎   **E125**
Nihon buyō meikyoku jiten 日本舞踊名曲事典 (Dictionary of famous Japanese dances) Sumoto, Asakawa Haruo, 1959. 361p.

Gives subjects, synopses, characteristics and pointers on appreciation of 200 classic dances, with many pictures of performances. Index of titles, including popular and abridged versions.

Atsumi, Seitarō 渥美清太郎   **E126**
Hōgaku buyō jiten 邦楽舞踊辞典 (Dictionary of Japanese music and dancing) Fuzanbō, 1956. 459p.

Covers all schools of traditional music and dancing from the 17th century, related theatrical matters, instruments and folk and popular songs, with introductory history. Illustrations. Index.

Zōtei Kojitsu Sōsho Henshūbu   **E127**
増訂故実叢書編集部
Bugakuzu bugaku zusetsu 舞楽図・舞楽図説 (Court dances, *bugaku*, illustrated) Yoshikawa Kōbunkan, 1930. 77, 10, 7p. 78 plates.

Album of color reproductions of 39 paintings by Chiharu Takashima of dances of the left style, 30 by Arisato Kitazume of dances of the right style, and of 25 masks. Explanations by Josetsu Otsuki of music for 37 dances of the left and 24 of the right and of 25 masks. Index.

THEATER

Waseda Daigaku Engeki Hakubutsukan   **E128**
早稲田大学演劇博物館
Engeki hyakka daijiten 演劇百科大事典 (Encyclopedia of theatrical arts) Heibonsha, 1960-62. 6v.

Includes Western and Oriental entertainment from ancient times to the present but strongest in Japanese court music, Nō drama, kabuki, modern drama and folk entertainment, with many portraits, stage sets and references. Chronology, world entertainment development chart, calendar of folk entertainments in each prefecture and bibliography appended in v.6. Index. Some 2,500 entries on Japanese plays selected from the above, with additional information on recent drama in the following:

Sōgō Nihon engeki jiten (General Japanese theatrical dictionary) ed. by Shigetoshi Kawatake. Heibonsha, 1964. 634, 23p. 17 plates. **E128a.**

Waseda Daigaku Engeki Hakubutsukan **E129**
早稲田大学演劇博物館
Geinō jiten 芸能辞典 (Dictionary of performing arts) Tokyodō, 1961. 794p.

Some 1,200 entries covering terms, forms, personalities, etc. in music, dance, drama, motion pictures and other entertainments from ancient times to the present, with genealogies of families, repertorial lists and bibliography. Classified table of topics. Index of persons, terms and subjects.

Iijima, Tadashi 飯島正 **et al.** **E130**
Engeki eiga hōsō buyō opera jiten 演劇映画 放送舞踊オペラ辞典 (Dictionary of drama, cinema, broadcasting, dance and opera) Hakusuisha, 1955. 1070p.

Explains terms, with emphasis on those in current use and of foreign origin. Entertainment chronology, bibliography and list of periodicals appended. Index.

Atsumi, Seitarō 渥美清太郎 **E131**
Nihon engeki jiten 日本演劇辞典 (Japanese theatrical arts dictionary) Shin Taishūsha, 1944. 687p.

Emphasis is on kabuki but includes related aspects of puppet drama, Nō, new-style drama, music and dance.

Waseda Daigaku Engeki Hakubutsukan **E132**
早稲田大学演劇博物館
Kokugeki yōran 国劇要覧 (Handbook of national drama) Azusa Shobo, 1932. 646p.

Gives illustrated historical summations of ancient and folk drama, Nō and related short comedies (Kyōgen) puppet drama, kabuki, new-style drama, variety shows, street performances and other popular entertainments, Okinawan, Korean, Formosan and Ainu folk dramas, and motion pictures. Bibliography. Index. Old but still useful.

Nippon Hōsō Kyōkai 日本放送協会 **E133**
Engeki gedai yōran 演劇外題要覧(Direcotry of Japanese play titles) 2d ed. Nippon Hōsō Shuppan Kyōkai, 1954. 544p.

Lists classical puppet and kabuki plays with correct readings and notes on variant titles, dates, writers and numbers of acts and scenes. Indexes of popular abridged titles and first characters of formal titles.

Kawatake, Shigetoshi 河竹繁俊 **E134**
Nihon engeki zuroku 日本演劇図録 (Japa-

nese theatrical arts illustrated) Asahi Shinbunsha, 1956. 152, 137, 13p.

Historical survey with about 400 pictures of actors, performances, masks, costumes, stage properties, theaters, etc. Chronology and English summary appended.

Nō · Kyōgen

Nogami Kinen Hōsei Daigaku Nōgaku **E135**
Kenkyūjo 野上記念法政大学能楽研究所
Zōsho mokuroku 蔵書目録 (Library catalogue annotated) 1954. 116p.

Lists and comments on early manuscripts and block-print books, facsimile editions of pre-17th century manuscripts and texts of Nō songs and associated comedies published since 1868 in a notable collection. List of Nō songs appended.

Shōda, Shōjirō 正田章次郎 **and** **E136**
Amagaya, Kan'ichi 雨谷幹一
Nōgaku yōkyoku daijiten 能楽謡曲大辞典 (Comprehensive dictionary of Nō plays and songs) Rev. by Shin'ami Nakamura. Yoshikawa Kōbunkan, 1931. 2v.

Divided into sections defining technical terms on the basis of manuscripts and oral traditions of the Kanze Nō school and interpreting difficult words and phrases in texts, with brief survey of masks and costumes appended. Supplementary volume shows masks, costumes, stage sets and properties.

Maruoka, Akira 丸岡明 **E137**
Nōgaku kanshō jiten 能楽鑑賞事典(Manual for appreciation of Nō drama) Kawade Shobō Shinsha, 1961. 475p.

Explains each of 255 songs in the repertoires of five schools, with notes on structures; includes ways of performance, styles, masks and costumes. List of songs and tables of extant and lost plays of each school appended. Index.

Kanzeryū Kaiteibon Kankōkai **E138**
観世流改訂本刊行会
Nōgaku goi 能楽語彙 (Glossary of Nō plays) 1931. 332p.

Defines technical terms concerning plays, including kyōgen, songs, performances, dances, rhythms, accompaniments, masks, costumes, stage sets and properties, etc. Identifies schools with which songs, plays and performance styles are associated.

Sanari, Kentarō 佐成謙太郎 **E139**
Nō yō zusetsu 能謡図説 (Pictures and explanations of Nō plays and songs) Meiji Shoin,

1948.   348p.

Color illustrations of the stage, masks, costumes, properties and reproductions of pages of old and new texts, accompanied by introduction to Nō drama and detailed study of songs. Originally published as the introductory volume of the same author's *Yōkyoku taikan* (General survey of Nō), 7v., Meiji Shoin, 1930-31.

Furukawa, Hisashi   古 川 久   **E140**
Kyōgen jiten   狂 言 辞 典   (Dictionary of *kyōgen*) Vocabulary. Tokyodō, ·1963.   548p.

Explains and gives examples of about 10,000 special words and phrases selected from texts. General remarks on *kyōgen* and list of sources of quotations appended. Indexes of proper nouns, poems and songs, and historical allusions.

Kabuki

Kawatake, Shigetoshi   河 竹 繁 俊   **E141**
Kabuki jiten   歌 舞 伎 事 典 (Kabuki dictionary) Jitsugyō no Nipponsha, 1957.   298p.

Briefly explains 1,100 items concerning kabuki, puppet drama, dance, music and related fields, with many illustrations. Appended are lists of *kyōgen*, with variant titles, specialties of schools and actors, with genealogies.

Kanazawa, Yasutaka   金 沢 康 隆   **E142**
Kabuki meisaku jiten   歌 舞 伎 名 作 事 典 (Dictionary of famous kabuki plays) Seiabō, 1959.   388p.

Outlines and explains, with emphasis on relationship to Japanese traditions, 400 currently performed plays, each with easily available references. Biographies of playwrights appended. Index of kabuki titles.

Ihara, Toshirō   伊 原 敏 郎   **E143**
Kabuki nenpyō   歌 舞 伎 年 表 (Kabuki chronology) Ed. by Shigetoshi Kawatake and Eiji Yoshida.   Iwanami Shoten, 1956-63.   8v.

Basic record of plays, performances and related events from 1559 to 1907, with parallel columns for Edo (later Tokyo) and other cities, especially Kyoto and Osaka, with many quotations from original sources. Indexes of plays, persons and subjects in v.8.

Shuzui, Kenji   守 随 憲 治   **and**   **E144**
Akiba, Yoshimi   秋 葉 芳 美
Kabuki zusetsu   歌 舞 伎 図 説 (Kabuki illustrated) Man'yōkaku, 1931.   1 case (171, 29p. 700 plates)

More than 700 photographs document kabuki history in four periods from 1596 to 1867, showing screens, other genre art, portraits, programs and wide range of books, with general introduction and detailed explanation of each illustration. Published in 1v. in 1934 from Chūbunkan. Explanatory volume was reprinted in 1943 by Kaizōsha.

Tanaka, Ryō   田 中 良   **E145**
Kabuki jōshiki butai zushū 歌 舞 伎 定 式 舞 台 図 集   (Collection of pictures of formal kabuki stages) Kōdansha, 1958.   358p.

Reproduces 153 color sketches by the author and 19 woodblock prints, with introductory history of stage designs, sets and preparations for performances. Chronology appended. Classified table of contents.

New drama

Ōki, Yutaka   大 木 豊   **E146**
Sengo shinsaku gikyoku jiten   戦 後 新 作 戯 曲 事 典   (Dictionary of new dramatic productions since the war)   Seiabō, 1960.   263p.

Lists 808 kabuki and other plays, musical shows and revues, giving outlines, casts and playwrights' introduction for 87.

Tanaka, Eizō   田 中 栄 三   **E147**
Meiji Taishō shingekishi shiryō   明 治 大 正 新 劇 史 資 料   (Materials on the history of the new drama in the Meiji and Taishō periods ⌈1868-1925⌋)   Engeki Shuppansha, 1964.   256p.

Records dates, places, plays, authors, actors and producers, with introductory history and photographs.

Rakugo

Imamura, Nobuo   今 村 信 雄   **E148**
Rakugo jiten   落 語 事 典 (Comic-story, *rakugo*, handbook)   3d ed., rev. and enl.   Seiabō, 1960. 355p.

Summarizes and explains about 500 famous stories from 17th century to the present, with brief history of storytelling, genealogy of schools, biographies of storytellers, observations on the art of storytelling and plays on words, and directory of contemporary storytellers.

Motion pictures

Iwasaki, Akira   岩 崎 昶   **et al.**   **E149**
Eiga hyakka jiten   映 画 百 科 辞 典 (Motion-

picture encyclopedia) Hakuyōsha, 1954. 638p.

Covers world film history to 1953, techniques, persons and the film industry, with many photographs. Surveys of motion-picture developments in major countries, record of prize-winning pictures in international festivals, chronology, references, American production code and Japanese code of film ethics appended. Indexes.

Eiga nenkan 映画年鑑 (Motion-picture yearbook) 1949- . Jiji Tsūshinsha, 1949- . 16v. **E150**

Gives statistics, chronicle of events, directory and survey of foreign developments. Indexes of subjects and film titles. Originally (1947-48) titled *Eiga geinō nenkan* (Motion-picture and entertainment yearbook).

Kinema junpō nenkan キネマ旬報年鑑 **E151**
(Kinema junpō yearbook) 1960- . Kinema Junpōsha, 1960-61, 1963- . 3v. Irregular.

Covers motion pictures, television and radio in Japan and abroad, with lists of prize-winning works and new films and directories of persons, companies, organizations, theaters, etc.

Nihon Eiga Rengōkai **E152**
日本映画連合会
Nihon gekieiga sakuhin mokuroku 日本劇映画作品目録 (Catalogue of Japanese dramatic motion pictures) 1956. 257p.

Covers all aspects of 2,308 feature films by production dates and producers, 1945-55. List of companies and their production totals appended.

PHYSICAL CULTURE

Noguchi, Iwasaburō 野口岩三郎 **E153**
Taiikusho kaidai 体育書解題 (Annotated bibliography of physical culture) Fumaidō, 1953. 287, 43, 32p.

Lists and comments on books published since 1868, with names of owners of rare titles. List of related newspapers and periodicals appended. Classified index with 44 headings, author index.

Ōtani, Buichi 大谷武一 **et al.** **E154**
Taiiku daijiten 体育大辞典(Comprehensive dictionary of physical culture) Rev. ed. Fumaidō, 1957. 1207, 130p.

Covers sports, gymnastics, games, military arts, related aspects of medicine and psychology, persons, statistics and records. Illustrations. Index of subjects and persons.

Udo, Masahiko 宇土正彦 **et al.** **E155**
Hoken taiikuka daijiten 保健体育科大事典 (Cyclopedia of education in health and physical culture) Kokudosha, 1960. 524p.

Guide to theory, instruction, teaching materials and extra-curricular activities from nursery school through high school. Many illustrations. Index.

Maekawa, Mineo 前川峯雄 **et al.** **E156**
Shin taiikuka jiten 新体育科事典 (New manual of physical education) Iwasaki Shoten, 1964. 876p.

Systematically explains teaching materials and methods, physiology, psychology, etc. for teachers.

Imamura, Yoshio 今村嘉雄 **E157**
Taiikushi shiryō nenpyō 体育史資料年表 (Chronology of physical culture) Fumaidō, 1963. 574, 108p.

Lists Japanese events from 38 B.C. to 1959, with parallel events in Western physical culture and general history. Sources given for pre-1868 events. List of sources appended, with dictionary of terms and information on traditional Japanese martial arts.

Ara, Motoi 荒基 **E158**
Gengo hon'i supōtsu hokengaku taiikugaku yōgo 原語本位スポーツ保健学体育学用語 The technical terms of sports, health and physical culture. Fumaidō, 1961. 204p.

Divided into sections on health and physical culture, with many terms of foreign origin. Japanese index.

Airyūdō 愛隆堂 **E159**
Supōtsu yōgo jiten スポーツ用語辞典 (Dictionary of sports terms) 1956. 302p.

Classified by sports, with illustrations.

E160
Supōtsu nenkan スポーツ年鑑 Annual of sports. 1962- . Bēsubōru Magajinsha, 1962- . 3v.

General survey of major sports, with chronicle of events and important foreign records. The period up to 1960 is covered in the following titles:

Asahi supōtsu nenkan (Asahi sports annual) Asahi Shinbunsha, 1954-58. **E160a.**

Continuation of *Undō nenkan* (Sports yearbook), published from 1916 through 1953.

Yomiuri supōtsu nenkan (Yomiuri sports yearbook) Yomiuri Shinbunsha, 1955-59. **E160b.**

Ōbunsha 旺文社   **E161**
Supōtsu rūrushū スポーツ・ルール集
(Collection of sports rules) 9th ed., rev. 1963.
445p. (Ōbunsha supōtsu series)

Revised whenever there are significant changes.

Mountaineering

Kobayashi, Yoshimasa 小林義正   **E162**
Yama to shomotsu 山と書物 Mountains and
books) Tsukiji Shoin, 1957-60. 2v.

v.1 contains bibliographical essays on Japanese
and foreign books from 1600 to 1912 with list of
pre-1868 major works, maps and drawings and v.2,
Zoku yama to shomotsu, to about 1930. Index covers
both volumes.

Kawasaki, Takaaki 川崎隆章   **E163**
Sangaku jiten 山岳事典 (Mountaineering
handbook) Yama to Keikokusha, 1960. 440p.
(Tozan kōza, supp.)

Gives altitude chart, chronology of mountain climb-
ing, evaluations of rock-climbing sites, bibliography,
list of 1:50,000 and 1:25,000 topographical maps,
glossaries of mountain-climbing, mountain-area folk
language and meteorological terms, etc. Index.

Martial arts

Watatani, Kiyoshi 綿谷雪 **and**   **E164**
Yamada, Tadachika 山田忠史
Bugei ryūha jiten 武芸流派辞典 (Dictiona-
ry of schools of martial arts) Jinbutsu Ōraisha,
1963. 508p.

Gives the founder, history and characteristics
of each of about 5,000 schools of traditional military
and naval sciences, swimming, fencing and shooting.
Name index.

TEA CEREMONY

See also **E84-E88** for utensils.

Kuwata, Tadachika 桑田忠親   **E165**
Chadō jiten 茶道辞典 (Tea-ceremony dictionary) Tokyodō, 1961. 714p.

Explains 4,500 entries on ceremonies, schools,
manners, architecture, gardens, scrolls, utensils,
food, books and persons. Brief history, outline of
etiquette, genealogies of teamasters, etc. appended.
Classified index of persons and index of terms and
subjects.

Sue, Sōkō 末宗広   **E166**
Chadō jiten 茶道辞典 (Tea-ceremony dictionary) Kyoto, Kōbunsha, 1949. 698p.

Identifies masters, makers of artistic utensils
and noted books, and defines wide range of terms.
Illustrations.

Sasaki, Sanmi 佐々木三味   **E167**
Chadō saijiki 茶道歳事記 (Book of tea-
ceremony seasonal events) Kyoto, Tankō Shinsha, 1960. 403p.

Gives for each month ceremonial observations,
memorial days of teamasters and appropriate flowers,
food, sweets, flavors and terms. Index.

FLOWER ARRANGEMENT

Ikenobō Gakuen Tanki Daigaku Toshokan E168
池坊学園短期大学図書館
Kadō bunken mokuroku 華道文献目録 (Bibliography of flower arrangement) Kyoto, Ikenobō
Gakuen Tanki Daigaku Kadō Bunka Kenkyūjo,
1957. 110p.

Union catalogue of holdings of 142 Japanese
libraries. Author index.

Kobayashi, Roshū 小林鷺州   **E169**
Ikebana kokon shoseki ichiran いけばな古
今書籍一覧 (Survey of ancient and modern
flower-arrangement books) Dai Nihon Kadōkai,
1924. 102, 25p.

Arranged chronologically and annotated. Title
index.

LANGUAGE

✤ Linguistic studies and language dictionaries are included. See also bibliographies and dictionaries of literature which usually cover the language.

LINGUISTICS

Monbushō Gakujutsu Bunken Sōgō   **F1**
Mokuroku Bunka Shingikai
文部省学術文献綜合目録分科審議会
Gengogaku bunken sōgō mokuroku sōan 言語
学文献綜合目録草案 (Draft of the union catalogue of linguistic literature) 1950. 156p.

Endō, Yoshimoto 遠藤嘉基 **et al.**   **F2**
Kotoba no kagaku 8: yōgo kaisetsu sōsakuin
コトバの科学 8 : 用語解説総索引
(Science of language. v.8, Glossary, general index) Nakayama Shoten, 1959. 154p.

Linguistic terms in Japanese arranged alphabetically, followed by the original word and meanings with cross references. Index of important words in the entire series included.

Ichikawa, Sanki 市河三喜 **et al.**   **F3**
Sekai gengo gaisetsu 世界言語概説 (Outline of the world languages) Kenkyūsha, 1956. 2v.

Some 40 major languages, Indo-European in v. 1, others, mainly Asian, in v. 2, described and analyzed, with bibliography at end of each chapter. Indexes in Roman and Russian letters. Japanese indexes for subjects and names, and titles.

Kobayashi, Chikahei 小林智賀平   **F4**
Gengogaku shoho 言語学初歩 (Introductory linguistics) Sōgensha, 1952. 226, 51p. (Sōgen sensho)

Appendixes giving a history of linguistic studies, a list of language periodicals, a bibliography, etc., and subject indexes (Japanese and foreign) with a detailed table of contents, make this useful as a handbook and dictionary.

EUROPEAN LANGUAGES

→ G15

The Japan Times   **F5**
Nihongo chūshin rokkakokugo jiten 日本語中心六ヵ国語辞典 The Japan Times' 6-language dictionary. Hara Shobō, 1958-60. 2v.

v. 1, Nich-Ei-Doku-Futsu-Ro-Chūgokugo. Rev. and enl. ed.

About 10,000 romanized words, arranged alphabetically, are given their English, German, French, Russian and Chinese equivalents, each with phonetic symbols. Appendixes explain pronunciation and grammar, give weights and measures, proper nouns, conversational forms and idiomatic phrases. English index.

v. 2, Nichi-Ei-Futsu-Sei-Po-I kokugo.

Otherwise like v. 1, but has English, French, Spanish, Portuguese and Italian equivalents of Japanese words, with indexes for locating Spanish and English words.

English

PHILOLOGY

✤ Bibliography of English dictionaries in Japan since the Edo period is given in "Nihon ni okeru Eigo jiten" (English dictionaries in Japan; its historical development, present and future) by Susumu Kuranaga, in the magazine

Bungaku, pub. by Iwanami Shoten, v. 30, no. 2, 1962. **F6.**

Araki, Ihei 荒木伊兵衛 **F7**
Nihon Eigogaku shoshi 日本英語学書誌 (Bibliography of English studies in Japan) Sōgensha, 1931. 407, 48p.

Works written and published in Japan from the Tokugawa period to about 1930 and translations for use as language textbooks are listed chronologically and annotated, with comments on developments in the study of English. Subject and title indexes.

Yamaguchi, Hideo 山口秀夫 **F8**
Eigogaku bunken sōran 英語学文献総覧 Bibliographia linguistica & anglistica. List of books chiefly on the English language. Shinozaki Shoin, 1952. 117p.

Divided into general linguistics, Indo-European languages, Germanic languages, English and other modern languages, each with sub-divisions for theory, semantics, grammar, etc. Includes books and periodicals, most of them in Shizuka Saitō's collection. Author and title indexes.

Ichikawa, Sanki 市河三喜 **F9**
Eigogaku: kenkyū to bunken 英語学：研究と文献 (English philology; studies and literature) Sanseidō, 1956. 324p.

Annotated briefly are popular and scholarly works in Japanese under the following headings: dictionaries and vocabulary, dialects, phonetics and style, and special studies. Names, subjects and titles indexed.

F10
Eigo nenkan 英語年鑑 Kenkyūsha yearbook of English. 1960- . Comp. by Eigo Seinen Henshūbu. Kenkyūsha, 1960-61, 1964- . 3v. Annual.

Lists scholars, courses in English language and literature in universities and colleges, books and articles published during the year, organizations and societies.

Kenkyūsha 研究社 **F11**
Eigogaku jiten 英語学辞典 The Kenkyūsha dictionary of English philology. Ed. by Sanki Ichikawa. 1958. 1188p.

Terms used in English philology, phonology, general linguistics, prosody, metrics, rhetoric and language teaching are explained, with special emphasis on grammatical and phonological terms, often with diagrams. Prominent philologists identified. An English index, a list of Japanese terms with their English equivalents and a classified bibliography are useful.

TEACHING

Gogaku Kyōiku Kenkyūjo 語学教育研究所 **F12**
Eigo kyōjuhō jiten 英語教授法事典 (Dictionary of English teaching methods) Kaitakusha, 1962. 514p.

Detailed discussion of English teaching in Japan under fifty-seven main headings, arranged in Japanese syllabic order, each with historical developments, conditions in foreign countries, related laws, systems, summaries of important literature, references, various views, and suggests desirable teaching methods. "The standard English vocabulary" (3,000 words) by Harold E. Palmer, his three theses, and brief biography appended.

Kenkyūsha 研究社 **F13**
Eigo kyōiku jiten 英語教育事典 The Kenkyūsha cyclopaedia of English. Ed. by Rintarō Fukuhara. 1961. 10,1167p.

Deals with terms, subjects and names of people related to English language teaching, and descriptions of culture and characteristics of English and American life. Appendix contains handbook of facts about the United States and Britain, and a chronological table.

Sanseidō 三省堂 **F14**
Eigo kyōjuhō jiten 英語教授法辞典 Sanseidō's dictionary of English language teaching. Ed. by Yoshio Ogawa. 1964. 17,765p.

Covers theory and practice, and discusses teaching method, psychology, English language study, evaluation system, teaching materials, and personal names. Outline of foreign language teaching in foreign countries, comments on teachers' guides published by Ministry of Education, annotated list of references, and chronological table of English language education, 1600-1963, appended. Index.

GRAMMAR

Sanseidō 三省堂 **F15**
Shin eibunpō jiten 新英文法辞典 Sanseidō's dictionary of English grammar. Ed. by Takanobu Ōtsuka. 1959. 1101p.

1,800 English grammatical terms explained, with quotations and reference sources. A table of classified topics, a list of Japanese terms and their English equivalents and a general index facilitate its use.

Irie, Iwae 入江祝衛 **F16**
Eisakubun jiten 英作文辞典 A dictionary of English composition. Rev. ed. Yūhōdō, 1953.

1391p.

Proper sentence structure demonstrated through numerous examples.

Inoue, Yoshimasa 井上義昌 **F17**
Ei-Beigo yōhō jiten 英米語用法辞典 A dictionary of English and American usage. Kaitakusha, 1960. 1308p.

With more clarification of subtleties than is usual in such compilations, examples of usage and explanations by Japanese and foreign authorities are given, all with sources indicated. List of reference books appended. Detailed index.

BILINGUAL DICTIONARIES

Fuzanbō 冨山房 **F18**
Dai Ei-Wa jiten 大英和辞典 Fuzanbō's comprehensive English-Japanese dictionary. Rev. and enl. Ed. by Sanki Ichikawa and others. 1951. 1855, 243p.

Contains some 140,000 words including 8,500 proper nouns. Postwar words and American words listed in the last 243 pages.

Fuzanbō 冨山房 **F19**
Sōkai Ei-Wa jiten 雙解英和辞典 Fuzanbō's English-Japanese dictionary on bilingual principles. Rev. and enl. Ed. by Shizuka Saitō. 1954. 124, 1918p.

Japanese meanings supplemented with English explanations. Derivation of each word shown. Includes 124p. list of new words.

F20
Iwanami Ei-Wa jiten 岩波英和辞典 Iwanami's simplified English-Japanese dictionary. Rev. new ed. by Morisuke Shimamura and others. Iwanami Shoten, 1958. 1140p.

Though of limited scope, it emphasizes essential meanings instead of giving many Japanese counterparts.

F21
Kenkyūsha shin Ei-Wa daijiten 研究社新英和大辞典 Kenkyūsha's new English-Japanese dictionary on bilingual principles. New ed., rev. and enl. by Tamihei Iwasaki and Jūjirō Kawamura. Kenkyūsha, 1960. 2204p.

A comprehensive standard dictionary with more than 140,000 words, including abbreviations, new scientific terms, proper nouns, synonyms, foreign words and phrases. Derivations and English and American pronunciations given.

F22
Kenkyūsha shin Wa-Ei daijiten 研究社新和英大辞典 Kenkyūsha's new Japanese-English dictionary. Entirely new ed. by Senkichiro Katsumata. Kenkyūsha, 1959. 2136p.

A standard dictionary with more than 100,000 romanized words, each with Japanese orthography, and copious examples of usage. Lists of abbreviations and names of Government offices appended.

Saitō, Shizuka 斉藤静 **F23**
Beigo jiten 米語辞典 (Dictionary of American English) Sanseidō, 1949. 551, 14p.

Words and phrases having specific meanings in the United States, including colloquialisms, explained. Pronunciation given when it differs from that in England.

DICTIONARIES

Ogawa, Yoshio 小川芳男 **F24**
Handei gogen Ei-Wa jiten ハンディ語源英和辞典 A handy dictionary of etymology and usage. Yūseidō, 1961. 694p.

Lists about 20,000 words.

Kenkyūsha 研究社 **F25**
Eigo gogen shōjiten 英語語源小辞典 Kenkyūsha's little etymological dictionary of English language. Ed. by Fumio Nakajima. 1962. 593p. (Kenkyūsha Eigo shōjiten series)

Lists 2,000 commonly used English words with date and author of first appearance in literature. Explains etymology, historical development, and synonyms. Outline of etymology appended.

Hitotsubashi Shobō 一橋書房 **F26**
Saishin Ei-Bei ryakugo jiten 最新英米略語辞典 Hitotsubashi Shobō's new dictionary of abbreviations and contractions. Ed. by Kenji Akutsu. 1953. 510p.

Lists about 20,000 words. Supplemented with about 3,000 words in 1956.

Kenkyūsha 研究社 **F27**
Jiji Eigo jiten 時事英語辞典 Kenkyūsha's current English dictionary. 1960. 790p.

English-Japanese and Japanese-English dictionary of new words used in newspapers and magazines. Includes lists of abbreviations, personal names, place names, American English and technical terms of politics, economics, medicine, etc. List of chief newspapers and magazines in the world appended.

Kobayashi, Norio 小林則雄 **F28**
Jiji Eigo jiten 時事英語辞典 (Dictionary of current English) Hara Shobō, 1963. 272p.

Explains new words appearing in newspapers; English-Japanese and Japanese-English sections. Appended are list of English translations of names of Japanese government offices and various organizations, major world cities, and various foreign currencies.

Inoue, Yoshimasa 井上義昌 **F29**
Eigo ruigo jiten 英語類語辞典 A dictionary of English synonyms. New enl. ed. Kaitakusha, 1956. 1075p.

Synonyms and synonymous phrases are explained with examples and notes on how they are used. Includes an annotated bibliography.

Hornby, Albert Sidney, et al. **F30**
Idiomatic and syntactic English dictionary. Kaitakusha, 1959. 1518p.

Lists about 20,000 words.

Saitō, Hidesaburō 斉藤秀三郎 **F31**
Jukugo hon'i Ei-Wa chūjiten 熟語本位英和中辞典 Saitō's idiomological English-Japanese dictionary. New ed., rev. and enl. Rev. by Minoru Toyota. Iwanami Shoten, 1960. 1786p.

Idiomatic expressions, translated and explained clearly; a useful supplement to other dictionaries.

F32
The Kenkyūsha dictionary of current English idioms. Ed. by Sanki Ichikawa and others. Kenkyūsha, 1964. 22, 849p.

Arranged by keywords and explained in English with many examples cited from authoritative sources. Index.

Kenkyūsha 研究社 **F33**
Eigo kan'yōku shōjiten 英語慣用句小辞典 Kenkyūsha's little dictionary of English idiomatic phrases. Ed. by Ryōichi Inui and Shigeru Ono. 1959. 521p. (Kenkyūsha Eigo shōjiten series)

Confined to standard phrases, primarily for student use.

Sanseidō 三省堂 **F34**
Eigo kan'yōhō jiten 英語慣用法辞典 Sanseidō's dictionary of current English usage. Ed. by Takanobu Ōtsuka. 1961. 1354p.

Lists and explains in detail words, compound words, synonyms, and words with similar spelling and pronunciations, giving examples of usage and comparing standard form with slang, American-English with English-English and literary form with colloquialism. Index.

F35
Kenkyūsha shin Ei-Wa katsuyō daijiten 研究社新英和活用大辞典 Kenkyūsha's new dictionary of English collocations. Ed. by Senkichiro Katsumata. Kenkyūsha, 1958. 1525p.

Proper linkage of nouns, verbs and adjectives with other words, arranged according to parts of speech with some 200,000 examples, translated into Japanese but not explained. Compound words, solid and hyphened, are listed. There is an abridged edition:

Handei Ei-Wa katsuyō jiten (Handy dictionary of English collocation) ed. by Senkichiro Katsumata. Kenkyūsha, 1960. 1016p. **F35a.**

Kenkyūsha 研究社 **F36**
In'yōku jiten 引用句辞典 The Kenkyūsha dictionary of English quotations. Ed. by Sanki Ichikawa and others. 1956. 968p.

Quotations from the Bible, English and American literary works, etc. are explained in English. Index of key words.

Inoue, Yoshimasa 井上義昌 **F37**
Ei-Bei koji densetsu jiten 英米故事伝説辞典 A dictionary of English-American phrase and fable. Fuzanbō, 1963. 104, 61p.

Sayings, songs, myths, poems, etc. alluded to in English and American literature explained, with reference sources and illustrations. Bibliography and detailed index of key terms appended.

Iwasaki, Tamihei 岩崎民平 **et al.** **F38**
Ei-Bei fūbutsu jiten 英米風物事典 (Dictionary of things English and American) Kenkyūsha, 1960. 232p. (Eigoka handobukkusu, supp. 2)

About 500 terms related to food, clothing and housing are explained with many illustrations. Tables of holidays, weights and measures, currencies, etc. appended. A handy guide for beginning students.

Tarumi Shobō 垂水書房 **F39**
Eigo hyakka shōjiten 英語百科小辞典 Tarumi Shobō's handbook of English. Rev. ed. Ed. by Takanobu Ōtsuka. 1961. 824p.

An encyclopedic handbook, explains not only phonetics, grammar, word structure, prosody, rhetoric, Roman letters, English and American differences, punctuation, symbols, etc., but also lists personal names, countries and states, weights and measures, national flowers, etc. Japanese and English indexes.

HANDBOOK

Kenkyūsha 研究社 **F40**
Beigo handobukku 米語ハンドブック Kenkyūsha's handbook on American English. Ed. by Yoshinobu Takabe. 1963. 564p. (Kenkyūsha Eigo shōjiten series)

A dictionary of usage of colloquial and idiomatic expressions. Includes a comparative table of American-English and English-English, commenting on differences of spelling and syntax, etc. Index to non-dictionary section.

German

Katayama, Masao 片山正雄 **F41**
Doitsu bunpō jiten 独逸文法辞典 Grammatisches Wörterbuch der deutschen Sprache. Rev. ed. Yūhōdō, 1956. 1054p.

Words are explained with examples of usage. Includes introduction to German grammar. Index.

Kenkyūsha 研究社 **F42**
Doitsu bunpō shōjiten ドイツ文法小辞典 Kenkyūshas Lexikon der deutschen Grammatik. Ed. by Takeo Maruyama. 1961. 703p. (Kenkyūsha Doitsugo shōjiten series)

Important grammatical terms explained in Japanese and German. Japanese and German indexes.

Katayama, Masao 片山正雄 **F43**
Sōkai Doku-Wa daijiten 雙解独和大辞典 Grosses deutsch-japanisches Wörterbuch. Rev. and enl. ed. Nankōdō, 1939. 2476p.

F44
Iwanami Doku-Wa jiten 岩波独和辞典 Iwanamis Wörterbuch deutsch-japanisch. 2d ed. Ed. by Takeo Komaki and others. Iwanami Shoten, 1955. 1668p.

A dictionary for beginners; emphasizes common meanings.

Satō, Tsūji 佐藤通次 **and** **F45**
Morinaga, Takashi 森永隆
Hyōon Doku-Wa jiten 標音独和辞典 Kleiner Wortschatz deutsch-japanisch. Hakusuisha, 1956. 630, 17p.

Pronunciation given in both phonetic symbols and Japanese syllabary. For selected words there

is a Japanese-German dictionary section. A similar dictionary follows:

Hyōon Doku-Wa (Pronouncing German-Japanese dictionary) Ed. by Sanshichi Sugiyama and Tomone Itakura. Sanshūsha, 1960. 941p. **F45a.**

Kenkyūsha 研究社 **F46**
Poketto Doku-Wa jiten ポケット独和辞典 Kenkyūshas deutsch-japanisches Wörterbuch. Ed. by Morio Sagara. 1961. 1322p.

Lists about 50,000 words.

Sagara, Morio 相良守峯 **F47**
Grosses deutsch-japanisches Wörterbuch. Hakuyūsha, 1958. 1801p.

Words of foreign origin, dialect and slang words, and proper nouns included with many usage examples. Derivatives and compounds entered separately. An abridged edition follows:

Shintei Doku-Wa jiten (Kimura-Sagara deutsch-japanisches Wörterbuch) Ed. by Kinji Kimura and Morio Sagara. Rev. ed. Hakuyūsha, 1963. 1639, 19, 24p.

Satō, Tsūji 佐藤通次 **F48**
Doku-Wa genrin 独和言林 Neuer deutscher Wortschatz. Rev. ed. Hakusuisha, 1961. 1564p.

Derivatives and compounds entered under the basic words, making this illustrated medium-sized dictionary useful for systematic understanding of meanings.

Kimura, Kinji 木村謹治 **F49**
Wa-Doku daijiten 和独大辞典 Grosses japanisch-deutsches Wörterbuch. Hakuyūsha, 1956. 2633p.

A standard dictionary. The vocabulary and usage examples exceed those in **F51**, but the explanations are in pre-war Japanese.

Sagara, Morio 相良守峯 **F50**
Japanisch-deutsches Wörterbuch. Sanshūsha, 1957. 600p.

Lists about 50,000 words.

Okutsu, Hikoshige 奥津彦重 **F51**
Wa-Doku jiten 和独辞典 Neues japanisch-deutsches Wörterbuch. Hakusuisha, 1959. 1934p.

Notable for the absence of out-of-date expressions.

Kenkyūsha 研究社 **F52**
Eigo taishō Doitsugo dōigo shōjiten 英語対照ドイツ語同意語小辞典 Kenkyūshas kleines Wörterbuch der Synonymen. Ed. by

Hisashi Kojima. 1961. 377p. (Kenkyūsha Doitsugo shōjiten series)

Sanshūsha 三修社 **F53**
Doitsugo dōshi gyakubiki jiten ドイツ語動詞逆引辞典 Zeitwörter mit all ihren Konjugationsformen nebst Grammatik. 1961. 259p.

Infinitives of irregular verbs and their conjugated forms are arranged in alphabetical order. Conjugated form entries are followed by irregular verbs with Japanese translations and irregular verbs by transitive, intransitive, and self-reflective verbs with Japanese translations. Outline of grammar appended.

Kenkyūsha 研究社 **F54**
Doitsugo koyū meishi shōjiten ドイツ語固有名詞小辞典 Kenkyūshas kleines deutsches Eigennames Wörterbuch. Ed. by Tatsuo Koike. 1964. 14, 396p. (Kenkyūsha Doitsugo shōjiten series)

Names of well-known places and persons of Europe and America arranged according to German spelling. Japanese index.

Finnish

Imaoka, Jūichirō 今岡十一郎 **F55**
Finrandogo jiten フィンランド語辞典 (Dictionary of Finnish language) Nikkō Bunka Kyōkai, 1963. 9,696p.

Gives Japanese translations of about 20,000 Finnish words. Phrases and idioms are not included.

Dutch

Takushoku Daigaku Nanshinkai **F56**
拓殖大学南親会
Ran-Wa daijiten 蘭和大辞典 Nederlandsch-japansch Woordenboek. Sōzōsha, 1943. 1246, 30p.

Asakura, Sumitaka 朝倉純孝 **F57**
Ran-Nichi jiten 蘭日辞典 Nederlandsch-japansch Woordenboek. Meiji Shoin, 1944. 203p.

Van de Stadt, P. A. **F58**
Nichi-Ran jiten 日蘭辞典 Japansch-nederlandsch Woordenboek. Nan'yō Kyōkai, 1934. 1311p.

French

Asakura, Sueo 朝倉季雄 **F59**

Furansu bunpō jiten フランス文法事典 Dictionnaire des difficultés grammaticals de la langue francaise. Hakusuisha, 1955. 403p.

Grammatically important words and technical terms explained with many usage examples. Japanese subject index.

Yanagawa, Katsuji 柳川勝二 **et al.** **F60**
Mohan Futsu-Wa daijiten 模範仏和大辞典 Nouveau dictionnaire français-japonais. Hakusuisha, 1950. 2176p.

Pronunciations based on those of Larousse.

Martin, Jean Marie **F61**
Marutan Futsu-Wa daijiten マルタン仏和大辞典 Dictionnaire français-japonais. Reprint ed. Comp. by E. Raguet. Hakusuisha, 1953. 1467p.

Designed for advanced students, about 100,000 words and their uses explained in romanized Japanese.

Inoue, Genjirō 井上源次郎 **and** **F62**
Tajima, Kiyoshi 田島清
Shin Futsu-Wa chūjiten 新仏和中辞典 Nouveau dictionnaire pratique français-japonais. Rev. by Hiroshi Okada and Toshio Nakahara. Hakusuisha, 1960. 1220, 29p.

Though less comprehensive than **F60**, it is more up-to-date in its words and meanings.

Suzuki, Shintarō 鈴木信太郎 **et al.** **F63**
Sutandādo Futsu-Wa jiten スタンダード仏和辞典 Dictionnaire STANDARD français-japonais. Taishūkan, 1957. 1587, 31p.

Contains some 70,000 words with emphasis on new words and new meanings of words. Archaic and technical terms omitted.

Cesselin, G. **F64**
Wa-Futsu daijiten 和仏大辞典 Dictionnaire japonais-français. Yokohama, Pari Gaikoku Senkyōkai, 1953. 2395p.

Lists about 30,000 words.

Miki, Osamu 三木治 **et al.** **F65**
Shin Wa-Futsu chūjiten 新和仏中辞典 Nouveau dictionnaire pratique japonais-français. Hakusuisha, 1963. 993p.

Gives detailed explanations of correct use of words.

Maruyama, Juntarō 丸山順太郎 **F66**
Hakusuisha Wa-Futsu jiten 白水社和仏辞典

Nouveau dictionnaire japonais-français. Rev. ed. Hakusuisha, 1959. 740p.

Spanish

Muraoka, Gen 村岡玄   **F67**
Sei-Wa jiten 西和辞典 Diccionario de la lengua española. New enl. ed. Tokyo Supein Gakkai, 1956. 820, 320p.
A Spanish-Japanese dictionary containing over 100,000 words. Few idiomatic phrases and usage examples included. Last 122p. contain new words, Central and South American words, slang, cant, etc.

Takahashi, Masatake 高橋正武   **F68**
Sei-Wa jiten 西和辞典 Diccionario español-japonés. Hakusuisha, 1958. 982, 33p.
About 68,000 words, including many used in Latin America, with a 33p. table of conjugations.

     F69
Daigaku Shorin Supeingo shōjiten 大学書林 スペイン語小辞典 Diccionario para estudiantes: español-japonés, japonés-español. Ed. by Michinori Watanabe. Daigaku Shorin, 1961. 2, 463p.
Spanish-Japanese section includes about 24,500 words; Japanese-Spanish section, about 6,000 words.

     F70
Daigaku Shorin Wa-Sei shōjiten 大学書林和西小辞典 Pequeño diccionario, japonés-español. Ed. by Yoshitarō Tai. Daigaku Shorin, 1962. 6, 369p.
Lists about 20,000 commonly used words with emphasis on the idioms of commerce, conversation, and correspondence.

Muraoka, Gen 村岡玄   **F71**
Sei-Wa jukugo kan'yōku jiten 西和熟語慣用句辞典 Diccionario de la lengua española. Hakusuisha, 1949. 565p.

Calvo, Juan   **F72**
Nis-Sei daijiten 日西大辞典 Diccionario japonés-español. Sanseidō, 1958. 1427p.
First printed in 1937, it is still useful.

Portuguese

Hoshi, Makoto 星誠   **F73**
Saishin Po-Wa jiten 最新葡和辞典 Novíssimo

dicionário português-japonês. Nippaku Bunka Kyōkai, 1955. 404p.
About 18,000 words, including dialect and colloquial expressions, given in their revised spellings. Usage examples limited.

Hoshi, Makoto 星誠   **F74**
Saishin Wa-Po jiten 最新和葡辞典 Novíssimo dicionário japonês-português. Nippaku Bunka Kyōkai, 1960. 1184p.
Small dictionary. Useful only for common words.

Noda, Ryōji 野田良治   **F75**
Nip-Po jiten 日葡辞典 Dicionário japonês-português. Yūhikaku, 1963- . 1v. (A-K) In progress.

Tomoda, Kinzō 友田金三   **F76**
Burajirugo shōjiten ブラジル語小辞典 Dicionário de bôlso português-japonês. Kyoto, Tomoda Jimusho, 1957. 657p.
Brazilian Portuguese words in the 1943 official spellings with Japanese equivalents.

Italian

Inoue, Seiichi 井上静一   **F77**
Itarīgo jiten 伊太利語辞典 Nuovo dizionario moderno- razionale- pratico italiano-giapponese. Daiichi Shobō, 1936. 1013p.
Lists about 38,000 words.

Yoshida, Yakuni 吉田弥邦 **and**   **F78**
Tōdō, Takaaki 藤堂高紹
I-Nichi jiten 伊日辞典 Vocabolario italiano-giapponese. I-Nichi Jiten Kankōkai, 1938. 1031, 81p.
Lists about 35,000 words.

Scalise, Guglielmo   **F79**
I-Nichi jiten 伊日辞典 Dizionario italiano-giapponese. Tokyo Ikuei Kōgei Gakkō, 1940. 823p.

Nogami, Soichi 野上素一   **F80**
Shin I-Wa jiten 新伊和辞典 Nuovo dizionario italiano-giapponese. Hakusuisha, 1964. 10, 888, 82p.
Covers current, technical terms, new words, and special terminologies associated with theology, medieval philosophy, and Catholic ceremonies. Appended are list of abbreviations, outline of Italian grammar, and table of verb conjugations.

Shimoi, Eiichi 下位英一 **and** **F81**
Sakamoto, Tetsuo 坂本鉄男
Itariago shōjiten イタリア語小辞典 Piccolo
dizionario italiano-giapponese, giapponese-
italiano. Daigaku Shorin, 1962. 484p.

Italian-Japanese section lists 21,000 words and
Japanese-Italian section, 6,000 words. Includes
outline of Italian pronunciation and syntax.

Russian

F82

Iwanami Roshiago jiten 岩波ロシア語辞典
Russko-iaponskii slovar'. Ed. by Sadatoshi
Yasugi. Iwanami Shoten, 1960. 1535p.

The only up-to-date dictionary with many scientific and technical terms. Gives list of post-in-
flections and pronunciation guide. Sanseidō's
concise Russo-Japanese dictionary, ed. by Sadatoshi Igeta gives less coverage, but also useful.

Fel'dman, N. I. **F83**
Wa-Ro jiten 和露辞典 Iaponsko-russkii
slovar'. Gogatsu Shobō, 1952. 828p.

Reprint of 1951 Russian edition. Includes about
34,000 words.

Matsuda, Mamoru 松田衛 **F84**
Matsuda Wa-Ro daijiten 松田和露大辞典
Polnyi iapono-russkii slovar'. Tokyodō, 1959.
181,542p.

Hungarian

Imaoka, Jūichirō 今岡十一郎 **F85**
Hangarīgo shōjiten ハンガリー語小辞典
Magyar-japánés, japán-magyar zsebszótár.
Daigaku Shorin, 1958. 150p.

Includes an introduction to Hungarian grammar.

Latin and Greek

Tanaka, Hidenaka 田中秀央 **F86**
Ra-Wa jiten 羅和辞典 Lexicon latino-japo-
nicum. Kenkyūsha, 1952. 650p.

Based mainly on Hermann Menge's *Langenscheidts
Tasehenwörterbuch der lateinischen und deutschen
Sprache*, Erster Teil, gives about 35,000 words,
including proper nouns and adjectives, and medical
and pharmaceutical terms.

Tanaka, Hidenaka 田中秀央 **and** **F87**
Ochiai, Tarō 落合太郎

Girisha Raten in'yōgo jiten ギリシア・ラテ
ン引用語辞典 Lexicon sententiarum graec-
arum et latinarum. Enl. ed. Iwanami Shoten,
1954. 158, 841, 111p.

Quotations from Greek (158p.) and Roman (841p.)
classics are explained with sources given. No
index.

Esperanto

Okamoto, Yoshitsugu 岡本好次 **F88**
Shinsen Esu-Wa jiten 新選エス和辞典 Nova
vortaro esperanto-japana. Enl. ed. Nihon Esuperanto Gakkai, 1960. 228, 34, 25p.

Elementary dictionary, with an introduction to
Esperanto syntax.

Okamoto, Yoshitsugu 岡本好次 **F89**
Shinsen Wa-Esu jiten 新選エス辞典 Nova
vortaro japana-esperanto. Nihon Esuperanto
Gakkai, 1960. 822p.

Includes a guide to writing Esperanto. Proper
nouns treated in separate section.

ORIENTAL LANGUAGES
→ G29

Chinese
BIBLIOGRAPHY

Chūgoku Gogaku Kenkyūkai **F90**
中国語学研究会
Chūgoku gogaku bunken mokuroku 中国語学
文献目録 (Bibliography of Chinese language)
No. 1- . 1957- . 2v. In progress.

Classified list of Japanese studies. Includes
monographs and articles. No. 1 covers Aug., 1945 -
July, 1957, published by Kōnan Shoin. No.2, Aug.,
1957 - Dec., 1961 includes Tibetan and a few other
minority languages.

DICTIONARIES

Ōbunsha 旺文社 **F91**
Ka-Nichi daijiten 華日大事典 (Chinese-
Japanese dictionary) 1950. 1412, 47p.

About 14,000 characters and 120,000 compounds
arranged by radicals and strokes. Pronunciation
given in Chinese phonetic script and Wade romanization for each character, with only the latter for
compounds. Phonetic script index.

Inoue, Midori 井上翠 **F92**
Inoue Chūgokugo shinjiten 井上中国語新辞典 Inoue's pocket Chinese-Japanese new dictionary. Rev. and enl. ed. Kōnan Shoin, 1954. 1111, 5, 63p.
Pronunciation shown in Wade romanization.

Miyajima, Yoshitoshi 宮島吉敏 **and F93 Yajima, Tōsuke** 矢島藤助
Chūgokugo jiten 中国語辞典 (Chinese dictionary) Rev. and enl. ed. Sakai Shoten, 1955. 1007p.
Arranged by radicals and strokes. Characters have Wade romanizations.

Kanegae, Nobumitsu 鐘ヶ江信光 **F94**
Chūgokugo jiten 中国語辞典 (Dictionary of Chinese language) Daigaku Shorin, 1960. 1157p.
Entries by romanized Chinese followed by characters. Stroke index. Good for modern simplified characters used in People's Republic of China.

Kōsaka, Jun'ichi 香坂順一 **and F95 Ōta, Tatsuo** 太田辰夫
Gendai Chū-Nichi jiten 現代中日辞典 (Current Chinese-Japanese dictionary) Kōseikan, 1961. 743, 22p.
Arrangement according to romanized pronunciations.

F96
Iwanami Chūgokugo jiten 岩波中国語辞典 (Iwanami's Chinese dictionary) Ed. by Takeshiro Kuraishi. Iwanami Shoten, 1963. 25, 914p.
Deals with contemporary conversational Chinese, Peking dialect. Arranged by romanized Chinese followed by Chinese characters and Japanese translations with usage examples. Indexes by characters and by topics such as animals, plants, houses, machines, weights and measures, etc. Useful for the modern language used in People's Republic of China.

Hiraoka, Ryūjō 平岡竜城 **et al. F97**
Nik-Ka daijiten 日華大辞典 Nipponese-Chinese dictionary. Tōyō Bunka Mikan Tosho Kankōkai, 1936-38. 3 v.
Contains some 100,000 words. Chinese pronunciation romanized in the Wade system. Many examples of usage.

Ch'ên, T'ao 陳濤 **F98**
Nik-Kan jiten 日漢辞典 (Japanese-Chinese dictionary) Daian, 1959. 2214p.
Lists about 80,000 words.

Harada, Minoru 原田稔 **F99**
Saishin Nit-Chū jōyō jiten 最新日中常用字典 (The newest Japanese-Chinese dictionary of characters for everyday use) Today's Chinese characters and language. Daian, 1960. 85, 209p.
Using only the simplified characters adopted in mainland China, gives common Japanese words and Chinese equivalents with pronunciation and usages. Pt.2 translates the *Hanzi pinyin jianzi*, a Shanghai dictionary of 8,000 common characters arranged separately by strokes and pronunciations.

Formosan

✤ Not a native language, but a dialect of Amoy, China.

Taiwan Sōtokufu 台湾総督府 **F100**
Tai-Nichi daijiten 台日大辞典 (Formosan-Japanese dictionary) Taipei, 1931-32. 2v.
Some 90,000 words of Amoy dialect family used in Formosa arranged according to their pronunciation as indicated by Japanese syllabary, followed by Chinese characters, Japanese translation, examples of usage, etc.

Wang, Yü-tê 王育徳 **F101**
Taiwango jōyō goi 台湾語常用語彙 The basic vocabulary of the Formosan dialect. Eiwa Gogakusha, 1957. 475p.
Lists about 5,000 romanized words. Each word given in Chinese characters, followed by part of speech, Japanese translation, grammatical explanation, examples of use. Introduction to Formosan dialect included.

Korean

Chōsen Sōtokufu 朝鮮総督府 **F102**
Chōsengo jiten 朝鮮語辞典 (Korean language dictionary) Seoul, 1920. 983p.
Lists about 20,000 characters, arranged by *onmon*. Each onmon is signified by Chinese characters, and phrases beginning with these characters listed with onmon. Indexes.

Chōsengo Kenkyūkai 朝鮮語研究会 **F103**
Chōsengo jiten 朝鮮語辞典 (Korean dictionary) Kaiseisha, 1953. 983p.
Reprint of **F102**.

Song, Jihak 宋枝学　　　　　　　　**F104**
Chōsengo shōjiten 朝 鮮 語 小 辞 典 (Small Korean dictionary) Japanese-Korean, Korean-Japanese. Daigaku Shorin, 1960. 400p.

Korean-Japanese part gives about 25,000 words arranged by Korean letters, each with pronunciation, Japanese meaning and usage examples. Japanese-Korean part has about 4,600 words. Korean grammar outlined.

Ainu

Batchelor, John　　　　　　　　　**F105**
Ainu-English-Japanese dictionary. 4th ed. Iwanami Shoten, 1938. 145, 581, 100p.

Ainu words, arranged alphabetically by romanized pronunciations, given their English and Japanese counterparts. Has a separate English-Ainu vocabulary. Ainu grammar explained. Notes and examples in English.

Chiri, Mashiho 知里真志保　　　　**F106**
Bunrui Ainugo jiten 分 類 ア イ ヌ 語 辞 典 (Classified dictionary of the Ainu language) Nihon Jōmin Bunka Kenkyūjo, 1953-62. 3v.

v.1, Botany, lists 500 words; v.2, Zoology, 500 words; and v.3, Human beings, 850 words. Japanese words are translated into Ainu, giving morphology, accents, definitions, etymology and feelings and faiths associated with the words. v.2 is an unfinished work published posthumously. Japanese and Ainu indexes in each volume.

Hattori, Shirō 服 部 四 郎　　　　　**F107**
Ainugo hōgen jiten ア イ ヌ 語 方 言 辞 典 An Ainu dialect dictionary, with Ainu, Japanese and English indexes. Iwanami Shoten, 1964. 43, 556p.

Expressions in the dialect of Hokkaido, the Kuriles, and Sakhalin. Collected by field investigations and classified into thirty-five categories, such as human body, society, clothes, food, dwelling, animal, plant, natural phenomena, etc. Arranged by romanized Japanese, giving briefly parts of speech, usage, meaning of each entry, and Ainu and English translations. Ainu, Japanese, and English indexes.

Chiri, Mashiho 知里真志保　　　　**F108**
Chimei Ainugo shōjiten 地 名 ア イ ヌ 語 小 辞 典 (Small geographical dictionary of Ainu) Sapporo, Nire Shobō, 1956. 169p. (Nire sōsho, 2)

Not a gazetteer. About 500-600 entries for topographical words, natural features of the earth, verbs, adjectives, adverbs, prefixes, suffixes, etc. as they appear in Ainu place-names. Entry words are romanized. Index to examples of usage.

Tibetan

Hōzōkan 法 蔵 館　　　　　　　　　**F109**
Zō-Kan jiten 蔵 漢 辞 典 Tibetan-Chinese dictionary. Kyoto, 1944. 116p. Mimeo.

Lists about 4,000 words.

Yoshimura, Shūki 芳 村 修 基　　　**F110**
Chibettogo jiten チ ベ ッ ト 語 辞 典 (Tibetan dictionary) Kyoto, Ryūkoku Daigaku Tōhō Seiten Kenkyūkai, 1956. 1119p.

Lists about 26,000 words.

Burmese

Ajia Afurika Gengo Kenkyūshitsu　**F111**
ア ジ ア ・ ア フ リ カ 言 語 研 究 室
Nihon Birumago shōjiten 日 本 ・ ビ ル マ 語 小 辞 典 (Japanese-Burmese small dictionary) 1960. 196p. Mimeo.

Lists about 1,200 words.

Siamese

Okuno, Kinzaburō 奥 野 金 三 郎　　**F112**
Tai-Nichi daijiten タ イ 日 大 辞 典 (Siamese-Japanese dictionary) Tōkō Shoin, 1958. 858p.

About 80,000 words, including those in classics and sutras, arranged according to Thai alphabet, with pronunciations, Japanese meanings and usage examples. Old spellings indicated.

Malay

Taketomi, Shōichi 武 富 正 一　　　**F113**
Maraigo daijiten 馬 来 語 大 辞 典 (Comprehensive Malay dictionary) Ōbunsha, 1942. 1074p.

Lists about 30,000 words.

Asakura, Sumitaka 朝 倉 純 孝　　　**F114**
Indoneshiago shōjiten イ ン ド ネ シ ア 語 小 辞 典 Kamus bahasa Indonésia-Djepang, Djepang-Indonésia. Daigaku Shorin, 1964. 523p.

Official Malay adopted by the Republic of Indonesia is used. Indonesia-Japanese section lists 28,000 terms and the other, 6,000 terms. May be used for Malay in different spellings by consulting the guide, included in the book.

Tagalog

Yamaga, Taiji 山鹿泰治 **and**   **F115**
Versoza, Paul Rodoriguez
Nip-Pi shōjiten 日比小辞典 (Little Japanese-Filipino dictionary) Manila, 1943. 234, 48p.

Manchu

Watabe, Kuntarō 渡部薫太郎   **F116**
Manshūgo tosho mokuroku 満州語図書目録 (Catalogue of books on the Manchu language) Osaka, Osaka Tōyō Gakkai, 1925. 32p. (Ajia kenkyū, no. 3)

Haneda, Tōru 羽田亨   **F117**
Man-Wa jiten 満和辞典 Manju zo-ben gisum kamcibuha bithe. Kyoto, Kyoto Teikoku Daigaku Man-Mō Chōsakai, 1937. 478p.
  Manchurian-Japanese dictionary. Lists about 29,000 words.

Mongolian

Rikugunshō 陸軍省   **F118**
Mōkogo daijiten 蒙古語大辞典 (Comprehensive Mongolian dictionary) Kaikōsha, 1933. 3v.
  v.1 and 2, Mongolian-Japanese. v.3, Japanese-Mongolian.

Abematsu, Gen'ichi 精松源一 **et al.**   **F119**
Mō-Wa jiten 蒙和辞典 (Mongolian-Japanese dictionary) 3d ed., rev. and enl. Osaka, Kōbundō, 1940. 495, 18p. Mimeo.
  Lists about 17,800 words.

Ishida, Kiyoshi 石田喜代司 **and**   **F120**
Khionin, A. P.
Saishin hyōon Mō-Ro-Nichi daijiten 最新標音蒙露日大辞典 Mongol'sko-russko-iaponskii slovar'. Rev. ed. Gakugeisha, 1941. 829p.
  Lists about 5,000 words.

Abematsu, Gen'ichi 精松源一   **F121**
Shin Mō-Nichi jiten 新蒙日辞典 Shine-mongol-iapon tol'. Osaka Gaikokugo Daigaku Dōsōkai, 1959. 574p.

In Russian scripts. New Mongolian-Japanese dictionary.

Osaka Gaikokugo Gakkō Mōkobu   **F122**
大阪外国語学校蒙古部
Wa-Mō jiten 和蒙辞典 (Japanese-Mongolian dictionary) Rev. ed. Osaka, Guroria Shobō, 1941. 432p.
  About 26,000 words.

Turkish

Nit-To Kyōkai 日土協会   **F123**
Nit-To To-Nichi daijiten 日土・土日大辞典 (Japanese-Turkish and Turkish-Japanese dictionary) 1936. 1009p.
  Japanese-Turkish section lists about 5,000 words, Turkish-Japanese section about 6,500 words. A comparative dictionary of new and old Turkish appended.

Sanskrit

Hagiwara, Unrai 萩原雲来   **F124**
Kan'yaku taishō Bon-Wa daijiten 漢訳対照梵和大辞典 (Comprehensive Sanskrit-Japanese dictionary with Chinese translation) Taishō Daigaku, 1940- . 7v. In progress.
  Covers A-Ni.

Pali

Kumoi, Shōzen 雲井昭善   **F125**
Pa-Wa shojiten 巴和小辞典 (Small dictionary of Pali-Japanese) Kyoto, Hōzōkan, 1961. 353p.
  Lists about 7,000 words.

JAPANESE LANGUAGE

❋ Works dealing with the national language together with literature, so often the case in Japan, are listed according to the custom, under literature. For the sake of convenience, Chinese-Japanese dictionaries which are used to translate Chinese classics into Japanese as well as to find meanings of Japanese words written in Chinese characters are listed here along with ordinary Japanese language dictionaries. Also dictionaries of characters are included in this section.

Philology

BIBLIOGRAPHY

Tōjō, Misao 東條操　**F126**
Saikin no kokugogaku to hōgengaku 最近の国語学と方言学 (The recent study of the Japanese language and dialects) Chikuma Shobō, 1960. 150, 7p.

Developments and problems outlined by introducing major studies from 1938 to 1957. Subject and title indexes.

Saeki, Umetomo 佐伯梅友 **et al.**　**F127**
Kokugogaku 国語学 (Japanese philology) Sanseidō, 1961. 807p. (Kokugo kokubungaku kenkyūshi taisei, 15)

History of Japanese language studies outlined with bibliographical emphasis under such headings as phonology, phonetics, use of *kana*, etymology, semantics, dictionaries and indexes, particles, conjugations, modernisms, syntax, honorifics, dialects and punctuation marks. 158p. appendix lists source materials. Title-subject index.

Tokyo Teikoku Daigaku 東京帝国大学 **F128**
Kokugogaku shomoku kaidai 国語学書目解題 (An annotated bibliography of Japanese language study) Yoshikawa Hanshichi, 1902. (858p.)

More than 600 pre-Meiji works, some of them no longer extant, are described but not evaluated. Chronology of studies to 1897 with author and subject indexes.

Doi, Tadao 土井忠生　**F129**
Meiji Taishō kokugogaku shomoku kaisetsu 明治大正国語学書目解説 (An annotated bibliography of Japanese language study in the Meiji and Taishō periods, 1867-1926) Iwanami Shoten, 1932. 106p. (Iwanami kōza: Nihon bungaku)

Forty major works annotated in detail.

Kameda, Jirō 亀田次郎　**F130**
Kokugogaku shomoku kaidai 国語学書目解題 (An annotated bibliography of Japanese language) Meiji Shoin, 1933. 110p. (Kokugo kagaku kōza, 3)

Under the headings of general and miscellaneous, phonology, etymology, *kana* usage, particles, letters, conjugations, dictionaries and grammar, 190 works are annotated. Studies by foreigners covered in an appendix. Title index.

Kokuritsu Kokugo Kenkyūjo　**F131**
国立国語研究所
Meiji ikō kokugogaku kankei kankō shomoku 明治以降国語学関係刊行書目 (Bibliography of works on Japanese language study published since the Meiji period) Shūei Shuppan, 1955. 301p. (Kokuritsu Kokugo Kenkyūjo shiryōshu, 4)

Listed without evaluation under 11 headings are 3,027 books on the Japanese language published from 1868 through 1952. Periodical articles not included. This is brought up to date each year in **F135.**

Nihon Gakujutsu kaigi 日本学術会議 **F132**
Bungaku tetsugaku shigaku bunken mokuroku. VI: Kokugogaku hen 文学·哲学·史学文献目録 VI : 国語学編 (Bibliography of literature, philosophy and history. VI: Japanese language) 1957. 281p.

Monographs, articles and other writings, including mimeographed works and reprints, published from August, 1945, through December, 1955, classified under twenty headings, each with sub-divisions. List of periodicals and an author index.

DICTIONARIES

Kokugo Gakkai 国語学会　**F133**
Kokugogaku jiten 国語学辞典 (Dictionary of Japanese language study) 7th ed., rev. Tokyodō, 1961. 1249p.

2,700 signed entries with bibliographies cover all aspects of Japanese language study, including minor and unorthodox views. Subject, title, name and foreign word indexes. Useful to supplement this is **G56.**

Zenkoku Kyōiku Tosho 全国教育図書 **F134**
Kokugo kokubungaku zukai daijiten 国語国文学図解大事典 (Illustrated dictionary of Japanese language and literature) 1962- . 1v. In progress.

Explains systematically historical developments from early times to the present with illustrations, charts and tables. v.1 deals not only with Japanese language in general, but also with related topics such as books and publishing, natural science, the calendar, life, politics, economics and industry. Lists of references.

YEARBOOK

F135
Kokugo nenkan 国語年鑑 (Japanese language yearbook) 1954- . Comp. by Kokuritsu Kokugo

Kenkyūjo. Shūei Shuppan, 1954- . 11v.

Lists books, magazine and newspaper articles on Japanese linguistics published the preceding year, reports activities of institutions and societies and lists scholars engaged in language studies.

Education

Shiraishi, Daiji 白石大二 **et al.**　**F136**
Kokugo kyōiku jiten 国語教育辞典 (Dictionary of Japanese language education) Rev. ed. Tokyodō, 1963. 762p.

Intended for teachers in elementary and secondary schools. Entries give bibliographical references. In appendixes are a list of Chinese characters in daily use, proofreading symbols and a language education and literature chronology from 1868. Detailed subject index.

Fujii, Nobuo 藤井信男 **et al.**　**F137**
Kokugo kyōiku jiten 国語教育辞典 (Dictionary of terms used in Japanese language teaching) Gakutōsha, 1963. 413p.

Explanations include important points in teaching and lists of references. Chronological table, list of teaching manuals for elementary, junior and senior high schools appended. Subject index.

Sakamoto, Ichirō 坂本一郎　**F138**
Kyōiku kihon goi 教育基本語彙 (Basic vocabulary for compulsory education) Maki Shoten, 1958. 377p.

The 22,500 words to be learned in elementary and secondary schools arranged according to Japanese orthography in current use. Grades in which they are to be taught indicated. Chinese characters for daily use are differentiated from those which there is need only to recognize.

Hirai, Masao 平井昌夫　**F139**
Kokugo kyōiku handobukku 国語教育ハンドブック (Handbook of Japanese language education) Maki Shoten, 1955. 782, 17p.

For comprehension of post-war language education, terms are defined, laws and regulations given, teaching materials explained and a bibliography provided. Japanese and English subject and name indexes.

History

Hiraoka, Tomokazu 平岡伴一　**F140**
Kokuji kokugo mondai bunken mokuroku 国字国語問題文献目録 (Bibliography of Japanese letters and language) Iwanami Shoten, 1932.　323p.

Monographs and magazine and newspaper articles on history of Japanese language and literature are listed chronologically under basic references, theory, practice and related problems with location and some with annotation. Title and name indexes.

Monbushō Kyōkashokyoku　**F141**
文部省教科書局
Kokugo chōsa enkaku shiryō　国語調査沿革資料 (Literature on the history of Japanese language surveys; with a bibliography of language and writing problems in foreign countries) 1949. 261p.

A collection of data of the national language research activities carried by the committees and boards of inquiries of the Ministry of Education since 1868. Reports and recommendations are not included. Chronological table of enforcements of policies of the national language and letter improvement and an annotated bibliography ed. by Yoshikata Uno appended. Trends after 1949 can be traced in *Monbushō Kokugo Shingikai hōkokusho* (Report of the Japanese Language Council, Ministry of Education) No. 1- . Shūei Shuppan, 1952- . Triennial.

Phonology

Terakawa, Kishio 寺川喜四男 **and**　**F142**
Kusaka, Miyoshi 日下三好
Hyōjun Nihongo hatsuon daijiten 標準日本語発音大辞典 (Standard Japanese pronouncing dictionary) Kyoto, Taigadō, 1956. 1067p.

Entered in *kana*, divided into syllables, each word has phonetic symbols and accent marks in an attempt to show standard pronunciation. There are detailed explanations of accent, timbre and quantity. Homonyms and dialect accents compared.

Nippon Hōsō Kyōkai 日本放送協会　**F143**
Nihongo akusento jiten　日本語アクセント辞典 (Japanese accent dictionary) Nippon Hōsō Shuppan Kyōkai, 1951. 803, 27p.

Indicates the standard pronunciation of about 50,000 Japanese words, with accent atlas and rules for determining accent.

Sanseidō 三省堂　**F144**
Meikai Nihongo akusento jiten　明解日本語アクセント辞典 (Precise Japanese accent dictionary) 1958. 926, 68p.

Standard pronunciation dictionary with about 60,000 words, including particles, adverbs, conjunctions, conjugation forms, compounds, surnames and place names, with comments on and rules of accent.

Hirayama, Teruo 平山輝男 **F145**
Zenkoku akusento jiten 全国アクセント辞典 (Dictionary of Japanese accents) Tokyodō, 1960. 950p.

Contains about 100,000 words. Entry words with standard accent notations compared with two major regional accents, i. e. Kyoto and Kagoshima. Includes compound words with standard accent notations and their uses. Distribution maps of accent, dialect and phonetic changes, introduction to accent, accents of numerals and family names included.

Orthography

❧ Since the study for improving the orthography of contemporary Japanese has not been completed, the most up-to-date dictionaries should be used.

Monbushō Kyōkashokyoku **F146**
文部省教科書局
Tōyō kanji gendai kanazukai ni kansuru bunken mokuroku 当用漢字現代かなづかいに関する文献目録 (Bibliography of literature on the newly adopted Chinese characters for daily use and orthography) 1949. 70p.

Monographs and newspaper and magazine articles from 1946, when the Government announced its list of 1,850 basic characters and new orthography through 1948.

Hirota, Eitarō 広田栄太郎 **F147**
Shinpen yōji yōgo jiten 新編用字用語辞典 (Newly compiled dictionary of syntax) Tokyodō, 1960. 364p.

A guide for writing sentences using the 1,850 basic characters, their derivatives and modern syllabic declensions.

Shiraishi, Daiji 白石大二 **F148**
Tōyō kanji okurigana hitsujun reikai jiten 当用漢字・送りがな・筆順例解辞典 (Dictionary of current Japanese orthography) Teikoku Chihō Gyōsei Gakkai, 1964. 11, 624p.

Lists common words and phrases in Japanese syllabic order and explains orthography of current Chinese characters with examples of correct and incorrect usage, synonyms and antonyms.

F149
Shinbun yōgoshū 新聞用語集 (Glossary of newspaper language) 1956- . Nihon Shinbun Kyōkai, 1956- . 9v. Annual.

A general newspaper stylebook listing standardized, technical and Imperial Household terms, Chinese characters for daily use, words of foreign origin, foreign personal and place names, etc. and giving rules for Japanese orthography.

Reading aid marks

Yoshizawa, Yoshinori 吉沢義則 **F150**
Tenpon shomoku 点本書目 (Bibliography of books with marks for the Japanese reading of Chinese writing) Iwanami Shoten, 1931. 150p. (Iwanami kōza: Nihon bungaku)

Lists, briefly annotates and locates copies of Chinese books and Buddhist scriptures with markings to aid Japanese readers, which throw light on early Japanese usage. Discussion of such books and their markings appended.

Endo, Yoshimoto 遠藤嘉基 **and** **F151**
Hirohama, Fumio 広浜文雄
Shinpan tenpon shomoku 新版点本書目 (New bibliography of books with reading aid marks) Meiji Shoin, 1957. 180p.

Lists books not in **F150**, arranged by the years in which the marks were made, with location of copies, colophons and references.

Dictionaries

→ **C17**

Ochiai, Naobumi 落合直文 **F152**
Nihon daijiten: Gensen 日本大辞典言泉 (Comprehensive Japanese dictionary: Fountain of words) Rev. by Yaichi Haga. Ōkura Shoten, 1927-29. 6v.

Includes ancient, dialectal, and technical terms, historical and literary allusions, titles of literary works, words found in poems, songs and dramas, etc., each given in old orthography, meanings and examples of use, with their sources. Some illustrations. Indexed by Chinese characters.

Ōtsuki, Fumihiko 大槻文彦 **F153**
Daigenkai 大言海 (Great sea of words) Fuzanbō, 1932-37. 5v.

An expanded revision of the 1891 *Genkai* (Sea of words), it is strong in archaic words but also gives modern, dialect and commonly used Chinese words and words of non-Chinese foreign origin, each with pronunciation, etymology, meanings and usage examples, with sources. Indexes of Chinese characters arranged by strokes, Japanese words in syllabic order and words of foreign origin. A one-volume edition without the indexes was published in 1956.

Ueda, Kazutoshi 上田万年 **and** **F154**
Matsui, Kanji 松井簡治
Dai Nihon kokugo jiten 大日本国語辞典 (Dictionary of the Japanese language) Rev. ed. Fuzanbō, 1939. 5v.

Gives more than 200,000 words, excluding dialects, proper nouns unless related to legends and folklore, with emphasis on ancient words. Etymology is mostly ignored, but usage examples, all with their sources, are extensive. Syllabic and character indexes. A 2376p. one-volume edition without the indexes was published in 1952.

Heibonsha 平凡社 **F155**
Daijiten 大辞典 (Great dictionary) 1953-54. 13v.

Of encyclopedic proportions, it combines more than 400,000 modern, classical, dialect and technical terms, including those of foreign origin, with nearly 300,000 personal and place names, literary titles, etc. Meanings are by specialists. Some illustrations. Introduction to grammar and indexes of Chinese characters arranged by strokes, difficult pronunciations and foreign personal and place names appended. Reduced-size reprint of 1934-37 edition in 26v. with additional entries.

Kindaichi, Kyōsuke 金田一京助 **F156**
Jikai 辞海 (Sea of words) Sanseidō, 1952. 2070p.

A standard one volume dictionary, with accent marks, contains about 130,000 modern and ancient words and technical terms in the natural and social sciences and humanities, with usage examples for common words. List of conjugations, orthography, and index of Chinese characters appended. There is also a reduced-size edition, first published in 1954.

Shinmura, Izuru 新村出 **F157**
Kōjien 広辞苑 (Wide garden of words) Iwanami Shoten, 1955. 2359p.

Semi-encyclopedic, including many personal and place names, book titles, poetic themes, set phrases, proverbs, etc., as well as scholarly terms in all fields, among its nearly 200,000 entries. Headings and explanations are in postwar orthography. Etymologically strong. Many illustrations. Appended are readings for characters used in personal names, romanization rules, etc. Revision of the same editor's *Jien* (Garden of words), 1935.

Kanazawa, Shōzaburō 金沢庄三郎 **F158**
Shinpan kōjirin 新版広辞林 (Newly published wide word forest) Sanseidō, 1958. 2158, 72p.

Compiled to supplant the once widely used semi-encyclopedic *Kōjirin* (Wide word forest), with 13,000 of its words dropped and 33,000 added, making a total of about 136,000. Explanations conform to the new orthography.

F159
Iwanami kokugo jiten 岩波国語辞典 (Iwanami's dictionary of national language) Ed. by Minoru Nishio and Etsutarō Iwabuchi. Iwanami Shoten, 1963. 1112p.

Lists 57,000 Japanese words and phrases and 2,400 Chinese characters in Japanese reading arranged in syllabic order. Useful and handy. Appendix includes tables on grammar and orthography.

Kindaichi, Kyōsuke 金田一京助 **et al.** **F160**
Meikai kokugo jiten 明解国語辞典 (Concise Japanese dictionary) Rev. ed. Sanseidō, 1959. 978p.

Emphasis on current words but also giving archaic and literary words pertinent to modern interests.

CHINESE-JAPANESE

✤ Useful as a bibliography of Chinese-Japanese dictionaries from ancient times is the article "Honpō jishoshi gaisetsu" (Outline of the history of Japanese dictionary) by Tadao Yamada in the magazine, *Kokugogaku*, pub. by Musashino Shoin. Series no. 39, 1959. **F161.**

Morohashi, Tetsuji 諸橋轍次 **F162**
Dai Kan-Wa jiten 大漢和辞典 (Great Sino-Japanese dictionary) Taishūkan Shoten, 1955-60. 13v.

Monumental compilation giving about 50,000 root Chinese characters, compared with 48,000 in the Imperial edition of the K'ang-hsi dictionary, and about 520,000 compounds, with explanations, many of them with illustrations, and exhaustive usage examples from identified sources arranged chronologically. Characters are given in all forms, and Japanese and Chinese pronunciations, ancient and modern, are indicated. v. 13 has indexes by strokes, Japanese readings and four-corner number arrangements, as well as lists of characters used in Japan and simplified characters used in China.

Ueda, Kazutoshi 上田万年 **et al.**   **F163**
Daijiten 大字典 (Great character dictionary)
7th rev. ed. Kōdansha, 1963. (2821p.)

Though relatively old and not in present-day Japanese, it retains usefulness because of its large number of compounds. Gives variant forms of basic characters and Chinese and Japanese pronunciations, including those used in personal names, and has a section on cursive writing. Indexed by strokes and by Japanese readings.

Hattori, Unokichi 服部宇之助 **and**   **F164**
Oyanagi, Shiketa 小柳司気太
Shōkai Kan-Wa daijiten 詳解漢和大辞典
(Comprehensive Sino-Japanese dictionary with detailed explanations) Rev. and enl. ed. Fuzanbō, 1956. 2180, 252p.

Gives for each character compounds beginning and ending with it. Ancient Japanese and Chinese court and military practices illustrated. Indexed by Wade phonetics.

Shionoya, On 塩谷温   **F165**
Shinjikan 新字鑑 (New mirror of characters)
3d ed., rev. and enl. Kōtō Kyōiku Kenkyūkai, 1961. 2423p.

Gives 11,000 Chinese characters arranged by number of strokes and their modern Chinese compounds, with pronunciation in Wade phonetics. Appended are a list of homonyms, a guide to Chinese, information about cursive writing and the composition of characters and a chronology of Chinese history and culture. Originally published in 1939 by Kōdōkan.

Kanno, Dōmei 簡野道明   **F166**
Jigen 字源 (Source of characters) Enl. ed.
Kadokawa Shoten, 1959. 2358, 234p.

Etymologies and homonyms of some entry characters given. Compounds arranged according to Japanese pronunciation of their second characters. Illustrations of ancient court and military customs and examples of cursive and ornamental characters appended.

Oyanagi, Shiketa 小柳司気太   **F167**
Shinshū Kan-Wa daijiten 新修漢和大辞典
(Newly compiled comprehensive Sino-Japanese dictionary) Hakuyūsha, 1953. 2117p.

Has cursive style of each character and 76p. list of homonyms. Originally published in 1932 by Hakubunkan.

CHARACTERS

Takada, Tadachika 高田忠周   **F168**
Kanji shōkai 漢字詳解 (Characters explain-

ed in detail) 2d ed., rev. Seitō Shobō, 1925. 3v.

Deals with etymology of characters on the basis of classical Chinese dictionaries, shows them in various styles and gives pronunciations and meanings. Abridged edition follows:

Taikei kanji meikan (Simplified explanation of characters) by Tadachika Takada. Rev. ed. Fuzanbō, 1940. 872, 91p.   **F168a.**

Itō, Tōgai 伊藤東涯   **F169**
Sōko jiketsu 操觚字訣 (Chinese thesaurus)
With supplement. Rev. by Tokujun Murayama.
Suharaya Shoten, 1885. 772p.

Gives meanings and different uses of synonymous Chinese characters.

Nagashima, Toyotarō 長島豊太郎   **F170**
Kojisho sōgō sakuin 古字書綜合索引 (Union index to old dictionaries) Nihon Koten Zenshū Kankōkai, 1958-59. 2v. (Koten bunko)

Chinese characters included in eight old Japanese dictionaries, *Shinsen jikyō, Wamyō ruijūshō, Honzō wamyō, Iroha jiruishō, Ruijū myōgishō, Jikyōshū, Ryūgan tekagami, Setsumon kaiji,* listed according to the order and the form used in K'ang-hsi Imperial dictionary, 1716, with variations of forms and locations in each dictionary.

Classical phrases and allusions

Ikeda, Shirojirō 池田四郎次郎   **F171**
Koji jukugo daijiten 故事熟語大辞典 (Comprehensive dictionary of Chinese historical allusions and compounds) Hōbunkan, 1960. 300, 1750, 204p.

Arranged by Japanese syllabary and explained with usage examples.

Kanno, Dōmei 簡野道明   **F172**
Koji seigo daijiten 故事成語大辞典 (Comprehensive dictionary of Chinese historical allusions and expressions) Meiji Shoin, 1929. 1851, 134p.

Arranges by Japanese syllabary facts and phrases found in Chinese classics relating to astronomy, seasonal events, government posts, politics, music, ethics, literature, science, weapons, human affairs, arts and accomplishments, food, dress, flowers, trees, bamboo, stones, etc. Sources given. Indexed by strokes.

Nakano, Yoshihei 中野吉平   **F173**
Rigen daijiten 俚諺大辞典 (Comprehensive dictionary of proverbs) Tōhō Shoin, 1933. 1507p.

Gives proverbs and sayings from Chinese and Japanese classics, including historical allusions, puns, etc., with meanings and sources, arranged in the following categories under each syllable of the Japanese syllabary: astronomy, geography, government orders, morals, religion, human affairs, the human body, arts and sciences, food, utensils, economics, court affairs, animals, plants and miscellaneous. General index.

Fujii, Otoo 藤井乙男   **F174**
Gengo daijiten 諺語大辞典 (Comprehensive dictionary of proverbs) Yūhōdō, 1953. 1159, 13, 254p.

Extensive compilation of Japanese proverbs, historical allusions, legends, puns, riddles, etc. not found in ordinary dictionaries, arranged in Japanese syllabic order, with explanations for those not self-explanatory. Sources of examples given. Includes many Western proverbs in English for comparison. Classified index, difficult to use. Reprint of 1925 edition.

Takahashi, Gen'ichirō 高橋源一郎   **F175**
Koji seigo gengo jiten 故事成語諺語辞典 (Dictionary of historical allusions, familiar phrases and proverbs) Meiji Shoin, 1962. 699p.

Lists about 7,000 items. Reprint of *Koji seigo gengo shūkai*, 1960.

Suzuki, Tōzō 鈴木棠三 **and**   **F176**
Hirota, Eitarō 広田栄太郎
Koji kotowaza jiten 故事ことわざ辞典 (Dictionary of historical allusions and proverbs) Tokyodō, 1956. 983p.

Gives meanings and examples from identified sources of Japanese historical allusions, proverbs, maxims, etc., including many of Chinese and Buddhist origin. Distinguished from earlier similar compilations in having explanations in postwar language. No index.

Zoku koji kotowaza jiten (Dictionary of historical allusions and proverbs, continued) by Tōzō Suzuki. Tokyodō, 1961. 456p. **F176a.**

Supplements **F176**, with emphasis on popular proverbs. Discussion of proverbs and old books of proverbs appended.

Ema, Tsutomu 江馬務   **F177**
Kokubun kojitsu fūzokugo shūshaku 国文故実風俗語集釈 (Terms for ancient practices, manners and customs in Japanese literature explained) Kyōritsusha, 1935. 502p.

Defines with examples the use of terms in 44 literary works of the Heian and Muromachi periods under the headings of coiffure, hair ornaments, makeup, headgear, dress, footwear and personal effects. Many illustrations. Bibliography and index.

Nomoto, Yonekichi 野本米吉   **F178**
Koten yōgo yūsokuzu jiten 古典要語有職図辞典 (Illustrated dictionary of classical terms and ancient court and military practices) Musashino Shoin, 1956. 530p.

Gives meanings and usage examples from identified sources of about 6,000 terms connected with ancient court customs, Buddhism and literature, conventional epithets in poetry, names of animals and plants, etc., with many illustrations of customs, dress, armor, utensils, plant and animals, and maps. Appended are an annotated bibliography with title entries, explanations of annual events, directory of numerical names, list of government posts and simple chronology of Japanese literature.

Synonyms and homonyms

Shida, Gishū 志田義秀 **and**   **F179**
Saeki, Tsunemaro 佐伯常麿
Nihon ruigo daijiten 日本類語大辞典 (Comprehensive dictionary of Japanese synonyms) Seikōkan, 1909) 1777, 50, 25p.

Common words and their meanings are followed by synonyms, including those requiring adjectives. Variants of place names and nicknames listed.

Hirota, Eitarō 広田栄太郎 **and**   **F180**
Suzuki, Tōzō 鈴木棠三
Ruigo jiten 類語辞典 (Dictionary of synonyms) Tokyodō, 1955. 746p.

Gives synonyms of Chinese and Japanese modern and archaic words, slang expressions, honorifics, dialect words, set phrases, etc. Cross-references inadequate, and shades of meaning not distinguished. Lists of floral language, seasonal themes, poetical epithets, etc. appended.

Kokuritsu Kokugo Kenkyūjo   **F181**
国立国語研究所
Bunrui goihyō 分類語彙表 Word list by semantic principles. Shūei Shuppan, 1964. 362p. (Kokuritsu Kokugo Kenkyūjo shiryōshū, 6)

Lists about 32,600 Japanese words currently in use, including nouns, verbs, adjectives, etc., classified in 798 categories. Serves as dictionary of synonyms and expressions, guide to the study of differences of expression by area and social class. Includes historical development of Japanese language and basic vocabularies. List of subjects. Index.

Shioda, Norio 塩田紀男 **and** **F182**
Nakamura, Kazuo 中村一男
Hantaigo jiten 反対語辞典 (Dictionary of antonyms) Tokyodō, 1958. 365p.

Lists about 13,000 words. Similar work follows:

Taishō kanren hantaigo jiten (Comparative dictionary of antonyms) ed. by Umetomo Saeki. Shūeisha, 1963. 429p. **F182a.**

Shūgiin Sokkisha Yōseijo **F183**
衆議院速記者養成所
Dōongo ruiongoshū 同音語・類音語集 (Vocabulary of homonyms and quasi-homonyms) 1954. 280p.

Kokuritsu Kokugo Kenkyūjo **F184**
国立国語研究所
Dōongo no kenkyū 同音語の研究 (Study of homonyms) Shūei Shuppan, 1961. 290p. (Kokuritsu Kokugo Kenkyūjo hōkoku, 20)

Includes 7,800 sets of homonyms.

Historical words

→ D59, D103

Sanseidō 三省堂 **F185**
Meikai kogo jiten 明解古語辞典 (Precise dictionary of archaic words) Rev. ed. 1958. 1156p.

Explains 36,000 words, including terms connected with ancient customs and practices and Buddhism, found in pre-1868 literature. Rich in usage examples from identified sources. Notes on grammar, chronology, maps and illustrations appended.

Kadokawa kogo jiten 角川古語辞典 (Kado- **F186**
kawa dictionary of archaic words) Ed. by Yūkichi Takeda and Sen'ichi Hisamatsu. Kadokawa Shoten, 1958. 1051p.

Words which must be known for understanding of classical literature are entered in their old orthography, followed by the postwar orthography, Chinese characters, meanings and usage examples. Some illustrations. Notes on grammar, lists of government posts, coins, etc. appended.

Ōbunsha kogo jiten 旺文社古語辞典 (Ōbunsha's dictionary of archaic words) Ōbunsha, **F187**
1960. 1312p.

Contains about 40,000 words.

Nakada, Norio 中田祝夫 **F188**
Shinsen kogo jiten 新撰古語辞典 (New dictionary of old words) Shōgakkan, 1963. 8,1335p.

Lists about 44,000 words.

Ishigami, Ken 石上堅 **F189**
Nihon koten bungakugo jiten 日本古典文学語辞典 (Dictionary of words in Japanese classical literature) Ipposha, 1955. 748p.

Contains about 5,000 important words in literary works to about 1710, including those of Chikamatsu and Saikaku, entered in historical orthography, with characters, grammatical notes, definitions, transliteration into modern Japanese, and examples of use in identified works. Briefly annotated list of literary works appended.

Matsuoka, Shizuo 松岡静雄 **F190**
Nihon kogo daijiten 日本古語大辞典 (Comprehensive dictionary of Japanese archaic words) Reprint ed. Tōkō Shoin, 1963. 2v.

Analyzes, explains and gives the sources of words in the earliest Japanese writings. v. 2 interprets difficult passages in the *Kojiki* and *Nihon shoki* and all the poems in them and the *Man'yōshū*. Outline of grammar appended. First ed. in 1929. An abridged one-volume edition appeared in 1962, entitled *Shinpen Nihon kogo jiten*, 32,608p.

Maeda, Isamu 前田勇 **F191**
Kinsei kamigatago jiten 近世上方語辞典 (Dictionary of pre-modern dialects of the Kyoto-Osaka area) Tokyodō, 1964. 1213p.

Explains words commonly used in Kyoto-Osaka area; selected from pre-modern literature with sources and examples of usage. Useful for study of Japanese literature of the period.

Satō, Tsurukichi 佐藤鶴吉 **F192**
Genroku bungaku jiten 元禄文学辞典 (Dictionary of Genroku literature) Shinchosha, 1928. 704p.

Comments on and gives the sources of words, sayings and allusions peculiar to the Genroku period (1688-1704) in the verse and prose of Saikaku and the plays of Chikamatsu, with quotation of passages in which they appear. Omits ordinary words found in usual dictionaries. References listed. Useful in conjunction with **G84** and **G179.**

Ōtsuka, Tatsuo 大塚竜夫   **F193**
Makurakotoba jiten 枕詞辞典 (Dictionary of *makurakotoba*, conventional attribute-words) Kazama Shobō, 1961.   303, 36p.

Pt.1 lists about 850 conventional attribute-words with their meanings and usage examples in 31-syllable poems.   Pt.2 lists words preceded by conventional attribute-words with their matching attribute-words.

Fukui, Kyūzō 福井久蔵   **F194**
Makurakotoba no kenkyū to shakugi 枕詞の研究と釈義 (The study and interpretation of *makurakotoba*, conventional attribute-words) Rev. and enl.   ed., by Tokuhei Yamagishi. Yūseidō, 1960.   748p.

An introduction is followed by a 558p. dictionary which gives after each attribute-word the words which it may modify and its source. A chronology of attribute-words studies appended. Indexes of personal names, titles, subjects, attribute-words and words modified by them.

Nakayama, Yasumasa 中山泰昌   **F195**
Nankunjiten 難訓辞典 (Dictionary of difficult character readings) Tokyodō, 1956.   579p.

Gives the correct special readings not found in ordinary dictionaries for characters and compounds, which are arranged by strokes in separate sections for common words and personal and place names. Lists of names including numbers, i. e., Sanpitsu (Three great calligraphers) and Rikkokushi (Six books of Japanese history) appended.   No index.

New words

→ M18

❧ Following titles are revised every year.

Asahi shinbunsha 朝日新聞社   **F196**
Shinbungo jiten 新聞語辞典 (Dictionary of newspaper words) 1964 ed.   1964.   640p.

Defines new names and other words found in current newspapers, with foreign spellings given when necessary. Some maps and illustrations. Brief who's who of foreign personages appended. Index.

Jiyū Kokuminsha 自由国民社   **F197**
Gendai yōgo no kiso chishiki 現代用語の基礎知識 (Basic current Japanese) 1965 ed. 1964.   1112p.

Defines 14,500 new terms in politics, economics, industry, sociology, etc.   Index.

Hōgaku Shoin 法学書院   **F198**
Jiji yōgo kaisetsu 時事用語解説 (Current words, annotated) 1965 ed.   1964.   463p.

Lists about 3,300 words.

Loanwords

Ueda, Kazutoshi 上田万年 **et al.**   **F199**
Nihon gairaigo jiten 日本外来語辞典 (Dictionary of loanwords in Japanese) Sanseidō, 1915.   426p.

Pioneer listing of about 7,000 Japanese words of non-Chinese foreign origin introduced from ancient times to about 1915, with their meanings and original words.

Arakawa, Sōbei 荒川惣兵衛   **F200**
Gairaigo jiten 外来語辞典 (Dictionary of loanwords)   Fuzanbō, 1941.   1208p.

Most comprehensive dictionary of its kind, giving the sources and meanings of about 10,000 words adopted into Japanese from foreign languages, excluding words of Chinese origin, with comments and about 60,000 usage examples. Chronologically arranged bibliography.

Kenkyūsha 研究社   **F201**
Gairaigo shōjiten 外来語小辞典 Kenkyūsha's little dictionary of loan-words in Japanese. Ed. by Yoshio Ogaeri. 1959.   481p. (Kenkyūsha shōjiten series)

Lists about 10,000 currently used words, including personal and place names, taken into Japanese, with original spellings and meanings or explanations. Markings indicate those "indispensable in daily usage". Borrowings from modern Chinese included. Foreign-language abbreviations found in Japanese writings appended.

Slang

Umegaki, Minoru 楳垣実   **F202**
Ingo jiten 隠語辞典 (Dictionary of cant, argot and slang) Tokyodō, 1956.   600p.

Most inclusive compilation of special expressions used by thieves, students, artists and other classes or groups since Nara period, listing about 17,000 words with their meanings, etymology, usage examples, indication of the groups and times in which they were used and cross references. Introduction to the formation of such language, list of secret words for numbers and annotated bibliography of cant studies appended. Classified indexes by social groups and of synonyms.

Grammar

Meiji Shoin 明治書院   **F203**
Nihon bunpō jiten 日本文法辞典 (Dictionary of Japanese grammar) 1958. 401p.

Explains Japanese grammatical terms and words with important grammatical functions, giving different theories and views and many usage examples from identified sources. Classified table of contents. Originally published as v.6 of *Nihon bunpō kōza* (Japanese grammar course).

Asano, Shin 浅野信   **F204**
Shinsen Nihon bunpō jiten
新撰日本文法辞典   (New dictionary of Japanese grammar) Spoken language, written language, composition. Enl. ed. Morikita Shuppan, 1950-54. 3v.

Explains sentence structure and words of grammatical importance. Useful in interpreting sentences.

Dialects

✽ Works only with nationwide coverage are included.

Nihon Hōgen Kenkyūkai   **F205**
日本方言研究会
Nihon no hōgen kukaku 日本の方言区画 (Distribution of Japanese dialects) Tokyodō, 1964. 708p.

A collection of theses on Japanese dialects. Appended: 1. List of books on dialects (p.541-547, 1943-63), 2. List of theses on dialects (p.576-662, 1943-63), and 3. List of literary works in dialects (p.664-684, 1868-1963). Nos. 1 and 2 are successors to "Kankō hōgen shomoku" (List of books on dialects) and "Hōgen ronbun mokuroku" (List of theses on dialects) which appear in the rev. ed. of *Hōgen to hōgengaku* (Dialects and dialectology) pub. by Shun'yōdō. No.3 covers literary works with expressions in dialect which are not listed in nos. 1 and 2. For basic works on dialects see **F126**.

Tōjō, Misao 東条操   **F206**
Zenkoku hōgen jiten 全国方言辞典 (Nationwide dialect dictionary) Tokyodō, 1951. 881p.

Only work of its kind; gives meanings and geographical usage distribution of about 40,000 dialect words selected from dialect studies and local histories, with usage examples and some source indicated. Includes dialect map and introduction to dialect studies. Indexed in **F207**.

Tōjō, Misao 東条操   **F207**
Hyōjungobiki bunrui hōgen jiten 標準語引分類方言辞典(Classified dictionary of dialect words listed by standard words) Tokyodō, 1954. 804p.

Indexes for both **F206** and **F207** in 14 categories, such as universe and the seasons, food and drinks, and society, within which standard words are followed by their dialect variants or synonyms. Complete syllabic index of both dialect and standard words also given. Map of dialect accents and bibliography appended.

Kokugo Chōsa Iinkai   **F208**
国語調査委員会
Kōgoho chōsa hōkokusho 口語法調査報告書 (Report on colloquial Japanese grammar) Kokutei Kyōkasho Kyōdō Hanbaijo, 1906. 2v.

Compiled from returns of questionnairs sent to prefectures by Japanese Language Research Committee. Covers 38 topics of grammatical importance on various dialects. 37 distribution maps of colloquialisms sppended. Basic material on distribution of dialects.

Monbushō 文部省   **F209**
On'in chōsa hōkokusho 音韻調査報告書 (Phonetic survey report) Nihon Shoseki, 1905. 511, 15p.

Gives a general view of pronunciation in each prefecture as revealed in the first nationwide phonetic survey, sponsored by the Japanese Language Research Committee, with 29 phonetic distribution maps corresponding to 29 items investigated for prolonged sounds, gradations and consonants.

Tōjō Misao Sensei Koki Kinenkai   **F210**
東条操先生古稀記念会

Nihon hōgen chizu 日本方言地図 (Japan dialect atlas) Yoshikawa Kōbunkan, 1956. 23p. 24 maps.

Gives 4 phonetic maps and 12 of colloquial expressions taken from **F208** and **F206**, a phonetic distribution map by Haruhiko Kindaichi, an intonation distribution map by Teruo Hirayama, a map of sentence-ending particles by Yoichi Fujiwara, a map showing distribution of dialect words for "heel" by Masanaka Oiwa, 4 foreign-language dialect maps and a map of Japanese dialect boundaries by Misao Tōjō. Explanatory text follows.

Ryukyuan language

Kokuritsu Kokugo Kenkyūjo   **F211**
国立国語研究所
Okinawago jiten 沖縄語辞典 (Dictionary of

Okinawa dialect) 1963. 854p. (Kokuritsu Kokugo Kenkyūjo shiryōshū, 5)

Gives Japanese translations and annotations to
dialect of Shuri area of Okinawa with close relationship to old Okinawan records and books. Covers
about 15,000 words, including colloquial words,
literary expressions, old words, and names of places.
Words adapted from Japanese since 1868 are excluded. Headings are in international phonetic
signs. For literary words, traditional ways of writing
by Chinese characters or Japanese syllabary are
also indicated. Standard Okinawan language index,
maps and list of place names.

Miyanaga, Masamori 宮良当壮   **F212**
Yaeyama goi 八重山語彙 (Vocabulary of
Yaeyama dialect) Tōyō Bunko, 1930. 135,
301, 203p.

Pt.1 is a collection of words indicated by Japanese syllabary with Japanese translation, and pt.2,
Japanese words with corresponding Yaeyama words.

Miyanaga, Masamori 宮良当壮   **F213**
Saihō nantō goi kō 採訪南島語彙稿

(Draft of the Southern Islands vocabulary collected on-the-spot) Kyōdo Kenkyūsha, 1926.
781p. Mimeo.

Dictionary of dialects collected at various places
in Ryūkyū Islands classified by parts of speech.
Contains 1,685 Japanese words with equivalents
in the dialects.

Kuwae, Yoshiyuki 桑江良行   **F214**
Hyōjungo taishō Okinawago no kenkyū 標準語
対照沖縄語の研究 (Study of Okinawa
dialect in comparison with standard Japanese)
Naha, Aoyama Shoten, 1930. 438p.

Iba, Fuyū 伊波普猷   **F215**
Ryūkyū gikyoku jiten 琉球戯曲辞典 (Dictionary of Ryūkyū plays) Kyōdo Kenkyūsha, 1938.
271p.

About 600 difficult words in Ryūkyū plays, arranged according to their pronunciation, are explained.

LITERATURE

❧ General works on literature usually contain bibliographical and biographical studies; histories of literature especially those with good indexes are useful as annotated bibliographies, biographical dictionaries, and for chronological tables often included. They are good reference sources.

GENERAL WORKS
BIBLIOGRAPHY

Kokuritsu Kokkai Toshokan　　　**G1**
国立国会図書館
Meiji Taishō Shōwa hon'yaku bungaku mokuroku
明治・大正・昭和翻訳文学目録　　A list of foreign literary works done into Japanese. Kazama Shobō, 1959.　779p.

Lists Japanese translations of European and American literary works (fiction, drama, poetry, criticism, essays, travel accounts, diaries and letters), as well as some Persian and Indian, but none of China or Korea, published from 1868 to 1955.　Pt.1, the main list, from 1912 to 1955, has author entries in Japanese transliterations with titles translated, different editions, translators, publishers and publication dates. Authors indexed in original spelling.　Pt.2, for 1868-1911, gives translations and adaptations, including those in newspapers and periodicals, by publication dates.

Yanagida, Izumi　柳田泉　　**G2**
Meiji shoki hon'yaku bungaku no kenkyū 明治初期翻訳文学の研究　(Studies of translated literature in early Meiji period) Shunjūsha, 1961.　493, 16p. (Meiji bungaku kenkyū, 5)

Bibliographical and biographical studies in the early translation of Western literature from 1868 to 1900.　Includes a Shakespeare translation bibliography and a chronological list of translations.

Author and title indexes.　Rev. ed. of *Meiji shoki no hon'yaku bungaku* (Translated literature of the early Meiji period), published by Shōhakukan in 1935.

DICTIONARIES

Yoshie, Takamatsu　吉江喬松　　**G3**
Sekai bungei daijiten　世界文芸大辞典 (World literature dictionary)　Chūō Kōronsha, 1935-37.　7v.

Explains authors, writings and literary terms and concepts of major countries from ancient times; also has entries on related arts, history, philosophy, and religion, with references in various languages for each subject.　v.7 gives national literary histories.　Dated but useful.

G4

Kenkyūsha sekai bungaku jiten　研究社世界文学辞典　Kenkyūsha dictionary of world literature.　Kenkyūsha, 1955.　1493p.

Entries cover authors, titles, subjects, including linguistics and the arts, for all countries, including Japan, China, and Korea from ancient times, with a literary chronology by countries and many illustrations.　Detailed indexes in Japanese, Western languages, and Chinese.

G5

Sekai bungei jiten　世界文芸辞典 (Dictionary of world literature)　Japan and Asia, the Western.　New ed., rev. Tokyodō, 1957-59.　2v.

Identifies writers and their works with annotations for major works and explains literary forms and related matters.　Terms given with English, German or French equivalents.　Each volume indexed for authors, titles and subjects.　Special index of waka and haiku quotations.

Suzuki, Yukio 鈴木幸夫 **et al.** **G6**

Sekai bungaku kanshō jiten 世界文学鑑賞
辞典 (Dictionary for the appreciation of
world literature) Tokyodō, 1962-64. 4v.

Lists representative works from ancient times
to the present by Japanese translated titles. Gives
for each title synopsis, criticism, points of appreciation, brief biography of the author, with title and
author's name in original language. Japanese index.

Tokyo Daigaku Gakusei Bunka Shidōkai **G7**
東京大学学生文化指導会
Bungei yōgo jiten 文芸用語辞典 (Dictionary
of literary arts terms) 1950. 406p.

Words used in criticism and related subjects are
explained, with some bibliographical referneces.
Entries of English, French, and German terms give
original spellings.

Fukuhara, Rintarō 福原麟太郎 **G8**
Bungaku yōgo jiten 文学要語辞典 A dictionary of literary terms. Kenkyūsha, 1960.
347p. (Kenkyūsha refarensu bukkusu)

English words encountered in the study of English
and American literature, including names of organizations and places listed alphabetically and explained in Japanese.

G9
Sekai gendaishi jiten 世界現代詩辞典 (A
dictionary of the modern poetry of the world)
Sōgensha, 1951, 615p.

About 1,200 poets of all countries active from
1868 to 1950 are identified, movements, techniques,
problems and terms explained. Table shows poets
and their works in chronological order. Subject
and term indexes.

G10
Gendaishi yōgo jiten 現代詩用語辞典 (A
dictionary of modern poetry) Kinseidō, 1950.
291p.

Explains poetic words and technical terms used
in poetics, indexed by their original languages.
Brief biographies of important 19th and 20th century
European and American poets in 103 pages.

Murano, Shirō 村野四郎 **and** **G11**
Sugawara, Katsumi 菅原克己
Gendaishi yōgo jiten 現代詩用語辞典 (Dic-
tionary of contemporary poetry terms) Iizuka
Shoten, 1956. 197, 28p.

Article-length explanations, with many quotations,
of about 200 important terms. Names, subjects,
quoted poems indexed.

Edogawa, Ranpo 江戸川乱歩 **G12**
Kaigai tantei shōsetsu: sakka to sakuhin
海外探偵小説：作家と作品 (Foreign de-
tective story writers and their works) Hayakawa
Shobō, 1957. 385, 91p.

Contains biographies of and comments on 80 European and American writers. Appended are a general
list of Western detective stories, a chronological
Sherlock Holmes bibliography and selected lists
of famous English and American detective stories.

CHRONOLOGY

Ichiko, Teiji 市古貞次 **et al.** **G13**
Kaisetsu sekai bungakushi nenpyō 解説世界
文学史年表 (A chronological table of the
history of the world literature with annotations)
Chūō Kōronsha, 1957. 886p.

Divided into 87 periods from 2500 B.C. to 1955,
Asian and Western literary history is outlined by
countries, with explanation of major developments.
Ainu, Korean and Ryūkyūan literatures covered in
appendix. Authors, titles, including newspapers
and magazines, and subjects indexed. Illustrated.

BIOGRAPHIES

Tokyo Daigaku Gakusei Bunka Shidōkai **G14**
東京大学学生文化指導会
Gendai bungaku jinmei jiten 現代文学人名
辞典 (Biographical dictionary of contemporary authors) 5th ed., rev. and enl. 1951. 368p.

Bio-bibliographies of about 1,000 post-1868 authors and literary scholars, divided into Japanese
and foreign sections. Western names given in original spelling. Appended are articles on Western
classics and modern Japanese literary thought,
chronology of modern literature, etc. Name index.

EUROPEAN

Nihon Gakujutsu Kaigi 日本学術会議 **G15**
Bungaku tetsugaku shigaku bunken mokuroku.
II: Seiyō bungaku gogaku hen 文学・哲学・
史学文献目録 II：西洋文学・語学編
(Bibliography of literature, philosophy and history. II: Western literature, linguistics) 1954.
138p.

Selected by academic societies for scholarly
value, Japanese monographs and articles on literature in general, the literatures of Western countries,
comparative literature and Western languages are
listed, with subject and author indexes. v.2 covers
those published from August, 1945, through June,

1952, and supplementary volume, *Bunkakei bunken mokuroku XII...* 1961. 257p., adds those published to the end of 1959.

Kure, Shigeichi 呉 茂一 **et al.** **G16**
Seiyō bungaku jiten 西 洋 文 学 辞 典 (Dictionary of Western literature) Koishikawa Shobō, 1950. 554, 33p.

Basic information about Western writers, literary terms and related subjects from the earliest times. Especially useful in working with literature available in Japanese translation. Major works have independent entries, but most titles are listed under their authors. Author and subject indexes.

Nakano, Yoshio 中 野 好 夫 **et al.** **G17**
Sekai bungaku jiten 世 界 文 学 辞 典 (Dictionary of world literature) Kawade Shobō, 1954. 581, 63p. (Sekai bungō meisaku zenshū, supp.)

Limited to Western literature. Outlines national literary histories, identifies writers and schools, explains forms, etc. Works, unless anonymus, are treated under their authors. References are given for major subjects.

English and American

→ **F10**

BIBLIOGRAPHY

Saitō, Takeshi 斉 藤 勇 **G18**
Igirisu bungakushi イ ギ リ ス 文 学 史 (A history of English literature) 4th ed., enl. Kenkyūsha, 1957. 850p.

A 186p. annotated bibliography and a comprehensive English index of names. Titles and terms give reference value to this general history from early Middle Ages to the 1950's.

Daiches, David **G19**
Gendai Eibungaku no tenbō 現 代 英 文 学 の 展 望 (Contemporary English literature, a survey) Tr. by Tsutomu Ueda and Keiichi Hirano. Kenkyūsha, 1960. 273, 244, 7p.

In translating "The present age after 1920", final volume of *Introduction to English literature*, ed. by Bonamy Dobrée, the translator has up-dated the 244-page bio-bibliography, which is divided by literary forms, and added works translated into Japanese, with an index of authors in both the history and the bibliography.

Ueda, Tsutomu 上 田 勤 **et al.** **G20**
Gendai Ei-Bei bungaku handobukku 現 代 英 米 文 学 ハ ン ド ブ ッ ク A handbook of modern British and American literature. Nan'undō, 1962. 544, 49p.

Annotated bio-bibliographies of 90 writers of this century, given in two parts, English and American, each with lists of general reference works including those by Japanese scholars, and notes on Japanese translations. Indexes.

DICTIONARY

G21
Kenkyūsha Ei-Bei bungaku jiten 研 究 社 英 米 文 学 辞 典 The Kenkyūsha dictionary of English and American literature. New ed., rev. and enl. Ed. by Takeshi Saitō. Kenkyūsha, 1961. 1604p.

Entries cover not only English and American literature, including many younger writers, but also contemporary European literature and Western culture in general, with citation of Japanese studies. Biographical entries give pronunciation and dates. A 349p. chronology from classical times to 1960 shows literary and social developments in England and America in parallel to those in Europe and Asia. The copious illustrations are indexed.

BIOGRAPHIES

G22
Kenkyūsha Ei-Bei bungaku hyōden sōsho 研 究 社 英 米 文 学 評 伝 叢 書 Kenkyūsha's series of critical biographies of figures in English and American literature. Kenkyūsha, 1933-39. 103v.

Representative authors predominate with life and works of one author in each volume. A chronology of English and American literature, *A dictionary of literary terms* **G8** and a general index issued as supplementary volumes.

Kanō, Hideo 加 納 秀 夫 **G23**
Gendai Ei-Bei bungaku jinmei jiten 現 代 英 米 文 学 人 名 辞 典 Literary who's who. Kenkyūsha, 1961. 333p. (Kenkyūsha refarensu bukkusu)

Compiled from 15 English reference books. Entries give briefly the careers, characteristics and major works of English and American writers of the present century.

German

Nihon Dokubungakkai 日 本 独 文 学 会 **G24**
Doitsu bungaku jiten ド イ ツ 文 学 辞 典 Deutshes Literatur-Lexikon. Kawade Shobō,

1956.   1101p.

Mainly a biographical dictionary of German writers to the present. Also has entries on subjects related to German literature and history. Some major works treated independently. General indexes in Japanese and German.

French

Doi, Hiroyuki 土居寛之 **et al.**   **G25**
Furansu bungaku jiten フランス文学辞典 (Dictionary of French literature) Genchōsha, 1963.   383p.

Under Japanese headings, lists French men of letters, writers, writings and literary thought since the Middle Ages with emphasis on the twentieth century. Japanese index.

Tokyo Daigaku Furansu Bungakkai   **G26**
東京大学フランス文学会
Furansu bungaku jiten フランス文学辞典 (Dictionary of French literature) Kyoto, Zenkoku Shobō, 1950.   439, 49p.

Entries on writers, their works and literary terms with a short history of French literature, a chronology (1040-1948) and a list of literary awards. Indexed by authors, titles and subjects.

Girard, Marcel   **G27**
Gendai Furansu bungaku jiten 現代フランス 文学辞典 Guide illustré de la littérature française moderne, 1918-49. Tr. by Jun Watanabe. Hakusuisha, 1951.   325p.

Divided into three periods, each sub-divided into poetry, fiction and drama, with a short introduction to each category. Biographical sketches of about 180 writers are followed by reference lists.

Russian

Yokemura, Yoshitaro 除村吉太郎   **G28**
Roshia bungaku techō ロシア文学手帖 (Notes on Russian literature) Osaka, Sōgensha, 1955.   278p. (Sōgen techō bunko)

Contains a brief history of Russian literature, a biographical dictionary of novelists, poets, critics, etc., information on art, publishers, libraries, newspapers, magazines, etc., and a survey of literature in East European countries. Includes lists of Stalin Prize awards and Russian literary works published in Japan since 1945, and a literary chronology. Names, titles and subjects indexed.

ORIENTAL

Nihon Gakujutsu Kaigi 日本学術会議   **G29**
Bungaku tetsugaku shigaku bunken mokuroku. III: Tōyō bungaku gogaku hen 文学 · 哲学 · 史学文献目録Ⅲ：東洋文学 · 語学編 (Bibliography of literature, philosophy and history. III: Oriental literature, language) 1954-58.   2v.

Japanese studies, translations, compilations and commentaries published from Aug., 1950 to Oct., 1956, extending from the Ainu and Giliak in the north to those of Southwest Asia and the Pacific area. Includes monographs and articles in journals, newspapers and collected works.

Chinese

Iida, Yoshirō 飯田吉郎   **G30**
Gendai Chūgoku bungaku kenkyū bunken mokuroku 現代中国文学研究文献目録 (Bibliography of studies on contemporary Chinese literature) 1919-45. Chūgoku Bunka Kenkyūkai, 1959.   87p.

Chronological list of Japanese monographs and periodical articles.

Tenri Daigaku Jinbun Gakkai   **G31**
天理大学人文学会
... Chūgoku gogaku bungaku ronbun mokuroku 中国語学文学論文目録 (Chinese periodical and newspaper index to Chinese literature and language) Tenri, Tenri Daigaku Shuppanbu, 1960- .   2v. (Tenri Daigaku Jinbun Gakkai series) In progress.

Classified list of items extracted from the Chinese monthly *Zenkoku shuyō hōkan shiryō sakuin* (National major periodical index) published in Shanghai. Covers 1957-58.

Kondō, Moku 近藤杢   **G32**
Chūgoku gakugei daijiten 中国学芸大辞典 (Dictionary of Chinese culture) Gengensha, 1959.   (1806p.)

Covers all aspects of literature up to the Chinese Republic in about 9,000 entries, each with references. Includes terms, names, titles of books, famous passages and phrases. Appendix contains lists of scholars, literary men, literary schools, chronologies of Chinese culture, Western Sinology, and Sino-Japanese cultural relations. Indexes of names and general indexes by pronunciation and by strokes. Rev. ed. of *Shina gakugei daijii* (Dictionary of Chinese culture) 1936.

Saku, Misao 佐久 節   **G33**
Kanshi taikan 漢詩大観 (Comprehensive collection of Chinese poems) Seki Shoin, 1936-39. 5v.

Poems found in 15 famous anthologies published up to the 13th century with marks to aid Japanese reading. Includes poems by T'ao Yüan-ming 365-427, Li Po, 701-762, Tu Fu, 712-770, Po Chü-i, 772-846, Su Shih, 1036-1101, and others. Index in v.4 and 5 by first lines arranged by strokes.

Yoshikawa, Kōjirō 吉川幸次郎 **and**   **G34**
Ogawa, Tamaki 小川環樹
Chūgoku shijin senshū sōsakuin 中国詩人選集総索引 (General index of selected works of Chinese poets) Iwanami Shoten, 1959. 359p.

Themes, lines and annotated words arranged by Japanese readings of 17 standard works, including the section on "Customs and manners of the states" in *Shih-ching* (Book of poetry) and the "selected works" of the following 11 poets: Ts'ao Chih, T'ao Yüan-ming, Han Shan, Wang Wei, Li Po, Tu Fu, Han Yu, Po Chü-i, Li Ho, Li Shang-yin and Li Yu, indexed separately. Supplementary volume gives an outline of T'ang poetry and a chronological table of T'ang poets.

Iijima, Tadao 飯島忠夫 **and**   **G35**
Fukuda, Fukuichirō 福田福一郎
Toshi sakuin 杜詩索引 (An index to the poems of Tu Fu) Shōundō, 1935. 339p.

Based on Ch'ou Chao-ao's Commentary on Tu Fu's Poetry and other sources, each line is indexed by its final character.

Kyoto Daigaku, Jinbun Kagaku Kenkyūjo **G36**
京都大学人文科学研究所
Tōdai kenkyū no shiori 唐代研究のしおり (T'ang civilization reference series) 1954- . 14v. In progress.

Basic materials on T'ang literature and its background are given in the following volumes:

Tōdai no koyomi (T'ang calendar) by Takeo Hiraoka. 1954. 28,383p. (v.1)

From 618 to 907 A.D. Lunar calendar, showing sexagenary cycles, is matched with Western dates on the basis of careful calculations. Era names are indexed.

Tōdai no gyōsei chiri (T'ang administrative geography) by Takeo Hiraoka and Kōkichi Ichihara. 1955. 42,382p. 2 maps. (v.2)

A gazetteer of states, counties and prefectures. Has all place-names mentioned in eight books published in or near the T'ang period and two books

of the Ch'ing dynasty. It is indexed by corner numbers.

Tōdai no shijin (T'ang poets) by Takeo Hiraoka and Kōkichi Ichihara. 1960. 16,178p. (v.4)

Based on the *Ch'üan T'ang shih* (Complete collection of T'ang poetry), published in 1707, and the supplement to this, *Zen Tō shi itsu*, published in Japan in 1804 by Seinei Ichikawa, the poets are listed by their real names. Other names , family connections, birthplace, period and works are given.

Tōdai no shihen (T'ang poems) by Takeo Hiraoka and others. pt.1. 1964. 26,889p. (v. 11)

Lists titles of more than 50,000 poems found in the *Ch'üan T'ang shih* and *Zen Tō shi itsu* and many other sources, under names of authors with locations cited. When completed in two parts this index will cover almost all the poems and poets and titles of books in which they are found, of the T'ang period.

Chōan to Rakuyō (Ch'ang-an and Lo-yang) by Takeo Hiraoka and Kiyoshi Imai. 1956. 3v. (v.5-7)

Consists of a volume reproducing seven basic gazetteers and related books, a volume indexing the names of residences, places, stores, graves, wells, trees, etc. mentioned in v.5 and a volume of 30 maps of the two capitals, with an explanatory pamphlet.

Rihaku kashi sakuin (Concordance to the poems of Li Po) by Hideki Hanabusa. 1957. 96,8, 522p.

Each word and phrase in the 1,049 poems in the 30-volume *Li T'ai-po wên-chi* is indexed, with indexes by titles, personal names and place-names.

Rihaku no sakuhin (Works of Li Po) by Takeo Hiraoka. 1958. 48,180p. (v.9)

Sung texts in the Seikadō Library, Tokyo, are reproduced, with a compilation of probable dates and places of composition by Huang Hsi-kuei and Chan Ying.

Tōdai no sanbun sakka (T'ang prose writers) by Takeo Hiraoka and Kiyoshi Imai. 1954. 28, 120p. (v.3)

Names, birthplaces and periods of some 3,500 writers of about 23,000 titles are listed. The titles are from the *Ch'üan T'ang-wên* (Complete collection of T'ang literary works), published in 1814, and its two supplements, *T'ang-wen shih-i* and *T'ang-wên hsü-shih*. Appended are an index of pseudonyms and chronological and genealogical tables.

Tōdai no sanbun sakuhin (T'ang prose works) by Takeo Hiraoka and others. 1960. 23, 887p. (v.10)

With bibliographical references to many other sources, all of the titles in the three books named in v.3 are listed. Personal names are indexed.

Monzen sakuin (Concordance to *Wên-hsüan*) by Rokurō Shiba. 1957-59. 4v.

Words and phrases of this oldest anthology of masterpieces since the Chou period, compiled by Prince Chao-ming, 501-531 A.D., which influenced Japanese literature from the ninth century, are entered by strokes. v.4 consists of indexes.

JAPANESE

❧ Titles are listed under headings: general, poetry, prose, Chinese language literature, individual authors and their works, juvenile literature. Since each topic is interrelated, cross reference should be made to other pertinent sections.

General

BIBLIOGRAPHY

Kondō, Tadayoshi 近藤忠義 **G37**
Nihon bungaku nyūmon 日本文学入門 (Introduction to Japanese literature) Nihon Hyōronsha, 1940. 492p.

Includes a discussion of research methods and a bibliographical guide divided by periods and literary forms. List of bibliographies on Japanese literature compiled by Yoshibumi Sakakibara appended. No index.

Saitō, Kiyoe 斎藤清衛 **G38**
Nihon bungaku kenkyūhō 日本文学研究法 (Japanese literary research methods) Kawade Shobō, 1956. 311p.

Gives outline of research methods, with many references, and lists by form literary works on which there has been research. References include monographs, articles in magazines and series published, 1868-1955. No index.

Asō, Isoji 麻生磯次 **and** **G39**
Shuzui, Kenji 守随憲次
Nihon bungaku kenkyū nyūmon 日本文学研究入門 (Introduction to the study of Japanese literature)　Tokyo Daigaku Shuppankai, 1956. 438p.

Divided into five periods, each with an introduction. Surveys contemporary studies and points out research problems, with many bibliographical references. Appended is a directory of libraries and collections containing important materials. No index.

Nihon Bungaku Kyōkai 日本文学協会 **G40**
Nihon bungaku kenkyū hikkei: koten hen 日本文学研究必携 古典編 (Handbook for the study of Japanese literature: classics) Iwanami Shoten, 1959. 387, 28p. (Iwanami zensho)

Useful as a bibliographical introduction. Gives the history of studies in classical literary forms, works and authors in 83 signed articles with references to source materials and names of interested scholars. Index inadequate.

G41
Kokugo kokubungaku kenkyūshi taisei 国語国文学研究史大成 (Complete works of the studies of Japanese language and literature) Comp. by Zenkoku Daigaku Kokugo Kokubungakkai. Sanseidō, 1959- . 14v. In progress.

The following volumes have been published: 1-2, Man'yōshū; 3-4, Genji monogatari; 5, Heian nikki; 6, Makura no sōshi, Tsurezuregusa; 7, Kokinshū, Shinkokinshū; 8, Yōkyoku, Kyōgen; 9, Heike monogatari; 10, Saikaku; 11, Chikamatsu; 12, Bashō; 13, Tōson, Katai; 15, Japanese literature. Each adequately surveys studies to date, gives annotated texts of major studies and a bibliography. Indexed. v.14 will cover Ōgai and Sōseki.

Ishiyama, Tetsurō 石山徹郎 **G42**
Nihon bungaku shoshi 日本文学書誌 (Bibliography of Japanese literature) Ōkura Kōbundō, 1934. 932p.

Classified and annotated list of literary works and books containing literary works published by the 16th century Muromachi period. Short stories and comic plays are listed under title. List of references includes commentaries, studies and periodical articles. Detailed table of contents. No index.

Kunaishō Shoryōbu 宮内庁書陵部 **G43**
Zushoryō tenseki kaidai 図書寮典籍解題 文学編 (Annotated catalogue of classical books in the Zushoryō) Literature. Kunitachi Shoin and Yōtokusha, 1948-50. 2v.

Rare poetry collections, narratives, diaries, travel books and other literary works in the Bureau of Books of the Imperial Household are described in detail. The comprehensive index is useful.

Hisamatsu Sen'ichi Hakushi Kanreki Ki- **G44** **nenkai** 久松潜一博士還暦記念会 Kokubungaku kenkyū shomoku kaidai 国文学 研究書目解題 (Annotated bibliography of Japanese literature studies) Shibundō, 1957. 506p.

About 2,000 scholarly works from the Middle Ages through 1955 on literature up to the Meiji period are listed by periods, with critical notes and references to related works. Title index.

Kaizōsha 改造社 **G45** Nihon bungaku kōza 日本文学講座 (Japanese literature lecture series) v.17, Chronology and bibliography. 1935. 416p.

Lists major literary works and studies on Japanese literature from ancient times through the Heian, Kamakura, Muromachi, Edo, Meiji and Taishō periods, ending in 1926, with annotations by authorities. Also gives annotated list of literary magazines, bibliography of language studies, chronology and brief biographies of literary figures.

Joshi Gakushūin 女子学習院 **G46** Joryū chosaku kaidai 女流著作解題 (Annotated works by women writers) 1939. 582p.

Under headings of women of the Imperial family, poets, novelists and essayists are separate entries for writers, with biographical details, and their works from the 1600's through the 1890's.

Naniwa Kōtō Gakkō 浪速高等学校 **G47** Kokugo kokubun kenkyū zasshi sakuin 国語 国文研究雑誌索引 (Periodical index on Japanese language and writing) Kyoto, Hoshino Shoten, 1933. (1254p.)

Originally published as special issues of *Kokugo kokubun* (Japanese language and literature), a Kyoto University journal, the three parts list articles in about 400 periodicals to 1931 under such headings as literature, language, legends, ancient customs, dance and music, literary geography, Shintō and other religions, literary art, and history of the book. Table of contents is detailed, and the periodicals covered are listed.

Saitō, Kiyoe 斎藤清衛 **G48** Kokugo kokubungaku ronbun sōmokuroku 国語 国文学論文総目録 (General catalogue of scholarly works on Japanese language and literature) Aug., 1945 - July, 1953. Shibundō, 1954. 315p.

Periodical articles and monographs listed in three sections: literature, language and language education, the first classified by periods and the others by subjects. Subject index for articles.

Nihon Gakujutsu Kaigi 日本学術会議 **G49** Bungaku tetsugaku shigaku bunken mokuroku. I: Nihon bungaku hen 文学哲学史学文献 目録 I：日本文学編 (Bibliography of literature, philosophy and history. I: Japanese literature) 1952-55. 2v.

Lists important monographs and periodical articles including reprints, critical reviews and foreign translations, published from Sept., 1945 through 1955. Author index, additional items, corrigenda in 35p. supplement.

Kyoto Teikoku Daigaku, Kokubun Gakkai **G50** 京都帝国大学国文学会 Edo bungaku zuroku 江戸文学図録 (Literature of the Edo period in illustration) Guroria Sosaete, 1930. 2v.

Contains photographs of important works. Detailed explanations in separate volume.

Murakami, Hamakichi 村上浜吉 **G51** Meiji bungaku shomoku 明治文学書目 (Catalogue of books on Meiji period literature) Murakami Bunko, 1937. 835p.

Inclusive enough for bibliographical use, it lists about 30,000 items collected by Hamakichi Murakami and now for the most part in the University of California's East Asiatic Library, with photographs of important works. Books related to Emperor Meiji are followed by histories and studies of Meiji period literature, the works of individual authors, sets, with notes on their contents, a chronological list of periodicals, pseudonyms, etc. Title index.

Okano, Takeo 岡野他家夫 **G52** Meiji bungaku kenkyū bunken sōran 明治文学 研究文献総覧 (Conspectus of research materials of Meiji period literature) Fuzanbō, 1944. 74, 21, 810p.

Publications from 1868 to 1943 are grouped and annotated under history, criticism, biographies, works of individual authors and periodicals, all listed chronologically, with research materials on authors, and many facsimile illustrations. Indexes not easy to use.

Kawashima, Gosaburō 川島五三郎 **and** **G53** **Yagi, Fukujirō** 八木福次郎 Choshabetsu shomoku shūran 著者別書目 集覧 (Authors and their works at a glance) Yagi Shoten, 1959. 537p.

A brief biography and a list of works arranged by publication dates to 1957, with notes for different editions, are given for each of 80 important modern writers. No index.

Kindai Bungaku Kondankai   **G54**
近代文学懇談会
Kindai bungaku kenkyū hikkei 近代文学研究
必携 (Vade mecum for the study of modern
literature) Enl. ed. Gakutōsha, 1963. 424p.

Guide to Japanese literature since 1868, in about
150 topics dealing with trends, literary schools,
principal writers, problems, controversies, etc.,
each with bibliographical references published up
to 1960. Index.

Japan P.E.N. Club   **G55**
Japanese literature in European languages,
a bibliography. 2d ed. 1961. 98p.

Lists books and articles published up to 1960,
including translations of literary and classical
works. Author and title index.

DICTIONARIES

Fujimura, Tsukuru 藤村 作   **G56**
Nihon bungaku daijiten 日本文学大辞典
(A large dictionary of Japanese literature) Rev.
and enl. ed. Shinchōsha, 1949-52. 8v.

Gives signed entries on literature, language and
such related subjects as art and foreign literature
to 1925, arranged according to the Japanese syllabary. The supplementary volume includes some
contemporary writers, a chronological table to 1950
and an index. Bibliographies. Illustrations. An
abridged 1,500p. edition was published in 1955.

Nishio, Minoru 西尾実 **and**   **G57**
Hisamatsu, Sen'ichi 久松潜一
Nihon bungaku jiten 日本文学辞典 (Dictionary of Japanese literature) Gakuseisha, 1954.
584p.

Though elementary, its approximately 1,200 entries
are well selected and carefully written, with some
reference titles. Chronological table covers period
to 1953.

Izui, Hisanosuke 泉井久之助 **et al.**   **G58**
Nihon bungaku jiten 日本文学辞典 (Dictionary of Japanese literature) Sūken Shuppansha,
1961. 537p.

For student use, contains about 2,000 entries on
literature, language and language teaching with
lists of references.

Washimi, Toshihisa 鷲見寿久   **G59**
Kokubungaku kenkyū jiten 国文学研究辞典
(Dictionary for the study of Japanese literature)
Meiji Shoin, 1961. 335p.

Works published before the 1920's listed with

annotations under poetry, prose, drama, language
and history. Contents given for collected works.
List of references. Index.

Yoshida, Seiichi 吉田精一 **et al.**   **G60**
Nihon bungaku sakuhin jinmei jiten 日本文学
作品人名辞典 (Dictionary of characters
in Japanese literary works) Kawade Shobō,
1956. 665, 34p.

Gives about 2,000 characters in tales, novels,
legends and plays from ancient times to the present,
those before 1868 entered by their first names and
later ones by family names with brief descriptions
of their roles. Chronological list of works, name
index.

Kondō, Tadayoshi 近藤忠義 **et al.**   **G61**
Nihon bungakushi jiten 日本文学史辞典
(Dictionary of the history of Japanese literature)
Nihon Hyōron Shinsha, 1960. 980, 84p.

Outlines literary periods from the classical to
the present. Also includes comparative literature,
folk literature and language studies. Gives biographies of authors and digests of works. List of
references. Index.

Yoshida, Seiichi 吉田精一   **G62**
Nihon bungaku kanshō jiten 日本文学鑑賞
辞典 (Dictionary of Japanese literature appreciation) Tokyodō, 1960. 2v.

Consists of a volume for 300 pre-1868 classical
works and a volume for 650 modern works from 1868
to 1960. Each work is described and evaluated with
information about the author. Author and title-subject
indexes.

Shiraishi, Daiji 白石大二 **et al.**   **G63**
Koten dokkai jiten 古典読解辞典 (Dictionary for reading the classics) Tokyodō, 1955.
850p.

To help in studying the pre-1868 classics, what
and how to read, style and rhetoric, social institutions and practices, etc. are explained with examples and references. Appended are a dictionary
of classical words, and a chronological table. Illustrations. Indexes of subjects and quotations.

Araki, Yoshio 荒木良雄   **G64**
Chūsei Kamakura Muromachi bungaku jiten
中世鎌倉室町文学事典 (Dictionary of Mid-
dle Age - Kamakura and Muromachi - Japanese
literature) Shunjūsha, 1961. 376, 62p.

Identifies and explains authors, works, literary
terms from 1200 to 1568 under poetry, essays, dia-

ries, novels and other forms of literature. Chronological and genealogical tables. Indexes of names, works and subjects.

Kindai Bungakusha 近代文学社　**G65**
Gendai Nihon bungaku jiten 現代日本文学辞典 (Dictionary of present-day Japanese literature) Rev. and enl. ed. Kawade Shobō, 1951. 597, 34, 25p.

Authors, major works, movements, schools and journals from 1868 to 1950 are covered in about 500 entries, each with references. Emphasis is on evaluation and appreciation. Persons and events are indexed.

Hisamatsu, Sen'ichi 久松潜一 **and** **G66**
Yoshida, Seiichi 吉田精一
Kindai Nihon bungaku jiten 近代日本文学辞典 (Dictionary of modern Japanese literature) Rev. and enl. ed. Tokyodō, 1965. 928p.

About 1,800 entries cover writers, with comments on their works, literary currents, events and magazines from 1868 to 1964. Classified bibliography and chronological table to 1963 appended. Author, title and subject indexes.

HANDBOOKS

Numazawa, Tatsuo 沼沢竜雄　**G67**
Nihon bungakushi hyōran 日本文学史表覧 (Tables for the history of Japanese literature) Meiji Shoin, 1934. 2v.

Divided into five periods to 1932, list works and their authors, each major literary form in a separate column, with developments in the fine arts, religion, etc. in a parallel column. Appended are chronological tables of works on literary history, linguistic studies and translations into foreign languages, lists of lecture series and the contents of anthologies, a guide to difficult readings and a general index. The supplementary volume contains folded charts of Japanese history, the genealogy of literary schools, the life spans of writers, etc.

Shida, Engi 志田延義　**G68**
Kokubungaku benran 国文学便覧 (Manual of Japanese literature) Shibundō, 1960. 550p.

Pt. 1 gives basic bibliographies on language, literature and history and lists of the contents of series and collected works, magazines, editions of major works, etc. Pt. 2 consists mainly of tables and charts on such matters as grammar, official ranks and titles and genealogies of poets and classical scholars. Though somewhat elementary and without an index, it brings together much useful information.

CHRONOLOGY

→ **G56**

Takano, Tatsuyuki 高野辰之 **and** **G69**
Honma, Hisao 本間久雄
Nihon bungaku nenpyō 日本文学年表 (Chronological tables of Japanese literature) New ed., rev. Tokyodō, 1953. 337p. (Nihon bungaku zenshi, v.15)

From 645 to 1912, four parallel columns show social events, writers and those associated with them, giving birth and death dates, works, and works about them with publication dates, first performances of plays, and developments in the fine arts. No index.

Ichiko, Teiji 市古貞次 **and** **G70**
Matsushita, Munehiko 松下宗彦
Nihon bungakushi nenpyō 日本文学史年表 (Chronological tables of Japanese literature) New ed., rev. Musashino Shoin, 1956. 227p.

Literary works and their authors from 551 to 1954 listed in parallel to Japanese and world events. Writers and titles indexed.

Saitō, Shōzō 斉藤昌三　**G71**
Gendai Nihon bungaku dainenpyō 現代日本文学大年表 (Chronological table of modern Japanese literature) Kaizōsha, 1931. 526p. (Gendai Nihon bungaku zenshū, supp.)

About 33,000 plays and novels, including translations of foreign works, listed in order of publication from 1868 to 1926, with names of authors, translators and publishers and magazines or newspapers in which they appeared. No index.

Yoshida, Seiichi 吉田精一　**G72**
Gendai Nihon bungaku nenpyō 現代日本文学年表 (Chronological table of modern Japanese literature) Chikuma Shobō, 1958. 422p. (Gendai Nihon bungaku zenshū, supp. 2)

By months from 1868 to 1957, five parallel columns list poems, novels and plays, criticisms, literary and artistic events, and social developments. Authors and names of newspapers and magazines in which works appeared given. Appended are an annotated list of major anthologies of modern literature, genealogical charts of poets and list of important writers with birth and death dates.

BIOGRAPHIES

→ **D24, D25**

Akabori, Matajirō 赤堀又次郎　**G73**
Nihon bungakusha nenpyō 日本文学者年表

(Chronological list of Japanese writers) Rev. and enl. ed. Musashino Shoin, 1926. 242, 30, 42p.

Lists writers, scholarly monks, etc. from ancient times to about 1800 by death dates, with major writings and other information. Bibliographies of Buddhist books on Sanskrit grammar and phonology, etc. Names, pseudonyms and titles indexed.

Supp. volume, by Kōzō Mori. Dai Nihon Tosho, 1919. 588, 40, 93p.

Adds persons who died between 1805 and 1912 and literary figures living in 1912. Names, titles indexed.

Matsumoto, Ryūnosuke 松本竜之助 **G74**
Meiji Taishō bungaku bijutsu jinmei jisho 明治大正文学美術人名辞書(Who's who of Japanese writers and artists of Meiji and Tai-shō periods, 1868-1926) Osaka, Tategawa Bun-meidō, 1941. 983p.

Including many neglected elsewhere, about 1,600 writers and artists are listed with brief biographies. Pen names indexed.

G75
Nihon bungaku arubamu 日本文学アルバム (Album of Japanese literature) Chikuma Shobō, 1954-61. 25v.

Pictorial biographies introduce the following modern writers: 1, Tōson Shimazaki; 2, Hakushū Kitahara; 3, Ichiyō Higuchi; 4, Tatsuo Hori; 5, Ōgai Mori; 6, Ryūnosuke Akutagawa; 7, Sōseki Natsume; 8, Takuboku Ishikawa; 9, Takeo Arishima; 10, Takiji Kobayashi; 11, Saneatsu Mushanokōji; 12, Naoya Shiga; 13, Writers of proletarian literature; 14, Yuriko Miyamoto; 15, Osamu Dazai; 16, Akiko Yo-sano; 17, Sakutarō Hagiwara; 18, Doppo Kunikida; 19, Kōtarō Takamura; 20, Fumiko Hayashi; 21, Kenji Miyazawa; 22, Yūzō Yamamoto; 23, Bokusui Wakayama; 24, Katai Tayama; 25, Mokichi Saitō.

G76
Kindai bungaku kenkyū sosho 近代文学研究叢書(Studies of modern Japanese liter-ature series) Shōwa Joshi Daigaku Kindai Bungaku Kenkyūshitsu, 1956- . 21v. In pro-gress.

Eventually to cover 477 writers and literature scholars since 1868 in 54 volumes; gives brief bio-graphies with evaluation of achievements, chrono-logical lists of works and reference bibliographies.

ILLUSTRATIONS

Hase, Akihisa 長谷章久 **G77**
Nihon bungakushi zukan 日本文学史図鑑

(Illustrated history of Japanese literature) Kawade Shobō, 1955. 156, 41, 6p.

Contains over 820 photographs of manuscripts and other illustrations helpful in appreciation of literature, arranged by literary forms. Selective bibliography, chronology and tables of *kana* forms with original Chinese characters appended. No index.

Sakakura, Tokutarō 阪倉篤太郎 **G78**
Nihon bungaku zue 日本文学図会 (Japa-nese literature in pictures) Kyoto, Sakakura Sensei Kiju Kinen Kankōkai, 1958. 247p.

Facsimiles of literary works, authors' portraits, examples of handwriting, etc. in 445 plates with explanatory text. Gives locations of the originals.

Nihon Kindai Bungakkan 日本近代文学館 **G79**
Nihon kindai bungaku zuroku 日本近代文学図録(Modern Japanese literature illus-trated) Mainichi Shinbunsha, 1964. 369, 21p.

Illustrations and notes related to authors and works from the 1860s to 1945, arranged chrono-logically. Includes theaters, juvenile and popular literature. Author and subject indexes.

INDEXES

Iwanami Shoten 岩波書店 **G80**
Nihon koten bungaku taikei sōsakuin 日本古典文学大系総索引(Index to the Library of Japanese classics) 1964. 602p. (Nihon koten bungaku taikei, supp.)

Indexes 66v. of the First Series, covering repre-sentative literature from the *Kojiki* to studies of linked-verses of the Edo period, edited with commen-taries based on the latest studies. Contains about 60,000 words and phrases explained in the texts. Useful as a dictionary of meanings and usage of words. First line index of *waka, haiku* and songs, and detailed table of contents.

G81
Yūhōdō Bunko sōsakuin sōkaidaisho 有朋堂文庫総索引総解題書(Yūhōdō Library; index and annotations) Yūhōdō, 1917. 540p. (Yūhōdō Bunko, supp.)

The Library consists of two series of 471 pre-1868 classical texts. The index covers persons, places and subjects in 261 texts in the 2d series and gives an annotated list of all the texts includ-ing the 210 texts in the 1st series.

Maruoka, Katsura 丸岡桂 **and** **G82**
Matsushita, Daizaburō 松下大三郎
Kokubun taikan 国文大観(Survey of Japa-

nese literature) v.10, Index. Itakuraya Shobō, 1906. 718p.

Lists and annotates with locations names of persons, places, books, official positions, and customs, in the survey of 47 important novels, essays, diaries and historical narratives of the Heian and Kamakura periods, 800-1400.

Hirabayashi, Harunori 平林治徳 **et al. G83**
Nihon setsuwa bungaku sakuin 日本説話 文学索引 (Index to Japanese narrative literature) Reprint ed. Osaka, Seibundō, 1964. 816p.

Summarizes narratives of the Heian-Kamakura period, 800-1400, found in 44 anthologies and collection in *Kokushi taikei* (Japanese history library) or *Nihon koten zenshū* (Japanese classical library) and indexes 15,000 items including persons, places and poems, with brief explanations and locations in texts.

Kōdansha 講談社 **G84**
Hyōshaku Edo bungaku sōsho sakuin 評釈江 戸文学叢書索引 (Annotated Edo literature series, index) 1938. 356p. (Hyōshaku Edo bungaku sōsho, supp.)

Its more than 45,000 terms taken from the headings and texts of the series can be used as a dictionary of Edo literature.

YEARBOOK

G85
Bungei nenkan 文芸年鑑 (Literary yearbook) 1929- . Comp. by Nihon Bungeika Kyōkai. 1929-37, 1939-40, 1943, 1948- . 29v.

Indispensable as a record of major literary and related events, publications, performances, etc. and directory of authors and organizations. It has been compiled by Association of Japanese Literary Men and issued by various publishers and since 1949 by Shinchōsha.

Poetry

WAKA

❖ Trends of the year in *Waka* poetry circles, directories of organizations, poets, and publications of the year are contained in **Tanka nenkan** (*Waka* poetry yearbook) 1950- , published as a supplement of the magazine, *Tanka Kenkyū*, by Tanka Kenkyūsha. **G86.**

Bibliography

Fukui, Kyūzō 福井久蔵 **G87**
Dai Nihon kasho sōran 大日本歌書綜覧 (General survey of books on Japanese poetry) Fuji Shobō, 1926-28. 3v.

Covers about 6,000 books and manuscripts to 1912, classified and arranged chronologically by dates of completion or publication, with brief explanations. v.1 gives studies of poetry and general anthologies, and v.2, collections of individual poets, records of poetry contests, songs, miscellaneous poems, etc. v.3 has a supplement, indexes titles and names, and clarifies difficult readings. There is a 5v. reprint, pub. in 1928.

Koizumi, Tōzō 小泉苳三 **G88**
Meiji Taishō kasho sōran 明治大正歌書 綜覧 (General suvey of the books on poetry of Meiji and Taishō periods, 1868-1926) Kyoto, Ritsumeikan Shuppanbu, 1941. 475, 65p. (Meiji Taishō tanka shiryō taisei, v.2)

About 2,200 books of poetry and related critical works, listed chronologically by publication dates and annotated. Appended are tables of contents of nine poetry series, with some notes, and a list of magazines referred to in **G101**, annotated on the basis of their first numbers. Indexes.

Dictionaries

Itō, Yoshio 伊藤嘉夫 **et al. G89**
Waka bungaku daijiten 和歌文学大辞典 (Dictionary of *waka* poetry) Meiji Shoin, 1962. 2038p.

Contains about 4,500 entries, explaining in detail the subject matter, expressions, personal names, and reference sources from ancient times to the present. Appendix lists poetical monuments and includes an extensive bibliography; libraries and collections (with descriptive notes); keys to the *Chokusen sakusha burui* and the *Man'yō sakusha burui*; chronological table, 660 B.C. - 1959. Index.

Nakamura, Kaoru 中村薫 **G90**
Tenkyo kensaku meika jiten 典処検索名歌 辞典 (A source finding dictionary of famous poems) Meiji Shoin, 1936. 632, 49, 102p.

Some 8,000 pre-1868 poems are arranged with identification of their authors and sources. Variations and some critical notes are given. Leading words and phrases are indexed.

Takeda, Yūkichi 武田祐吉 **G91**
Tsūkai meika jiten 通解名歌辞典 (Diction-

ary of famous poems, with transliterations into spoken language) Morikita Shuppan, 1958. 745p.

Authors, sources and transliterations into spoken Japanese, given for some 3,000 pre-1868 poems, with notes on difficult words. There is a separate listing of selected post-1868 poems under names of authors. Indexing of the first lines of the second part. Appended are a list of annotated books of poetry, brief biographies, an outline history of *waka*, a chronological table, and a genealogy of schools of poets.

Terms

Makura kotoba → **F193, F194**

Kimata, Osamu 木俣修 et al.　　**G92**
Kindai tanka jiten 近代短歌辞典 (Modern *tanka* dictionary) Shinkō Shuppansha, 1956. 12, 521, 46p.

Covers technical terms, important poets, anthologies, books on *tanka*, groups and their journals, from about 1890 to about 1955 in 650 signed entries, most of them with references. Chronology from 1868 to 1955. Names, subjects indexed.

Watanabe, Junzō 渡辺順三 and　　**G93**
Miyagi, Ken'ichi 宮城謙一
Shiki bunrui sakka jiten 四季分類作歌辞典 (Dictionary of terms used in writing poetry, classified by the four seasons) Iizuka Shoten, 1957-59. 5v.

Classified under the headings of spring, summer, autumn, winter and non-seasonal, terms related to such matters as natural phenomena, personal events, animals and plants, explained with examples of their use in modern *waka*. No index. v.5 explains and gives examples of the use of words other than nouns, arranged according to the parts of speech.

Kimata, Osamu 木俣修 and　　**G94**
Watanabe, Junzō 渡辺順三
Gendai sakka yōgo jiten 現代作歌用語辞典 (Dictionary of modern poetic terms) Hokushindō, 1954. 337, 17p.

Defines 2,300 terms selected from poems in books and magazines published from 1868 to 1951, with usage examples from identified sources. Poems, authors indexed.

Biographies

G95
Kōchū Kokka taikei 校註国歌大系 (Collated and annotated collection of Japanese poetry)

v.23. Kokumin Tosho, 1930. 792p.

The last part of the volume has reference value because it indexes the names and/or pen names of all poets represented in the collection and gives biographical data, official positions, genealogies, titles of books in which poems are found, and their numbers. Listing is by radicals and stroke numbers. Chronological table of history of *waka* to 1889.

Indexes

Matsushita, Daizaburō 松下大三郎 and **G96**
Watanabe, Fumio 渡辺文雄
Kokka taikan 国歌大観 (A comprehensive survey of *waka* poetry) Reprint ed. Kadokawa Shoten, 1951-58. 4v.

Indispensable for identifying poems, determining authors and tracing references to places and subjects. Given in one volume are the complete texts of the *Man'yōshū*, the 21 anthologies compiled by Imperial command and the *Shin'yōshū* and the poems in 30 major pre-1400 histories, diaries, and narratives, such as the *Kojiki* and *Genji monogatari*. Each poem is numbered, and this numbering has been found so convenient that it has been adopted widely. The companion volume is a concordance of the words and phrases in the poems, arranged in Japanese syllabic order. The *Zoku kokka taikan* (Second series of *Kokka taikan*) continues the survey, listing some 41,000 poems in 112 anthologies, individual collections, and other sources, also numbered consecutively. The indexing is by the first and fourth phrases of *waka*, more selective in coverage and therefore less helpful than the concordance in the *Kokka taikan*.

G97
Kōchū Kokka taikei 校註国歌大系 (Collated and annotated collection of Japanese poetry) v.24-28. General indexes. Kokumin Tosho, 1931. 5v.

About 200,000 poems and songs in 147 anthologies from ancient times to the 1870's are indexed by the first and third phrases of *waka*, the first and fourth of *sedōka* and the first of *chōka* and other forms. Though more comprehensive, it does not supplant **G96**. At the end of v.28 are an index to annotations and a general table of contents of the set. For quick checking, each volume has an index to the works in the general collection.

G98
Nihon kagaku taikei 日本歌学大系 (Collection of Japanese poetics) v.10. Ed. by Hitaku Kyūsojin and Yoshimaro Higuchi. Kazama Shobō, 1963. 451p.

Lists about 180 important works on poetics, from ancient times to the Edo period. v.10 contains indexes of titles, personal names, verses of poems, and poems in Chinese. Terms and subjects not indexed.

Nagasawa, Mitsu 長沢美津 **G99**
Nyonin waka taikei 女人和歌大系 (Collection of poems by women) Kazama Shobō, 1962- . 2v. In progress.

Arranged by authors, with a list of references. v.1 is divided into periods: early songs, *Man'yōshū*, Imperial anthologies (Heian and Kamakura periods) and other anthologies (Muromachi and Edo periods). Brief biographies, author and first line indexes.

Takeda, Yūkichi 武田祐吉 **G100**
Zoku Man'yōshū 続万葉集 (Continuation of the *Man'yōshū*) Kokin Shoin, 1926. 334p.

Texts of poems prior to the Nara period not in the *Man'yōshū* arranged chronologically with annotations. Indexes.

Chronology

Koizumi, Tōzō 小泉苳三 **G101**
Meiji Taishō tanka dainenpyō 明治大正短歌大年表 (Comprehensive chronology of *tanka* literature in the Meiji and Taishō periods) Kyoto, Ritsumeikan Shuppanbu, 1942. 494p. (Meiji Taisho tanka shiryō taisei, 3)

Anthologies, individual collections, books on poetry, and newspaper and magazine articles and commentaries are listed chronologically from 1868 to 1926. List of newspapers and magazines with first and last publication dates.

RENGA (Linked verses)

→ G110, G111

Fukui, Kyūzō 福井久蔵 **G102**
Renga no shiteki kenkyū 連歌の史的研究 (A historical study of *renga*) Seibidō, 1930-31. 2v.

v.1 gives a history of *renga* and a chronological table, with indexes of names, titles, and subjects. v.2 is an annotated list of about 2,400 books classified into scholarly works, anthologies, and forms of *renga*, arranged chronologically, with indexes of titles and dates.

Yamada, Yoshio 山田孝雄 **and** **G103**
Hoshika, Sōichi 星加宗一
Renga hōshiki kōyō 連歌法式綱要 (Principal rules for composing *renga*) Iwanami Shoten, 1936. 342p.

Gives rules for linked poems with glossary of terms. A compilation for use by specialists.

Yamada, Yoshio 山田孝雄 **G104**
Renga gaisetsu 連歌概説 (General outline of *renga*) Iwanami Shoten, 1937. 295p.

An introductory guide, explains the composition and appreciation of *renga*, technical terms, etc. General index.

KYŌKA (Satirical poems)

Kan, Chikuho 菅 竹浦 **G105**
Kyōka shomoku shūsei 狂歌書目集成 (Collection of books of *kyōka* poetry) Kyoto, Hoshino Shoten, 1936. 231p.

Lists chronologically 1,181 *kyōka* anthologies from 1630 to 1867 and gives for each the size, author, illustrations, illustrator, publication date, and publisher. Titles which are not self-explanatory are explained. Titles and names with pronunciations indexed.

Kanō, Kaian 狩野快庵 **G106**
Kyōka jinmei jisho 狂歌人名辞書 (A biographical dictionary of *kyōka* poets) Bunkōdō, 1928. 273p.

About 3,000 comic poets, novelists, and illustrators from the 18th to the early 1920's, listed by their pseudonyms, with reference sources. Indexes by regions and periods. → **G140.**

HAIKU

❀ Trends of the year in *Haiku* poetry circles, directories of organizations, poets, and books of the year are in **Haiku nenkan** (*Haiku* poetry yearbook) 1955- , published as a supplement of the magazine, *Haiku*, by Kadokawa Shoten. **G107,** and in **Haiku nenkan** (*Haiku* poetry yearbook), a supplementary issue of *Haiku Kenkyū* (*Haiku* studies), by Haiku Kenkyūsha. **G107a.**

G108
Haiku kōza 俳句講座 (*Haiku* lecture series) Kaizōsha, 1932-33. 10v.

Exhaustively covers all aspects of *haiku*, including poets and their groups, their works, studies, versification and appreciation, with such useful reference materials as list of poets in v.2, annotations of books on *haiku* in v.6, list of major *haiku* magazines in the Meiji, Taishō and Shōwa periods in v.8, chronology and biographies of poets in v.9. Supplemented by **Zoku haiku kōza** (Second series of *haiku* lectures) published in 1934 in 8v. with genealogies of poets, bibliographies, glossary of terms, etc.

Bibliography

Kawanishi, Waro 川西和露 **and** **G109**
Ebara, Taizō 頴原退蔵
Waro Bunko haishomoku 和露文庫俳書目
(Catalogue of *haiku* books in the Waro Library) Kobe, Himurosha, 1938. 24, 671, 6p.

Gives bibliographical descriptions, including notes on contents and backgrounds, of 3,000 books collected by Tokutarō (Waro, pseud.) Kawanishi, now in Tenri University Library. Title index. Printed serially from 1926 to 1938 in the magazine *Himuro*.

Tenri Toshokan 天理図書館 **G110**
Wataya Bunko renga haikaisho mokuroku 綿屋文庫連歌俳諧書目録 (Wataya Library catalogue of *renga* and *haiku*) 1954. 465, 75p. (Tenri Toshokan sōsho, 17)
Renga books published before 1868 which the Library has acquired by 1953 listed under classifications, and *haiku* books listed chronologically. Title index. The Wataya Library, taken over from the family of *Shinbashira* Nakayama by Tenri University Library in 1937 and augmented by four other poetry collections, is without parallel for *renga* and *haiku* materials. A mimeographed index of its *haiku* books and the pen names, house names and full names of poets was privately circulated in 1955 by Katsutada Suzuki.

Dictionaries

Ijichi, Tetsuo 伊地知鉄男 **et al.** **G111**
Haikai daijiten 俳諧大辞典 (Comprehensive dictionary of *haikai*) Meiji Shoin, 1957. 1008p.

About 5,000 entries on *renga*, *haiku*, and *senryū*, including technical terms and seasonal words, poets and their works, with references. Chronological table of *renga* and indexes of titles, persons, and seasonal words. Location of books given.

Takagi, Sōgo 高木蒼梧 **G112**
Haikai jinmei jiten 俳諧人名辞典 (Who's who of *haiku* poets) Meiji Shoin, 1960. 660p.

Brief biographies, descriptions of styles, comments on major works, and evaluations of poets from Sōkan (d.1553) to 1959, classified by periods and schools. Index of pen names and annotated bibliography appended.

Asō, Isoji 麻生磯次 **and** **G113**
Kodaka, Toshirō 小高敏郎
Hyōkai meiku jiten 評解名句辞典 (Diction-

ary of famous *haiku* with critical annotations) Sōmeisha, 1955. 459p.

About 1,500 *haiku* briefly explained with notes on authors, sources and seasons. A brief history of *haiku*, biographies of poets, annotated list of major works, and an index of *haiku* second lines are included.

Yamamoto, Kenkichi 山本健吉 **et al.** **G114**
Gendai haiku jiten 現代俳句事典 (Dictionary of modern *haiku*) Kawade Shobō, 1954. 377, 16p.

Concerned chiefly with twentieth century poets, their schools and movements, major works, vocabulary, and literary magazines. Detailed table of contents, arranged in historical order, is useful in grouping poets by schools. List of *haiku* seasonal words and chronological table for 1887-1954 given. Index.

Seasonal terms

Zusetsu haiku daisaijiki 図説俳句大歳時記 **G115**
(Illustrated book of seasonal topics of *haiku* poetry) Kadokawa Shoten, 1964- . 2v. In progress.

Each volume lists more than 1,000 seasonal terms, classified under 26 sections, e.g. weather, heaven, earth, man, religion, animals, plants, etc. and gives historical studies of the development of seasonal topics with reference to 132 classics, and poetical examples. Illustrated with photographs and reproductions of famous paintings. Classified table of contents and index of topics and subtopics. A sono-sheet recording of songs of wild birds is attached.

Heibonsha ban haiku saijiki 平凡社版俳句 **G116**
歳時記 (Glossary of seasonal *haiku* terms) Spring, summer, autumn, winter, New Year. Comp. by Fūsei Tomiyasu and others. Heibonsha, 1959. 5v.

Gives explanations and citations to sources and other references. The New Year volume has an annotated list of glossaries published since pre-1600, a table of memorial days of poets. Subject index.

Yamamoto, Kenkichi 山本健吉 **G117**
Shin haiku saijiki 新俳句歳時記 (New glossary of seasonal *haiku* terms) Spring, summer, autumn, winter, New Year. Kōbunsha, 1956. 5v. (Kappa library)

Each volume lists terms appropriate for a season.

Tables of seasons according to the lunar calendar and memorial days, a history of records of annual events, explanations of seasonal themes, and a general subject index are found in volume on the New Year.

Chronology

Hirabayashi, Hōji 平林鳳二 **and** **G118**
Ōnishi, Ichigai 大西一外
Shinsen haikai nenpyō 新選俳諧年表 (Newly selected chronology of *haikai*) with a directory of *haiku* poets. Osaka, Shoga Chinpon Zasshi-sha, 1923. 150, 594p.

About 7,000 poets with brief biographies arranged by their death dates from 1501 to 1923. Books listed chronologically by date of publication. Index to pen names and a list of poets whose death dates are unknown appended.

Indexes

G119

Nihon haisho taikei 日本俳書大系 (Comprehensive collection of *haiku* literature) v.16 Index. Nihon Haisho Taikei Kankōkai, 1928. 313, 289p.

Standard reference set containing 330 anthologies, studies, some of them written especially for this collection, and other materials on *haiku* of the Edo period. v.15 brings together 17 key sources for genealogical and biographical reference. v.16 has an index of poets mentioned in v.15, an index of place names in the entire collection and an index of opening lines of all *haiku* in the collection by Bashō, Buson, and Issa. There is a 34v. reprint of the collection titled *Haisho taikei*, published by Shunjūsha.

Sassa, Masakazu 佐々政一 **G120**
Sanku sakuin haiku taikan 三句索引俳句大観 (Collection of *haiku* indexed by three lines) Meiji Shoin, 1916. 762p.

Indexes by each of their three lines, with authors and sources, about 12,000 pre-1868 *haiku* from 12 well-known anthologies. Gives complete list of Bashō's poems.

Andō, Hidekata 安藤英方 **G121**
Kinsei haiku daisakuin 近世俳句大索引 (Comprehensive index of pre-Meiji *haiku*) Meiji Shoin, 1959. 1200p.

More inclusive than **G120**, it indexes, but only by their first lines, about 60,000 pre-1868 *haiku* from about 100 collections, giving their authors, sources, and seasons.

SENRYŪ

Ōmagari, Kuson 大曲駒村 **G122**
Senryū daijiten 川柳大辞典 (Comprehensive senryū dictionary) Takahashi Shoten, 1962. 2v.

Explains words, including slang peculiar to *senryū* poetry, each with unidentified pre-1868 examples of use. Identifies persons and places associated with *senryū*. Originally printed privately as *Senryū jii* (*Senryū* vocabulary) and reprinted by Hakutō Shobō in 1948 and Nichibunsha in 1955.

Negishi, Senryū 根岸川柳 **G123**
Kosenryū jiten 古川柳辞典 (Dictionary of old senryū) Nihon Shinbunsha, 1955- . 5v. In progress.

Explains special and difficult words in *senryū* of the Edo period, giving identified examples of use. To be completed in 8v.

Karai, Senryū 柄井川柳 **G124**
Shodai Senryū senkushū 初代川柳選句集 (Poems selected by Senryū, the *First*) Rev. by Osamu Chiba. Iwanami Shoten, 1960. 2v. (Iwanami bunko)

Contains six books of *senryū* poems selected and commented upon by Senryū I. Index in v.2 facilitates location of individual poems. Together with **G182** includes almost all the better poems of his selection.

MODERN POETRY

❀ Trends of the year, directories of organizations, poets, and books of the year are to be found in **Gendai shijin nenkan** (Modern poetry yearbook), a supplement of the magazine, *Gendaishi techō*, published by Shichōsha, **G125** and in **Shigaku nenkan** (Poetics yearbook), a supplement of *Shigaku*, by Shigakusha. **G125a.**

Sangū, Makoto 山宮允 **G126**
Meiji Taishō shisho sōran 明治大正詩書綜覧 (Bibliography of literature on new-style poetry in the Meiji and Taishō periods) Keiseisha, 1934. 2v.

Lists in order of publication, some briefly annotated, about 4,000 books and selected newspaper and magazine articles on new-style poetry and related subjects from 1868 through 1926, prefaced with a history of new-style poetry. List of magazines, list of collections, etc. appended. Title index. Companion volume has photographs of about 500 books.

Iizuka Shoten 飯塚書店 **G127**
Gendaishi jiten 現代詩辞典 (Dictionary of contemporary poetry) 1951. 301, 27p.

About 1,000 entries cover poets, books, movements and groups, terms, etc. since 1868. Appended is an 1868-1950 chronology including cultural and social events. Subjects, names indexed.

Kubota, Masafumi 久保田正文 **and** **G128**
Shidai, Ryūzō 司代隆三
Nihon gendaishi jiten 日本現代詩辞典 (Dictionary of modern Japanese poetry) Hokushindō, 1955. 367, 28p.

Explains trends, movements, organizations and technical terms in poetry from about 1850s and identifies poets and publications, including magazines. Selective bibliography and 1843-1954 chronology appended. Name and subject indexes.

Prose

BIBLIOGRAPHY

Kindai Nihon bungaku taikei 近代日本文 **G129**
学大系 (Compilation of Edo period Japanese literature) v.25. Kokumin Tosho, 1929. 896p.

Gives a complete table of contents to 370 Edo literary texts of almost all genres, a chronology of narrative literature from earliest times to 1867, a revised expansion of Musei Asakura's *Shinshū Nihon shōsetsu nenpyō* (Newly compiled chronology of Japanese fiction), published by Shun'yōdō in 1926. Titles before 1600 arranged chronologically, and those of the Edo period divided into types, and arranged chronologically, with brief annotations. Title index. Also includes a biographical dictionary of fiction writers and illustrators by Fumoto Yamazaki.

Yokoyama, Shigeru 横山重 **and** **G130**
Ohashi, Raizō 巨橋頼三
Monogatari sōshi mokuroku 物語草子目録 (Catalogues of story books) Ōokayama Shoten, 1937. 526p.

Contains eight annotated catalogues of story books from ancient times to the 16th century. Annotations and locations of story books are found in: **Muromachi jidai monogatarirui genzaibon kanmei mokuroku** (A brief catalogue of extant story books of the Muromachi period) by Takanobu Matsumoto. Inoue Shobō, 1962. 67p. (Keiō Gijuku Daigaku Shidō bunko shoshi sōkan, 2) **G130a.**

Ichiko, Teiji 市右貞次 **G131**
Mikan chūsei shōsetsu kaidai 未刊中世小

説解題 (Survey of unpublished medieval fiction) Reprint ed. Rakurō Shoin, 1942. 317p.

Outlines about 40 stories written between 1200 and 1600 not yet in print by 1942 (several of which have since been published), with notes and locations of manuscripts. List of fictions of the same period published since 1868 appended. Index of titles, names, technical terms.

G132
Shin gunsho ruijū 新群書類従 (Classified lists of books, new series) v.7, Bibliography. Kokusho Kankōkai, 1906. 752p.

Contains 16 catalogue books of popular literature of the Edo period, including those on *kyōka*, *haiku*, stories, novelettes, illustrated books, etc. listing more than 6,500 titles, some with annotations.

Ozaki, Hisaya 尾崎久弥 **G133**
Edo jidai shōsetsu kyakuhon jōruri zuihitsu honkokumono sakuin 江戸時代小説脚本浄瑠璃随筆翻刻物索引 (Index of reprints of Edo fiction, drama, *jōruri* and essays) Shun'yōdō, 1927. 270p.

Classified index of works in series published before 1927, giving authors, titles and volume numbers. Title index.

Sasakawa, Tanerō 笹川種郎 **G134**
Kinsei bungeishi 近世文芸志 (History of Edo period literature) Meiji Shoin, 1931. 450p.

Revised expansion, with material on *jōruri*, of annotated lists in **G129**, classified under such headings as *kabuki*, fiction of Edo, and of the Kyoto-Osaka area. Detailed table of contents. No index.

Teruoka, Yasutaka 暉峻康隆 **G135**
Edo bungaku jiten 江戸文学辞典 (Dictionary of Edo literature) Fuzanbō, 1940. 551p.

Lists chronologically about 900 works of all genres of Edo fiction, with annotations and indications of available editions. Some shown in illustrations. Prefaced by a survey of Edo fiction. Notes on about 87 writers in chronological order appended. Detailed index, with list of difficult readings by strokes.

Takagi, Bun 高木文 **G136**
Meiji zen shōsetsu gikyoku taikan 明治全小説戯曲大観 (General survey of all fiction and drama of the Meiji period) Juhōkaku, 1925-26. 2v.

Contains a survey of Meiji literature, a chronological listing of about 9,000 titles published in periodicals, and a genealogical table of literary schools. Supplementary volume lists works of individual authors, excluding translations, by date of publication, with author index.

Ishikawa, Iwao 石川 巌 **G137**
Meiji shoki gesaku nenpyō 明治初期戯作年表 (Chronologies of light literature of the early Meiji period) Jūgoshokōsha, 1927. 156p. (Shomotsu ōrai sōsho, supp.)

Divided into translated novels, composite volumes of stories with pictures, new and old novels, manners and customs in the licensed quarters, humor and miscellaneous works. Listed chronologically from 1868 to 1888, with some annotations and illustrations.

Yoshida, Seiichi 吉田精一 **G138**
Gendai bungakuron taikei 現代文学論大系 (Compilation of contemporary essays on literature) v.8. Kawade Shobō, 1955. 352, 26p.

Gives in chronological order the titles of articles on literature from 1885 to 1935, with authors' names and the titles and issues of the newspapers and magazines in which they appeared. Useful, though poetics excluded. Author index.

DICTIONARY

Yoshida, Seiichi 吉田精一 **G139**
Kindai meisaku moderu jiten 近代名作モデル事典 (Dictionary of characters in famous modern literary works) Shibundō, 1960. 348p.

Outlines well-known modern works of fiction and identifies the persons on whom their characters were based, with references. Revision of material in Oct., 1959 issue of *Kokubungaku kaishaku to kanshō* (Japanese literature: interpretation and appreciation).

BIOGRAPHIES

Nakamura, Tsurukichi 中村鶴吉 **G140**
Gesakusha denki shūsei 戯作者伝記集成 (Collections of biographies of authors of light literature) Edo Bungaku Ruijū Kankōkai, 1929. 432p. (Edo bungaku ruijū; Denki bu, 1)

Reprints of three biographical sources, published in 1830-56, covering writers of popular fiction and *kyōka* satirical poems, who lived in the 16th to mid-19th century.

Suzuki, Kōzō 鈴木行三 **G141**
Gikyoku shōsetsu kinsei sakka taikan 戯曲小説近世作家大観 (General survey of Edo period writers of drama and fiction) Chūbunkan Shoten, 1933. 20, 666p.

Short biographies with quotations from various sources on authors' lives and works chronologically arranged, covering period from 1558 to date. Detailed list of contents, but no index.

Chinese language literature

→ **D21, D22**

Okada, Masayuki 岡田正之 **G142**
Nihon Kanbungakushi 日本漢文学史 (History of Chinese language literature in Japan) Rev. and enl. by Tokuhei Yamagishi and Kikuya Nagasawa. Yoshikawa Kōbunkan, 1954. 458, 10p.

Table of contents and indexes of names, titles, schools and temples permit use as annotated bibliography of writings in Chinese by Japanese from the 7th to the mid-16th century. Annotated list of research materials appended.

Uemura, Kankō 上村観光 **G143**
Gozan bungaku shōshi 五山文学小史 (Short history of literature of the five principal Zen temples) Shōkabō, 1906. 242, 40p.

Recounted through biographies of writer priests. Bibliography of their works, lists of priests and place-names and chronology appended.

Kitamura, Sawakichi 北村沢吉 **G144**
Gozan bungakushi kō 五山文学史稿 (Draft history of literature of the five principal Zen temples) Fuzanbō, 1941. 876p.

Gives the lives and doctrines and evaluates the literary abilities and works of 99 authors, divided into those belonging to and those outside the temples, from the 13th through the 16th century.

Individual authors and works

MAN'YŌSHŪ

→ **G41**

Heibonsha 平凡社 **G145**
Man'yōshū taisei 万葉集大成 (Comprehensive *Man'yōshū* materials) 1953-56. 22v.

Covers all aspects of the *Man'yōshū*, textual,

bibliographical, historical, linguistic, interpretive, aesthetic, etc. in studies by more than a hundred experts. Especially valuable for reference are:

v.2, Bibliography by Mokichi Saitō, surveying and commenting on *Man'yō* studies from the Heian period.

v.12-19, Facsimile of the 1643 edition of the *Man'yōshū* (3v.), with variant readings, and comments by Hisataka Omodaka and Umetomo Saeki in footnotes, and detailed indexes (5v), revised from Atsuo Masamune's *Man'yōshū sōsakuin* (General index to the Man'yōshū), published in 4v., 1929-31, giving all words, with examples of their use and the *Kokka taikan* **G96** numbers. Includes an index of variant words and phrases taken from 25 reference works and an index of all Chinese characters, with notes on their readings and locations in the anthology.

v.22, Bibliography, edited by Tomoo Fujimori, classifying and annotating *Man'yōshū* manuscripts, printed editions, commentaries and related books to the end of 1950, and chronology, 313-788 A.D., compiled by Yoshio Matsuda, bringing together details from histories of the period and the *Man'yōshū*.

Maeno, Sadao 前野貞雄 **G146**
Man'yō shoshigaku 万葉書誌学 (Bibliographical studies of the Man'yōshū) Shinobu Shoin, 1956. 436p.

Annotated bibliography of books mentioned in the *Man'yōshū*, different editions, and works on the *Man'yōshū*; with chronological and classified list of books related to the *Man'yōshū* to 1947. Title index.

Sasaki, Nobutsuna 佐々木信綱 **G147**
Man'yō jiten 万葉辞典 (*Man'yō* dictionary) Rev. and enl. ed. Yūhōdō, 1953. 608p.

Keyed to the *Shinkun Man'yōshū* (New reading text of the *Man'yōshū*) in the Iwanami Bunko series, gives words and phrases, with examples and *Kokka Taikan* **G96** numbers of the poems in which they appear. Illustrations.

Sasaki, Nobutsuna 佐々木信綱 **G148**
Man'yōshū jiten 万葉集事典 (*Man'yōshū* dictionary) Heibonsha, 1956. 801p.

Sections for poetical words, personal names, place-names, animals, plants, etc.; gives profuse examples and locations in the text. Appended are a chronology from 200 to 799 A.D., an annotated bibliography of about 1,200 texts and studies. Title and name indexes, a detailed table of contents of the *Man'yōshū* and tables of grammatical terms and pronunciations peculiar to *Man'yōshū*.

Origuchi, Shinobu 折口信夫 **G149**
Man'yōshū jiten 万葉集辞典 (*Man'yōshū* dictionary) Rev. ed. Chūō Kōronsha, 1956. 429p.

(Origuchi Shinobu zenshū, v.6)

Gives meanings, usage, etc. of some 3,000 terms. Revision of edition published in 1919 by Bunkaidō Shoten.

Sasaki, Nobutsuna 佐々木信綱 **G150**
Man'yō nenpyō taisei 万葉年表大成 (Comprehensive *Man'yō* chronology) Tanbaichi, Yōtokusha, 1947. 319, 57p.

Divided into the period when the *Man'yō* poems were written and the period to 1912 to cover *Man'yō* research. Classified list of poets appended.

KOKIN WAKASHŪ

→ **G41**

Matsumoto, Jin 松本仁 **G151**
Kokin wakashū jiten 古今和歌集辞典 (*Kokin wakashū* dictionary) Kyoto, Ritsumeikan Shuppanbu, 1939. 288p.

Explains ornate and special words, phrases and sentences and pivot-words and identifies place-names. List of poets with poems and brief biographies appended.

Nishishita, Kyōichi 西下経一 **and** **G152**
Takizawa, Sadao 滝沢貞夫
Kokinshū sōsakuin 古今集総索引 (*Kokinshū* general index) Meiji Shoin, 1958. 246p.

Gives all words and locates them by the *Kokka taikan* **G96** numbers of the poems in which they appear, with separate indexes for the words of the kana preface, poetical expressions, notes, variants, personal names, etc.

DIARIES

Saeki, Umetomo 佐伯梅友 **and** **G153**
Imuta, Tsunehisa 伊牟田経久
Kagerō Nikki sōsakuin かげろふ日記総索引 (Index to the *Kagerō Nikki*) Kazama Shobō, 1963. 805p.

Contains a text based on the Katsura no Miya edition owned by the Imperial Household Library; concordance of all words, classified under particles, auxiliary verbs, and general words.

Tokyo Kyōiku Daigaku, Chūko Bungaku **G154**
Kenkyū Bukai
東京教育大学中古文学研究部会
Murasaki Shikibu nikki yōgo sakuin 紫式部日記用語索引 (Concordance of *Murasaki Shikibu nikki*) Nihon Gakujutsu Shinkōkai, 1956. 390p.

Indexes all words in the text of the diary as edited by Kikan Ikeda for the Iwanami Bunko series from a 1682 manuscript, with a table collating this with the *Gunsho ruijū* text printed in 1820, on which most commentaries are based, and an index of variant readings. Also summarizes and indexes theories about the diary.

Azuma, Setsuo 東　節夫 **et al.**　　　**G155**
Izumi Shikibu nikki sōsakuin 和泉式部日記
総索引 (Complete index to *Izumi Shikibu nikki*) Musashino Shoin, 1959.　78, 84p.

Parallel texts of the 1414 manuscript of the diary held by Kyoto University and the Sanjō Nishi family's manuscript now in the Imperial Household Library. Indexes all words in both texts. Pivot-words and poems indexed separately.

Yoshida, Kōichi　吉田幸一　　　**G156**
Izumi Shikubu kenkyū 和泉式部研究 (Studies of Izumi Shikibu) v.1, Complete works of Izumi Shikibu. Koten Bunko, 1959.　784, 287p. (Heian bungaku sōsho, 4)

Edited by the Society for Literary Language Study, with general index of the Kangen (1243-46) text and a word index of the Ōei (1397-1427) and Sanjō Nishi family texts.

Azuma, Setsuo　東　節夫 **et al.**　　**G157**
Sarashina nikki sōsakuin　更級日記総索引
(General index to the *Sarashina nikki)*
Musashino Shoin, 1956.　80, 94p.

Index to the text of the Imperial Household edition.

Mabuchi, Kazuo 馬淵一夫　　　**G158**
Sanuki Tenji nikki sakuin 讃岐典侍日記
索引 (Index to *Sanuki Tenji nikki*) Kyoto, 1954.　58p.

MONOGATARI (The 9th-16th century stories)

Yamada, Tadao 山田忠雄　　　**G159**
Taketori monogatari sōsakuin　竹取物語総
索引 (General index to "The bamboo-cutter's story") Musashino Shoin, 1958.　446p.

With facsimile of old movable type text, gives all words, with phrases in which they appear.

Ikeda, Kikan 池田亀鑑　　　**G160**
Ise monogatari ni tsukite no kenkyū　伊勢物
語に就きての研究 (Studies of the *Ise monogatari*) Yūseidō, 1958-61.　3v.

v.1 contains 43 important texts, collated and with variant readings. Also contains a list of variant styles of characters, comparative table of pas-

sages in different editions, and index of all lines of the *waka* poems. v.2 contains bibliographical studies on the composition of the story and variant editions. v.3 is a supplement containing texts of five other editions, supplementary studies and index of words in all editions, classified under headings of particles, auxiliary verbs and general words. Illustrated with 35 photographs of old manuscripts and old printed editions.

Ikeda, Toshio 池田利夫　　　**G161**
Hamamatsu Chūnagon monogatari sōsakuin 浜松
中納言物語総索引　　(Index of Tales of Counsellor Hamamatsu) Musashino Shoin, 1964. 22, 300p.

Indexes entire vocabulary in the text edition of *Shinchū kokubungaku sōsho* (New annotated national literature series) published by Kōdansha in 1951. Comparative paging to Iwanami edition in *Nihon koten bungaku taikei* appended.

GENJI MONOGATARI
→ G41

Fujita, Tokutarō 藤田徳太郎　　　**G162**
Genji monogatari kenkyū shomoku yōran 源氏
物語研究書目要覧　(Bibliographical survey of the study of the *Genji monogatari*) Riku-bunkan, 1932.　260p.

Lists and annotates works on the Tale of Genji, classified under 16 topics such as commentaries, terminology, outlines, chronologies, etc., with locations.

Fujita, Tokutarō 藤田徳太郎　　　**G163**
Kokan Genji monogatari shomoku 古刊源氏
物語書目　(Bibliography of materials on the *Genji monogatari*)　Shunnansha, 1934.　271p. (Kosho kenkyū sōsho)

Annotates manuscripts and books to 1931 in sections on commentaries, outlines, historical studies, illustrated materials, etc., with notes on location of those not easily accessible. Chronology of studies and table showing interrelationship of studies appended.　Title index.

Ikeda, Kikan 池田亀鑑　　　**G164**
Genji monogatari jiten 源氏物語事典 (*Genji monogatari* dictionary)　Tokyodō, 1960.　2v.

v.1 explains about 3,000 terms for ancient court practices, customs and manners, personal and place names, etc., with examples keyed to the collated text of **G167** and notes from various reference books. v.2 gives general comments, annotated bibliographies of commentaries, editions, outlines, lists of quoted poems and Buddhist literature, with indexes, information about characters, including genealogies and court ranks, a chronology of studies to 1960, and pictorial materials.

Kitayama, Keita 北山谿太　　　**G165**
Genji monogatari jiten 源氏物語辞典 (*Genji monogatari* dictionary) Heibonsha, 1957. 978, 111p.

Lists and comments on all words, phrases and poems, with copious examples and their location in the texts in the Yūhōdō Bunko series and **G168.** Appended are a chronology of developments in the story, genealogies of the characters and a list of characters in each section of the story.

Sanari, Kentarō 佐成謙太郎　　　**G166**
Genji monogatari sōran 源氏物語総覧 (*Genji monogatari* handbook) Meiji Shoin, 1953. 291p. (Taiyaku Genji monogatari, supp.)

Comments on the story and its author, explanations of court offices, customs, manners, etc., illustrations, list of characters with their genealogies and locations in the story, and chronology of Genji's life.

Ikeda, Kikan 池田亀鑑　　　**G167**
Genji monogatari taisei 源氏物語大成 (*Genji monogatari* study series) Chūō Kōronsha, 1953-56. 8v.

Compares editions textually, gives indexes, lists research materials and reproduces illustrations from picture scrolls.

Yoshizawa, Yoshinori 吉沢義則 **and**　**G168**
Kinoshita, Masao 木之下正雄
Taikō Genji monogatari shinshaku　対校源氏物語新釈 (New commentaries on *Genji monogatari* with collated texts) Heibonsha, 1952. 8v.

Shows variant readings in detail by collating Kigin Kitamura's *Kogetsushō* text of 1674 with the Kawachi edition. Gives comments on words. v.7 and 8 index all words in both texts.

SAIGYŌ, 1118-90

Osaka Shidankai 大阪史談会　　　**G169**
Saigyō Hōshi bunken mokuroku 西行法師 文献目録 (Bibliography of Priest Saigyō) Osaka, 1940. 106p.

TSUREZUREGUSA

→ **G41**

Hirao, Mitsuko 平尾美都子　　　**G170**
Tsurezuregusa jiten 徒然草辞典　　(*Tsure-*

zuregusa dictionary) Kigensha, 1957. 474p.

Matsuo, Satoshi 松尾聡 **and**　**G171**
Okada, Shōtarō 岡田正太郎
Shōkai Tsurezuregusa jiten　詳解徒然草辞典 (*Tsurezuregusa* dictionary with detailed explanations) Meiji Shoin, 1957. 805p.

Tokieda, Motoki 時枝誠記　　　**G172**
Tsurezuregusa sōsakuin 徒然草総索引 (Complete index to *Tsurezuregusa*) Shibundō, 1955. 541p.

Standard index to words in the essays of Kenkō Yoshida (1283-1350), keyed to the Mitsuhiro edition in the Imperial Household Library, with variant readings in the Shōtetsu edition shown in upper margins.

MATSUO, BASHŌ, 1644-94

→ **G41**

Iino, Tetsuji 飯野哲二　　　**G173**
Bashō jiten 芭蕉辞典 (Bashō lexicon) Tokyodō, 1959. 734p.

Discusses the poetry and prose in sections on sources, diction, poetic interpretations, etc., and identifies his disciples and friends. Annotated bibliography and chronology appended. General index of headings, awkward to use because many of them are phrases and lines of poems.

Sakuragi, Shunkō 桜木俊晃　　　**G174**
Bashō jiten 芭蕉事典　　 (Bashō dictionary) Seiabō, 1963. 480p.

Lists and annotates *haiku* poems, prose works and study of poetry by Bashō, technical terms, seasonal expressions, related personal names, and about 800 items of pre-Meiji works related to Bashō. Also contains important letters. Biography and chronological table appended. Indexes.

Abe, Masami 阿部正美　　　**G175**
Bashō denki kōsetsu 芭蕉伝記考説 (Bashō biography) Meiji Shoin, 1960. 1146p.

Chronology of the poet, listing writings and events, collated on the basis of dependable sources. Indexes of personal names, works and sources cited.

Meguro, Yachō 目黒野鳥　　　**G176**
Bashōō hennenshi 芭蕉翁編年誌 (Annals of the venerable Bashō) Seiabō, 1958. 693p.

A chronology from 1644 to 1698, when his posthumous *Zoku sarumino* (Sequel to "Monkey's straw raincoat") was published. Chronology of books related to his works published before 1865 appended.

Yamamoto, Yuiitsu 山本唯一 **G177**
Bashō shichibushū sosakuin 芭蕉七部集総索引 (Complete index to the seven anthologies of the Bashō school) Kyoto, Hōzōkan, 1957. 487p.

Gives texts, taken from the first editions, with the poems numbered consecutively, followed by indexes of all words, first lines under authors' variant names.

Imoto, Nōichi 井本農一 **and** **G178**
Haraoka, Hideto 原岡秀人
Oku no hosomichi sōsakuin 奥の細道総索引 (Index to *Oku no hosomichi*) Meiji Shoin, 1962. 32, 184p.

Contains a reprint of the manuscript copy of Soryū, and indexes all the words in the text. Variant readings in other editions are given in upper margin.

CHIKAMATSU, MONZAEMON, 1653-1724

→ G41

Ueda, Kazutoshi 上田万年 **and** **G179**
Higuchi, Yoshichiyo 樋口慶千代
Chikamatsu goi 近松語彙 (Glossary of Chikamatsu) Fuzanbō, 1930. 771p.

Explains important words, phrases and passages in all the works of Monzaemon Chikamatsu, giving sources and relating them to social conditions and events. Listed separately are place and personal names, animals, plants, diseases, medicines, laws, economic matters, etc. Short biography, bibliography, chronology, list of research materials, index to difficult words, etc. appended.

IHARA, SAIKAKU, 1642-93

→ G41

Takita, Sadaji 滝田貞次 **G180**
Saikaku no shoshigakuteki kenkyū 西鶴の書誌学的研究 (Bibliographical studies of Saikaku) Taipei, Noda Shobō, 1941. 488p. (Taihoku Daigaku Bungakuka kenkyū nenpō, 5)

Annotated bibliography of works by Saikaku, various editions, commentaries, studies and literary works influenced by Saikaku. Includes chronological list of works to 1940.

Noma, Kōshin 野間光辰 **G181**
Saikaku nenpu kōshō 西鶴年譜考証 (Research on Saikaku chronology) Chūō Kōronsha, 1952. 32, 413p.

Events during the author's lifetime are listed year by year, and after his death to 1812 pertinent years only with emphasis on books and collated references. Includes lists of chronological tables of works by and on Saikaku.

YANAGIDARU

Karai, Senryū 柄井川柳 **G182**
Haifū yanagidaru 誹風柳多留 (*Haifū yanagidaru* ⊏senryū collections⊐) Iwanami Shoten, 1950-56. 5v. (Iwanami bunko)

Reproduces the first editions of the first 24 (1765-91) of the *senryū* collections bearing this title, including poems by Senryū I (1718-90), with notes on sources, variant readings, etc. Index of first lines and second lines, compiled by Ryūtei Sugimoto.

TSUBOUCHI, SHŌYŌ, 1859-1935

Takita, Sadaji 滝田貞次 **G183**
Shōyō shoshi 逍遙書誌 (Bibliographical study of Shōyō) Yoneyamadō, 1937. 451, 53p.

Includes works by and about the dramatist published up to 1934. Chronology and index.

SHIMAZAKI, TŌSON, 1872-1943

→ G41

Ishikawa, Iwao 石川巌 **G184**
Tōson shoshi 藤村書誌 (Bibliography of Tōson) Taikandō Shoten, 1940. 187p.

Writings of Tōson, excluding contributions to newspapers, listed under six categories, with some annotations and references to his works. Illustrations.

ISHIKAWA, TAKUBOKU, 1885-1912

Yoshida, Koyō 吉田孤羊 **G185**
Takuboku kenkyū bunken 啄木研究文献 (Bibliography of Takuboku) Meiji Bungaku Danwakai, 1934. 120p. (Meiji Bungaku Danwakai pamphlet, 1)

Includes works by and about the poet.

YOSANO, AKIKO, 1878-1942

Irie, Haruyuki 入江春行 **G186**
Yosano Akiko shoshi 与謝野晶子書誌 (Bibliography of Akiko Yosano) Osaka, Sōgensha, 1957. 121p.

Lists chronologically the writings of Akiko Yosano, including those in magazines and newspapers, and materials about her published through 1955, with brief comments on major books. Short biography appended. Index of titles, excluding reference materials, names and subjects.

HAGIWARA, SAKUTARO, 1886-1942

Maebashi Shiritsu Toshokan 前橋市立　**G187**
図書館
Hagiwara Sakutarō shoshi 萩原朔太郎書誌
(Bibliographical study of Sakutarō Hagiwara)
As of March, 1964.　1964.　137, 10p.
　Lists works by and about the poet. Gives locations. Author index.

Juvenile literature

Wakuri, Eiichi 和久利栄一　**et al.**　**G188**
Sekai jidō bungaku jiten 世界児童文学事典
(Dictionary of children's literature of the world)
Kyōdō Shuppansha, 1955.　347p.
　Covers all countries except Japan, listing works chronologically by countries with outlines, critical remarks, indication of Japanese translations and brief biographies of authors. Short history of children's literature appended. Titles, authors indexed.

Furuya, Tsunatake 古谷綱武　**et al.**　**G189**
Gendai jidō bungaku jiten 現代児童文学
辞典 (Dictionary of contemporary juvenile literature)　Rev. ed.　Hōbunkan, 1958.　452, 60p.
　Article-length entries discuss aspects of Japanese and foreign juvenile literature, mythology and folklore, authors, etc., with references. Chronology of foreign and Japanese developments, from early times to date. Classified table of contents and indexes of names and subjects.

Hasegawa, Seiichi 長谷川誠一　**G190**
Nihon jidō bungaku jiten 日本児童文学事典
(Dictionary of Japanese juvenile literature)
Kawade Shobō, 1954.　377, 23p.
　Major Japanese books, magazines and other materials, chronologically arranged from early times to date, with comments and notes about the authors. General study of juvenile literature, summaries of 12 histories of juvenile literature, notes on writers' groups and chronology appended. Indexes of names and subjects.

HISTORY

✤ Includes biography, family crests, historical geography, cultural geography and travel.

BIOGRAPHIES

✤ Biographies of religious workers, statesmen, technicians, artists, men of letters and others are given in the sections on their fields of activity. Specialized dictionaries and year-books often include biographical notes.

World · Europe

Heibonsha 平 凡 社　　　　　　　　**H1**
Dai jinmei jiten 大人名辞典 (Comprehensive biographical dictionary) 1953-55. 10v.

Standard work, especially useful for brief factual accounts of the lives and achievements, including writings, of historical figures, covering about 50,000 Japanese of the past (v.1-6), 8,000 living Japanese (v.7) and 8,000 foreigners (v.8-9), with references for each entry. Japanese surnames, personal names and pseudonyms indexed by strokes; foreign names indexed in original spelling. Imperial genealogy and list of traditional number-designated groups, such as the Six Master Poets, appended.

Tokyodō　東 京 堂　　　　　　　　**H2**
Sekai jinmei jiten 世界人名辞典 (Biographical dictionary of the world) 1961. 2v.

v.1 covers 6,000 Occidentals and v.2, 6,300 Orientals; but the listing among Occidentals of Orientals closely associated with the West and vice versa complicates use. Occidentals indexed in original spelling. v.2 has a list of unusual names, an index of personal names appearing in comments and an index of Europeans and Europeanized names of Orientals.

Kōjunsha　交 詢 社　　　　　　　　**H3**
Gendai kokusai jinmei jiten 現代国際人名辞典 (Present-day international biographical dictionary) 1957. 280, 26p.

Lists in Japanese syllabic reading persons prominent in countries other than Japan, giving for each his nationality, position, date and place of birth, career and any writings. Names indexed in original spelling and in Japanese reading arranged by countries.

　　　　　　　　　　　　　　　　　H4
Iwanami Seiyō jinmei jiten　岩波西洋人名辞典 (Iwanami biographical dictionary of the West) Comp. by Hideo Shinoda. Iwanami Shoten, 1956. 1962p.

Standard dictionary of basic information on 23,000 persons of past and present prominence in Europe, the Americas, Near and Middle East, Africa, Oceania and India, listed by Japanese syllabic reading. Especially strong in persons associated with Japan and China. Includes major fictional characters and deities. Comparative table of personal and place—names in various languages and lists of Nobel Prize recipients and sovereigns appended. Indexes of names in original spelling and names for which there are readings in Chinese characters.

Senda, Masao 仙田正雄 **et al.**　　　**H5**
Kan'yaku Kanmei Seiyō jinmei jiten 漢訳漢名西洋人名字典 (Dictionary of Chinese transcriptions of Western names and Chinese names adopted by Westerners) Tenri, Tenri Daigaku Shuppanbu, 1964. 100p.

The first comprehensive compilation of its kind, showing a special effort to include those linked with Japanese cultural history, it lists the names of Westerners as given in Chinese sources, with original spelling, birth and death dates, nationalities and specialties or occupations. Indexed by Chinese characters and original names. Useful in identifying persons referred to by different transcriptions and adopted Chinese names.

Kasumigasekikai   霞 関 会   **H6**
Gendai Soren jinmei jiten 現代ソ連人名辞典 (Who's who of contemporary Soviet Union) Kōnan Shoin, 1957. 220p.

Gives the full names, with Russian spelling, and careers of Russians prominent as of Feb., 1957. Similar is *Sorenpō yōjin meiroku 1961* (Directory of Soviet government personages, 1961), published by Kyokutō Tsūshinsha, 1960.

China and Korea

Nanba, Tsuneo 難 波 常 雄 **et al.**   **H7**
Shina jinmei jisho 支那人名辞書 (Chinese biographical dictionary) Yoshikawa Kōbunkan, 1910. (1856p.)

Covers briefly about 24,000 persons from ancient times to 1903, arranged by sound of the first character. Stroke index. Index of aliases and pseudonyms and list of numeral-prefixed groups.

Hashikawa, Tokio   橋 川 時 雄   **H8**
Chūgoku bunkakai jinbutsu sōkan 中 国 文 化 界 人 物 総 鑑 (Complete directory of Chinese cultural personages) Peking, Chūka Hōrei Hen'inkan, 1940. (863p.)

Brief biographies of about 4,000 leaders in Chinese science, education, literature and arts, with portraits of 400. Chronology of Chinese culture from the mid-19th century to date, list of universities, etc. appended.

Kasumigasekikai   霞 関 会   **H9**
Gendai Chūgoku jinmei jiten 現 代 中 国 人 名 辞 典 (Who's who in contemporary China) 1962 ed. Gaikō Jihōsha, 1962. 116, 789, 6p.

Lists about 8,500 persons. Indexed in Japanese and Chinese.

Chōsen Sōtokufu, Chūsūin   **H10**
朝 鮮 総 督 府 中 枢 院
Chōsen jinmei jisho 朝 鮮 人 名 辞 書 (Korean biographical dictionary) Seoul, Chōsen Insatsu, 1938. 2v.

Gives short biographies, with sources, of about 13,000 Koreans from ancient times to about 1930, with separate section for priests; entered in standard Chinese dictionary order. Appended are a reference list, index of pseudonyms, list of 15,000 successful candidates in examinations for official appointments under the Li dynasty, outline of

government organization, and comparative table of year names.

Kasumigasekikai   霞 関 会   **H11**
Gendai Chōsen jinmei jiten 現 代 朝 鮮 人 名 辞 典 (Who's who of contemporary Korea) 1962 ed. Sekai Jānarusha, 1962. (509p.)

Describes briefly the lives of about 1,600 prominent South and 830 North Koreans. Charts of political structures of North and South Korea, government directories and chronology from Aug., 1945 to Mar., 1962. Indexes by Japanese readings, Chinese characters and romanized Korean.

Japan

✤ Directories of learned societies and associations, business firms, etc., are listed under pertinent subjects. See also yearbooks and periodicals for contemporary biographies.

BIBLIOGRAPHY

✤ In the absence of adequate bibliography of biographical literature, use must be made of such tools as **A9**, **A10** and **A33**. Also helpful, though somewhat outdated, is:

Tokyo Shiritsu Hibiya Toshokan   **H12**
東 京 市 立 日 比 谷 図 書 館
Denki shiryō sakuin 伝 記 資 料 索 引 (Index of biographical articles) Tokyo Shiyakusho, 1928-38. 5v.

H13
Denki kenkyū sankōsho   伝 記 研 究 参 考 書
(List of reference works on biographical studies) Yūzankaku, 1938. 186p. (Kokushi sankō sōsho, 3)

Itō, Kazuo   伊 藤 一 男   **H14**
Zasshi ni okeru tsuitōgō shomoku 雑 誌 に 於 け る 追 悼 号 書 目 (List of memorial numbers of periodicals) Osaka, Kazuo Shoten, 1929. 40p.

Nihon Gakujutsu Kaigi   **H15**
日 本 学 術 会 議
Bunkakei bunken mokuroku. XIV: Nihon kindai-shi, denki hen 文 化 系 文 献 目 録 XIV：日 本 近 代 史 伝 記 編 (Bibliography of literature, philosophy and history. XIV: Modern Japanese history, biography) 1963. 65p.

Lists books and magazine articles (1935-61) in Japanese on persons prominent in modern history, with separate section for foreigners.

Takanashi, Kōji 高梨光司 **H16**
Ishin shiseki kaidai denki hen 維新史籍解題伝記編 (Bibliographical introduction to historical works on the Meiji Restoration: Biographies) Meiji Shoin, 1935. 13, 17, 342p.

Lists and annotates biographies published from 1868 to Sep., 1934, of scholars who contributed to the background of the Restoration, including those concerned with Western learning, leading participants in the Restoration and foreign visitors and- residents. Magazine articles and collected essays listed separately without annotation. Indexes of persons and titles.

DICTIONARIES

→ **H1**

H17
Dai Nihon jinmei jisho 大日本人名辞書 (Japan biographical dictionary) New ed., rev. Dai Nihon Jinmei Jisho Kankōkai, 1937. 5v.

Brief notes, with references, on about 35,000 Japanese in all walks of life from earliest times to date, with chronology, genealogies of prominent families. Index.

Haga, Yaichi 芳賀矢一 **H18**
Nihon jinmei jiten 日本人名辞典 (Japanese biographical dictionary) Ōkura Shoten, 1914. 1174p.

Though not detailed, useful in that it includes persons not in **H1** as well as pseudonyms, aliases and nicknames. Listing is by personal names in Japanese syllabic order. Stroke indexes of personal names and syllabic index of surnames.

Takeuchi, Rizō 竹内理三 **et al.** **H19**
Nihon kodai jinmei jiten 日本古代人名辞典 (Biographical dictionary of Japan in ancient times) Yoshikawa Kōbunkan, 1958- . 4v. In progress.

Gives all known facts about all persons, regardless of status, mentioned in documents to 781, with sources for each entry.

Names

Nippon Hōsō Kyōkai 日本放送協会 **H20**
Nandoku seishi 難読姓氏 (Unusual surnames) 5th ed. Nippon Hōsō Shuppan Kyōkai, 1964. 144p.

Character listing of unusual Japanese surnames gathered from previous publications of this kind, directories and other sources and gives their readings in Japanese syllabary. Originally published in two parts with the same title in 1935 and 1938. Index by Sinico-Japanese reading of first character.

Yajima, Genryō 矢島玄亮 **H21**
Nandoku seishi 難読姓氏 (Unusual surnames) No.1. Sendai, 1953. 125,7p. Mimeo.

Ono, Shirō 大野史朗 **H22**
Nandoku seishi shūsei 難読姓氏集成 (Compilation of unusual names) Tokyo Nōgyō Daigaku Toshokan, 1964. 22, 204p. (Nōdai Toshokan sōsho, 2)

Names arranged by strokes; gives readings based on 20 reference works, including dictionaries and directories.

Araki, Ryōzō 荒木良造 **H23**
Nanori jiten 名乗辞典 (Dictionary of personal names) supplemented with dictionary of hard-to-read surnames. Tokyodō, 1959. 306p.

Dictionary for finding possible readings of Japanese names written in Chinese characters. Pt.1 lists characters in phonetic order with examples of combinations with other characters and Japanese readings. Pt.2 lists in Japanese syllabic order, the examples mentioned in pt.1 with corresponding characters. Includes lists of names composed of characters of Japanese origin, official names used as personal names and foreign names written in characters. Dictionary of unusual surnames appended.

Wakimizu, Ken'ya 脇水謙也 **H24**
Senken meika betsugō besshō jiten 先賢名家別号別称辞典 (Dictionary of other names and pseudonyms of past sages and masters) Ishizaki Shoten, 1960. 278p.

Especially useful for art connoisseurs, it lists in syllabic order the pseudonyms and other names, with the real names, of calligraphers, artists and those associated with them, including patrons, writers, tea masters and craftsmen. Indexed by first characters.

Suzuki, Tōzō 鈴木棠三 **H25**
Gijinmei jiten 擬人名辞典 (Dictionary of made-up names) Tokyodō, 1963. 446p.

Cites about 2,000 slang terms, such as ebicha-shikibu for girl students, nukesaku for simpleton and goheida for coal, with general survey of such usage.

DIRECTORIES

H26
Bunka jinmeiroku 文化人名録 (Names in the arts and sciences) 1st ed. (1951)- . Comp. by Nihon Chosakuken Kyōgikai. 1951- . 11v.

Lists authors, artists, journalists, organizations, schools, libraries, museums, galleries, members of the Japan Copyright Council, etc., with comprehensive indexes of names, pseudonyms, etc. The most convenient reference source for contemporary Japanese copyright holders.

H27
Nihon jinjiroku 日本人事録 (Japan directory) 1st ed.- . Chūō Tanteisha, 1956- . 13v. Annual.

Gives for 200,000 persons occupation, place and date of birth, address(es), education, achievements, religion, interests, family members, etc.

H28
Nihon shinshiroku 日本紳士録 (Directory of distinguished Japanese) 1st ed.- . Kōjunsha, 1889- . 53v. Annual.

Covers leaders in business, politics, government, education, art and other fields, with positions, addresses, family members, birth dates and places, education and interests. Appended are staff directories of public offices, universities, major banks and companies and directory of Japanese living abroad.

H29
Taishū jinjiroku 大衆人事録 (Popular who's who) 1st ed.- . Teikoku Himitsu Tanteisha, 1925- . 24v.

Latest edition gives basic facts about approximately 100,000 prominent persons. Revised at intervals of from one to three years.

H30
Jinji kōshinroku 人事興信録 (⌐Japan⌐ directory of persons) 1st ed.- . Jinji Kōshinjo. 1903- . 35v. Biennial.

Standard listing of about 85,000 statesmen, company executives, professors, religious leaders, artists, etc., and prominent foreign residents, with their occupations, permanent and present addresses, family members and relatives, careers, writings or studies, hobbies and religion. The Imperial Family and its relatives given separately.

H31
Zen Nihon shinshiroku 全日本紳士録 (All-Japan who's who) 1950- . Jinji Kōshinjo, 1951- . 7v. Biennial from 1953.

Covers about 100,000 persons, including foreign residents, with information limited to birth year, permanent and present addresses, occupations and last school attended.

H32
Nihon shokuinroku 日本職員録 (Directory of Japanese officials) 1947- . Jinji Kōshinjo, 1947- . 9v. Biennial from 1950.

Gives the executives, organizational structure, locations of main and branch offices, and outlines the history, management and, where applicable, financial condition, of 35,000 national and local government offices and institutions, public corporations, universities, companies and banks.

H33
Sankei Nihon shinshi nenkan 産経日本紳士年鑑 (Sankei yearbook of Japanese personages) 1st ed. (1957)- . Sangyō Keizai Shinbunsha, 1957- . 8v. Annual.

Records the places and dates of birth, careers, tastes, any writings or artistic works, relatives and addresses of prominent persons in all parts of the country. Directory of government offices, universities, banks and companies in supplementary volume.

WOMEN

H34
Takamure, Itsue 高群逸枝 Dai Nihon josei jinmei jisho 大日本女性人名辞書 (Biographical dictionary of Japanese women) 3d ed., rev. Kōseikaku, 1942. 16, 690p.

Contains brief accounts of about 2,000 famous women, both fictions and real, appearing in Japanese historical literature. The accounts are based on established or prevailing versions, with notes on reliable variants and notes on source materials. Appendix lists empresses, empress dowagers, princesses in religious orders. Indexes by character, occupation, and special abilities.

FOREIGNERS IN JAPAN

H35
The Japan Times directory of foreign residents. 1951- . Japan Times, 1951- . 17v. Annual.

Convenient guide to addresses and phone numbers

of many foreign residents in Tokyo and elsewhere and of firms and other organizations with which they are associated; limited to those requesting to be listed. Includes Japanese offices, firms, restaurants, etc. of interest to foreigners.

❧ Many Europeans and Americans who came to Japan before the 1890s contributed to its modernization. For information about them, the following are useful:

Meiji bunka ni kiyo-seru Ōbei-jin no ryakureki (Brief lives of Europeans and Americans who contributed to Meiji culture) 1924. Special issue of *Bunmei taikan* (Survey of civilization) v.6. **H36**

Covers about 400 persons.

Meiji Taishō Shōwa keizai bunka tenrankai mokuroku (Catalogue of exhibition on the economy and culture of the Meiji, Taishō and Shōwa periods). Tōyō Keizai Shinpō Sha, 1940. **H36a**

Summarizes the lives and lists the writings of about 110 persons.

Meiji igo honpō doboku to gaijin (Foreigners and Japanese in public works from the Meiji period). By Magoichi Nakamura. 1942. **H36b**

Biographical information on 77 foreign civil engineers.

Meiji bunka kankei Ōbei jinmeiroku (Who's who of Europeans and Americans related to Meiji culture). By Tokutarō Shigehisa. *Toshokan kenkyū* (Library studies) v.10, no.4, Oct., 1937. **H36c**

Gives nationality, length of stay in Japan, occupation, etc. of about 750 persons.

"Oyatoi gaikokujin ichiran" (List of foreigners employed by the government). **H36d** See H170 v.16.

COURT NOBLES AND MILITARY FAMILIES

Sakamoto, Takeo 坂本武雄 **H37**
Kuge jiten 公卿辞典 (Dictionary of court nobles) Shichijō Shoin, 1944. 111, 183p.

Gives the lineage, rank, achievements and death year of about 2,000 court nobles from the Middle Ages whose official posts are recorded, classified by the rank of their families, with cross references. Indexes of family names, titles, religious names, pseudonyms and other names.

Kugyō bunin 公卿補任 (Appointment of **H38** Court nobles) Reprint ed. Yoshikawa Kōbunkan, 1964- . 3v. (Shintei zōho Kokushi taikei, 53, 54- , supp.1) In progress.

Gives chronologically from the time of Emperor Jinmu to 1868 all known appointments to posts upward from imperial advisers (*Sangi*) and conferments of ranks upward from the junior third. Indexes of personal, posthumous and religious names and titles.

Hashimoto, Hiroshi 橋本博 **H39**
Kaitei dai bukan 改訂大武鑑 (Revised comprehensive directory of military families) Dai Bukan Kankōkai, 1940. 6v.

Tabulates in chronological order from the Kamakura to the Meiji period, name, native province, castle, amount of fief, court-rank, official duties, ancestry, inherited fortunes, marital relations, service in Edo, gifts to and from shōgun, family crests, flags, banners, important retainers, etc. of the daimyōs. First published in tabular form in 1647, issued annually from 1716.

PORTRAITS

Morisue, Yoshiaki 森末義彰 **and** **H40**
Tani, Shin'ichi 谷信一
Kokushi shōzō shūsei 国史肖像集成 (Collection of Japanese historical portraits) Meguro Shoten, 1940-44. 6v.

Reproduces portraits of emperors and other members of the imperial family, shōguns, warriors and priests. Only six of 10 projected volumes published.

Nara Teishitsu Hakubutsukan **H41**
奈良帝室博物館
Nihon shōzōga zuroku 日本肖像画図録 (Japanese portraits: collection of paintings) Kyoto, Benridō, 1938. 2v.

GENEALOGIES

Ōta, Akira 太田亮 **H42**
Seishi kakei daijiten 姓氏家系大辞典 (Comprehensive dictionary of surnames and genealogies) Reprint ed. Kadokawa Shoten, 1963. 3v.

Exhaustive listing of family names found in pre-1868 documents and records, with notes on the origin and distribution of families and relations between their main lines and branches. Reproduces available crests. First published by Seishi kakei Dai-jiten kankōkai, 1934-36, in 3v. and reprinted by Kokuminsha, 1942-44, in 6v.

Hioki, Shōichi 日置昌一 **H43**
Nihon keifu sōran 日本系譜総覧 (General survey of Japanese family trees) Kaizōsha, 1936. 36,984p.

Gives lines of succession of the imperial and other prominent families, Buddhist sects and schools of art, learning, martial arts, etc., from ancient times to date. Appended are a 150p. chronology of Japanese history and tables of court ranks, important posts, administrative structures and daimyōs. No index.

Kokusho Kankōkai 国書刊行会 **H44**
Keizu sōran 系図綜覧 (General survey of genealogies) 1925. 962p.

Contains more than 150 important genealogies based on those in Yoshizumi Maruyama's *Shoka keizu san* (Compilation of the lineages of many houses), of the late 17th century, and in the collection of the Historiographical Institute of Tokyo University, with titles, birth and death dates and achievements of each individual. First published in 1915 in 2v.

H45
Sonpi bunmyaku 尊卑分脈 (Genealogies of main and branch families) Rev. ed. reprinted. Yoshikawa Kōbunkan, 1958-64. 5v. (Shintei zōho Kokushi taikei, 58-60, supp. 2)

Best printed edition of the compilation of genealogies of the Imperial Family and aristocratic families to about the 14th century originally made by Kinsada Tōin (1340-99), based on the revised version owned by the Maeda family and collated with 11 other editions, supplemented with material from early books. Gives briefly the life of each individual included. Indispensable for study of the Minamoto, Taira, Fujiwara, Tachibana and other ancient families. Useful with it is *Sonpi bunmyaku datsuru* (Addenda to Sonpi bunmyaku), in the genealogical section of the series titled *Zoku Gunsho ruijū* (Sequel to the Gunsho ruijū).

H46
Shintei Kansei chōshū shokafu 新訂寛政重修 諸家譜 (Kansei collated genealogies of many houses) Newly rev. ed. Zoku Gunsho Ruijū Kanseikai, 1964- . 9v. In progress.

Basic document, completed in 1812 under Masaatsu Hotta; gives the genealogies of daimyō, warriors, physicians and others of prominence in the Tokugawa hierarchy to 1798, with notes on family histories and relations between main and branch houses and brief accounts of individuals. Based on Eishinsha ed., 1917-18, 9v. To be completed in 25v., the last 3v. of which will contain indexes. Also indexed in **H128** by government offices and by fiefs.

Ōta, Akira 太田亮 **H47**
Dōjōke keifu taisei 堂上家系譜大成 (Compilation of genealogies of court nobles) Sōgensha, 1941. 18,296p.

Gives brief genealogies to 1868 of the families of nobles who in the Tokugawa period had access to the Emperor or performed important functions, with ranks, histories, positions, addresses, burial place, and notes on individuals.

Masamune, Atsuo 正宗敦夫 **H48**
Jige kaden 地下家伝 (Family histories of lowranking court officials) Nihon Koten Zenshū Kankōkai, 1937-38. 6v. (Nihon koten zenshū, 6th series)

Lists court officials below the 5th rank from ancient times to 1852, arranged by family names, with birth and death dates, appointments, etc. Compiled originally by Kagebumi Mikami (Hata) at the end of the Tokugawa period. General table of contents and index of names by strokes.

Jinji Kōshinjo 人事興信所 **H49**
Zaikai kakeizu 財界家系図 (Genealogies of families in the financial world) Rev. ed. 1963. 700p.

Gives the family trees and connections through marriage of 306 contemporary financial leaders, with photographs and accounts of their careers. Index.

IMPERIAL HOUSE AND PEERAGE

Ihara, Yoriaki 井原頼明 **H50**
Kōshitsu jiten 皇室事典 (Cyclopedia of the Imperial House) enl. ed. Fuzanbō, 1941. 483p.

Explains, article by article, the provisions of the former Imperial Household Law and other regulations, including much information about practices and ceremonies. Genealogies related to the Imperial Family and various rescripts appended. Indexes.

Nishimura, Kiichi 西邑木一 **H51**
Kazoku taikan 華族大観 (Directory of noble families) Rev. 2d ed. Kazoku Taikan Kankōkai, 1940. 726p.

HERALDRY

Numata, Raisuke 沼田頼輔 **H52**
Nihon monshōgaku 日本紋章学 (Japanese

heraldry) Meiji Shoin, 1926. 1486p.

Most authoritative survey of the subject, with general introduction and catalogue of family crests, each with its name and notes on its significance, type, relation to the family name and the families using it. See also **H39** and **H42**.

ARCHAEOLOGY

BIBLIOGRAPHY

Nihon kōkogaku nenpō 日本考古学年報 **H53**
(Japan annual of archaeology) No.1 (1948)- .
Comp. by Nihon Kōkogaku Kyōkai. Seibundō Shinkōsha, 1951- . 12v. Irregular.

Outlines developments, reports on excavations and lists books and articles.

Okamoto, Isamu 岡本勇 **and** **H54**
Asō, Masaru 麻生優
Nihon sekki jidai sōgō bunknen mokuroku 日本石器時代綜合文献目録 (Comprehensive bibliography of Stone Age Japan) Yamaoka Shoten, 1958. 194p.

Lists chronologically books and articles published from 1868 to 1955. Chronology of Stone Age studies and list of magazines cited appended. Index classified by prefectures and author index.

Tomoyori, Eiichirō 友寄英一郎 **H55**
Ryūkyū kankei kōkogaku bunken mokuroku 琉球関係考古学文献目録
(Bibliography of Ryūkyū archaeology) Komiyama Shoten, 1962. 158p.

Lists 946 pre-1962 books and magazine articles, arranged under magazine titles, and 1951-61 newspaper articles, arranged by years. Directory of research organizations and their publications appended. Subject and personal name indexes.

DICTIONARIES

Mizuno, Seiichi 水野清一 **and** **H56**
Kobayashi, Yukio 小林行雄
Zukai kōkogaku jiten 図解考古学辞典
(Illustrated cyclopedia of archaeology) Tokyo Sōgensha, 1959. 1056, 46p.

Covers prehistoric and later remains, including those relevant to Japan in China, Korea and other nearby areas, with many entries on history, geography, local customs, biology, etc. Major topics receive detailed attention, with references. Chronology of early Japanese culture based on types of earthenware and chronology of world archaeology appended. Index.

Nihon Kōkogaku Kyōkai **H57**
日本考古学協会
Nihon kōkogaku jiten 日本考古学辞典
Dictionary of Japanese archaeology. Tokyodō, 1962. 652p.

About 3,600 entries, many with illustrations, on historic sites, relics, personal names, book titles and terms, including some related foreign topics. Lists of government designated cultural properties, historical sites, coins, inscriptions and references appended, with earthenware chronology and map of state-established provincial temples. Index.

SITES

Tokyo Teikoku Daigaku 東京帝国大学 **H58**
Nihon sekki jidai ibutsu hakken chimeihyō 日本石器時代遺物発見地名表 (Japanese Stone Age sites) 5th ed. Oka Shoin, 1928. 544p.

Sakazume, Nakao 酒詰仲男 **H59**
Nihon kaizuka chimeihyō 日本貝塚地名表 (Japanese shell mound sites) Kyoto, Doyōkai, 1959. 207p.

Gives alternative names, locates, describes the condition, contents, etc. of and gives references for 2,428 mounds in Saghalien, the Kuriles, Hokkaidō, Honshū, Ryūkyū, Formosa and the Chinese mainland. Name index.

Morimoto, Rokuji 森本六爾 **H60**
Nihon seidōki jidai chimeihyō 日本青銅器時代地名表 (Japanese Bronze Age sites) Oka Shoin, 1929. 25, 230p.

Gives places where Aëneolithic remains have been found, arranged by provinces and also by the kinds of objects excavated. Illustrations and distribution map appended.

Saito, Tadashi 斉藤忠 **H61**
Nihon kofun bunka shiryō sōran 日本古墳文化資料綜覧 (Survey of materials on Japan's ancient tomb culture) Yoshikawa Kōbunkan, 1953-56. 3v. Mimeo.

Pt.1 lists literature on the Tomb period, which is supplemented through 1955 in pt.3. Pt.2 surveys tombs, kilns, lepidary and other sites of the period, classified by areas, with notes on their locations, characteristics and objects unearthed from them. Omitted are imperial mausoleums and ritual sites, which are covered in *Ryōbo yōran* (Handbook of Imperial tombs), Shoryōryō, 1934, and Iwao Ōba's "Jōdai saishi iseki chimeihyō" (List of sites of ancient rites), in *Shintō kōkogaku ronkō* (Shintō archaeological studies), Ashime Shobō, 1943. 692p.

ILLUSTRATIONS

Heibonsha 平凡社 **H62**
Sekai kōkogaku taikei　世界考古学大系
(Compendium of world archaeology) 1958- .
15v. In progress.

Surveys early cultures in various parts of the
world, with profuse illustrations of sites and
objects, maps, chronologies and references.

Umehara, Sueji 梅原末治 **and** **H63**
Fujita, Ryōsaku　藤田亮策
Chōsen kobunka sōkan　朝鮮古文化綜鑑
(Ancient Korean culture, illustrated) Tenri,
Yōtokusha, 1947- . 2v. In progress.

v.1 shows and explains archaeological relics of
the pre-Lolang period, and v.2, Lolang period, 108
B.C. to 313 A.D. with general survey. To be completed in 3v.

Saitō, Tadashi 斉藤忠 **H64**
Nihon kōkogaku zukan　日本考古学図鑑
(Japanese archaeology illustrated) Yoshikawa
Kōbunkan, 1955. 8, 25, 6p. 160 plates.

An introductory guide from 1700 B.C. to 800 A.D.
(Jōmon to Nara periods), classified by periods,
and arranged by topics such as dwellings, occupations, decoration, ritual, etc. Notes on each
plate (subject, location, place of discovery,
measurements) appear on the verso. Bibliography,
indexes of sites and subjects.

Tokyo Kokuritsu Hakubutsukan **H65**
東京国立博物館
Nihon kōko zuroku　日本考古図録 (Japanese
archaeology in illustrations) Asahi Shinbunsha,
1953. 62p. 96 plates.

Shows representative relics from the Jōmon
period to the late bomb period. Notes and essay
by Ichirō Yawata appended.

Kobayashi, Yukio 小林行雄 **and** **H66**
Sugihara, Shōsuke 杉原荘介
Yayoishiki doki shūsei　弥生式土器集成
(Collection of Yayoi-type pottery) Yayoishiki
Doki Shūsei Kankokai, 1961- . 1v. In
progress.

About 2,000 pieces, of which those found in
western Japan are in v.1. To be completed in 2v.

Kobayashi, Yukio 小林行雄 **and** **H67**
Sugihara, Shōsuke 杉原荘介
Yayoishiki doki shūsei　弥生式土器集成
(Collection of Yayoi-type pottery) Tokyodō,
1964- . 1v. In progress.

v.1 shows on a 1:6 scale pieces not in **H66** from
Kyūshū, Shikoku and Chūgoku, with notes and
references.

Nihon Kōkogaku Kyōkai **H68**
日本考古学協会
Nihon nōkō bunka no seisei　日本農耕文化
の生成 The origin and growth of farming communities in Japan. Tokyodō, 1960-61. 2v.

Reports research on 25 Yayoi period sites excavated in western Japan, with diagrams and bibliography. Photographs of sites and relics in separate
volume.

WORLD HISTORY

BIBLIOGRAPHY

Endō, Motoo 遠藤元男 **et al.** **H69**
Kokushi Tōyōshi Seiyōshi shiseki kaidai
国史東洋史西洋史史籍解題 (Bibliogra-
phical introduction to materials on Japanese,
Oriental and Western history) Heibonsha,
1940. 682p.

The parts on Japan (Superseded by **H113**) and
the Orient list by titles books, including some in
Western languages, and annotated documents.
The Western part gives by author European and
American works classified by period, area and
subject. Title index in each part.

Kokusai Rekishigaku Kaigi, Nihon **H70**
Kokunai Iinkai
国際歴史学会議日本国内委員会
Nihon ni okeru rekishigaku no hattatsu to genjō
日本における歴史学の発達と現状
(The development and present state of Japanese
historiography) Tokyo Daigaku Shuppankai,
1959. 514, 22p.

Signed surveys cover significant Japanese
studies, mainly since 1945, in various fields of
Japanese history, arranged by period; in the history
of the Orient by country or area; in the history of
the West by period and country; and in the international relations; titles of books and articles
appear in notes at the end of each section. Author
index. A translation, in English despite its French
title, *Le Japon au XIe Congres International des
Sciences Historiques a Stockholm*, was published
by the Nippon Gakujutsu Shinkōkai in 1960. A
similar early work is *Meiji igo ni okeru rekishigaku
no hattatsu* (Progress of historiography since the
Meiji period), 680p., edited by the Rekishi Kyōiku
Kenkyūkai and published as a special issue of
Rekishi kyōiku (Teaching of history), v.7, no.9,
1932.

Chiyoda, Ken 千代田謙 **et al.**   **H71**
Shigaku meicho kaidai   史学名著解題
(Important historiographical works annotated)
Kyōritsusha, 1931.   137, 149, 75p.   (Gendai
shigaku taikei, v.15)

In three sections: section on West by Ken
Chiyoda, is arranged by historians and their works;
section on Japan by Hikojiro Matsumoto discusses
writings as they occur in the development of historiography. Section on China by Hitoshi Matsui, is
arranged by title or subject with comments on
related works and reference works. Although in
no sense exhaustive, a useful study of historiography.

Shigakkai   史学会   **H72**
Shigaku bunken mokuroku   史学文献目録
(Bibliography of historiography)   1946-1950.
Yamakawa Shuppansha, 1951.   204p.

Lists Japanese books, articles and essays
on general, Asian and Western history, each subdivided into period, country, and subject. Author
index.

DICTIONARIES

Heibonsha   平凡社   **H73**
Sekai rekishi jiten   世界歴史事典
(Encyclopedia of world history)   1951-55.
25v.

Gives a broad survey of Japanese, Oriental and
Western history in signed articles by specialists,
with references and many illustrations and maps.
Headings are not exhaustive, and the general index
omits many details. Indexes of Chinese characters,
Western-language terms and illustrations. For the
last four volumes, on historical materials, see
H122, Japan, **H87**, the Orient, and **H84**, the West.

Inoue, Kōji 井上幸治 **et al.**   **H74**
Sōgō Sekai rekishi jiten 総合世界歴史事典
(Comprehensive dictionary of world history)
Rev. ed. Jiji Tsūshinsha, 1957. 810p.

Outlines selected topics with some articles
giving references. Illustrations and maps. Comparative chronology showing events in Japan, the
Orient and the West to 1945, comparative calendars
and table of reigns appended. Personal names
and subjects indexed with brief identifications
or explanations.

Sōbunsha   創文社   **H75**
Gendaishi jiten 現代史事典 (Dictionary of
contemporary history) Supplement: Chronology
of contemporary history. 1955. 328p. (Gendaishi kōza, v.6)

Explains major events and identifies prominent

persons, excluding living Japanese, with original
spelling of foreign terms and names. Subject and
personal name indexes. The chronology, from
1830 to 1954, has separate columns for the West,
Asia, Japan, and thought and culture.

CHRONOLOGY

Kyoto Daigaku Bungakubu   **H76**
京都大学文学部
Sekaishi dainenpyō 世界史大年表 (Comprehensive chronology of world history) Tōindō
Shoten, 1955. 789p.

Detailed chronology with emphasis on Europe,
listing political and cultural events for each
country or area from 5000 B.C. to 1941, with brief
annotation of the more important. No index. Two-
volume edition published by Meguro Shoten,
1947-49.

Sanseidō   三省堂   **H77**
Saishin Sekai nenpyō 最新世界年表(Up-to-
date chronology of the world) Rev. ed. 1958.
427, 217, 65p.

Concentrates extensive information from ancient
times to 1957 into parallel columns for Japan, the
Orient and the West, with listing by months of
events from 660 A.D. and with full dates for some
from 1868. Genealogies, lists of personal names
and era names appended. Indexes of Japanese,
Oriental and Western events.

Honjō, Kasō   本荘可宗   **H78**
Sekai bunka nenpyō 世界文化年表
(Chronology of world culture, newly edited)
Seirinsha, 1955. 364, 88p.

Gives events from 4500 B.C. to 1955 relating
to philosophy, education, literature, arts, law,
politics, economy, industry, the natural sciences,
commerce, navigation, exploration, etc. Index.

Gendaishi Taikei Henshūbu   **H79**
現代史大系編集部
Gendaishi nenpyō 現代史年表 (Chronologies of contemporary history) Misuzu
Shobō, 1957. 322p. (Gendaishi taikei, 12)

Following an introductory chronology from the
mid-19th century to 1914, there are interpretive
chronologies of political and economic events from
1914 to 1954 in international affairs and the history
of Europe, America, Africa, Asia and Oceania,
subdivided by period and country. Based on
Auszug aus der Geschichte, by Karl Ploetz, 1956.
Major topics indexed.

ATLAS

Kamei, Takayoshi 亀井高孝 **and** **H80**
Mikami, Tsugio 三上次男
Teihon sekaishi chizu 定本世界史地図
(Standard historical atlas of the world) Yoshi-
kawa Kōbunkan, 1954. 128, 62p.

Contains maps of states, ancient sites, cities,
trade routes, battles, etc., from pre-historic times
to date, with place–names and subjects both
in Japanese and original spelling. General index.

ILLUSTRATIONS

Kadokawa Shoten 角川書店 **H81**
Zusetsu Sekai bunkashi taikei 図説世界文化
史大系 (Illustrated compendium of world
cultural history) 1958-61. 27v.

A bibliography at end of each volume and ex-
cellent illustrations distinguish this set of general
histories of individual countries, including five
volumes on Japan. General index, maps and chronologies in final volume.

Seibundō Shinkōsha 誠文堂新光社 **H82**
Sekaishi taikei 世界史大系 (Compendium of
world history) 1957-60. 18v.

Notable for many illustrations. Supplementary
volume has general index, extensive bibliography,
lists of Western personal and place names and
table of old and new names of major Chinese cities.

Europe

Inoue, Kōji 井上幸治 **and** **H83**
Hayashi, Kentarō 林健太郎
Seiyōshi kenkyū nyūmon 西洋史研究入門
(Introduction to the study of Western history)
Tokyo Daigaku Shuppankai, 1954. 461p.

Bibliographical survey of Japanese studies and
Western-language materials, divided into chapters
on the ancient period, Middle Ages, histories of
individual countries, international relations and
problems of historiography.

Heibonsha 平凡社 **H84**
Seiyō shiryō shūsei 西洋史料集成 (Western
historical materials) 1956. 1166p. (Sekai
rekishi jiten, v. 24, 25)
Consists of historical materials and annotated
bibliography sections. Materials in translated
excerpts are arranged chronologically from ancient
times to the present and classified by subject.
The bibliography section lists standard refer-

ence works, and periodicals with annotations,
arranged by period and subdivided by subject,
except that modern-age subdivision is by country.
Title index.

Igirisushi Kenkyū Sentā **H85**
イギリス史研究センター
Igirisu kakumei bunken mokuroku イギリス
革命文献目録 (A bibliography of the English
Revolution) Nagoya, Nagoya Daigaku Keizai-
gakubu Toshoshitsu, 1963. 60p.

Lists by author bibliographies, documents, books
and microfilms, covering the 17th and 18th centuries,
in the library of the Economics Department, Nagoya
University, as of Sept., 1963.

Kyoto Daigaku Bungakubu **H86**
京都大学文学部
Seiyōshi jiten 西洋史辞典 (Dictionary of
Western history) Tokyo Sōgensha, 1958.
881, 107p.

Covers the period from ancient times to 1945
in about 5,000 entries in Japanese with brief explanation. Appendix contains a comparative table
of names with different spellings, lists of sovereigns,
genealogies, administrative maps. Index in
Japanese.

Asia
Bibliography

Heibonsha 平凡社 **H87**
Tōyō shiryō shūsei 東洋史料集成 (Oriental
historical materials) 1956. 556p. (Sekai
rekishi jiten, v. 23)

Lists and annotates standard works, translated
excerpts of historical materials, and reference
books, in Chinese, Japanese and Western languages;
arranged by areas, subdivided by periods or
countries. Author index and index of Chinese
titles.

H88
Tōyōshi kenkyū bunken ruimoku 東洋史研究
文献類目 Annual bibliography of Oriental
studies. 1934- . Comp. by Kyoto Daigaku,
Jinbun Kagaku Kenkyūjo. Kyoto, Kyoto Jinbun
Gakkai, 1935- . 17v. Annual since 1957.

Lists Oriental studies in Japanese, Chinese
and Western languages, limited originally to holdings of the Tōhō Bunka Gakuin (forerunner of the
Institute) but expanded since 1940. Author index.
Published biennially from 1938 to 1956, with 1946-50
covered in a single issue.

Tōyōshi Kenkyū Ronbun Mokuroku **H89**
Henshū Iinkai
東洋史研究論文目録編集委員会

Nihon ni okeru Tōyōshi ronbun mokuroku
日本における東洋史論文目録
Japanese studies on Asian history; a catalogue
of articles concerning the history of Asia
(excluding Japan) in periodicals and other
collections published in Japan from c.1880 to
1962. Nihon Gakujutsu Shinkōkai, 1964- .
1v. In progress.

Lists articles, book reviews, bibliographical
lists, etc., in chronological order under the titles
of 190 periodicals and 270 transactions and
memoirs. Final volume is to have author index.

Ōtsuka Shigakkai 大塚史学会 **H90**
Hōbun rekishigaku kankei shozasshi Tōyōshi
ronbun yōmoku 邦文歴史学関係諸雑誌
東洋史論文要目 (List of studies on Oriental
history in Japanese history journals) Rev.
and enl. ed. 1936. 362p.

Classifies articles published from 1868 to 1935,
preceding those in **H88**. No index.

Dictionaries

Heibonsha 平凡社 **H91**
Tōyō rekishi daijiten 東洋歴史大辞典
(Cyclopedia of Oriental history) 1937-39.
9v.

Covers the area from Mongolia and Manchuria
to Southeast Asia and West Asia with emphasis
on recent times. References with each article.
Indexes (v.9) in Chinese characters, Japanese
syllabary and Western languages; index of Chinese
personal and place names in modern readings.

Heibonsha 平凡社 **H92**
Ajia rekishi jiten アジア歴史事典 (Cyclopedia of Asian history) 1959-62. 10v.

New standard compilation giving attention not
only to China but also to Southeast and Southwest
Asia, Africa and East-West relations, with many
illustrations and maps. References with each
article. Tables including chronology of Asian
history appended to v.9. General index in v.10.

Kyoto Daigaku Bungakubu **H93**
京都大学文学部
Tōyōshi jiten 東洋史辞典 (Dictionary of
Oriental history) Tokyo Sōgensha, 1961. 994p.

Covers Asia except Japan from ancient times
to 1958; about 5,000 topics. Emphasis is on India,
West and Southeast Asia. Appendix contains lists
of sovereigns, era-names, Chinese government posts,
unusual names, Chinese weights and measures,
principal currencies, and historical maps. Index.

Atlas

Yanai, Watari 箭内亘 **H94**
Tōyō dokushi chizu 東洋読史地図 (Histori-
cal atlas of the Orient) Rev. ed., by Sei Wada.
Fuzanbō, 1943. 64p. 37 maps.

Consists largely of maps showing changes in
political conditions and battles in China, from
ancient to modern times, with some maps of cities
and roads. Notes on the maps at the end. No
index.

Illustrations

Ishida, Mikinosuke 石田幹之助 **and** **H95**
Iwai, Hirosato 岩井大慧
Tōyō rekishi sankō zufu 東洋歴史参考
図譜 (Illustrations of Oriental history) Sankō
Zufu Kankōkai, 1924-30. 6v.

Consists of 15 series of illustrations in 3v. showing mainly Chinese historical sites, portraits,
calligraphy, painting, tombs, inscriptions, and
other social and economic conditions, with citation
to sources; and accompanied by explanatory pamphlets for each series bound separately in 3v..

CHINA

Tōhō Gakujutsu Kyōkai **H96**
東方学術協会
Chūgoku shigaku nyūmon 中国史学入門
(Introduction to the study of Chinese history)
Kyoto, Heian Bunko, 1951. 692p.

Bibliographical guide to books on history from
before the Ch'in dynasty to the Ch'ing, with
sections on archaeology, historical geography and
East-West relations.

Wada, Sei 和田清 **H97**
Chūgokushi gaisetsu 中国史概説 (Outline
of Chinese history) Iwanami Shoten, 1951.
2v. (Iwanami zensho)

Useful for its chapter references and annotated
bibliography in v.2.

Nakatani, Hideo 中谷英雄 **H98**
Tōdaishi kenkyū bunken mokuroku 唐代史
研究文献目録 (Bibliography of studies in
T'ang history) Wakayama, Wakayama Kōtō
Gakkō, 1956. 82, 13p. Mimeo.

Classified list of books and articles published
in Japan from 1868 and in China from 1912 to Mar.,
1956.

Sōshi Teiyō Hensan Kyōryoku Iinkai H99
宋史提要編纂協力委員会
Sōdai kenkyū bunken mokuroku 宋代研究
文献目録 (Bibliography of Sung Dynasty
studies) Tōyō Bunko, 1957-59. 2v.

Classifies books and articles by Japanese and
articles by foreign scholars in Japanese journals
published from 1868 to 1956 on the Five Dynasties,
the Sung Dynasty and border states. English
table of contents appended. Author index. Supplement extends coverage to 1957.

Sōshi Teiyō Hensan Kyōryoku Iinkai H100
宋史提要編纂協力委員会
Sōdai kenkyū bunken teiyō 宋代研究文献
提要 Abstracts of Japanese books and articles
concerning the Sung. Tōyō Bunko, 1961.
842, 11p.

Classifies under 16 headings and abstracts
about 3,000 studies listed in H99 with some supplementary titles. Author index.

Yamane, Yukio 山根幸夫 H101
Mindaishi kenkyū bunken mokuroku 明代史
研究文献目録 (Bibliography of studies in
Ming history) Tōyō Bunko, 1960. 258p.
Mimeo.

Classified list of magazines and newspaper
articles by Japanese from 1868 to 1960 and by
Chinese from 1900 to 1960, with chronology, 1368-
1909. Indexes of Japanese and Chinese authors;
of Chinese, Manchurian, Korean, and Japanese
priests with Chinese-style names referred to in
the articles; of famous non-Chinese who visited
or resided in China during the late Ming period.

Chūgoku Kindaishi Kenkyūkai H102
中国近代史研究会
Chūgoku kindaishi ronbun sakuin kō 中国近代
史論文索引稿 (Provisional index of articles
on modern Chinese history) 1840-1949. 1957.
65p.

Classifies Chinese articles published from Oct.,
1949, to Aug., 1956, covering the period from the
Opium War of 1839-42 to the founding of the People's
Republic in 1949. No index.

Kojima, Shōtarō 小島昌太郎 H103
Shina saikin daiji nenpyō 支那最近大事
年表 (Chronology of recent major events in
China) Yūhikaku, 1942. 980p.

Events from 1840 to 1941 under such headings as
internal politics, diplomacy, industry, society
and culture, followed by explanatory notes and
references. Detailed general index.

Baba, Akio 馬場明男 H104
Shina mondai bunken jiten 支那問題文献
辞典 (Dictionary of literature on the China
problem) Keiō Shobō, 1940. 350p.

Lists and annotates Japanese works and translations published from 1926 to 1940 on contemporary
China, classified under social, economic and political affairs.

H105
Shina mondai jiten 支那問題辞典 (Dictionary
on the China problem) Chūō Kōronsha, 1942.
776p.

Deals with events from about 1926 to 1940 under
some 50 topics. Chinese biographical dictionary
and chronological table of Chinese cultural history
appended. Subject index.

Baba, Akio 馬場明男 H106
Shina seiji keizai nenpyō 支那政治経済
年表 (Chronological table of Chinese politics
and economy) Keiō Shobō, 1943. 684p.

Lists historical events from 1839 to 1940 with
brief explanations. Name and subject index.

MANCHURIA

Manshūkokushi Hensan Iinkai H107
満州国史編纂委員会
Manshūkokushi nenpyō 満州国史年表
(Chronology of the history of Manchukuo) Man-
Mō Dōhō Engokai, 1956. 204p.

Lists events from Sept. 18, 1931, to Aug. 15,
1945, with citation to official Manchukuo publications, newspapers and other sources. No
index.

SOUTHEAST ASIA

Ide, Tokuo 井出徳雄 H108
Annanshi nenpyō 安南史年表 (Chronology
of Annamese history) Nan'yō Keizai Kenkyūjo,
1944. 98p. (Nan'yō shiryō, 386)

Extends from early times to 1941.

Osaka Gaikokugo Daigaku Biruma H109
Gogaku Kenkyūshitsu
大阪外国語大学ビルマ語学研究室
Birumashi nenpyō ビルマ史年表 (Chronology
of Burmese history) 1960. 101p.

Chronology from 850 B.C. to 1960.

PACIFIC ISLANDS

Tōa Kenkyūjo 東亜研究所 H110
Nanpō shokuminshi bunken mokuroku 南方植

民史文献目録 (A bibliography of the history of colonies in the South Pacific) 1942. 823p.

Lists by colonizing countries, with area and subject subdivision, pre-1930 foreign books in the libraries of Tokyo, Kyoto, Hokkaido and Taihoku Imperial Universities, as well as some in the Library of Congress, Dutch National Institute of Colonial Studies and East Asian Economic Research Institute of the South Manchuria Railway Company. No. index.

Japan

Bibliography

→ M29, M30

Tōyama, Shigeki 遠山茂樹 **and** **H111**
Satō, Shin'ichi 佐藤進一
Nihonshi kenkyū nyūmon 日本史研究入門 (Introduction to research in Japanese history) Rev. ed. Tokyo Daigaku Shuppankai, 1954-62. 2v.

Signed articles divided by period, on various aspects of historiography and significant books and articles. Outline of feudalism and capitalism; lists of dictionaries and chronologies, unpublished manuscripts with location, and research institutions. v.2 covers 1955-60 publications. Further volumes projected at five-year intervals.

Kurita, Motoji 栗田元次 **H112**
Sōgō kokushi kenkyū 綜合国史研究 (General studies in Japanese history) Dōbunkan, 1935-36. 3v.

Useful annotated bibliography of studies and reference works, excluding local history, published from 1868 to 1934 arranged by periods and fields, with introductory survey of pre-Meiji historical materials. Collected essays and periodicals annotated in v.2, and documents in v.3. Title and author indexes.

Endo, Motoo 遠藤元男 **and** **H113**
Shimomura, Fujio 下村富士男
Kokushi bunken kaisetsu 国史文献解説 (Annotated bibliography of Japanese history) Asakura Shoten, 1957. 644, 72p.

Expanded from the Japanese section of **H69**, it fully annotates, and evaluates important Japanese and foreign historical materials, including manuscripts, with their location, and series and collections, with their contents. Title index.

Ōtsuka Shigakkai 大塚史学会 **H114**
Sōgō kokushi ronbun yōmoku 綜合国史論文

要目 (Comprehensive subject list of articles on Japanese history) Tōkō Shoin, 1939. 627p.

Articles published in magazines and symposia from 1868 to April, 1938, classified by archaeology, folk manners, language, etc., and listed by author. List of magazines cited arranged in the order of foundation.

Tsukubake Kokushi Kenkyūbu **H115**
筑波家国史研究部
Kokushigaku kai 国史学界(Historical studies in Japan) 1929-1943. 1930-45. 15v.

Reviews progress in historiography and lists and annotates each year's books and articles; classified by subject.

Takagi, Shintarō 高木真太郎 **H116**
Kokushi shincho kaidai 国史新著解題 (Annotated list of new works on Japanese history) Shunjūsha, 1943-44. 2v.

Limited to 1942-43 publications but gives detailed attention to a few outstanding books and lists others in each field, including general history, the Imperial Court and Shintō, bibliographies and documents, archaeology and ethnology. v.2 adds 1943 articles. No index.

Koizumi, Yasujirō 小泉安次郎 **H117**
Nihon shiseki nenpyō 日本史籍年表 (Chronological list of Japanese historical materials) Reprint ed. Yoshikawa Kōbunkan, 1911. 716p.

Gives for each year from 888 to 1867 records, diaries and other documents, some of them in compilations, which contain references to events, with indications of location. Those to 1602 are based largely on *Shiseki nenpyō* (Chronological list of historical materials), compiled by Nobutomo Ban (1773-1846). Those for later years are divided into Imperial Court materials, Edo materials and compilations. Title index for each part. First published in 2v. in 1903-04.

Kunaichō, Shoryōbu **H118**
宮内庁書陵部
Zushoryō tenseki kaidai 図書寮典籍解題 (Annotated catalogue of Zushoryō-Government Library; history) Yōtokusha, 1950-51. 2v.

Lists historical materials exhibited for a time by the Imperial Household Library with detailed annotations. v.1, classified by historical works, records to about 1400, documents and genealogies with bibliographical survey and general index; and v.2 by law, court ceremonies, appointments of officials, events at court, mausolea and miscellany with title index.

H119

Tokyo Daigaku Shiryō Hensanjo tosho mokuroku
東京大学史料編纂所図書目録
(Library catalogue of Tokyo University Historiographical Institute) Pt.2. Japanese and Chinese books and manuscripts. No.2. Historical materials. Shiryō Hensanjo, 1961. 351p.

Lists old documents and other materials available in photographic reproduction, registered by the Institute through 1960, giving their owners when reproduced, reproduction dates, etc.

H120

Shiryōkan shozō shiryō mokuroku 史料館所蔵 史料目録 (Catalogue of historical materials in the Shiryōkan) Shiryōkan, 1952- . 10v. In progress.

Documents from the early 17th century to 1868, arranged by subject under pertinent families and villages.

Kinsei Shomin Shiryō Chōsa Iinkai   **H121**
近世庶民史料調査委員会
Kinsei shomin shiryō shozai mokuroku 近世 庶民史料所在目録 (Catalogue of private collections of modern history) Nihon Gakujutsu Shinkōkai, 1952-55. 3v.

Lists village records, histories, school documents, and legal instruments from 1600 to the 1860s; arranged by prefectures, entries include name and address of owner, original location, size of collection, inclusive dates and general nature of materials included. Geographical index.

Heibonsha   平凡社   **H122**
Nihon shiryō shūsei 日本史料集成 (Collection of Japanese historical materials) 1956. 32,601, 49p. (Sekai rekishi jiten, v.22)

Useful as a documented outline history, divided by period, subdivided by topic (politics, economy, diplomacy, etc.). Includes excerpts of documentary materials. Tables. Title and subject indexes.

Tōyō Bunko Kindai Nihon Kenkyūshitsu **H123**
東洋文庫近代日本研究室
Kindai Nihon kankei bunken bunrui mokuroku 近代日本関係文献分類目録
Classified catalogue of books in the Tōyō Bunko on modern Japan - Japanese books and microfilms. 1961-63. 3v.

Lists some 6,000 titles, including works donated to the Seminar on Modern Japan. No periodicals or books on literature and art. Title index.

Tokyo Daigaku, Shiryō Hensanjo   **H124**
東京大学史料編纂所
Nihon kankei kaigai shiryō mokuroku 日本 関係海外史料目録 Historical documents relating to Japan in foreign countries. 1963- . 3v. In progress.

Detailed catalogue of microfilms collected by the Historiographical Institute of unpublished documents concerning not only Japan but also other East Asian countries in foreign archives and libraries. First five volumes (1, 2 and 4 published) devoted to documents in the Netherlands, mostly about the East India Company. To be completed in 14v.

Dictionaries

Kawade Shobō Shinsha   **H125**
河出書房新社
Nihon rekishi daijiten 日本歴史大辞典 (Encyclopedia of Japanese history) 1956-60. 24v.

Exceptionally comprehensive in factual coverage from prehistoric times to the present, including politics, economy, folklore, archaeology, art, literature and personages, with separate entries for even minor topics. Numerous illustrations. Index (v.20) classified under personal names, place names, bibliography, politics and law, society, and economy. For supplementary volumes, see **H135** and **H139**.

Kyoto Daigaku Bungakubu   **H126**
京都大学文学部
Nihonshi jiten 日本史辞典 (Dictionary of Japanese history) Tokyo Sōgensha, 1954. 983p.

Ranges from early times to postwar period; about 3,000 topics with brief explanations. Classified table of contents of personal names, politics and law, society and economy, culture, place – names and terminology, and general index. Appendix contains many tables, illustrations and a classified catalogue of documentary materials.

Wakamori, Tarō   和歌森太郎   **H127**
Nihon rekishi jiten 日本歴史事典 (Dictionary of Japanese history) Rev. and enl. ed. Jitsugyō no Nipponsha, 1958. 601p.

Good for succinct information, with references, under about 2,700 headings, emphasizing socioeconomic history, folklore and culture.

Handbooks

Tokyo Teikoku Daigaku, Shiryō Hensanjo H128
東京帝国大学史料編纂所
Dokushi biyō 読史備要 (Handbook of Japanese history) Naigai Shoseki, 1942. 2154p.

Authoritative compilation of reference data, including comparative table of dates, chronology to 1932, lists of emperors, shōguns, daimyōs and office-holders, administrative charts, histories of provinces and counties, calendar of annual observances, fluctuations in currency and rice prices, genealogies, tables of religious sects, national studies, and cultural and martial arts, and ·indexes of biographical literature. Chart of calendar signs appended.

Kyoto Daigaku Bungakubu H129
京都大学文学部
Nihonshi kenkyū jiten 日本史研究事典 (Manual for the study of Japanese history) Osaka, Sōgensha, 1955. 409p.

Contains useful tables, lists and illustrations, simpler than H128 but better for modern history. Expanded from the appendix to H126.

Chronology

Tsuji, Zennosuke 辻善之助 H130
Dai Nihon nenpyō 大日本年表 (Japanese chronological table) Dai Nihon Shuppan, 1942. 390, 84p.

Gives for each year from 660 B.C. to 1940 calendar information helpful in equating lunar and solar dates, the calendar signs of the first day of each month, the number of each year counted backwards from 1940 and information about leading personages, major events, including deaths, with source materials indicated to 1868. Genealogy of the Imperial Family, lists of important office-holders and table of era names appended. No index. Revised ed., but only v.1, to 1600, follows:

Nihon bunkashi nenpyō (Chronology of Japanese cultural history) v.1, by Zennosuke Tsuji. Shunjūsha, 1956. 322p. **H130a**.

Nishioka, Toranosuke 西岡虎之助 H131
Shin Nihonshi nenpyō 新日本史年表 (New chronology of Japanese history) Chūō Kōronsha, 1955. 633p.

From 601 to 1955, gives events, primarily in Japan but also abroad, Japanese, Chinese and Korean era names, emperors, ministers, etc. Supplementary materials include archaeological tables, chronologies of the *Kojiki* and *Nihon Shoki* covering the pre-601 period, and lists of offices, officials, political parties and leaders. Index.

Ōkubo, Toshiaki 大久保利謙 **and** H132
Shimomura, Fujio 下村富士男
Nihon hyakka nenpyō 日本百科年表 (Encyclopedic chronologies of Japan) Asakura Shoten, 1956. 362p.

Separate chronologies to 1955 give events in 64 fields, including the Diet, politics, diplomacy, agriculture, social movements, art, disasters and population, preceded by a simple general chronology. Tables on other subjects and bibliography of chronologies by date of publication appended.

Ōmori, Kingorō 大森金五郎 **and** H133
Takahashi, Shōzō 高橋昇造
Saishin Nihon rekishi· nenpyō 最新日本歴史年表 (Up-to-date Japanese historical chronology) Sanseidō, 1945. 484p.

Gives the number of each year counted backwards from 1945, the era name, the reigning emperor and important Japanese, Chinese and Western events, with the more important in bold type in margins. Various lists and bibliography of studies and reference works on historical periods appended. Indexes.

Kuroita, Katsumi 黒板勝美 H134
Kokushi kenkyū nenpyō 国史研究年表 (Chronology for the study of Japanese history) Rev. and enl. by Jirō Maruyama. Iwanami Shoten, 1955. 277p.

Gives dates for events from 667 B.C. to 1954. Indexes of personal names, subjects and place names.

Kawade Shobō Shinsha H135
河出書房新社
Nihon rekishi nenpyō 日本歴史年表 (Chronology of Japanese history) 1960. 373, 59p. (Nihon rekishi daijiten, supp.)

Shows for each year from 1 to 1959 the calendar signs, era name, emperor, principal ministers and political, economic, social and cultural events, with their dates (according to the lunar calendar to 1872). There is also a chart of changes in local institutions to Feb., 1958. Source materials listed in editorial note. Archaeological tables appended. No index.

Tokyo Daigaku, Shiryō Hensanjo H136
東京大学史料編纂所
Shiryō sōran 史料綜覧 (Survey of historical materials) 1923- . 17v. In progress.

The most accurate and detailed chronology of important events from 887 to 1867, so far carried to 1639, citing primary source materials in the monumental *Dai Nihon shiryō* (Japanese historical materials) of the Historiographical Institute.

Tahara, Shinsaku 田原新作 **H137**
Rekishi nikkan 歴史日鑑 (Book of historic dates) Rekishi Nikkan Kankōsho, 1937. 363p.

Lists for each day of the year anniversaries of historical events, including a few foreign ones, and observances at famous shrines and temples. Pre-1872 dates are according to the lunar calendar. No index. There is no more recent work of its kind.

Atlases

Nishioka, Toranosuke 西岡虎之助 **and** **H138**
Hattori, Shisō 服部之総
Nihon rekishi chizu 日本歴史地図
(Japanese historical atlas) Zenkoku Kyōiku Tosho, 1956. 482p.

Contains 75 maps illustrating politics, industry, trade routes, education and military affairs. Arranged chronologically from early times to the present. Each map is accompanied by a related selection map, distribution map and notes. Indexes of place-names in the *Man'yōshū*, foreign place names; lists of principal sites and monuments, Japanese era names; five contemporary maps appended.

Kawade Shobō Shinsha **H139**
河出書房新社
Nihon rekishi chizu 日本歴史地図 (Historical atlas of Japan) 1961. 58p. 60 maps. (Nihon rekishi daijiten, supp.)

Shows the places of major events in each period, including such information as the location of manors, ruling families, uprisings, temples, popular theatricals, etc. General index.

Yoshida, Tōgo 吉田東伍 **H140**
Dai Nihon dokushi chizu 大日本読史地図
(Historical atlas of Japan) Rev. and enl. by Koreto Ashida. Fuzanbō, 1935. 27p. 82 maps.

National, regional, city, political and military, from ancient times to about 1930 with brief notes and insets.

Illustrations

Nishioka, Toranosuke 西岡虎之助 **H141**
Shin Nihonshi zuroku 新日本史図録
(Illustrations of new Japanese history) v.1. Chūō Kōronsha, 1952. 479p.

Emphasizes socio-economic aspects of life,

especially of the common people, with reproductions of paintings, drawings, relics, old sites and records in chronological order from primitive times through early feudalism. No index. Only v.1 published.

Shōgakkan 小学館 **H142**
Zusetsu Nihon bunkashi taikei 図説日本
文化史大系 (Illustrated compendium of Japanese cultural history) 1958-59. 13v. and supp.

Standard cultural history from prehistoric times to date with signed articles by specialists and numerous reliable illustrations. Further reference to illustrations, selected documents with comments and general annotated bibliography in supplementary index volume. Similar works follow:

H143
Kokushi daizukan 国史大図鑑 (Compendium of illustrations of Japanese history) Yoshikawa Kōbunkan, 1933. 6v.

Nihon Kindaishi Kenkyūkai **H144**
日本近代史研究会
Shashin zusetsu sōgō Nihonshi 写真図説
総合日本史 (General history of Japan in photographs) Kokusai Jōhōsha, 1955-57. 10v.

Chūō Kōronsha 中央公論社 **H145**
Zusetsu Nihon rekishi 図説日本歴史
(Pictorial history of Japan) 1960-61. 8v.

Kōdansha 講談社 **H146**
Shashin zusetsu Nihon hyakunen no kiroku 写真図説日本百年の記録 (Photographic record of Japan's past century) 1960-61. 2v.

Documents

Aida, Jirō 相田二郎 **H147**
Nihon no komonjo 日本の古文書 (Old documents of Japan) Iwanami Shoten, 1949-54. 2v.

Standard guide to pre-1600 documents, explaining where and in what condition they exist, their kinds and forms, with 862 examples in v.2. Index of terms relating to such documents, chronological list of documents.

Tokyo Teikoku Daigaku, Shiryō **H148**
Hensangakari 東京帝国大学史料編纂掛
Komonjo jidai kagami 古文書時代鑑

(Documents of the ages) 1925-27. 4 cases.

About 450 sheets of collotype facsimiles of pages of letters, documents, books, etc., from early times to 1868 selected to show calligraphic styles, including those of famous persons, with transcriptions into modern language and notes. Helpful in familiarization with old handwriting.

Signatures

Kinoshita, Keifū　木下桂風　**H149**
Nihon kaō taikan 日本花押大観 (Survey of Japanese signatures) Shūhōen, 1933. 311p. Japanese style binding.

Useful until **H150** is completed.

Tokyo Daigaku, Shiryō Hensanjo　**H150**
東京大学史料編纂所
Kaō kagami 花押かがみ (Signature facsimiles) Yoshikawa Kōbunkan, 1964- . 1v. In progress.

Reproduces in actual size the signatures of important persons arranged chronologically by death dates from 845 to 1185 in v.1, with sources. Index.

ANCIENT

Nihon Gakujutsu Kaigi　**H151**
日本学術会議
Bungaku tetsugaku shigaku bunken mokuroku. VIII: Nihon kodaishi hen　文学哲学史学
文献目録 VIII: 日本古代史編 (Bibliography of literature, philosophy and history. VIII: Ancient Japanese history) 1959. 122p.

Lists monographs and articles published from 1946 to 1957. Author index.

Takagi, Ichinosuke 高木市之助 and　**H152**
Tomiyama, Tamizō　富山民蔵
Kojiki taisei 古事記大成 (Complete study of the *Kojiki*) Index. Heibonsha, 1958. 2v.

Although part of the 8v. set, an independent work with its own collated text, based on the *Kōtei Kojiki* (The collated and revised Kojiki) published by the Kōten Kōkyūjo in 1911, the content and vocabulary of which are indexed exhaustively.

Murabayashi, Magoshirō　**H153**
村林孫四郎
Kojiki jiten 古事記辞典 (Kojiki dictionary) Kinseisha, 1943. 817p.

Explains briefly deities, persons, places, and subjects in the Kojiki.

Zōho Rikkokushi　増補六国史　(The six　**H154**
Japanese national histories) Enl. ed. Comp. by Ariyoshi Saeki. Asahi Shinbunsha, 1940-41. 12v.

The texts, with headnotes and reading aids, of the series of officially compiled chronicles from early times to 887 are followed by v.11, a chronology showing where events are recorded in the six chronicles and v.12, indexes of names of deities, personal names, place names and miscellany.

Rikkokushi Sakuin Henshūbu　**H155**
六国史索引編集部
Nihon sandai jitsuroku sakuin　日本三代
実録索引 (Index to Nihon sandai jitsuroku ⌐History of three Japanese reigns⌐) Yoshikawa Kōbunkan, 1963. 414p. (Rikkokushi sakuin, 4)

Divided into personal names, offices and posts, subjects, place names, and shrines, temples and mausolea, keyed by date to the text of the official chronicle for the period from 858 to 887.

Yashiro, Kuniji　八代国治　**H156**
Shōen mokuroku 荘園目録 (Catalogue of manors) Iwai Reimeidō, 1933. 146p.

Divided into imperial and nonimperial, subdivided by prefecture, lists names of manors with notes on feudal overlords, locations, reference sources. Index, arranged in Japanese syllabic order with reference sources, includes also names of manors in the *Shōen kō* (Study of shōen), by Hiroshi Kurita, Useful as a guide to basic sources on Japanese manors.

Shimizu, Masatake　清水正健　**H157**
Shōen shiryō 荘園志料 (Materials on manors) Teito Shuppansha, 1933. 2v.

Lists and gives notes on the origin and development of manors (*shōen*), arranged by provinces, on the basis of documents and other sources.

15TH - MID 19TH CENTURIES

Inagaki, Shisei　稲垣史生　**H158**
Sengoku buke jiten　戦国武家事典
(Cyclopedia of samurai families in the period of civil wars) Seiabō, 1962. 551p.

Explains how the warrior class was organized, lived and fought in the 15th and 16th centuries. References and chronology of battles appended. Index.

Tochinai, Sōjirō　栃内曾次郎　**H159**
Yōjin Nihon tanken nenpyō
洋人日本探検年表

(Chronology of Westerners' contacts with Japan) 2d ed., rev. and enl. Iwanami Shoten, 1929. 179p.

Covers visits, diplomatic relations, trade and propagation of Christianity from 1501 to 1875, with entries from Japanese and Western sources on facing pages. Major events explained in detail, Quotations from original documents on the order to repel foreign ships, the Russian invasion of the Kuriles, etc. appended. Bibliography of Western books on Japan. Index.

Kaikoku Hyakunen Kinen Bunka   **H160**
Jigyokai 開国百年記念文化事業会
Sakoku jidai Nihonjin no kaigai chishiki 鎖国時代日本人の海外知識 (Knowledge of the Japanese about Western countries during the period of national isolation) Kangensha, 1953. 498p.

Classified bibliography of books on geography, maps, and books on Western history by Japanese published from 1615 to 1867, with a general survey of each class and detailed annotations. Some illustrations. Chronological list of titles appended. Names, titles indexed.

MEIJI RESTORATION

Rekishigaku Kenkyūkai   **H161**
歴史学研究会
Meiji Ishinshi kenkyū kōza 明治維新史研究講座 (Series on study of the Meiji Restoration) v.6. Heibonsha, 1959. 266, 87p.

Lists and annotates source materials and works concerning the period from 1830 to the promulgation of the Meiji Constitution in 1889, under ten classifications, arranged chronologically. Name and subject indexes for the series.

Irimajiri, Yoshinaga 入交好脩   **H162**
Meiji Ishinshi kenkyū no hatten 明治維新史研究の発展 (Development in the study of the Meiji Restoration) Dōbunkan, 1949. 199p.

Chapters surveying studies in important aspects of the Restoration give critical comments on reference works. Bibliography and table of changes from provinces to prefectures appended.

Nihon Rekishi Chiri Gakkai   **H163**
日本歴史地理学会
Ishinshi kenkyū shiryō sakuin 維新史研究資料索引 (Index to studies in Restoration history) 1919. 220p.

Lists by subject and author articles on the 1844-71 period in 30 important periodicals from

Mar., 1876, to Dec., 1914.

Monbushō, Ishin Shiryō Hensan   **H164**
Jimukyoku 文部省維新史料編纂事務局
Ishinshi 維新史 (History of the Restoration) Meiji Shoin, 1939-41. 6v.

The 5v. history of the 1846-71 period compiled by the Education Ministry's Secretariat for the Editing of Meiji Restoration Materials. v.6, Indexes include list of court, shogunate and Meiji government appointments, list of feudal domains and their lords, and index of names in these lists. Useful as a handbook.

Monbushō, Ishin Shiryō Hensan   **H165**
Jimukyoku 文部省維新史料編纂事務局
Ishin shiryō kōyō 維新史料綱要 (Outline of materials on the Restoration) 1937-39. 10v.

Lists Restoration events by month from 2d month, 1846 to 7th month, 1869 with notes on source materials, providing incidentally the most detailed and reliable chronology of the period. Compiled as summary index to *Dai Nihon Ishin shiryō* (Materials relating to the Japanese Restoration), an exhaustive collection of primary materials that was suspended indefinitely after the publication of 19v.

MODERN

Kyoto Daigaku Bungakubu   **H166**
京都大学文学部
Nihon kindaishi jiten 日本近代史辞典 (Dictionary of modern Japanese history) Tōyō Keizai Shinpōsha, 1958. 990p.

About 3,300 entries, each with references, explain events from about 1850 to 1958, with considerable attention to postwar changes. Tables and statistics, with notes on sources, appended. General index.

    H167
Nihon kokusei jiten 日本国政事典
(Cyclopedia of Japanese politics) Rengō Shuppansha, 1953- . 10v. In progress.

Gives extracts from the "Official Gazette", newspapers and authoritative books concerning developments under successive cabinets, starting with the Itō Cabinet of 1885, arranged chronologically in sections on the Imperial Family, politics, institutions, diplomacy, military affairs, education, finance, industry and economics, communications, culture, labor and society. v.10 carries the work through the first Konoe Cabinet to 1939.

Tsumaki, Chūta 妻木忠太   **H168**
Ishin go dainenpyō 維新後大年表 (Com-

prehensive post-Restoration chronology) Rev. and enl. ed. Yūhōdō Shoten, 1925. (791p.)

Detailed chronology of events from 1867 to Apr., 1925, preceded by brief chronology from 1846 to 1867. List of Tokugawa fiefs, names of governors, prefectural changes and directory of peers appended. Classified index under laws, official posts, political parties, inventions, banks, companies, foreign visitors, foreign employees of the Japanese government, wars and uprisings, and calamities.

Shinobu, Seizaburō 信夫清三郎 **H169**
Gendai seijishi nenpyō 現代政治史年表 (Chronology of contemporary political history) Kyoto, San'ichi Shobō, 1960. 252p. (Nihon gendaishi nenpyō)

Lists events from 1853 to 1959, with comments on facing pages. Index.

Yoshino, Sakuzō 吉野作造 **et al.** **H170**
Meiji bunka zenshū 明治文化全集 (Complete collection on Meiji culture) Nihon Hyōronsha, 1927-30. 24v. Reprint ed. 1955-59. 16v.

Valuable collection of materials to about 1890, in an original edition of 24v. and a new edition consisting of material selected from the former and three new volumes, embodying bibliographies, arranged chronologically, on the following: (I = 1st ed.; II = 2d ed. Arabic numerals denote volumes.) Constitutional documents (I-4, II-1), popular rights (I-5, II-2), foreign relations (I-6, II-11), politics (I-7, II-3), law (I-8, II-13), economics (I-9, II-12), education (I-10), religion (I-11), literature (I-12), novels on current themes (I-13), translations of foreign literary works (I-14), thought (I-15), foreign culture (I-16, II-7), newspapers (I-17, II-4), magazines (I-18, II-5), civilization and enlightenment (I-20), social affairs (I-21, II-6), miscellaneous historical writings (I-22), science (I-24) and women's problems (II-16). Also included are chronologies of imperial visits (I-1), military affairs (I-23) and transportation (I-23, list of government-employed foreigners (I-16, II-7) and chronological table of changes in manners and customs (I-19, II-8).

Kaikoku Hyakunen Kinen Bunka **H171**
Jigyōkai 開国百年記念文化事業会
Nichi-Bei bunka kōshōshi 日米文化交渉史 History of Japanese-American cultural relations, 1853-1926. Yōyōsha, 1954-56. 6v.

v.1, Japan-American diplomatic relations in the Meiji-Taishō era, 1845-1922; v.2, Japanese trade and industry in the Meiji-Taishō era; v.3, Educational relations; v.4, Japanese literature: manners and customs in the Meiji-Taishō era; v.5, Japanese emigration, 1853-1930. Each volume includes chronology and indexes. Vols.1, 2 and 3 are

available in English translations.

Kaikoku Hyakunen Kinen Bunka **H172**
Jigyōkai 開国百年記念文化事業会
Meiji bunkashi 明治文化史 Cultural history of the Meiji era, 1868-1912. Yōyōsha, 1953-57. 14v.

Consists of a general introduction with separate volumes on literature, thought, religion, fine arts, etc., each edited by an authority; 10 volumes are available in English translations or adaptations. General index of subjects and plates in v.14.

Kinoshita, Sōichi 木下宗一 **H173**
Nihon hyakunen no kiroku 日本百年の記録 (Record of a century in Japan) Jinbutsu Ōraisha, 1960. 2v.

Annotated excerpts from official reports and newspaper accounts of important events from 1868 through 1941. Each volume indexed.

H174
Shinbun shūsei Meiji hennenshi 新聞集成 明治編年史 (Chronicle of the Meiji period compiled from newspapers) Zaisei Keizai Kenkyūkai, 1934-36. 15v.

Brings together articles on a wide range of subjects from some 200 newspapers from 1862 to 1912, with chronology of major events and classified list of source materials, arranged chronologically, in each volume. General index of about 130,000 entries in v.15.

H175
Shinbun shūsei Shōwa hennenshi 新聞集成 昭和編年史 (History of Shōwa period through newspapers) Comp. by Shinbun Shūsei Taishō Shōwa Hennenshi Kankōkai. 1955- . 6v. In progress.

Compiled in the same style as **H174**. Includes important events in both national and local papers. To be completed in 33v., corresponding to the number of years of Shōwa (e.g., v.5 lists events of the fifth year of Shōwa). 5, 6, 7, 8, 23, and 24 in publication.

LOCAL HISTORY

Kokugakuin Daigaku, Shigakkai **H176**
国学院大学史学会
Zenkoku chihōshi bunken mokuroku kō 全国 地方誌文献目録稿 (Checklist of Japanese local histories) 1960. 299p. Mimeo.

Lists by geographical area, with annotation of important items, histories, published 1868-1959, of the old provinces, feudal clans (*han*), prefectures, towns and villages, materials related to historic and scenic sites, catalogues and bibliographies of local histories, local chronologies, etc. No index.

Ōtsuka Shigakkai　大塚史学会　**H177**
Kyōdoshi jiten　郷土史辞典　(Cyclopedia of local history) Asakura Shoten, 1955. 919p.

Explains objectively 1,290 entries, each with a few references, primarily on Tokugawa socio-economic history but including folklore, archaeology, entertainment and general culture. Illustrations. Tables and indexes.

Chihōshi Kenkyū Kyōgikai　**H178**
地方史研究協議会
Chihōshi kenkyū hikkei　地方史研究必携 (Manual for the study of local history) Iwanami Shoten, 1952. 316p. (Iwanami zensho)

Useful introduction, with explanation of the best approaches to local studies from primitive times to the present, references, maps and plates. No index.

Chihōshi Kenkyū Kyōgikai　**H179**
地方史研究協議会
Kinsei chihōshi kenkyū nyūmon　近世地方史研究入門 (Introduction to the study of Tokugawa period local history) Iwanami Shoten, 1955. 316p. (Iwanami zensho)

Explains how to use and evaluate documents on village administration, with facsimiles, notes on reading them, examples of village picture-maps, land registers, directories, records of religious conversions and five-man groups, etc. Annotated bibliography and chronology appended. Index.

HISTORICAL GEOGRAPHY

China

Yoshida, Tora 吉田寅 and　**H180**
Tanada, Naohiko　棚田直彦
Chūgoku rekishi chiri kenkyū ronbun mokuroku 中国歴史地理研究論文目録 (List of studies on Chinese history and geography) Tokyo Kyōiku Daigaku Bungakubu, 1960. 161p. Mimeo.

Classified bibliography of books and articles by Japanese and Chinese scholars from 1868 to 1957, with a few later titles.

H181
Kokuritsu Kokkai Toshokan zō Chūgoku chihō-shi sōroku kō　国立国会図書館蔵中国地

方志綜録稿 (Checklist of Chinese local gazetteers in the National Diet Library) Kokuritsu Kokkai Toshokan, 1950- . 18v. In progress. Mimeo.

Includes holdings of the National Diet Library, Tōyō Bunko, Seikadō Library, Cabinet Library, the Imperial Household Library, Sonkeikaku Library and the Research Institute for Humanistic Studies, Kyoto University.

H182
Tōyō Bunko chihōshi mokuroku　東洋文庫
地方志目録　(Catalogue of local gazetteers in the Oriental Library) China, Manchuria, Formosa. Tōyō Bunko, 1935. 237, 36p.

Lists 2,550 titles collected systematically since 1920, arranged by provinces. Title index. For gazetteers of towns, mountains, temples, mausolea, rivers and embankments, see **B35.**

Tenri Toshokan　天理図書館　**H183**
Chūbun chishi mokuroku　中文地志目録 (Catalogue of Chinese local gazetteers) Tenri, Tenri Daigaku Shuppanbu, 1955. 138, 276p. (Tenri Toshokan sōsho, 19)

Classified list of about 2,400 ancient and modern Chinese local gazetteers in the Tenri Library as of Aug., 1955. Title index.

Aoyama, Sadao　青山定雄　**H184**
Dokushi hōyo kiyō sakuin, Shina rekidai chimei yōran　読史方輿紀要索引支那歴代地名要覧 (Index to Tu-shih fang-yu chi-yao: Geographical essentials for the reader of history; manual of Chinese historical place names) Tōhō Bunka Gakuin, 1939. 721, 89p.

Lists in Japanese syllabic order the names of mountains, rivers, barriers, fortresses, cities, temples, etc., from ancient times to about 1630 in the compilation of Ku Tsu-yü (1631-82), with their present names, locations in the text and comments. Indexes.

Japan

Akioka, Takejirō　秋岡武次郎　**H185**
Nihon chizushi　日本地図史　(History of Japanese maps) Kawade Shobō, 1955. 217p.

Useful as bibliography of pre-1868 maps, which it lists with years of preparation and publication, cartographers, styles and present owners. Many illustrations and maps.

Takagi, Toshita　高木利太　**H186**
Kazō Nihon chishi mokuroku 家蔵日本地誌

目録 (Catalogue of Japanese geographical books in the author's possession) Ōyama-mura (Hyōgo Pref.), 1927-30. 2v.

Lists about 3,000 topographical descriptions, travel guides and accounts, historical studies, etc. from early times, with emphasis on the 17th and 18th centuries, some with annotations. Title index in each volume.

Wada, Mankichi 和田万吉 **H187**
Kohan chishi kaidai 古版地誌解題 (Annotated bibliography of old geographical descriptions) Rev. ed. Ōokayama Shoten, 1933. 229p.

Gives full bibliographical details of, and comments on 108 titles of the 17th and early 18th centuries, with many photographic reproductions, including maps. Title index.

Naimushō Chirikyoku 内務省地理局 **H188**
Chishi mokuroku 地誌目録 (Catalogue of geographical descriptions) Ōokayama Shoten, 1935. 202p.

Originally published in 1884 by the Geography Bureau, Ministry of Home Affairs, classifies by locality and gives full bibliographical details of old works, with indication of whether they are in the *Henshū chishi biyō tenseki kaidai* (Annotated bibliography of books concerned with geographical descriptions), a listing of about 2,000 titles owned by the Shogunate, compiled by Shishin Mamiya about 1825. No index.

Kishii, Yoshie 岸井良衛 **H189**
Gokaidō saiken 五街道細見 (Guide to the five highways) Seiabō, 1959. 274p.

Based on Tokugawa period guidebooks and maps, it traces the Tōkaidō, Kōshu-kaidō, Nakasendō, Ōshu-kaidō and Nikkō-kaidō and their branches. Map from Shirakawa to Osaka, 1:750,000, appended.

HUMAN GEOGRAPHY

World

BIBLIOGRAPHY

Uyama, Yasuo 宇山保雄 **H190**
Jinbun chiri bunken mokuroku 人文地理文献目録 (Bibliography of cultural geography) Yamaguchi, Yamaguchi Kōtō Gakkō, 1951. 179p.

Classified index of articles in 17 journals, including *Chirigaku Hyōron* (Geographical review) and *Chirigaku* (Geography), from 1923 to 1950, with appended list of monographs.

Jinbun Chiri Gakkai 人文地理学会 **H191**
Chirigaku bunken mokuroku 地理学文献目録 (Bibliography of geography) Kyoto, Yanagiwara Shoten, 1953-63. 3v.

Classified list of books, series and articles. v.1 covers 3,500 titles, 1945-51; v.2, 15,000 titles, 1952-56; v.3, 12,000 titles, 1957-61.

Fujioka, Kenjirō 藤岡謙二郎 **H192**
Jinbun chirigaku kenkyūhō 人文地理学研究法 (How to study cultural geography) Asakura Shoten, 1957. 332p.

Outlines the history and methodology of research with many references and annotated list of major foreign journals. Personal name and subject indexes.

Keiō Gijuku Daigaku, Bunka Chiri Kenkyūkai 慶応義塾大学文化地理研究会 **H193**
Sekai kunibetsu chishi mokuroku 世界国別地誌目録 (Catalogue of geographies of the world) Kōgakusha, 1959. 552p.

Studies of history, politics, economy and society relevant to geography, of 80 countries published in the West, Japan and China from 1901 to 1959, giving for holdings of the National Diet Library, Keiō University Library, Hibiya Library and Hideo Nishioka.

Monbushō Daigaku Gakujutsukyoku 文部省大学学術局 **H194**
Gakujutsu tosho sōgō mokuroku ... 学術図書総合目録人文地理学欧文編 (Union catalogue of scientific books) Books on cultural geography in European languages. 1961 ed. Nihon Gakujutsu Shinkōkai, 1961. 326p.

Gives about 8,700 titles in the collections of 81 national, prefectural, municipal and private universities as of Dec., 1956.

DICTIONARIES

Kudō, Chōsu 工藤暢須 **H195**
Jinbun chiri jiten 人文地理辞典 (Dictionary of human geography) Tokyodō, 1957. 724p.

Simply written and illustrated.

Asai, Tokuichi 浅井徳一 **H196**
Sōgō chiri jiten 総合地理事典 (General geographical dictionary) Meiji Tosho, 1957. 498p.

About 4,000 entries related to physical and cultural geography and place-names, simply explained.

Fujioka, Kenjirō 藤岡謙二郎 **H197**
Saishin taikei chiri jiten 最新体系地理

辞典 (Up-to-date systematic geographical dictionary) Taimeidō, 1960. 398p.

Classifies and briefly explains terms under nature, history, population and communities, economy, etc., with emphasis on human geography. Illustrations and tables. Subject index.

GAZETTEERS

Heibonsha 平凡社   **H198**
Sekai chimei jiten 世界地名事典 (World gazetteer) 1950-52. 6v.

Describes places, with geographical and geological characteristics, and gives their histories, including postwar changes. Atlas (v.6) has 33 maps, each with key index on reverse. General index lists all place-names in original spelling, Japanese reading and, for Chinese and Korean names, pronunciation.

Kokin Shoin 古今書院   **H199**
Sekai chimei jiten 世界地名辞典 (World gazetteer) 1954. 637p.

Locates countries, cities, towns, mountains, rivers, lakes, oceans, etc., with, where pertinent, data on topography, population, products and history. Chinese and Korean names given in original pronunciation, with Japanese reading. Selection of entries differs considerably from that in **H200**.

Tokyodō 東京堂   **H200**
Sekai chimei jiten 世界地名辞典 (World gazetteer) 1955-58. 2v.

v.1, Japan and the Orient; v.2, the Occident. Includes historical and literary place names and gives more emphasis to political, economic and cultural matters than to physical geography. Tables show populations and areas of Japanese towns and counties, sizes of lakes, lengths of rivers and tunnels and heights of mountains and volcanoes. Administrative divisions of major countries given in v.2. Each volume indexed.

Hōsō Bunka Kenkyūjo   **H201**
放送文化研究所
Gaikoku chimei hatsuon jiten 外国地名発音辞典 (Pronunciation dictionary of foreign place names) 1956. 522p.

Gives the Japanese reading of about 18,000 names of countries, local administrative units, cities and natural objects throughout the world, excluding Japan, China, Korea and Formosa, with brief identifications. Index in original spelling. Appended are an outline of foreign languages, notes on how to read and write them, distribution charts, meanings of generic elements of place names and explanations of geographical terms.

ATLASES

Zenkoku Kyōiku Tosho   **H202**
全国教育図書
Shin Sekai chizu 新世界地図 New world atlas. 1964. 62 maps. 120p.

Most detailed Japanese atlas of its kind, with 20 of its 62 maps devoted to Asia. Place names, totaling about 70,000, given in both Japanese (kana or romanized) and vernacular. Descriptive information and maps of large cities on reverse of main maps. Indexes of names in Western languages and Chinese characters.

Heibonsha 平凡社   **H203**
Sekai chizuchō 世界地図帖 World atlas. 1963. 276p.

Handy atlas of 114 maps, including 34 of Japan, ranging in scale from 1:1,000,000 to 1:350,000, with index of about 50,000 places.

ILLUSTRATIONS

Heibonsha 平凡社   **H204**
Sekai bunka chiri taikei 世界文化地理大系 (World cultural geography) 1954-58. 28v.

Useful country-by-country description of people, life, industry, economy and customs about evenly divided between text and photographs, many of them in color. Japanese part (v.2-6) available separately. Similar works follow:

Shashin Sekai chiri taikei (World geography in photographs) Zenkoku Kyōiku Tosho 1953. 360p. **H204a**

Sekai shashin chiri zenshū (Complete collection of world geographical photographs), comp. by Zayūhō Kankōkai. Kawade Shobō, 1954-55. 9v. **H204b**

Japan

BIBLIOGRAPHY

Keiō Gijuku Daigaku, Bunka Chiri   **H205**
Kenkyūkai 慶応義塾大学文化地理研究会
Nihon kenbetsu chishi mokuroku 日本県別地誌目録 (Catalogue of Japanese prefectural geographies) Kōgakusha, 1955. 244p.

Lists about 5,000 titles, excluding government publications, published since 1868, arranged by prefectures with subdivisions for bibliographies, prefectural, municipal, county, town and village records, natural characteristics, population, economy, transportation, education, religion, folklore, history, tourism, etc.

GAZETTEERS

Yoshida, Tōgo 吉田東伍 **H206**
Dai Nihon chimei jisho 大日本地名辞書 (Dictionary of Japanese place names) Fuzanbō, 1937-40. 7v.

Comprehensive compilation, divided by regions, giving names of provinces, counties, domains, villages, noted temples and shrines, scenic spots, rivers, mountains, etc., with detailed information about their geographical aspects and history, including poems and other quotations from old books. Indexed by Japanese syllabary and characters. Hokkaidō, Ryūkyū and Taiwan covered separately. Basic for historical geography.

Nihon Shobō 日本書房 **H207**
Nihon chimei daijiten 日本地名大辞典 (Comprehensive dictionary of Japanese place names) 1937-38. 6v.

Gives geographical and historical data on prefectures, cities, towns, villages, provinces, counties, mountains, rivers, lakes, etc., with subordinate units, shrines, temples and scenic spots covered under cities, towns and villages. Includes old names.

Asakura Shoten 朝倉書店 **H208**
Nihon chimei jiten 日本地名事典 (Cyclopedia of Japanese place names) 1954-56. 4v.

Divided into regions: v.1, Hokkaidō, Tōhoku and Kantō; v.2, Chūbu and Kinki; v.3, Chūgoku, Shikoku and Kyūshū, and prefectures, each with a chapter on physical features, geology, climate, history, manners and customs, etc., it lists and identifies cities, villages and other administrative units as of Oct. 1, 1954, mountains, rivers, lakes, highways, etc., with maps and photographs. v.4, Index facilitates use as geographical dictionary.

Nippon Hōsō Kyōkai 日本放送協会 **H209**
Nihon chimei hatsuon jiten 日本地名発音 辞典 (Pronunciation dictionary of Japanese place names) Nippon Hōsō Shuppan Kyōkai, 1959- . 4v. Loose-leaf.

v.1, Kantō and Kō-Shin-Etsu; v.2, Chūbu; v.3, Kinki; v.4, Chūgoku; each divided into two parts, the first giving by prefectures the names of cities, counties, towns, villages and village sections and the second giving names of mountains, rivers, capes, islands, railway stations, airports, light-houses, etc., each with pronunciation, characters and location. Pt.1 has syllabary and character indexes; pt.2 an index of unusual names.

Ōkurasho Insatsukyoku 大蔵省印刷局 **H210**
Shinkyū taishō saishin zenkoku shi-chō-son meikan 新旧対照最新全国市町村名鑑 (Up-to-date comparative list of new and old names of Japanese cities, towns and villages) 1964 ed. 1964. 180, 73p.

Gives name changes arranged by prefectures and districts. Revised yearly. Index.

Nisuikaku 二水閣 **H211**
Saishin zenkoku shi-chō-son meikan 最新 全国市町村明鑑 (Up-to-date directory of Japanese cities, towns and villages) 1963 ed. 1963. 720p.

Lists counties, cities, towns and villages under prefectures, with streets and village sections, as of May 1, 1963. Indexes.

HANDBOOK

Kokudo Chiri Kyōkai 国土地理協会 **H212**
Kyōzai kokudo genseishi 教材国土現勢誌 (Teaching materials on present territorial conditions) 1955- . 7v. Loose-leaf.

Gives the history, physical geography, climate, transportation, industry, special products, historical sites and tourist facilities of each prefecture, followed by less detailed information about cities, counties, towns and villages. Supplementary volume has gazetteer, charts and statistics on population, industry, etc. Index.

ATLASES

Nihon Shoin 日本書院 **H213**
Shōmitsu Nihon chizu 詳密日本地図 (Detailed maps of Japan) 1956. 20p. 16 maps.

Sixteen general and regional maps, with table of old and new names of cities, towns and villages. No index.

Zenkoku Kyōiku Tosho 全国教育図書 **H214**
Hyōjun Nihon chizu 標準日本地図 (Standard atlas of Japan, with gazetteer) 1956. 450p. (50 maps)

Individual prefectural maps with reverse-side outline maps of administrative divisions and brief surveys of history, geography, climate, transportation and cities, are accompanied by gazetteers classified by counties, cities, towns and villages.

Nitchi Shuppan 日地出版 **H215**
Saishin Nihon bunken chizu 最新日本分縣 地図 (Latest Japanese prefectural atlas)

1965 ed.   1964.   58p.   47 maps.

Comprehensive index and separate index arranged by prefectures, cities and villages. Revised yearly.

Tōsei Shuppan   統正出版   **H216**
Dai Nihon bunken chizu   大日本分縣地図 (Prefectural maps of Japan)   1965 ed.   1964. Various paging.

Together with gazetteers.   Revised yearly.

Jinbunsha   人文社   **H217**
Nihon bunken chizu chimei sōran   日本分県地図地名総覧 (Prefectural atlas and gazetteer of Japan)   1965 ed.   1964.   various paging.

Together with manual of public institutions. Revised yearly.

Jinbunsha   人文社   **H218**
Nihon toshi chizu zenshū   日本都市地図全集   (Complete atlas of Japanese cities) 1958- .   3v.   In progress.

v.1 has spread-out maps of Tokyo, the 45 prefectural capitals, Hakodate and Kawasaki, varying in scale from 1:8,000 to 1:20,000; v.2, of other cities with more than 100,000 population, and v.3, of smaller cities. Indexes of street names. To be completed in 8v.

ILLUSTRATIONS

H219
Nihon chiri fūzoku taikei   日本地理風俗大系   (Japanese geography and customs) Seibundō Shinkōsha, 1959-60.   13v.

Emphasis is on cultural geography, presented by regions, divided about evenly between text and plates, charts and tables.   v.13 contains general survey and detailed name and subject index to all volumes, including illustrations, making it useful as a manual.

Asaka, Yukio   浅香幸雄   **et al.**   **H220**
Zusetsu Nihon bunka chiri taikei   図説日本文化地理大系   (Compendium of Japanese cultural geography, illustrated)   Shōgakkan, 1960-63.   18v.

Surveys physical features, history and social life in each region, with more emphasis on tourist attractions and manners than in **H219.** Many photographs. Detailed index in v.18.

Tokyo Daigaku Rigakubu   **H221**
東京大学理学部
Shashin chishi Nihon   写真地誌日本 (Japan; a photographic geography)   Kōdansha, 1952. 286p.

With Japanese and English captions, 769 photographs show topography, climate, settlements, land utilization, customs and modernization. Index map, land utilization charts and general survey appended. Index of photographs.

Travel

Nihon Kōtsū Kōsha   日本交通公社   **H222**
Gaikoku ryokō annai   外国旅行案内 (Guide to travel abroad)   19th ed.   1964.   1168p.

Explains procedures for going abroad, transportation facilities, routes and fares, and travel preparations and cautions, with guide to studying abroad and lists of foreign holidays and weights and measures, followed by sections on individual countries, and exit procedures, noted places and the time and cost of tours.   First published in 1952.   Revised yearly.   4v. edition available.

Nihon Kōtsū Kōsha   日本交通公社   **H223**
Ryotei to hiyō   旅程と費用 (Journeys and costs)   20th ed., rev.   1964.   988, 132p.

Standard guide for travel in Japan, with detailed information about cities, towns, mountains, resorts, etc., including how to get to them, where to stay and what to see and buy.   Indexed map for each district.   Appended are guides to national and other parks, hotels and hostels and use of the national railways and other facilities.   First published in 1919 and revised yearly.   An English adaptation, *Japan: The official guide* is revised every few years.

HISTORICAL SITES

Bunkazai Hogo Iinkai   **H224**
文化財保護委員会
Tokubetsu shiseki meishō tennen kinenbutsu mokuroku   特別史跡名勝天然記念物目録 (Catalogue of special historical sites, scenic spots and natural monuments)   Daiichi Hōki Shuppan, 1963.   330p.

Large, clear plates, with notes, show places of major importance designated by the Cultural Properties Protection Commission from 1951 to date, with complete list, including those designated earlier, appended.

SOCIAL SCIENCES

Section

J

❧ In addition to social sciences in general, this section includes statistics, political science, military affairs, law, economics including population, social affairs, including labor, folklore, customs, and education. For convenience, the economic aspects of industry and agriculture are covered under Technology and Industry (R) and Agriculture (T). Emphasis is placed on works published since World War II and on publications of governments and international organizations.

GENERAL WORKS

BIBLIOGRAPHY

Amano, Keitarō 天野敬太郎　　　　**J1**
Hōsei keizai shakai ronbun sōran　法政・経済・社会論文総覧　(Index to articles on law, politics, economics and sociology) Tōkō Shoin, 1927-28.　2v.

   Articles in about 100 journals, nearly all of any importance, on law, politics, economics and sociology, from their first issues to June, 1926, are listed according to subjects in the main volume, and those in more than 50 journals, monographic series, etc., from their first issues to the end of 1927, in the supplementary volume.　Author index.

Kōbe Kōtō Shōgyō Gakkō, Shōgyō　　**J2**
Kenkyūjo 神戸高等商業学校商業研究所
Keizai hōritsu bunken mokuroku　経済・法律文献目録　A bibliography of law and economics. Osaka, Hōbunkan, 1927-31.　2v.

   Based on compilations originally published in the *Kokumin keizai zasshi* (National economics journal), it gives books, pamphlets, statistical data and articles in major journals and newspapers on economics, industry, sociology, politics, diplomacy and law from 1916 to 1925 under 36 headings in v. 1 and from 1926 to 1930 under 32 headings in v. 2. Each volume has a list of journals and newspapers and a subject index.

Kokuritsu Kokkai Toshokan, Chōsa　　**J3**
Rippō Kōsakyoku 国立国会図書館　調査立法考査局
Refarensu bunken yōmoku　レファレンス文献要目　(Bibliographical references concerning principal subjects handled by the Legislative Reference Department, National Diet Library). 1960-　.　3v.　In progress.

   Useful as a bibliographical guide for contemporary topics in law, diplomacy, economics, industry, sociology, labor and education.　v.1 gives the texts of national constitutions as of 1959; v.2 has a table of publications of national legislatures as of 1960. Selected titles annotated briefly.

Osaka Shiritsu Daigaku, Keizai　　**J4**
Kenkyūjo 大阪市立大学経済研究所
Shakai kagaku bunken kaisetsu　社会科学文献解説　(An annotated bibliography of social sciences) Nihon Hyōron Shinsha, 1947-53.　10v.

   A revival of the prewar *Bunken nenpō* (Bibliography annual) of the former Osaka Shōka Daigaku (Osaka University of Commerce), it is almost the only bibliographical guide in this field for the seven years from Sept. 1945, to June, 1952.　Though the emphasis is on economics, each volume has bibliographies of, and comments on books and articles on other subjects.　After publication ceased, a similar guide for 1955 was published independently as *Keizaigaku bunken kaidai 1955* **M2**.　Materials published in subsequent years are listed without annotation at end of each monthly issue of *Keizai hyōron* (Economic review).

Nihon Yunesuko Kokunai Iinkai   **J5**
日本ユネスコ国内委員会
Shakai kagaku bunken kaidai 社会科学文献
解題 (Annotated bibliography of social sciences). Nihon Gakujutsu Shinkōkai, 1962. 296p.

Lists books and articles published from 1945 through 1959 on sociology, law, politics, economics and cultural anthropology with annotations and remarks on academic trends in each field. No index.

Seiwadō 清和堂   **J6**
Sengo Nihon zasshi sōran: shakai kagaku no bu 戦後日本雑誌総覧社会科学の部 (Directory of postwar Japanese magazines: social sciences) 1963. 161p.

Lists about 1,000 magazines, mainly on economics and politics, being published as of Mar. 31, 1963, with references to former titles, dates of first issues and suspension periods. Editors and publishers listed in appendix.

DICTIONARIES

Shakai kagaku yōgo jiten   社会科学用語 **J7**
辞典 (Dictionary of social science terms) 2d ed., rev. and enl. Kyoto, San'ichi Shobō, 1960. 326, 30p.

Nakayama, Ichirō 中山伊知郎 **et al.**   **J8**
Shakai kagaku shinjiten 社会科学新辞典 (New social science dictionary) Rev. ed. Kawade Shobō, 1946. 429, 30p.

Ukai, Nobushige 鵜飼信成   **J9**
Hōritsu keizaigo daijiten 法律経済語大辞典 (Comprehensive dictionary of legal and economic terms) Kōbun Shoin, 1962. 1048, 79p.

Explains legal terms in relation to economics and economic terms in legal contexts. Appended are a chart of the national administrative structure and outlines of civil and penal procedures.

Nihon Keizai Kikō Kenkyūjo   **J10**
日本経済機構研究所
Seiji keizai daijiten 政治経済大辞典 (Comprehensive dictionary of politics and economics) Iwasaki Shoten, 1953. 560, 55p.

CHRONOLOGY

Yamada, Hideo 山田秀雄 **et al.**   **J11**
Shakai kagaku nenpyō 社会科学年表 Annals of the social sciences. v.1. Dōbunkan, 1956. 560p.

In six columns, five for areas (Britain and America; France, Italy and Belgium; Germany, Austria, and Netherlands; Russia and other countries; and Japan) and one for events, important works related to the social sciences, including titles on politics, law, economics, sociology, historiography, pedagogy, philosophy, literature and natural sciences, usually their first printed editions, are listed chronologically from 1401 to 1750. Locations of copies have been ascertained from library catalogues. Only v.1 has been published.

STATISTICS

❦ General works on and of statistics and almanacs are listed here. For statistics on special subjects, see names of individual subjects.

BIBLIOGRAPHY

Sōrifu Tōkeikyoku Toshokan zōsho   **J12**
mokuroku: washo no bu 総理府統計局図書
館蔵書目録 和書の部 (Prime Minister's Office, Bureau of Statistics, catalogue of the Library: Japanese books) 1955. 568p.

Pt.1, Publications of the Bureau; pt.2, General publications; pt.3, Old materials; Title index. Inclusion as of Nov. 1, 1954.

Sōrifu Tōkeikyoku Toshokan zōsho   **J13**
mokuroku: yōsho no bu 総理府統計局図書
館蔵書目録 洋書の部 (Prime Minister's Office, Bureau of Statistics, catalogue of the Library: Western books) 1961. 553, 125p.

Pt.1, Statistical publications held at the end of Aug. 1960; pt.2, General publications. Author index.

Keizai Dantai Rengōkai   **J14**
経済団体連合会
Minkan tōkei chōsa shiryō ichiran 民間統計
調査資料一覧 (Catalogue of non-governmental statistical materials) 3d ed., rev. 1962. 293p.

Covers economic organizations, industrial and business companies and banks. List of materials of government organizations appended. Index of organizations.

Gyōsei Kanrichō Tōkei Kijunkyoku   **J15**
行政管理庁統計基準局
To-Dō-Fu-Ken tōkei kankōbutsu mokuroku 都道
府県統計刊行物目録 (Catalogue of prefectural statistical publications) 1959 ed. 1960. 151p.

Union Catalogues

Kokuritsu Kokkai Toshokan　　　**J16**
国立国会図書館
Meiji ikō To-Dō-Fu-Ken tōkeisho sōgo mokuroku
明 治 以 降 都 道 府 県 統 計 書 総 合 目 録
(Union catalogue of prefectural statistical materials since the Meiji period) 1958. 123p.

Lists the holdings of 73 institutions as of June 1956, with appendix giving annual prefectural industrial reports in Ueno Library (now in the National Diet Library).

Kokuritsu Kokkai Toshokan　　　**J17**
国立国会図書館
Nihon kyūgaichi kankei tōkei shiryō mokuroku
日 本 旧 外 地 関 係 統 計 資 料 目 録　　(Catalogue of statistical materials on former territories of Japan) 1964. 191p.

Covers the period to September, 1945 and the territories: Formosa, Southern half of Sakhalin, Korea, South Pacific Islands and Manchuria. Japanese basic and secondary source materials were collected from various catalogues of special libraries (including defunct libraries) with locations. Subject Index.

Ajia Keizai Kenkyūjo　　　**J18**
アジア経済研究所
Tōnan Ajia tōkei shiryō mokuroku　東 南 ア ジ ア 統 計 資 料 目 録　　(Catalogue of statistical materials on Southeast Asia) 1961. 66p.

Materials for the area and its separate countries in the collections of 24 Japanese institutions, for which it serves as a union catalogue, are listed.

Senmon Toshokan Kyōkai　　　**J19**
専門図書館協会
Kakkoku bunken mokuroku shūsei　各 国 文 献 目 録 集 成　　第 1 集　欧 文 総 合 統 計 年 鑑 編 (Collected list of foreign materials) v. 1: General statistics and annuals in European languages. 1943. 273p.

Union catalog of the foreign statistical collections of 12 major institutions, including Mitsubishi Economic Institute, Research Division of the Bank of Japan, Ministry of Finance Library, Tokyo Chamber of Commerce Library, Ohara Sociological Institute and Economic Research Department of the South Manchuria Railway Company. Though some of these collections have been lost or dispersed because of the war, the catalog has value in showing the prewar availability and location of basic foreign statistics.

Annotated Bibliography

Gotō, Teiji　後 藤 貞 治　　**J20**
Honpō tōkei shiryō kaisetsu　本 邦 統 計 資 料 解 説　(Annotated list of statistical materials of Japan) Sōbunkaku, 1936. 249, 20p. (Jitsumu tōkeigaku kōza, v. 18)

Pt. 1 lists the materials by the institutions which published them; pt. 2 classifies by subjects.

Naikaku Tōkeikyoku　内 閣 統 計 局　　**J21**
Tōkei shiryō kaidai　統 計 資 料 解 題　　(A bibliographical introduction to statistical materials) Zenkoku Keizai Chōsa Kikan Rengōkai, 1936. 643p.

Most basic survey of prewar statistical materials in Japan, with comments as well on statistical tables published by government offices, educational and private research institutions, etc. First issues of periodical publications are dated. Subject index.

Yūshōdō Firumu Shuppan Yūgen Kaisha　　**J22**
雄 松 堂 フ イ ル ム 出 版 有 限 会 社
Meiji nenkan Fu-Ken tōkeisho shūsei　マ イ ク ロ フ イ ル ム 版　明 治 年 間 府 県 統 計 書 集 成　解 説　収 録 書 総 目 録　(Collection of prefectural statistical records during the Meiji period, microfilm edition) Commentary and complete catalogue of contents. 1964. 61p.

Kazuo Yamaguchi explains the materials in the collection, and the catalogue is followed by 12 charts showing boundary changes of the 46 prefectures, Hokkaiko and Okinawa. The institutions possessing the records are listed in **J16**.

J23
Nihon tōkei geppō: shiryō kaisetsu hen　日 本 統 計 月 報　資 料 解 説 編　Supplement to the Monthly Statistics of Japan; explanatory notes 1962-　. Comp. by Gyōsei Kanrichō, Tōkei Kijunkyoku. 1962-　. 3v. Annual.

An annual commenting on data in the *Nippon tōkei geppō*, published by the Bureau of Statistics, Office of the Prime Minister, and on Japanese statistics in general. Each of twelve chapters on such topics as climate, population and family income and expenditure is divided into remarks on pertinent data of importance and explanations of statistics in the monthly.

DICTIONARY

Gyōsei Kanrichō Tōkei Kijunkyoku　　**J24**
行 政 管 理 庁 統 計 基 準 局
Shitei tōkei chōsa yōgo teigishū　指 定 統 計

調査用語定義集 (Definitions of terms in research on government-required statistics) 1962. 367p.

Defines terms found in research from 1951 to 1960 on government-required statistics.

HANDBOOKS

Masaki, Chifuyu 正木千冬 **and**　　　　**J25**
Matsukawa, Shichirō 松川七郎
Tōkei chōsa gaidobukku 統計調査ガイド ブック (Guidebook for statistical research) Tōyō Keizai Shinpōsha, 1951. 288p.

Explains 335 government statistical surveys conducted under the U.S. occupation of Japan from the end of the War to the Peace Treaty in 1951, based on the so-called Rice reports of the first American statistical mission.

Minobe, Ryōkichi 美濃部亮吉 **and**　　　**J26**
Matsukawa, Shichirō 松川七郎
Tōkei chōsa sōran 統計調査総覧 統計 利用者への手びき (Handbook of statistical research) A guide for the user of statistics. Tōyō Keizai Shinpōsha, 1956. 466p.

Pt.1 contains 1957 statistical surveys conducted by government offices, non-government organizations and research institutions; pt.2 contains 197 surveys by labor unions. Pt.1 is divided into labor, agricultural and mining industries, each with comments on history, purpose, contents and methods of publications. Lists of statistical publications and of statistical reports required by the government. Index.

CHRONOLOGY

Nōrin Tōkei Kyōkai 農林統計協会　　**J27**
Nihon tōkei chōsa nenpyō 日本統計調査 年表 (Chronological table of statistical research in Japan) 1952. 69p.

Sets forth development from 1868 to 1950 under 7 headings: institutions and organizations, population, labor, agriculture-forestry-marine industries, industries, commerce and trade, miscellaneous. The last 34p. contains an outline history.

INDEX

Senmon Toshokan Kyōgikai　　　　　**J28**
専門図書館協議会
Nihon tōkei sōsakuin 日本統計総索引 General index of Japanese statistics. Tōyō Keizai Shinpōsha, 1959. 41, 1483p.

Using a unique classification system, shows what statistical research has been done and where the results have been published. Compiled with the help of many organizations, including the National Diet Library and the Bureau of Statistics of the Prime Minister's Office. Appended are lists of statistical research projects and statistical materials arranged by organs.

Statistical science

Tōkei Sūri Kenkyūjo 統計数理研究所　**J29**
Statistical bibliography in Japan. 1958. 58p.

Lists in English books and articles on statistics published in Japan from the end of the war to the autumn of 1957. No index.

Nakayama, Ichirō　中山伊知郎　　**J30**
Tōkeigaku jiten 統計学辞典 (Dictionary of statistical science) 2d ed., enl. Tōyō Keizai Shinpōsha, 1957. 1304p.

Entries, many of which are long articles, give comprehensive information about the history, concepts, definitions, etc. of statistics and statistical science. Subject index facilitates use as glossary. Important reference works listed in appendix.

Nakayama, Ichirō　中山伊知郎　　**J31**
Gendai tōkeigaku daijiten 現代統計学大 辞典 (Comprehensive dictionary of modern statistics) Tōyō Keizai Shinpōsha, 1962. 1036p.

Supplementing **J30**, reflects recent developments in statistical theories and practices in sections on modern statistics, basic mathematics, methods of statistical estimation, research methods, special methods in various fields of science, economic statistics, operations research, data processing, teaching of statistics and statistical organizations. Explanatory notes on statistical tables, list of Japanese source materials and general bibliography appended. Subject and name indexes.

Statistics

WORLD

J32
Sekai tōkei nenkan 世界統計年鑑 Statistical yearbook. 1952- . Comp. by the United Nations 1953- . 12v.

Japanese version of the *Statistical yearbook*, issued by the Statistical Office of the United Nations, accepted as the most authoritative digest of world statistics. English headings.

J33
Kokusai tōkei yōran 国際統計要覧 (Manual of international statistics) 1951- . Comp. by

Sōrifu, Tōkeikyoku. Ōkurashō Insatsukyoku, 1954- . 12v. Annual.

A revival of the prewar *Rekkoku kokusei yōran* (Manual of conditions of various countries), published by the Cabinet's Statistical Bureau, it gives a-bridgements of miscellaneous international statistics.

Tokyo-to Sōmukyoku 東京都総務局 **J34**
Sekai daitoshi hikaku tōkei nenpyō 世界大都市比較統計年表 (Comparative annual statistical tables of major world cities) 2d ed. 1964. 45p.

Gives various statistics of cities of more than 2,000,000 in population.

JAPAN

J35
Nihon tōkei nenkan 日本統計年鑑 Japan statistical yearbook No. 1, 1949- . Comp. by Sōrifu Tōkeikyoku. Nihon Tōkei Kyōkai, 1950- . 14v.

Most comprehensive official compilation of basic Japanese statistics, continuing the *Nihon Teikoku tōkei nenkan* (Statistical yearbook of the Japanese Empire, 1-59, 1882-1940, which Tokyo Ripurinto-sha is reprinting). Gives figures for the decade preceding the title year, which is the year before the year of issuance. War-damage statistics given in no.1. From no.2, basic international statistics are appended.

J36
Kokkai tōkei teiyō 国会統計提要 Statistical abstracts of Japan 1949- . Comp. by Kokuritsu Kokkai Toshokan, Chōsa Rippō Kōsakyoku. 1949- . 15v. Annual

Abridges major statistics in various fields.

J37
Nihon kokusei zue 日本国勢図会 (A charted survey of Japan) 1927- . Comp. by Yano Tsuneta Kinenkai. Kokuseisha, 1928- . 19v. Annual.

English ed.: *Nippon; a charted survey of Japan.* No. 1, 1936, no. 2, 1955, no. 3, 1957- . 10v. Annual.

J38
Daitoshi hikaku tōkei nenpyō 大都市比較統計年表 (Comparative annual statistical tables of big cities) 1936- . Comp. by Daitoshi Tōkei Kyōgikai. 1938- . 13v.

Statistics for Tokyo, Osaka, Kyoto, Nagoya, Kobe and Yokohama, comp. by each city in turn. Four issues from 1938 to 1942; revived in 1955.

Yearbooks
FOREIGN COUNTRIES

J39
Sekai nenkan 世界年鑑 World manual 1949- . Comp. by Kyōdō Tsūshinsha. 1949- . 16v. Annual.

Only Japanese yearbook specializing in world affairs. Chapters on world trends, international organizations, current affairs by countries, space programs, missiles and atomic energy, with documentary materials. Problems of importance to Japan are commented on in detail. Pictures and maps in text. Basic statistics and international who's who appended.

J40
Ajia Afurika nenkan アジア・アフリカ年鑑 (Afro-Asian yearbook) 1962-63- . Comp. by Ajia Afurika Kenkyūjo and Chūgoku Kenkyūjo. Kyokutō Shoten, 1963- . 1v.

Covers conditions in Asian and African countries other than Japan and China, with chronology of important Afro-Asian events since 1945, documents and statistics. Biennial publication intended. Issued by the same publisher is *Shin Chūgoku nenkan* (New China yearbook) **J42**.

J41
Sobieto Nenpō ソヴィエト年報 (Annual report on the Soviet Union) 1958- . Comp. by Naikaku Chōsashitsu. Nikkan Rōdō Tsūshinsha, 1958- . 6v.

Important aspects of the Soviet Union and East European satellite states covered in some detail with statistics, chronological tables, brief biographies, etc. Subjects and personal names indexed. Successor to the *Sobieto-nenkan* (Soviet yearbook), which was suspended after 1954 and 1955 issues.

J42
Shin Chūgoku nenkan 新中国年鑑 (New China yearbook) 1962- . Comp. by Chūgoku Kenkyūjo. Kyokutō Shoten, 1962- . 3v.

Former title: *Chūgoku nenkan* (China yearbook), 1955-1961. Ishizaki Shoten. 6v.

Facts about the People's Republic of China (excluding Taiwan) given in sections on general survey of the preceding year, land and people, foreign relations, politics, economy, society and culture, statistics, documentary materials, organizations and institutions, who's who, etc. Subject and personal name indexes.

JAPAN

J43

Asahi nenkan 朝日年鑑 (Asahi yearbook) 1925- . Asahi Shinbunsha, 1924- . 40v.

Respected for its accuracy and timeliness, it is divided into chronological tables, world trends, domestic affairs, culture (including since 1962, bibliographies on major cultural and social topics), statistics and directories. Since 1955, unlike other yearbooks, it has covered the whole of the preceding calendar year. Subject index. With the 1964 ed. is a separate volume, *Nihon hyakunen no ayumi* (Japan's footprints over a century: a history of the Meiji, Taishō and Shōwa periods), commemorating the 40th issue of the yearbook.

J44

Jiji nenkan 時事年鑑 Jiji almanac 1948- . Jiji Tsūshinsha, 1947- . 17v.

Covers in detail events and developments of the preceding Sept.-Aug. year in sections on Japan and the world, documents, directories and statistics. Subject and name indexes. Started by the newspaper Jiji in 1917, it was suspended in 1936 and continued by the Dōmei Jiji Tsūshinsha as the *Dōmei Jiji nenkan* until taken over and given again its original name by the Jiji Tsūshinsha in 1947.

J45

Mainichi nenkan 毎日年鑑 (Mainichi yearbook) 1920- . Mainichi Shinbunsha, 1919- 45v.

Similar to **J43**, but each section is more minutely divided and the coverage is for the preceding Sept.-Aug. year. To the economic statistics stressed in early issues, social and cultural statistics have been added. Subject index and glossarial index of current terms.

J46

Yomiuri nenkan 読売年鑑 (Yomiuri yearbook) 1950- . Yomiuri Shinbunsha, 1949- . 15v.

World affairs, Japanese affairs, local trends, science and culture, and law and treaties are covered for the preceding Sept.-Aug. year, followed by a directory of prominent Japanese and foreigners, a calendar, statistics, etc. Titled *Yomiuri seiji nenkan* (Yomiuri political yearbook) from 1946 to 1949, with emphasis on political developments. Subject index.

J47

Nihon gensei 日本現勢 Japan manual 1952- . Kyōdo Tsūshinsha, 1951- . 13v.

Political, financial, industrial, social and cultural developments in the nation and each prefecture (including Okinawa) are surveyed, with documentary materials, statistics and a directory.

J48

Nihon toshi nenkan 日本都市年鑑 (Yearbook of Japanese cities) 1931- . Comp. by Zenkoku Shichōkai. 1931- . 24v.

Based on the findings of the Japan Association of Mayors, with statistics from official and private sources, it has a general survey and sections on area and population, administration, finances, planning, housing, social welfare, health, education and culture, public enterprises, disasters, transportation and communications, and economy.

POLITICAL SCIENCE

❧ Political conditions· of various governments, foreign relations, legislatures, local government and military affairs are included. For background materials reference should be made to political history as well as to special subjects.

Bibliography

Kyōto Kokuren Kitaku Toshokan　　　**K1**
京都国連寄託図書館
Kokuren shiryō　国連資料　利用の手引
と国連刊行物目録 (United Nations materials) A guide to users and a catalogue of U. N. publications.　Kyōto, 1962.　124p.
　　Pt.1 outlines U. N. materials in general, and pt. 2 lists materials published from 1945 to April 1962.

Kokuritsu Kokkai Toshokan　　　**K2**
国立国会図書館
Gikai seiji bunken mokuroku　議会政治文
献目録　A bibliography on parliamentary government.　1961.　444p.
　　Exhaustive listing of literature on parliamentarianism, political parties, elections, etc., divided into Japanese books and articles published from 1868 to May, 1960, foreign literature, including Russian, and documents concerning the establishment of the Japanese Diet. Indexes of authors, foreigners, titles of Meiji period publications, parliamentary materials, party organs, etc.

Kokuritsu Kokkai Toshokan　　　**K3**
国立国会図書館
Kenseishi Hensankai shūshū bunsho mokuroku 憲政史編纂会収集文書目録 (Catalogue of documents collected by the editorial board

for compilation of a history of constitutional government)　1960.　224p. (Kensei Shiryōshitsu shozō mokuroku, no. 1)
　　Indispensable for study of the history of constitutional government in Japan.　Lists about 700 titles of manuscripts and documents in 1,000 volumes (now in the National Diet Library) assembled from 1938 to 1941 by the board which the House of Representatives had set up to compile a history.

Hanabusa, Nagamichi　英　修道　　**K4**
Nihon gaikōshi kankei bunken mokuroku　日本
外交史関係文献目録　(List of literature on Japanese diplomatic history)　Keiō Gijuku Daigaku, Hōgaku Kenkyūkai, 1961.　485p.
(Keiō Gijuku Daigaku Hōgaku Kenkyūkai sōsho, 9)
　　Gives about 4,870 Japanese, 680 Chinese and 2,470 Western-language books and 6,000 Japanese magazine articles through Dec., 1960, on not only diplomatic history but also politics, economy and other aspects of society related to diplomacy. Japanese books are arranged by titles, with an author-translator index;　Chinese books by the Japanese readings of their titles, and Western books by their authors in alphabetical order. Articles are listed by titles under the names of magazines. Use handicapped by lack of subject index. A supplement giving Japanese and Western books to May, 1963, and Japanese magazine articles through 1962 is in the magazine *Hōgaku kenkyū* (Law research)　v.36,　no.12, Dec.,　1963.

Dictionaries

Heibonsha　平凡社　　　**K5**
Seijigaku jiten 政治学事典 (Dictionary of political science)　1954.　1416, 80p.
　　The article-length entries in this first authoritative Japanese dictionary on the subject, each with references, reflect recent concepts in political science

and an international viewpoint. There are short-comings in the selection of synonyms, handling of abbreviations and cross references between foreign and Japanese terms.

Sasaki, Hideo 佐々木英夫 **et al.** **K6**
Chihō jichi yōgo jiten　地方自治用語辞典
(Dictionary of local government terms) Gakuyō Shobō, 1961.　378p.

Ueda, Toshio 植田捷雄 **et al.** **K7**
Chūgoku gaikō bunsho jiten: Shin-matsu hen 中国外交文書辞典　清末編　A glossary of Chinese diplomatic documents.　Gakujutsu Bunken Fukyūkai, 1954.　139p.

Handbooks

Nihon Kokusai Rengō Kyōkai **K8**
日本国際連合協会
Kokusai Rengō taikan　国際連合大観
(Comprehensive survey of the United Nations) Kokuren Shuppansha, 1950.　2v.
　　v.1 gives the objectives, principles, structure and activities of the United Nations and the Inter-national Court of Justice, with the United Nations Charter and other documents appended.　v.2 does the same for the specialized agencies and other organizations concerned with labor, finance, agri-culture, telecommunications, science, culture, etc. Major reference works listed at end of each chapter.

Kaigai Jijō Chōsajo 海外事情調査所 **K9**
Amerika yōran アメリカ要覧 (Handbook of America) Nikkan Rōdō Tsūshinsha, 1962. 615p.
　　Covers briefly American politics, economics, foreign policy and culture, with who's who, chro-nology, etc.

La Sociedad Latino-Americana **K10**
ラテン・アメリカ協会
Raten Amerika jiten ラテン・アメリカ事典 (Encyclopedia of Latin America) 3d ed., rev. 1964.　798p.
　　Following a general survey of the area are details of individual countries, the Charter of the Organi-zation of American States, and a map. A useful book.

Chūgoku Kenkyūjo 中国研究所 **K11**
Gendai Chūgoku jiten 現代中国事典 (Diction-ary of contemporary China) 2d ed., rev. and enl.　Iwasaki Shoten, 1959.　742, 155p.
　　Grouped under subjects, the entries give detailed information about and comment on the present con-ditions, history and personages of the People's Re-

public of China.　Appended are Sino-Japanese non-official agreements and joint statements, economic statistics, lists of government organizations and officials, a chronology of modern Chinese history, etc.　Subject index.

Ajia Seikei Gakkai アジア政経学会 **K12**
Chūgoku seiji keizai sōran　中国政治経済綜覧　(Handbook of Chinese politics and economy) 3d ed., rev.　Nikkan Rōdō Tsūshin-sha, 1962.　1440p.
　　Covers the geography, recent history, politics, military affairs, diplomacy, economic construction, industry, foreign trade, economic aid and culture of the People's Republic of China, with condensed information about Mongolia, South Korea and North Korea.　Texts of documents, a chronology of Chinese Communism, and a list of reference books appended. Index of subjects, personal names.　Because of the many changes, the editions of 1954 and 1960 retain value.

JAPAN

K13
Kokkai benran　国会便覧　(National Diet handbook) 1954- .　Comp. by Nihon Seikei Shinbunsha.　1954- .　11v.　Annual.
　　Gives brief biographies of members of both Houses, lists Ministers, Vice-Ministers, chairmen and members of standing committees and party officers, etc.

Fujiwara, Hirotatsu 藤原弘達 **K14**
Kokkai giin senkyo yōran　国会議員選挙要覧 (Manual of National Diet elections) Kō-bundō, 1959.　447p.
　　Through the 28th general election of May, 1958, postwar elections of members to both Houses of the Diet are described and analyzed on the basis of official and non-official materials.　For each election are given the pre-election situation, candidates, press views, party policies and financial circum-stances, voting, analysis of results and outstanding features.

Asahi Shinbunsha 朝日新聞社 **K15**
Senkyo taikan　選挙大観 (Comprehensive sur-vey of elections) 1949-55.　1949-55.　4v.

Sōrifu 総理府 **K16**
Kanchō benran 官庁便覧 (Government office handbooks)　Ōkurashō Insatsukyoku, 1958-60. 17v.
　　v.1, Prime Minister's Office I, Cabinet, Prime Minister's Secretariat, auxiliary organs, committees; v.2, *Ibid* II, National Police Agency, Fire Defense Headquarters, Imperial Household Agency; v.3, *Ibid*.

III, Defense Agency, Procurement Agency; v.4, *Ibid.* IV, Administrative Management Agency, Hokkaido Development Agency, Autonomy Agency; v.5, *Ibid* V, Economic Planning Agency, Fair Trade Commission, Scientific and Technical Agency; v.6, Justice Ministry; v.7, Ministry of Foreign Affairs; v.9, Education Ministry; v.10, Welfare Ministry; v.11, Agriculture and Forestry Ministry; v.13, Transportation Ministry; v.14, Postal Services Ministry; v.15, Labor Ministry; v.17, Japan Monopoly Corporation; v.18, Japanese National Railways; v.19, Nippon Telegraph & Telephone Corporation; v.20, Board of Audit, National Personnel Authority. (v.8, Finance Ministry, v.12, Ministry of International Trade and Industry, and v.16, Construction Ministry, not to be issued.)

Give history, structure, responsibilities and functions of each office and its sub-divisions.

K17

Jichi benran 自治便覧 (Self-government manual) 1959- . Comp. by Jichichō. 1959- . 6v. Annual.

Cover title: Chihō jichi benran (Local self-government manual).

Handy compendium of statistics and other information about local self-governing bodies, their personnel, amalgamation of towns and villages, rehabilitation of the Amami Islands, elections, assemblies, taxes, finances, etc.

Tōyama, Shigeki 遠山茂樹 **and** **K18**
Adachi, Shizuko 安達淑子
Kindai Nihon seijishi hikkei 近代日本政治史必携 (Handbook of modern Japanese political history) Iwanami Shoten, 1961. 251p.

Convenient compilation of facts needed in basic research, including the composition of, changes in and high officials under each national administration since 1868, changes in territorial and local administration, with lists of governors and high colonial officials, the composition of each Diet, changes in the strength of Diet factions, Imperial appointments to the House of Peers and lists of party officers. No index.

Chronology

Gaimushō Jōhō Bunkakyoku **K19**
外務省情報文化局
Kokusai shuyō jikō nenpyō 国際主要事項年表 (Annual chronology of major international events) Series 1-2. 1959-62. 2v.
Series 1 (1945-58); series 2 (1959-61)

Gaimushō Bunshōka 外務省文書課 **K20**
Nihon gaikō nenpyō ... 日本外交年表並主要

文書 (Chronology of Japanese diplomatic history and basic documents 1840-1945) Nihon Kokusai Rengō Kyōkai, 1955. 2v.

Gives many treaties and other documents from the closing years of the Tokugawa Shogunate to the end of the Pacific War, some of them hitherto unpublished and not found in **K34**. Continued by **K19**. Appended are tables showing the office terms of Foreign Ministers and foreign diplomats in Japan, members of successive cabinets, establishment dates of embassies and legations abroad, etc.

Okamoto, Seiichi 岡本清一 **and** **K21**
Tōma, Ryūtarō 藤馬竜太郎
Nenpyō gikai seijishi 年表議会政治史 (Chronologies of parliamentary government) Shiseidō, 1960. 349, 24p.

Very detailed chronologies of Japanese and foreign parliamentary government and institutions, the former from 1867 to Feb. 1, 1960, the latter from the sixth century to Nov. 15, 1958. Also lists Diet Speakers and Vice-Speakers, standing committees, chairmen of special committees, legislative organizations of major countries and reference works.

Yearbooks

K22

Kokusai nenpō 国際年報 (Annual report on international affairs) No. 1 (1945-57) - . Comp. by Nihon Kokusai Mondai Kenkyūjo. 1961- . 5v.

Analyzes political and economic developments in the world as a whole, Japan, America, Asia, the Near East, Africa, Europe and Communist countries. Appended are major treaties and agreements and a chronology. Subject and name indexes.

K23

Nihon Soren kōryū nenshi 日本・ソ連交流年誌 (Annual record of Japan-USSR relations) 1960- . Comp. by Minshushugi Kenkyūkai. 1960- . 4v.

Summarizes developments, with official statements, list of visitors and statistics on Soviet-seized vessels and crews and trade.

K24

Nihon Chūkyō kōryū nenshi 日本・中共交通年誌 (Annual record of relations between Japan and Communist China) 1949- . Comp. by Minshushugi Kenkyūkai. 1957- . 6v.

Similar to **K23** in organization and scope.

K25

Kokkai nenkan 国会年鑑 (The National Diet yearbook) 1959- . Kokkai Nenkan Kankōkai. 1959- 5v.

Compiled from records of the Diet, political parties and Government and with the collaboration of these bodies to enlighten the public on their activities, it gives much information not easily found elsewhere. The 1963 edition has a special study on local government, sections on the Diet, the parties, important issues and deliberations, and Diet, party and Government directories. The 1959 edition gives Diet regulations and records of past Diet sessions, cabinets, etc.

K26

Senkyo nenkan 選挙年鑑 (Election yearbook) 1949-63. Comp. by Jichishō Senkyokyoku. 1953-64. 5v.

K27

Kokumin jichi nenkan 国民自治年鑑 (Yearbook of popular self-government) 1964- . Nihon Shakaitō Kikanshikyoku, 1963- . 1v. Annual.

Compiled to stimulate interest in local government, it covers conditions and issues in two parts, the first on villages, towns and cities and the second on prefectures, with a chronology of local self-government since the war and lists of organizations concerned with local self-government and their publications. Subject index.

K28

Kokumin seiji nenkan 国民政治年鑑 (People's political yearbook) 1962- . Nihon Shakaitō Kikanshikyoku, 1962- . 3v.

Gives the views of the Japan Socialist Party on the international situation, the United States-Japan Security Treaty, neutrality, the "struggle for peace and democracy", the "monopoly structure" in Japan, labor issues, the "class struggle", the political structure, etc. A postwar chronology and list of organizations appended.

Index

Kokuritsu Kokkai Toshokan Chōsa Rippō Kōsakyoku **K29**

国立国会図書館調査立法考査局
Kaigiroku sōsakuin 会議録総索引 (General index to the records of the Diet) The 39th Session (Extra Session, 1961)- . 1962- . 6v. In progress.

Records of the Diet sessions and committees of both House of Representatives and House of Councillors are indexed by subjects, by names of speakers, by bills (in the orders of presentation, names and dates of promulgation) and by inquiries and questions. Index by each session.

There is no index of the prewar records of the Imperial Diet for the House of Representatives, the House of Peers and their committees, 1890-1947, nos. 1-92, or for the postwar records beginning from "No.1 Diet" for House of Representatives, House of Councillors and their committees, 1947-61.

Directories

Directories **K30**

Shokuinroku 職員録 (Directory of government officials) 1886- . Comp. by Ōkurashō Insatsukyoku. 1886- . 98v. Annual.

v.1, Central government offices, public corporations, etc.; v.2, Prefectural offices.

Preceded by the privately published *Kan'inroku* (Official register) from 1868 to 1887. During the war years, 1944-48, *Shokuin shōroku*, one volume abridged edition was published.

K31

Nihon kankai meikan 日本官界名鑑 (Who's who of Japanese officialdom) 1937- . Comp. by Nihon Kankai Jōhōsha. 1936- . 15v.

Lists key personnel of the Cabinet, Prime Minister's Office, Ministries, including their local offices, public corporations and prefectural offices.

Source materials

Shugiin 衆議院 **and Sangiin** 参議院 **K32**

Gikai seido shichijū nenshi 議会制度七十年史 (A history of 70 years of parliamentary government) Ōkurashō Insatsukyoku, 1960-63. 12v.

v.1, Directory of members of House of Peers and House of Councillors; v.2, Titles of bills presented to the Imperial Diet; v.3-4, History of the National Diet (from 1947); v.5, Titles of bills presented to the National Diet; v.6, Political parties and factions; v.7 Documents; v.8, Chronology of parliamentary history; v.9-10, History of the Imperial Diet; v.11, Directory of members of the House of Representatives; v.12, Outline of constitutional history.

Jichishō 自治省 **K33**

Kōiki gyōsei no shiori 広域行政のしおり (Guide to local administration) Teikoku Chihō Gyōsei Gakkai, 1963. 174p. (Jichi Jihō, Aug., 1963, supp.)

Divided into a report by the Chihō Seido Chōsakai (Local Autonomy Research Society), with opinions of related organizations, laws and proposals, newspaper views, a chronology from abolition of the *han* governments to establishment of the prefectural system, and a bibliography of books and articles on local government published from May, 1936, to 1963.

Gaimushō 外務省　　　　　　　**K34**
Nihon gaikō bunsho 日本外交文書 (Japanese diplomatic documents) 1867- . Nihon Kokusai Rengō Kyōkai, 1936- . In progress.

Indispensable for research in Japanese diplomacy, the collection contains all correspondence between the Japanese and other governments and additional documents in the files of the Ministry of Foreign Affairs from 1867 through 1912, spanning the Meiji period. The main series of 63 volumes, extra series of 17 and supplements of 11 make a total of 91 volumes, each of which is indexed by dates. Series on Taishō period is in progress (1v. has been published).

MILITARY AFFAIRS

Morisawa, Kikaku 森沢亀鶴　　　**K35**
Bei-Ei-Wa Gunji yōgo shinjiten 米・英・和 軍事用語新辞典 Anglo-American-Japanese dictionary of military terms. Kōyōsha, 1953. 348p.

Bōei nenkan 防衛年鑑　　(National defense **K36**

yearbook) 1955- . Bōei Nenkan Kankō-kai. 1955- . 10v.

Surveys the defense strength of Japan and other countries and related developments, with special studies, documents, defense budgets, evaluations of weapons, directories of the Defense Agency and Self-Defense Corps and a list of military literature. Subject index. The 1955 issue summarizes defense developments from 1950.

K37
Jieitai nenkan 自衛隊年鑑 (Self-Defense Corps yearbook) 1956- . Comp. by Bōei Sangyō Kyōkai. 1956- . 9v.

Sets forth the organization, budget, equipment and auxiliaries of the land, sea and air branches of the Self-Defense Corps, with chronologies, directories and lists of registered dealers in defense materials and places where divisions and other units of the Corps are located. Each issue has a special study, such as that on guided missiles.

Bōeichō, Jieitai Jūnenshi Hensan Iinkai **K38**
防衛庁自衛隊十年史編集委員会
Jieitai jūnenshi 自衛隊十年史 (A history of ten years of the Defense Corps) Ōkurashō Insatsukyoku, 1961. 435p.

Gives the background of the establishment of the National Police Reserve Force in 1950 and developments to 1960, with texts of related documents and notes on them. Also covered are the Procurement Agency, American advisory groups and Diet debates on defense.

LAW

Bibliography

Hōritsu Jihō Henshūbu   **L1**
法律時報編集部
Sengo hōgaku bunken sōmokuroku　戦後法学
文献総目録　(Comprehensive list of postwar
legal literature)　Nihon Hyōron Shinsha, 1954-
55.　2v.

Lists books, 54 essay collections and articles
from 463 periodicals published from Sep., 1945,
through 1953 in 21 sections, each with books and
articles arranged separately by titles.　Some important works in politics, economy and sociology
included.　Not indexed.　Similar listing of materials
published from 1954 through June, 1956, is lacking,
but subsequent materials to 1959 are in **L49.**

     L2
The Japan science review: law and politics.
No. 1- .　Comp. by Nihon Gakujutsu Kaigi.
1950- .　12v.　Annual.

In English, the first issue reports on the state of
legal and political scholarship in Japan.　Subsequent
issues list, with brief descriptions or summations,
books and articles "which are considered to be important and appropriate enough to be introduced to
. . . foreign countries".

     L3
The Japan annual of law and politics.
No. 1- .　Comp. by Nihon Gakujutsu Kaigi.
1952- .　11v.

Contains treatises, mostly in English, with a few
in French and German, by Japanese jurists and
political scientists directed at learned circles a-
broad.　Emphasis is on all aspects of law.　Reports
on the activities of relevant Japanese societies
appended.

Saikō Saibansho Toshokan   **L4**
最高裁判所図書館
Hōritsu tosho mokuroku:　Washo no bu　法律
図書目録　和書の部　(Catalogue of law
books; Japanese)　1963- .　1v.　In progress.

Very useful because of extensive coverage and
detailed bibliographical references, it lists books
published before April, 1963, in the Supreme Court
Library.　A second volume is intended.

Hōritsu Kankei Shiryō Renrakukai   **L5**
法律関係資料連絡会
Gaikoku hōreishū sōgō mokuroku　外国法令
集総合目録　(Union catalogue of collections
of foreign laws)　January 1956.　Saikō Saibansho
Toshokan, 1957.　Supp. I, 1958.　2v.

Includes 5 government libraries:　Supreme Court,
National Diet Library, House of Councillors, Legis-
lative Bureau, Cabinet Legislative Bureau, and the
Ministry of Justice.

Asahi Shinbunsha　朝日新聞社　**L6**
Kyokutō Kokusai Gunji Saiban kiroku　極東国
際軍事裁判記録：目録及び索引
Records of the International Military Tribunal for
the Far East:　Catalogue and index, 1953. 314p.

Lists in comprehensive detail and indexes fully
the materials in the unique collection of the newspaper firm, *Asahi*, including the written indictments,
stenographic records of the preliminary procedures
for the trials, evidence admitted, evidence rejected,
decisions and attached documents, etc.　Indispensable for historical study of the period from the
Manchurian Incident to the end of the Pacific War.
The editor Kyōzō Mori was on the research　staff
of the *Asahi.*

Hōmu Toshokan　法務図書館　**L7**
Hōritsu kankei zasshi kiji sakuin　法律関係

雑誌記事索引 (Index of periodical articles on law) No. 1- . 1952- . 6v. In progress.

Indispensable in conjunction with **L8** for locating legal materials in periodicals, especially for years not covered in **L1** and **L49**. Indexed by subjects and authors. No. 1 spans 1945-51, with two more years in each subsequent number. Nos. 5 and 6 include commemorative collections of papers.

L8

Saikō Saibansho Toshokan hōbun hōritsu zasshi kiji sakuin 最高裁判所図書館邦文法律雑誌記事索引 (Supreme Court Library index of Japanese periodical articles on law) 1957- . Saikō Saibansho Toshokan, 1958- . 6v. Annual.

Divided into classified index of articles, index to comments on judicial precedents and author index.

HISTORY

Hōseishi Gakkai 法制史学会 **L9**
Hōseishi bunken mokuroku 法制史文献目録 (A bibliography of the history of laws) 1945-1959. Sōbunsha, 1962. 290p.

Lists Japanese books, magazines, collections of essays and book reviews published from August, 1945, through 1959 on the history of law in general and of Japanese, other Oriental, Roman and other Occidental law.

Ikebe, Gishō 池辺義象 **L10**
Nihon hōseishi shomoku kaidai 日本法制史書目解題 (Annotated bibliography of history of Japanese law) Daitōkaku, 1918. 2v.

Concerned with legal matters in the broad sense from early times to 1868, pt. 1 lists and annotates major legal documents and commentaries on them; pt. 2 enumerates and comments on materials useful in research, including bibliographies, dictionaries, popular writings, sources and periodicals, and pt. 3 comments on miscellaneous writings under such headings as deities, Imperial House, rites, foreign relations, military affairs and education.

Tōyōshi Kenkyūkai 東洋史研究会 **L11**
Bunken tsūkō goshu sōmokuroku 文献通考五種総目録 付通典・通志 (Complete list of contents of five *Wen-hsien t'ung-k'ao*) Appendix: *T'ung-tien, T'ung-chih*. Kyoto, 1954. 113p.

Lists all articles in the *Wen-hsien t'ung-k'ao* and the successive *Wang Ch'i hsü wen-hsien t'ung-k'ao, Ch'in-ting hsü wen-hsien t'ung-k'ao, Ch'in-ting huang-ch'ao wen-hsien t'ung-k'ao* and *Huang-ch'ao hsü wen-hsien t'ung-k'ao*, with those in two other cyclopedia-like compilations appended.

Dictionaries

GENERAL

Suekawa, Hiroshi 末川博 **L12**
Hōgaku jiten 法学辞典 (Law dictionary) New ed., rev. Nihon Hyōron Shinsha, 1956. 1090, 120p.

Though primarily legal, includes political, economic, diplomatic and historical entries, with many cross-references. Indexes of foreign terms, personal names.

Wagatsuma, Sakae 我妻栄 **et al.** **L13**
Shin hōritsugaku jiten 新法律学辞典 (New dictionary of jurisprudence) Yūhikaku, 1952. 1205p.

With about 10,000 entries, covers terms and concepts in all branches of law, including aspects of legal philosophy and history and foreign law pertinent to current Japanese law. Major changes since the peace treaty came into force in 1952 are given in a supplement.

Nakagawa, Zennosuke 中川善之助 **et al. L14**
Hōritsugaku shōjiten 法律学小事典 (Small dictionary of jurisprudence) Yūshindō, 1961. 800, 31p.

Suehiro, Izutarō 末弘厳太郎 **and** **L15**
Tanaka, Kōtarō 田中耕太郎
Hōritsugaku jiten 法律学辞典 (Dictionary of jurisprudence) Iwanami Shoten, 1934-37. 5v.

Most authoritative prewar dictionary on the subject, with terms explained comprehensively by law faculty professors of Tokyo Imperial University, each with listing of Japanese and foreign reference works. v. 5 has complete table of contents, systematic table of items and indexes of subjects, law texts and foreign terms. Obsolete in part because of postwar changes but still useful.

Hōritsu Kenkyūkai 法律研究会 **L16**
Saishin hōritsu jiten 最新法律辞典 (New revised dictionary of law) Hōgaku Shoin, 1963. 464p.

Hyōronsha 評論社 **L17**
Hōgaku yōgo jiten 法学用語辞典 (Dictionary of legal terms) 1960. 510p. (Shōkai hōgaku benran, supp.)

Tezuka, Yutaka 手塚豊 **et al.** **L18**
Nyūmon hōritsugaku jiten 入門法律学辞典

(The beginner's law dictionary) Rev. and enl. ed. Senbundō, 1964. 395, 54p.

Uzaki, Michiya 鵜崎充矢 **L19**
Hōritsu ruigo jiten 法律類語辞典 (A thesaurus of legal terms) Daiyamondosha, 1956. 285p.

CONSTITUTIONAL LAW

Satō, Isao 佐藤功 and **L20**
Wada, Hideo 和田英夫
Kenpō jiten 憲法辞典 (Dictionary of the Constitution) Ichiryūsha, 1960. 333p. (Hōritsu shōjiten zensho, 1)
Comments on important points of the Constitution of Japan.

Kiyomiya, Shirō 清宮四郎 **L21**
Kenpō jiten 憲法事典 (Dictionary of the Constitution) Seirin Shoin, 1959. 472p.
An article by article commentary on the Japanese constitution.

Miyata, Yutaka 宮田豊 **L22**
Kenpō shōjiten 憲法小辞典 (A concise dictionary of the Constitution) Yūshindō, 1957. 281p. (Yūshindō zensho)
Annotated glossary of about 300 terms used in the Japanese constitution. Bibliography of works on the constitutions of foreign countries and list of major collections of foreign constitutions appended.

CIVIL LAW

Suekawa, Hiroshi 末川博 et al. **L23**
Minji hōgaku jiten 民事法学辞典 (Dictionary of civil law) Yūhikaku, 1960. 2v.
With technical emphasis, about 2,000 entries cover not only the Civil, Commercial and Civil Procedure Codes but also related social and economic matters, international private law, etc. Important theories differing from those commonly accepted and representative judicial precedents are cited. List of references. Extensive index.

Nakagawa, Zennosuke 中川善之助 **L24**
Minpō jiten 民法事典 (Cyclopedia of civil law) Seirin Shoin, 1959. 941, 23p.

Wagatsuma, Sakae 我妻栄 et al. **L25**
Minpō jiten 民法事典 (Dictionary of civil law) Ichiryūsha, 1959. 384p. (Hōritsu shōjiten zensho, 3)

COMMERCIAL LAW

Izawa, Kōhei 伊沢孝平 **L26**
Shōhō jiten 商法事典 (Dictionary of commercial law) Yūshindō, 1956. 420p.

Suzuki, Takeo 鈴木竹雄 et al. **L27**
Shōjihō jiten 商事法辞典 (A dictionary of commercial laws) Ichiryūsha, 1962. 430p. (Hōritsu shōjiten zensho, 4)

CRIMINAL LAW

Takigawa, Yukitoshi 滝川幸辰 **L28**
Keiji hōgaku jiten 刑事法学辞典 (Dictionary of criminal law) Enl. ed. Yūhikaku, 1962. 836, 33, 78p.
About 900 articles explain provisions of the Criminal, Criminal Procedure and Penal Codes and related matters, with notes on important judicial rulings and dissenting opinions. Reference works listed. Under subheadings within entries, about 4,000 topics are treated in detail. There is a systematic index of the three codes, with separate indexes of subjects, names and foreign terms.

Kimura, Kameji 木村亀二 **L29**
Keihō jiten 刑法事典 (Cyclopedia of criminal law) Seirin Shoin, 1959. 470, 17p.

Hirano, Ryūichi 平野竜一 et al. **L30**
Keijihō jiten 刑事法辞典 (A dictionary of criminal law) Ichiryūsha, 1961. 264p. (Hōritsu shōjiten zensho, 6)

PROCEDURES

Kikui, Tsunahiro 菊井維大 et al. **L31**
Minji soshōhō jiten 民事訴訟法辞典 (A dictionary of civil procedure codes) Ichiryūsha, 1962. 293p. (Hōritsu shōjiten zensho, 5)

Kimura, Kameji 木村亀二 **L32**
Keiji soshōhō jiten 刑事訴訟法事典 (Dictionary of the Code of Criminal Procedure) Seirin Shoin, 1959. 285, 10p.

ANGLO-AMERICAN LAW

Takayanagi, Kenzō 高柳賢三 and **L33**
Suenobu, Sanji 末延三次
Ei-Beihō jiten 英米法辞典 Anglo-Ameri-

can law dictionary Yūhikaku, 1952. 742p.

With about 7,200 entries designed to facilitate understanding of British and American laws, legal documents and legal literature. Names indexed. Appended are lists of abbreviations, legal maxims, important laws, prominent jurists, courts of law, Japanese and English legal terms, etc.

Masujima, Rokuichiro 増島六一郎 **L34**
Eihō jiten 英法辞典 (Dictionary of English law) 8th ed. Yūhikaku, 1952. 296p.

INTERNATIONAL LAW

Taoka, Ryōichi 田岡良一 **L35**
Kokusaihō kokusai seiji jiten 国際法・国際政治事典 (Dictionary of international law and politics) Seirin Shoin, 1956. 340p.

LABOR LAW

Ariizumi, Tōru 有泉亨 **and** **L36**
Sotoo, Ken'ichi 外尾健一
Rōdōhō jiten 労働法辞典 (Dictionary of labor law) Ichiryūsha, 1961. 261p. (Hōritsu shōjiten zensho, 7)

ADMINISTRATIVE LAW

Sonobe, Satoshi 園部敏 **and** **L37**
Yano, Katsuhisa 矢野勝久
Gyōseihō jiten 行政法事典 (A dictionary of administrative law) Yūshindō, 1954. 190p. (Yūshindō bunko)

TERMS

Itō, Jujirō 伊藤重治郎 **L38**
Wa-Ei hōritsugo jiten 増補和英法律語辞典 (Japanese-English dictionary of legal terms) Enl. ed. Daigaku Shobō, 1953. 1242p.

Satō, Tatsuo 佐藤達夫 **and** **L39**
Hayashi, Shūzō 林修三
Hōrei yōgo jiten 法令用語辞典 (Dictionary of terms in laws and ordinances) Gakuyō Shobō, 1959. 779p.

More than 2,000 terms in the Constitution and current laws and ordinances explained, with examples of their use and notes clarifying distinctions between similar terms. Subject index.

Azumagawa, Tokuji 東川徳治 **L40**
Shina hōsei daijiten 増訂支那法制大辞典 (Comprehensive dictionary of Chinese law) Rev. and enl. ed. Shōundō, 1933. 1150, 20p.

Only dictionary explaining modern as well as past Chinese legal and economic terms. Originally published in 1930 as *Tenkai* (Ocean of law) by the Hōsei University Press, to which errata and supplement (20p.) of further terms have been added.

Handbooks

Tōkyō Daigaku, Gakusei Bunka Shidōkai **L41**
東京大学学生文化指導会
Hōgaku kenkyū no shiori 法学研究の栞 (Handbook of legal studies) 1950. 2v.

Outlines the problems and issues in all branches of law, Japanese and foreign, and gives basic literature relating to them. Appended to v.2 are notes on periodicals, dictionaries, yearbooks, newspapers, collected works, series, collections of laws, statutes and judicial decisions, statistical materials, etc. Useful for basic research.

L42
Hōgaku annai 法学案内 (Introduction to jurisprudence) 1963- . Yūhikaku, 1963- . 2v. Annual.

Issued by the magazine *Jurisuto* (Jurist) as a study guide for university students, covers various fields of domestic law, with bibliography which, though limited, usefully supplements that in **L41.**

Noguchi, Masaichi 野口政一 **and** **L43**
Fukuoka, Mitsuji 福岡光次
Shoshiki zenshū 書式全集 (Complete manual of forms of legal documents) Rev. ed. Seirin Shoin, 1958. 4v.

Revision of *Saishin shoshiki taizen* (1954-55, 3v.). v.1, Civil laws; v.2, Finance and taxation; v.3, Intangible property, industry and labor; v.4, legal procedure.

Hōsōkai 法曹会 **L44**
Shihō taikan 司法大観 (Comprehensive survey of administration of justice) 1957. 1183p.

Indexes

Kokuritsu Kokkai Toshokan Chōsa Rippō **L45**
Kōsakyoku 国立国会図書館 調査立法考査局

Nihon hōrei sakuin 日本法令索引 Index to the Japanese laws and regulations in force. 1963. 515p.

Lists all laws, excluding administrative notifications (*kokuji*), in force on July 1, 1963, with explanations of how they were enacted, amended, rescinded, promulgated, put in force and applied. Indexed by years and subjects. Preceded by the *Hōrei sakuin* (Index of laws), published by the Library in 1949, which gave laws in force from Dec. 17, 1945, to Aug. 1, 1949, and ordinances from May 3, 1947, to Aug. 1, 1949, it was published every three years from 1951, with half-yearly supplements of amendments, until becoming an annual in 1961, giving laws as of Jan. 1 of the year of issuance until changed to July 1 with the 1963 issue.

Shūgiin Hōseikyoku 衆議院法制局 **L46**
Hōritsu no seitei kaisei oyobi haishi no gojūonjun sakuin 法律の制定・改正及び廃止の五十音順索引 (Index by Japanese syllabary to laws legistered, revised and abolished) No.1- . 1949- . 16v.

Gives brief explanations or summations of new, revised and abolished laws, with appended listing of new laws according to the numbers on promulgation documents, enforcement dates, names of proposers, etc. The first issue covers the period from Jan., 1944, to Jan. 15, 1949, but from the 1952 issue the coverage is for the preceding Oct. - Sep. period.

Kokuritsu Kokkai Toshokan **L47**
国立国会図書館
Chūka Jinmin Kyōwakoku hōrei sakuin 中華人民共和国法令索引 (Index to laws of the People's Republic of China) Oct., 1949 -Dec., 1953. 1954. 145p.

Classified in 17 sections, beginning with "Organic Law", titles and promulgation dates are given. Separately, the laws are listed chronologically with the agencies which promulgated them and the publications in which they appeared.

Aichi Daigaku, Kokusai Mondai **L48**
Kenkyūjo 愛知大学国際問題研究所
Chūka Jinmin Kyōwakoku hōrei mokuroku 中華人民共和国法令目録 (Catalogue of laws of the People's Republic of China) v.1, 1949 - June, 1954. Toyohashi, 1954. 80p.

Yearbooks

L49
Hōritsu nenkan 法律年鑑 (Law yearbook) 1935-60. Comp. by Hōritsu Jihō Henshūbu.

Nihon Hyōron Shinsha, 1935-43, 1958-59. 12v.
Pt.1 outlines academic, legislative, judicial, administrative and world legal developments in the previous year, with comments on new literature on the various branches of law. Pt.2 indexes by serial numbers new laws, treaties, ordinances, etc. and lists comments on them. Pt.3 covers new judicial precedents, and pt.4 is a classified list of new books and magazine articles on law and related subjects. The 1943-58 gap is filled in part by **L1**, *Hōrei kaihai sōran* (Manual of laws amended and rescinded), 1945-56, *Minji hanrei tenbō, keiji hanrei tenbō* (Surveys of civil and criminal cases), 1948-53, and *Hanrei kaiko* (Precedents in retrospect), 1955-58.

L50
Hōmu nenkan 法務年鑑 (Yearbook of legal affairs) 1949- . Comp. by Hōmushō. 1950- . 14v.

Successor from 1949 to the prewar *Hōmu nenkan* (Yearbook of justice), compiled by the Justice Ministry, *Shihō ichiran* (Manual of judicial administration), 1945-47, and *Hōmu ichiran* (Manual of justice), 1948.

L51
Keisatsu jiji nenkan 警察時事年鑑 (Police yearbook) 1964- . Keisatsu Bunka Kyōkai, 1964- . 1v.

Contains summary of police activities and public safety trends, chapters on felonies, misdemeanors, social movements, traffic, source materials on police history, important court decisions, criminal statistics, and relevant activities of the fire departments, Maritime Safety Agency, Ministry of Health and Welfare and Ministry of Labor, and directory of police personnel.

STATISTICS

L52
Shihō tōkei nenpō 司法統計年報 Annual report of judicial statistics 1952- . Comp. by Saikō Saibansho. 1953- . 40v.

Divided into civil, criminal, family and juvenile affairs. Successor from 1952 to *Minji saiban tōkei nenpō* (Annual statistical report on civil trials) 1950-51, and *Keiji saiban tōkei nenpō* (Annual statistical report on criminal trials), 1948-51, also compiled by the Supreme Court.

L53
Kensatsu tōkei nenpo 検察統計年報 (Annual statistics of public prosecution) No.77 (1951)- . Comp. by Hōmushō. 1953- . 13v.

Gives statistics on criminal cases handled by public procurators. First published as *Keiji sōkeihyō* in 1873, changed to *Keiji tōkei nenpō*, and *Keiji tōkei yōshi*, covering the period to 1950 in 75v.

L54

Hanzai tōkeisho 犯罪統計書 (Book of criminal statistics) 1947- . Comp. by Keisatsuchō. 1948- . 17v. Annual.

1947-52 editions compiled by Kokka Chihō Keisatsu (National Rural Police Headquarters).

Collections

L55

Genkō Nihon hōki 現行日本法規 (Japanese laws and regulations currently in force) Comp. by Hōmushō. Teikoku Chihō Gyōsei Gakkai, 1949- . Loose-leaf.

Divided under the following 18 headings: Constitution, Diet and elections, administrative system, statistical materials, local government, justice, police and fire services, land and construction, finance, education and culture, industry, economic control, transportation, postal services, labor, welfare, foreign affairs, national defense. Publications containing related regulations listed. Indexed.

L56

Genkō hōrei shūran 現行法令輯覧 (Collection of laws and orders currently in force) Comp. by Naikaku Kanbō. Teikoku Chihō Gyōsei Gakkai, 1948- . Loose-leaf.

Grouped under the following 18 headings: Constitution and Imperial Family, Diet and elections, administrative system and civil service, uniforms and badges, awards and pensions, documents, statistics and national census, religion, local government, public safety and hygiene, society, land, finance, justice, education, industry, transportation and electricity, and foreign affairs.

L57

Genkō hōki sōran 現行法規総覧 (Conspectus of laws and regulations in force) Comp. by Shūgiin Hōseikyoku and Sangiin Hōseikyoku. Daiichi Hōki Shuppan, 1950- . Loose-leaf.

Grouped under subject, lists names of laws, orders, and regulations with cross references and dates of their revision and/or invalidation.

L58

Iwanami roppō zensho 岩波六法全書 (Book of "Six Laws") 1930- . Ed. by Hiroshi Suekawa. Iwanami Shoten, 1930-43, 1947- . 32v. Annual.

A basic compendium of major laws, including the Constitution and the six codes, 589 in force on Jan. 8, 1964. Detailed subject index.

L59

Roppō zensho 六法全書 (Book of 'Six Laws') 1948- . Ed. by Sakae Wagatsuma and Toshiyoshi Miyazawa. Yūhikaku, 1948- . 17v. Annual.

Former title: Teikoku roppō zensho, 1906-1931. 15v.

Divided into public, civil, penal and social and economic laws and treaties. All texts have headings to indicate content, and major laws are accompanied by reference texts and separate subject indexes. General and classified tables of contents and index of law titles. Gives 618 laws in force on Jan. 1, 1964.

L60

Hōrei zensho 法令全書 (Complete collection of laws and regulations) Oct. 1876- . Ōkurashō Insatsukyoku.

A monthly cumulation in two parts, intended for binding annually with a table of contents and index, of laws, regulations, treaties, public notices, etc. in the *Kanpō* (Official gazette) classifying them by subjects and by the Government offices concerned. Coverage complete from 1867, with those from that date to 1884 in 18 special volumes with subject index.

Cases

L61

Meiji zenki Daishin'in minji hanketsuroku 明治前期大審院民事判決録 (Record of the Great Court of Judicature civil judgements in the first part of the Meiji period) No. 1- . Comp. by Meiji Zenki Daishin'in Hanketsuroku Kankōkai. Kyoto, Sanwa Shobō, 1957- . 11v. In progress.

From the establishment of the Great Court in 1875 to 1885. The publication is in progress to cover the period to 1895.

L62

Daishin'in minji hanketsuroku 大審院民事判決録 (Record of the Great Court of Judicature civil judgements) No. 1-27. Comp. by Chūō Daigaku. 1895-1922. 32v.

From 1895 through 1921. Each volume in Series 1-8 and 21-27 has a general list of contents, and the supplement (3v.) lists comprehensively the decisions for 1903-21. Series 1-10 was published by Tokyo Hōgakuin.

L63

Daishin'in minji hanreishū 大審院民事判例集 (Collection of the Great Court of Judi-

cature civil cases) Comp. by Hōsōkai. 1951
-54. 46v.

A photographic reprint in reduced size, includes cases from Nov. 1922 to Jan. 1946. Subject index.

L64

Daishin'in keiji hanketsuroku 大審院刑事判
決録 (Record of the Great Court of Judicature criminal judgements) No. 1-27. Comp. by Chūō Daigaku. 1896-1922. 30v.

From 1895 through 1921. Each volume in Series 1-8 and 21-27 has a general index, and the supplement (2v.) indexes all decisions for 1904-21. Series 1-10 was published by Tokyo Hōgakuin.

L65

Daishin'in keiji hanreishū 大審院刑事判例
集 (Collection of the Great Court of Judicature criminal cases) Comp. by Hōsōkai. 1951-54. 31v.

A photographic reprint in reduced size, includes cases from 1922 to Mar. 1947. Subject index.

L66

Saikō Saibansho hanreishū 最高裁判所判例
集 (Collection of Supreme Court cases) v. 1, no. 1, May, 1947- . Comp. by Saikō Saibansho. 1948- . monthly.

Covers cases from May, 1947, with yearly indexes of laws concerned, case numbers and trial dates.

L67

Hanrei taikei 判例体系 (Systematic collection of cases) Daiichi Hōki Shuppan, 1953- . 127v. In progress.

Divided into 15 groups, beginning with the Constitution, cases are given with the laws concerned and marginal notes on major points. Subsequent cases provided in loose-leaf supplements. Compiled by Noboru Inoue, Saburō Iwamatsu and Sakae Wagatsuma.

L68

Saikō Saibansho 最高裁判所
Saibanshohō shikōgo ni okeru minji saibanrei sōsakuin 裁判所法施行後における民事
裁判例総索引 (General index to court decisions in civil cases since enforcement of the Court Organization Law) 1959. 3v.

Classifies and arranges according to the articles of the Civil Code decisions from 1947 to 1957, excluding those in administrative and labor cases. Bibliography lists collections of cases heard by the Supreme Court and lower courts and legal periodicals. Cases indexed by courts and dates.

Treaties

Gaimushō, Jōyakukyoku 外務省条約局 **L69**
Genkō jōyaku ichiran 現行条約一覧 (Tables of current treaties) 1964. 77p.

Convenient tool for ascertaining treaties in force as of Feb. 1, 1964, the texts of most of which may be found in **L70**, **L71**, and **L74**. Divided into bilateral and multilateral treaties, each subdivided by subjects, with columns giving titles, dates of coming into force, location of original texts, etc. May be supplemented with **L73** for information about invalidated and abortive treaties from 1854 to 1957.

L70

Genkō jōyaku shūran: nikokukan jōyaku 現行
条約集覧　二国間条約 (Collection of current treaties: bilateral) Gaimushō Jōyakukyoku, 1952- . Loose-leaf.

Arranged by names of countries. No index, but **L69** may be used as a substitute. A selective collection of important treaties, entitled *Nikokukan jōyakushū*, was published in 1962. 1123p.

L71

Genkō jōyaku shūran: tasūkokukan jōyaku 現
行条約集覧　多数国間条約 (Collection of current treaties: multilateral) Gaimushō Jōyakukyoku, 1954- . Loose-leaf.

Consists of politics (2v.), economy (4v.), transportation (2v.), culture and society (2v.). Arranged chronologically by dates of effectuation. Important treaties are collected under the title, *Tasūkoku jōyakushū*, v. 1 of which was published in 1962. v. 2 is in preparation.

L72

Jōyakushū 条約集 (Collection of treaties) 1st series, v. 1- . Gaimushō Jōyakukyoku, 1922- . 1556v.

Gaimushō Jōyakukyoku 外務省条約局 **L73**
Jōyaku benran: nikokukan jōyaku 条約便覧
二国間条約 (Treaty manual: bilateral) 1958. 656p.

A guide to treaties concluded from 1854 to 1957. → **L69**.

Tabata, Shigejirō 田畑茂二郎 **and** **L74**
Takabayashi, Hideo 高林秀雄
Kokusai jōyaku shiryōshū 国際条約・資料
集 (Collection of international treaties and documents) Yūshindō, 1960. 424p. (Hōgaku shiryō taikei, 10)

Includes both treaties and declarations and decisions of international organizations. United Nations organization chart, list of cases submitted to the International Court of Justice and map showing areas covered by security pacts appended.

Constitutions

Miyazawa, Toshiyoshi 宮沢俊義 **L75**
Sekai kenpōshū 世界憲法集 (Collection of constitutions of the world) Iwanami Shoten, 1960. 344p. (Iwanami bunko)

Ōishi, Yoshio 大石義雄 **L76**
Shintei Sekai kakkoku no kenpōten 新訂世界各国の憲法典 (Constitutions of the world) New rev. ed. Yūshindō, 1959. 740p.

Shūgiin Hōseikyoku 衆議院法制局 **L77**
Wayaku Kakkoku kenpōshū 和訳各国憲法集 (Constitutions of the world translated into Japanese) 1955- . 84v.

Translated and compiled by the Legislative Bureaus of both Houses of the Diet, the National Diet Library and the Legislative Bureau of the Cabinet, the current constitutions of 84 countries are given.

ECONOMICS

❧ Economic theory, economic conditions of various countries, population, management, money and banking, commerce and trade are included under this heading. Labor is included in **N** section.

GENERAL WORKS

BIBLIOGRAPHY

Keizaigaku bunken kihō　経 済 学 文 献 季 報　**M1**
Quarterly bibliography of economics. v.1, no.1, 1956- .　Comp. by Keizai Shiryō Kyōgikai. Yūhikaku, 1956- .　30v.

Best current Japanese bibliography of not only economics but also social sciences in general, including American, Soviet, other European and Chinese (only to 1960) periodical articles.　Entries, each with a serial number, are grouped in 16 classes. There is a list of periodicals covered.　Author index.

Osaka Shiritsu Daigaku, Keizai Kenkyūjo　**M2**
大 阪 市 立 大 学 経 済 研 究 所
Keizaigaku bunken kaidai　経 済 学 文 献 解 題 (Annotated bibliography of economics) 1955. Nihon Hyōron Shinsha, 1957.　279p.

Bridges the gap between **J4** and **M1** with a selective survey for 1952-54 and a listing of 1955 publications classified in much the same way as the entries in **M1**.

Osaka Shōka Daigaku, Keizai Kenkyūjo　**M3**
大 阪 商 科 大 学 経 済 研 究 所
Keizaigaku bunken taikan　経 済 学 文 献 大 鑑 (Great mirror of economic bibliography) Osaka, 1934-39.　4v.

Lists exhaustively books and articles in both learned and popular journals published in Japan and major foreign countries (excepting the Soviet Union) from 1933 to 1936.　Divided into finance (v.1), currency and banking (v.2-3) and commerce and industry (v.4).　Contents of important books given.　Subject and author indexes at the end of each volume.

Osaka Shōka Daigaku, Keizai Kenkyūjo　**M4**
大 阪 商 科 大 学 経 済 研 究 所
Keizai shiryō sōran　創 立 十 周 年 記 念　経 済 資 料 総 覧 (Handbook of economic materials) Jan. 1928 - Dec. 1937.　Osaka, 1940. 505, 125p.

Useful with **M3**, lists reports of government offices and companies and statistics published from 1928 to 1937.　Titles given of series, yearbooks, documentary journals, bibliographies.　Subject and author indexes.

M5
The Japan science review: economic sciences.
No.1- .　Comp. by Nihon Keizai Gakkai Rengōkai.　Nihon Gakujutsu Shinkōkai, 1953- . 9v.　Annual.

Lists in English significant articles by Japanese economists.　Author index.

Economic geography

Kokushō, Iwao　黒 正　厳　and　**M6**
Kikuta, Tarō　菊 田 太 郎
Keizai chirigaku bunken sōran　経 済 地 理 学 文 献 総 覧 (Handbook of literature on economic geography)　Sōbunkaku, 1937.　33, 478, 320p.　(Keizai chirigaku kōza, supp.)

Lists Japanese and foreign books and articles from 1868 to 1935, divided into Japanese, Chinese and Western parts, each with the following categories: bibliographies, dictionaries, encyclopedias, yearbooks, statistics, series, collected articles, general geography, human geography, political geography, economic geography, communications geography, industrial geography, commercial geography, studies of merchandise, world economy, international economic relations, colonies, trade, international finance, cartography, maps, charts, Japanese geographical records and world geographical records. No index.

Kokuritsu Kokkai Toshokan   M7
国立国会図書館
Keizai keikaku bunken mokuroku 経済計画文献目録 (Bibliography on economic planning, with special reference to long-term projects). 1962. 208p.

Classified list of about 2,000 foreign prewar and postwar books and magazine articles through 1961 and about 1,600 parallel Japanese publications to Sep. 1962. No index.

Hokkai Gakuen Daigaku, Kaihatsu   M8
Kenkyūjo 北海学園大学開発研究所
Kaihatsu kankei bunken shiryō mokuroku 開発関係文献資料目録 (Catalogue of documents and source materials on economic development) No. 1. Sapporo, 1962. 196p.

Especially strong in Hokkaido materials, it lists about 6,000 books, research reports, magazine articles, chiefly in Japanese, in the collections of the Hokkaido Development Bureau, for which it was compiled, and the Development Institute of Hokkai Gakuen University. No index. There is a separate edition published by the Hokkaido Development Bureau.

DICTIONARIES

Nakayama, Ichirō 中山伊知郎 et al.   M9
Keizaigaku daijiten 経済学大辞典 (Comprehensive dictionary of economics) Tōyō Keizai Shinpōsha, 1955. 3v.

Most exhaustive postwar economic dictionary, grounded in modern concepts and including many basic industrial and commercial terms. Explanations average five pages in length, each with listing of Japanese and foreign reference works. Indexes of subjects, personal names and titles of tables.

Nakayama, Ichirō 中山伊知郎   M10
Keizai jiten 経済事典 (Dictionary of economics) Seirin Shoin Shinsha, 1964. 855p.

Entries classified under 14 headings, each with reference list. Appended are a 1516-1961 chronology of political economy and charts of the life spans of major economists and the lineage of schools of economic thought. Subject and name indexes.

Heibonsha 平凡社   M11
Keizaigaku jiten 経済学事典 (Dictionary of economics) 1954. 1759, 80p.

Covers exceptionally large number of terms, with those of importance explained in detail. Both Marxian and modern economic ideas included. Listed with each entry are a few reference works. Subjects and personal names indexed.

Osaka Shiritsu Daigaku, Keizai Kenkyūjo   M12
大阪市立大学経済研究所
Keizaigaku shōjiten 経済学小辞典 (Little dictionary of economics) 2d. ed., rev. and enl. Iwanami Shoten, 1956. 1434p.

Intended less for quick consultation than for reading, it explains basic concepts and on such subjects as "value" and "capital" gives both Marxist and opposing theories. References with each entry. Subjects, personal names indexed.

Takahashi, Taizō 高橋泰蔵 and   M13
Masuda, Shirō 増田四郎
Taikei keizaigaku shōjiten 体系経済学小辞典 (Small systematic dictionary of economics) 3d ed., rev. Tōyō Keizai Shinpōsha, 1956. 32, 1002p.

Entries of medium length, each with references, under the following headings: social economic thought, social economic system, schools of economic thought, economic theories and personages, the last of which covers the careers, ideas and principal writings of about 160 scholars. Appended are a list of important Japanese and foreign literature (162p.) and a chronology matching economic theories with economic and political developments. Subjects, foreign terms and names indexed.

Osaka Shōka Daigaku, Keizai Kenkyūjo   M14
大阪商科大学経済研究所
Keizaigaku jiten 経済学辞典 (Dictionary of economics) Iwanami Shoten, 1930-36. 7v.

Covers not only national economy but also related aspects of law, politics and thought, though considerably out-of-date, with little on modern economy. The information in the first five volumes, completed in 1932, is brought up to 1936 in a supplemental volume. Final volume contains a general table of contents and indexes of subjects, personal and place names and foreign terms.

Yamada, Yūzō 山田雄三   M15
Kindai keizaigaku jiten 近代経済学辞典 (Dictionary of modern economics) Shunjūsha, 1954. 394p.

Extensive and systematic compilation of modern economic terms but increasingly inadequate with the passage of time. Each entry gives the work in which the term first was used, lists references and calls attention to related entries. Subject and name indexes.

Kozlov, G. A. and Pervushin, S. P.   **M 16**
Keizaigaku shōjiten 経済学小辞典 (Little dictionary of economics) Tr. by Sobieto Kenkyū-sha Kyōkai. Aoki Shoten, 1960. 32, 378, 15p.

Translation of *Kratkii ekonomicheskii slovar'*, 1958, arranged by Japanese translated terms.

Kuruma, Samezō 久留間鮫造 **et al.**   **M 17**
Shihonron jiten 資本論辞典 (*Das Kapital* dictionary) Aoki Shoten, 1961. 18, 766p.

A handbook on Marx's *Das Kapital*, classifies and explains Marx's ideas, comments on scholars and writers, outlines the history of the composition of *Das Kapital* with a chronology, and gives notes on editions in different languages. Subject and name indexes.

Terms

Nihon Keizai Shinbunsha   **M 18**
日本経済新聞社
Keizai shingo jiten 経済新語辞典 (Dictionary of new economic terms) 1964 ed. 1964. 345, 12, 31p.

This publication is kept up-to-date by adding new terms on economics and current affairs every year. The 1964 edition lists 2,700 terms.

The Oriental Economist   **M 19**
Keizai yōgo Wa-Ei jiten 経済用語和英辞典 Japanese-English dictionary of economic terms. Tōyō Keizai Shinpōsha, 1963. 626p.

About 45,000 terms listed alphabetically in Hepburn romanization. Appended are English translations and abbreviations of the names of government offices, economic organizations and labor unions.

Shinomiya, Kyōji 四宮恭二   **M 20**
Doku-Wa keizaigo jiten 独和経済語辞典 Deutsch-japanisches Wörterbuch der Wirtschaft. Yūhikaku, 1960. 541p.

Approximately 40,000 entries, including industrial, legal, political, administrative and statistical terms, as well as abbreviations and foreign terms.

Hisatake, Masao 久武雅夫 **and**   **M 21**
Koizumi, Akira 小泉 明
Kindai keizaigaku kihon yōgo jiten 近代経済

学基本用語辞典 (Dictionary of basic terms in modern economics). 2d ed., rev. and enl. Shunjūsha, 1961. 250, 24p.

Subject and name indexes.

HANDBOOK

Hitotsubashi Daigaku, Shinbunbu   **M 22**
一橋大学新聞部
Keizaigaku kenkyū no shiori 経済学研究の栞 (Handbook of economic studies) 2d ed. Shunjūsha, 1953. 1179p.

Divided into sections on the history of economic theories, economic policies, Western economic history and Oriental economic history, it introduces concepts and issues and points out basic literature. The first edition, 1949, was published in 4v. The book of the same title which the same compiler published in 1935 is entirely different in content.

HISTORY

Adamu Sumisu no Kai   **M 23**
アダム・スミスの会
Honpō Adamu Sumisu bunken 本邦アダム・スミス文献 (Literature on Adam Smith in Japan) Catalogue and annotation. Kōbundō, 1955. 227p.

Catalogues chronologically literature relating to Adam Smith from 1869 to 1952, listing under each year books, magazine and newspaper articles, histories of theories, collected essays, bibliographies, proceedings of learned societies, etc., with annotation of important items. No index.

Amano, Keitarō 天野敬太郎   **M 24**
Bibliography of the classical economics. Science Council of Japan, 1961-64. 5v. (Economic series, no. 27, 30-33)

Comprehensive bibliography of books and articles by and about Adam Smith, Malthus, Ricardo, J. S. Mill, British economists and general description, with notes on Japanese translations.

Takahashi, Seiichirō 高橋誠一郎   **M 25**
Kohan Seiyō keizaisho Kaidai 古版西洋経済書解題 (Notes on early printed editions of Western economic books) Keiō Shuppansha, 1943. 715p.

Full explanatory notes on 35 early editions of major works from the end of the sixteenth century to the first half of the nineteenth. Originally in the magazine *Mita gakkai zasshi*, Mita Journal of Economics.

Hori, Tsuneo 堀 経夫   **M 26**
Keizai shisōshi jiten 経済思想史辞典

(Dictionary of economic thought) 2d ed., rev. and enl. Osaka, Sōgensha, 1959.   823, 70p.

Subjects and persons are itemized under 14 stages or peaks in the evolution of economic thought in Europe and America, followed by special studies on employment, cycle of prosperity, economic planning, etc. Subject and name indexes.

Kobayashi, Noboru 小林　昇　　**M 27**
Keizaigakushi shōjiten 経済学史小辞典
(Little dictionary of the history of economics) Gakuseisha, 1963.   320p.

Mainly biographies of Japanese and foreign economists and leaders in related fields, with an annotated list of their principal works. Appended outline of schools of thought and a brief chronology. Name and title indexes.

Economic history

BIBLIOGRAPHY

Ōtsuka, Hisao 大塚久雄 **et al.**　　**M 28**
Seiyō keizaishi koza. V. Shiryō bunken kaidai
西洋経済史講座 V. 史料文献解題
(Lecture series on Western economic history. V. Annotated list of historical materials and literature) Iwanami Shoten, 1962.   327, 34p.

Gives about 2,300 basic titles on the transition from feudalism to capitalism in three parts, general, Middle Ages and modern times. Annotated list of major Japanese and foreign journals. Name index.

Honjō, Eijirō 本庄栄治郎　　**M 29**
Nihon keizaishi bunken 日本経済史文献
(Bibliography of Japanese economic history) Nihon Hyōron Shinsha, 1953-59.   4v.

The most comprehensive bibliography of monographs and articles on not only economic history but all the social sciences, including Western works on Japanese social and economic history. Appended are a bibliography of local histories, a title index and a list of journals used.

Dai-ichi bunken (Bibliography no. 1) covering materials from 1868 to 1931, originally published in 1933 as *Kaihan* (Revised) *Nihon keizaishi bunken.*

Dai-ni bunken (Bibliography no. 2) with 1932-40 materials, first published in 1942 as *Nihon keizaishi shin* (new) *bunken.*

Dai-san bunken (Bibliography no. 3) with 1941-50 materials, compiled by Eijirō Honjō and others.

Dai-shi bunken (Bibliography no. 4) with 1951-57 materials, compiled by Eijirō Honjō and others.

Nihon Keizaishi Kenkyūjo　　**M 30**
日本経済史研究所
Keizaishi bunken kaidai 経済史文献解題
(Annotated bibliography of the history of economics) 1959- . Nihon Hyōronsha, 1960- . 4v.

Exhaustively lists Japanese books and articles related to economic history in Japan, the rest of the Orient and the West, with brief annotations. Book titles indexed. Preceded by the prewar *Keizaishi nenkan* (Yearbook of economic history), limited to Japanese economic history, which was an annual special issue of the magazine *Keizaishi kenkyū* (Study of economic history), three volumes for 1951-53 with the same title published independently, and the *Keizaishi bunken* (Bibliography of economic history) for 1957 and 1958.

Iwanami Shoten 岩波書店　　**M 31**
Nihon shihon shugi hattatsushi shiryō kaisetsu
日本資本主義発達史資料解説 (Annotated bibliography of materials on the development of Japanese capitalism) 1932-33. 4v. (Nihon shihon shugi hattatsushi kōza)

Annotated bibliography of literature on the development of world capitalism, by Kinnosuke Ōtsuka, 1932, 82p.; Literature on the financial and economic history of the Meiji period, by Hyōe Ōuchi and Takao Tsuchiya, 1933, 107p; Notes on materials on the history of peasants, by Takeo Ono, 1933, 62p.; Notes on literature on socialism in Japan, by Karoku Hosokawa, 1932, 120p.

Takimoto, Seiichi 滝本誠一　　**M 32**
Nihon keizai tenseki ko 日本経済典籍考
(Studies on Japanese economic writings) Nihon Hyōronsha, 1928. 25, 454p.

Explanatory notes on works of the Tokugawa period.

Keizaishi Kenkyūkai 経済史研究会　　**M 33**
Nihon keizaishi jiten 日本経済史辞典
(Dictionary of Japanese economic history) Nihon Hyōron Shinsha, 1954. 3v.

Includes extensive coverage of social, political and legal matters related to economic history but is confined largely to developments before 1868, with emphasis on the Tokugawa period. Indexes in separate volume. Published originally by Nihon Hyōronsha in 1940.

CHRONOLOGY

Osaka Shōka Daigaku, Keizai Kenkyūjo　　**M 34**
大阪商科大学経済研究所
Sekai keizai nenpyō 世界経済年表 (Chronology of world economy) Iwanami Shoten, 1937.

1064p.

From before the Christian era to 1935, with Japanese and foreign-language indexes.

Tōyō Keizai Kenkyūjo 東洋経済研究所 **M 35**
Sakuin seiji keizai dainenpyō 索引政治経済大年表 (Comprehensive chronology of politics and economy, with index) Tōyō Keizai Shimpō-sha, 1943. 2v.

Yoshida, Hideo 吉田英雄 **M 36**
Nihon shakai keizai hennenshi 日本社会経済編年史 (Annals of Japanese society and economy) Kaizōsha, 1928. 681p.

A socio-economic chronology from 660 B.C. to 1926, with source materials cited. No index.

M 37
Nihon shihon shugi nenpyō 日本資本主義年表 (Chronology of Japanese capitalism) Aoki Shoten, 1955. 245p. (Aoki bunko)

From 1848 to 1954, with subject index.

Kajinishi, Mitsuhaya 楫西光速 **et al.** **M38**
Nihon ni okeru shihon shugin no hattatsu - nenpyō 日本に於ける資本主義の発達一年表 (Chronology of the development of capitalism in Japan) Tokyo Daigaku Shuppankai, 1953. 312p.

For each year from 1858, when the first Japan-American commercial treaty was concluded, to 1951, when the peace treaty was signed, major economic, political and social events are listed, as well as figures on population, companies, factories, factory workers, banks, trade, and rice and other commodity prices. Classified index with subjects arranged in chronological order.

Okazaki, Jirō 岡崎次郎 **et al.** **M 39**
Nihon shihon shugi hattatsushi nenpyō 日本資本主義発達史年表 (Chronology of the development of Japanese capitalism) Enl. ed. Kawade Shobō, 1954. 450p. (Nihon kindaishi sōsho, supp.)

From 1868 to 1933, with events classified by subjects. Statistical tables cover major economic indicators.

Horie, Eiichi 堀江英一 **M 40**
Gendai keizaishi nenpyō 現代経済史年表 (Chronology of modern economic history) San'ichi Shobō, 1962. 251p. (Nihon gendaishi nenpyō)

Covers Japanese economic developments from 1860 to 1959, with important events in other fields on facing pages. Subject index.

Usami, Seijirō 宇佐美誠次郎 **M 41**
Sengo Nihon shihon shugi nenpyō 戦後日本資本主義年表 (Chronology of capitalism in postwar Japan) Iwanami Shoten, 1954. 431p. (Nihon shihon shugi kōza, supp.)

Most detailed chronology of political and economic developments from 1945 to 1953, with parallel columns for international affairs, political and economic events, and other national developments, the most important of which are in bold type. For each year, a brief political and economic summary is given.

Matsuo, Hiroshi 松尾 弘 **and** **M 42**
Yamaoka, Kikuo 山岡喜久雄
Sengo Nihon keizai seisakushi nenpyō 戦後日本経済政策史年表 (Chronology of Japanese postwar economic policies) 2d ed., rev. and enl. Keisō Shobō, 1962. 552p.

A general survey for each year is followed by separate columns for political developments, industrial, financial, monetary, trade, labor, and social policies. Reference list. The first edition, mimeographed in 2v., was compiled by the Nihon Keizai Seisaku Gakkai.

SOURCE MATERIALS

Ōkurashō 大蔵省 **M 43**
Nihon zaisei keizai shiryō 日本財政経済史料 (Materials on the financial and economic history of Japan) Zaisei Keizai Gakkai, 1922-25. 11v.

Materials on the Tokugawa period are arranged in chronological order in sections on finance, economy, public engineering, population, etc. Detailed subject index and chronological table of contents in supplementary volume.

Ōuchi, Hyōe 大内兵衛 **and** **M 44**
Tsuchiya, Takao 土屋喬雄
Meiji zenki zaisei keizai shiryō shūsei 明治前期財政経済史料集成 (Collection of materials on the financial and economic history of the early Meiji period) Kaizōsha, 1931-36. 21v.

Important basic compilation of government records, memorials and reports concerning the establishment and functioning of various agencies in the first few decades of the Meiji period, including official histories of the Finance and Public Works Ministries, the views of the Agriculture Ministry on promotion of industry, the financial policies of Count Masayoshi Matsukata, Finance Ministry reports on reforms in the monetary system and the land tax, and a directory of companies. No index. A reprint is being published by the Meiji Bunken Shiryō Kankōkai (Society for Reprinting Literature and Documents of the Meiji Period).

Tōyō Keizai Shinpōsha M 45
東洋経済新報社
Shōwa sangyōshi 昭和産業史 (Shōwa industrial history) 1950. 3v.

v. 1-2 outline developments in all significant industries from 1926, with emphasis on wartime changes. v. 3 gives statistics on banking, commodity prices, commodity supply and demand, trade, finance, labor, agriculture and forestry, overseas affairs and war damages. Wartime statistics especially useful. No index.

Economic conditions

Gaimushō 外務省 M 46
Kokusai keizai kikō ABC 国際経済機構 ABC (ABC of international economic organizations) Noda Keizaisha, 1963. 374p.

Brief descriptions with appended lists of the member nations of each organization and an organization chart of the United Nations. Subject index.

United Nations. Department of Economic and Social Affairs M 47
Afurika keizai gaikan アフリカ経済概観 (General survey of African economy) Tr. by Afurika Kyōkai. (Africa Society of Japan) Hara Shobō, 1961. 248p.

A translation of Economic survey of Africa since 1950, 1959.

Ajia Tsūshinsha 亜細亜通信社 M 48
Chūgoku sangyō bōeki sōran 中国産業貿易総覧 (Manual of Chinese industry and trade) 1963. 356p.

Surveys the industry and trade of China, excluding Taiwan, with statistics of the productive capacities of the metallurgical, power, mechanical, chemical, textile, paper-making and ceramic industries. Many statistics.

YEARBOOKS

Sekai keizai nenpō 世界経済年報 (Annual report on world economy) 1957- . Comp. by the United Nations. Nihon Kokusai Rengō Kyōkai, 1957- . 7v. M 49

Japanese translation of the World economic survey, published yearly by the United Nations Secretariat, giving a general survey and discussion of specific problems. Began with the edition for 1957, corresponding to the original edition for 1956. Published until the 1959 edition by Tōyō Keizai Shimpō Sha.

Kokumin shotoku tōkei nenkan 国民所得統計年鑑 (Yearbook of national income statistics) 1959- . Comp. by the United Nations, Statistical Office. Tr. by Keizai Kikakuchō. Hara Shobō, 1961- . 4v. M 50

Gives side by side with the original English text a Japanese translation of the Yearbook of national accounts statistics, published since 1957 by the United Nations.

Sekai keizai no gensei 世界経済の現勢 (Present situation of world economy) 1958- Comp. by Keizai Kikakuchō, Chōsakyoku. 1958- 6v. M 51

Surveys general world movements and area problems, with statistics appended. 'White-paper on world economy' is the trade title, published by Shiseidō since 1958.

Keizai yōran 経済要覧 (Manual of economics) 1954- . Comp. by Keizai Kikakuchō, Chōsakyoku. 1954- . 10v. M 52

Digests Japanese and foreign economic statistics.

Sekai keizai nenpō 世界経済年報 (Annual report on world economy) 1948-1960. Comp. by Sekai Keizai Kenkyūjo. Nihon Hyōron Shinsha, 1948-61. 18v. M 53

For each three-month period from 1948 through 1960, economic and political events in the world and major individual countries are recorded, together with discussion of special problems and statistics. Discontinued with the issue for the last quarter of 1960. Publisher varies, by Nihon Hyōronsha since 1957.

Gaikoku keizai tōkei nenpō 外国経済統計年報 (Yearly report on foreign economic statistics) 1946- . Comp. by Nihon Ginkō, Tōkeikyoku. 1947- . 18v. M 54

Former title: Gaikoku keizai tōkei. 1924-1941. 15v. Arranges statistics of foreign countries and areas under subjects.

Ajia keizai nenpō アジア経済年報 (Annual report on Asian economy) 1955- . Comp. by the United Nations, Economic Commission for Asia and the Far East. Tr. by Nihon ECAFE Kyōkai. Tōyō Keizai Shinpōsha, 1955- . 9v. M 55

Translation of the *Economic survey of Asia and the Far East,* issued by ECAFE (Economic Commission for Asia and the Far East), of each preceding year, covering general developments and special problems. Statistics on population, employment, national accounts, production, transportation, foreign trade, prices and wages, currency and banking. Lists titles, periods, merchandise covered and accounting methods of trade agreements signed the previous year.

M 56

Keizai tōkei nenkan　経済統計年鑑
(Yearbook of economic statistics)　1952- .
Tōyō Keizai Shinpōsha, 1952- .　13v.

Former title: *Keizai nenkan* (Economic yearbook) 1917 - 1944.　27v.

Japan

M 57

Nenji keizai hōkoku　年次経済報告　(Yearly economic report) 1949- .　Comp. by Keizai Kikakuchō.　1949- .　16v.

Most authoritative general survey of Japanese economy, published each year about July.　Trade title: *Keizai hakusho* (White paper on economy). There is an English edition: *Economic survey of Japan,* 1952-53 - .　1953- .　11v.　Annual.

M 58

Kokumin shotoku hakusho　国民所得白書
(White paper on national income) 1957- .　Comp. by Keizai Kikakuchō.　1959- .　6v.

Sequel to 1954, 1955, 1956 editions, entitled *Shōwa . . . nendo no kokumin shotoku* (3v.).　Covers special problems, quarterly national income accounts, details of principal items in the accounts, incomes of individuals by prefectures, the national incomes of other countries, etc.

M 59

Keizai kyōryoku no genjō to mondaiten　経済協力の現状と問題点　(Present state and problems of economic cooperation).　1958-
Comp. by Tsūshō Sangyōshō.　Tsūshō Sangyo Chōsakai, 1958- .　6v.

A general survey of developments in the preceding year is followed by description of policies and activities with regard to individual countries in Southeast and Southwest Asia.　As "economic cooperation" is used in a broad sense, it provides a good summation of Japanese policy on foreign economic matters other than trade.　Known also as *Keizai kyōryoku hakusho* (White paper on economic cooperation).

M 60

Honpō keizai tōkei　本邦経済統計　(Eco-
nomic statistics of Japan).　1920- .　Comp. by Nihon Ginkō, Tōkeikyoku.　1920- .　34v.

Emphasis on banking and finance.

M 61

Nihon keizai nenkan　日本経済年鑑　(Japan economic yearbook)　1950-1963.　Nihon Keizai Shinbunsha, 1950-62.　13v.

Gives a general survey of the fiscal year ending in March before the year of issuance and separate chapters on national income, production, agriculture and fisheries, trade, etc., with related statistics. No index.　Compiled through the 1952 edition by the Statistics and Research Division, Ministry of International Trade and Industry.

M62

Nihon keizai nenpō　日本経済年報　(Annual report on Japanese economy)　No. 1-102.　Tōyō Keizai Shinpōsha, 1930-44, 1948-59.　102v.

Points out and. comemnts on major topics in Japanese and world economy in each three-month period. Some issues report on serious economic studies. Suspended from Aug., 1944, to April, 1948.

M63

Asahi keizai nenshi　朝日経済年史
(Asahi yearbook of economic history)　Asahi Shinbunsha, 1928-1955.　1928-55.　28v.

Each edition surveys economic activities in the preceding calendar year under the headings of finance, banking, enterprises, mining, fisheries, transportation, trade, special procurements, commerce, national life, labor and world economy, followed by statistics, a chronicle and a directory of companies and organizations.

STATISTICS

United Nations. Statistical Office　　**M64**
Sekai no keizai seichō to sangyō kōzō 世界の経済成長と産業構造 (World economic growth in relation to industrial structure)　Tr. by Keizai Kikakuchō Sōgō Keikakukyoku.　Hara Shobō, 1960.　471p.

A translation of *Patterns of industrial growth 1938-1958,* giving statistics and other data on mining, industry, construction, electricity and gas in 75 countries, as well as a general world survey.

United Nations. Statistical Office　　**M65**
Sekai no keizai seichō to sangyō kōzō 世界の経済成長と産業構造 (World economic growth in relation to industrial structure).　1938-1961.　Tr. by Saburō Ōkita.　Hara Shobō, 1964.　849p.

A translation, together with English text, of *The growth of world industry 1938-1961*, which rearranges the data in **M64** and extends the coverage to 1961, with the number of countries increased to about 100.

U.S.S.R. Tsentral'noe Statisticheskoe Upravlenie   M66

Soren kokumin keizai tōkeishū ソ連国民経済統計集 (Collection of national economic statistics of the Soviet Union) 1956. Tr. by Sangyō Keizai Kenkyūjo, 1956. 273p.

Gives the first Soviet statistics published after the war, inadequate but indicative of the Soviets' own estimate of their economic strength at that time. Newer and better statistics have been published, but they have not yet become available in Japanese.

Tsūsho Sangyō Chōsakai   M67
通商産業調査会

Sorenken shokoku no keizai tōkei ソ連圏諸国の経済統計 (Economic statistics of Soviet satellite nations) 1957. 136p.

Japan

Hitotsubashi Daigaku, Keizai Kenkyūjo   M68
一橋大学経済研究所

Kaisetsu keizai tōkei 解説経済統計 (Annotated economic statistics) Iwanami Shoten, 1953. 207p.

Statistics from 1929 to 1951 or 1952 which are pertinent to advanced study or analysis of Japanese economy are given in nine sections, including national income, population and labor, production, and trade, accompanied by directions on their use, comparison with foreign statistics, citation of reference literature, etc. Subject index.

Hitotsubashi Daigaku, Keizai Kenkyūjo   M69
一橋大学経済研究所

Kaisetsu Nihon keizai tōkei 解説日本経済統計 (Annotated economic statistics of Japan) Iwanami Shoten, 1961. 192p. (Keizai Kenkyūjo sōsho, supp.)

Carries on from **M68**, with additional sections on commerce, enterprise and business operations, transportation, employment, and wages and analyses of trade relations, monetary flow, etc. Statistical literature listed with brief annotations. Subject index.

Asahi Shinbunsha 朝日新聞社   M70
Nihon keizai tōkei sōkan 日本経済統計総観 (General view of Japanese economic statistics)

Osaka, 1930. 1280p.

Basic for minutely itemized statistics from the early years of the Meiji period into the Taishō period.

Tōyō Keizai Shinpōsha   M71
東洋経済新報社

Meiji Taishō kokusei sōran 明治大正国勢総覧 (Outline of national conditions, Meiji and Taishō periods) 2d ed., enl. 1929. 764p.

Most detailed standard collection of statistics on banking, securities, commodities, trade, industry and society from the first recorded early in the Meiji period to 1924 or 1925, supplemented with statistics to 1914 on miscellaneous matters not covered in the main compilation.

Nihon Tōkei Kenkyūjo   M72
日本統計研究所

Nihon keizai tōkeishū: Meiji·Taishō·Shōwa 日本·経済統計集 明治·大正·昭和 (Collection of Japanese economic statistics. Meiji, Taishō, Shōwa periods) Nihon Hyōron Shinsha, 1958. 407p.

Statistical tables from 1868 to 1956, with comments and notes on sources, in sections on land, population, mining and industry, transportation and communication, agriculture, trade and balance of international payments, banking, finance, commodity prices, national life, national wealth and income, class structure and former colonies. Chronology of the history of statistics in Japan from 1869 to 1957 lists statistical studies and related matters.

Keizai Kikakuchō Chōsakyoku   M73
経済企画庁調査局
Kihon Nihon keizai tōkei 基本日本経済統計 (Basic Japanese economic statistics) Shiseido, 1959. 264, 16p.

Cumulative principal Japanese economic statistics from the Meiji period to about 1958, with appended chronology of Japanese economy.

Okurashō Rizaikyoku 大蔵省理財局   M74
and Nihon Ginkō 日本銀行
Zaisei keizai tōkei nenpō 財政経済統計年報 (Annual report on financial and economic statistics) Ōkura Zaimu Kyōkai, 1948. 847p.

Cumulative statistics from 1926 to about 1945 and detailed statistics from 1946 to 1948 on finance, banking and economy in general. Especially useful for war and early postwar years.

Nakayama, Ichiro 中山伊知郎   M75
Nihon no kokufu kōzō 日本の国富構造 (Structure of Japanese national wealth) Tōyō Keizai Shinpōsha, 1959. 632p.

The first half explains the principles and methods of the Economic Planning Agency in its investigation, completed in 1958, of national wealth in 1955, the first such postwar investigation, and the second half outlines the results, with statistics which include prewar and foreign estimates of national wealth.

M76

Tsūshō sangyō tōkei yōran 通商産業統計要覧 (Manual of statistics on trade and industry) 1957- . Comp. by Tsūshō Sangyōshō. Tsūshō Sangyō Chōsakai, 1957- . 8v. Annual.

Yamada, Yūzō 山田雄三 **M77**
Nihon kokumin shotoku suikei shiryō 日本国民所得推計資料 (Materials for estimating the national income of Japan) Enl. ed. Tōyō Keizai Shinpōsha, 1957. 220p.

ATLASES

Sekai Keizai Kenkyūjo **M78**
世界経済研究所
Sekai seiji keizai chizu 世界政治経済地図 (Atlas of world politics and economy) Ōtsuki Shoten, 1949. 165p.

Zenkoku Kyōiku Tosho 全国教育図書 **M79**
Nihon keizai chizu 日本経済地図 Economic atlas of Japan. 1954. 227p.

Sixty-one multi-colored maps show natural features, geology, commerce, industry, banking, etc., with 147 pages of explanation and 56 statistical tables.

Chihō Chōsa Kikan Zenkoku Kyōgikai **M80**
地方調査機関全国協議会 **and Tōhoku Kaihatsu Kenkyūkai** 東北開発研究会
Nihon chiiki gensei zusetsu 日本地域現勢図説 (Illustrated book of current regional conditions in Japan) Kawade Shobō, 1952. 224p.

Regional economic differences are pointed out and explained in maps and graphs.

POPULATION

BIBLIOGRAPHY

Sōrifu Tōkeikyoku Toshokan **M81**
総理府統計局図書館
Hōbun jinkō kankei bunken narabini shiryō kaidai 邦文人口関係文献並資料解題 (Japanese literature on population, with comments) 1951. 407p.

Compiled as of Aug. 1, 1951.

Nihon Yunesuko Kokunai Iinkai 日本ユ **M82**
ネスコ国内委員会 **and Nihon Gakujutsu Kaigi** 日本学術会議
Jinkō mondai kankei bunken mokuroku 人口問題関係文献目録Literature on population problems in Japan, 1945-1951. 1952. 46, 67, 20p.

DICTIONARY

Heibonsha 平凡社 **M83**
Jinkō daijiten 人口大事典 (Comprehensive cyclopedia of population) 1957. 940p.

Chapters 1-3 explain basic theories; chapter 4 covers population statistics; chapter 5 discusses population problems in foreign countries; chapter 6 does the same for Japan, and chapters 7-12 take up population and economy, population and society, population biology, family planning, emigration and population policies. Lists of organizations concerned with population and important reference works, statistics and population maps appended. Japanese and foreign terms indexed.

STATISTICS

United Nations. Statistical Office **M84**
Sekai Jinkō nenkan 世界人口年鑑 (World population yearbook). No. 12, 1961. Hara Shobō, 1961. 571p.

Japanese translation of v.12, 1960, of the *Demographic yearbook*, compiled by the Statistical Office of the United Nations, explaining how population statistics are computed and giving official statistics on population, births, deaths, marriages, etc. There is a special study of migration.

M85

Kokusei chōsa hōkoku 国勢調査報告
Population census of Japan. 1920- . 1920-35, 182v., Temporary census, 1939, 6v. published by Naikaku Tōkeikyoku; Temporary census, 1947, 7v., 1950, 54v. in 8 parts, 1955, 54v. in 5 parts, 1960, 54v. in 5 parts, by Sōrifu Tōkeikyoku (Bureau of Statistics, Office of the Prime Minister)

Report of the total population of Japan, geographical distribution, characteristics of occupation as well as age groups. Used as basic data for national policy making. A major census is taken every 10 years and a simple census half-way between; methods of collecting and enumerating items vary. Since World War II (re: 1950 Population census of Japan, v. 8) data for the intermediate census are about the same as for the major census. The last major census in 1960 was the 9th, the third regular census since the War.

M86

Jinkō dōtai tōkei 人口動態統計 Vital statistics. 1899- . Comp. by Kōseishō. 1903-42, 1946- . (126v. +) Annual.

v. 1 describes and explains compilation procedures and gives statistics on births, stillbirths, deaths, marriages and divorces. v. 2 covers causes of deaths, including those of foreigners in Japan and Japanese abroad. Key details also in English. Published by the Statistical Bureau of the Cabinet from 1899 through 1942. Republished in 1946 by the Welfare Ministry.

MANAGEMENT

BIBLIOGRAPHY

Sakamoto, Fujiyoshi 坂本藤良 **M87**
Keiei no meicho 経営の名著 (Famous books on management) How to select and study them. Keirin Shobō, 1962. 2v.

A selective bibliography of recent outstanding Japanese and foreign works with annotations. Lists of Japanese books are from 1946 to July, 1962.

DICTIONARIES

Takamiya, Susumu 高宮普 **M88**
Taikei keieigaku jiten 体系経営学辞典 (Systematic dictionary of management science) Daiyamondosha, 1962. 1509p.

Explains more fully than other dictionaries such new terms as "industrial engineering" and "research development" classified in 18 sections covering all aspects of management theories and practices. Appended are brief biographies of prominent authorities, abbreviations, research institutions and reference literature. Subject and name indexes.

Hirai, Yasutarō 平井泰太郎 **M 89**
Keieigaku jiten 経営学辞典 (Dictionary of business management) Daiyamondosha, 1952. 1304p.

Standard dictionary systematically covering both theories and practical matters, with references at the end of each entry. Brief biographies of Japanese and foreign management scholars. Indexes of Japanese and foreign terms and personal names.

Yamashiro, Akira 山城章 **M90**
Shinsen Keieigaku jiten 新撰経営学辞典 (New dictionary of management) Chūō Keizaisha, 1958. 515p.

General survey precedes annotated titles. Japanese authors listed.

Keiei Keizai Kenkyūjo **M91**
経営経済研究所
Keieigaku nyūmon jiten 経営学入門辞典 (Primer on management) Iwasaki Shoten, 1952. 388, 47p.

A handbook designed for both those wanting to study management and those engaged in management, covering the various branches of management economy, including Marxist theories and Soviet enterprise management problems. Indexes of subjects in Japanese and foreign languages and of personal names. Originally published as *Gendai keieigaku jiten* (Dictionary of modern management) by the same publisher in 1950.

Nakamura, Tsunejirō 中村常次郎 **M 92**
Kindai keieigaku kihon yōgo jiten 近代経営学基本用語辞典 (Dictionary of basic terms of modern management science) Shunjūsha, 1962. 290p.

Kigyō Keiei Kyōkai 企業経営協会 **M93**
Ei-Wa keiei keiri jiten 英和経営理辞典 (English-Japanese dictionary of management and accounting) Chūō Keizaisha, 1962. 214p.

Gives about 12,000 English terms related to management, bookkeeping, accounting, labor control, etc., including a few trade and insurance terms. Lists abbreviations, major foreign journals, and organizations.

HANDBOOKS

Furukawa, Eiichi 古川栄一 **et al.** **M94**
Keiei handobukku 経営ハンドブック (New management handbook) Rev. ed. Dōbunkan, 1956. 1212p.

Theoretical and practical management explained in 184 entries under the headings of general survey, finance, production, labor, business operations, accounts and clerical work. Japanese and foreign references listed. General index.

Keiei Keizai Kenkyūjo **M95**
経営経済研究所
Keiei zensho 経営全書 (Complete book of management) Zeimu Keiri Kyōkai, 1959. 1016p.

Manual of theories. Japanese and foreign terms and personal names indexed.

M96
Keiei rōmu handobukku 経営労務ハンドブック (Handbook of management and labor) Maruzen, 1963. 1300p.

Covers relations with labor from the standpoint of management in 42 chapters. Japanese and foreign reference list. Subject index.

M97

Jōhō kanri benran 情報管理便覧 (Documentation manual) Nikkan Kōgyō Shinbunsha, 1963. 1330, 49p.

Explains uses of reference materials in business management. Lists major international organizations concerned with documentation. Subject index.

M98

Chōsa keikaku benran 調査計画便覧 (Manual of research projects) Nikkan Kōgyō Shinbunsha, 1963. 1674, 13p.

Explains statistical, credit and other kinds of research for business enterprises, with list of statistical publications of government offices and public corporations and list of major foreign research institutions. Subject index.

M99

Shanai hyōjunka benran 社内標準化便覧 (Manual of company standardization) Nikkan Kōgyō Shinbunsha, 1964. 1520p.

Gives procedures for adoption and application of management regulations and standards for control of materials, quality, personnel, clerical work, etc. Subject index.

Tanaka, Yōjin 田中要人 **M100**
Saishin kaisha gyōmu kitei bunshū 最新会社業務規定文集 (Newest comprehensive collection of company regulations) Fujisawa, Ikeda Shoten, 1960. 1374p.

Gives model regulations, each with notes on the kind of company for which suited, on general affairs, documents, accounting, duties, wages, production, techniques, sales, purchases, materials, etc.

Chūshō Kigyō Shindan Kyōkai **M101**
中小企業診断協会
Kigyō shindan handobukku 企業診断ハンドブック (Handbook on diagnosis of enterprises) 1959. 2v.

v.1 covers theories of diagnosing commercial enterprises, with list of reference works. v. 2 describes in detail the diagnosis of retail shops and shopping centers and gives general diagnoses for other retail, wholesale and service enterprises.

Isobe, Kiichi 磯部喜一 **et al.** **M102**
Chūshō kōgyō keiei benran 中小工業経営便覧 (Manual on management of small- and me-

dium-scale industries) Morikita Shuppan, 1955. 699p.

Practical guidance for managers and administrators.

Zenkoku Chūshō Kigyō Dantai Chūōkai **M103**
全国中小企業団体中央会
Chūshō kigyō kumiai sōran 中小企業組合総覧 (Manual on unions in small- and medium-scale industries) 1960. 1136p.

Surveys the history, present state and finances of unions on the basis of information from the Smaller Enterprise Board, Central Bank of Commercial and Industrial Unions and Federation of Cooperative Unions, with pertinent statistics, a list of reference books and articles from 1932 to 1959, a directory of about 450 organizations and a directory of 1,700 representative men.

Chushō Kigyō P.R. Sentā **M104**
中小企業Ｐ．Ｒ．センター
Chūshō kigyō tōkei yōran 中小企業統計要覧 (Manual of statistics on small- and medium-scale industries) 1964. 334p.

Gives important statistics in surveying the scope of medium-scale and small enterprises, the structure and distribution of industries, manufacturing, commerce, service industries, unions, the money market, management, exports, labor, government investment in and loans to medium-scale and small industries, annual expenditures for commerce and industry, private loans, chambers of commerce and industry and developments in the diagnosis of medium-scale and small enterprises.

STATISTICS

M105

Shuyō kigyō keiei bunseki 主要企業経営分析 Analysis of financial statements of main industrial corporations in Japan. 1951- . Comp. by Nihon Ginkō Tōkeikyoku. Nihon Ginkō, 1952- . 26v. Biennial.

Former title: *Honpō shuyō kigyō keiei bunseki chōsa*, 1951-1959. English edition since 1962. 3v.

Zenkoku kigyō zaimu shohyō bunseki **M106**
tōkei 全国企業財務諸表分析統計 (Analytical statistics of financial statements of Japanese enterprises) 1958- . Comp. by Teikoku Kōshinjo. 1958- . 6v. Annual.

Like the analysis of financial statements by Dun & Bradstreet, in the United States, analyzes the statements of about 8,400 companies, classified by industries. Gives general survey and examples of management analysis. Indispensable for business reference and study of management analysis.

MONEY

Gaikoku Kawase Bōeki Kenkyūkai   M107
外国為替貿易研究会
Shitei gaikoku tsūka zuroku 指定外国通貨図
録 (Pictorial book of authorized foreign
currencies) 1963. 130p.

   Shown are the currencies of 14 countries authorized for acceptance in Japanese transactions by the
Finance Ministry. Appended are descriptions of trav-
eler's checks, related laws, etc.

Fujisawa, Masaru 藤沢優   M108
Sekai no kahei 世界の貨幣 (Coins of the
world) Nihon Kahei Chōsakai, 1961. 272p.
   Plates followed by notes.

Bankoku Kahei Kenkyūkai   M109
万国貨幣研究会
Nihon shihei katarogu 日本紙幣型録 (Catalogue of Japanese paper money) Bankoku Kahei
Yōkō, 1958. 3v.
   v.1 Government and Bank of Japan notes; v.2
Notes of Japanese banks abroad; v.3 Military currency.

Ōhashi, Yoshiharu 大橋義春   M110
Ishin ikō Nihon shihei taikei zukan 維新以降
日本紙幣大系図鑑 (Systematic presen-
tation in pictures of Japanese paper money after
the Meiji Restoration) Bankoku Kahei Kenkyūkai,
1957. 271p.

Ōkura Zaimu Kyōkai 大蔵財務協会   M111
Nihon tsūka hensen zukan 日本通貨変遷図
鑑 (Illustrated book of Japanese currency
changes) 1955. 24,124p.

Ōkurashō 大蔵省   M112
Dai Nihon kaheishi 大日本貨幣史 (History
of Japanese currency) Reprint ed. Naikaku
Insatsukyoku Chōyōkai, 1936-37. 8v.
   Basic work on currency from ancient times to early
in the Meiji period. Separate volumes on coins,
paper money and local money are followed by three
reference volumes on *hansatsu* (paper money issued
by *han* governments), loans, buying and selling,
prices of commodities, gold and silver, and foreign
trade. v. 7 gives weights and measures and exchange
rates. In the supplementary volume are a table of
contents for the set, currency tables, a chronology
and a subject index. Published originally, without
the supplement, in 1876-78 and reprinted in 1925-26.

Banking

BIBLIOGRAPHY

Sumitomo Shintaku Ginkō, Shintaku   M113
Kenkyūkai 住友信託銀行信託研究会
Shintaku kankei bunken mokuroku 信託関係文
献目録 (Bibliography of literature on
trust companies) Ōsaka, 1960. 177p.

   Lists books and articles published before Jan.,
1958, classified under general, law, economy, business and dictionaries. Appended are foreign materials grouped by languages, including Chinese.

DICTIONARIES

Takagaki, Torajirō 高垣寅次郎 **et al.**   M114
Taikei kin'yū jiten 体系金融辞典 (Systematic
dictionary of money) Tōyō Keizai Shinpōsha,
1953. 1080p.
   Covers terms related to monetary theories, systems,
policies and practices, with references at the end
of each entry. A list of important Japanese and
foreign literature (104p.) is appended, together with
a chronology of the money market from 1868 to 1952,
etc. Subject and personal name indexes.

Yamaguchi, Shigeru 山口茂 **and**   M115
Okinaka, Tsuneyuki 沖中恒幸
Gendai kin'yū jiten 現代金融辞典 (Dictionary
of present-day money market) Shunjūsha, 1959-
61. 5v.
   A manual compiled for those in the money market.
v.1-2 cover operations and laws; v.3, management
and supervision; v.4, systems and organs; v. 5,
administration and policies.

Suzuki, Kazunori 鈴木一憲   M116
Kin'yū yōgo jiten 金融用語辞典 (Dictionary of
financial terms) Kindai Sērususha, 1963.
290, 26p.
   Covers about 1,400 terms related to banking, securities, insurance and other financial matters, with
emphasis on those in current use. Indexes of terms
classified under banking, insurance and securities
and of Western-language terms.

HANDBOOK   DIRECTORY

Uehara, Satoshi 上原聡   M117
Kin'yū keizai benran 金融経済便覧 (Manual
of monetary economy) 1965 ed. Gakuyō Shobō,
1964. 480p.
   Financial, tax, and legal aspects.   Major Japa-

nese and foreign economic indicators and other information appended.   Subject index.

Nihon kin'yū meikan 日 本 金 融 名 鑑 (Directory **M118**
of Japanese finance) 1960- . Comp. by Nihon
Kin'yū Tsūshinsha.   1960- . 4v.   Annual.
Lists banks of all types, related institutions and
official agencies.

YEARBOOKS

Sekai kin'yū keizai nenpō 世 界 金 融 経 済 年 **M119**
報   (Annual report on the international money
market and economy) 17th, 1946-47 - . Comp.
by the Bank for International Settlements.   Tr.
by Tokyo Ginko Chōsabu.   Shiseidō, 1948-
17v.
Japanese translation of the annual report of the
Bank for International Settlements, surveying its
activities and world monetary trends. The first report translated is the 17th, for 1946-47. Since the
18th, the Research Division of the Bank of Tokyo
has done the translation.

Kawase seigen ni kansuru Kokusai Tsūka Kikin **M120**
nenji hōkoku 為 替 制 限 に 関 す る 国 際 通 貨
基 金 年 次 報 告   (Annual report of the International Monetary Fund on exchange restrictions)
No. 2, 1951- . Comp. by the International Monetary Fund. 1951- . 17v.
Japanese translation of the *Report on exchange
restrictions . . . .* of the International Monetary Fund,
beginning with that for 1951, giving a general survey
and trustworthy details of the exchange policies and
regulations of individual countries. Also published
in recent years as a supplement to the magazine *Gaikoku kawase* (Foreign exchange).

Ginkōkyoku kin'yū nenpō 銀 行 局 金 融 年 報 **M121**
(Annual report of the Banking Bureau on the
money market) No. 1, 1952- . Kin'yū Zaisei
Jijō Kenkyūkai, 1952- . 12v.
Basic for information on yearly developments.
Supplemented with "Current regulations of the Bank-
ing Bureau, Ministry of Finance".

CHRONOLOGY

Nihon Ginkō Chōsakyoku **M122**
日 本 銀 行 調 査 局
Nihon kin'yū nenpyō 日 本 金 融 年 表 (Chronolo-

gy of Japanese money market) 1868-1960.   Enl.
ed. 1961. 196p.

SOURCE MATERIALS

Nihon Ginkō Chōsakyoku **M123**
日 本 銀 行 調 査 局
Nihon kin'yūshi shiryō 日 本 金 融 史 資 料
(Sources on the history of the Japanese money
market) 1955- . 36v. In progress.
Documents on the money market, mainly from the
archives of the Bank of Japan, compiled since 1942
by the Economics Department of Tokyo University
under the direction of Takao Tsuchiya. The volumes
on the Meiji and Taishō periods were completed in
1961, and seven on the Shōwa period had been published by April, 1964.

Insurance

Ōbayashi, Ryōichi 大 林 良 一 **and** **M124**
Mizusawa, Kenzō 水 沢 謙 三
Hoken Jiten 保 険 辞 典   (Insurance dictionary)
Yūhikaku, 1962. 616p.
Though giving only 4,500 terms and briefer in its
explanations than **M125**, handy for general reference.

Yokoo, Tomeo 横 尾 登 米 雄 **et al.** **M125**
Hoken Jiten 保 険 辞 典   (Insurance dictionary)
Hoken Kenkyūjo, 1961-62. 2v.
Covers about 7,000 technical and common terms,
as well as some persons, connected with all
types of insurance. Reference list.

M126
Hoken nenkan 保 険 年 鑑   (Insurance yearbook) 1960- . Comp. by Seimei Hoken Kyōkai
and Nihon Songai Hoken Kyōkai. Ōkura Zaimu
Kyōkai, 1906-43, 1951- . 78v.+
Gives basic insurance statistics, to which are
added from the edition for 1957 a survey of insurance
activities, regulations and related statistics.   Key
details also in English in postwar editions. Compiled originally by the Ministry of Agriculture and Commerce and then by the Insurance Bureau, Ministry of
Commerce and Industry, until taken over by the
Banking Bureau, Ministry of Finance. Suspended
1940-1948 editions.

M127
Nihon hoken meikan 日 本 保 険 銘 鑑 (Japan in-
surance directory) 1952- . Comp. by Hoken
Hyoronsha. Nishinomiya, 1952- . 9v. Annual.
Lists companies with names of officers and busi-
ness summaries.

FINANCE

BIBLIOGRAPHY

Masui, Mitsuzō 増井光蔵   **M128**
A bibliography of finance. Keigyōsha, 1935.
1614, 116p.

Exhaustive listing of British, French, German
and American books and articles. Author index.

DICTIONARIES

Hayashi, Shūzō 林修三 **and**   **M129**
Morinaga, Teiichirō 森永貞一郎
Zaisei kaikei jiten 財政会計辞典 (Dictionary
of finance and accounting) Gakuyō Shobo, 1959.
511p.

Explains 813 common terms in current laws and
regulations on finance and accounting.

Inoue, Kanae 井上 鼎   **M130**
Taikei kanchō kaikei jiten 体系官庁会計辞
典 (Systematic dictionary of accounting in
government offices) Ōhama Shoten, 1959. 998p.

Arranged under 16 headings, accounting matters
are explained with cross references. List of important Japanese reference literature appended. Subject index.

Miyamoto, Yoshio 宮元義雄   **M131**
Chihō zaimu yōgo jitsumu jiten地方財務用語
実務辞典 (Practical dictionary of terms
used in local finances) Gakuyō Shobo, 1960.
231p.

Nihon Senbai Kōsha 日本専売公社 **M132**
Wa-Ei taiyaku Senbai yōgo jiten 和英対訳専
売用語辞典 (Japanese-English dictionary
of terms relating to monopolies) 1955. 903p.
Bibliography: p. 897-903.

YEARBOOKS

                      M133
Kuni no yosan 国の予算   (The country's
budget) 1949- . Comp. by Zaisei Chōsakai.
Dōyū Shobo, 1949- . 16v.

Compiled yearly by Finance Ministry officials to
make the national budget more easily comprehensible
than in the form in which it is enacted by the Diet.
With explanatory notes, revenue and expenditure in
the general and special accounts, Government invest-

ments and loans and the final budget of the preceding
fiscal year are given.

                      M134
Kokuzeichō jigyō nenpōsho 国税庁事業年
報書 (Annual report of the National Tax
Agency) 1949- . Comp. by Kokuzeichō.
1952- . 11v.

A general report on tax administration. Detailed
tax statistics are in the *Kokuzeichō tōkei nenpōsho* (Annual statistical report of the National Tax
Agency).

                      M135
Chihō kōei kigyō nenkan 地方公営企業年鑑
(Yearbook of local public enterprises) No. 1- .
Comp. by Jichishō.   Chihō Zaimu Kyōkai,
1955- . 10v.

Gives the size, finances and personnel of water,
gas, electricity and transportation systems, hospitals and other local public enterprises, with details
of their financial statements.

STATISTICS

                      M136
Zaisei keizai tōkei yōran   財政経済統計
要覧 (Manual of financial and economic statistics) 1951- .   Comp. by Ōkurashō.
1951- . 25v. Annual.

Expanded in recent editions to include wide range
of statistics. Published twice yearly until made an
annual in 1963. Preceded by *Zaimu keizai yōran-
tōkeihen*, 1950.

Tōyō Keizai Shinpōsha   **M137**
東洋経済新報社
Meiji Taishō zaisei shōran 明治大正財政
詳覧 (Detailed survey of finance in the Meiji
and Taishō periods) 1926. 760p.

Comprehensive basic collection of Meiji-Taisho
statistics on national and local finances, with tax
rates, a chronology, a list of officials concerned
with finance and a general survey of national and
local public property. Subject index. Can be used
advantageously with **M71**.

SOURCE MATERIALS

                      M138
Meiji zaiseishi 明治財政史 (Financial history of the Meiji period) Maruzen, 1904-5. 15v.

Written by officials directly concerned, its volumes
cover in detail financial organs, the accounts system,
the budget and settlement of accounts, treasury income and expenditure, taxation, the tobacco mo-

nopoly, national bonds, reserve funds, deposits, awards and allowances, emergency grants, currency and banking from 1868 to 1902. Subtitled *Matsukata zaisei jireki* (Matsukata's financial achievements).

Ōkurashō 大蔵省   **M139**
Meiji Taishō zaiseishi 明治大正財政史 (Financial history of the Meiji and Taishō periods) Keizai Ōraisha, 1955-59. 20v.

Finance Ministry officials, under the editorship of Shūzō Yoshikawa, cover the period from early Meiji through 1925 with emphasis since 1902, with a general survey and volumes on financial organs, the accounts system, annual accounts, taxation, customs duties, monopolies, national bonds, currency, deposits, banking, the money market, overseas finances, etc. There is a general table of contents. Reprinted from the 1936-40 edition of the Zaisei Keizai Gakkai.

Ōkurashō 大蔵省   **M140**
Showa zaiseishi 昭和財政史 (Financial history of the Shōwa period). Tōyō Keizai Shinpōsha, 1956- . 16v. In progress.

Continues **M138** and **M139** to 1945 under the editorship of Hyōe Ōuchi, with such scholars as Takeo Fujita, Seijirō Usami and Kiyoshi Ōshima collaborating with Finance Ministry officials. Volumes, each with a general survey, laws and regulations, cover the following topics: financial organs, annual accounts, extraordinary war expenditures, taxes, national bonds, national enterprises, public property, construction and repairs, currency, prices, the money market, government deposits, government investments, the international money market, foreign trade, local finances, overseas finances and the accounts system. Yet to be published as of April, 1964, are a general introduction and a volume of chronological tables and indexes.

Ōkurashō 大蔵省   **M141**
Dai Nihon sozeishi 大日本租税史 (History of Japanese taxation) Naikaku Insatsukyoku Chōyōkai, 1925-27. 3v.

Classifies and lists materials from ancient times to 1880 in sections on cultivated fields, land taxes, taxes in kind, unpaid labor, forced labor, etc. Compiled at the order of Finance Minister Masayoshi Matsukata in 1881 to provide background information for tax policies. Originally published in 30 volumes bound in Japanese style in 1882-85.

COMMERCE

BIBLIOGRAPHY

Tōhoku Gakuin Daigaku, Keiri   **M142**
Kenkyūjo 東北学院大学経理研究所

Kaikeigaku bunken mokuroku 会計学文献目録 (Bibliography of accountancy) Sendai, 1955. 171p.

Japanese books and articles and foreign books published from 1949 to 1953 are listed.

DICTIONARIES

Fukami, Giichi 深見義一 **et al.**   **M143**
Gendai shōgaku jiten 現代商学事典 (Dictionary of modern commercial science) Shinkigensha, 1961. 741, 35p.

Kōsaka, Torizō 上坂酉三   **M144**
Shōhin daijiten 商品大辞典 (Comprehensive dictionary of commodities) 2d ed., rev. and enl. Tōyō Keizai Shinpōsha, 1964. 1684p.

Classifies commodities in 31 major groups, each subdivided into categories, with separate section on commodity packaging. Lists of dealer organizations and institutions for the inspection of commodities appended. Glossary index.

Watanabe, Susumu 渡辺進   **M145**
Kijun kaikeigaku jiten 基準会計学辞典 (Standard accounting dictionary) Chūō Keizaisha, 1962. 425p.

Explains 1,105 terms in common use selected by the Accounting Terms Subdivision of the Economic Terms Division, Council for the Promotion of Science, Ministry of Education. Index of terms in European languages.

Kōbe Daigaku Kaikeigaku Kenkyūshitsu   **M146**
神戸大学会計学研究室
Kaikeigaku jiten 会計学辞典 (Dictionary of accounting) Enl. ed. Dōbunkan, 1961. 1200p.

Standard dictionary, with the length of entries in proportion to their importance. Literature in Japanese and European languages listed. Subject index.

Yokohama Shiritsu Daigaku Shōgakubu   **M147**
横浜市立大学商学部
Kaikei jiten 会計事典 (Accounting dictionary) Rev. new ed. Dōbunkan, 1964. 463p.

Satō, Kōichi 佐藤孝一   **M148**
Shinsen Boki kaikei jiten 新撰簿記会計事典 (New dictionary of bookkeeping and accounting) Chūō Keizaisha, 1958. 415p.

Terms in Western languages are indexed.

Yokohama Shiritsu Daigaku Shōgakubu   **M149**
横浜市立大学商学部

Boki jiten 簿記事典 (Bookkeeping cyclopedia) Rev. ed. Dōbunkan, 1964. 456p.

Emphasizes commercial bookkeeping. Reference list. Subject index.

Yokohama Shiritsu Daigaku Shōgakubu **M150**
横浜市立大学商学部

Genka keisan jiten 原価計算事典 (Dictionary of cost accounting) Rev. new ed. Dōbunkan, 1964. 467p.

Nihon Keizai Shinbunsha **M151**
日本経済新聞社

Kabushiki yōgo jiten 株式用語事典 (Dictionary of stock market terms) 1958. 215p.

HANDBOOKS

Yokohama Shiritsu Daigaku Shōgakubu **M152**
横浜市立大学商学部

Kindai kaikeigaku handobukku 近代会計学ハンドブック (Modern accounting handbook) Dōbunkan, 1958. 820p.

Emphasis is on financial accounting. Japanese and foreign reference literature given. Subjects, personal names indexed.

Ōta, Tetsuzō 太田哲三 **et al.** **M153**
Kaikei handobukku 会計ハンドブック (Handbook of accounting) 1958 ed., rev. and enl. Chūō Keizaisha, 1957. 1520p.

Explains the theory and practice of modern accounting in 27 chapters on bookkeeping principles, how to keep books, financial statements, profit and loss statements, depreciation, capital, cost accounting, etc. Pertinent laws and regulations appended. Japanese reference literature listed. Subject index.

Iwata, Iwao 岩田巌 **et al.** **M154**
Boki kaikei handobukku 簿記会計ハンドブック (Bookkeeping and accounting handbook) Dōbunkan, 1952. 2v.

Gives basic information in 36 chapters, with accounting tables, English and American accounting terms and a list of Japanese and foreign references (95p.) in a supplementary volume. General index. One-volume edition, published in 1957, with slight revisions but without the contents of the supplementary volume except for the index.

Kōbe Daigaku Kaikeigaku Kenkyūshitsu **M155**
神戸大学会計学研究室

Genka kaikei handobukku 原価会計ハンドブック (Cost accounting handbook) Zeimu Keiri Kyōkai, 1959. 1240p.

Genka kanri benran 原価管理便覧 (Manual of cost control) Nikkan Kōgyō Shinbunsha, 1963. 1580p. **M156**

General survey of the theory and practice with chapters on cost accounting, control techniques, cost reduction, cost accounting in relation to taxation, etc. Reference list. Subject index.

Shōken Shijō Kenkyūkai **M157**
証券市場研究会

Shōken handobukku 証券ハンドブック (Securities handbook) Daiyamondosha, 1959. 764p.

Twelve chapters on the securities system, securities exchanges, etc., are followed by a list of reference literature. Subject index.

Nihon Mākettingu Kyōkai **M158**
日本マーケティング協会

Mākettingu benran マーケティング便覧 (Marketing handbook) Maruzen, 1962. 1286p.

Standard handbook of theory and practice in 29 chapters, further subdivided. Subject index.

Hayashi, Hisakichi 林久吉 **et al.** **M159**
Mākettingu handobukku マーケティング・ハンドブック (Marketing handbook) Dōbunkan, 1961. 880p.

Covers marketing techniques, controls, advertising, laws, etc. Subjects and personal names indexed.

Shimizu, Akira 清水晶 **et al.** **M160**
Hanbai jiten 販売事典 (Marketing dictionary) Dōbunkan, 1956. 402p.

Explains in 26 chapters sales theories, sales planning, sales systems, salesmanship, packaging, etc. Appended are excerpts of pertinent laws and a list of Japanese and foreign reference literature. Subject index.

Keiō Gijuku Kōkokugaku Kenkyūkai **M161**
慶応義熟広告学研究会

Gendai kōkoku handobukku 現代広告ハンドブック (Modern advertising handbook) Dōbunkan, 1958. 598p.

Explains the theory of advertising in 12 sections written mainly by scholars and its practice in 21 sections written by company experts. Japanese and foreign reference literature listed. Subject index.

Shimizu, Akira 清水晶 et al. **M162**
Kōkoku jiten 広告事典 (Dictionary of advertising) Dōbunkan, 1956. 399p.

Explains the theories and practice of advertising in 28 chapters on advertising and management, advertising and market research, costs and effects of advertising, analysis of advertising budgets, etc. Japanese reference literature listed. Subject index.

DIRECTORIES

M 163

Kaisha nenkan 会社年鑑 (Yearbook of companies) 1949- . Comp. by Nihon Keizai Shinbunsha. 1949- . 16v.

Lists 1,660 companies by categories and gives for each its head office, branches, capital, officers, history, assets, income and expenditure, business conditions, stock prices, major stockholders, labor conditions, bank affiliations, etc.

M 164

Kaisha sōkan 会社総鑑 (General survey of companies) 1960- . Comp. by Nihon Keizai Shinbunsha. 1960- . 5v. Annual.

With emphasis on those not in **M163**, covers about 3,400 companies, including newspapers , advertising, broadcasting and publishing agencies and other enterprises of which the financial statements ordinarily are not made public.

M 165

Kabushiki kaisha nenkan 株式会社年鑑 (Japanese corporations yearbook) 1950- . Comp. by Yamaichi Shōken. 1949- . 15v.

Covers 1,388 companies listed on Japanese security exchanges, with table of contents classifying the companies by kinds and index. English edition published since 1960. 4v.

M166

Jōjō kaisha sōran 上場会社総覧 (Survey of listed companies) 1949- . Comp. by Tokyo Shōken Torihikijo. Nihon Shōken Shinbunsha, 1951- . 15v. Annual.

Describes the structure and operations of 709 companies listed in the First Section of the Tokyo Stock Exchange, divided into 25 categories. Quotations of their stocks, stock distribution, summaries of their financial statements, etc., appended.

M 167

Daiyamondo kaisha yōran ダイヤモンド会社要覧 (Diamond survey of companies) 1934- . Comp. by Daiyamondosha. 1934- . 42v. Semiannual.

Former title: *Poketto Kaisha yōran*, 1934-1943. Suspended: 1944-49.

The latest issue lists 1,560 companies.

M 168

Nihon kigyō yōran 日本企業要覧 (Manual of Japanese enterprises) 1960- . Comp. by Shokuryō Keizai Shinbunsha, 1961, 1963- . 3v. Annual.

Differs from other such manuals and directories in listing companies in six groups according to the dates of their settlement of accounts. Company names indexed.

M 169

Teikoku ginkō kaisha yōroku 帝国銀行会社要録 (Digest of the Empire's banks and companies) 1st ed. - . Comp. by Teikoku Kōshinjo. 1912- . 43v. Annual.

Lists 83,122 enterprises.

M 170

Tōyō Keizai kaisha jinjiroku 東洋経済会社人事録 (Tōyō Keizai directory of company personnel) 1963- . Comp. by Tōyō Keizai Shinpōsha, 1963- . 2v. Annual.

Lists about 100,000 officers of 1,404 Japanese companies, including virtually all of importance. Table of contents groups companies by types of business. Company names indexed.

M 171

Daiyamondo kaisha shokuinroku ダイヤモンド会社職員録 (Diamond directory of company officers) No. 1- . Daiyamondosha, 1935-42, 1950, 1952- . 22v. Semiannual since 1964.

Standard listing of the officers of about 750 companies arranged by types of business. Company names indexed.

COMPANY HISTORIES

Kin'yū Keizai Kenkyūjo 金融経済研 **M172** 究所 **and Ōhara Shakai Mondai Kenkyūjo** 大原社会問題研究所

Honpō kaishashi mokuroku 本邦会社史目録 (Catalogue of Japanese company histories) Kin'yū Keizai Kenkyūjo, 1962. 146p.

Supersedes all earlier catalogue of this kind. The histories are classified by branches of industry and types of enterprise, with indexes for types of enterprise, corporate names, subjects and titles. Locations of copies noted.

Keizai Dantai Rengōkai **M 173** 経済団体連合会

Shashi keizai dantaishi mokuroku 社史・経済団体史目録 (Catalogue of histories of companies and economic organizations) 1961.

88p.

Lists 918 histories, mostly in the collection of the secretariat of the Federation of Economic Organizations (Keizai Dantai Rengōkai).

Tsūshō Sangyōshō 通商産業省 **M 174**
Nihon kaishashi sōran 日本会社史総覧 (Historical survey of Japanese companies) Keizai Ōraisha, 1954. 906p.

Gives a general history of different branches of industry and the histories to April, 1954, of about 1,000 major companies.

YEARBOOKS

M 175
Sekai shōhin nenpō 世界商品年報 (Annual report on world commodities) 1959- . comp. by the United Nations. Tr. by Nihon ECAFE Kyōkai. Tōyō Keizai Shinpōsha, 1959- . 4v.

Japanese translation of the annual *Commodity survey*, compiled by the United Nations, giving world commodity trends and surveying important commodity markets, with statistics. Each issue dated one year later than the original.

M 176
Nihon chūshō kigyō nenkan 日本中小企業年鑑 (Yearbook of Japanese small- and medium-scale industries) 1957, 1960. Comp. by Chūshō Kigyō Kenkyūjo. 1957, 60. 2v.

Despite the title, issued only in 1957 and 1960. Gives a general survey, detailed descriptions, list of pertinent organizations, chronological record of developments (from Aug., 1945, to Sep., 1956, in the 1957 issue; from 1957 to June, 1959, in the 1960 issue), list of books and articles (from before the war to 1956 in the 1957 issue; from 1957 in the 1960 issue) and statistics.

M 177
Chūshō kigyō hakusho 中小企業白書 (White paper on small- and medium-scale industries) 1963- . Comp. by Chūshō Kigyōchō. 1964- . 1v.

Gives trends, statistics and plans for succeeding year for enterprises incorporated with capital of less than ¥50,000,000 or fewer than 300 employees or are privately owned with fewer than 300 employees.

M 178
Shōken nenkan 証券年鑑 (Securities yearbook) 1958- . Comp. by Tokyo Shōken Torihikijo. Nihon Shōken Shinbunsha, 1958- . 7v.

Standard reference on operations, policies and organization of the Japanese security market, with statistics on major Japanese and foreign market indicators. Index of terms. Established with the merger in 1958 of *Tōshō nenkan* (Tōshō yearbook), *Shōken nenpō* (Annual report on securities) and *Shōken nenkan* (Securities yearbook).

M 179
Kōkoku nenkan 広告年鑑 (Advertising yearbook). 1925- . Comp. by Mannensha. Osaka, 1924-42, 1952- . 31v.

Oldest in the field. Covers advertising ethics, editing of advertising copy, magazines, newspapers (including trade and student papers), commercial broadcasting and overseas media. Directory of organizations and companies. Reference materials listed.

M 180
Dentsū Kōkoku nenkan 電通広告年鑑
Dentsū AD annual 1956- . Comp. by Dentsū. 1956- . 9v.

A general survey is followed by sections on media, techniques, marketing research, advertising statistics, publicity, foreign advertising, organizations and companies, reference literature, etc.

STATISTICS

M 181
Shōgyō tōkeihyō 商業統計表 (Commercial statistical tables) 1952- . Comp. by Tsūshō Sangyōshō. 1954- . 12v. Annual.

Gives the findings in the nationwide commercial census carried out every two years since 1952. Those for 1952, 1954 and 1956 are each in 2v., the first on prefectures and cities and the second on different types of industry, with each volume divided into general statistics, statistics on shops organized as legal persons and private shops employing permanent workers, and statistics on shops not employing permanent workers. The 1958 findings are in 3v., one on industries and two on commodities.

Hakuhōdō, Chōsabu 博報堂調査部 **M 182**
Shijō shihyō 市場指標 消費市場の府県別特性 (Market indicators) Characteristics of prefectural consumer market. 2d ed., rev. 1964. 466p.

Outlines the Japanese consumer market, gives market indicators for each prefecture and explains the use of indicators.

Sōrifu Tōkeikyoku 総理府統計局 **M 183**
Jūnen no kouri kakaku... 10年の小売価格 小売物価統計調査総合報告 (Ten years of retail prices; comprehensive report on investi-

gation of retail price statistics) 1962. 387p.

Gives statistics on retail prices in 54 Japanese cities from 1950 to 1960, with notes, supplementary tables and prices of selected commodities in villages. Headings also in English.

Nihon Ginkō Tōkeikyoku   **M184**
日本銀行統計局
Oroshiuri bukka shisu 卸売物価指数 (Wholesale price indexes) 1887-1962. 1964. 486p.

Gives wholesale price indexes since 1887 with adjustment for revisions to facilitate comparisons. Major headings also in English.

Trade

BIBLIOGRAPHY

    M185

Kaigai shiryōshū 海外資料輯 Overseas market research sources. 1961- . Comp. by Nihon Bōeki Shinkōkai. 1962- . 3v. Annual.

A catalogue of the library of the Nihon Bōeki Shinkōkai (Japan External Trade Recovery Organization) popularly known as JETRO, includes books on the economy of foreign countries or trade chiefly in foreign languages, tariff tables, directories, statistics, newspapers and magazines. Title and country indexes.

DICTIONARIES

Kōsaka, Torizō 上坂酉三   **M186**
Bōeki jitsumu jiten 貿易実務辞典 (Dictionary of foreign trade operations) Seirin Shoin Shinsha, 1964. 836p.

Brief explanations with international regulations and special laws appended. Classified table of contents and indexes of Western and Japanese terms.

Tokyo Ginkō Chōsabu   **M187**
東京銀行調査部
Bōeki kawase jiten 貿易為替辞典 (Dictionary of foreign trade and exchange) Shiseidō, 1960. 347, 73p.

Covers special trade and exchange terms and related political and economic terms. List of world currencies appended. Index in Japanese and European languages (73p.).

Fujita, Jintarō 藤田仁太郎   **M188**
Ei-Wa bōeki sangyō jiten 英和貿易産業辞典 Kenkyūsha's English-Japanese dictionary of trade and industry. Kenkyūsha, 1955. 1012p.

Explains terms related to trade, commodities and pertinent organizations and regulations. Weights and measures appended.. Japanese-English index.

Nihon Yūsen Kabushiki Kaisha   **M189**
日本郵船株式会社 **and**
Kaiun Bōeki Kenkyūkai 海運貿易研究会
Kaiun bōeki shōjiten 海運貿易小辞典
Shipping and foreign trade vocabulary. Izumi Shobō, 1962. 298p.

Japanese equivalents and brief explanations of English and a few other foreign shipping and trade terms, with list of abbreviations and tables of tonnage conversion, currency par values, etc.

YEARBOOKS

    M190

Tsūshō hakusho 通商白書 (White paper on international trade) 1949- . Comp. by Tsūshō Sangyōshō. Tsūshō Sangyō Chōsakai, 1949- . 24v.

Gives the yearly trade statistics of the Ministry of International Trade and Industry. Divided since the 1958 issue into 2v., the first of which is a general survey. Titled *Nihon bōeki no genjō* (Present state of Japanese trade) before 1955.

    M191

Kaigai shijō hakusho 海外市場白書 (White paper on overseas markets) 1957- . Comp. by Nihon Bōeki Shinkōkai. 1957- . 8v.
Special issue of *Kaigai Shijō* (monthly), published by JETRO.

Surveys and statistics of trade potentialities of markets, divided by geographical areas, with a separate section for Communist countries. Commodities indexed.

STATISTICS

    M192

Bōeki tōkei nenkan 貿易統計年鑑 (Trade statistics yearbook) 1953- . Comp. by the United Nations, Statistical Office. Tr. by Ryōkichi Minobe. Hara Shobō, 1955- . 4v.

Japanese translation, with the English text also given, of the *Yearbook of International Trade Statistics*, compiled by the United Nations, giving comprehensive world trade statistics. Only the 1953 and 1961 editions translated in full. v.2 of 1956 has been translated independently as *Kokusai Rengō bōeki yōran* (United Nations trade survey), and only v.1 of 1958 has been translated.

M 193

Bōeki nenkan 貿易年鑑 (Foreign trade year-book) 1961- . Comp. by Nihon Kanzei Kyōkai. 1961- . 3v.

A general survey of trade in the preceding year is followed by sections on commodity and market trends, trade and tariff policies, trade negotiations, activities of international bodies, etc., and such reference data as statistics and lists of non-liberalized commodities.

M 194

Soren bōeki tōkei nenkan ソ連貿易統計年鑑 (Statistical yearbook of Soviet trade) 1956- . Comp. by U.S.S.R., Ministerstvo Vneshnei Torgovli. Tr. by Kokusai Jijō Kenkyūkai. Japan Puresu·Sābisu, 1958- . 7v.

Ajia Keizai Kenkyūjo   **W 195**
アジア経済研究所
Ajia bōeki tōkei アジア貿易統計 Asian trade statistics; statistics on foreign trade between the Asian countries and industrial nations classified by commodities. 1956-1958. 1961. 503p.

M 196

Nihon gaikoku bōeki nenpyō 日本外国貿易年表   Trade of Japan ... country by commodity. 1882- . Comp. by Ōkurashō Shuzeikyoku. 1882-1939, 1940-47, 1948- . (215v.+) Annual.

Gives official trade statistics year by year. Issues before 1940, when it was suspended, have separate tables for commodities, countries and ports. From 1948 to 1954 and again since 1962, there are only two divisions, imports and exports. Issues from 1955 through 1961 have tables of commodities by countries and two tables of countries, one of imports from them and the other of Japanese exports to them. Headings in postwar issues are also in English. Prewar title: *Dai Nihon gaikoku bōeki nenpyō.* Prior to 1882 statistical records can be traced back to 1867 in *Dai Nihon kakukō yushitsunyū buppin nenpyō* and other titles.

Tōyō Keizai Shinpōsha   **M 197**
東洋経済新報社
Nihon bōeki seiran 日本貿易精覧 (Detailed survey of Japanese trade) Enl. ed. 1935. 708p.

Standard for trade statistics from 1868 to 1933, including exports from Sakhalin, Formosa and Korea to Japan proper and foreign countries. Introduction points out trade changes in this period.

SOCIETY · FOLKLORE

❧ Includes sociology, labor, social welfare, folklore, manners and customs, and legends.

SOCIOLOGY

Fukutake, Tadashi 福武直 **et al.** **N 1**
Shakaigaku jiten 社会学辞典 (Dictionary of sociology) Yūhikaku, 1958. 977, 83p.
  Standard work with good coverage of such recently conspicuous social phenomena as *mura-hachibu* (village ostracism) and *chiiki tōsō* (local strikes or "struggles"). Includes terms in related sciences. Many cross-references. Subject and personal name indexes.

Kanba, Toshio 樺俊雄 **N 2**
Shinsen shakaigaku jiten 新撰社会学辞典 (New dictionary of sociology) Chūō Keizaisha, 1959. 350p.

Shinmei, Masamichi 新明正道 **N 3**
Shakaigaku jiten 社会学辞典 (Cyclopedia of sociology) Kawade Shobō, 1944. 801, 134p.
  Pt.1 surveys the nature and content of sociology; pt.2 gives the history of its development as a science, with details of its progress in individual countries and a chronology. Subject and personal name indexes.

Fukutake, Tadashi 福武直 **et al.** **N 4**
Kōza Shakaigaku 講座社会学 (Lecture series: Sociology) Supp. Tokyo Daigaku Shuppankai, 1958. 288p.
  Contains glossary and chronological tables.

Shimizu, Ikutarō 清水幾太郎 **N 5**
Masu komyunikēshon kōza マス・コミュニ ケーション講座 (Lectures on mass communication) v. 6, Kawade Shobō, 1955. 397p.
  Reference literature listed.

Yasuda, Saburō 安田三郎 **N 6**
Shakai chōsa handobukku 社会調査ハンドブック (Handbook of social research) Yūhikaku, 1960. 249p.
  Includes annotated list of social research literature, annotated statistics, examples of questionnaires, etc. Glossary index.

N 7
Dokusho yoron chōsa 読書世論調査 (Survey of public opinion on reading) No. 1 (1947)- . Mainichi Shinbunsha, 1948- . 17v. Annual.
  Report of annual sampling survey of reading plans, opinions of good books, purchases of books and periodicals, hours spent watching television, etc. of Japanese over 16, with diagrams and tables. Also summarizes results of similar surveys among elementary, junior and senior high school students. Survey of bestsellers of various book-stores appended. The first survey was titled *Donna hon ga yomareruka* (What books do people read?).

Social thought · Socialism

❧ Some entries under philosophy, religion and economics are useful.

Ōhara Shakai Mondai Kenkyūjo **N 8**
大原社会問題研究所
Nihon shakai shugi bunken 日本社会主義文献 (Literature on socialism in Japan) To 1914. Dōjinsha Shoten, 1929. 255p.
  Chronological listing from 1882 to 1914 of liter-

ature on socialism in the broad sense, including related fields. Pt. 1 covers books, pamphlets, declarations and handbills; pt. 2, periodicals. Indexes of authors, translators and newspapers and magazines. Basic for study of social thought.

Watanabe, Yoshimichi 渡部義通 **and** **N 9**
Shioda, Shōbei 塩田庄兵衛
Nihon shakai shugi bunken kaisetsu 日本社会主義文献解説 (Annotated bibliography of Japanese socialism) From the Meiji Restoration through the Pacific War. Ōtsuki Shoten, 1958. 339, 31p.

Notable as first such compilation not restricted by official policies. Covers more years than **N8** but includes fewer materials of the Meiji period. Divided into five periods, each with general survey. Brief chronological table of Japanese literature on socialism appended. Personal name and title indexes.

Shinmei, Masamichi 新明正道 **and** **N 10**
Kanba, Toshio 樺俊雄
Shakai shisōshi jiten 社会思想史辞典 (Dictionary of history of social thought) New ed., rev. Osaka, Sōgensha, 1962. 667, 80p.

Describes and explains social ideas in the order of their development, with supplementary entries on subjects and persons, each with references. Subject and personal name indexes.

Labor

BIBLIOGRAPHY

Koyama, Hirotake 小山弘健 **N 11**
Nihon rōdō undō shakai undō kenkyūshi 日本労働運動社会運動研究史 戦前・戦後の文献解説 (History of Japanese studies of labor and social movements) An annotated bibliography of prewar and postwar literature. Kyoto, Sangatsu Shobō, 1957. 296p.

Classified arrangement of books and articles from the Meiji period to mid-1956, with general explanations. Pt. 1 covers general studies; pt. 2, specific studies; pt. 3, biographies, records of incidents, related reference works and bibliographies. Indexed.

Rōdō Kagaku Kenkyūjo **N 12**
労働科学研究所
Fujin rōdō ni kansuru bunken shōroku 婦人労働に関する文献抄録 (Abstracts of literature on women's labor) 1941. 2v. (Rōdō Kagaku Kenkyūjo hōkoku, pt. 1)

v. 1, Japanese materials; v. 2, European materials.

Each volume gives a bibliography, followed by abstracts. Compiled for the Cabinet Planning Board, which issued its own edition.

Rōdō Kagaku Kenkyūjo **N 13**
労働科学研究所
Shōnen rōdō ni kansuru bunken shōroku 少年労働に関する文献抄録 (Abstracts of literature on child labor) 1943. 2v. (Rōdō Kagaku Kenkyūjo hōkoku, pt. 3)

v. 1, Japanese materials; v. 2, European materials.

Parallels **N12**.

Nihon Ōyō Shinri Gakkai **N 14**
日本応用心理学会
Nihon sangyō shinri kankei bunken mokuroku 日本産業心理関係文献目録 (Bibliography of industrial psychology in Japan) Rōdō Kagaku Kenkyūjo. 1963. 143p.

Publications from the Meiji period are listed in three parts: works by psychologists, works by non-psychologists and publications of government offices, universities, institutes and other organizations. Biographical data for authors. Indexes, cumbersome because divided into three parts, of names of persons and organizations, magazines, and books.

DICTIONARIES

Rōdō Kagaku Kenkyūjo **N 15**
労働科学研究所
Rōdō kagaku jiten 労働科学辞典 (Cyclopedia of the science of labor) Kawade Shobō, 1949. 327, 59p.

With emphasis on labor-management problems, 208 topics are arranged in 12 chapters. Subject index.

Rōdōshō Shokugyō Anteikyoku **N 16**
労働省職業安定局
Shokugyō shōjiten 職業小辞典 (Small dictionary of occupations) Koyō Mondai Kenkyūkai, 1957. 1567p.

Rōdōshō Shokugyō Anteikyoku **N 17**
労働省職業安定局
Shokugyō jiten 職業辞典 (Dictionary of occupations) Koyō Mondai Kenkyūkai, 1953. 2v.

Pt. 1 classifies occupations from the most general to the most specific, some of them with explanations. Pt. 2 lists and explains occupational names and gives the duties associated with them. Compiled for use by Public Employment Security agencies.

Rōdōshō 労働省 **N 18**
Saishin rōdō yōgo jiten 最新労働用語辞典
(Newest dictionary of labor terms) Nikkan Rōdō
Tsūshinsha, 1962. 722p.

About 3,000 terms covered.

Sangyō Rōdō Chōsajo **N 19**
産業労働調査所
Chingin jiten 賃金辞典 (Dictionary of wages)
2d ed., rev. Rōdō Shūhōsha, 1963. 436p.

Entries classified in 12 sections. Diagrams and
tables indexed apart from subject index.

HANDBOOKS

Nakayama, Ichirō 中山伊知郎 **N 20**
Chingin kihon chōsa 賃金基本調査 (Basic
research on wages) Their composition, form and
organization. Tōyō Keizai Shinpōsha, 1956.
1392p.

A guide to wage problems giving the findings of
the Committee for Basic Research on Wages of the
Statistical Research Society. Bibliography of postwar literature on wages, wage statistics and chronology of wage problems appended.

Nihon Ōyō Shinri Gakkai **N 21**
日本応用心理学会
Sangyō shinri handobukku 産業心理ハンド
ブック (Handbook of industrial psychology)
Dōbunkan, 1958. 1316p.

Designed for use by those working with industrial
workers, summarizes the results of recent research,
including that of the Industrial Psychology Division
of the Psychology Society during the war, in a general survey and chapters on administration, labor,
occupations, operations, safety and sales. Emphasis is on human problems. Reference literature
listed and major research organs described. General
and personal name indexes.

Rōdōshō 労働省 **N 22**
Shokugyō handobukku 職業ハンドブック
(Handbook of occupations) Nakayama Shoten,
1956. 557p.

Rōdō Chōsa Kyōgikai **N 23**
労働調査協議会
Rōdō kumiai jitsumu benran 労働組合実務
便覧 (Manual of labor union affairs) Rev. ed.
Ōtsuki Shoten, 1961. 984p.

Provides practical guidance for union officers and
members in sections on the nature of unions, union

activities, workers' conditions and union demands,
welfare, and social security. Lists of major unions
and other labor organizations appended. Detailed
table of contents, but no index.

YEARBOOKS

N 24
Kokusai rōdō keizai tōkei nenkan 国際労働
経済統計年鑑 (International yearbook of
labor economy statistics) 1955- . Comp. by
the International Labor Organization. Tr. by
Ichiro Nakayama. Nihon ILO Kyōkai, 1956- .
8v.

Japanese version of the *Yearbook of labour statistics*, published by the International Labor Organization, giving basic statistics on labor in all
countries, with list of reference works and sources.
Headings also in English.

N 25
Rōdō nenkan 労働年鑑 (Labor yearbook)
1947-1963. Comp. by Katsura Rōdō Kankei Kenkyūjo. 1946-62. 17v.

Covers not only labor but also general economic
matters in sections on Japan and foreign countries,
followed by chronicles of Japanese and foreign labor
developments from April to March, lists of government offices and organizations concerned with labor,
and statistics.

N 26
Nihon rōdō nenkan 日本労働年鑑 (Japan
labor yearbook) No. 1- . Comp. by Ōhara
Shakai Mondai Kenkyūjo. Tōyō Keizai Shinpōsha, 1920-1940, 1949- . 36v.

Gives a year's record of Japanese labor developments and surveys labor conditions, movements and
policies. Reference works listed. Directories of
unions and related organizations.

N 27
Rōdō hakusho 労働白書 労働経済の分析
(White paper on labor) Analysis of labor economy.
1948- . Comp. by Rōdōshō Rōdō Tōkei Chōsabu.
Rōdō Hōrei Kyōkai, 1950- . 16v.

Covers developments during the year in a general
survey and sections, with many statistical tables,
on employment and unemployment, wages, working
hours and accidents, living conditions of workers
and labor-management relations. Titled *Rōdō
keizai no bunseki* (Analysis of labor economy) until
1953.

N 28

Rōdō tōkei nenpō 労働統計年報 Yearbook of labor statistics 1948- . Comp. by Rōdōshō Rōdō Tōkei Chōsabu. Rōdō Hōrei Kyōkai, 1950- . 15v.

Former title: *Rōdō tōkei chōsa nenpō* (Annual report on investigation of labor statistics)

Basic official statistics under headings of labor economy indicators, employment and unemployment, productivity, wages, working hours, accidents, living costs, social insurance, unions and disputes. Major details also in English.

N 29

Rōmu nenkan 労務年鑑 (Labor yearbook) 1963- . Comp. by Nihon Rōmu Kenkyūkai. 1963- . 2v.

Edited, unlike **N27**, **N28** and *Rōdō gyōsei yōran**, from an entirely non-official viewpoint, it has sections on labor and economic trends, labor policies, labor management, labor-management relations, working hours, wages, education and training, and health and welfare. Appended are a chronology and lists of references and labor officers of major companies.

* **Rōdō gyōsei yōran** 労働行政要覧 (Survey of labor administration) 1954- . Comp. by Rōdōshō. Rōdō Hōrei Kyōkai, 1954- . 9v.

DIRECTORIES

Shakai Rōdō Kyōkai 社会労働協会 **N 30**
Rōdō jinji meikan 労働人事名鑑 (Who's who of labor) 2d ed., rev. 1960. 1361, 102p.

CLASSIFICATION OF OCCUPATIONS

Gyōsei Kanrichō Tōkei Kijunkyoku **N 31**
行政管理庁統計基準局
Nihon hyōjun sangyō bunrui 日本標準産業分類 (Standard classified table of Japanese industries) Ōkurashō Insatsukyoku, 1959. 2v.
See **R13**.

Gyōsei Kanrichō Tōkei Kijunkyoku **N 32**
行政管理庁統計基準局
Nihon hyōjun shokugyō bunrui 日本標準職業分類 (Standard classified table of Japanese occupations) 1960. 244p.
Gives the classification used in the 1955 and 1960 national censuses and the standard international classification of occupations of 1958.

International Labor Organization **N 33**
Kokusai hyōjun shokugyō bunrui 国際標準職業分類 (Standard international classification of occupations) Tr. by Kokusai Rōdō-kyoku Nihon chūzaiin. Kokusai Kōronsha, 1950. 279p. (ILO sōsho, 6)

CHRONOLOGY

N 34

Sekai rōdō undōshi minzoku undōshi nenpyō
世界労働運動史民族運動史年表 (Chronology of the history of world labor and race movements) Aoki Shoten, 1955. 215p. (Aoki bunko)

Charts major labor, political and race movements from 1848 to 1953 outside Japan, with national and subject headings under each year. Pertinent political and economic matters in parallel column. Important terms and phrases in bold type. Subject index.

N 35

Nihon rōdō undōshi shakai undōshi nenpyō
日本労働運動史社会運動史年表 (Chronology of the history of Japanese labor and social movements) Aoki Shoten, 1956. 250p. (Aoki bunko)

Watanabe, Yoshimichi 渡部義通 **and** **N 36**
Shioda, Shōbei 塩田庄兵衛
Nihon shakai undōshi nenpyō 日本社会運動史年表 (Chronology of Japanese social movements) Ōtsuki Shoten, 1956. 229p. (Kokumin bunko)
Covers from 1868 to 1956, with genealogy of proletarian parties and subject index.

Rōdō Sōgi Chōsakai **N 37**
労働争議調査会
Rōdō nenpyō 労働年表 (Labor chronology) August, 1945 - August, 1955. 1956. 128p.

Rōsei Kenkyūkai 労政研究会 **N 38**
Nenpyō Nihon rōdō undōshi 年表日本労働運動史 (Chronology of history of Japanese labor movements) Suibunsha, 1961. 235p.

Watanabe, Tōru 渡部徹 **N 39**
Gendai rōnō undōshi nenpyō 現代労農運動

史年表 (Chronology of modern farmer-labor movements) Kyoto, San'ichi Shobō, 1961. 256p. (Nihon gendaishi nenpyō).

Mitsui, Reiko 三井礼子 **N40**
Gendai fujin undōshi nenpyō 現代婦人運動史年表 (A chronology of modern women's movements) San'ich Shobō, 1963. 260p. (Nihon gendaishi nenpyō)

The first comprehensive chronology of its kind, running from 1868 to 1959, covering not only women's movements in Japan but also related matters, with explanatory notes on facing pages. Subject index.

Rōdōshō 労働省 **N41**
Shiryō rōdō undōshi 資料労働運動史 (Materials on the history of the labor movement) 1945- . Rōdō Gyōsei Kenkyūjo, 1951- . 16v. In progress.

Except for two years in the first, each volume covers a single year with more than 1,000 pages of objective and detailed information about labor trends, organizational problems, major union meetings, labor administration, radical political movements, major prefectural disputes, etc. Directories of major unions and managerial bodies appended, with chronicles and statistics.

Rōdō Undō Shiryō Iinkai **N42**
労働運動史料委員会
Nihon rōdō undō shiryō 日本労働運動史科 (Historical materials on the Japanese labor movement) 1962- . 4v. In progress.

Including hitherto little known documents obtained with the help of librarians and foreign scholars, it is to be a basic collection extending from 1868 to 1945. Of the 4v. so far published, v. 1-2 cover 1868-1907, v.7, 1932-36 and v.10, statistics for the entire period. v. 11 is to have a table of contents and lists of persons, major unions, other labor organizations and union newspapers and magazines, with annotations.

Social welfare

DICTIONARIES

Ōkawa, Hidekichi 大川秀吉 **et al.** **N43**
Shakai hoshō jiten 社会保障辞典 (Social security dictionary). Shakai Hoken Hōki Kenkyūkai, 1958. 401p.

Covers common terms relating to social welfare, social insurance, public aid, etc., with signed articles on such topics as "Social security and finance". Variant terms given in index.

Shakai Jigyō Kenkyūjo **N44**
社会事業研究所
Shakai jigyō yōgo jiten 社会事業用語事典 (Glossary of social work terminology) 1958. 266p.

DIRECTORY

Shakai Jigyō Kenkyūjo **N45**
社会事業研究所
Nihon shakai jigyō sōran 日本社会事業総覧 (Directory of social work in Japan) Nihon Shakai Jigyō Chōsakai, 1954. 616p.

CHRONOLOGY

Shakai Jigyō Kenkyūjo **N46**
社会事業研究所
Nihon shakai jigyō dainenpyō 日本社会事業大年表 (Comprehensive chronological table of social work in Japan) Tōkō Shoin, 1936. 306p.

YEARBOOKS

N47
Shakai hoshō nenkan 社会保障年鑑 (Social security yearbook) 1950- . Comp. by Kenkō Hoken Kumiai Rengōkai. Tōyō Keizai Shinpōsha, 1954- . 9v.

Surveys Japanese and foreign developments from July of the preceding year through June, with emphasis each year on a special topic. List of laws and ordinances, chronicle, bibliography, list of organizations and institutions, and statistics appended.

N48
Shitsugyō taisaku nenkan 失業対策年鑑 (Yearbook of unemployment countermeasures) 1951- . Comp. by Rōdōshō Shokugyō Anteikyoku. Rōdō Hōrei Kyōkai, 1952- . 12v.

Japanese and foreign employment and unemployment developments surveyed, with chronicle and statistics.

N49
Kokumin seikatsu hakusho 国民生活白書 (White paper on national living standards) 1956- . Comp. by Keizai Kikakuchō. 1956- . 8v.

Emphasizes a different special topic each year, i. e., "National livelihood under the business adjustment policy and the status of the living reform movement" in the 1962 issue.

N 50

Seishōnen hakusho 青少年白書 (White paper on youth) 1956- . Comp. by Chūō Seishōnen Mondai Kyōgikai. 1956, 1959- . 6v.

Former title: *Seishōnen jidō hakusho* (White paper on youth and juveniles), 1956. 1v.

Surveys not only delinquency but also youth problems in education, labor, welfare, etc., activities of the Central Council on Youth Problems and appropriations. Related organizations listed.

STATISTICS

N 51

Shakai fukushi tōkei nenpō 社会福祉統計年報 Annual report of the social welfare statistics, 1951-59. Comp. by Kōseishō. 1952-61. 10v.

From 1960 published annually under three separate titles: *Shakai fukushi gyōsei gyōmu hōkoku* (Survey of social welfare administration), *Shakai fukushi shisetsu chōsa hōkoku* (Survey of social welfare facilities), and *Seikatsu hogo dōtai chōsa hōkoku* (Survey of livelihood protection). Major details also in English.

N 52

Shakai hoshō tōkei nenpō 社会保障統計年報 (Annual report of social security statistics) No. 1, 1959- . Comp. by Sōrifu, Shakai Hoshō Seido Shingikai. Shakai Hoken Hōki Kenkyūkai, 1959- . 5v.

N 53

Kakei chōsa nenpō 家計調査年報 Annual report on the family income and expenditure survey, 1953- . Comp. by Sōrifu Tōkeikyoku. 1954- . 10v.

Former titles: *Shōhisha kakaku chōsa nenpō* (Annual report of consumer price survey). 1946-50. 4v. *Shōhi jittai chōsa nenpō* (Annual report of family income and expenditure survey). 1951-53. 3v.

Major details also in English.

Sōrifu Tōkeikyoku 総理府統計局 **N 54**
Sengo jūnen no kakei 戦後10年の家計
Family income and expenditure in post-war Japan, 1946-55 1956. 193p.

Text also in English.

Sōrifu Tōkeikyoku 総理府統計局 **N 55**

Kakei chōsa sōgō hōkokusho 家計調査総合報告書 (Comprehensive report on investigation of household economy) 1946-62. 1964. 550p.

Statistical tables give the findings in surveys of household budgets over 16 years, followed by analytical tables, correlative tables of the results of special or short-term investigations and tables of the price indexes of consumers' goods. Headings also in English.

FOLKLORE

BIBLIOGRAPHY

Nihon Gakujutsu Kaigi 日本学術会議 **N 56**
Bungaku tetsugaku shigaku bunken mokuroku 文学・哲学・史学・文献目録 V. 日本民俗学編 (Bibliography of literature, philosophy and history) V. Japanese folklore. 1955. 138p.

Nihon Gakujutsu Kaigi 日本学術会議 **N 57**
Bunkakei bunken mokuroku 文化系文献目録 XIII 文化人類学編 (Bibliography of literature, philosophy and history) XIII, Cultural anthropology. 1962. 95p.

Lists monographic works and periodical articles published 1945-61 under 13 topics and 22 regions.

Nihon Minzokugaku Kyōkai **N 58**
日本民族学協会
Minzokugaku kankei zasshi ronbun sōmokuroku 民族学関係雑誌論文総目録 (Complete list of periodical articles related to ethnology) 1925-59. Seibundō Shinkōsha, 1961. 199p.

Indexes articles published in 9 periodicals of ethnology, folklore and anthropology.

Yanagida, Kunio 柳田国男 **N 59**
Nochi no karikotoba no ki 後狩詞記 Comp. by Yanagida Kunio Sensei Kiju Kinenkai. Jitsugyō no Nippon sha, 1951. 131p.

This reprint of the first book of the eminent folklorist, Yanagida, a folklore collection originally published in 1909, gives a bibliography of his folklore writings and a chronology of his life from 1875 to 1951.

Gusinde, Martin and Sano, Chiye **N 60**
An annotated bibliography of Ainu studies by Japanese scholars. Heibonsha, 1962. 109p. (Collectanea universitatis Catholicae Nanzan, series 3)

Lists 349 titles in English translations of Japanese studies on Ainu under names of authors. Original Japanese titles are noted. Pt. 1 covers archeology, race, linguistics and ethnology and pt. 2, anthropology. No index.

DICTIONARIES

Kitamura, Nobuyo 喜多村信節   **N 61**
Kiyū shōran 嬉遊笑覧 Ryokuen Shobō, 1958. 673p.

A cyclopedia of Edo manners and customs classified in 28 sections with such headings as dwellings, manners, costume, utensils, prostitution, sodomy, language, food and drink, fire and lighting, merchants, beggars, birds and insects, fishing and hunting and plants with explanations citing historical documents and old traditions. No index. Originally published about 1830 in 12v. and a supplement; reprinted in 2v. in 1927.

Minzokugaku Kenkyūjo 民俗学研究所 **N 62**
Minzokugaku jiten 民俗学辞典 (Folklore dictionary) Tokyodō, 1951. 714p.

Basic work explaining 897 items on customs, festivals, mythology, social patterns, house types, etc., in articles with references. Classified table of contents; subject index. Plates and maps. Old-style *kana* used to facilitate coordination with **N66-78**.

Nakayama, Tarō 中山太郎   **N 63**
Nihon minzokugaku jiten 日本民俗学辞典 (Dictionary of Japanese folklore) Shōwa Shobō, 1933-35. 2v.

Nihon Minzokugaku Kyōkai   **N 64**
日本民俗学協会
Nihon shakai minzoku jiten 日本社会民俗 辞典 (Cyclopedia of Japanese society and folklore) Seibundō Shinkōsha, 1952-60. 4v.

Classified under 24 headings, such as race and population and climate and disasters, articles by outstanding scholars, with references, cover many basic aspects of Japanese life from the viewpoints of cultural anthropology and sociology. Detailed table of contents; general index.

Minzokugaku Kenkyūjo 民俗学研究所 **N 65**
Sōgō Nihon minzoku goi 綜合日本民俗語彙 (Comprehensive vocabulary of Japanese folklore terms) Heibonsha, 1955-56. 5v.

Reliable dictionary of about 35,000 terms not found in ordinary dictionaries, with illustrations and quotations. v. 5 gives general index, bibliography. Good substitute for **N66-78**.

Yanagida, Kunio 柳田国男 **et al.**
Bunrui minzoku goishū 分類民俗語彙集 (Collection of classified vocabularies of folkways)

⚜ The following 13 titles known collectively as the *Bunrui minzoku goishū*, were compiled by Kunio Yanagida and his associates on the basis of inquiries throughout the country. The terms given have been in common oral use, but not many of them are in the usual dictionaries. See **N65**.

     N 66
San'iku shūzoku goi 産育習俗語彙 (Vocabulary of childbirth and rearing of children) Aiikukai, 1935. 119p.

     N 67
Kon'in shūzoku goi 婚姻習俗語彙 (Vocabulary of marriage customs) Minkan Denshō no Kai, 1937. 339p.

     N 68
Sōsō shūzoku goi 葬送習俗語彙 (Vocabulary of funeral customs) Minkan Denshō no Kai, 1937. 233p.

     N 69
Bunrui nōson goi 分類農村語彙 (Classified vocabulary of farm villages) Nagano, Shinano Kyōikukai, 1937. 417p.

     N 70
Bunrui gyoson goi 分類漁村語彙 (Classified vocabulary of fishing villages) Minkan Denshō no Kai, 1938. 443p.

     N 71
Fukusō shūzoku goi 服装習俗語彙 (Vocabulary of clothing customs) Minkan Denshō no Kai, 1938. 207p.

     N 72
Kinki shūzoku goi 禁忌習俗語彙 (Vocabulary of taboo customs) Kokugakuin Daigaku, Hōgen Kenkyūkai, 1938. 138p.

     N 73
Kyojū shūzoku goi 居住習俗語彙 (Vocabulary of dwelling customs) Minkan Denshō no Kai, 1939. 328p.

     N 74
Saiji shūzoku goi 歳時習俗語彙 (Vocabulary of seasonal customs) Minkan Denshō no Kai, 1939. 703, 43p.

Bunrui saishi shūzoku goi 分類祭祀習俗語彙 (Classified vocabulary of worship and festivals) Kadokawa Shoten, 1963. 508p. **N 75**

Bunrui sanson goi 分類山村語彙 (Classified vocabulary of mountain villages) Nagano, Shinano Kyōikukai, 1941. 410p. **N 76**

Bunrui jidō goi 分類児童語彙 (Classified vocabulary of children) v.1 Tokyodō, 1949. 223p. **N 77**

Zokusei goi 族制語彙 (Vocabulary of the family system) Nihon Hōri Kenkyūkai, 1943. 274p. **N 78**

ILLUSTRATIONS

Minzokugaku Kenkyūjo 民俗学研究所 **N 79**
Nihon minzoku zuroku 日本民俗図録 (Pictorial record of Japanese folk customs) Asahi Shinbunsha, 1955. 325p. (Asahi Shinbunsha zuroku series)

Arranged to show historical changes and local differences, reproductions of 744 photographs of customs taken from about 1925 to 1955 are followed by explanatory notes (148p.). Subject index.

Honda, Yasuji 本田安次 **N 80**
Zuroku Nihon no minzoku geinō 図録日本の民俗芸能 (Japanese folk theatre in pictures) Asahi Shinbunsha, 1960. 290p. 168 plates.

Manners and customs

DICTIONARIES

Morisue, Yoshiaki 森末義彰 **and** **N 81**
Hinonishi, Sukenori 日野西資孝
Fūzoku jiten 風俗辞典 (Dictionary of manners and customs) Tokyodō, 1957. 830p.

Fourteen hundred entries, with emphasis on clothing, food and shelter. Many illustrations. Lists of festivals and other observances and of color combinations in apparel, a genealogy of martial arts, etc., appended. Classified table of contents; subject index.

Aono, Hisao 青野寿郎 **et al.** **N 82**
Kyōdo shakai jiten 郷土社会事典 (Cyclo-

pedia of the national community) Kaneko Shobō, 1956. 603p.

Information in the fields of geography, history, folklore, pedagogy and sociology helpful in the study of national life is summarized in scholarly articles, most of which have bibliographical notes. Classified table of contents; subject index.

Mitamura, Engyo 三田村鳶魚 **N 83**
Buke jiten 武家事典 (Dictionary of the warrior class) Ed. by Fumio Inagaki. Seiabō, 1958. 459p.

Convenient source of information about the manners and customs of the warrior class in the Tokugawa period extracted from the writings of Engyo Mitamura (1870-1952), an authority on the subject. Chronology of the Tokugawa period, table of important posts in the Tokugawa administration, etc., appended. Subject index.

Mitamura, Engyo 三田村鳶魚 **N 84**
Edo seikatsu jiten 江戸生活事典 (Dictionary of Edo life) Ed. by Fumio Inagaki. Seiabo, 1959. 541p.

Companion to **N83**, covering all aspects of life in Edo under such headings as travel, women, hoodlums and beggars, economy, and fire brigades. Taken from the writings of Engyo Mitamura and other authorities. Table of currencies, chronology of manners and table of hours of daily practices appended. Subject index.

Miyoshi, Ikkō 三好一光 **N 85**
Edo Tokyo seigyō bukka jiten 江戸東京生業物価事典 (Cyclopedia of trades and prices in Edo and Tokyo) Seiabō, 1960. 461p.

Brings together references in the works of such playwrights as Mokuami Kawatake (1816-93) and Nanboku Tsuruya IV (1755-1829) to trades, commodity prices, diseases, medicine, religion, food and drink, and famous shops in Edo and then Tokyo early in the Meiji period. Companion to **N86**.

Miyoshi, Ikkō 三好一光 **N 86**
Edo Tokyo fūzokugo jiten 江戸東京風俗語事典 (Dictionary of vocabulary of Edo and Tokyo manners and customs) Seiabō, 1959. 449p.

CHRONOLOGY

Suzuki, Kōzō 鈴木行三 **N 87**
Sandai shakai fūzoku nenpyō 三代社会風俗年表 (Chronological table of social manners of the three eras: Meiji, Taishō and Shōwa) Nihon Jōmin Bunka Kenkyūjo, 1956. 131, 88p.

(Nihon Jōmin Bunka Kenkyūjo note, 29) Mimeo. From 1868 to 1955.

ILLUSTRATIONS

Ema, Tsutomu 江馬務 **N 88**
Zusetsu Nihon fūzokushi 図説日本風俗史 (Illustrated history of Japanese manners) Seibundō Shinkōsha, 1956. 244p.

Divided into eight periods from earliest times, manners are shown in pictures with captions in English and Japanese. A brief history of Japanese dress, with an English digest, appended.

Kawabata, Sanehide 河鰭実英 **N 89**
Yūsoku kojitsu zufu 有職故実図譜 (Illustrated book of ancient court and military usages) Reprint ed. Kyoto, Jinbun Shoin, 1949. 483p.

Costumes, armor, dwellings, furniture and vehicles related to the Imperial Court and the warrior class are shown in 170 plates with explanatory notes. Classified table of contents. Originally published in 1941.

Takahashi, Kenji 高橋健自 **N 90**
Rekisei fukushoku zusetsu 歴世服飾図説 (Illustrated book of costumes of successive ages) Shūseidō Shoten, 1929. 2v.

Pictures, usually from sources of the periods concerned, show dress from ancient times to the late middle period in v.1 and to modern times in v.2. Subject index.

Sōma, Akira 相馬皓 **N 91**
Nihon keppatsu fūzoku zusetsu 日本結髪風俗図説 (Illustrated book of Japanese coiffure) Ningyō Bunka Kenkyūjo, 1959, 67p.

INDEXES

N 92
Kojitsu sōsho 故実叢書 (Ancient court and military usages series) New rev. and enl. ed. No. 39, Index. Meiji Tosho Shuppan, 1957. 497, 43p.

Indexes subjects taken mainly from the tables of contents of the 39 volumes in the series, which bring together 64 studies and manuals written mostly by scholars of the Tokugawa period. First published in 1899-1906; revised and enlarged edition in 1928-31.

Miyao, Shigeo 宮尾しげを **N 93**
Fūzoku gahō sakuin 風俗画報索引 (Index to *Fūzoku gahō*) Seiabō, 1959. 129p.

Facilitates use of the extensive materials on local customs in the Meiji period, noted places, songs, dialects, etc., in the 479 issues of the *Fūzoku gahō* (Pictorial magazine of manners and customs) from Feb., 1889, to Apr., 1916.

ANNUAL EVENTS

Nishitsunoi, Masayoshi 西角井正慶 **N 94**
Nenjū gyōji jiten 年中行事辞典 (Dictionary of annual events). Tokyodō, 1958. 972p.

Explains past and present annual events, Japanese and foreign, including many of special interest to scholars, with lists of annual observances at the Imperial Court and among the warrior class, calendars of folk events and festivals, etc. Index.

Minzokugaku Kenkyūjo 民俗学研究所 **N 95**
Nenjū gyōji zusetsu 年中行事図説 (Annual events illustrated) Iwasaki Shoten, 1954. 286p. (Zusetsu zenshū, 6)

Current and recent Japanese annual events pictured with explanations. Reference list. Index.

Fujisaki, Hiroshi 藤崎弘 **N 96**
Kankon sōsai jiten 冠婚葬祭事典 (Dictionary of ceremonies of coming of age, marriage, funerals and ancestral worship) Tsuru Shobō, 1957. 388p.

Legends
→ D47, D48

Iwaya, Sazanami 巌谷小波 **and** **N 97**
Iwaya, Eiji 巌谷栄二
Daigoen 大語園 (Great garden of words) Heibonsha, 1935-36. 10v.

Most comprehensive collection of myths, legends, oral traditions, fables and allegorical stories of Japan, China, Korea and India, arranged under 25 headings, including Shintō deities, Buddhist deities, shrines and temples, kings and emperors, dragons and snakes, and demons. v.10 gives a classified table of contents, list of sources and classified name index.

Nippon Hōsō Kyōkai 日本放送協会 **N98**
Nihon mukashibanashi meii 日本昔話名彙 (Index of old tales of Japan) Reprint ed. Nippon Hōsō Shuppan Kyōkai, 1954. 323p.

Tales collected by Kunio Yanagida and his associates are listed in two main groups, primary and derivative, subdivided into types, with summaries of their standard versions and local variants. Source materials given. Subject index.

Nippon Hōsō Kyōkai 日本放送協会 **N99**
Nihon densetsu meii 日本伝説名彙
(Index of Japanese legends) Nippon Hōsō Shuppan Kyōkai, 1950. 481p.

Gives the titles and summaries of legends in various parts of Japan classified under the headings of wood, stones and rocks, water, sepulchres, slopes and mountain passes, and shrines. Bibliography. Companion to **N98**.

EDUCATION

❦ Works on education, directories of research organizations, associations and biographical directories are included.

Bibliography

Kokuritsu Kyōiku Kenkyūjo   **P1**
国立教育研究所
Kyōiku bunken sōgō mokuroku　教育文献総合目録 (Union catalogue of literature on education) 1950-54. 2v.

Pt.1, "Union catalog of literature on education from the Meiji period", classifies and locates works published in Japan from 1868 to 1949 held by major libraries, research institutions and individuals in Tokyo. See **P2** for index. Pt.2, "Union catalogue of literature on local education", groups works by prefectures, divided into materials on the history of schools and data on local education. Author index.

Kokuritsu Kyōiku Kenkyūjo   **P2**
国立教育研究所
Meiji ikō kyōiku bunken sōgō mokuroku sakuin　明治以降教育文献総合目録索引 (Index to union catalogue of literature on education from the Meiji period) 1954. 292p.

Arranged by authors and subjects, it compensates for some of the short-comings of the classified arrangement of pt.1 of **P1**.

Nihon Gakujutsu Kaigi 日本学術会議　**P3**
Bungaku tetsugaku shigaku bunken mokuroku　文学・哲学・史学　文献目録 Ⅶ 教育学編 (Bibliography of literature, philosophy and history) Ⅶ Education. 1958. 317p.

Nihon Shakaika Kyōiku Gakkai   **P4**
日本社会科教育学会
Shakaika kyōiku bunken mokuroku　社会科教育文献目録 (Bibliography of social education) 1946-1961. Tōyōkan Shuppansha, 1962. 97p.

Books and articles classified in 18 sections, including general, history of social education, and curriculums in various countries. No index.

Ishikawa, Matsutarō　石川松太郎　**P5**
Kyōikushi ni kansuru bunken mokuroku narabini kaidai　教育史に関する文献目録並に解題 (Annotated bibliography of history of education) Kōdansha, 1953. 242, 33p.

Classifies, annotates and locates about 2,000 titles published from the start of the Meiji period through Oct., 1953. Titles arranged by publication dates under the following headings: 1, History of educational development, historical views, methodology; 2, History of education in Japan; 3, History of education in the rest of the Orient; 4, History of education in the West; 5, Collections of dissertations, memoirs, periodicals; 6, Dictionaries, chronologies, bibliographies. Author and title index.

Keiō Gijuku Daigaku　慶応義塾大学　**P6**
Fukuzawa Yukichi kyōiku kankei bunken sakuin　福沢諭吉教育関係文献索引　(Index to literature on education by Yukichi Fukuzawa) 1955. 112p.

Dictionaries

Abe, Shigetaka　阿部重孝　**and**   **P7**
Kido, Mantarō　城戸幡太郎
Kyōikugaku jiten 教育学辞典 (Dictionary of education) Iwanami Shoten, 1936-39. 5v.

Useful prewar compilation, including topics from

related fields, with more detailed explanations than in **P9**. References with each article. v. 5 gives general and name indexes, classified list of subject headings, a chronology and list of Japanese and foreign education periodicals. v. 4 includes "Statistical materials concerning the history of education in the prefectures" (200p.) based on the annual report of the Ministry of Education.

Aoki, Seishirō 青木誠四郎 **and**   **P8**
Munakata, Seiya 宗像誠也
Kyōiku kagaku jiten 教育科学辞典 (Dictionary of educational science) Asakura Shoten, 1952. 816p.

Heibonsha 平凡社   **P9**
Kyōikugaku jiten 教育学辞典 (Cyclopedia of education) 1954-56. 6v.

Standard compilation, rich in content, with many illustrations and statistics. Japanese and foreign reference works given at end of articles. v. 6 contains a survey of the educational systems and problems of foreign countries, a chronology of the history of education, a classified table of contents and subject and name indexes.

Ishiyama, Shūhei 石山脩平 **and**   **P10**
Umene, Satoru 梅根悟
Kyōiku kenkyū jiten 教育研究事典 (Cyclopedia of educational research) Kaneko Shobō, 1954. 1570p.

Modeled after Monroe's *Encyclopedia of educational research*, synthesizes Japanese educational research to 1951-52, with references at end of articles and supplementary bibliography. Subject index.

Ishiyama, Shūhei 石山脩平 **and**   **P11**
Umene, Satoru 梅根悟
Kyōiku shōjiten 教育小辞典 (Little dictionary of education) Kaneko Shobō, 1955. 688p.

Japanese and foreign educational terms from ancient times explained briefly.

Itō, Hideo 伊藤秀夫 **et al.**   **P12**
Gendai kyōiku jiten 現代教育事典 (Cyclopedia of modern education) Meiji Tosho Shuppan, 1961. 619p.

Covers 431 topics, each with reference list. Subject and name indexes.

Kobayashi, Sumie 小林澄兄   **P13**
Kyōiku hyakka jiten 教育百科辞典 (Encyclopedia of education) 2d ed., enl. Fukumura Shoten, 1954. 1300p.

Covers major topics related to education, with references at end of main articles. Bibliography.

Subject and personal name indexes. Except for supplement (9p.), same as Keiō Shuppansha edition of 1950.

Toyosawa, Noboru 豊沢登 **and**   **P14**
Nagai, Itsuo 永井五男
Taikei kyōikugaku daijiten 体系教育学大辞典 (Systematic dictionary of education) 5th ed., enl. Iwasaki Shoten, 1952. 1159, 66p.

Sections on the philosophy of education, science of education, educational policies and systems, educational administration and finance, trends in world education and education in individual countries, and social psychology include entries on subordinate topics. Detailed table of contents, subject and name indexes and classified reference list, mostly of postwar publications.

R. S. F. S. R. Akademiia Pedagogicheskikh   **P15**
Nayk
Sobieto kyōiku kagaku jiten ソビエト教育科学辞典 (Dictionary of Soviet educational science) Tr. by Sobieto Kyōikugaku Kenkyūkai. Meiji Tosho Shuppan, 1963. 941p.

Selected from the 2,240 in the original, published in 1960, 1,550 entries are grouped under such headings as pedagogy, educational systems, personages and education in different countries. Indexed by subjects, names and countries.

Ushijima, Yoshitomo 牛島義友 **and**   **P16**
Sakamoto, Ichirō 阪本一郎
Kyōiku shinrigaku jiten 教育心理学辞典 (Cyclopedia of educational psychology) Kaneko Shobō, 1961. 689p.

Emphasis is on recent achievements in educational psychology, but general psychology and related fields are also covered in comparatively detailed articles, each with reference list. Biographical entries on persons associated with educational psychology grouped together. Lists of educational research institutions, child consultation centers and tests appended with bibliography of publications from 1868 to 1955. Classified table of contents.

Sakamoto, Ichirō 阪本一郎 **et al.**   **P17**
Taikei kyōiku shinrigaku jiten 体系教育心理学辞典 (Systematic dictionary of educational psychology) 2d ed., enl. Iwasaki Shoten, 1958. 294, 12, 10p.

Gives basic explanations of technical terms classified in 26 chapters, with Japanese and Western references at the end of each chapter and some internal sections. Directory of psychologists and list of standard tests. Subject and personal name indexes. Omits bibliography given in 1951 edition.

Sagara, Iichi 相 良 惟 一 **et al.** **P18**
Gakkō gyōsei jiten 学 校 行 政 事 典 (Cyclopedia of school administration) Seibundō Shin-kōsha, 1958. 768p.

Covers present-day administration and management and related matters with citation of laws and regulations and reading references. Classified table of contents, but no index. Major references listed.

Yamauchi, Kazuo 山 内 一 夫 **et al.** **P19**
Kyōiku hōki jiten 教 育 法 規 辞 典 (Dictionary of educational laws and regulations) Gakuyō Shobō, 1961. 565p.

Aoki, Shōshin 青 木 章 心 **and** **P20**
Arimitsu, Shigenori 有 光 成 徳
Shichōkaku kyōiku jiten 視 聴 覚 教 育 事 典 (Cyclopedia of audio-visual education) Meiji Tosho Shuppan, 1956. 615, 15p.

Major headings include theory, broadcasts, recordings, films, slides, picture shows (kamishibai), photographs and models. Directories given of Japan Broadcasting Corporation and other related organizations, with bylaws, codes, etc. Subject index.

Kowada, Takeki 小 和 田 武 紀 **et al.** **P21**
Shakai kyōiku jiten 社 会 教 育 事 典 (Cyclopedia of social education) Iwasaki Shoten, 1955. 637, 36p.

First half covers practical aspects of social education; second half gives theory, the history of social education in major countries and the administration and financing of social education, the last of which must be used with caution because of important changes in 1959 in the Social Education Law. Bibliography lists Japanese and Western titles without publication dates. Index.

Kobe Daigaku Kyōiku Gakubu **P22**
神 戸 大 学 教 育 学 部
Kyōiku yōgo jiten 教 育 用 語 辞 典 (Dictionary of educational terms) San'ichi Shobō, 1960. 334p.

Covers about 1,000 basic terms and prominent educators. Subject index.

Handbook

Komiyama, Eiichi 小 見 山 栄 一 **P23**
Kyōiku hyōjun kensa handobukku 教 育 標 準 検査ハンドブック (Handbook for inspection of educational standards) Tōyōkan Shuppansha, 1959. 665p.

Yearbooks

P24
Sekai no kyōiku 世 界 の 教 育 (World education) 1952- . Comp. by UNESCO. Tr. by the Japanese National Commission for Unesco. 1955- . 9v.

Translation of *International yearbook of education*, published by the International Bureau of Education and UNESCO, giving developments in many countries and statistics. The issues for 1952-54 are abridged.

P25
Nihon kyōiku nenkan 日 本 教 育 年 鑑 (Japan education yearbook) 1961- . Comp. by Nihon Kyōiku Shinbunsha. 1960- . 4v.

Chronicles developments of the year and has descriptive surveys under the following headings: outlook; school education; social education; organizations and trends; policies, administration and finance; local education, and world education. Historical chronology of Japanese education, laws and regulations and statistics included. Subjects, statistics indexed. Similar to the yearbook of the same title published from 1948 to 1952 by the Association for the Advancement of Educational Culture and may be supplemented for 1952-56 with *Kyōiku nenkan* (Education yearbook), published by Jiji Press.

P26
Monbushō nenpō 文 部 省 年 報 (Annual report of the Ministry of Education) No. 1 (1873) - . Comp. by Monbushō Chōsakyoku. Ōkurashō Insatsukyoku, 1875- . 142v.

Mainly statistical until publication of **P27** from 1951 resulted in broadening of it into a descriptive survey with enlarged documents section. Issued in second year after the year covered.

English abridged ed.: Education in 1955- . 8v.

P27
Gakkō kihon chōsa hōkokusho 学 校 基 本 調 査 報 告 書 (Summary report on basic school statistics) 1951- . Comp. by Monbushō Chōsakyoku. 1952- . 12v.

Gives numbers of schools, students and faculty and staff members, organization of classes, and other basic information from kindergartens to universities, with introductory graphs. Cumulative statistics at end. Comparable statistics for 1948-51 are in **P26**.

Directories

SCHOOLS

P28

Zenkoku gakkō meikan 全国学校名鑑
(Nationwide school directory) 1953- . Comp.
by Bunka Kenkyūsha. 1953- . 11v. Annual.

A directory of the same title was compiled for
1949 and 1959 by the Japan Teachers' Association.

P29

Zenkoku gakkō sōran 全国学校総覧
(Directory of schools in Japan) 1959- . Comp.
by Tokyo Kyōiku Kenkyūjo. Hara Shobō,
1959- . 5v. Annual.

Yomiuri Shinbunsha Fujinbu **P30**
読売新聞社婦人部
Zenkoku shokugyō gakkō annai 全国職業学
校案内 (Nationwide guide to vocational
schools) 1955 ed. Nihon Bunka Tsūshinsha,
1954. 656p.

ACADEMIC ORGANIZATIONS

Nihon Gakujutsu Kaigi 日本学術会議 **P31**
Kokusai gakujutsu dantai 国際学術団体
(International learned organizations) 1962 ed.
1962. 435p.

Lists 173 organizations with data obtained by the
Japan Science Council in response to questionnaires
or from the *Yearbook of international organizations.*
1963 supp. (mimeographed) adds 33 organizations.

Monbushō Daigaku Gakujutsukyoku **P32**
文部省大学学術局
Zenkoku kenkyū kikan tsūran 全国研究機関
通覧 (Nationwide directory of research institutions) 3d ed. Nihon Gakujutsu Shinkōkai,
1963. 525p.

Describes briefly on the basis of reports to the
government about 2,800 institutions divided into
two groups, natural sciences and humanities, each
subdivided into government, private, and university.
Names of institutions indexed.

Nihon Gakujutsu Kaigi 日本学術会議 **P33**
Zenkoku kenkyū kikan sōran 全国研究機関
総覧 (Nationwide directory of research institutions) Nihon Gakujutsu Shinkōkai, 1959. 604,
22p.

Alphabetical listing of more than 1,700 institutions

not under the direct jurisdiction of the Ministry of
Education or universities. Though dated, still useful
because more detailed than **P32** in giving names of
leading researchers and descriptions of past and
present research. Names of institutions and publication titles in English.

Nihon Gakujutsu Shinkōkai **P34**
日本学術振興会
Zenkoku gakkyōkai yōran 全国学協会要覧
人文科学・自然科学 (Nationwide di-
rectory of learned societies and associations)
Humanities, natural sciences. 1958 ed. 1958.
167p.

Based on a 1957 survey by the Ministry of Education, gives for each body its location, president's
name, date of founding, purposes, history, size of
membership, expenditures, activities, affiliations,
publications. Names of organizations, titles of
periodicals are also given in English. Index to
organizations and periodicals.

SCHOLARS

Kyōiku Gyōsei Kenkyūjo **P35**
教育行政研究所
Nihon hakushiroku 日本博士録 (Directory of
Japanese doctorates) 1956- . 8v. Annual.

v. 1 lists some 40,000 arranged under subjects in the
order in which their degrees were conferred from
May, 1888, through 1955, giving their universities
and dissertation titles. Prefaced by a history of
Japanese academic degrees. Classified index of
names. Became an annual after v. 2.

Hanabusa, Yoshitarō 花房吉太郎 **and** **P36**
Yamamoto, Genta 山本源太
Nihon hakushi zenden 日本博士全伝 (Com-
plete biographies of Japanese doctorates) Hakubunkan, 1892. 364p.

Covers briefly the 121 pioneers who received
doctorates from 1881 to 1892.

P37

Dai Nihon hakushiroku 大日本博士録
(Directory of Japanese doctorates) Hattensha, 1921-
30. 5v.

Superseded by **P35**, though more biographical information is given on individuals.

Nihon Gakujutsu Shinkōkai **P 38**
日本学術振興会
Senmonbetsu daigaku kenkyūsha kenkyū daimoku
sōran 専門別大学研究者研究題目総覧
(Directory of university research scholars and
subjects, classified by fields) 2d ed., rev. 1961.
2v.

v.1 covers, as of June 1, 1959, literature, history and philosophy; law and politics; economics, commerce, business administration, and miscellaneous. v.2 covers physical sciences, technology, agriculture, and medicine, dentistry, pharmacy. Names indexed. In the 1956 edition, classification is by universities and institutions.

Centre for East Asian Cultural Studies　　P39
Japanese researchers in Asian studies. 1963. 281p.

Lists about 4,000 scholars, covering all fields of research.

Kokusai Kankei Chiiki Kenkyū　　P40
Genjō Chōsa Iinkai 国際関係・地域研究 現状調査委員会
Nihon no daigaku ni okeru kokusai kankei oyobi chiiki kenkyū no genjō chōsa hōkoku 日本の 大学における国際関係および地域研究 の現状調査報告 (A survey of international and area studies in Japan) Kokusai Bunka Kaikan, 1962. 43,335p.

Tabulates findings in a survey made from 1958 through March, 1962. Lists alphabetically 881 scholars of 89 universities and 26 research institutions, giving for each his specialty, publications and other achievements, present projects, languages, etc. Indexed by geographical areas and fields of study.

Kyōiku jinmei jiten 教育人名辞典　P41
(Who's who in education) Risōsha, 1962. 927p.

Gives biographical data, summaries of their ideas and significance and lists of works by and about them for about 2,000 Japanese and foreign educators, philosophers, psychologists, etc. Various education chronologies appended.

Zenkoku daigaku shokuinroku 全国大学職員 P42
録 (Nationwide university staff directory) 1959- . Comp. by Daigaku Shokuinroku Kankōkai. Kōjunsha, 1959, 1961- . 4v. Annual.

Source materials

United Nations. Educational,　　P43
Scientific and Cultural Organization
Sekai no shotō kyōiku 世界の初等教育 (World primary education) Tr. by the Japanese National Commission for Unesco. Minshu Kyōiku Kyōkai, 1961. 1241p.

Translation of *World survey of education: II. Primary education*, published in 1958, with sections on primary education in all but a few countries in 1950-54, school-age and school-going populations and the progress of primary education since 1930.

United Nations. Educational,　　P44
Scientific and Cultural Organization
Sekai no chūto kyōiku 世界の中等教育 (World secondary education) Tr. by the Japanese National Commission for Unesco. Minshu Kyōiku Kyōkai, 1963. 1454p.

Translation of *World survey of education: III. Secondary education*, published in 1961, giving the status and problems of secondary education in 106 countries. The Japanese version of the reference list in Chapter 8 of the original is a separate volume.

Monbushō 文部省　　P45
Gakusei hachijūnenshi 学制八十年史 (Eighty years of the school system) Ōkurashō Insatsukyoku, 1954. 1182, 38p.

Surveys educational developments from 1872 to Aug., 1952, with a third of the text given to postwar changes. Includes laws and regulations, excerpts of resolutions of educational conferences, directives of the Supreme Commander for the Allied Powers, summaries of the reports of American education missions, organizational charts, statistics based on **P26**, and a chronology. Subject and name indexes. *Gakusei 90 nenshi* (Ninety years of the school system), published in 1964, abridges the prewar information and emphasizes the decade from 1952.

Kyōikushi Hensankai 教育史編纂会　P46
Meiji ikō kyōiku seido hattatsushi 明治以降 教育制度発達史 (History of progress in the educational system from the Meiji period) Ryūginsha, 1938-39. 12v.

Traces, mainly through official documents and statistics, developments in education, exclusive of the training of army and navy officers and government officials, from the promulgation of the educational system in 1872 to 1932, with introductory survey of education from ancient times and special section on education in Korea, Formosa and other possessions. No index.

Kindai Nihon kyōiku seido shiryō 近代日本 P47
教育制度史料 (Historical materials on the modern Japanese educational system) Kōdansha, 1956-59. 35v.

Continues **P46** from Jan., 1932, to the coming into force of the Peace Treaty in April, 1952, divided into 35 sections, each with an introductory survey. Postwar materials begin with section 22 (v.16). Background materials include basic policies of the postwar occupational forces, political, economic, social and administrative documents and Diet proceedings. v. 35 gives a chronology (455p.) and general index (227p.).

SCIENCE AND TECHNOLOGY

❧ General works on science and technology and works on physical sciences are included. Technology of specific industry is treated together with economic works under Technology and Industry **R** section. As a matter of convenience works on home economics are included at the end of **R** section. See also Biological sciences section **S**.

SCIENCE

BIBLIOGRAPHY

Yuasa, Mitsutomo 湯浅光朝　　　**Q1**
Shizen kagaku no meicho　自然科学の名著 (Great works of natural science) Mainichi Shinbunsha, 1954.　392, 12p.　(Mainichi Library)
　Summarizes and evaluates the historical significance of 158 classic works arranged chronologically under mathematics, astronomy, physics, chemistry, geology, biology, medicine, technology and scientific thought, with brief biographies of their authors and reference lists.

Kokuritsu Kokkai Toshokan　　　**Q2**
国立国会図書館
Directory of Japanese science periodicals: natural sciences, medical sciences and industry. 1962.　229p.
　Lists 2,241 titles as of 1962, arranged by Universal Decimal Classification. Entries by romanized title with Japanese title, English translation, publisher and address. Indexes of romanized titles and translated titles.

Sōrifu Shigen Chōsakai　　　**Q3**
総理府資源調査会
Nihon shigen bunken mokuroku　　日本資源

文献目録　(Bibliography of natural resources in Japan) 1956-57.　4v.
　Lists about 220,000 research articles in journals and memoirs from 1880 to 1950, classified by Universal Decimal Classification. Concerned mainly with Japanese resources, but resources in the Pacific area closely related to Japan are also included. Universal Decimal Classification table with relative index adjusted for this book appended.

Kagaku Gijutsuchō Shigenkyoku　　　**Q4**
科学技術庁資源局
Nihon kaiyō shigen bunken shōrokushū　日本 海洋資源文献抄録集　Abstracts of oceanographic works in Japan. 1963- .　4v.　In progress.
　Collected extensively from Japanese periodical articles and memoirs since 1945, classified and abstracted; v.1, Chemical resources in sea water, 1945-61; v.2, Submarine geology, 1945-62; v.3, Marine fisheries resources, 1945-61, in 2v.

DICTIONARIES

　　　Q5
Rikagaku jiten　理科学辞典　(Dictionary of science) Rev. and enl. ed.　Fuzanbō, 1957. 938, 105p.
　Useful for the general reader, it explains in popular language and with illustrations scientific terms found in secondary-school textbooks, excluding those in biology and mathematics.

Fujimoto, Haruyoshi 藤本治義　　　**Q6**
Hakubutsu jiten　博物辞典　(Dictionary of natural history) Sanseidō, 1938.　1080p.
　Covers about 15,000 terms, including names of plants, animals and minerals, found in textbooks, monographs, academic journals and dictionaries,

with classification tables and indexes of Japanese and foreign names of plants and animals. Identifies famous scientists, excluding those still living.

Heibonsha 平凡社 **Q7**
Rika jiten 理科辞典 (Cyclopedia of science) 1953-54. 19v.

Explains in detail, with many illustrations, about 2,000 fundamental terms, principles and experimental procedures in all the natural sciences for self-study by secondary-school students and more advanced readers. v.18 is a comprehensive index, and v.19 **Q22** gives chronologies of developments in all major fields of science and technology, as well as tables and formulas.

Q8
Iwanami rikagaku jiten 岩波理科学辞典 (Iwanami's dictionary of physics and chemistry) Rev. and enl. ed. Comp. by Bun'ichi Tamamushi and others. Iwanami Shoten, 1958. 1762p.

Standard dictionary for advanced students and professional scientists, including major terms in such other fields as mathematics, astronomy, geophysics, geology and mineralogy. Gives English, German and French equivalents of each term. Tables, explanations of nomenclature, etc. appended. Index.

Iwanami Shoten 岩波書店 **Q9**
Kagaku no ziten (Dictionary of science) 2d ed. 1964. 1274p.

Though designed for reading by secondary-school students, with detailed explanations of about 167 topics drawn from all the sciences, it can be used as a dictionary of technical terms through its index. Chronology of science and technology appended.

Q10
Rikōgaku jiten 理工学事典 (Dictionary of science and technology) Morikita Shuppan, 1950-54. 7v.

With emphasis on the connection between science and technology, it gives more technological but fewer biological terms than **Q7**.

Ōsuga, Yasuhiro 大須賀康広 et al. **Q11**
Rika kiki kōzō sōsa zukai daijiten 理科機器構造操作図解大辞典 (Illustrated dictionary of experimental scientific apparatus) Zenkoku Kyōiku Tosho, 1957. 480p.

Shows and explains the structure and use of apparatus for scientific demonstrations and experiments in primary and secondary schools. Includes laws regarding promotion of science education. General index.

Fujita, Tamiaki 藤田黎明 **and** **Q12**
Kitamura, Kazuyuki 喜多村和之
Kagaku gijutsu bunken ryakugo jiten 科学技術文献略語辞典 World list of abbreviations in scientific and technical literature. Rev. and enl. ed. Hirakawa Bunken Seminā. 1963. 538p.

Provides the full titles of reference works and names of institutions for which abbreviations are found in scientific literature. Technical abbreviations excluded. Lists about 10,000 abbreviations.

Terms

Satō, Jūhei 佐藤重平 **et al.** **Q13**
Chūkai Ei-Wa kagaku yōgo jiten 注解英和科学用語辞典 (An annotated English-Japanese science dictionary) Kyōritsu Shuppan, 1952. 592p.

Gives Japanese equivalents and brief definitions of about 12,000 basic English scientific terms in handy pocket-size volume. Names of scientists included. Japanese-English index.

Kuroya, Masahiko 黒屋政彦 **and** **Q14**
Tomita, Gunji 富田軍二
Eigo kagaku ronbun yōgo jiten 英語科学論文用語辞典 (Dictionary of terms for scientific papers in English) Asakura Shoten, 1960. 328p.

Definitions and examples of use of about 1,500 English words, exclusive of technical terms, commonly used in the writing of scientific reports in English.

Nichi-Futsu Rikōkakai 日仏理工科会 **Q15**
Futsu-Wa rikōgaku jiten 仏和理工学辞典 Dictionnaire français-japonais des termes techniques et scientifiques. Hakusuisha, 1961. 484p.

Japanese equivalents approved by scientific and technological societies for about 40,000 French terms.

Saitō, Hideo 斉藤秀夫 **Q16**
Rikō Roshiyago jiten 理工ロシヤ語辞典 Russko-iaponskii slovar' nauchnykh terminov. Sankyō Shuppan, 1964. 513p.

Gives 20,000 Russian terms in mathematics, physics, chemistry, biology, geology, etc., with their Japanese equivalents.

HANDBOOKS

Q17
Rikagaku benran 理化学便覧 (Manual of

physics and chemistry) Kyōritsu Shuppan, 1949. 219p.

Brings together for easy reference physical and chemical constants, diagrams and tables and such related information as meteorological and astronomical tables, weights and measures, characteristics of common medicines and broadcasting wave lengths.

Kagaku Gijutsuchō Shigen Chōsakyoku   **Q18**
科学技術庁資源調査局
Nihon no shigen 日本の資源 (Japan's resources) Daiyamondosha, 1962. 20, 1202p.

Discusses the state of Japan's resources, including land, foodstuffs, energy, marine resources, and regional planning, with historical background and present conditions. Illustrated with maps, statistics and graphs. No index.

Q19
Rika nenpyō 理科年表 (Annual of science tables) No.1, 1925- . Comp. by Tokyo Tenmondai. Maruzen, 1924- . 37v.

Gives the annual ephemeris and other astronomical calculations of the Tokyo Astronomical Observatory and the Hydrographic Office of Japan, data of the Weather Bureau, and basic constants and diagrams in physics, chemistry and the earth sciences, with formulas, mathematical and conversion tables, etc. appended. General index.

MATHEMATICAL TABLES

Shiba, Kamekichi 芝亀吉 **et al.**   **Q20**
Rikagaku teisūhyō 理化学定数表 (Constants in physics and chemistry) Iwanami Shoten, 1952. 139p.

Convenient compilation, including many constants required in highly specialized fields of chemistry.

History

Kamo, Giichi 加茂儀一 **et al.**   **Q21**
Zukai kagaku gijutsushi jiten   図解科学技術史事典 (Illustrated cyclopedia of the history of science and technology) Kōbundō, 1954. 229p.

Divided into the primitive age, ancient times, the Middle Ages and the Renaissance, the manufacturing era, the time of the industrial revolution and the present, it describes scientific and technological developments with many illustrations. Names and terms indexed.

Sugai, Jun'ichi 菅井準一 **et al.**   **Q22**
Kagaku gijutsushi nenpyō   科学技術史年表

(Chronologies of science and technology) Heibonsha, 1956. 438p.

Separate publication, with minor revisions, of v.19 of **Q7**.

Yuasa, Mitsutomo 湯浅光朝   **Q23**
Kaisetsu kagaku bunkashi nenpyō 解説科学文化史年表 (Annotated chronology of science) Enl. 1960 ed. Chūō Kōronsha, 1960. 266p.

Parallels scientific and technological developments in the West and East, as well as related developments in the social sciences, with brief notes. Includes many figures and photographs. Terms and names of Japanese and Western scientists indexed. Bibliography on the history of science and technology. Covers from the prehistoric period to the present.

Yuasa, Mitsutomo 湯浅光朝   **Q24**
Gendai kagaku gijutsushi nenpyō   現代科学技術史年表 (Chronology of modern science and technology) San'ichi Shobō, 1961. 277p.

Pocket-size chronology of Japanese science and technology from 1853 to 1959 with major events explained in parallel column. Index.

Tokyo Kagaku Hakubutsukan   **Q25**
東京科学博物館
Edo jidai no kagaku 江戸時代の科学 (Science in the Edo period) Hakubunkan, 1938. 9, 345, 49p.

Compiled as a catalogue for the first anniversary exhibit of the Tokyo Science Museum, covering mathematics, astronomy and calendars, herbs and natural history, medicine, geography, mining and geology, firearms, electricity, printing and photography, railways and shipbuilding, architecture, and miscellaneous subjects, each with a chronology, genealogy of scholars, list of references, illustrations and names of owners. Well indexed.

MATHEMATICS

DICTIONARIES

Q26
Iwanami sūgaku jiten 岩波数学辞典 (Iwanami's mathematics dictionary) Rev. and enl. ed. Comp. by Nihon Sūgakukai. Iwanami Shoten, 1954. 591, 89, 90p.

Covers pure and applied mathematics in physics, astronomy, engineering, etc. Historical development of terms, biographies of important mathematicians included. Each Japanese entry includes its English, French, German equivalents with brief explanations and list of references. Mathematical formulas, tables and annotated list of periodicals and other serials appended.

Riron enshū sūgaku shinjiten 理論演習数 **Q27**
学新事典 (New Handbook of mathematics with exercises) 10th ed. Tōyōkan Shuppansha, 1964. 858, 23p.

Covers pure and applied mathematics, explained with historical survey, exercises and answers. Mathematical tables and index.

Ishitani, Shigeru 石谷茂 **et al.** **Q28**
Sūgaku kyōiku jiten 数学教育事典 (Dictionary of mathematics and mathematics education) Meiji Tosho Shuppan, 1961. 638p.

Explains history and psychology of arithmetic education, integers, decimals, fractions, applied problems, algebra, figures, statistics, etc. Important terms and names of persons in the explanation printed in gothic type and indexed. Annotated lists of equations, formulas, notations appended. Useful guide to principles and rules of mathematics education.

Monbushō 文部省 **Q29**
Gakujutsu yōgoshū: sūgaku hen 学術用語集 数学編 Japanese scientific terms: mathematics. Dai Nihon Tosho, 1954. 146p.

Japanese-English and English-Japanese glossaries compiled to simplify and coordinate usage, with similar glossaries of terms in statistical mathematics.

HANDBOOKS

Tannaka, Tadao 淡中忠郎 **and** **Q30**
Komatsu, Yūsaku 小松勇作
Sūgaku handobukku 数学ハンドブック (Handbook of mathematics) Asakura Shoten, 1961. 655p.

Covers algebra, geometry, differential and integral calculus, functional equations, theory of functions, probability and statistics, and applied mathematics.

Yoshida, Kōsaku 吉田耕作 **Q31**
Ōyō sūgaku benran 応用数学便覧 (Handbook of applied mathematics) Maruzen, 1960. 520p.

The most comprehensive collection of mathematical formulas related to science and technology, including linear algebra, group theory, representation of groups, analytical geometry and projective geometry, with brief explanations and reference lists. Index.

Sūgaku Handobukku Henshū Iinkai **Q32**
数学ハンドブック編集委員会
Rikōgaku no tameno sūgaku handobukku 理工学のための数学ハンドブック (Handbook of mathematics for science and technology) Maruzen, 1960. 546p.

Moriguchi, Shigeichi 森口繁一 **et al.** **Q33**
Sūgaku kōshiki 数学公式 (Mathematical formulas) Iwanami Shoten, 1956-60. 3v. (Iwanami zensho)

Gives formulas for differential and integral calculus, plane curves, series, Fourier analysis and special functions, with descriptions of notations. Simple numerical tables and bibliography appended.

MATHEMATICAL TABLES

Boll, Marcel **Q34**
Bannō sūchihyō 万能数値表 Tables numeriques universelles. Rev. and enl. ed. Tr. by Shōkichi Iyanaga and Kentarō Yano. Hakusuisha, 1960. 920p.

Compilation of tables used in pure mathematics, physics, chemical engineering, statistics, etc., divided into sections on arithmetic and algebra, trigonometry, exponents, probability, complex numbers, and units and constants, with many graphs and figures. Includes tables of elliptic and Bessel functions and some relating to special fields, such as $1/\sqrt{1-\beta^2}$ for relativity.

Q35
Maruzen shichiketa taisūhyō 丸善七桁 対数表 (Maruzen's seven-place logarithm tables) Maruzen, 1961. 524p.

Standard tables of trigonometrical functions and their logarithms, natural logarithms, hyperbolic and exponential functions, squares, cubes and roots of integers, as well as of stadia, longitude and latitude distances and weight-and-measure conversion. Pocket-size edition and "Maruzen's five-place logarithm tables", 1962, 106p., also available.

Kasugaya, Nobumasa 春日屋伸昌 **Q36**
Jitsuyō sūhyō taikei 実用数表大系 (Series of practical mathematical tables) Gihōdō, 1961- . 2v. In progress.

Compilation of frequently used tables calculated by electronic computer, including tables of normal trigonometric functions and radian-minute-second conversion.

Rikō Tosho 理工図書 **Q37**
Seisū no keisanhyō 整数の計算表 (Numerical tables for integers) Squares, cubes, square

and cube roots and reciprocals. 1960. 216p.

Gives tables for integers up to 10,000. Formulas used in algebra, trigonometry, analytical geometry and differential and integral calculus appended.

Barlow, Peter   **Q38**
Bārō no sūhyō バーローの数表 Barlow's tables. 12th ed. Morikita Shuppan, 1961. 216p.

Reprint of standard work, giving squares, cubes and square and cube roots from 1 to 9,999 and square and cube roots of ten times the integer.

Hayashi, Keiichi   林桂一   **Q39**
Kōtō kansūhyō 高等関数表 (Tables of higher functions) Iwanami Shoten, 1961. 234p.

Covers circular, hyperbolic, gamma, spherical, Bessel, elliptic functions, etc. The accuracy being eight figures for circular functions and five figures for Bessel and elliptic functions. See **Q40**.

Hayashi, Keiichi   林桂一   **Q40**
Besseru kansūhyō ベッセル関数表 (Tables of Bessel functions) Rev. and enl. ed. Iwanami Shoten, 1949. 114p.

Covers the functions $j_0(x)$, $j_1(x)$, $Y_0(x)$ and $Y_1(x)$ with tables for $x = 0.00 \setminus 25.00$, based on the British Association's *Mathematical tables*, v.6, 1937, and $x = 25.00 \setminus 50.00$, calculated by the author.

Shibagaki, Wasao   柴垣和三雄   **Q41**
0.01% henkei Besseru kansūhyō to sono sūchi keisanhō 0.01 % 変形ベッセル関数表とその数値計算法 (Tables of 0.01% modified Bessel functions and methods of numerical calculation) Baifūkan, 1955. 21, 129p.

Modified Bessel functions of $\sqrt{x} In(x)$ and $\sqrt{x} Kn(x)$ for integer n, tabulated to an accuracy of 0.01%, with explanations of tables, numerical calculation methods, characteristics of modified Bessel functions, asymptotic approximation and numerical analysis of ordinary differential equations. Table of coefficients of Bessel's interpolation formula appended.

Ishida, Yasushi   石田保士   **Q42**
Hokan keisūhyō 補関係数表 (Tables of coefficients of interpolation) Baifūkan. 1953. 291p.

Coefficients of interpolation presented in cases from 3 point to 9 point methods with 0.01 steps. Contains detailed introduction for users without preliminary knowledge.

Kitagawa, Toshio   北川敏男   **Q43**
Poason bunpuhyō ポアソン分布表 (Tables

of Poisson distribution) Baifūkan, 1951. 261p.

Describes several methods in statistical analysis of rare phenomena, beginning with basic models of probability. Lists of references and index.

Moriguchi, Shigeichi   森口繁一   **Q44**
... Jukketa sankaku kansūhyō 10 ケタ三角関数表 (Tables of trigonometric functions to ten places) Tokyo Daigaku Shuppankai, 1960. 87p.

Gives sines, cosines and tangents to ten places at a ten-thousandth and a millionth of a right angle, calculated and typed by electronic computer.

Shibagaki, Wasao   柴垣和三雄   **Q45**
Hachiketa kansūhyō 八桁関数表 (Eight-place functional tables) v.1. Maruzen, 1949. 104p.

Based on H. W. Holtappel's *Tafels van e^x*, tabulates to eight significant figures. Useful for utilizing power and asymptotic series and for numerical analysis of differential equations.

History

Teikoku Gakushiin   **Q46**
Wasan tosho mokuroku 和算図書目録 (Catalogue of books on Japanese mathematics) 1932. 822p.

Lists 12,270 pre-1868 items classified under generalia; collected works; plans; essays; biographies; surveying; astronomy, fortunetelling, almanacs and navigation; Chinese mathematics; European mathematics; Dutch mathematics; instruments; portraits and photographs, and miscellaneous books.

Hagino, Kōgo   萩野公剛   **Q47**
Nihon sūgakushi kenkyū benran 日本数学史研究便覧 (Research handbooks of history of Japanese mathematics) Fuji Tanki Daigaku Shuppanbu, 1961. 162p.

Consists of chronological tables arranged by subject with a list of references, index of biographies of mathematicians mentioned in 22 books on Japanese mathematics published before 1868, and a list arranged by prefectures, of extant plaques with mathematical figures presented to shrines.

PHYSICS

✤ For Nuclear physics see **R154-R161**.

Monbushō   文部省   **Q48**
Gakujutsu yōgoshū: butsurigaku hen   学術

用語集 物理学編 Japanese scientific terms: physics. Dai Nihon Tosho, 1954. 221p.

Equates about 3,700 terms in Japanese-English and English-Japanese sections.

Toda, Morikazu 戸田盛和 **and** **Q49**
Miyajima, Tatsuoki 宮島竜興
Butsurigaku handobukku 物理学ハンド
ブック (Handbook of physics) Asakura Shoten, 1963. 497p.

Relatively simple presentation of all branches of physics for anyone with knowledge of high school physics.

Ōyō Butsuri Gakkai 応用物理学会 **Q50**
Butsuri jikken pokettobukku 物理実験
ポケットブック (Pocket book of physics experiments) Morikita Shuppan, 1956. 717p.

Practical guide to instruments, materials and techniques for experiments in sound, heat, electricity, radioactive rays, vacuums, etc. Subject index.

Shiba, Kamekichi 芝亀吉 **Q51**
Butsuri jōsūhyō 物理常数表 (Tables of physical constants) 3d ed. Iwanami Shoten, 1948. 346p.

Based on the Landolt-Börnstein-Roth-Scheel tables and F. Henning's *Wärmetechnische Richtwerte*, tabulates 136 constants in physics and chemistry, with notes distinguishing degrees of reliability. Measured values of important constants appended. No index.

CHEMISTRY

ABSTRACTS · INDEXES

Nakazawa, Kōichi 中沢浩一 **Q52**
Yūki kagaku bunken no shirabekata 有機化学
文献の調べ方 (Guide to the literature of organic chemistry) 2d ed., rev. Hirokawa Shoten, 1960. 175p.

Use of abstract journals, patent journals, foreign and domestic research and technical journals, explained for engineers and beginning researchers. Abbreviations, nomenclature of organic compounds, and chronological tables of technical journals and patent numbers appended. Indexes of Japanese and foreign names.

Q53
Nihon kagaku sōran 日本化学総覧 Complete chemical abstracts of Japan. 1927- .
Comp. by Nihon Kagaku Gijutsu Jōhō Sentā,

1927- . Monthly.

Continued from Series 1, 1877-1926, comp. by Nihon Kagaku Kenkyūkai. Shōkabō, 1927-34. 7v. Became monthly, numbered as Series 2, v.1; from v.37, 1964, the compiler changed to Nihon Kagaku Gijutsu Jōhō Sentā. About 20,000 articles a year in about 950 Japanese technical and patent journals in chemistry and related fields are abstracted currently. Classified in 34 sections. Indexed twice a year. For cumulative index see **Q54.**

Nihon Kagaku Kenkyūkai **Q54**
日本化学研究会
Nihon kagaku sōran sōsakuin 日本化学総
覧総索引 Complete chemical abstracts of Japan: indexes. Nihon Kagaku Gijutsu Jōhō Sentā, 1953-59. 6v. (2 parts)

Pt.1 is an index to Series 1 and Series 2, v.1-14, covering the period 1877-1940, published by Gihōdō in 1953-54. Pt.2 continues from v.15 to v.29 for the period 1941-1955, published by the Japan Information Center of Science and Technology (JICST) in 1958-59. Index of Japanese and foreign names of authors, index of patent numbers, and subject indexes by Japanese terms and by Western terms, mainly German.

DICTIONARIES

Q55
Kagaku daijiten 化学大辞典 Encyclopaedia chimica. Kyōritsu Shuppan, 1960-64. 10v.

Comprehensive coverage of compounds, systems of matter, theoretical systems, industries, phenomena, reactions, laws, experimental methods, biographies of personages in chemistry, etc. in about 70,000 entries, concise in text but supplemented with figures and tables. Subject index; index of inorganic compound formulas.

Q56
Kagaku jiten 化学辞典 (Chemical dictionary) Rev. and enl. ed. Maruzen, 1954. 797p.

For research workers, engineers and students, it explains terms briefly and gives their English, German and French equivalents, with English-Japanese and German-English indexes. Lists and tables appended.

Q57
Shin kagaku jiten 新化学辞典 (New chemical dictionary) Nikkan Kōgyō Shinbunsha, 1958. 1341p.

Contains about 20,000 words, mainly names of compounds with English equivalents. Appended are data sheets, tables of chemical symbols and abbreviations. Index in English.

Sōda, Tokurō 左右田徳郎 **et al.**   **Q58**
Kagōbutsu jiten 化合物事典 (Dictionary of chemical compounds) Kyōritsu Shuppan, 1954. 456, 28p.

Designed for workers in chemistry, pharmacology and medicine, lists about 10,000 compounds alphabetically by their English names and gives Japanese name, properties and references to Beilstein's *Handbuch der organischen Chemie*. Shows many structural formulas. Index of Japanese names.

Hashimoto, Yoshirō 橋本吉郎   **Q59**
Ei-Doku-Ra-Nichi kagaku ryakugo kigō jiten 英独羅日化学略語記号辞典 (English-German-Latin-Japanese dictionary of abbreviations and symbols used in chemistry) Sankyō Shuppan, 1962. 280p.

Includes about 4,000 common and technical abbreviations related to physics, chemistry, agricultural chemicals, and pharmacy, giving original words, parts of speech, equivalents in English, German, Latin and Japanese, and chemical formulas. Symbols in chemistry, pharmacy and mathematics, prefixes to organic compounds, etc. also included.

Terms

Monbushō 文部省   **Q60**
Gakujutsu yōgoshū: kagaku hen 学術用語集 化学編 Japanese scientific terms: chemistry. Rev. ed. Nankōdō, 1964. 457p.

Equates about 7,500 terms in Japanese-English and English-Japanese.

Q61
Kakaku yōgo jiten 化学用語辞典 (Glossary of chemical terms) Gihōdō, 1958. 650p.

Based on **Q60**, defines technical terms in basic and applied chemistry and the chemical industry. Arranged by their romanized Japanese with its English or German equivalent. Index of terms in English and German.

Hashimoto, Yoshirō 橋本吉郎   **Q62**
Ei-Wa Wa-Ei shin kagaku yōgo jiten 英和和英新化学用語辞典 New English-Japanese, Japanese-English dictionary of chemical terms. Sankyō Shuppan, 1964. 484p.

Defines some 10,000 words.

Matsuda, Michio 松田道夫   **Q63**
Ei-Wa kagaku yōgo shinjiten 英和化学用語新辞典 (New English-Japanese chemical dictionary) Rev. ed. Keibunsha, 1964. 1124, 163p.

Brief definitions of 17,000 English terms in theoretical and applied chemistry, pharmacy and industry. Uses and trade names given for chemical substances. Index of Japanese terms.

Hashimoto, Yoshirō 橋本吉郎   **Q64**
Kagaku Doitsugo shinjiten 化学ドイツ語新辞典 (New German-Japanese dictionary for chemists) Sankyō Shuppan, 1958. 653p.

About 20,000 words with Japanese equivalents and chemical formulas where necessary. Lacks some recent terms.

Q65
Shinkyū Ei-Doku taishō hyōjun gakujutsu yōgo jiten 新旧英独対照標準学術用語辞典 化学編 (Standard dictionary of new and old technical terms with English and German equivalents) Chemistry. Seibundō Shinkōsha, 1961. 473p.

Gives synonyms, English and German equivalents and brief explanations of terms in **Q60**.

HANDBOOKS

Nihon Kagakukai 日本化学会   **Q66**
Kagaku benran 化学便覧 (Chemical handbook) Rev. ed. Maruzen, 1958. 2075, 156p.

Most extensive Japanese compilation of chemical constants and properties of elements and compounds, giving also mathematical formulas, units, and tables used in special fields of chemistry, with definitions, usage and references. Section on applications includes inorganic-chemical and ceramic industries, chemical equipment and materials, production techniques, test methods, etc. Directory of manufacturers appended. Index.

Q67
Jōyō kagaku benran 常用化学便覧 (Chemical handbook for laboratory use) Seibundō Shinkōsha, 1960. 748p.

Contains some 7,000 tables of properties and nomenclature of organic and inorganic compounds, basic constants, thermochemistry, chemical equilibrium, reactions, electrochemistry, analytical methods using radioactivity, polymer and biochemistry, etc. Indexes.

Q68
Jikken kagaku nenran 実験化学便覧 (Handbook of experimental chemistry) Rev. ed. Kyōritsu Shuppan, 1963. 620p.

Considers solutions, density, heat and temperature, optics, physical chemistry, electrochemistry, geochemistry, analysis, reagents, chemical reactions, and photography. Tables and index.

Q69

Kagaku jikken handobukku 化学実験ハンドブック (Handbook for chemical experiments) Gihōdō, 1964. 600p.

Tabulates properties of important compounds and explains numerical values used in chemistry and pharmacology. Subject index.

Q70

Kagaku jikken sōsahō benran 化学実験操作法便覧 (Handbook for chemical experiments) Seibundō Shinkōsha, 1960. 700p.

Describes in a manner easy to follow general experimental operations, separation and purifying procedures, measurement, analysis, and operations using radioactivity. References. Illustrations of apparatus, tables of solvents and reagents, guide to accident prevention, list of important journals, appended. Subject index.

Nihon Bunseki Kagakukai **Q71**
日本分析化学会
Bunseki kagaku benran 分析化学便覧 (Handbook of analytical chemistry) Maruzen, 1961. 1428p.

Explains fundamental principles, practical operations in inorganic and organic analysis and applications, with tables and references. Analytical methods established under the Japan Industrial Standards (JIS) and the Japanese pharmacopoeia described briefly. List of apparatus and its makers appended. Index.

Hirano, Shizō 平野四蔵 **et al.** **Q72**
Kagaku bunsekihō handobukku 化学分析法ハンドブック (Handbook of chemical analysis) Sangyō Tosho, 1961. 297p.

Describes basic and typical analytical methods as a guide to engineers in laboratories and plants, with references, in sections on organic and inorganic qualitative and quantitative analyses.

Denki Kagaku Kyōkai 電気化学協会 **Q73**
Denki kagaku benran 電気化学便覧 (Handbook of electrochemistry) Maruzen, 1953. 1219p.

Fundamental theories including mathematics, chemistry, measurement, equipment and materials, and their applications in electrochemical industries and plant maintenance. Statistics and references included. Index.

Nihon Hōshasei Dōi Genso Kyōkai **Q74**
日本放射性同位元素協会

Aisotōpu benran アイソトープ便覧 (Isotopes Handbook) Maruzen, 1962. 950p.

Detailed explanations of basic facts, methods of utilization, and techniques of handling. Index.

Q75

Muki kagaku handobukku 無機化学ハンドブック (Handbook of inorganic chemistry) Gihōdō, 1960. 1205p.

Sections on elements and important compounds, basic chemistry, basic analysis, and industry give detailed information, with many figures and references, for research workers and engineers.

Yūki Gōsei Kagaku Kyōkai **Q76**
有機合成化学協会
Yūki kagaku handobukku 有機化学ハンドブック (Handbook of organic chemistry) Rev. ed. Gihōdō, 1959. 1551p.

Explains for research workers and engineers, with references, such matters as reactions, experimental operations, analysis of organic compounds, natural products, the organic-chemical industry, and constants. Indexed in Japanese and English.

MATHEMATICAL TABLES

Bukkagaku Dōkōkai 物化学同好会 **Q77**
Jōyō kagaku teisūhyō 常用化学定数表 (Tables of chemical constants for laboratory use) Rev. and enl. ed. Hirokawa Shoten, 1963. 596p.

Includes properties of important compounds, spesific gravity and concentration, solubility, viscosity and refraction indices, thermodynamic properties, optics and electrochemistry, experimental chemistry, tables for analytical calculation, nomenclature, and a conversion table of units. Technical terms used in the book are those adopted by the Japan. Chemical Society, and English names are used for chemical compounds.

Kotake, Munio 小竹無二雄 **Q78**
Yūki kagaku teisū benran 有機化学定数便覧 (Handbook of constants of organic compounds) Asakura Shoten, 1963. 765p. (Dai yūki kagaku series, supp. 2)

Includes ultraviolet and infrared absorption, optical rotatory dispersion, parachor, proton magnetic resonance, nuclear quardrupole coupling constants and asymmetry parameters, molecular diamagnetism, electric dipole moment, molecular diagrams, bond dissociation energy, thermochemical constants, dissociation constants, etc. Names of compounds given in English and indexed.

Organic syntheses

Yamada, Keisuke　山田桂輔　　**Q79**
Yūki gōsei kagaku handobukku　有機合成化
学ハンドブック (Handbook of organic syntheses)　Kōgakkan, 1958.　591p.

Names of 1,043 organic compounds, arranged alphabetically, each described with its synthetic methods, properties, uses, instructions, etc.

　　　　　　　　　　　　　　　　Q80
Yūki kagōbutsu gōseihō　有機化合物合成法
(Methods for syntheses of organic compounds)
No.1- .　Comp. by Yūki Gōsei Kagaku Kyōkai.
Gihōdō, 1949- .　14v.　Annual.

Annual results in the field of organic syntheses
in Japan, selected and reproduced, following the
style of *Organic Syntheses* (annual, 1921-). Each
item contains descriptions of the methods of preparation, instruction, properties, reactions, test
methods, and references. The quantity handled in
the preparation is kept within the range of an ordinary
laboratory. When literature indicates different values
of a property, all of them are cited. Indexes of items,
compounds and authors.

Kameya, Tetsuji　亀谷哲治　　**Q81**
Jinmei sakuin yūki hannō　　人名索引有機
反応　Name index of organic reactions. Kanehara Shuppan, 1954.　150p.

About 300 examples of general and well known
organic reactions and basic terms. Examples of
reactions are given with outlines, references and
a few experiments.　Index.

Murakami, Masuo　村上増雄　**and**　**Q82**
Yukawa, Yasuhide　湯川泰秀
Jinmei yūki hannōshū　人名有機反応集 (Collection of organic compounds arranged by types
of reactions and names)　Asakura Shoten, 1957-
58.　2v.

Chemical reactions classified according to types,
such as substitution, condensation, rearrangement,
oxydation, and reduction, and subdivided by names.
Each item described with an outline and experimental procedures in relation to electronic theory
with examples and references. Supp. volume summarizes special syntheses, decomposition, and other
reactions in chemical formulas. Name and subject
indexes.

Urushibara, Yoshiyuki　漆原義之　**Q83**
Yūki kagaku meimeihō　有機化学命名法
(Nomenclature of organic chemistry)　Rev. new

ed.　Asakura Shoten, 1962.　210p.

Includes the *Nomenclature of Organic Chemistry*
recommended by the International Union of Pure and
Applied Chemistry (IUPAC), 1957, with Japanese
and European equivalents and a list of chemical
group names in English and Japanese arranged alphabetically with chemical formulas.　Name index.

Hirayama, Kenzō　平山健三　**et al.**　**Q84**
Kagōbutsu meimeihō　化合物命名法 (Nomenclature of chemical compounds)　3d ed., rev.
Nankōdō, 1960.　394p. (Kagaku no ryōiki, zōkan
no.39)

An article-by-article translation of the conventions recommended by the IUPAC, 1957, with detailed
explanations and comments. Former recommendations, other rules and committee reports included.
Appended are tables of miscellaneous prefixes, symbols, signs and abbreviations, pronunciation of chemical words, Japanese transliteration of chemical
words, and guide to use of *Chemical Abstracts*.
Index of terms in Japanese and English.

ASTRONOMY

Heibonsha　平凡社　　**Q85**
Chikyū tenmon jiten　地球天文事典 (Handbook of the earth sciences and astronomy)　1958.
632p.　(Taikei rika jiten, 1)

Explains terms in astronomy, geophysics, meteorology, oceanography, geology, mineralogy and geography with illustrations and tables.　Detailed index.

Araki, Toshima　荒木俊馬　**and**　**Q86**
Araki, Yūgō　荒木雄豪
Gendai tenmongaku jiten　現代天文学事典
(Guidebook to modern astronomy)　Rev. and enl.
ed.　Kōseisha Kōseikaku, 1959.　727p.

Provides university students and secondary-school
teachers with systematic knowledge of all branches
of astronomy, including celestial mechanics, extragalactic nebulae and modern cosmology, as well
as such related matters as elementary differential
calculus.　Fuller and more specialized information
is given in the same publisher's 15-volume *Shin
tenmongaku kōza* (New course in astronomy).

Bizony, M. T.　　**Q87**
Uchū kūkan no hyakka jiten　宇宙空間の
百科事典　The space encyclopaedia.　Tr.
by Sadao Murayama.　Hōsei Daigaku Shuppankyoku, 1961.　280p.

Explains basic aspects of astronomy, atomic and
nuclear physics and rocket engineering related to
space research in language understandable to am-

ateur scientists and journalists as well as experts, with many photographs and other illustrations.

Hirose, Hideo 広瀬秀雄 **and Q88**
Nakano, Shigeru 中野繁
Zenten kōseizu 全天恒星図 (Map of stars and constellations) New ed. Seibundō Shinkō-sha, 1964. 75p.

Shows all stars of more than the sixth magnitude. Appended are instructions for use, names of constellations and other information helpful to amateur astronomers.

Nakano, Shigeru 中野繁 **Q89**
Hyōjun seizu 標準星図 (Standard celestial map) 4th ed. Chijin Shokan, 1960. 130p.

Similar to **Q88** but including all stars to 7.5 magnitude.

✿ A planisphere edited by the Astronomical Society of Japan and published by Sanseidō in 1958 locates stars at any hour on any date.

Calendars

Naimushō Chirikyoku 内務省地理局 **Q90**
Sansei sōran 三正綜覧 (Tabular comparison of Eastern and Western calendars) Teito Shuppansha, 1932. 424p.

The most reliable tabular comparison from 214 B.C. to 1903 A.D. of Japanese, Chinese, Islamic, and European calendars. It also contains the lunar calendar of Japan, Roman, and Julian Calendars.

Gaimushō 外務省 **Q91**
Kindai in'yōreki taishōhyō 近代陰陽暦 対照表 (Tabular comparison of modern solar and lunar calendars) 1951. 214p.

Compares dates from 1700 to 1911 A.D. Appendix includes the tabular comparison of the 60th year cyclic calendar and the Christian era from 1912 to 1970. Although it is duplicated up to 1903 by **Q90**, it is easier to use.

EARTH SCIENCES

BIBLIOGRAPHY

Kōgyō Gijutsuin, Chishitsu Chōsajo **Q92**
工業技術院地質調査所
Chishitsu Chōsajo Shuppanbutsu mokuroku 地質調査所出版物目録 (Catalogue of publications of the Geological Survey Institute)

1880-1952. Kawasaki, 1952. 124p.

In two parts for Japanese and foreign-languages, with maps classified under morphology, geology or minerals, reports listed under names of journals in which they appear. Geological map and map of coal and oil fields appended. Indexes of geographical areas, subjects and foreign-language reports.

Kōgyō Gijutsuin, Chishitsu Chōsajo **Q93**
工業技術院地質調査所
Chigaku bunken mokuroku 地学文献目録 (Bibliography of earth sciences) 1945-1955. III. Author index. Kawasaki, 1957. 696p.

Lists about 4,500 items selected from about 600 monograph collections, journals and memoirs.

Fujimoto, Haruyoshi 藤本治義 **Q94**
Nihon chishitsu bunken mokuroku 日本地質 文献目録 (Bibliography of Japanese geological studies) 1873-1955. Rev. ed. Chijin Shokan, 1956. 711p.

Classifies about 8,000 articles from 174 periodicals by subjects under regions. No index.

Suibun Chishitsu Kenkyūkai **Q95**
水文地質研究会
Chikasui onsen bunken mokuroku 地下水温泉 文献目録 (Bibliography of underground water and hot springs) Kokin Shoin, 1958. 124p.

Lists chronologically pre-1956 publications by Japanese under subjects and also geographical areas. References and foreign titles appended.

Yoshimura, Shinkichi 吉村信吉 **Q96**
Nihon koshōgaku bunken mokuroku 日本 湖沼学文献目録 (Bibliography of Japanese limnology) Chijin Shokan, 1944. 131p.

Chronologically arranged articles from scientific journals and reports published from 1883 to 1942.

DICTIONARIES

Watanabe, Tōru 渡辺貫 **Q97**
Chigaku jiten 地学辞典 (Dictionary of earth sciences) 4th ed. Kokin Shoin, 1948. 2026p.

A standard dictionary, extensive in coverage and precise in information. Gives English, German and/or French equivalents of terms. Charts. Index of foreign words.

Kudō, Chōsu 工藤暢須 **Q98**
Chigaku jiten 地学辞典 (Dictionary of earth sciences) Tokyodō, 1958. 530p.

Profusely illustrated. Appended lists of volcanoes, rivers, lakes, temperatures, amounts of precipitation, and chronological tables of geology and typhoons. Index.

Fujimoto, Haruyoshi 藤本治義 and **Q99**
Suzuki, Keishin 鈴木敬信
Chigaku kyōiku jiten 地学教育辞典 (Dictionary for education in earth sciences) Asakura Shoten, 1957. 488, 132p.

Primarily for use by teachers. Many diagrams, tables, photographs. Appended lists of laboratories, societies, research institutes, museums, and chronology.

Nihon Chishitsu Gakkai **Q100**
日本地質学会
Chisōmei jiten 地層名辞典 Index of stratographic names of Japan: Cenozoic erathem. Tokyo Daigaku Shuppankai, 1959-62. 4v.

Analyzes strata named before 1950 in Hokkaidō, Shikoku, Kyūshū and various small islands, followed by bibliography and chart of strata of Cenozoic zones.

Nihon Kōtsū Kōsha 日本交通公社 **Q101**
Nihon onsen jiten 日本温泉事典 (Dictionary of hot springs in Japan) 1957. 975p.

Guide to nature, use and development of hot springs, with pertinent information on medical science, chemistry, earth sciences, technology, biology, laws and business management. Reference list includes 1600-1868 publications. Indexes.

Fujimoto, Haruyoshi 藤本治義 **Q102**
Chishitsugaku benran 地質学便覧 (Handbook of geology) 5th ed. Kokin Shoin, 1941. 125p.

Chapters on geology, earth, elements, mineralogy, petrology, paleontology and historical geology.

SOURCE MATERIALS

Musha, Kinkichi 武者金吉 **Q103**
Nihon jishin shiryō 日本地震史料 (Historical materials on earthquakes in Japan) Mainichi Shinbunsha. 1951. 1119p.

Lists materials for Japan, Formosa and Korea from 1848 to 1867, continuing *Dai Nihon jishin shiryō*, 520 B.C. - 1847 A.D. (comp. by Monbushō, Shinsai Yobō Hyōgikai. 1941-43. 3v. Mimeographed) and gives chronology of earthquakes, volcanic eruptions, disasters, unusual colors of solar and lunar lights, changes in the water of springs, etc. from 520 B.C. to 1867, arranged by Japanese calendar years, with notes on where and the time of day they occurred. Map showing epicenters of major earthquakes from ancient times to 1950 appended.

Meteorology

BIBLIOGRAPHY

Arakawa, Hidetoshi 荒川秀俊 et al. **Q104**
Nihon kishō shiryō mokuroku 日本気象資料目録 (Bibliography of Japanese meteorological materials) Chūō Kishōdai, 1954. 457p. Mimeo.

A comprehensive list of research articles in monthlies, yearbooks, reports published by meteorological stations and weather bureaus, and scholarly journals from 1875 to 1941, arranged chronologically under publishing organizations.

Nihon Seppyō Kyōkai 日本雪氷協会 **Q105**
Seppyō kanrei ni kansuru bunken shōroku 雪氷寒冷に関する文献抄録 (Abstracts of literature on snow, ice and coldness) Nōgyō Sōgō Kenkyūjo, 1960. 186p. (Nōgyō Sōgō Kenkyūjo kankōbutsu, 201)

Abstracts 1,500 papers published from 1935 to 1950 covering agriculture, forestry, civil engineering, railways, electric power, architecture, public welfare. Continuation of *Yuki ni kansuru bunken shōroku* (Abstracts of literature on snow) 1920-35, comp. by Sekisetsu Kagaku Kenkyūjo, 1939.

DICTIONARIES

Q106
Kishō jiten 気象辞典 The cyclopedia of weather and climate. Rev. and enl. ed. Tennensha, 1957. 393, 24, 60p.

Coverage includes allied matters concerning agriculture, oceanography, and natural disasters, with forms of snow crystals and radar pictures of meteorological phenomena among illustrations. Weather charts. Index of foreign terms.

Wadachi, Kiyoo 和達清夫 **Q107**
Kishō no jiten 気象の事典 A meteorological dictionary. Enl. ed. Tokyodō, 1964. 600p.

Detailed explanations of meteorological phenomena, giving causes, classifications and measurements. Tables, charts and index appended.

Nippon Hōsō Kyōkai 日本放送協会 **Q108**
Kishō yōgoshū 気象用語集 (Glossary of meteorological terms) Nippon Hōsō Shuppan Kyōkai, 1964. 261p.

Defines for broadcasters terms covering general weather conditions, observations of the upper atmosphere, extraordinary atmospheric phenomena, earthquakes and volcanic eruptions and special reports for farmers and fishermen. Maps of observatories and trajectories of major typhoons, list of disasters and table of annual mean temperatures appended.

Sakuraba, Shin'ichi 桜庭信一 **Q109**
Nichi-Ei-Futsu-Ro kishōgaku yōgo jiten 日英仏露気象学用語事典 Meteorological vocabulary: Japanese-English-French-Russian. Izumi Shobō, 1960. 166p.

Briefly explains each term with English, French, Russian equivalents. English index.

HANDBOOK

Q110
Kishōgaku handobukku 気象学ハンドブック (Meteorology handbook) Gihōdō, 1959. 1580p.

For practical use by technicians. Covers not only weather and climate but also such related subjects as mathematics, physics, chemistry and astronomy, with formulas, diagrams and tables. Lists of terms used by international stations and weather symbols and trajectories of typhoons appended. Index.

CHRONOLOGY

Okada, Takematsu 岡田武松 **Q111**
Sekai kishōgaku nenpyō 世界気象学年表 (World chronological table of meteorology) Enl. by Hidetoshi Arakawa. Chijin Shokan, 1956. 229p. (Kishōgaku kōza, supp.)

Covers the period, 1441-1956.

Q112
Nihon kishō saigai nenpyō 日本気象災害年表 (Chronological table of meteorological disasters in Japan)

1900-47. Comp. by Chūō Kishōdai. Keizai Antei Honbu, 1949. 172p. (Shigen Chōsakai shiryō, 17)

1948-59. Comp. by Kishōchō. Kishō Kyōkai, 1960. 175p.

These two volumes and **Q114** cover the histroy of unusual weather phenomena from 176 B.C. to 1959 except the period 1888-1899. The 1900-47 volume consists of dates, kinds, extent of disasters, meteorological elements, and written sources; the 1948-59 volume gives in addition detailed figures on extent of disasters.

ILLUSTRATIONS

Ishimaru, Yūkichi 石丸雄吉 **Q113**
Kumo no shashin to zukai 雲の写真と図解 Cloud atlas. Hokuryūkan, 1953. 251p.

Contains 119 photographs of various kinds of clouds with analytical explanations based on photographic measurements.

SOURCE MATERIALS

Chūō Kishōdai 中央気象台 **Q114**
Nihon kishō shiryō sōran 日本気象史料綜覧 (Survey of Japanese meteorological source materials) Chijin Shokan, 1943. 248p.

Chronological table (176 B.C. - 1887 A.D.) listing localities, subjects and titles of source materials, based on *Nihon Kishō shiryō* (Japanese meteorological source materials) and supplement published in 1939. Contains a list of books cited in the table.

Oceanography

Terada, Kazuhiko 寺田一彦 **et al.** **Q115**
Kaiyō no jiten 海洋の事典 (Cyclopedia of oceans) Tokyodō, 1964. 671p.

About 1,600 entries on all aspects of oceanography, including marine products, with tables and diagrams. Tables of tides around Japan and water temperatures and directory of oceanographic institutes appended. Index.

Chūō Kishōdai 中央気象台 **Q116**
Kaiyō kansoku jōyōhyō 海洋観測常用表 (Tables for oceanographic observations) 1955. 96p. (Kaiyō kansoku shishin, supp.)

Thirty-three tables, including ones for calibration of Akanuma standard hydrometer, specific gravity and harmonic analysis.

Mineralogy

BIBLIOGRAPHY

Naikaku Shigenkyoku 内閣資源局 **Q117**
Jūyō kōbutsu shigen shiryō mokuroku 重要鉱物資源資料目録 (Bibliography of important mineral resources) 1936. 263p.

Lists Japanese and foreign periodical articles published from 1929 to 1934, classified by name of minerals.

Q118

Nihon san kōbutsu bunkenshū 日 本 産 鉱 物 文 献 集 (Bibliography on minerals produced in Japan) 1872-1956. Sapporo, Kōbutsu Bunkenshū Henshū Iinkai, 1959. 412p.

Lists periodical articles published from 1872 to 1956, classified under names of minerals.

DICTIONARIES

Kinoshita, Kameki 木 下 亀 城 **Q119**
Kōbutsu gakumei jiten 鉱 物 学 名 辞 典 (Dictionary of mineralogy terms) Kazama Shobō, 1960. 1002p.

Briefly explains technical terms in mineralogy, petrology and related subjects and gives Japanese equivalents.

Okamoto, Yōhachiro 岡 本 要 八 郎 **and** **Q120**
Kinoshita, Kameki 木 下 亀 城
Kōbutsu wamei jiten 鉱 物 和 名 辞 典 (Dictionary of Japanese names of minerals) Kazama Shobō, 1959. 874p.

Gives old and new terms, including those of foreign origin and popular and dialect terms of minerals, jewels, rocks, stoneware, quarries and mines.

Kume, Takeo 久 米 武 夫 **Q121**
Shin hōseki jiten 新 宝 石 辞 典 (New dictionary of jewels). Rev. and enl. ed. Kazama Shobō, 1962. 480p.

Describes jewels and allied subjects for jewelers. Tables give weights and styles of cutting.

ILLUSTRATIONS

Kinoshita, Kameki 木 下 亀 城 **Q122**
Genshoku kōseki zukan 原 色 鉱 石 図 鑑 Coloured illustrations of economic minerals. Rev. and enl. ed. Osaka, Hoikusha, 1962. 229p. (Hoikusha no genshoku zukan, 14)

About 300 representative ores in color, and about 100 microphotographs, classified under precious metals, radioactive metals, crude jewels, etc. References and tables, including microscopic properties of economic minerals, and list of mines by prefectures appended. Index.

Supp. volume, ed. by Kameki Kinoshita and Hideo Minato. 1963. 300p. (Hoikusha no genshoku zukan, 31) Describes forms and crystallographic and chemical properties of some 350 ores. A method of examining opaque minerals by reflecting microscope appended.

Masutomi, Hisanosuke 益 富 寿 之 助 **Q123**
Genshoku ganseki zukan 原 色 岩 石 図 鑑 Coloured illustrations of rocks. Osaka, Hoikusha, 1955. 158p. (Hoikusha no genshoku zukan, 13)

Contains color photographs of 288 rocks and 61 rock minerals and 86 microphotographs, classified and explained, with notes on how to prepare specimens, microscopic examinations, the mechanism of the polarized microscope and visual methods of rock appraisal. Tables of optical properties of rock minerals and refractive indexes of anisotropic metals appended.

Shibata, Hidekata 柴 田 秀 賢 **and** **Q124**
Sutō, Toshio 須 藤 俊 男
Genshoku kōbutsu ganseki zukan 原 色 鉱 物 岩 石 図 鑑 Keys to the illustrated manual of minerals and rocks in full colour. Hokuryūkan, 1956. 280p.

Water-color paintings of 370 minerals, including crystal forms of important ones, and 200 rocks, with microscopic properties of some. Methods of collecting rocks, properties of crystals and minerals, classification, etc. appended.

Shikama, Tokio 鹿 間 時 夫 **Q125**
Nihon kaseki zufu 日 本 化 石 図 譜 Index fossils of Japan. Rev. ed. Asakura Shoten, 1964. 287p.

Lists about 2,000 fossils under animals and plants, giving for each its size, name of discoverer, time and place of discovery, period of fossilization. Appendixes include tables showing distribution of geological eras and formations in East Asia and technical terms of forms of fossils. Index of generic names.

Endō, Seidō 遠 藤 誠 道 **Q126**
Nihon san kaseki shokubutsu zufu 日 本 産 化 石 植 物 図 譜 Icones of fossil plants from Japanese Islands. Sangyō Tosho, 1955. 104p.

Contains 51 plates of fossil plants with their scientific names and places and strata where they were excavated. List of references.

Ōishi, Saburō 大 石 三 郎 **Q127**
Tōa koshokubutsu bunrui zusetsu 東 亜 古 植 物 分 類 図 説 Illustrated catalogue of East-Asiatic fossil plants. Kyoto, Chigaku Shuppan Shiseisha, 1950. 2v.

Describes 320 plants, mostly extinct, arranged by botanical classification. Appended list of about 180 fossil plants without illustrations, and list of references. Index of scientific names.

TECHNOLOGY AND INDUSTRY

GENERAL WORKS

BIBLIOGRAPHY

R1

Kagaku gijutsu bunken sokuhō　科学技術文献速報 (Bulletins on scientific and technical literature) Nihon Kagaku Gijutsu Jōhō Sentā, 1958- .

Chemistry and chemical engineering series. v.1- . 1958- . semimonthly.

General engineering and mechanical engineering series. v.1- . 1958- . semimonthly.

Electrical engineering series. v.1- . 1958- semimonthly.

Metal engineering, mining engineering, earth sciences series. v.1- . 1958- . semimonthly.

Civil engineering, architectural engineering series. v.1 - . 1958- . semimonthly.

Physics and applied physics series. v.1- 1959- . semimonthly.

Atomic power abstracts (Isotope and radiation chemistry series). v.1- . 1961- . monthly.

Management and supervision series. v.1- 1963- . monthly.

Very useful with **R2** and **R16** for searching foreign sources. Combined series abstract yearly about 150,000 articles from foreign journals kept on file by the Japan Science and Technology Information Center except for "Atomic power abstracts", which includes Japanese. Author and subject indexes since 1960. List of journals consulted published yearly.

R2

Gijutsu bunken nyūsu　技術文献ニュース Current technical literature. Kokuritsu Kokkai Toshokan, Etsuranbu, 1961- . monthly.

Indexes reports of European and American national research institutes, American university dissertations and theses, English translations of Soviet literature, etc. Succeeds *Saiensu raiburari* (Science library), published by PB Report-sha, v.1, 1955- v.6, no. 8, 1960.

DICTIONARIES

Heibonsha　平凡社　　**R3**
Kōgyō daijiten　工業大事典　(Encyclopedia of industry) 1959-62. 18v.

Covers all branches of industrial engineering, with emphasis on manufacturing. Photographs, diagrams and English equivalents of key terms.

Mizuno, Tsunekichi　水野常吉　**R4**
Ei-Wa-Doku, Doku-Ei-Wa kōgyō yōgo shinjiten 英和独　独英和　工業用語新辞典 Neues Technisches Wörterbuch: englisch-japanisch-deutsch, deutsch-englisch-japanisch. 4th ed. Keibunsha, 1956. 486p.

Each part equates about 10,000 terms.

Kōgyō Kyōiku Kenkyūkai　　**R5**
工業教育研究会
Zukai kōgyō yōgo jiten　図解工業用語辞典 (Illustrated dictionary of technical terms) Nikkan Kōgyō Shinbunsha, 1961. 446p.

Explains about 4,000 terms, including popular words and words of foreign origin, with 700 illustrations. Abbreviations and symbols listed. Western language - Japanese index.

R6

Gendai sangyō yōgo no kiso chishiki　現代産業用語の基礎知識　(Principles of current industrial terminology) 1964- . Jiyū Kokuminsha, 1964- . 1v. Annual.

Classified dictionary of terms, manufacturing processes, and names of new products, related to building construction, various industries, and public works, with simple explanations for common use. Illustrated with many diagrams and charts. Index of terms and illustrations.

DIRECTORIES

Nihon Gakujutsu Kaigi 日本学術会議 **R7**
Kōgaku kenkyūsha meibo 工学研究者名簿 (Directory of engineering research workers) 1953- . Nikkan Kōgyō Shinbunsha, 1953-57, 1961- . 6v.

Classified listing of workers in research institutes, limited to university graduates with at least seven years of experience, and their specialties. Issues for 1953, 1955, 1957 give workers in university and government research institutes; those for 1954, 1956, 1961, workers in private companies and institutes.

R8
Zenkoku kōjo tsūran 全国工場通覧 (National survey of factories) 1931- . Comp. by Tsūshō Sangyōshō. 1931- . 21v. Biennial.

Compiled from replies to industrial census questionnaires from owners of all factories with ten or more workers. Gives addresses, capital assets, main and branch establishments, etc., classified according to kinds of business and localities. Public corporation establishments, research institutes, associations and related financial enterprises listed in appendixes. Trade edition published by Nikkan Kōgyō Shinbunsha.

STATISTICS

R9
Kōgyō tōkeihyō 工業統計表 Census of manufactures 1939- . Comp. by Tsūshō Sangyōshō 1942- . 20v. Annual.

Former title: *Kōjō tōkeihyō*, 1909, 1914, 1919-1938. 22v.

Official statistics on production, number of employees, facilities, etc. of factories with three or more workers. Products listed by categories and localities. The first 14 volumes of *(Kōjō tōkeihyō)* (1909-29) are being reprinted by Keiō Shobō. To compensate for the three-year lag in publication the following title gives rough statistics on factories with 30 or more workers:

Kōgyō tōkei sokuhō (Advance report on industrial statistics) 1948- . Comp. by Tsūshō Sangyōshō. 1949- . 16v. Annual **R9a.**

Tsūshō Sangyōshō 通商産業省 **R10**
Kōgyō tōkei gojūnenshi 工業統計50年史

History of the census of manufactures (for 1909-1958) 1961-63. 3v.

Gives statistics for industries and individual products from the time the regulations for census reports by manufacturers were promulgated, with general survey of industrial development and historical outlines of each segment of industry, different scales of industry and regional industries. Tables have both Japanese and English headings.

YEARBOOKS

R11
Kagaku gijutsu nenkan 科学技術年鑑 (Yearbook of science and technology) 1958-62. Comp. by Nihon Kagaku Gijutsu Shinkō Zaidan. Gihōdō, 1958-62. 4v.

Reports developments in research, including important reports and studies, in education and in government policies and appropriations. Also covers major developments in other countries. Appended are laws and regulations, recommendations of official bodies, directory of learned societies, information on research funds and list of government publications. Developments in preceding prewar years summarized in 1958 edition.

R12
Nihon sangyō no genjō 日本産業の現状 (The present state of Japanese industry) 1959-1960. Comp. by Tsūshō Sangyōshō. Tsūshō Sangyō Chōsakai, 1959-60. 2v.

Gives detailed data on production, capital investments, consumption, imports and exports, the international trade structure, industrial growth factors and rate changes, etc., with analyses and many tables. Tables indexed. Discontinued.

R13
Kagaku gijutsu hakusho 科学技術白書 (White paper on science and technology) 1958- . Comp. by Kagaku Gijutsuchō. Ōkurashō Insatsukyoku, 1958- . 3v. Irregular.

Explains general trends in science and technology in Japan and discusses important topics of the year.

INDUSTRIAL STANDARDS

Nihon Kikaku Kyōkai 日本規格協会 **R14**
JIS kikaku sōmokuroku ＪＩＳ規格総目録 (A complete catalogue of JIS standards) As of March 31, 1964. 1964. 162, 68p.

Gives the Japanese industrial standards established by Mar. 31, 1964, in the following 17 categories, each subdivided by products: civil engineering and construction, railways, shipbuilding, iron and steel, non-ferrous metals, chemical reagents, textiles, mining, paper and pulp, ceramics, daily necessities, medical apparatus, aircraft, and sundries. Industrial Standardization Law appended. Index.

Gyōsei Kanrichō Tōkei Kijunkyoku **R15**
行 政 管 理 庁 統 計 基 準 局
Nihon hyōjun sangyō bunrui 日 本 標 準 産 業 分 類 (Japanese standard industrial classification) 5th rev. ed. 1959. 2v.

Explains the basic principles of classification and lists with their classification numbers about 16,500 products of representative industries. Useful for compilers and users of industrial statistics.

PATENTS · TRADEMARKS

R16
Gaikoku tokkyo sokuhō: kagakuhen 外 国 特 許 速 報 化 学 編 Foreign patent news: chemistry. v.1, no.1- . Comp. by Nihon Kagaku Gijutsu Jōhō Sentā. Apr. 25, 1958- weekly.

Includes abstracts from the *Official gazette* of the U.S. Patent Office. Index of American patent applicants and indexes of British and West German patents.

Tokkyochō 特 許 庁 **R17**
Tokkyo bunruibetsu sōmokuroku 特 許 分 類 別 総 目 録 (Complete classified patent catalogue) Aug., 1885-Dec., 1956. Gihōdō, 1958. 1044p.

Lists 778,508 patents registered in Japan from Aug., 1885, through 1956, divided into 14,993 categories, with registration or notification numbers. Kept up-to-date annually since 1957 under the same title. 5v.

Tokkyochō 特 許 庁 **R18**
Hatsumei oyobi jitsuyō shin'an no bunruihyō 発 明 及 び 実 用 新 案 の 分 類 表 (Classification system of inventions and utility models) As revised in Jan., 1962. Gihōdō, 1962. 426p.

Tokkyochō 特 許 庁 **R19**
Hatsumei oyobi jitsuyō shin'an bunrui no sakuin 発 明 お よ び 実 用 新 案 分 類 の 索 引 (Index to the classification of inventions and utility models) Rev. ed. Gihōdō, 1963. 346p.

Over 21,000 entries, including terms used in **R18** and popular synonyms.

Tokkyochō 特 許 庁 **R20**
Jitsuyo shin an bunruibetsu sōmokuroku 実 用 新 案 分 類 別 総 目 録 (Complete classified

catalogue of utility models) July, 1905-Dec., 1956. Gihōdō, 1958-59. 3v.

Classifies and lists by registration numbers all models entered in the *Jitsuyo shin'an kōhō* (Utility model gazette) from 1905 through 1956. Kept up-to-date by an annual since 1957 under the same title. 4v.

Shōhyō Kenkyūkai 商 標 研 究 会 **R21**
Nihon shōhyō daijiten 日 本 商 標 大 事 典 (Encyclopedia of Japanese trademarks) Chūō-sha, 1959. 1460p.

Surveys the history, principles and applications of trade-mark laws, international treaties and systems in other countries and lists famous and important trade-marks, signs and slogans. Directory of patent attorneys appended. Detailed tables of contents; index of trademark owners.

Statistical engineering

Tokyo Kōgyō Daigaku, Tōkei Kōgaku **R22**
Kenkyūkai 東 京 工 業 大 学 統 計 工 学 研 究 会
Tōkei kōgaku handobukku 統 計 工 学 ハ ン ド ブ ッ ク (Handbook of statistics and engineering) Gihōdō, 1953-54. 2v.

Explains statistical techniques and their application in production control and non-industrial fields. Bibliography and index. Numerical tables in supplementary volume.

Measurement and control

Seiki Gakkai 精 機 学 会 **and Nihon** **R23**
Keisoku Gakkai 日 本 計 測 学 会
Kōgyō sokutei benran 工 業 測 定 便 覧 Technical measurement handbook. Rev. ed. Koronasha, 1964. 1258p.

Covers measurement concepts, mechanical and electrical measuring instruments, measurement of length and angles, testing of materials, measurement of sounds, vibrations, fluids and temperatures, chemical analysis, optical and electromagnetic measurements, aeronautic instruments and automatic controls, each with reference list. Index.

Chūō Keiryō Kenteijo **R24**
中 央 計 量 検 定 所
Keiryō gijutsu handobukku 計 量 技 術 ハ ン ド ブ ッ ク (Handbook of measurement techniques) 2d ed., rev. Koronasha, 1959. 857p.

For use by workers. Explains weights and measures, with tables and reference lists. Index.

R25
Seigyo kōgaku handobukku 制 御 工 学 ハ ン ド

ブック Control engineering handbook. Asakura Shoten, 1964. 1299p.

Provides simple documented and illustrated explanations of basic machine tool and calculating machine principles and applications. For students and technicians.

Jidō Seigyo Kenkyūkai   **R26**
自動制御研究会
Jidō seigyo benran 自動制御便覧 (Automatic control manual) Koronasha, 1959. 1064, 74p.

Explains fundamentals, equipment and techniques. Directory of manufacturers appended. Index.

    R27
Purosesu keisoku seigyo benran プロセス計測制御便覧 (Process measurement and control manual) Nikkan Kōgyō Shinbunsha, 1960. 1289p.

Deals with the principles, means and techniques of measuring and testing materials, energy, operations and products, with sections on cost-cutting and safety and health controls. Index.

Industrial materials

Nagai, Shōichirō 永井彰一郎   **R28**
Muki yūki kōgyō zairyo benran 無機有機工業材料便覧 (Manual of inorganic and organic industrial materials) Tōyō Keizai Shinpōsha, 1960. 1749p.

Emphasis on plastics and other new synthetics, special ceramic products, etc. in 33 classifications, with notes on conventional materials improved by new processing methods and detailed descriptions of new materials of high potentialities. Index of raw materials and products.

Nihon Zairyō Shiken Kyōkai   **R29**
日本材料試験協会
Zairyō shiken benran 材料試験便覧 (Materials testing manual) Maruzen, 1957. 1110, 168p.

Practical information in simple terms on how to plan and carry out tests, with many illustrations. References. Index.

Shizai Kikaku Chōsa Kenkyūkai   **R30**
資材規格調査研究会
Shizai benran 資材便覧 (Industrial materials handbook) 1964 ed. Hakua Shobō, 1964. 1235p.

Guidance in the selection, purchase and handling of coal and petroleum products, iron and steel, nonferrous metals, chemicals, ceramic products, oils and fats, paints, rubber, leather, textiles, paper, wood, building materials, electrical appliances and plastics. Tables. Index.

Industrial management

    R31
Kōgyō keiei benran 工業経営便覧 (Industrial management handbook) Nikkan Kōgyō Shinbunsha, 1960. 2129p.

Explains procedures, with many tables and illustrations. Reference lists. Index.

PRODUCTION CONTROL

    R32
Seisan kanri benran 生産管理便覧 (Handbook of production control) Rev. ed. Maruzen, 1962. 1919p.

Covers controls in relation to research, technology, patents, production planning and organization, facilities, processes, sub-contracting, transportation, work studies, standardization, quality maintenance, metallurgy, measurement, automation, machinery and tools, packaging, power, labor management, education and training, safety, sanitation, plant accounting, profit management, office work, etc., with photographs, diagrams, documentary materials and references. Index. See also **R33**.

International Labor Organization   **R33**
Wāku sutadei benran ワークスタディ便覧 (Handbook of work studies) Tr. by Nihon Seisansei Honbu. 1959. 437p.

Suitable for textbook use in training for productivity, research and work measurement studies. Bibliography. Index in English and Japanese.

Chūshō Kigyō Shindan Kyōkai   **R34**
中小企業診断協会
Kigyō shindan handobukku: kōgyō hen 企業診断ハンドブック 工業編 (Business diagnosis handbook: industrial section) Dōyūkan, 1960-62. 2v.

Based on experience of the small- and medium-sized industries agency since 1948, it covers diagnosis of management, finances, purchasing, production, sales, labor, processing, power, quality and operational controls, materials, equipment, designing, work areas, subcontracting, etc., with guidance in reporting diagnoses.

    R35
Kōtei kanri benran 工程管理便覧 (Handbook of process controls) Rev. and enl. ed. Nikkan Kōgyō Shinbunsha, 1961. 927p.

Explains fundamental principles and ways to plan and improve production, with examples and illustrations. Index. Useful with **R32**.

Hinshitsu kanri benran 品質管理便覧 (Handbook of quality controls) Nihon Kikaku Kyōkai, 1962. 986p. **R36**

Information for factory owners on principles and applications of quality controls from receipt of materials to sale of products, including testing methods and use of statistics, with tables, glossary and bibliography. Index with English equivalents of terms.

Chūō Netsu Kanri Kyōgikai **R37**
中央熱管理協議会
Netsu kanri benran 熱管理便覧 (Heat control manual) Rev. ed. Maruzen, 1963. 794, 93p.

Explains in detail heat calculations, thermodynamics, fuels, including measurement and chemical analysis, and equipment, with illustrations, tables, practice problems and references. Brief index.

Osaka Furitsu Sangyō Nōritsu **R38**
Kenkyūjo 大阪府立産業能率研究所
Shikisai kanri handobukku 色彩管理ハンドブック (Color control handbook) Gihōdo, 1953. 263p.

Covers plant facilities, equipment and techniques for color control, with standard industrial color control terms, Japan Color Research Institute symbols, and revised Munsell color notation system.

INDUSTRIAL SAFETY

Takeuchi, Toshisuke 武内敏介 **R39**
Sangyō anzen yōgo kaisetsu 産業安全用語解説 (Industrial safety terms explained) Zen Nihon Sangyō Anzen Rengōkai, 1955. 155p.

Detailed explanations of a limited number of terms.

R40
Sangyō anzen nenkan 産業安全年鑑 Industrial safety yearbook. 1957- . Zen Nihon Sangyō Anzen Rengōkai, 1957- . 8v. Annual.

Reports Japanese and foreign developments in prevention of industrial accidents, with statistics.

LABOR MANAGEMENT

Uchida, Tomoji 内田知二 **et al.** **R41**
Kōjō kantokusha pokettobukku 工場監督者ポケットブック (Pocket book for factory supervisors) OHM-sha, 1959. 235p.

Explains, with illustrations and tables, improvement of productivity, modernization of facilities and rationalization of management and work.

Rōmu Kanri Kenkyūkai **R42**
労務管理研究会
Saishin rōmu kanri sōran 最新労務管理総覧 (Up-to-date survey of labor management) Nihon Keieisha Dantai Renmei, 1959. 713p.

Gives postwar developments in labor supervision, on-the-job training, workshop management, welfare facilities, etc., with reports on labor management in major concerns and bibliography. Lists local labor management organizations.

CIVIL ENGINEERING

DICTIONARIES

Monbushō 文部省 **R43**
Gakujutsu yōgoshu: doboku kōgaku hen 学術用語集 土木工学編 Japanese scientific terms: civil engineering. Doboku Gakkai, 1960. 395p.

Japanese-English and English-Japanese dictionary of standard terms.

R44
Hyōjun gakujutsu yōgo jiten (shinkyū Ei-Doku taishō) Doboku kōgaku hen 標準学術用語辞典 新旧英独対照 土木工学編 (Standard dictionary of technical terms: civil engineering section, with new and old terms and English and German equivalents) Seibundō Shinkōsha, 1962. 508p.

Based on **R43**, gives the historical development, synonyms and colloquial equivalents of each term. Strong in terms for new methods, materials and equipment.

HANDBOOKS

Doboku Gakkai 土木学会 **R45**
Doboku kōgaku handobukku 土木工学ハンドブック (Civil engineering handbook) Rev. ed. Gihōdo, 1964. 3v.

Each of 38 sections has reference list. Useful because of extensive reference data, including excerpts of the Japan industrial standards, and calculation examples. Index.

R46
Doboku kōgaku pokettobukku 土木工学ポケットブック (Civil engineering pocket book) Junior ed. OHM-sha, 1962. 1173p.

Reliable information for on-site engineers of technical highschool graduate level.

Construction works

Sudō, Makane 須藤真金　　　　　**R47**
Wa-Ei kensetsu jiten　和英建設辞典
(Japanese-English construction glossary)　Rikō
Tosho, 1958.　165p.

Entries in Japanese syllabary are given their e-
quivalents in Chinese characters and in English.

　　　　　　　　　　　　　　　　　　R48
Kensetsu gyōmu tōkei nenpō 建設業務統計
年報 (Annual statistical report on construction work)　1955- .　Comp. by Kensetsushō.
1956- .　9v.　Annual.

Former title: *Kensetsu tōkei nenpyō* (Annual
statistical report on construction) 1949-54.　6v.

Gives findings in annual surveys made by national and local public agencies.

　　　　　　　　　　　　　　　　　　R49
Kokudo kensetsu no genkyō 国土建設の現
況 (Present state of land development and
construction) 1951- .　Comp. by Kensetsushō.
1951- .　14v.　Annual.

Surveys facilities, technical levels, and immediate
and projected objectives in riparian works, road
building, city planning, housing, public buildings,
development planning, overseas co-operation, surveying, map revision and research in construction
techniques. Trade edition titled *Kensetsu hakusho*
(Construction white paper).

　　　　　　　　　　　　　　　　　　R50
Jitsuyō kensetsu meikan　実用建設名鑑
(Practical construction directory)　1959- .
Nikkan Kensetsu Tsūshinsha,　1959, 1961- .
5v.　Annual.

Gives names of responsible persons in governmental agencies, public corporations, universities,
architectural offices, construction companies and
other agencies concerned with construction. Classified index.

Nikkan Kensetsu Kōgyō Shinbunsha　　**R51**
日刊建設工業新聞社
Kensetsu gyōsha yōran　建設業者要覧
(Directory of construction companies)　1963 ed.
1962.　1193p.

Lists all companies registered with the Ministry
of Construction, architectural and designing offices
and suppliers of construction equipment and materials.

DISASTERS AND RECONSTRUCTION

　　　　　　　　　　　　　　　　　　R52
Saigai tōkei 災害統計 (Disaster statistics)

1954- .　Comp. by Kensetsushō, Kasenkyoku.
1955- .　10v.　Annual.

Tables on the year's disasters, classified by
types, with reconstruction or rehabilitation expenditures. Appended are meteorological records, maps
showing typhoon routes, estimates of government
aid, etc. The first volume covers the 1946-53 period.

Kensetsushō Kasenkyoku　　　　　**R53**
建設省河川局
Saikin jukkanen no saigai tōkei　最近 10 ヶ
年の災害統計 (Disaster statistics for the
past ten years)　1959.　128p.

Combines statistics for 1948-57 taken from **R52**,
including national and prefectural expenditures on
public civil engineering for disaster rehabilitation.
Appended are tabulation of government disaster-
relief grants since 1868, meteorological records,
typhoon routes, etc.

MATERIALS

Doshitsu Kōgakkai 土質工学会　　　**R54**
Doshitsu kōgaku yōgoshū　土質工学用語集
(Soil engineering glossary)　Gihōdō, 1957.　46,
3, 7p.

English-Japanese and Japanese-English sections
equate about 1,000 terms taken mainly from the
glossary published by the 1953 3rd World Congress
on Fundamental Soil Engineering.　Symbols given.

U. S. Bureau of Reclamation　　　**R55**
Doshitsu benran: doshitsu chōsa, shiken kikaku
hen　土質便覧 土質調査試験規格編
(Earth manual: section on soil investigation
and test specifications)　Kyoto Daigaku Doboku-
kai, 1963.　421p.

Translation of the 1960 edition of *Earth Manual:
A guide to the use of soil as foundations and as
construction materials for hydraulic structures*, covering on-site and laboratory tests and work supervision,
for which Japanese standards have not yet been developed.

U. S. Bureau of Reclamation　　　**R56**
Doboku zairyō shiken benran 土木材料試験
便覧　Material testing procedures manual. Tr.
by Yasuo Kondō.　Kokumin Kagakusha, 1962.
303p.

With nothing comparable of Japanese authorship,
this translation is indispensable for construction
specialists and manufacturers of materials. Gives
detailed information on the handling of samples,
testing apparatus and methods,　interpretation of
results, report forms, etc.

Concrete

Kondō, Yasuo 近藤泰夫 **R57**
Konkurīto jiten コンクリート辞典 (Concrete dictionary) Nihon Semento Gijutsu Kyōkai, 1959. 254p.
　Explains in simple terms about 3,000 words, including brand names. English-Japanese index.

U.S. Bureau of Reclamation **R58**
Konkurīto manyuaru
コンクリートマニュアル
Concrete manual. Tr. by Yasuo Kondō. Kokumin Kagakusha, 1963. 427, 17p.
　Translation of *Concrete manual: A detailed handbook covering all aspects of the raw materials and applications of concerete*, 6th ed. Index.

Kondō, Yasuo 近藤泰夫 **and** **R59**
Ban, Shizuo 坂静雄
Konkurīto handobukku コンクリートハンドブック (Concrete handbook) Asakura Shoten, 1957. 745p.
　Gives simple explanations of materials, mixing and laying methods and designing of reinforced concrete, with much reference data on testing and construction. Lists companies and products. Index.

Surveying

Kensetsushō, Chiri Chōsajo **R60**
建設省地理調査所
Sokuryō chizu benran 測量地図便覧 (Handbook of surveying and maps) Kensetsu Kyōkai, 1950. 213p.
　Outlines the history of the Geographical Survey Institute and describes in detail its surveying, cartographic, photographic, plate-making and map-printing operations. Reference tables and pertinent legislation appended.

Hayashi, Ikkan 林一幹 **and** **R61**
Kasugaya, Nobumasa 春日屋伸昌
Sokuryō benran 測量便覧 (Surveying handbook) Morikita Shuppan, 1959. 888p.
　Describes techniques and gives tables, relevant legislation, list of abbreviations and glossary of technical terms. Index.

Kasugaya, Nobumasa 春日屋伸昌 **R62**
Shūsei sokuryōhyō 集成測量表 (Compilation of surveying tables) Morikita Shuppan, 1958. 697p.
　Gives traverse, grade conversion, curve function

and other tables, each with detailed explanation and examples of its use. Short list of abbreviations appended.

DESIGN MANUALS

Doboku sekkei benran 土木設計便覧 (Civil **R63**
engineering design manual) Rev. ed. Maruzen. 1961. 1330p.
　Covers dynamics, hydrography, designing of temporary structures, etc., with many formulae, tables and graphs. Reference data on bridges and roads appended. Index.

Kinoshita, Yōzaburō 木下洋三郎 **R64**
Genba katsuyō doboku sekkei handobukku 現場活用土木設計ハンドブック (On-site practical civil engineering design handbook) Rikō Tosho, 1957. 2v.
　v.1 gives basic formulae and mathematical data arranged to facilitate rapid calculations; v. 2, design reference materials, including tables and graphs.

R65
Doboku sekkei dēta bukku 土木設計データブック (Civil engineering design data book) Morikita Shuppan, 1960. 772p.
　Broad range of designing information in 22 chapters with 350 subdivisions.

R66
Doboku sekō dēta bukku 土木施工データブック (Civil engineering works data book) Morikita Shuppan, 1964. 1106p.
　Complements **R65** with coverage of surveying, earthwork, machinery, work methods and special undertakings, giving cost and other data.

MACHINERY

R67
Kensetsu kikai zairyō benran 建設機械材料便覧 (Manual of construction machinery and materials) Sankaidō, 1963. 633p. (Saishin doboku sekōhō kōza, supp.)
　Surveys up-to-date construction methods, machinery and materials, with directory of construction companies.

Nihon Kensetsu Kikaika Kyōkai **R68**
日本建設機械化協会
Nihon kensetsu kikai yōran 日本建設機械

要覧 (Survey of Japanese construction machinery) 1964. 1399p.

Confined to machinery and equipment which have passed exacting inspection and have good performance records.

Roads

Dōro sōran 道路総覧 (General survey of roads) 1957- . Comp. by Keizai Seisaku Kenkyūkai, 1956- . 7v. Annual.   **R69**

Annual review of road and highway administration, traffic, roads and the national livelihood, present state of roads, reorganization and consolidation of roads, highway planning, based on materials of the Ministries of Construction and Transportation, Japan Public Highway Corporation and Construction Bureau of the Tokyo Metropolitan Government.

Nihon Dōro Kyōkai 日本道路協会   **R70**
Dōro benran 道路便覧 (Road manual) Koronasha, 1959. 1105p.

Describes new techinques, with emphasis on reference data, for building roads, earthwork, paving, maintenance, auxiliary facilities, etc. Index.

Dōro tōkei nenpō 道路統計年報 Road statistics. 1949- . Comp. by Kensetsushō Dōrokyoku. 1951- . 14v. Annual.   **R71**

Data on roads, bridges and construction expenditures based on surveys by prefectural governments and local construction bureaus, with percentage of the national budget spent on roads, road income, automobile taxes and vehicle registrations appended.

Rivers

Suematsu, Sakae 末松栄   **R72**
Kasen kōgaku benran 河川工学便覧 (Manual of river engineering) Koronasha, 1954. 2v.

Gives detailed information on planning and operations, with relevant legislation and river map appended. Index.

Sanitary engineering

Denryoku Chūō Kenkyūjo   **R73**
電力中央研究所
Taiki osen ni kansuru bunken mokuroku 大気汚染に関する文献目録 (Bibliography of atmospheric pollution literature) No. 1- .

1963- . 2v. In progress.

No. 1: Classified listing of 1960-62 articles in 73 Western-language and 23 Japanese periodicals. No.2: Articles from 1963 through Mar., 1964, in 93 periodicals.

Taiki Osen Kenkyūkai Zenkoku **R74**
Kyōgikai 大気汚染研究会全国協議会
Jojin sōchi handobukku 除塵装置ハンドブック (Handbook of dust-removal equipment) Koronasha, 1963. 352p.

Surveys atmospheric pollution and various kinds of equipment for removal of dust, smoke and soot.

Tokyoto Suidōkyoku, Suidō Kenkyūkai **R75**
東京都水道局水道研究会
Jōge suidō jitsumu handobukku 上下水道実務ハンドブック (Handbook of water supply and drainage services) Asakura Shoten, 1962. 1025p.

Comprehensive coverage of technical and practical details. Index.

                                      R76
Suidō nenkan 水道年鑑 (Water system yearbook) 1960- . Suidō Sangyō Shinbunsha, 1960- . 5v.

Based on documents and statistics of the year, covers all aspects of utilization of water resources, city water, industrial and agricultural water supply, protection of water supply and sewage disposal. Directory of related government offices and companies appended.

ARCHITECTURE

BIBLIOGRAPHY

                                      R77
Nihon Kenchiku Gakkai sōritsu shichijusshūnen kinen Kenchiku Zasshi, ronbunshū, kenkyū hokoku sōmokuroku 日本建築学会創立七十周年記念建築雑誌論文集研究報告総目録 (In commemoration of the 70th anniversary of the founding of the Architectural Institute of Japan: General list of contents of the "Architectural Journal", essay series, and research reports) 1936-55. 1957. 368p.

Classified listing of about 1,600 articles and studies. Sequel to *Kenchiku zasshi sōmokuroku*, a general list of articles in v.1-49, 1886-1935. Articles since 1956 listed annually in Jan. or Feb. issue.

Kyoto Teikoku Daigaku Kōgakubu **R78**
京都帝国大学工学部
Dai Tōa kenchiku ronbun sakuin 大東亜建築
論文索引 (Index to articles on East Asian
architecture) Kyoto, Seikansha, 1944. 468p.
Lists articles in Japanese and foreign periodicals
from 1868 to 1942 on Oriental architecture, arranged
by country or region.

DICTIONARIES

Monbushō 文部省 **R79**
Gakujutsu yōgoshū: kenchikugaku hen 学術
用語集 建築学編 Japanese scientific
terms: architecture. Nihon Kenchiku Gakkai,
1955. 360p.
Japanese-English section contains 6,234 terms;
and English-Japanese section, 5,401 terms.

R80
Kyōritsu kenchiku jiten 共立建築辞典
(Kyōritsu dictionary of architecture) Kyōritsu
Shuppan, 1959. 533p.
Defines and comments briefly on about 1,000 fre-
quently used terms, with their foreign equivalents,
many of them not in ordinary dictionaries. Tables
and list of architectural journals appended. Index.

Nihon Kenchiku Gakkai 日本建築学会 **R81**
Kenchiku jutsugoshu 建築術語集 (Glossary
of architectural terms) Rev. ed. Maruzen, 1959.
265, 92, 37p.
Standard dictionary defining and giving English
equivalents of 2,733 terms classified under such
subjects as applied dynamics, construction materials, design and style, installations, city planning
and building laws, and gardens. Illustrations.
Glossary of housing terms appended. Index.

Tsugawa, Toshio 津川俊夫 **R82**
Ei-Wa kenchiku yōgo jiten 英和建築用語字
典 English-Japanese dictionary of architectural terms. Sagami Shobō, 1955. 360p.
Translates into Japanese about 10,000 English
terms covering a wide range, including building
equipment, civil engineering, landscape designing,
sports buildings, etc.

Nakamura, Tatsutarō 中村達太郎 **R83**
Nihon kenchiku jii 日本建築辞彙 (Japanese
architectural glossary) Rev. and enl. ed. Maruzen, 1953. 422, 92, 30p.
Especially strong in terms found in architectural
history, many with English, German and French
equivalents and illustrations. Chronology of architecture appended. Index.

HANDBOOKS

Hirayama, Takashi 平山嵩 **R84**
Kenchikugaku pokettobukku 建築学ポケッ
トブック (Pocket book of architecture) OHM-
sha, 1962. 1604p.
Practical information on construction, architectural
dynamics, planning, drawing, materials, equipment,
specifications, laws, etc., with formulas and tables.
Index with English equivalents of terms.

R85
Kenchiku sekkei seizu benran 建築設計製
図便覧 (Manual of architectural design and
drafting) Rikōgakusha, 1963. 1512p.
Has chapters on materials, drawing, structural
dynamics and planning, equipment, construction,
specifications, making of estimates, contracts, laws,
civil engineering, and data. Tables appended. Index.

Nihon Kenchiku Gakkai 日本建築学会 **R86**
Kenchiku sekkei shiryō shūsei 建築設計資
料集成 (Collection of materials on architectural design) Rev. and enl. ed. Maruzen,
1963- . 3v. In progress.
Gives detailed information, well illustrated, on
such general aspects of designing as modular coordination, space for movement, weather considerations, earthquakes, sunshine, heat, ventilation,
sound and use of color, as well as on specific types
of buildings, including homes, apartment houses,
hotels, restaurants, stores and shops, theaters and
other public halls, hospitals, garages, office buildings, banks, studios and stations. Each volume
indexed. v. 4 projected.

YEARBOOKS

R87
Kenchiku nenkan 建築年鑑 Annual of architecture in Japan. 1960- . Bijutsu Shuppansha,
1960- . 5v.
Surveys trends in construction and has biographical directory of Japanese architects, list of completed buildings and list of new publications. Index.

R88
Jūtaku nenkan 住宅年鑑 Housing yearbook.
1964- . Nihon Jūtaku Kyōkai, 1964- . 1v.
Comprehensive compilation of materials and statistics on housing conditions and policies. v. 1
covers 1951-63. Index. Coverage for immediate
postwar years given in volume of same title published in 1950 by the Housing Bureau of the Ministry
of Construction.

Kenchiku tōkei nenpō 建築統計年報 (Statistical survey of construction) 1950- . Comp. by Kensetsushō. 1950, 1952- . 13v. Annual. **R89**

Based on reports to the government, giving general trends, charts, statistics.

Kenchiku keizai tōkei shiryō 建築経済統計資料 (Statistical data on construction economy) 1951- . Comp. by Nihon Kenchiku Gakkai. 1951- . 13v. Annual. **R90**

Covers trends, housing construction, materials, labor, costs, management, accidents, with list of major projects, statistics and bibliography.

BUILDINGS

Yokoyama, Shin 横山信 **and** **Takahashi, Hitoshi** 高橋仁 **R91**
Nihon kenchiku nenpyō 日本建築年表 (Chronology of Japanese architecture) Taiyōdō, 1931. 109, 96p. 47 plates.

Comprehensive list of buildings with Japanese, Western and Chinese completion dates. Directory by prefectures of legally protected buildings appended. Building names indexed.

Tokyo Kensetsugyō Kyōkai **R92**
東京建設業協会
Shuyō kenzōbutsu nenpyō 主要建造物年表 (Chronology of important constructions) 1958-62. 3v.

Gives sites, beginning and completion dates, builders, designers, construction supervisors, descriptions, including dimensions, and costs of important construction works from 1868 to 1958 divided into buildings, bridges, dams, tunnels, railroads, harbor developments, irrigation and drainage works, airports, and others.

STRUCTURAL MECHANICS

Watanabe, Kōsaku 渡辺耕策 **R93**
Mondai kaihō kōzo rikigaku poketto jiten 問題解法構造力学ポケット事典 (Question and answer pocket dictionary of structural mechanics) 2d ed., enl. Rikōgakusha, 1961. 334p. (Kenchiku gengyō bunko)

Explains 50 topics by means of illustrated questions and answers. Tables of functions and Greek-letter symbols appended.

Mizuhara, Akira 水原旭 **et al.** **R94**
Kōzo keisan benran 構造計算便覧 (Structural calculation manual) Sangyō Tosho, 1963. 1940p.

Explains basic principles and their applications with many tables and charts. Detailed references. Index.

Okamura, Masao 岡村雅夫 **R95**
Jitsuyō rāmen keisan benran 実用ラーメン計算便覧 (Practical manual of *Rahmen* framework calculations) Rev. ed. Sangyō Tosho, 1951. 493p.

Gives 512 diagrams of and formulas for use in calculating structural framework, arranged by forms of structure.

Tanaka, Masayoshi 田中正義 **R96**
Tekkotsu danmen santeihyō 鉄骨断面算定表 (Tables for calculation of steel framework sections) Rev. ed. Kōgaku Tosho, 1961. 144p.

Covers steel, structural sections, and rivets, bolts and welding, with 0.01 step calculations for I shape sections and angle sections and moments of inertia of cover and web plates and rivet holes.

Building materials

Kanō, Harukazu 狩野春一 **R97**
Kenchiku zairyō handobukku 建築材料ハンドブック (Handbook of building materials) Chijin Shokan, 1959. 751, 62p.

Surveys all kinds of materials used in construction, including wood, bamboo fibers, stone, clay and clay products, cement, concrete, glass, plastics, asphalt, paints, linoleum, adhesives, iron and steel, etc. Comments on production of building materials and the Japan industrial standards appended.

Saishin kenchiku shizai sōran 最新建築資材総覧 (Up-to-date survey of building materials) 1964 ed. Kenchiku Shizai Kenkyūkai, 1964. (1485)p. **R98**

Covers almost all materials on the market and their uses, with specifications, standards, diagrams, tables and statistics. List of manufacturers and their products appended.

Masudo, Norio 増戸憲雄 **and** **Fukunishi, Seiji** 福西清治 **R99**
Shin kenchiku zairyō 新建築材料 (Manual of new construction materials and fixtures) Ariake Shobō, 1959. 334, 70p.

Gives technical explanations of materials and fixtures and tells how to use or install them.

Soshiroda, Saburō 十代田三郎 **R100**
Kenchiku naisō handobukku 建築内装ハンドブック (Handbook of interior design) Asakura Shoten, 1963. 826p.

Explains materials and techniques of flooring, finishing of walls and ceilings, insulation, acoustical control, fireproofing, painting, masonry, and discusses fixtures, equipment, furniture, etc. Gives laws and regulations. Index.

Uchida, Yoshiya 内田祥哉 **R101**
Kenchiku no tameno garasu 建築のためのガラス Glass handbook for architecture. Asahi Garasu Kabushiki Kaisha, 1964. 391p.

Handbook on glass in building apertures, relationship of apertures to walls, metallic sash and other aperture fittings, designing and installation, and maintenance. Laws, Japanese architectural standard specifications (JASS) and Japanese industrial standards (JIS) appended.

WOODEN BUILDINGS

Ōkawa, Akira 大川彰 **R102**
Jitsuyō zukai mokuzō kenchiku poketto jiten 実用図解木造建築ポケット事典 (Practical illustrated pocket cyclopedia of wooden building construction) Rikōgakusha, 1957. 254p.

Explains preparation of site, temporary construction, foundation laying, selection of timber and other materials, construction, and installation of fixtures, with many charts, tables and glossary of construction terms. Index.

Kitao, Harumichi 北尾春道 **R103**
Sukiya zukai jiten 数寄屋図解事典 (Illustrated dictionary of *Sukiya* style architecture) Shōkokusha, 1959. 466p.

Explains terms relating to the style of "artless" simplicity found in buildings for the tea ceremony and reflected in dwellings since the 15th century. Many diagrams. Classified index.

STEEL AND LIGHT METAL

Kōzai Kurabu 鋼材倶楽部 **R104**
Kōkōzō jiten 鋼構造事典 (Steel construction dictionary) Shōkokusha, 1960. 305p.

Defines about 2,000 technical terms concerning materials, dynamics, welding, machinery, towers, and bridges. Relevant laws appended.

R105
Keiryō katakō kenchiku benran 軽量形鋼建築便覧 (Manual of construction with lightweight steel shapes) Gihōdō, 1961. 2v.

Covers structural planning, effective widths of sections, flexural and torsional conditions, designing of girders and columns, bracing, and welding.

Keikinzoku Kyōkai 軽金属協会 **R106**
Keikinzoku kenchiku handobukku 軽金属建築ハンドブック (Light metal construction handbook) 1955. 512p.

Gives information on production of aluminum, standard sizes, processing, welding, surface treatment, construction methods and trends abroad in the use of aluminum, with standard specifications and directory of producers.

Architectural acoustics

Nihon Onkyō Zairyō Kyōkai **R107**
日本音響材料協会
Kenchiku onkyō kōgaku handobukku 建築音響工学ハンドブック (Handbook of acoustical engineering in construction) Gihōdō, 1963. 936p.

Practical information for architects and building engineers on basic principles, room acoustics, noise, acoustic materials and designing, and sound-effects equipment. Lists laboratory-tested materials and notable acoustical projects with completion dates, sites, architects and designers. To be revised every three years.

Construction

Tanahashi, Makoto 棚橋諒 **et al.** **R108**
Kenchiku sekō handobukku 建築施工ハンドブック (Construction work handbook) Asakura Shoten, 1960. 1061, 112p.

Covers preparations, all stages of construction, finishing, installation of equipment and use of machinery, with glossary, weights and measures and catalogue of machinery and equipment. Index.

Kanō, Harukazu 狩野春一 **R109**
Kenchiku sekōhō pokettobukku 建築施工法ポケットブック (Pocket manual of construction work) OHM-sha, 1962. 1289p.

Tells how to select and use materials and equipment. Index.

Equipment

Watanabe, Kaname 渡辺要 **and** **R110**

Yanagimachi, Masanosuke 柳町政之助
Kenchiku setsubi handobukku 建築設備ハンドブック (Building equipment handbook) Asakura Shoten, 1959. 973, 114p.

Explains heating, air-conditioning, plumbing, gas, electricity and other installations, with illustrations, graphs and formulas. Index.

Inoue, Uichi 井上宇市 **R111**
Kenchiku setsubi pokettobukku 建築設備ポケットブック (Pocket book of building equipment) Rev. ed. Sagami Shobō, 1964. 454p.

Tells how to select and install heating and air-conditioning equipment, refrigerators, plumbing and other fixtures, electric wiring, etc. and how to estimate costs. Charts, tables, bibliography appended.

Inoue, Uichi 井上宇市 **R112**
Kūki chōwa handobukku 空気調和ハンドブック (Air-conditioning handbook) Maruzen, 1956. 278p.

Explains planning, equipment, including freezers, and installation methods, with examples and diagrams.

Nihon Kikaku Kyōkai 日本規格協会 **R113**
Eisei danbō yōgoshū 衛生暖房用語集
Japanese engineering terms: plumbing, heating, and ventilation. 1955. 176p.

Equivalents of about 2,800 terms in Japanese-English section and 3,000 in English-Japanese section.

Matsuo, Tetsuo 松尾徹男 **and** **R114**
Saitō, Hideo 斉藤英夫
Kenchiku denki setsubi poketto jiten 建築電気設備ポケット事典 (Pocket dictionary of electrical installations in buildings) Rikō-gakusha, 1960. 390p. (Kenchiku gengyō bunko)

Tells, with diagrams and tables, how to plan and put in installations.

Tokyoto Suidōkyoku 東京都水道局 **R115**
Kyūsui sōchi handobukku 給水装置ハンドブック (Handbook on water-supply installations) Asakura Shoten, 1963. 472p.

Gives technical information on measurement of water sources, planning, materials, tools, meters and hot-water equipment, as well as legal requirements in Tokyo metropolitan area.

Sakurai, Shōgo 桜井省吾 **R116**
Kenchiku kyūhaisui setsubi benran 建築給排水設備便覧 (Manual of water-supply and drainage installations for buildings) 3d ed.,

rev. Shōkokusha, 1962. 244p.

Covers plans, tools, faucets, traps, pipes, hydrants, pumps, boilers, tanks, sewage disposal. Bibliography appended.

FIRE PREVENTION

Nihon Kasai Gakkai 日本火災学会 **R117**
Kasai benran 火災便覧 (Fire handbook) Rika Shoin, 1955. 1549, 68p.

Basic information on relationship between weather conditions and fires, fire hazards, fires in buildings, fire alarms, fire-fighting, city and forest fires, arson, and fire laws, with catalogue of fire-fighting equipment and bibliography. Index.

R118
Bōka nenkan 防火年鑑 (Fire prevention yearbook) 1963- . Comp. by Nihon Kagaku Bōka Kyōkai. Kōgyō Chōsakai, 1963- . 1v.

Covers 1961-63 statistics, policies, weather conditions, fire phenomena, preventive measures and equipment, fire-resistant and fireproof building materials, fire-fighting equipment, city planning, insurance, laws, research and experiment.

MECHANICAL ENGINEERING

BIBLIOGRAPHY

R119
Nihon Kikai Gakkaishi oyobi Ronbunshū sōsaku-in 日本機械学会誌および論文集総索引 (General index to the Journal and Transactions of the Japan Society of Mechanical Engineering) Series 1- . 1933- . 4v.

Covers the Journal from no. 1, published in Dec., 1897 and the Transactions from no. 1, published in 1935. Author and subject indexes.

Nihon Gakujutsu Shinkōkai **R120**
日本学術振興会
Jikuuke bunkenshū 軸受文献集 (Bibliography on bearings) 1952. 232p.

Entries under mechanics cover the period to 1941, under metallurgy to 1949, under physics to 1940, and under chemistry to 1939. Some entries include abstracts.

DICTIONARIES

R121
Kikai kōgaku jiten 機械工学辞典 (Diction-

ary of mechanical engineering) Nikkan Kōgyō Shinbunsha, 1958. 772, 52p.

Explains about 9,600 technical terms, with English equivalents, proper names and symbols. Many drawings and photographs. Formulas, tables and list of JIS standards appended. English index.

Kikai kōgaku yōgo jiten 機械工学用語辞典 **R122**
(Dictionary of mechanical engineering terms) Gihōdō, 1958. 760p.

Explains about 8,000 terms selected from **R121**.

Kōgyō Gijutsuin, Keiryō Kenkyūjo **R123**
工業技術院 計量研究所
Keisoku jiten 計測辞典 (Measurement dictionary) Nikkan Kōgyō Shinbunsha, 1962. 563p.

Explains terms in detail with many illustrations. Appendix includes descriptions of how units are determined and coefficients for unit conversions. English index.

Monbushō 文部省 **R124**
Gakujutsu yōgoshū: kikai kōgaku hen 学術用語集：機械工学編 Japanese scientific terms: mechanical engineering. Rev. ed. Nihon Kikai Gakkai, 1962. 564p.

Todoroki, Tokushige 等々力徳重 **R125**
Kōhan kikai yōgo jiten 広範機械用語辞典
Technical terms dictionary for mechanical engineers. Rev. ed. Kikai Kyōkai, 1964. 1110p.

Defines 45,000 mechanical engineering terms and related terms in physics, electricity, metallurgy, chemistry, auto mechanics, railroading, civil engineering, shipbuilding, architecture, and industrial management. English-Japanese and Japanese-English sections.

HANDBOOKS

Nihon Kikai Gakkai 日本機械学会 **R126**
Kikai kōgaku benran 機械工学便覧 (Mechanical engineer's handbook) 4th rev. ed. 1960. (2038)p.

Deals with numerical tables, units, physical constants, mathematics, dynamics, strength of materials, measurement methods, machine elements, hydraulics, hydrodynamics, hydraulic and pneumatic machinery, heat, thermodynamics, combustion, fuels, and furnaces, steam power, internal combustion engines, transportation, lifting and carrying, machine processing, industrial machinery, factory design and management, and electricity. Many illustrations. Index with English equivalents.

Nihon Kōgyō Gakkai 日本工業学会 **R127**
Kikai kōgyō benran 機械工業便覧 (Machine industry handbook) Morikita Shuppan, 1958. 1741p.

Data and standards for field engineers, concisely covering industrial mathematics and dynamics, materials, machine designing, machining, measurement, automatic controls, hydraulic machinery, heat and heat engines, electricity and electric machines, cost analysis, productivity, etc. Index with English equivalents.

R128
Kikai kōgaku pokettobukku 機械工学ポケットブック (Mechanical engineer's pocket book) Junior ed. OHM-sha, 1957. 1332p.

Abridgment of **R126** for students, with explanations in simple words.

R129
Kikai sekkei benran 機械設計便覧 (Machine design handbook) Maruzen, 1958. 1944, 128p.

Contains basic data on properties of metallic and non-metallic materials, fatigue and creep, beams, columns, stress of structures, vibrations, screws and rivets, shafts, bearings, springs and vibration-proofing, transmissions, gears, fluids, heat and machining.

R130
Kikai sekkei handobukku 機械設計ハンドブック (Machine design handbook) Kyōritsu Shuppan, 1955. 1141p.

Data on fastening methods, pressure pipes and valves, springs and shock absorbers, brakes, shafts, shaft couplings, bearings, friction gearing, gears, cams and swash plates, link mechanisms, automatic control devices, etc., using the terminology of **R124** with many diagrams and tables. Basic formulas and tables concerning strength of materials and dimensional standards appended. General index.

R131
Kyōdo sekkei dēta bukku 強度設計データブック (Design and strength data book) Shōkabō, 1962. 1180p.

Explains for machine designers the fundamentals of stress analysis, breakdown and fatigue of materials and permissible stress and the properties of materials and characteristics of shapes, with data on beams, columns, notches, bars with irregular cross sections, impacts, shafts, plates, frameworks, thin plate structures, and rotating bodies. Index.

R132
Jidō seigyo kiki benran 自動制御機器便覧 (Handbook of automatic control equipment) OHM-

sha, 1962. 1685p.

Explanations are brief, but coverage is wide, including common electrical and mechanical elements, detectors, indicators and recorders, controllers, electrical amplifiers, operating and measurement devices, testing, calculation, and instrumentation work.

Kōsaku Kikai Kenkyūkai   **R133**
工作機械研究会
Kikai kōsaku handobukku　機械工作ハンド
ブック (Machining handbook) Yōkendō, 1958. 958p.

Explains cutting, grinding, gear-cutting, threading, jig mountings, manual finishing, assembling, the inspection, transportation and installation of machine tools, tool parts, machining accuracy, precision measurement and shop management. Conversion tables, units, industrial standards and lists of tool manufacturers and importers appended. Index.

     R134
Sessaku kakō gijutsu benran　切削加工技術
便覧 (Handbook of cutting techniques) Nikkan Kōgyō Shinbunsha, 1962. 1550p.

Covers theories, cutting and machining processes, the machinability of metals and non-metallic materials, machining methods for shafts, gears and lenses, inspection and tool management. Japanese industrial standards for cutting tools, grinding wheels, and machine-tool inspections appended.

     R135
Jikuuke junkatsu benran 軸受潤滑便覧
(Bearing and lubrication handbook) Nikkan Kōgyō Shinbunsha, 1961. 963p.

Emphasizes practical aspects of abrasion and wear, lubrication, bearings for various types of machinery, testing and standards. Reference at end of each chapter.

Iwanami, Shigezō 岩波繁蔵 **and**   **R136**
Chikamori, Tokushige 近森徳重
Pakkin gijutsu benran パッキン技術便覧
(Handbook of packing engineering) Sangyō Tosho, 1962. 386p.

Deals with packing materials, self-sealing packings, gaskets, diaphragms, mechanical seals, metal packings, oil seals and related questions of inspection and lubrication. List of references.

Tsūshō Sangyōshō Jūkōgyōkyoku   **R137**
通商産業省重工業局
Kokusan kikai sōran 国産機械総覧 (Directory of machinery made in Japan) 1964 ed. Tokyo Tosho, 1963. 1206p.

Classifies about 5,000 types of machines and appliances according to the Standard Commodity

Classifications of the Statistics Bureau of the Prime Minister's Office, with general production conditions, chief dimensions and approximate prices. Index of names of machinery and equipment. List of machinery associations and manufacturing companies appended.

     R138
Zen Nihon kikai kōgu hyōjun katarogu 全日本
機械工具標準型録 (All-Japan machine and tool standard catalogue) 1962. Zen Nihon Kikai Kogushō Rengōkai, 1962. (700)p.

Covers cutting, measuring, machining, working, motor-driven and pneumatic tools, construction machinery, parts for power transmissions, valves and cocks, rivets and screws, and grinding wheels, with shapes, dimensions, and prices. Tables of weights and measures, descriptions of systems of fit, and material standards appended. Index.

YEARBOOKS

     R139
Kikai kōgaku nenkan 機械工学年鑑
(Mechanical engineering yearbook) 1934-
Nihon Kikai Gakkai, 1934-39, 1941, 1943, 1945, 1959- 15v.

Gives information on conditions in mechanical engineering and the machine industry in Japan and abroad during the year. Engineering section describes trends in research in industrial mathematics and engineering materials, mentioning many research publications. Industrial section gives data on technological levels and industrial productivity. Record-breaking products are introduced.

     R140
Kikai to kōgu nenkan　機械と工具年鑑
(Machinery and tool yearbook) 1958- . Kōgyō Chōsakai, 1958-60, 1962- . 5v.

Former title: *Kōsaku kikai to kōgu nenkan*, 1958.

Reports production, imports and exports, etc. of the previous year in detail, with many statistics. Review of new models and company directory appended.

     R141
Kikai tōkei nenpō 機械統計年報 Annual
machine statistical report. 1953- . Comp. by Tsūshō Sangyōshō. Tsūshō Sangyō Chōsakai, 1953- . 12v.

Surveys developments in Japan's machine industry, based mainly on reports of factories with 20 or more workers.

Gears

R142

Haguruma benran 歯車便覧 (Gear handbook)
Nikkan Kōgyō Shinbunsha, 1962. 1346p.

Treats fundamental principles, design fundamentals, applications, machining, measurement and inspection. Index.

R143

Haguruma Sekkei Kenkyūkai 歯車設計研究会
Haguruma sekkei handobukku 歯車設計ハンドブック (Gear design handbook) Nikkan Kōgyō Shinbunsha, 1961. 455p.

Tables for use by gear designers, cutters, purchasers and suppliers.

Heat engines

Tanishita, Ichimatsu 谷下市松 **R144**
Netsukōgaku handobukku 熱工学ハンドブック (Thermal engineering handbook) Sankaidō, 1958. 234p.

Collection of constants and data covering such fields as thermodynamics, heat transmission, fuels, combustion, air conditioning, solar heat, and atomic power. Useful for engineers. Index.

Hatta, Keizo 八田桂三 **and** **R145**
Asanuma, Tsuyoshi 浅沼強
Nainen kikan handobukku 内燃機関ハンドブック (Internal combustion engine handbook) Asakura Shoten, 1960. 1149p.

Describes heat engines, displacement-type and velocity-type internal combustion engines, and measuring and testing methods. References, list of manufacturers and products, and tables appended. General index.

Nihon Boira Kyōkai 日本ボイラ協会 **R146**
Boira benran ボイラ便覧 (Boiler handbook)
Rev. ed. Maruzen, 1959. 722p.

Explains in detail principles and problems of boiler construction and operation for boilermen. List of manufacturers appended. Index.

Refrigeration

Nihon Reitō Kyōkai 日本冷凍協会 **R147**
Reitō kūchō benran 冷凍空調便覧 (Refrigeration and air conditioning handbook) 1963. 1400p.

Covers in detail all aspects of refrigeration engineering and its applications. Many illustrations.

Unno, Shūichi 海野修一 **et al.** **R148**
Kūki chōwa reitō gijutsu benran 空気調和・冷凍技術便覧 (Handbook of air-conditioning and refrigeration engineering) Sangyō Tosho, 1961. 605p.

A technical manual explaining principles and operation of equipment. Index.

Hydraulic machinery

R149

Suiryoku kikai kōgaku benran 水力機械工学便覧 (Handbook of hydraulic machine engineering) Koronasha, 1962. 1030, 89p.

Deals with fundamentals of physical properties of fluids and their applications in hydroelectric power plants, turbines, various types of pumps and other hydraulic mechanisms. Many tables and illustrations. Lists products of 37 manufacturers of hydraulic machinery. Indexes in Japanese and European languages.

Barubu Kenkyūkai バルブ研究会 **R150**
Jitsuyō barubu benran 実用バルブ便覧 (Practical valve handbook) Sangyō Tosho, 1961. 678, 27p.

Covers the selection, handling, functions, and efficiency of valves used in equipment handling liquids. Section on metallic and non-metallic materials and packings. Index.

R151

Yuatsu gijutsu benran 油圧技術便覧 (Hydraulic engineering handbook) Nikkan Kōgyō Shinbunsha, 1959. 943, 17p.

Explains the hydraulic properties of oils, their application to machine tools, automobiles, ships, etc. and pertinent devices, with comparison of American and JIS standards, formulas, conversion tables and list of manufacturers. Each chapter has references to 1957. Japanese and European-language indexes.

R152

Kūki kikai kōgaku benran 空気機械工学便覧 (Handbook of pneumatic machine engineering) Koronasha, 1958. 714p.

Considers aerodynamics, calculation of the strength of materials, various types of compressors and other pneumatic machinery and their handling, with figures and photographs. Laws and regulations and illustrated testing instructions appended. General index.

Precision machinery

Seiki Gakkai　精機学会　　　　**R153**
Seimitsu kōsaku benran　精密工作便覧
(Precision machining handbook) Rev. ed. Ko-
ronasha, 1958.　1386p.

Explains machining by cutting tools, grinding
wheels, abrasive grains, etc. and machining of special
materials. Many photographs and other illustrations.
Index.

ATOMIC ENERGY

Kokuritsu Kokkai Toshokan　　　　**R154**
国立国会図書館
Amerika Genshiryoku Iinkai kizō bunken mokuroku　アメリカ原子力委員会寄贈文献
目録 (Catalogue of documents presented by
the American Atomic Energy Commission) 1955-　.
1955-64.　8v.　In progress.

Lists AEC materials in the National Diet Library,
classified as in *Nuclear science abstracts*.

Nihon Genshiryoku Sangyō Kaigi　　　**R155**
日本原子力産業会議
Genshiryoku jiten　原子力事典 (Dictionary of
atomic energy) OHM-sha, 1957.　258p.

Covers about 1,300 terms in nuclear science and
instrumentation, names of prominent persons and
organizations and titles of laws and regulations.
Laws, tables of symbols and unit conversions and
list of radio-isotopes appended.　English index.

Amamiya, Yōzō　雨宮庸蔵　**et al.**　　**R156**
Genshiryoku yōgo kaisetsu　原子力用語解説
(Dictionary of atomic energy terms) Nakayama
Shoten, 1957.　121p.　(Kyōyō genshiryoku kōza,
supp.)

Briefly explains and gives English equivalents
of selected terms in literature on atomic energy,
nuclear physics and engineering and related matters.

Nihon Genshiryoku Sangyō Kaigi　　　**R157**
日本原子力産業会議
Nichi-Ei-Futsu-Ro　genshiryoku　yōgo　jiten
日英仏露原子力用語辞典 (Glossary of
atomic energy terms; Japanese-English-French-
Russian) Kinokuniya Shoten, 1956.　330p.

Based on the *Provisional glossary on atomic energy*,
comp. by the United Nations, about 3,000 English
terms are arranged alphabetically with French, Russian and Japanese equivalents.　List of thermal
neutron cross-sections for elements and table of
basic constants appended. Indexes of French, Russian
and Japanese terms.

Miyake, Yasuo　三宅泰雄　**et al.**　　**R158**
Hōsha kagaku handobukku　放射化学ハンド
ブック (Handbook for radiation chemistry)
Asakura Shoten, 1962.　789p.

Explains basic principles of nuclear reactions,
radiation effects on materials, radiation measurements, isolation, and high molecular polymerization
by radiation and their application to chemical
analysis, geophysics, biochemistry, agriculture, medical science, and engineering.　Also covers chemical
problems occurring in nuclear reactors, and radiation safety. Methods of obtaining radiation materials
and list of radiation measurement equipment appended.　Index.

Kagaku Gijutsusha　科学技術社　　**R159**
Nihon genshiryoku kankei kiki sōran 日本原子
力関係機器総覧 (General survey of Japanese atomic energy equipment) 1957.　201p.

Chapters on nuclear reactors, radiation measurement equipment, radioactive material-handling facilities and equipment, shielding materials, radio
isotopes and related devices, nuclear research instruments, chemical equipment for atomic research and
miscellaneous equipment. Many diagrams and photographs.

R160
Genshiryoku nenkan　原子力年鑑 (Yearbook
of atomic energy) 1957-　.　Comp. by Nihon
Genshiryoku Sangyō Kaigi. 1957, 1959-　. 7v.

Covers international and national developments
and activities of organizations including laws, international agreements, financial assistance for research, list of applications for patents and bibliography.　Subject index.

R161
Genshiryoku nenpō 原子力年報 Annual report of the Atomic Energy Commission　No. 1,
1956-　.　Comp. by Genshiryoku Iinkai. 1957-　.
8v.

Reviews basic laws and policies, summarizes the
utilization of atomic power and reports recent developments in atomic energy, construction of nuclear
reactors, development of nuclear engineering techniques and nuclear fuel, investigation of nuclear
radiation, and international cooperation on nuclear
energy. The trade title of this report is *Genshiryoku
hakusho* (Atomic energy white paper).　An English
edition has been available since 1960.

TRANSPORTATION

R162
Kōtsū nenkan 交通年鑑 (Transportation almanac) 1947-　.　Comp. by Kōtsū Kyōryokkai,

1947, 1949- . 17v. Annual.

Surveys national and private railways, automobiles, municipal traffic, marine transportation, ports and harbors, aviation, tourism and rolling-stock industry. Lists of public corporations and companies, directory of governmental agencies, etc. appended. No index.

R163

Un'yu keizai tōkei yōran 運輸経済統計要覧 (Statistical abstracts of transportation and economy) 1960- . Comp. by Un'yushō. 1961- . 4v. Annual.

Gives statistics from 1936 of facilities, production, management, tourism and world transportation. Appended are world population statistics, areas and coastline lengths of Japanese prefectures, etc.

R164

Rikuun tōkei yōran 陸運統計要覧 (Statistical survey of land transportation) 1963- . Comp. by Un'yushō. 1964- . 1v. Annual.

Former title: *Jidōsha tōkei nenpō* (Automobile statistical yearbook), 1959-62. 4v.

Deals with such topics as railway and other cargo and passenger transportation, tourism, rolling stock, roads, accidents, and labor.

Railways

R165

Tetsudō gijutsu bunken shōroku 鉄道技術文献抄録 (Railway engineering abstracts) v. 1, no. 1, 1959- . Comp. by Nihon Kokuyū Tetsudō, Tesudō Gijutsu Kenkyūjo. Ken'yūsha, 1959- . Monthly.

Selected from 180 foreign and domestic journals and classified according to the Universal Decimal Classification. Appendixes include abstracts of patents and designs and bibliography.

Nihon Kokuyū Tetsudō 日本国有鉄道 **R166**
Tetsudō jiten 鉄道辞典 (Railway dictionary) 1958. 2v.

Defines 4,456 terms, many of them illustrated.

Kitada, Isao 北田勲 **R167**
Tetsudō hyakka jiten 鉄道百科事典 (Railway encyclopedia) Nagoya, Kōyūsha, 1952. 1037p.

Concerned solely with the Japan National Railways, with entries classified under generalia, transportation, operations, rolling stock, installations, electric power, signals, communications, personnel and administration. Profusely illustrated. Tables appended. Index.

Suita Tetsudō Kyōshujo **R168**
吹田鉄道教習所
Tetsudō yōgo jiten 鉄道用語辞典 (Dictionary of railway terms) Nagoya, Kōyūsha, 1955. 227p.

Briefly defines 3,000 technical, legal and commonly used terms, giving English equivalents.

Nihon Kokuyū Tetsudō Un'yu **R169**
Chōsakyoku 日本国有鉄道運輸調査局
Nichi-Ei-Bei-Doku-Futsu-Ro-Ka-taiyaku tetsudō jiten 日英米独仏露華対訳鉄道辞典 (Railway dictionary: Japanese, English, American, German, French, Russian and Chinese) 1952. 870p.

Defines 8,619 terms concerning railway operations, traffic technology and transportation and related aspects of road, automobile and marine transportation, listed first in Japanese, with English, German, French, Russian and Chinese equivalents and then in English, German and French, with Japanese equivalents. Illustrated.

R170

Tetsudō yōran 鉄道要覧 (Railway survey) 1947- . Comp. by Nihon Kokuyū Tetsudō. 1948- . 16v. Annual.

Annual report of the Japanese National Railways, with summary of general developments and sections on operation, administration, personnel, facilities, and construction, including maps. Index.

R171

Denki tetsudō benran 電気鉄道便覧 (Electric railway handbook) OHM-sha, 1956. 1426p.

Covers structure, maintenance and repair with many illustrations.

R172

Sekai kakkoku tetsudō tōkei 世界各国鉄道統計 (World railway statistics) 1926- . Comp. by the International Union of Railways. Nihon Kokuyū Tetsudō, 1927-40, 1954- . 21v. Annual

Based on English and French editions of *International railway statistics*, covering tracks, locomotives, passenger and freight cars, workers, train and car mileages, passengers and freight, income and expenditure, accidents, taxes, etc.

Nihon Kokuyū Tetsudō 日本国有鉄道 **R173**
Tetsudō ryaku nenpyō 鉄道略年表 (Brief chronology of railways) Rev. and enl. ed. 1962. 522p.

Covers 1825 to Mar., 1962 with emphasis on Japan. Name and subject indexes.

Automobiles

Jidōsha Kyōkai 自動車協会 **R174**
Shashin zukai jidōsha gijutsu yōgo jiten 写真・図解自動車技術用語辞典 (Illustrated dictionary of automobile technical terms) Kin'ensha, 1963. 452p.

Explains about 3,200 terms with help of diagrams. English and Japanese indexes.

Yamamoto, Mineo 山本峯雄 **et al.** **R175**
Jidōsha handobukku 自動車ハンドブック (Automobile handbook) Asakura Shoten, 1962. 893p.

A how-to-do-it manual with many diagrams giving a resumé of the development of automobiles, speed records, statistics and information on traffic problems, and automobile shows. Index.

Jidōsha Gijutsukai 自動車技術会 **R176**
Jidōsha kōgaku handobukku 自動車工学ハンドブック (Automobile engineering handbook) Rev. and enl. ed. 1962. 362p.

Basic data for specialists on fuels, strength and properties of materials, strength standards, testing methods, and parts. Three-wheel and other special vehicles, manufacturing processes, maintenance and servicing, laws and regulations, and statistics, also covered. Diagrams. English and Japanese indexes.

Iimure, Nagisa 飯牟礼渚 **R177**
Jidōshayō sekiyu seihin handobukku 自動車用石油製品ハンドブック (A handbook of petroleum products for automotive use) Sangyō Tosho, 1960. 399p.

Covers engines and their functions, lubricants, engine servicing, with information on recent models of automobiles. Detailed diagrams and tables. Index.

Sugiura, Kan 杉浦乾 **R178**
Jidōsha kōgu benran 自動車工具便覧 (Automobile tool handbook) Machines and tools for servicing, testing, and inspection. Natsumesha, 1961. 562p.

Descriptions and instructions for use. Appended are lists of equipment and tools based on the Standards for Equipment for Automobile Repair and Maintenance Shops, a table giving dimensions of wrenches and socket openings, and private standards for automobile servicing equipment. Index.

Sasagawa, Tarō 篠川太郎 **R179**
Jidō sanrinsha handobukku 自動三輪車ハンドブック (Handbook of three-wheeled motor vehicles) Nishizawa Kōbundō, 1958. 253p.

Covers construction and servicing, driving instructions, licenses and laws and regulations. Operational requirements for various types of vehicles, conversion tables, study guide for automobile mechanic examinations, specifications of vehicles and glossary appended. Illustrated.

R180
Sekai no jidōsha 世界の自動車 Cars of the world. 1958- . Asahi Shinbunsha, 1958- . 7v. Annual.

Photographs of new automobiles of the year, giving types and names, comparative tables of engine sizes, design features, road performance, etc. Tables of specifications and directory of manufacturers appended.

R181
Nihon no jidōsha kōgyō 日本の自動車工業 (Automotive industry of Japan) 1957- . Comp. by Tsūshō Sangyōshō Jūkōgyōkyoku. Tsūshō Sangyō Kenkyūsha, 1957-58, 1960-62, 1964- . 6v. Annual.

Surveys production and distribution and the effects on the industry of foreign economic conditions. Lists laws and regulations, import statistics, export inspections, and techniques introduced from foreign countries. Appended are lists of Japanese automobiles and major companies and manufacturers.

R182
Jidōsha tōkei nenpyō 自動車統計年表 (Annual automobile statistics) 1953- . Jidōsha Kōgyōkai, 1953- . 11v.

Gives statistics, mainly from the Ministry of Commerce and Industry, on the production, distribution and use of automobiles in Japan.

Jidōsha Gijutsukai 自動車技術会 **R183**
Kokusan jidōsha shogenhyō 国産自動車諸元表 (Tables of basic data for Japanese-made motor vehicles) 1963. 137p.

Gives the type, popular name, shape and year, dimensions and weight, performance characteristics, gear system and other details for each Japanese-made passenger car, bus, truck, etc. Published under supervision of Highway Transportation Section, Ministry of Transportation.

Aeronautics

Kimura, Hidemasa 木村秀政 **R184**
Kōkūgaku jiten 航空学辞典 (Dictionary of aeronautics) Chijin Shokan, 1959. 792p.

Based on the "Aeronautical glossary" compiled by the Industrial Standard Terminology Committee of the Science Encouragement Council. Includes many English terms. Chronology of world aeronautics, world who's who, illustrations of tools, list of abbreviations and tables appended. Classified table of contents and index of English words.

Hōbun Shorin 鳳文書林 **R185**
Kōkū yōgo jiten 航空用語辞典 (Dictionary of aviation terms) 1963. 177p.

Simple definitions of 2,000 English terms covering aerodynamics, meteorology, plane construction, operation, laws and regulations, rocket engineering and aerospace technology. Appended are definitions of terms in "Instructions for airworthiness examination", illustrations of aircraft parts and list of English abbreviations.

Nozawa, Tadashi 野沢正 **R186**
Nihon kōkuki sōshū 日本航空機総集 (Complete directory of Japanese aircraft) Shuppan Kyōdōsha, 1958- . 5v. In progress.

Each volume lists in order of production the planes of one or more makers, i. e., Mitsubishi, Aichi, Kawasaki, etc., with their Japanese and English names, detailed design and production records, comprehensive achievement records, performance characteristics, etc. Emphasis on history rather than technical data. Further volumes projected. Rev. ed. of v.1, 1961, has changes in illustrations.

Izumiyama, Ryūzō 泉山隆三 **R187**
Kōkūki kakubu meishōzu 航空機各部名称図 (Nomenclature of aircraft parts in diagrams) Kobe, Kaibundō, 1962. 91p.

Gives Japanese and English names of the parts of aircraft bodies, engines and equipment shown in diagrams, as well as the marks of 76 major airlines, English index.

Sekai kōkuki nenkan 世界航空機年鑑 (World aircraft annual) 1955- . Kantōsha, 1954- . **R188**
11v.

With drawings on facing pages, it gives for each model of the principal Japanese and foreign planes currently in service, its history, special features in design and performance, a comparison with other models and an estimate of its prospects, as well as its size, weight, speed, flight range, crew and any weapons. The 1959 edition indexes all models in previous editions.

Kōkū nenkan 航空年鑑 Air annual: Japan. **R189**
1930- . Nihon Kōkū Kyōkai, 1930-42, 1954- . 23v.

Gives national aviation expenditures, transportation statistics, performance statistics of main types of aircraft, engine data, lists of airports and major airlines, and directory of government agencies, research institutes, overseas agencies, associations, companies and personages.

Kōkū gensei 航空現勢 (Current trends in aviation) 1959- . Kōkū Kenkyūkai, 1959- . **R190**
6v. Annual.

Summarizes conditions, trends and problems in civil aviation, aviation industry, defense aviation, rockets and aeronautical engineering. Includes lists of aviation companies, airports and registered aircraft and statistical data.

Minkan kōkū no genkyō 民間航空の現況 **R191**
(Current report on civil aviation) 1952- . Un'yushō Kōkūkyoku, 1952- . 12v. Annual.

Summary statistics of Japanese and foreign civil aviation and air safety problems.

Kōkū kōgyō nenkan 航空工業年鑑 (The aircraft industry yearbook) 1954- . Nihon Kōkū Kōgyōkai, 1954- . 11v. **R192**

Useful compilation of laws, regulations and statistics, with survey of developments in Japan and directory of organizations. Detailed table of contents.

Kōkū tōkei nenpō 航空統計年報 Annual statistics of civil aviation. 1956- . Un'yushō, 1957- . 7v. **R193**

Covers air transportation, aircraft, personnel, airports and air safety facilities. Lists aviation companies and routes. Text in both English and Japanese.

Naval architecture

Sumita, Shōji 住田正二 **R194**
Kaiji kankei bunken sōmokuroku 海事関係文献総目録 (General bibliography of maritime

literature) Nihon Kaiji Shinkōkai, 1957. 443p.

Lists monographs, compilations of data and periodical articles from 1868 to 1956 classified under maritime transportation in general, shipping, maritime law, ships, routes and navigation, harbors and canals.

Tennensha 天 然 社 **R195**
Senpaku jiten 船 舶 辞 典 (Shipbuilding dictionary) 1963. 598p.

Defines technical shipbuilding terms, with index of foreign terms. Shipping laws and regulations, statistical data, JIS symbols, chronology of vessels, directories appended.

Kobe Shōsen Daigaku 神 戸 商 船 大 学 **R196**
Ei-Wa kaiji yōgo jiten 英 和 海 事 用 語 辞 典
English-Japanese dictionary of marine terms. Kobe, Kaibundō, 1963. 577p.

About 25,000 terms, including idioms and phrases on shipbuilding, shipping, and commerce.

Monbushō 文 部 省 **R197**
Gakujutsu yōgoshū: senpaku kōgaku hen 学 術 用 語 集 船 舶 工 学 編 Japanese scientific terms: naval architecture and marine engineering. Zōsen Kyōkai, 1958. 530p.

Includes approximately 9,200 words. Beaufort wind scale and swell, wave and visibility scales appended.

Tokyo Shōsen Daigaku 東 京 商 船 大 学 **R198**
Wa-Ei Ei-Wa senpaku yōgo jiten 和 英 英 和 船 舶 用 語 辞 典 (Dictionary of marine engineering terms: Japanese-English and English Japanese) Seizandō Shoten, 1962. 591p.

Briefly explains about 8,300 terms selected from **R197**. Tables of weights and measures, lists of multiples, etc. appended.

Yamaguchi, Masuto 山 口 増 人 **R199**
Zōsen yōgo jiten 造 船 用 語 辞 典 (Ship and shipbuilding technical dictionary) Kobe, Kaibundō, 1953. 306p.

In two parts, English-Japanese and Japanese-English, it explains terms used in shipbuilding and related matters. Many illustrations.

Yaoi, Hideyasu 矢 追 秀 保 **R200**
Saishin Ei-Wa Wa-Ei zōsen yōgoshū 最 新 英 和 和 英 造 船 用 語 集 (New English-Japanese, Japanese-English dictionary of naval architecture) Kobe, Kaibundō, 1961. 277p.

About 12,000 words with their equivalents in Japanese and English listed but not defined.

Masuda, Masakazu 升 田 政 和 **R201**
Ei-Wa Wa-Ei hakuyō kikan yōgoshū 英 和 · 和 英 舶 用 機 関 用 語 集 (English-Japanese, Japanese-English dictionary of marine engines) Seizandō Shoten, 1960. 215p.

An English-Japanese section of 2,800 words and a Japanese-English section of 2,600 words cover engines, shipbuilding and meteorology. List of abbreviations and English glossary concerning operation of engines appended.

Zōsen Kyōkai 造 船 協 会 **R202**
Senpaku kōgaku benran 船 舶 工 学 便 覧 (Shipbuilding engineering handbook) Rev. ed. Koronasha, 1962- . 2v. In progress.

v.1 covers physics, materials, strength of hulls, etc.; v.2, types of ships, shipbuilding and launching; v.3, yet to appear, engines, with appendixes on shipyard facilities and legal requirements. Each volume indexed. Supersedes the same publisher's *Senpaku kōgaku benran* (5v.).

Kansai Zōsen Kyōkai 関 西 造 船 協 会 **R203**
Zōsen sekkei benran 造 船 設 計 便 覧 (Handbook of naval architecutre) Kobe, Kaibundō, 1960. 714p.

Covers mathematics, dynamics and thermodynamics related to shipbuilding, as well as materials, designing, strength of hulls, fittings, meteorology and hydrography. Index.

Ikeda, Masaru 池 田 勝 **R204**
Sentai kakubu meishōzu 船 体 各 部 名 称 図 (Nomenclature of ship parts in diagrams) Kobe, Kaibundō, 1962. 80p.

Gives Japanese and English names of types of ships and the parts of their structures and fittings shown in diagrams, with color plates of the funnel markings of 40 major shipping companies. English index.

R205
Nihon senpaku meisaisho 日 本 船 舶 明 細 書 (Specifications of Japanese ships) 1929-30 - Kobe, Nihon Kaiun Shūkaijo, 1929-42, 1946- 31v. Annual.

Gives launching date, tonnage, speed, size, owner, radio equipment, etc. of each Japanese steel ship of more than 100 gross tons.

R206
Nihon senmeiroku 日 本 船 名 録 (Japanese ship directory) 1885- . Nihon Kaiji Kyōkai, 1887-1943, 1951- . 72v. Annual.

Lists each Japanese ship of more than 80 gross tons, with its type, name and number, code signal, class and grade, gross and net tonnages, size, launching date, builder, main engine, port of registry and owner. International signal flags in color and table of code signals appended. Compiled by the Government before 1901.

NAVIGATION

Shinomiya, Hiroshi 四之宮博 **R207**
Ei-Wa kōkai yōgo jiten 英和航海用語辞典 (English-Japanese dictionary of navigation terms) Seizandō Shoten, 1962. 285p.

Explains and gives examples of the use of words and phrases selected from **R197**.

Denpa Kōhō Kenkyūkai **R208**
電波航法研究会
Denpa kōhō yōgo jiten 電波航法用語辞典 (Dictionary of radio navigation terms) Kobe, Kaibundō, 1959. 643p.

Explains matters essential to understanding of radio navigation, with emphasis on electronics, under English and Japanese headings. Abbreviations listed. Index.

Kōkai benran 航海便覧 (Navigation handbook) Kobe, Kaibundō, 1956. 785, 29p. **R209**

Provides ships' officers with detailed chapters on mathematics, dynamics, mechanics, electricity, meteorology, navigation, loading systems, shipping practices, ship's English, signals and labor matters, each with list of references published before 1954. English and Japanese indexes.

Sakai, Susumu 酒井進 **R210**
Kōkaishi pokettobukku 航海士ポケットブック (Navigator's pocketbook) Rev. and enl. ed. Kobe, Kaibundō, 1963. 319p.

Practical information for maritime navigators on such matters as radio plotting of locations, signals and markers, hydrographic charts, deviation coefficients, routes through the Inland Sea, collision prevention, seamanship, cargo handling, inspection and certification of vessels, weather observation reports and logbook entries. Tables and formulas appended.

Maritime affairs

Takahashi, Masahiko 高橋正彦 **R211**
Kaiun jiten 海運事典 (Shipping dictionary) Kobe, Kaiji Kenkyūkai, 1955. 303p.

Emphasizes maritime law. Indexes of subjects, judicial precedents and laws and legal forms.

Nihon Yūsen Kabushiki Kaisha, Kaiun Bōeki Kenkyūkai 日本郵船株式会社 **R212**
海運貿易研究会
Kaiun bōeki shōjiten 海運貿易小辞典 Shipping and foreign trade vocabulary. Kyoto, Izumi shobō, 1962. 298p. **M189**.

Kaiji nenkan 海事年鑑 (Maritime affairs yearbook) 1952- . Nihon Kaiji Shinkōkai, 1952- . 12v. **R213**

Surveys Japanese maritime administration and business, routes, cargo movements, market conditions, labor, shipbuilding, harbors and warehouses, casualties, safety and laws. Overseas section includes major countries, their shipping and shipbuilding conditions and policies, owners, labor, fleets, harbors, canals, maritime organizations, etc.

Kōwan nenkan 港湾年鑑 (Harbor almanac) 1954- . Daidō Tsūshinsha, 1954-58, 1961- 7v. Biennial since 1961. **R214**

Conditions, facilities, etc. of Japanese harbors, with statistics and lists of companies, government agencies and related organizations.

Cargo handling

Kuniyuki, Ichirō 国行一郎 **R215**
Niyaku kikai kōgaku benran 荷役機械工学便覧 (Engineering handbook for cargo handling machinery) Koronasha, 1961. 888p.

Explains systematically, with illustrations, tables, specifications, JIS standards, laws and regulations, all engineering aspects of the design, operation, maintenance and supervision of cargo-handling machinery and equipment. Advertisements describe the products of 50 companies.

Minamigawa, Toshio 南川利雄 **R216**
Niyaku unpan kiki setsubi benran 荷役運搬機器設備便覧 (Handbook of cargo handling and carrying machinery and equipment) Yakumo Shoten, 1960. 1172p.

Describes machines, rolling stock, ships, auxiliary equipment, scales and balances, prime movers, etc., with criteria for selecting machinery and equipment, design data, estimates and tests, safety precautions, industrial standards and machinery classifications. Directory of companies appended. Brief index.

Niyaku Kenkyūjo 荷役研究所 **R217**
Saishin niyaku kikai katarogushū 最新荷役機械カタログ集 (Latest catalogues of

cargo-handling machinery) 1957. 298p.

Introducing catalogues of various makers, a general discussion of cargo handling with machinery is followed by a guide to the selection, installation and operation of equipment, JIS standards and laws and regulations. Bibliography of Japanese and foreign books, list of manufacturers, and equipment prices appended.

Niyaku Kenkyūjo 荷役研究所 **R218**
Saishin niyaku kikai katarogushū: shiryō hen 最新荷役機械カタログ集 資料編 (Latest catalogues of cargo-handling machinery: reference material section) 1960. 433p.

Continuation of **R217**, with data on types of equipment, protection of cargo, freight forwarding, ports and harbors, warehouses, labor, etc. Drawings, specifications, laws, reference list and various tables appended. Index.

ELECTRICAL ENGINEERING

DICTIONARIES

R219
Denki yōgo jiten 電気用語辞典 (Dictionary of electrical terms) Koronahsa, 1960. 1016p.

Explains briefly, with English and German equivalents, the terms in **R220** and 1,500 more. Symbols and signs appended. English and German indexes.

Monbushō 文部省 **R220**
Gakujutsu yōgoshū: denki kōgaku hen 学術用語集 電気工学編 Japanese scientific terms: electrical engineering. Denki Gakkai, 1957. 685p.

Glossary of 12,000 words in Japanese-English and English-Japanese sections, based on "JEC-55, Standard electrical terms" (1949).

R221
Denki kōgaku yōgo jiten 電気工学用語辞典 (Dictionary of electrical engineering) Gihōdō, 1962. 922p.

Explains technical terms, including those in **R220**, with illustrations, giving English, German and/or French equivalents. Numerical tables, units and symbols appended. English and German index.

Uchida, Tomoji 内田知二 **R222**
Denki jutsugo jiten 電気術語辞典 (Dictionary of technical terms in electricity) OHM-sha,

1960. 521p.

Briefly defines 5,000 terms in common use.

Ishibashi, Yūichi 石橋勇一 **R223**
Ei-Wa-Doku-Ro denki jutsugo daijiten 英和独露電気術語大辞典 English-Japanese-German-Russian dictionary of electro-technics. OHM-sha, 1964. 568p.

25,000 English terms, with their Japanese, German and Russian equivalents, including many on mechanical and nuclear engineering and other related fields. Abbreviations, units, etc. appended. Japanese, German and Russian indexes.

HANDBOOKS

Denki Gakkai 電気学会 **R224**
Denki kōgaku handobukku 電気工学ハンドブック (Electrical engineering handbook). 1960. 2128p.

Gives most recent domestic and foreign data on basic principles and their applications, including those in mechanical and civil engineering. List of references.

Denki Gakkai 電気学会 **R225**
Denki kōgaku pokettobukku 電気工学ポケットブック (Electrical engineering pocket book) Junior edition. Rev. and enl. ed. OHM-sha, 1959. 1902p.

Emphasizes practical information in simple terms on theories and their applications. Includes nuclear engineering and electronics.

Yamauchi, Jirō 山内二郎 **R226**
Denki keisoku benran 電気計測便覧 (Handbook of electrical measurements) OHM-sha, 1956. 1277p.

Data on recent techniques useful for field engineers in mechanical and applied chemical engineering. Information about manufacturers appended. Index of terms with English equivalents.

Denki Gakkai 電気学会 **R227**
Hōden handobukku 放電ハンドブック (Electric discharge handbook) 1958. 494p.

Systematically covers discharges in gases, solids and liquids, using standard terms in **R220** and **Q60**. Lists of references. Index.

Denki Gakkai 電気学会 **R228**
Denki zairyō benran 電気材料便覧 (Electric materials manual) 1961. 540p.

Explains and gives examples of bare conductors, insulators, resistive, magnetic, nuclear reactor and special materials, application of materials to devices, etc. Directory of manufacturers and their products appended. Index.

Nihon Densetsu Kōgyōkai R229
日 本 電 設 工 業 会
Shin denzai yōran 新 電 材 要 覧 (Manual of new electrical materials) 1962. (1200p.)

For use by engineers in design, construction and maintenance and by salesmen of electrical equipment, it describes and gives specifications of and uses for apparatus, materials and tools. List of manufacturers. Index.

R230
Denryoku kensetsu benran 電 力 建 設 便 覧
(Electric power construction manual) OHM-sha, 1958-59. 2v.

Explains transmission and distribution lines, power measurements, materials, planning and substations. Guide to manufacturers and their products and annotated list of symbols appended. Each volume indexed.

Yamashita, Hideo 山 下 英 男 R231
Denryoku kiki benran 電 力 機 器 便 覧 (Power apparatus manual) OHM-sha, 1960. 1078p.

Gives design, structure, materials, characteristics, testing methods, installation, operation, and maintenance.

Omoto, Yoshikazu 尾 本 義 一 **and** R232
Miyamoto, Yoshimi 宮 本 慶 巳
Dendōki ōyō handobukku 電 動 機 応 用 ハ ン ド ブ ッ ク (Handbook of electric-motor applications) Denki Shoin, 1961. 1002p.

Explains basic principles of use and operation of motors in industry and describes motors used in mining, the iron industry, shipbuilding, etc. Lists of references, technical standards and catalogue of motors of different manufacturers appended.

Yamashita, Hideo 山 下 英 男 R233
Jidō den'atsu chōsei sōchi benran 自 動 電 圧 調 整 装 置 便 覧 (Handbook of automatic voltage regulators) OHM-sha, 1955. 600p.

Comprehensive description of various methods of automatic voltage regulators and their parts, with practical examples. Few references on semi-conductors.

General Electric Company R234
Shirikon seigyo seiryūki benran シ リ コ ン 制 御 整 流 機 便 覧 Silicon-controlled rectifier manual. Tokyo Shibaura Denki, 1961. 260p.

Explains principles, circuit designs, protection circuits, cooling systems and testing methods and gives practical circuit examples. Table of specifications and diagrams appended.

Denki Shoin 電 気 書 院 R235
Kogata kaitenki handobukku 小 型 回 転 機 ハ ン ド ブ ッ ク (Handbook of small rotary machines) 1959. 752p.

Gives use, choice, performance, design, automatic control, tests, maintenance, standards, etc. Theory and methods of analysis are applicable to general rotary machines of larger sizes as well. Data on business firms appended.

Biwasaka, Minoru 枇 把 阪 実 **and** R236
Yamane, Hirotarō 山 根 弘 太 郎
Jikayō henden setsubi handobukku 自 家 用 変 電 設 備 ハ ン ド ブ ッ ク (Handbook on private electric installations) Denki Shoin, 1962. 768p.

Practical handbook on the designing and installation of private substations with large load capacity, information including chapters on basic planning, circuits, apparatus, protective devices, generation and testing methods. Related laws and regulations, list of abbreviations, numerical tables, statistics and data on manufacturers appended.

Nihon Densetsu Kōgyōkai R237
日 本 電 設 工 業 会
Denki kōji sekkei handobukku 電 気 工 事 設 計 ハ ン ド ブ ッ ク (Handbook on electric installation design) Rev. ed. Taiyōkaku, 1963. 341p.

Covers the designing of equipment for factories, offices, schools, stores and public buildings.

Shōmei Gakkai 照 明 学 会 R238
Shōmei no dēta bukku 照 明 の デ ー タ ブ ッ ク (Illumination data book) Rev. and enl. ed. OHM-sha, 1958. 733p.

Contains principles and practical data, including standards and regulations. Directory of business firms appended. Index.

YEARBOOK

R239
Denki kōgaku nenpō 電 気 工 学 年 報 (Annual report on electrical engineering) 1952- . Denki Gakkai, 1953- . 12v.

Includes electrical communications, nuclear engineering, developments in education, with references and statistics. Directory of major manufacturing companies and their products appended.

LAWS

Tsūshō Sangyōshō Kōeki Jigyōkyoku　　R240
通商産業省公益事業局
Denki yōhin torishimarihō kankei hōreishū
電気用品取締法関係法令集　(Laws and regulations on electrical appliances)　Nihon Denki Kyōkai, 1963.　521p.

Explains standardization laws in force in 1962.

MATHEMATICAL TABLES

Uchida, Tomoji 内田知二 **and**　　R241
Okamoto, Hisanobu 岡本久信
MKS denki kōgaku kōshikishū　　MKS 電気工学公式集 (MKS electrical engineering formulas)　OHM-sha, 1955.　315p.

Covers all aspects, with MKS rational system of units adopted for the formulas. Tables of conversions, units and chemical elements appended.

Electrical industry

Tsūshō Sangyōshō 通商産業省　　R242
Denki kikai sōgō meikan 電気機械綜合名鑑 (Comprehensive directory of electromechanical manufacturers) 1961 ed. Kōgyō Shuppansha, 1961.　541p.

Gives addresses, branch offices, names of products, trademarks, capital, size of factories, standardized merchandise, and affiliations with industrial groups for 2,420 manufacturing companies. Index.

R243
Denki nenkan 電気年鑑　(Electrical almanac) 1953- .　Nihon Denki Kyōkai, 1953-55, 1957- . 12v.　Annual.

Consists of annual report on power, equipment and labor force, and a directory of 3,500 manufacturers, government offices concerned with electricity, power companies, universities having electrical engineering courses and associations.

R244
Denki jigyō no genjō 電気事業の現状 (Present status of electrical industry) 1951-
Comp. by Tsūshō Sangyōshō Kōeki Jigyōkyoku. Nihon Denki Kyōkai, 1951- .　7v.　Biennial.

Former title: *Shin denryoku jigyō meikan.* Nikkan

Kōgyō Shinbunsha, 1951.

Includes current trends, international cooperation in electrical engineering, and outline of electrical industry in foreign countries. Statistics appended.

ELECTRICAL COMMUNICATION ENGINEERING

BIBLIOGRAPHY

R245
Denki Tsūshin Gakkai zasshi sōmokuji 電気通信学会雑誌総目次　(Index to the Journal of the Institute of Electrical Communications Engineers of Japan) No. 1 - 4 (1917-62) Denki Tsūshin Gakkai, 1937-64.　4v.

Papers and data arranged chronologically under subjects, with author index. Subject index of reviews of foreign papers and author index of transactions of research committees included.

Kōno, Tokuyoshi 河野徳吉　　R246
A bibliography on transistors.　P. B. Repōtosha, 1959.　288p.

Papers published in various countries and American patents registered in the *Official Gazette* since 1949, classified by subject. A history of transistors, survey of current trends, etc. appended. Author index.

DICTIONARIES

R247
Erekutoronikusu daijiten エレクトロニクス大事典 (Comprehensive dictionary of electronics)　Chijin Shokan, 1961.　831p.

Headings are in Japanese, followed by original spelling and explanations. Western language index.

Yūseishō Denpa Kanrikyoku　　R248
郵政省電波監理局
Denpa yōgo jiten　電波用語辞典 (Glossary of radio terms)　Denpa Shinkōkai, 1958.　107p.

Supplement of *Denpa Jihō* (Radio Journal), v. 13, no. 6, it explains for laymen about 650 technical terms in radio and broadcasting.

Kātō, Yoshio 加藤芳雄　　R249
Musen yōgo jiten 無線用語辞典 (Glossary of wireless terms)　Rev. and enl. ed.　Denshi Kō-

gakusha, 1962. 482p.

Explains about 2,500 technical and legal terms. Illustrations.

HANDBOOKS

Denki Tsūshin Gakkai 電気通信学会 **R250**
Tsūshin kōgaku handobukku 通信工学ハンド
ブック (Handbook of electric communication
engineering) Maruzen, 1962. 2210p.

Covers basic theories, materials, components of
equipment and systems and administrative matters.
Tables and diagrams. Indexes of subjects and personal names.

R251
Musen kōgaku handobukku 無線工学ハンド
ブック (Radio engineering handbook) OHM-
sha, 1964. 2351p.

Brought up-to-date by additional chapters on semi-
conductors, special circuits, information theory, and
automatic control. Index.

Kumagai, Saburō 熊谷三郎 **R252**
Denshi kōgaku handobukku 電子工学ハンド
ブック (Electronics handbook) Asakura
Shoten, 1961. 690p.

Basic theories of gas and solid electronics,
their application to electronic circuits, measurement
and control, electronic computers, devices for industrial use, medical instruments, etc. References
at the end of each chapter. Directory of manufacturers and products. Index.

R253
Denshi kōgaku pokettobukku 電子工学ポケ
ットブック (Electronics pocket book) Junior ed. OHM-sha, 1957. 1342p.

Elementary explanation of formulas, numerical
tables, measurement methods, electrons and their
functions, electron tubes and circuits, radio devices,
high-frequency measurement and testing, and industrial application. Index.

R254
Chōonpa gijutsu benran 超音波技術便覧
(Supersonics technology manual) Nikkan Kōgyō
Shinbunsha, 1960. 1425p.

Gives basic theory and applications, including
supersonics as a research tool in physics and chemistry. Tables, lists and references appended. Index.

Yamashita, Hideo 山下英夫 **et al.** **R255**
Denshi keisanki handobukku 電子計算機ハ
ンドブック (Electronic computer handbook) 2d ed. Koronasha, 1962. 795p.

Comprehensively describes digital and analogue
computers, explains their application to business
management, numerical analysis and programming,
and gives the characteristics of commercially a-
vailable domestic and foreign computers. Index of
technical terms.

R256
Handōtai handobukku 半導体ハンドブック
(Semi-conductor handbook) OHM-sha, 1963. 1264p.

Explains all aspects, from solid state physics
and materials to various applications and power
supplies. References and table of characteristics
of Japanese-made transistors and diodes appended.

R257
Tōshiba denshikan handobukku 東芝電子管
ハンドブック (Tōshiba electron-tube
handbooks) Comp. by Tōshiba Shōji Kabushiki Kaisha. Seibundō Shinkōsha, 1962- .
3v. In progress.

Comprehensive presentation of technical standards,
operational directions and applications, with many
examples, for receiving and cathode-ray tubes (2v.)
and special tubes (1v.).

Tōshiba handōtai handobukku (Tōshiba semi-conductor handbook) series, (1962-) is another
publication of this type.

R258
Denshi kairo handobukku 電子回路ハンド
ブック (Electronic circuit handbook) Maruzen, 1963. 988p.

Detailed and illustrated explanations for practical use, including sections on parts, meters and
other elements.

R259
Denshi kiki zairyō buhin handobukku 電子機
器材料部品ハンドブック (Handbook of
materials and parts for electronic apparatus)
Komine Kōgyō Shuppan, 1964. 584p.

Describes characteristics of various materials
under 14 headings. Index.

Nihon Gakujutsu Shinkōkai **R260**
日本学術振興会
Hakumaku kōgaku handobukku 薄膜工学ハン

ドブック (Thin film engineering handbook) OHM-sha, 1964. 917p.

Describes fabrication techniques, physics, and applications of thin film microelectronics essential for microminiaturization of elements and circuits, reduction of weight, and increased reliability. Related technology, basic solid state physics, and numerical tables, as well as an index are included in the appendix.

YEARBOOK

R261

Denshi kōgyō nenkan 電子工業年鑑 (Electronics industry almanac) 1959- . Comp. by Tsūshō Sangyōshō. Denpa Shinbunsha, 1959, 1962- . 4v.

Surveys present status and developments in technology, management, overseas activities, policies, communication and automation equipment, electronic computers and other devices, parts and materials. List of firms and institutions appended.

Telephone and Telegraph

Nihon Denshin Denwa Kōsha **R262**
Toshokan 日本電信電話公社図書館 Denshin denwa jigyō kankei zasshi kiji sakuin 電信電話事業関係雑誌記事索引 (Index of periodical articles on telephone and telegraph affairs) 1960. 159p.

Subject and author indexes to 44 journals.

Broadcasting

Nippon Hōsō Kyōkai 日本放送協会 **R263**
Terebijon yōgo jiten 「技術演出」テレビジョン用語辞典 (Glossary of television terms) Rev. and enl. ed. Nippon Hōsō Shuppan Kyōkai, 1963. 266p.

Terminology guide of about 2,000 terms, for use by specialists in the field. English index.

R264

Terebijon kōgaku handobukku テレビジョン工学ハンドブック (Television engineering handbook) OHM-sha, 1959. 1446p.

Detailed, practical explanations of principles, channel problems, pickup and receiving electron tubes, recent transistorized television circuits, studio

and transmitting facilities, telecasting and relaying techniques for servicemen, transmitting and receiving antennas and wave propagation, receiving sets and their operation, color television systems and devices, industrial television, measurement techniques in 21 chapters. References and directory of firms appended. Index.

Funakoshi, Akira 船越章 **R265**
Rajio hōsō handobukku ラジオ放送ハンドブック (Radio broadcasting handbook) Dabiddosha, 1958. 198p.

Describes daily services, operation and administrative organization of the Japan Broadcasting Corporation and commercial radio stations. Directories of commercial radio broadcasting companies, organizations and agents appended. Index.

MINES AND MINING ENGINEERING

Asai, Kazuhiko 浅井一彦 **R266**
Doku-Wa-Ei kōgyō yōgo jiten 独和英鉱業用語辞典 (German-Japanese-English dictionary of mining terms) Nihon Sekitan Kyōkai, 1961. 430, 11p.

Wide in range. Symbols, abbreviations and data on the organization of mining in Germany appended.

Monbushō 文部省 **R267**
Gakujutsu yōgoshū: saikō yakingaku hen 学術用語集 採鉱ヤ金学編 Japanese scientific terms: mining and metallurgy. Nihon Kōgyōkai, 1954. 263p.

English-Japanese and Japanese-English dictionary of standard terms.

Asano, Gorō 浅野五郎 **R268**
Kōzan chishitsu handobukku 鉱山地質ハンドブック (Mining geology handbook) Asakura Shoten, 1962. 484p.

For specialists, with sections on mining, mine appraisal, development and management, ore dressing, smelting, etc. Index.

Ogata, Otomaru 緒方乙丸 **R269**
Jitsuyō kōzan sekkei benran 実用鉱山設計

便覧 (Practical mine design handbook) Asakura Shoten, 1961. 536p.

Contains formulas and data, with graphs and tables. Bibliography.

Sayama, Sōhei 佐山総平 **R270**
Saikō saitan handobukku 採鉱・採炭ハンドブック (Handbook of ore and coal mining) Asakura Shoten, 1962. 742p.

Covers all aspects of mine planning and operations, including safety and supervision, with references at end of each section. Index. Revision of the author's *Jitsugi keikaku saikōgaku handobukku* (Mining handbook: Planning and practice), 1955.

Suzuki, Toshio 鈴木俊夫 **R271**
Kōzan kikai benran 鉱山機械便覧 (Handbook of mine machinery) Sangyō Tosho, 1961. 409p.

For those engaged in the selection, handling, repairing and simple designing of mine machinery and equipment. Index.

Kagamiyama, Toshio 鏡山俊夫 **R272**
Kōzan dōryoku benran 鉱山動力便覧 (Mine power handbook) OHM-sha, 1956-61. 3v.

Covers motor, compressed air and steam power machinery and other equipment, safety precautions etc. Each volume indexed.

Nihon Kōgyō Hyōjun Chōsakai **R273**
日本工業標準調査会
JIS Kōzan kikaku benran J I S 鉱山規格便覧 (JIS mine standards handbook) Nihon Kikaku Kyōkai, 1958. 1210p.

Gives Japanese and foreign mining standards and explains their formulation.

Kōzan Yōhin Kenkyūkai 鉱山用品研究会 **R274**
Kōzan yōhin shōkai 鉱山用品詳解 (Detailed explanation of mining equipment) 2d ed. Hakua Shobō, 1958. 385p.

Based on a survey by the Resources Research Institute of the Agency of Industrial Science and Technology, it describes and gives systematic explanations of mining machines, electrical equipment and explosives approved by testing laboratories or certified to be of superior quality after testing. Excerpts from safety regulation, regulations con-

cerning inspection of equipment for use in mine shafts, and standards for mining equipment appended.

Yamada, Yuzuru 山田穣 **R275**
Kōzan hoan handobukku 鉱山保安ハンドブック (Mine safety handbook) Asakura Shoten, 1958. 591,20p.

Discusses mine disasters, including explosions, fires and cave-ins, principles of mine safety and the duties of safety specialists.

Tsūshō Sangyōshō 通商産業省 **R276**
Kōkōgyō shisū sōran 鉱工業指数総覧 (Conspectus of mining and industrial indexes) Hokuetsu Bunka Kōgyō, 1964. 262p.

Compiled on the basis of surveys by the Ministry of International Trade and Industry. With 1960 as the base year, the indexes are computed by calendar and fiscal years, quarters and months.

R277
Honpō kōgyō no sūsei 本邦鉱業の趨勢 (Trends in Japanese mining) 1906- . Comp. by Tsūshō Sangyōshō. 1907- . 52v. Annual.

Statistical survey of the production, supply and demand, and imports and exports of metals, nonmetals, coal and petroleum and the management and equipment of mines and wells. Issuing agency has changed several times.

Tsūshō Sangyōshō 通商産業省 **R278**
Honpō kōgyō no sūsei gojūnenshi 本邦鉱業の趨勢50年史 (Fifty years of trends in Japanese mining) 1963-64. 2v.

Gives 1905-60 statistics abridged from **R277** and *Honpō kōgyō ippan* (Survey of Japanese mining), published in 1905, with charts and notes on development of the industry (v.2). Chronology and other data appended.

METALLURGY

DICTIONARIES

Kawaguchi, Toranosuke 川口寅之輔 **R279**
Kinzoku zairyō jiten 金属材料辞典 (Dictionary of metal substances) Nikkan Kōgyō Shinbunsha, 1963. 581p.

Names of metals and related terms in Japanese, English and German with descriptions and illustrations. Clark's number, electron structures of elements, components of Seger cones and temperature tables are appended. Indexes in English and German.

Nihon Keikinzoku Kabushiki Kaisha   **R280**
日本軽金属株式会社
Aruminyūmu jiten アルミニューム事典
(Aluminum cyclopedia) 1960. 428p.

Covers domestic and foreign production, exports and imports, consumption, prices, manufacturing processes, etc. of aluminum and its products and alloys. Tables and concise dictionary of terms appended.

Ōwaku, Shigeo 大和久重雄 **and**   **R281**
Terasawa, Masao 寺沢正男
Kinzoku jutsugo jiten 金属術語辞典
(Dictionary of technical terms concerning metals) Rev. and enl. ed. Agune Shuppansha, 1959. 378p.

About 2,200 words, with their English equivalents. Tables appended. English index.

HANDBOOKS

Hashiguchi, Ryūkichi 橋口隆吉   **R282**
Kinzokugaku handobukku 金属学ハンドブック (Metal science handbook) Asakura Shoten, 1958. 885p.

Explains such fundamentals as the structures and properties of metals, smelting of ferrous and non-ferrous metals, metallurgy methods, and the making of iron and steel, non-ferrous materials and such special materials as semi-conductors and materials for aircraft and nuclear reactors. Index.

    R283
Jitsuyō kinzoku benran 実用金属便覧 (Practical metals handbook) Rev. ed. Nikkan Kōgyō Shinbunsha, 1962. 1327p.

Defines terms and gives smelting principles, properties, methods, data for measurements and tests, tables, diagrams and standards, including private standards of Japanese metal working companies. List of manufacturers' products. Index.

Nihon Kinzoku Gakkai 日本金属学会 **R284**
Kinzoku benran 金属便覧 (Handbook of metals) Rev. and enl. ed. Maruzen, 1960. 1388p.

Covers the properties, structures, casting, working and testing of metals in general, iron and steel, non-ferrous metals, rare metals, reactor materials, etc. Lists manufacturers. Index.

Keikinzoku Kyōkai 軽金属協会   **R285**
Aruminyūmu handobukku アルミニウムハンドブック (Aluminum handbook) Asakura Shoten, 1963. 1307p.

Guide to all aspects of production, giving JIS standards, and testing methods. Bibliographies. Index.

Hampel, Clifford A.   **R286**
Rea metaru handobukku レアメタルハンドブック Rare metals handbook. Tr. by Genshiryoku Kinzoku Konwakai. Kinokuniya Shoten, 1957. 772p.

Outlines production, smelting, physico-chemical properties, etc. of the alkaline-earth, platinum, rare-earth and other metals.

Yamanaka, Hideo 山中秀男   **R287**
Kinzoku zairyō jūryō benran 「実用標準」金属材料重量便覧 (Standard practical handbook of weights of metal materials) Nakamura Shoten, 1963. 252p.

Gives tables for calculating gauge, weight and volume, formulas, and JIS standards.

YEARBOOKS

    R288
Kinzoku gyōran 金属業覧 (Directory of metal companies) 1957- . Sangyō Shinbunsha, 1957-61, 1963- . 7v.

Summarizes business of about 4,500 companies grouped under seven geographical regions. Index. See **M163.**

    R289
Hitetsu kinzoku seihin tōkei nenpō 非鉄金属製品統計年報 (Annual statistical report of non-ferrous metal products) 1948- . Comp. by Tsūshō Sangyōshō, 1949- . 16v.

Outlines production and supply of the aluminum smelting and rolling, copper elongation and electric wire industries and gives statistics on aluminum oxide, aluminum, reclaimed aluminum, rolled Al-products, copper elongation, electric wires, cables and Pb-products and on the demand and supply of non-ferrous metals by both calendar and fiscal years, with imports and exports by countries.

Iron and Steel

Nihon Tekkō Kyōkai 日本鉄鋼協会 **R290**
Tekkō benran 鉄鋼便覧 (Iron and steel handbook) 3d rev. ed. Maruzen, 1962. 1935p.

Covers theories, methods and materials of manufacture, testing and inspection, safety and sanitation. Tables and a list of products of domestic manufacturers appended. Indexes.

Hasegawa, Masayoshi 長谷川正義 **R291**
Sutenresukō benran ステンレス鋼便覧
(Stainless steel handbook) Rev. and enl. ed.
Nikkan Kōgyō Shinbunsha, 1960. 1373, 41p.

Considers stainless steel as well as corrosion- and heat-resisting high alloys in four parts: principles, manufacture, application (chemical, aircraft, atomic energy, shipbuilding, rolling stock and construction industies, household articles, etc.) and data (standards and statistics). Indexes of terms and names of alloys.

Nihon Yōsetsu Kyōkai, Atsuryoku Yōki **R292**
Kenkyūkai 日本溶接協会 圧力容器研究会
Kōchōryokukō benran 高張力鋼便覧 (High-tension steels handbook) Sanpo, 1964. 204p.

Gives chemical composition, mechanical properties and other characteristics of various kinds, classified by manufacturers, species, tensile strengths. Includes diagrams, detailed table of contents.

R293
Tekkō nenkan 鉄鋼年鑑 (Iron and steel yearbook) 1955- . Tekkō Shinbunsha, 1954- .
9v.

Summarizes production, raw materials and fuels, equipment, technology, labor, finances and accounts, demand and supply, exports and imports, prices, wholesalers, overseas conditions. List of manufacturers and related organizations with statistics. Data index.

R294
Tekkō niji seihin nenkan 鉄鋼二次製品年鑑
(Iron and steel secondary products yearbook) 1953- . Comp. by Kōzai Kurabu. Tekkō Shinbunsha, 1953- . 11v.

Surveys economic aspects on the basis of data gathered by the Kōzai (steel materials) Club and the Ministry of International Trade and Industry, with sections on administrative control, pertinent laws and domestic and foreign statistics. Business chronicle and directory of manufacturers and related organizations appended.

R295
Tekkō tōkei nenpō 鉄鋼統計年報 (Iron and steel statistical yearbook) 1951-52 - . Comp. by Tsūshō Sangyōshō. Nihon Tekkō Renmei, 1953- . 12v.

Contains government-required statistical data presented by the Japan Iron and Steel Federation, Customs Division of the Ministry of Finance and the Bank of Japan, including indexes and tables on equipment, employees, raw materials, demand and supply, and production, with business chronicle.

Metal working

Suzuki, Hiroshi 鈴木弘 **and** **R296**
Hibino, Fumio 日比野文雄
Kinzoku kakō sōbunkenshū 金属加工総文献 集 (General bibliography of metal working) Seibundō Shinkōsha, 1960. 687p.

Scholarly papers and technical reports from Japan, U.S.A., U.K., and Germany, 1921-53, chronologically listed under 24 subject categories.

Nihon Imono Kyōkai 日本鋳物協会 **R297**
Imono yōgo jiten 鋳物用語辞典 (Glossary of casting terms) Nikkan Kōgyō Shinbunsha, 1957. 105, 15, 22p.

Explains terms and gives English equivalents. English index.

Matoba, Yukio 的場幸雄 **et al.** **R298**
Kinzoku seiren gijutsu handobukku 金属製錬 技術ハンドブック (Handbook of metal smelting techniques) Asakura Shoten, 1963. 818p.

Covers iron, steel, alloys and non-ferrous metals, including copper, aluminum, magnesium, beryllium and tungsten. Index.

R299
Kinzoku netsushori gijutsu benran 金属熱処 理技術便覧 (A handbook of metal heat-treatment techniques) Nikkan Kōgyō Shinbunsha, 1961. 1048p.

Explains terms, treatment theories and methods, testing and inspection, equipment, automation, plant layouts and quality control. Index.

R300
Nihon Imono Kyōkai 日本鋳物協会
Imono benran 鋳物便覧 (Foundry manual) Rev. ed. Maruzen, 1961. 1447, 96p.

Detailed information, with illustrations and tables, on melting, casting and other foundry processes, materials, equipment, chemical analyses, tests, standards, management, etc. Lists of references. Comprehensive index.

Nihon Chūzō Kikai Kōgyōkai 日本鋳造 **R301**
機械工業会
Chūzō kikai setsubi gaidobukku 鋳造機械設 備ガイドブック (Casting machine and

equipment guidebook) Nikkan Kōgyō Shinbunsha, 1963. 528p.

Describes machinery, tools and other equipment for melting, molding, sand treatment, dusting, special casting, heat treatment, conveyance, etc., with rating of the efficiency of testing and measuring apparatus. Illustrations. Lists of manufacturers appended.

Nihon Imono Kyōkai 日本鋳物協会 **R302**
Kyupora handobukku キュポラハンドブック (Cupola handbook) Maruzen, 1959. 471p.

Covers the structure and operation of cupola furnaces, with sections on theories, materials and methods. Includes bibliographies and tables. Index.

Nihon Shindō Kyōkai 日本伸銅協会 **R303**
Shindō handobukku 伸銅ハンドブック (Brass handbook) 1957. 736p.

Gives standards, production trends, consumption, import trends, prices, tax rates, etc. Lists of members of the Japan Brass Makers' Association and related organizations, dealers and trade unions appended.

Sosei Kakō Kenkyūkai **R304**
塑性加工研究会
Puresu benran プレス便覧 (Press handbook) Maruzen, 1958. 765, 19, 85p.

Explains plastic-working machines and techniques. Includes diagrams, tables, and lists of references.

Welding

Okada, Minoru 岡田実 **R305**
Yōsetsu gijutsu handobukku 溶接技術ハンドブック (Welding technique handbook) Asakura Shoten, 1960. 650p.

Gives principles and welding methods for various metals. Bibliographies and index.

Suzuki, Haruyoshi 鈴木春義 **R306**
Saishin yōsetsu handobukku 最新溶接ハンドブック (New welding handbook) Enl. ed. Sankaidō, 1964. 858p.

Covers methods, metallurgy, tests and inspections. Includes references, JIS tables and a table of Japanese-English-German-French welding terms. Index.

Kihara, Hiroshi 木原博 **R307**
Yōsetsu dēta bukku 溶接データブック (Welding data book) Sanpō, 1964. 1082p.

Indispensable for structural designers, manufacturers of welding material, welders, and engineers. Index.

Yōsetsu Gakkai 溶接学会 **R308**
Yōsetsu benran 溶接便覧 (Welding handbook) Maruzen, 1959. 1228p.

Explains in detail theories, methods, materials, applications of welding and standards. Includes list of technical terms with English equivalents and illustrations. Index.

Nihon Yōsetsu Kyōkai, Kikaku Iinkai **R309**
日本溶接協会規格委員会
Yōsetsu kikaku yōran 溶接規格要覧 (Manual of welding standards) Sanpō, 1964. 250p.

Gives JIS standards for welding iron, steel and non-ferrous materials, electric machinery and tools, gas fittings, fuels, etc., technical terms, symbols, testing methods and related data.

Surface treatment

Kinzoku Hyōmen Gijutsu Kyōkai **R310**
金属表面技術協会
Kinzoku hyōmen gijutsu benran 金属表面技術便覧 (Handbook of metal surface techniques) Rev. ed. Nikkan Kōgyō Shinbunsha, 1963. 1680, 172p.

Discusses physicochemical properties of metal surface and methods of coating, etc. Includes formulas and tables. Indexes in Japanese and western languages.

Nihon Gakujutsu Shinkōkai, Fushoku Bōshi Iinkai **R311**
日本学術振興会腐蝕防止委員会
Kinzoku bōshoku gijutsu benran 金属防蝕技術便覧 (Handbook of metal corrosion prevention techniques) Nikkan Kōgyō Shinbunsha, 1959. 821p.

Covers corrosion phenomena, corrosion-proof materials, and methods of testing, etc. Glossary of terms. Index.

Kinzoku Hyōmen Gijutsu Kyōkai **R312**
金属表面技術協会
Rainingu benran ライニング便覧 (Lining handbook) Nikkan Kōgyō Shinbunsha, 1961. 565p.

Explains materials and methods, dealing with prevention of rust. Lists of references. Index.

R313
Tokin gijutsu benran 鍍金技術便覧 (Plating technique handbook) Nikkan Kōgyō Shinbunsha, 1961. 740p.

Covers basic theory, techniques, mills and production data, with diagrams, tables and references. A list of plating mills and their products appended. Index.

Nihon Bōshō Gijutsu Kyōkai   **R314**
日本防錆技術協会
Bōshō gijutsu benran 防錆技術便覧 (Handbook of rust prevention techniques) Nikkan Kōgyō Shinbunsha, 1958. 860p.

Deals with rust-prevention in manufacturing, storage, transportation and use. Includes a list of recommended materials and tables of temperature and humidity at various places in Japan and abroad. Index.

Tajima, Sakae 田島栄   **R315**
Hyōmen shori handobukku 表面処理ハンドブック (Handbook of surface treatment) Sangyō Tosho, 1955. 1041, 42p.

Covers basic techniques, chemicals and standards. Surveys techniques in western countries. Bibiliography and index.

CHEMICAL INDUSTRY

Oka, Shunpei 岡俊平 **and**   **R316**
Nagai, Hideo 永井秀男
Kagaku kōgyō jiten 化学工業辞典 (Handbook of chemical industry) Tokyodō, 1959-60. 2v.

Volume on inorganic chemistry includes atomic energy engineering, equipment, measurements, industrial instrumentation, quality control and industrial hygienics, etc. Volume on organic chemistry covers both raw and synthetic materials, with appendix containing tables and data. English and German terms indexed in each volume.

Kagaku Kikai Kyōkai 化学機械協会   **R317**
Kagaku kōgaku jiten 化学工学辞典 (Dictionary of chemical engineering) Maruzen, 1953. 243p.

Contains about 1,700 terms of which 600 are explained and others are given synonyms with source references, covering chemical engineering, mathematics, physical and industrial chemistry, mechanical engineering, automatic controls, statistics and production control. Commonly used abbreviations and English and German equivalents included. Index.

Kagaku Kōgaku Kyōkai 化学工学協会 **R318**
Kagaku kōgaku benran 化学工学便覧 (Handbook of chemical engineering) Rev. ed. Maruzen, 1964. 1184, 237p.

Describes unit operations with many examples of calculation for designing, planning and operation of equipment. Physicochemical constants included. Appended are list of materials for constructing equipment, anticorrosive methods, various standards. Catalogue of equipment by domestic manufacturers included.

Kaigai kagaku kōgyō sōran 海外化学工業   **R319**
総覧 (Survey of foreign chemical industry) 1961- . Kagaku Keizai Kenkyūjo, 1960- . 4v. Annual.

Reviews annual reports of about 40 well-known foreign companies and deduces from them the economic status, industrial structure and engineering levels of the countries they represent.

Kagaku kōgyō tōkei nenpō 化学工業統計   **R320**
年報 (Annual report on statistics of the chemical industry) 1954- . Comp. by Tsūshō Sangyōshō. Tsūshō Sangyō Chōsakai, 1954- . 11v.

Surveys trends and economic conditions and gives statistics on production, production capacity, exports and imports, prices, labor, etc., including those for related industries.

Kagaku kōgyō nenkan 化学工業年鑑 (Chemical industry annual) 1948- . Kagaku Kōgyō Nippōsha, 1948, 1952-53, 1955- . 13v.   **R321**

Gives statistics based on those of the Research and Statistics Division of the Ministry of International Trade and Industry; lists chemicals, manufacturers, and agencies.

Tsūshō Sangyōshō Keikōgyōkyoku   **R322**
通商産業省軽工業局
Kagaku kōgyō: sono genjō to tenbō 化学工業 その現状と展望 (Chemical industry, present and future) Rev. ed. Tokyo Tosho, 1964. 444p.

Covers domestic and foreign trends in the chemical and related industries, including structural changes, raw materials, investments, technology and cartels, and describes branches of the chemical industry and their products.

Nihon Kagakukai 日本化学会   **R323**
Kagaku oyobi kagaku kōgyō no tameno bōsai shishin 化学および化学工業のための防災指針 (Safety guide in chemistry and the chemical industry) Series 1, 2. Maruzen, 1962- . Loose-leaf.

Each part takes up a hazardous chemical, giving its properties, toxic effects or other hazards, methods of testing, directions for safe handling, how to deal with accidents, examples of hazards, references and pertinent laws and regulations. Originally published serially in *Kagaku to kōgyō* (Chemistry and industry) of the Japan Chemical Society. Further parts projected.

Iimure, Nagisa 飯牟礼渚 **R324**
Kikenbutsu toriatsukaisha hikkei 危 険 物 取 扱
者 必 携 (Guidebook on handling dangerous
materials) Rev. and enl. ed. Sangyō Tosho,
1960. 316p.

Safety regulations for licensed operators. Index.

Chemical equipment

Fujita, Shigefumi 藤 田 重 文 **R325**
Kagaku sōchi benran 化 学 装 置 便 覧 (Handbook of chemical equipment) Rev. ed. Kanazawa, Kagaku Gijutsusha, 1958. 234, 22p.

Provides engineers with basic information on designing and operation, with many examples and references. Appended data include scale for calculating
logarithmic mean values and humidity chart.

Kagaku Sōchi Kenkyūkai **R326**
化 学 装 置 研 究 会
Kagaku sōchi sekkeisha hikkei 化 学 装 置 設
計 者 必 携 (Handbook for chemical equipment designers) Sangyō Tosho, 1960. 510p.

Gives mathematical tables and basic design
equations and explains materials and designs of con-
tainers, buildings, rotating machines, piping, linings,
towers, kettles, conical ball mills, etc. Subject
index.

Kagaku Sōchi Kenkyūkai **R327**
化 学 装 置 研 究 会
Kagaku sōchi toriatsukaisha hikkei 化 学 装 置
取 扱 者 必 携 (Handbook for chemical equipment operators) Rev. ed. Sangyō Tosho, 1962.
502p.

Explains, with many tables and illustrations,
physicochemical constants and materials, unit operations and design calculations. List of manufacturers appended. Lists of references.

Kazumori, Toshirō 数 森 敏 郎 **R328**
Kōatsu gasu gijutsu benran 高 圧 ガ ス 技 術
便 覧 (Handbook of high-pressure gas technology) Sangyō Tosho, 1961. 456, 21p.

Explains properties of gas; describes production
method; and gives excerpts of pertinent regulation.
Directory of manufacturers appended. Index.

Kagaku Kōgaku Kyōkai 化 学 工 学 協 会 **R329**
Bussei teisū 物 性 定 数 (Physicochemical
constants) Series 1, 1963- Maruzen,
1963- . 1v. In progress.

Reviews research (in the 1959-61 period in this
first issue) in establishing experimental values in

physicochemical constants and methods of determining properties, introduces new values and
methods, and gives such data as recommended values
of properties of aliphatic hydrocarbons tabulated
by the Japan Chemical Industry Association and
constants approved by Le Bureau international
d'etalons physico-chimiques, *Brussels*. Annotated
bibliography.

Industrial water

Nihon Kōgyō Yōsui Kyōkai **R330**
日 本 工 業 用 水 協 会
Kōgyō yōsui benran 工 業 用 水 便 覧 (Handbook of industrial water) Rev. ed. Sangyō Tosho, 1963. 946, 231p.

Considers science of water, water resources,
troubles caused by water, water treatment, anticorrosive treatments, tests and data sheets. Catalogues of equipment and chemicals of various manufacturers appended.

R331
Kōgyō yōsui tōkeihyō 工 業 用 水 統 計 表 (Sta-
tistical tables of industrial water) 1958- .
Comp. by Tsūshō Sangyōshō. Nihon Kōgyō Yōsui
Kyōkai, 1960- . 2v.

Published every four years, giving statistics on
industrial water sources and consumption by purposes, prefectures, types of industry, etc.

Electrochemistry

Denki Kagaku Kyōkai 電 気 化 学 協 会 **R332**
Denki kagaku benran 電 気 化 学 便 覧 (Handbook of electrochemistry) New rev. ed. Maruzen, 1964. 1310, 34p.

Covers the theory, related mathematics, chemistry, measurements, equipment and materials, individual electrochemical industries, maintenance of
plants and statistics. Bibliographies. Catalogue of
products grouped by manufacturers. Subject index.

Kase, Hirotoshi 加 瀬 敬 年 **et al.** **R333**
Denki kagaku kiki toriatsukaisha hikkei 電 気
化 学 機 器 取 扱 者 必 携 (Handbook for
electrochemical equipment operators) Sangyō
Tosho, 1961. 463p.

Includes also other electrical equipment, measurement apparatus using electron-tube circuits, and
tools. Tables and selected bibliography appended.
Index.

Ceramic industry

Yōgyō Kyōkai 窯業協会 **R334**
Yōgyō jiten 窯業辞典 (Ceramic dictionary)
Maruzen, 1963. 354p.

Explains terms related to porcelain, earthenware, glass, cement, refractories, enamels, abrasives, carbon products, gypsum and lime, each with its English and German equivalents. English index.

Yōgyō Kyōkai 窯業協会 **R335**
Yōgyō kōgaku handobukku 窯業工学ハンド
ブック (Handbook of ceramic engineering)
Gihōdō, 1964. 1066, 35p.

Explains principles and techniques. Includes diagrams and tables. References at end of each chapter. Index.

Moriya, Tarō 森谷太郎 **et al.** **R336**
Garasu kōgaku handobukku ガラス工学ハ
ンドブック (Glass engineering handbook)
Asakura Shoten, 1963. 918, 20p.

Covers structure and properties, measurement methods, manufacturing, fabrication and special glasses, including devitroceramics and glass for measuring radioactive rays. References. List of makers and their products appended. Index.

R337
Yōgyō tōkei nenpō 窯業統計年報 (Annual statistical report on the ceramic industry) 1955–
Comp. by Tsūshō Sangyōshō. Hokuetsu Bunka Kōgyō, 1955-59, 1961- . 9v.

Gives statistics of national production, shipments, inventories of specific ceramics, production by regions and enterprises, and raw materials. Brief business chronicle appended.

Chemical products

Ryūsan Kyōkai 硫酸協会 **R338**
Ryūsan kōgyō benran 硫酸工業便覧 (Handbook of the sulphuric acid industry) Kawade Shobō, 1951. 1186p.

Includes basic mathematics, physics and chemistry, analysis, construction and maintenance of plants, catalogues of products of various manufacturers, and directories, with selected references and list of patents. English-Japanese dictionary of technical terms appended. To be revised.

R339
A-kei seihin nenkan ア系製品年鑑 (Yearbook of ammonia products) 1950- . Anmonia-

kei Seihin Kyōkai, 1950- . 14v.
Gives statistics, standards, and regulations.

Fuels

Nenryō Kyōkai 燃料協会 **R340**
Nenryō benran 燃料便覧 (Fuel handbook)
Maruzen, 1953. 648, 66p.

Covers mathematics, raw materials, transportation and storage, combustion and furnaces, etc. Index.

COAL

Tsūshō Sangyōshō 通商産業省 **R341**
Sekitan yōgo jiten 石炭用語事典 (Dictionary of coal terminology) Sekitan Keizai Kenkyūjo, 1959. 293p.

Defines technical terms and idioms. Classified index.

Nihon Tāru Kyōkai 日本タール協会 **R342**
Tāru kōgyō benran タール工業便覧 (Handbook of the coal-tar industry) 1960. 725p.

Describes technology and merchandising, with mathematical tables, statistics, chronology, references and list of terms. Index.

PETROLEUM

Tsutsumi, Shigeru 堤繁 **et al.** **R343**
Sekiyu kagaku jiten 石油化学事典 (Cyclopedia of petrochemistry) Kemikaru Mākettingu Sentā, 1962. 1306, 26p.

Gives separate dictionaries of technical and economic terms, process flow sheets and statistics and describes processes and the petrochemical industry, with discussion of its problems. Index of terms in the dictionaries.

Iimure, Nagisa 飯牟礼渚 **R344**
Sekiyu seihin jiten 石油製品事典 (Petrochemicals handbook) Sangyō Tosho, 1962. 262p.

Gives the history and properties of petrochemicals and explains, explicitly and with many cross references, terms relating to testing, petroleum combustion, lubricants and sales. References. Index.

Andō, Shingo 安東新午 **et al.** **R345**
Sekiyu kagaku kōgyō handobukku 石油化学
工業ハンドブック (Handbook of petrochemical industry) Asakura Shoten, 1962. 835, 56p.

Covers resources, cracking, conversion, products,

etc., with references. Data on manufacturers included. Subject index.

Iimure, Nagisa 飯牟礼渚 **R346**
Sekiyu seihin gaidobukku 石油製品ガイド
ブック (Guidebook to petrochemicals) Sangyō Tosho, 1960. 416p.

Systematically describes properties and uses and gives standards. Tables. Index.

Nihon Sekiyu Kabushiki Kaisha **R347**
日本石油株式会社
Sekiyu benran 石油便覧 (Petroleum handbook) Sekiyu Keizai Kenkyūkai, 1959. 519p.

Surveys production and marketing situation in Japan and abroad. Regulations, data sheets, statistics and supplementary tables appended. Index.

Sekiyu Kagaku Shinbunsha 石油化学 **R348**
新聞社
Puropan butan benran プロパンブタン便覧
(Propane and butane handbook) Rev. ed. 1962. 960p.

Deals with basic chemistry, properties, manufacturing, uses, apparatus and equipment, marketing, safety regulations and standards. Excerpts of laws and regulations and lists of related organizations in Japan and the United States appended. Index.

R349
Sekiyu tōkei nenpō 石油統計年報 (Annual statistical report on petroleum) 1948- . Comp. by Tsūshō Sangyōshō. Sekiyu Keizai Kenkyūkai, 1949- . 16v.

1948-51 ed.: *Sekiyu tōkei nenkan*, comp. by Shigenchō.

Gives general trends and statistics on production, and marketing. Lists of regulations and government-required statistics appended.

EXPLOSIVES

Kimura, Makoto 木村真 **R350**
Kayaku yōgo jiten 火薬用語辞典 (Dictionary of explosives terminology) Sangyō Tosho, 1959. 419p.

Lists about 3,000 words, including trade names and firework terms. Explanations inadequate, but this is the only work of its kind.

Oils and Fats

Nihon Yukagaku Kyōkai **R351**
日本油化学協会

Yushi kagaku benran 油脂化学便覧 (Handbook of the chemistry of oils and fats) Maruzen, 1958. 702p.

Deals mainly with oil and fat components and testing methods and, to a lesser extent, with manufacturing. List of terms and English index.

Nishi, Ichirō 西一郎 **et al.** **R352**
Kaimen kasseizai benran 界面活性剤便覧
(Handbook of surface active agents) Sangyō Tosho, 1960. 1149p.

Explains physical properties and applications. List of trade products (200p.) useful. Subject index in English and Japanese.

PERFUMES

Horiguchi, Hiroshi 堀口博 **R353**
Kōryō jiten 香料辞典 (Dictionary of perfumes) Kyōritsu Shuppan, 1955. 338, 29p.

Lists about 1,200 English terms, with Japanese equivalents and synonyms. For odors, gives examples; for substances, gives properties, odor and uses.

PAINT

Matsumoto, Toku 松本十九 **R354**
Toryō jiten 塗料辞典 (Paint dictionary) Gihōdō, 1956. 492p.

Gives English equivalents of about 3,000 entries, with glossary of painters' slang appended. Handbook section has tables and notes on treating and painting methods, etc.

Iwai, Shinji 岩井信次 **et al.** **R355**
Toryō handobukku 塗料ハンドブック
(Paint handbook) 3d ed., enl. Sangyō Tosho 1958. 959p.

Discusses pigments of various paints, testing methods and standards with tables. Index.

R356
Tosō gijutsu benran 塗装技術便覧 (Handbook of coating and painting techniques) Rev. and enl. ed. Nikkan Kōgyō Tsūshinsha, 1958. (700)p.

Covers both general and special techniques, including ingredients and film structures. Figures and tables include data on safety and hygienics, properties and uses of paints. Includes glossary of painters' slang, price list, dictionary of trade names, and a list of licensed factories and organizations. Index of 1,000 terms.

Toryō nenkan 塗料年鑑 (Paint yearbook) 1955- . Toryō Hōchi Shinbunsha, 1955- . 10v. **R357**

Surveys trends of the industry, production, technology, raw materials, exports and imports and the activities of trade groups and gives statistics on production, shipments, inventories, consumption, price trends, etc., with standards and directories of manufacturers and sales agencies.

PIGMENTS

Nihon Ganryō Gijutsu Kyōkai **R358**
日本顔料技術協会
Ganryō benran 顔料便覧 (Pigments handbook) Seibundō Shinkōsha, 1959. 360, 30, 22p.

Lists pigments with their chemical structures, physicochemical properties, testing methods, uses and synthetic vehicles. Short dictionary of terms, bibliography and Japanese Industrial Standards included. Outline of ASTM testing methods, and lists of Japanese pharmacopoeia compounds related to pigments, Japanese patents and organizations and manufacturers appended. Japanese and English indexes.

Dyes

Yūki Gōsei Kagaku Kyōkai **R359**
有機合成化学協会
Senryō benran 染料便覧 (Dye handbook) Maruzen, 1959. 1140, 75p.

Explains testing, processing and application of domestic and imported dyes, with useful lists and tables. Glossary and list of references. Subject and trade name indexes.

R360
Senryō senshoku nenpō 染料染色年報 (Annual report on dyes and dyeing) No. 1-7. Comp. by Yūki Gōsei Kagaku Kyōkai. Gihōdō, 1953-62. 7v.

Surveys trends and lists new commercial dyestuffs and fiber-treating agents.

HIGH MOLECULAR CHEMICAL INDUSTRY

Rubber

Kanbara, Shū 神原周 **et al.** **R361**

Gōsei gomu handobukku 合成ゴムハンドブック (Synthetic rubber handbook) Asakura Shoten, 1962. 783p.

Deals with synthetic rubber industry in Japan, with references at end of each chapter. Inadequate index.

Nihon Gomu Kyōkai 日本ゴム協会 **R362**
Gomu kōgyō benran ゴム工業便覧 (Rubber industry handbook) 1959. 852p.

Covers properties of natural and synthetic rubber, processing and products. Includes chronology of the industry, statistics and lists of references. Index.

Plastics

R363
Purasuchikkusu yōgo jiten プラスチックス用語辞典 (Glossary of plastics terms) Kōgyō Chōsakai, 1959. 553p.

Glossary of about 10,000 foreign terms relating to raw materials, processing and applications with index of Japanese equivalents and list of about 10,000 trade names of domestic and foreign products. Diagrams, tables, list of abbreviations.

Gōsei Jushi Kōgyō Gijutsu Kenkyūkai **R364**
合成樹脂工業技術研究会
Gōsei jushi benran 合成樹脂便覧 (Synthetic resins handbook) Rev. and enl. ed. Sangyō Tosho, 1959. 1047p.

Explains chemistry and uses, molding processes and fabrication tests. Tables, references and glossary appended. Index.

Mizutani, Kyūichi 水谷久一 **R365**
Purasuchikku kakō gijutsu benran プラスチック加工技術便覧 (Handbook of plastics processing) Nikkan Kōgyō Shinbunsha, 1960. 901p.

Explains in detail primary and secondary processing techniques. Conversion tables and comparison of characteristics of plastics appended. Index.

Nihon Biniru Kōgyōkai **R366**
日本ビニル工業会
Enka biniru jushiyō anteizai benran 塩化ビニル樹脂用安定剤便覧 (Vinyl chloride resins stabilizer handbook) Kōgyō Chōsakai, 1959. 116p.

Deals with properties of various stabilizers and classification of foreign stabilizers for vinyl chloride resins. Includes tables, diagrams, references and list of patents and a directory of manufacturers apended.

Kōgyō Chōsakai 工業調査会　　**R367**
Purasuchikkusu shōhinmei yōran プラスチックス商品名要覧 (Trade-name index of plastics) 1961. 873p.

Domestic and foreign sections list trade names of raw materials, products, processing aids and machines, etc., with constituents of materials, uses and names of manufacturers.

R368
Purasuchikkusu nenkan プラスチックス年鑑 (Plastic yearbook) 1960- . Kōgyō Chōsakai, 1959- . 5v.

Surveys molding materials, plasticizers, colorants, fillers and other processing aids and methods. Trade statistics, list of patents and laws and regulations.

Cellulose

Sofue, Hiroshi 祖父江寛 **and**　**R369**
Migita, Nobuhiko 右田伸彦
Kagaku kōgyō serurōzu handobukku 化学・工業セルローズハンドブック (Chemical and industrial cellulose handbook) Asakura Shoten, 1958. 654p.

Covers history, raw materials, refining, structure, uses, resolution and swelling, microstructures, decomposition and degradation and testing methods. Fully illustrated. References and index.

Adhesives

Setchaku Kenkyūkai 接着研究会　　**R370**
Setchaku benran 接着便覧 (Adhesives handbook) Kōbunshi Kagaku Kankōkai, 1964. 730p.

Analyzes commercial adhesives and gives guidance in their selection for specific purposes. List of domestic and foreign products and directory of domestic manufacturers appended.

R371
Setchaku gijutsu benran 接着技術便覧 (Handbook of adhesion technology) Nikkan Kōgyō Shinbunsha, 1962. 1112p.

Explains theory of adhesion and describes types of adhesives and their applications. History of adhesion technology and annotated glossary appended.

MISCELLANEOUS INDUSTRIES

Leather and Woodwork

Andō, Noriyuki 安藤紀之　　**R372**
Naigai hikaku bunken mokuroku 内外皮革文献目録 (International bibliography on leather) Meiji Seikaku Kabushiki Kaisha, 1953. 103p.

Lists Japanese books from ancient times to 1950; Japanese articles and foreign books from 1900 to 1950.

R373
Hikaku tōkei nenpō 皮革統計年報 (Annual report of leather statistics) 1955- . Comp. by Tsūshō Sangyōshō. Hokuetsu Bunka Kōgyō, 1955- 10v.

Covers production, raw materials and labor.

R374
Mokkō benran 木工便覧 (Woodworking handbook) Nikkan Kōgyō Shinbunsha, 1958. 710p.

Covers woods, and woodworking design, processing techniques, business mangement, etc. Simple explanations with many illustrations, and a few representative references at end of each chapter. Lists of related organizations, schools, testing stations, and publications appended. Index.

Paper

Isoda, Seizō 磯田清蔵　　**R375**
Wa-Ei-Doku taiyaku seishi jiten 和英独対訳製紙辞典 (Japanese-English-German dictionary of paper manufacture) Maruzen, 1953. 247p.

Defines technical terms, chiefly relating to pulp paper. Illustrated.

Narita, Kiyohide 成田潔英　　**R376**
Shigyō teiyō 紙業提要 (Papermaking manual) 6th rev. ed. Maruzen, 1961. 333p.

Deals with characteristics, products, quality tests, fibers, printing, weights and measures, financial problems, and marketing of both Western and Japanese paper. Appendixes include English paper classifications, standard dimensions and glossary of terms, and paper used for scrolls and Japanese interiors, ceremonial paper wrappings and ornaments.

Shigyō nenkan 紙業年鑑 (Paper and pulp industry almanac) 1948- . Shigyō Shinbunsha, 1948- . 10v. Biennial from 1952. **R377**

Surveys the industry, gives foreign and Japanese statistics and lists companies and associations.

Kami parupu tōkei nenpō 紙パルプ統計年報 (Annual report of paper and pulp statistics) 1952- . Comp. by Tsūshō Sangyōshō. Kami Parupu Rengōkai, 1953- . 12v. **R378**

Summary of production, industrial indexes and statistical data, based on the annual survey made by the Japan Paper and Pulp Association.

Yōshi ryūtsū tōkei nenpō 洋紙流通統計年報 (Annual statistical report on paper movements) 1959- . Comp. by Tsūshō Sangyōshō. Kami Purupu Rengōkai, 1959- . 5v. **R379**

Emphasizes supply and demand conditions from the maker to the retailer or consumer, with statistics on raw materials, finished products, labor conditions and distribution. For pre-1959 data, see **R378**.

Textiles

Matsuda, Kunio 松田国夫 **R380**
Kiji jiten 生地辞典 (Dictionary of fabrics) Senken Shinbunsha, 1959-60. 2v.

Lists 1,500 types on the market and in everyday use. The etymology, Egnlish equivalent, thread structure, texture, and uses of each fabric are described in detail. Index.

Ōno, Ichirō 大野一郎 **R381**
Keorimono jiten 毛織物事典 (Dictionary of woolen fabrics) Maruzen, 1953. 413p.

Terms from a variety of sources are arranged in alphabetical order and explained briefly. A list of standard woolen fabrics and their names, and a table showing the processes in wool carding and the manufacture of woolen fabrics are appended. Index of Japanese terms.

Orimono senshoku jiten 織物染色辞典 **R382**
(Dictionary of textiles and dyeing) Senmon Tosho, 1953. 974p.

Lists about 10,000 terms relating to raw materials, machinery and equipment, processing methods, business transactions, and synthetic fibers. Illustrations, tables, and English equivalents. Dated but useful.

Nihon Gakujutsu Shinkōkai **R383**
日本学術振興会
Sen'i senshoku kakō jiten 繊維染色加工辞典 (Textile dyeing dictionary) Nikkan Kōgyō Shinbunsha, 1962. 645p.

Defines some 5,300 terms with English equivalents. Includes tables, bibliography, lists of testing and research institutes, inspection organizations, universities giving courses on textiles, JIS standards, and English index of JIS technical terms.

Yōmō senshoku benran 羊毛染色便覧 (Handbook of wool dyeing) Sen'i Gijutsu Kenkyūjo, 1959. 552p. **R384**

Contributions from some 40 manufacturers of dyes and surface active agents in Japan and six other countries. Lists about 3,000 wool dyestuffs and 900 refining, bleaching, and auxiliary agents in tabular form; and describes their properties, uses, processes, criteria for testing and judging fastness. Detailed table of contents. No index.

Sakurada, Ichirō 桜田一郎 **R385**
Gōsei sen'i handobukku 合成繊維ハンドブック (Synthetic fiber handbook) Asakura Shoten, 1959. 585, 28p.

For use by manufacturers and users of synthetic fibers. Discusses dyeing processes, precautions for mixed spinning, suitable applications and sewing methods. Instructions for laundering, ironing, storing and identifying synthetic fibers are given. Brief index.

Sen'i Gakkai 繊維学会 **R386**
Kasen benran 化繊便覧 (Synthetic fiber handbook) Maruzen, 1963. 1254p.

A technical manual for specialists dealing with production, spinning, knitting, weaving, dyeing, inspection and testing. Statistics. Index.

Sen'i nenkan 繊維年鑑 Textile yearbook. 1948- . Nihon Sen'i Kyōgikai, 1948- . 16v. **R387**

Discusses progress in all aspects of staple and synthetic fiber industry, exports and imports, raw materials and products. Includes directories of companies, organizations, testing agencies, etc. and pertinent laws and regulations.

Sen'i tōkei nenpō 繊維統計年報 Yearbook of textile statistics. 1953- . Comp. by Tsūshō Sangyōshō. Sen'i Nenkan Kankōkai, 1954- . 11v. **R388**

Covers production, market conditions, raw materials, equipment, and labor conditions.

Foodstuff industry

DICTIONARIES

Meidiya 明治屋　　　　　　　　　**R389**
Meidiya shokuhin jiten 明治屋食品辞典 (Meidiya encyclopedia of food)　1963- ．3v.

A volume on liquor, 2 volumes on food (to be completed in 3v.) have been published.

R390
Hakkō kōgyō yōgo jiten 発酵工業用語辞典
(Dictionary of fermentation terms) Gihōdō, 1960. 372p.

Lists and defines 3,200 terms including words used in connection with the making of *sake*, *shōyu*, *miso* and other Japanese specialties. Classified list of fermentation microorganisms appended. Foreign language terms indexed.

HANDBOOKS

R391
Shokuhin seizō handobukku 食品製造ハンドブック　(Foodstuff processing handbook) Chikyū Shuppan, 1963.　1068p.

Pt.1 describes some 900 types of common foodstuffs. Pt.2 deals with packaging materials, factory management standards, sanitation, the standard composition of Japanese foodstuffs, export inspection methods, regulations, and the standardization law. Useful in the home as well as for specialists.

Futakuni, Jirō　　二国二郎　　　**R392**
Denpun handobukku デンプンハンドブック
(Starch handbook) Asakura Shoten, 1961. 742p.

Discusses chemical, physicochemical, enzyme chemical research results, and recent technological developments in Japan's starch industry. Indexes of personal names and subjects.

Kajū Gijutsu Kenkyūkai 果汁技術研究会 **R393**
Kajū handobukku 果汁ハンドブック　(Fruit juice handbook) Kōyō Shoten, 1955.　2v.

Covers in detail the production of fruit juice, commenting on the chemistry of juices, testing and inspection, etc. Tables, food sanitation laws, bibliography appended in v. 2.　Subject index.

Honda, Norimoto　　本多紀元　　**R394**
Arukōru handobukku　アルコールハンドブック　(Alcohol handbook)　Rev. and enl. ed.　Hakkō Kyōkai, 1963.　440p.

Deals with prices, constituents, standards, raw materials, production units, products, manufacturing processes, etc.

Ōeda, Masayoshi　大条方義　　**R395**
Gyūnyū nyūseihin handobukku 牛乳・乳製品ハンドブック　(Handbook of milk and dairy products) Asakura Shoten, 1958.　613p.

Covers not only products but also machinery, by-products, and inspection. Laws and regulations, standards, and equipment design data appended. Subject indexes in Japanese and European languages.

Hashimoto, Yoshio 橋本吉雄 **et al.** **R396**
Shokuniku nikuseihin handobukku 食肉・肉製品ハンドブック (Meat and meat products handbook)　Asakura Shoten, 1963.　698p.

Explains production and properties, packing materials, sanitation, management, and other items. Laws, regulations and a list of machinery and products of related companies appended. Subject index.

Zenkoku Suisan Neriseihin Kyōkai　**R397**
全国水産煉製品協会
Suisan neriseihin handobukku 水産煉製品ハンドブック　(Handbook of processed marine products)　1959.　846p.

Practical guide to the chemistry of fish, methods of making fish cakes and sausages, decomposition, laws and regulations, quality inspection standards, implements and machinery, and management.　No index.

YEARBOOKS

R398
Nihon nyūgyō nenkan 日本乳業年鑑　(Japanese dairy industry yearbook) 1951- ．Nihon Nyūseihin Kyōkai, 1951, 1956- ．6v. Biennial from 1956.

Surveys production and consumption and gives laws and regulations, statistics, references concerning production techniques, and directory of manufacturers and material suppliers.

R399
Nihon jōkai nenkan　日本醸界年鑑　(Japan brewing yearbook) 1953- ．Nihon Jōkai Shinbunsha, 1953- ．12v.

Reviews developments in the industry, lists source materials.　A 230p. directory of organizations and their members.

SUGAR INDUSTRY

Higuchi, Hiroshi 樋口弘   **R400**
Tōgyō jiten 糖業事典 (Dictionary of the sugar industry) Naigai Keizai Kenkyūjo, 1959. 3v.

Covers details about beet sugar, cane sugar, crystal glucose, artificial sweetening industrial agents, distribution and market transactions. Includes bibliography and many illustrations. The supplementary volume lists 1,750 world sugar companies and organizations, a map of world sugar production and tables showing the uses of sugar and its by-products. No index.

Kokuzeichō 国税庁   **R401**
Satō kankei yōgoshū 砂糖関係用語集 (Glossary of terms related to sugar) 1955. 238p.

Lists and defines terms relating to industry, manufacturing processes and commercial transactions. Tables. Index. The *Satō yōgo benran* (Handbook of sugar terms) published by the Sōgō Shuppansha is a reprint of this glossary.

Seitō Gijutsu Kenkyūkai   **R402**
精糖技術研究会
Seitō benran 製糖便覧 (Sugar refining handbook) Rev. and enl. ed. Asakura Shoten, 1962. 703p.

Discusses process controls, plant facilities, and general analytical methods. Tables and a glossary of standard sugar refinery terminology appended. Index.

  R403
Satō tōkei nenkan 砂糖統計年鑑 (Sugar statistical yearbook) 1957- . Nihon Seitō Kōgyōkai, 1957- . 5v. Triennial.

Covers domestic and overseas market conditions and statistics. Tables of supply and demand, regulations, and a directory of organizations appended. In the 1962 edition the metric system was adopted.

DOMESTIC SCIENCE

Nihon Kasei Gakkai 日本家政学会   **R404**
Nihon kaseigaku bunkenshū 日本家政学文献集 (Japanese bibliography of home economics) 1959. 338p.

Classified list of books and articles published from 1949 to 1959 and about 1,500 general American titles. No index.

  R405
Kateika daijiten 家庭科大事典 (Cyclopedia of home economics) Kokudosha, 1960. 765p.

Based on the teaching guides for primary and high schools, it covers fundamentals, practices and materials. References listed. Food analysis table appended. Subject, name indexes.

  R406
Kateika jisshū shiryō zukai daijiten 家庭科実習資料図解大事典 (Illustrated dictionary of home economics: practice and teaching) Zenkoku Kyōiku Tosho, 1961. 484p.

Consists mainly of illustrations with comments and notes for teaching, covering all aspects of home economics. Subject index to illustrations.

Daigo, Yoshiyasu 大後美保 **and**   **R407**
Shōji, Hikaru 庄司光
Seikatsu kagaku handobukku 生活科学ハンドブック (Handbook of domestic science) Asakura Shoten, 1964. 630p.

Scientific discussion of clothing, food, shelter and related matters, with tables, diagrams and bibliography of Japanese books.

Clothing

Hifuku Bunka Kyōkai 被服文化協会   **R408**
Hifuku daijiten 被服大事典 (Cyclopedia of costume) Rev. ed. Bunka Fukusō Gakuin Shuppankyoku, 1960. 978p.

Describes costumes from ancient to modern times in about 200 illustrated articles. Reference list of old Japanese and Western books. Detailed table of contents, but no index.

Tanaka, Chiyo 田中千代   **R409**
Zukai fukushoku jiten 図解服飾事典 (Illustrated dressmaking dictionary) Fujin Gahōsha, 1955. 805, 72p.

About 10,000 entries, many with illustrations, in some of which the styles are outmoded, and about 50 articles explaining key terms in detail. Foreign terms have original spellings.

Tanaka, Chiyo 田中千代   **R410**
Fukushoku jiten 服飾事典 (Dictionary of dressmaking) Fujin Gahōsha, 1957. 690, 16, 50p.

Reduced-size reprint of **R409** without its photographs but with additional terms appended.

Narita, Jun 成田順 **et al.**   **R411**
Yōsai shugei jiten 洋裁手芸事典 (Diction-

ary of dressmaking and handicrafts) Kasei Kyō-
ikusha, 1964.   389p.

Explains technical terms simply and clearly, often
with illustrations, in sections on dressmaking, handicrafts, materials and fashion changes, each also
available as a separate pamphlet.

Satō, Hikoo   佐藤彦雄   **R412**
Wa-Yō fukushoku yōgo   和洋服飾用語   (Japa-
nese and foreign vocabulary of dressmaking)
Meigen Shobō, 1960.   493p.

Defines Japanese terms and their foreign equivalents.

R413
Fukushoku nenkan   服飾年鑑   (Apparel yearbook) 1960- . Comp. by Yōhinkai Henshūbu.
Tokyo Yōhin Oroshishō Rengōkai   1960, 63- .
2v.

Contains events of the year, an exhaustive,
illustrated dictionary of terms with foreign equivalents, a management handbook and an index of ad-
vertisers. Published as a supplement to the magazine *Yōhinkai*.

Tanaka, Kaoru   田中薫   **and**   **R414**
Tanaka, Chiyo   田中千代
Genshoku Sekai ifuku daizukan   原色世界衣
服大図鑑   World folk costumes.   Osaka,
Hoikusha, 1961.   114, 64p.   (Hoikusha no gen-
shoku daizukan, 9)

Representative costumes of many countries (excluding the Soviet Union, mainland China, Australia
and Africa) shown in color photographs with cultural, historical and geographical notes. Short survey
of folk costumes appended. Brief index.

Food

Motoyama, Tekishū   本山荻舟   **R415**
Inshoku jiten   飲食事典   (Dictionary of food
and drink) Heibonsha, 1958.   604p.

Extensive coverage, with illustrations. More
important Japanese dishes explained in detail, with
histories and methods of preparation.

Tamura, Gyosai   田村魚菜   **R416**
Zairyōbetsu ryōri jiten   材料別料理事典
(Cooking dictionary arranged by materials) Shin-
jusha, 1961.   1153, 23p.

Explains with illustrations the preparation of
about 3,000 foodstuffs divided into such categories
as fish, meats, vegetables, dried stuffs, etc. Also
covers festival and tea-ceremony meals, condiments,
spices, table settings and manners, and kitchen
utensils.

Yamamoto, Naoyoshi   山本直文   **R417**
Shokumotsu jiten   食物事典   (Food   dictionary)
Shibata Shoten, 1958.   323p.

Defines Japanese, Western and Chinese culinary
terms, with appendix on table etiquette.

Okazaki, Seiichirō   岡崎整一郎   **and**   **R418**
Yasunaga, Yukio   安永幸生
Ryōri yōgo kihon gijutsu jiten   料理用語基本
技術事典   (Dictionary of cooking terms and
basic techniques)   Rev. ed.   Daiichi Shuppan,
1962.   228p.

Especially detailed on Japanese terms. Techniques explained with photographs.

Yamamoto, Naoyoshi   山本直文   **R419**
Futsu-Ei-Wa ryōri yōgo jiten   仏英和料理用
語辞典   Dictionnaire des termes de la cui-
sine.   Hakusuisha, 1962.   290p.

Useful in reading cookbooks and writing menus
by equating terms in two sections, French-English-
Japanese and Japanese-French-English. Examples
of menus, diagrams of cuts of meat, appended.

Nihon Joshi Daigaku Shokumotsugaku   **R420**
Kyōshitsu 日本女子大学食物学教室
Chōri kagaku sōten   調理科学綜典   (Complete
book of science of cooking) Asakura Shoten,
1959.   466p.

For home use. Discusses dietetics, the manufacture, preservation, analysis and inspection of
food, food hygiene, Japanese and Western dishes,
food for infants and invalids, table manners, kitchen
efficiency, etc. Standard Japanese table of food
components appended.

BIOLOGICAL SCIENCES

✤ Biology, zoology, botany and related subjects, such as biochemistry, microbiology and genetics are included. Works on garden plants, wood, and the fishery industry are listed under Agriculture **T** and medicinal plants under Medical section **U.**

BIOLOGY

BIBLIOGRAPHY

S1

Japan science review: biological section. No. 1- . Comp. by Nihon Gakujutsu Kaigi. Gihōdō, 1949- . 13v. Annual.

Classified index of articles in Japanese biological periodicals. Gives titles of English translations and abstracts of important articles.

DICTIONARIES

Usui, Masuo 碓井益雄 **et al.** **S2**
Seibutsu kagaku jiten 生物科学辞典 (Dictionary of the biological sciences) Misuzu Shobō, 1956. 474p.

Emphasizes physiology and the life sciences in detailed articles on medicine, agricultural botany, fisheries, livestock breeding, etc. Classification tables of animals and plants appended. Indexes in Japanese and European languages of personal names, with biographical notes on important persons, and subjects.

Tsuge, Hideomi 柘植秀臣 **et al.** **S3**
Seibutsu no jiten 生物の辞典 (Dictionary of biology) Iwasaki Shoten, 1956. 575p.

About 10,000 concise entries, with English,

German and Latin equivalents, useful for specialists as well as students. Lists of symbols, abbreviations, and animal and plant names appended. European-language index.

S4

Iwanami seibutsugaku jiten 岩波生物学辞典 (Iwanami dictionary of biology) Ed. by Tsuneo Yamada and others. Iwanami Shoten, 1960. 1278p.

Defines technical terms in medicine, agriculture and related sciences, with examples of use and equivalents in English, German, French, Russian and Latin. Animal and plant classification tables, etc. appended. Foreign terms, personal names indexed.

HANDBOOKS

Nihon Dōbutsuen Suizokukan Kyōkai **S5**
日本動物園水族館協会
Nihon dōbutsuen suizokukan yōran 日本動物園水族館要覧 (Guide to Japanese zoological gardens and aquariums) 1962. 237p.

Lists all fauna in zoos and aquariums. Gives history of the Japan Association of Zoological Gardens and Aquariums, directory and statistics.

Honjō, Ichijirō 本城市次郎 **S6**
Seibutsugaku Handobukku 生物学ハンドブック (Handbook of biology) Iwanami Shoten, 1953. 250p. (Iwanami zensho)

Reference data on biology and related sciences, including tables, guidance in collecting specimens and testing formulas, abbreviations and statistics.

S7

Suisan dōshokubutsu kan'yōmei shūran
水産動植物慣用名集覧
(Glossary of common names of marine animals

and plants) Nōrin Kyōkai, 1953. 445p.

Each common name is followed by its standard Japanese name and the area in which it is used. Also given is the index number of the family to which the plant or animal belongs, as well as its position in the appended classification table of Japanese standard names for important marine products of wide distribution. The classification table shows scientific names and has brief notes on distribution. Indexed by common and standard Japanese names.

Amamiya, Ikusaku 雨宮育作 **and**   **S8**
Kuroda, Nagamichi 黒田長礼
Yūyō yūgai kanshō suisan dōshokubutsu zusetsu 有用有害観賞水産動植物図説 (Useful, harmful and ornamental aquatic animals and plants, illustrated) Reprint ed. Daichi Shoin, 1933. 716p.

Gives the scientific name, morphology, ecology and economic value of each of 1,700 varieties of Japanese marine and fresh-water animals and plants, including ornamental fishes and birds.

CHRONOLOGY

Shirai, Kōtarō 白井光太郎   **S9**
Nihon hakubutsugaku nenpyō 日本博物学年表 (Chronology of the history of natural history in Japan) Reprint of the rev. and enl. ed. Ookayama Shoten, 1943. 437p.

Lists events from early times in zoology, botany and geology, including dates of scholars, establishment of facilities and introduction of animals and plants into Japan. Indexes to subjects, names and book titles.

Biochemistry

Nakazawa, Ryōji 中沢亮治   **S10**
Hakkō oyobi seibutsu kagaku bunkenshū 醸酵及生物化学文献集 Bibliography of fermentation and biological chemistry. Nihon Gakujutsu Shinkōkai, 1950- . 11v. In progress.

Lists alphabetically under English headings Japanese and foreign publications from 1800 to 1940 on fermentation, agricultural industry, fertilizers, biochemistry and food chemistry.

    S11
Kokusai Seikagaku Rengō Kōso Iinkai hōkoku
国際生化学連合酵素委員会報告 Report of the Commission on Enzymes of the International Union of Biochemistry. Tr. by Nobuo

Tamiya. Kyōritsu Shuppan, 1963. 163p.

Japanese translation of the Report published by Pergamon Press in 1961, discussing definition and application of terms and symbols, classification and nomenclature of enzymes and cytochromes.

Takada, Ryōhei 高田亮平 **and**   **S12**
Katsura, Eisuke 桂英輔
Nihon bitamin bunkenshū 日本ビタミン 文献集 (Bibliography of vitaminology in Japan) 1884-1960. Bitamin Gojusshūnen Kinen Jigyōkai, 1962. 1687p.

About 17,500 items on vitamins and related subjects, compiled by combining three previously published bibliographies by the Committee for comprehensive study of vitamins under the same title, with subtitle: Vitamin B group, 1950; Vitamins soluble in oil, 1952, and supplement, 1956.

    S13
Seibutsu kagaku handobukku 生 物 化 学 ハ ン ド ブ ッ ク (Biochemistry handbook) Rev. ed. Gihōdō, 1962. 1126, 24p.

Emphasizes recent findings in biochemistry and such related fields as bacteriology and medicine, including those found in *Seibutsu kagaku saikin no shinpo* (Recent progress in biochemistry), 1955-60, 6v., with constants and applications.

Miyake, Yasuo 三宅泰雄 **et al.**   **S14**
Hōsha kagaku handobukku 放射化学ハンド ブ ッ ク (Handbook of radiation chemistry) Asakura Shoten, 1962. 819p.

For research specialists. Information on obtaining radioactive substances, standard radioactive solutions, etc.

Nihon Hōshasei Dōi Genso Kyōkai   **S15**
日 本 放 射 性 同 位 元 素 協 会
Bunken shōrokushū 文献抄録集 (Abstracts)
Kōgyō riyō hen (Series on industrial applications) 1958- . 24v.
Nōgaku seibutsugaku riyō hen (Series on agricultural and biological applications) 1959- . 26v.
Igaku riyō hen (Series on medical applications) 1964- . 4v.

Includes almost all Japanese and selected foreign research reports. Printed in card form.

Microbiology

    S16
Biseibutsugaku handobukku 微生物学ハンド ブ ッ ク (Handbook of microbiology) Rev. ed.

Gihōdō, 1964. 1500p.

Covers bacteriology, food and soil microbiology, microbial genetics, problems in the handling of micro-organisms, etc., with references, list of micro-organic cultures, list of periodicals and 'International code of bacteriological nomenclature'. English, Japanese indexes.

Abe, Shigeo　阿部重雄　　**S17**
Biseibutsu zufu 微生物図譜 (Micro-organisms illustrated): The Penicillia. Kanehara Shuppan, 1957. 319p.

Comprehensive study of Penicillium in English and Japanese, including sections on identification of species, culture media and techniques, isolation and taxonomy. Lists antibiotics and penicillium products. No index.

Genetics

Menderukai　メンデル会　　**S18**
Idengaku saibōgaku bunken sōsetsu 遺伝学・細胞学文献総説 (Introduction to literature on heredity and cytology) Hokuryūkan, 1948-50. 2v.

Lists about 12,000 Japanese and foreign books and articles published from 1940 to 1946 on eugenics, breeding, cytology and evolution.

S19
Idengaku handobukku 遺伝学ハンドブック (Heredity handbook) Gihōdō, 1956. 1205p.

Covers all living organisms, with chapters on such subjects as genetics, gene analysis and symbols, chromosomes, cytoplasm, eugenics, experimental methods, and teaching practices and materials. Surveys geneticists and their achievements, research institutions, societies and publications. Glossary and tables. Subject, personal name indexcs.

Planktons

Kokubo, Seiji　小久保清治　　**S20**
Fuyū seibutsu bunruigaku 浮游生物分類学 (Classification of planktons) Rev. ed. Kōseisha Kōseikaku, 1959. 439, 37p.

Briefly describes fresh-water and salt-water planktons, with illustrations and references.

Yamaji, Isamu　山路　勇　　**S21**
Nihon purankuton zukan 日本プランクトン図鑑 Plankton of Japanese coastal waters. Osaka, Hoikusha, 1959. 252p. 8 plates.

(Hoikusha no genshoku daizukan, 5)

Gives representative planktons in not only Japanese waters but also the Arafura Sea, Antarctic and North Pacific, with illustrations, some in color. Systematic listing of those in Tanabe Bay, Kii Peninsula. Name indexes.

BOTANY

DICTIONARIES

Honda, Masaji　本田正次　　**S22**
Nihon shokubutsu meii 日本植物名彙 Nomina plantarum japonicarum. New ed., rev. Kōseisha Kōseikaku, 1963. 498p.

Lists by Latin family name, with Japanese name(s) appended, indigenous wild ferns and spermatophytes in the four main Japanese islands. Latin and Japanese name indexes.

Murakoshi, Michio　村越三千男　　**S23**
Genshoku zusetsu shokubutsu daijiten 原色図説植物大辞典 (Color illustrated encyclopedia of plants) Chūbunkan, 1938. 472, 139p.

Illustrations of over 6,000 indigenous and non-Japanese plants in color, with glossary of botanical terms and list of medicinal plants. Indexes of Japanese, Chinese and scientific names.

Satake, Yoshisuke　佐竹義輔 et al.　　**S24**
Shokubutsu no jiten 植物の事典 A cyclopedia of plants. Tokyodō, 1957. 594p.

About 4,000 entries, including 800 names of Japanese and exotic plants, with about 600 illustrations. Classification table of vascular plants, list of medicinal and other useful plants and list of reference books and slides.

Monbushō　文部省　　**S25**
Gakujutsu yōgoshū: shokubutsugaku hen 学術用語集・植物学編 Japanese scientific terms: botany. 3d ed., rev. and enl. Dai Nihon Tosho, 1959. 155p.

Equivalents of botanical terms, in romanized Japanese, listed in three sections, Japanese-English, English-Japanese and Latin-Japanese.

Hyōjun Gakujutsu Yōgo Jiten Henshū　　**S26**
Iinkai 標準学術用語辞典編集委員会
Shinkyū Ei-Doku taishō hyōjun gakujutsu yōgo jiten 新旧・英独対照標準学術用語辞典 植物学編 (Standard dictionary of new and old technical terms with English and German equivalents) Botany. Seibundō Shinkōsha,

1964. 460p.

Defines all terms in **S25** and others, with synonyms, including localisms, and English and German equivalents. Classification tables, etc. appended. Subject, English, and Latin name indexes.

ILLUSTRATIONS

Murakoshi, Michio 村越三千男 **S27**
Genshoku shokubutsu daizukan 原色植物大図鑑 (Comprehensive flora in color) Rev. by Tomitarō Makino. Seibundō Shinkōsha, 1955-56. 5v.

Describes, with information on morphology, ecology and distribution, about 10,000 species of indigenous and exotic plants, arranged according to Engler's classification; 5,000 color plates, 4,000 line drawings. Indexes.

Kitamura, Shirō 北村四郎 **et al.** **S28**
Genshoku Nihon shokubutsu zukan 原色日本植物図鑑 Coloured illustrations of herbaceous plants of Japan. Osaka, Hoikusha, 1960-64. 3v. (Hoikusha no genshoku zukan, 15-17)

Shows 297 species of Sympetalae, 600 of Choripetalae and 600 of Monocotyledoneae indigenous to Japan, with keys for identification of genera and species. Appendixes on techniques for preparing and preserving specimens and information on distribution. Indexes.

Makino, Tomitarō 牧野富太郎 **S29**
Shin Nihon shokubutsu zukan 新日本植物図鑑 Makino's new illustrated flora of Japan. Rev. ed. Hokuryūkan, 1961. 1057p.

Illustrates and describes representative phanerogams, gymnosperms, pteridophytes, cryptogams, etc., mainly indigenous to Japan, listed according to Engler's system. Glossary. Indexes.

Terazaki, Tomekichi 寺崎留吉 **S30**
Nihon shokubutsu zufu 日本植物図譜 Terazaki's illustrated flora of Japan. Shun'yōdō, 1933-38. 2v.

v.1 shows and briefly describes 2,100 species of plants native to Japan, Sakhalin, the Ogasawara and Ryūkyū islands and Taiwan, 1,700 of them classified by such seasonal appearances as blossoms or fruits and the rest divided into Gramineae, Cyperaceae, Juncaceae, Pinales and Pteriodophyta. v.2 has 1,900 species, chiefly of agricultural or ornamental plants, arranged according to Engler's system. Indexes.

Okuyama, Shunki 奥山春季 **S31**
Genshoku Nihon yagai shokubutsu zufu 原色日

本野外植物図譜 Coloured illustrations of wild plants of Japan. Seibundō Shinkōsha, 1957-63. 7v.

Color photographs, arranged in seasonal order, of about 3,000 varieties of common Japanese wild plants, excluding alpines, each with its common Japanese, alternate, and scientific name, general information, flowering season, distribution and names of similar plants. Supp. 1 adds about 500 varieties arranged by season. Supp. 2 is a general index, giving Japanese, Latin and local names.

Tanabe, Kazuo 田辺和雄 **S32**
Genshoku Nihon shokubutsu seitai zukan 原色日本植物生態図鑑 Plants of Japan in their environment. v.1, Horizontal and vertical distribution. Osaka, Hoikusha, 1960. 141p. 40 plates. (Hoikusha no genshoku daizukan, 11)

Plates, many in color, with simple explanations in Japanese and English, illustrate plant life in the hills, low mountains, semi-high mountains and high mountains of Japan's tropical, subtropical, temperate and subfrigid regions, as well as in swamps and seaside and volcanic areas. 27p. supplementary explanations. Index.

Yano, Tasuku 矢野佐 **and** **S33**
Ishido, Tadashi 石戸史
Genshoku shokubutsu kensaku zukan 原色植物検索図鑑 (Keys to plant life illustrated in color) Hokuryūkan, 1962. 108p. 118 plates.

Gives scientific name, distribution, habitat, habits and gross morphology of 575 species of herbaceous plants indigenous to Japan, including Polypetalae, Gamopetalae and Monocotyledoneae, arranged from lower to higher, with classification keys appended..

Plant chemistry

Hirao, Nenokichi 平尾子之吉 **S34**
Nihon shokubutsu seibun sōran 日本植物成分総覧 (Survey of Japanese plant components) Sasaki Shoten, 1949-56. 3v.

Bibliography of chemical studies of indigenous plants from about 1870 to 1944, arranged by plant names and their components and uses. Indexes.

Kariyone, Tatsuo 刈米達夫 **S35**
Annual index of the reports on plant chemistry. Hirokawa Shoten, 1961- . 4v. In progress.

Abstracts of articles on phytochemistry in about 100 world chemical journals, arranged according to botanical classification. In English, but Japanese names have Chinese characters. Indexes of scientific and Japanese common names of plants and names of chemical compounds.

Alpine plants

Honda, Masaji 本田正次 **and** **S36**
Kiyosu, Yukiyasu 清棲幸保
Genshoku kōzan shokubutsu 原色高山植物
Coloured illustrations of the alpine plants of Japan. 3d ed., rev. Sanseidō, 1958. 104, 48p.

Shows plants indigenous to Japan, divided into alpine, subalpine and montane, with scientific and Japanese common names and habitats. National protection of alpine plants outlined in appendix. Indexes.

Takeda, Hisayoshi 武田久吉 **S37**
Genshoku Nihon kōzan shokubutsu zukan 原色日本高山植物図鑑 Coloured illustrations of alpine flora of Japan. Osaka, Hoikusha, 1960-62. 2v. (Hoikusha no genshoku zukan, 12, 38)

Covers about 550 plants, with scientific names and notes on distribution, habitats and flowering periods. Names indexed.

Takeda, Hisayoshi 武田久吉 **et al.** **S38**
Nihon kōzan shokubutsu zukan 日本高山植物図鑑 Illustrated manual of alpine plants of Japan. Rev. and enl. ed. Hokuryūkan, 1961. 347p. 16 plates.

Shows about 800 species, including Hepaticae, Musci, Fungi, fresh-water Algae, Lichenes, Pteridophyta, Gymnospermae and Angiospermae, with notes on habitats, distribution, ecology and morphology. Methods of collecting, processing and preserving specimens and of cultivation appended. Index of Japanese common names.

Useful plants

Kadokura, Hajime 角倉一 **S39**
Yūyō shokubutsu no gakumeikai 有用植物の学名解 Explanation of the scientific names for useful plants. Hirokawa Shoten, 1959. 234p.

Covers names of agricultural crop, medicinal and ornamental plants, and trees used for timber. Biographical list of men whose names occur in plant names. Species names indexed.

Shibata, Keita 柴田桂太 **S40**
Shigen shokubutsu jiten 資源植物事典 A

cyclopedia of useful plants and plant products. Rev. and enl. ed. Hokuryūkan, 1957. 804, 252p.

Outlines for 1,300 plants their geographical distribution, growing conditions, morphology, useful components and cultivation, propagation, preservation and utilization methods. Indexes.

Algae

Okada, Yoshiichi 岡田喜一 **S41**
Genshoku Nihon kaisō zukan 原色日本海藻図鑑 Natural coloured icones of Japanese seaweeds. Kazama Shobō, 1956. 178, 42p. 84 plates.

Gives the uses, distribution and morphology of 300 species of indigenous marine Algae, including rare and harmful ones, with color plates made from dry specimens. Notes on collecting and processing specimens appended. Index.

Okamura, Kintarō 岡村金太郎 **S42**
Nihon kaisōshi 日本海藻誌 (Records of Japanese algae) 2d ed., rev. Uchida Rōkakuho, 1956. 964, 11p.

Compilation of authoritative studies by Japanese and foreign scholars on the characteristics, morphology, phytogeny, reproductive systems and distribution of Japanese species of Chlorophyceae, Phaeophyceae and Rhodophyceae.

Okamura, Kintarō 岡村金太郎 **S43**
Nihon sōrui zufu 日本藻類図譜 Icones of Japanese algae. Kazama Shobō, 1951-52. 7v.

Illustrates the form and structure of representative marine Algae, with notes in English and Japanese, including distribution, maturity period of spores and uses. Indispensable for Japanese algology.

Segawa, Sōkichi 瀬川宗吉 **S44**
Genshoku Nihon kaisō zukan 原色日本海藻図鑑 Coloured illustrations of seaweeds of Japan. Rev. ed. Osaka, Hoikusha, 1959. 175p. 72 plates. (Hoikusha no genshoku zukan, 18)

Shows about 600 species of Chlorophyceae, Phaeophyceae and Rhodophyceae, mostly indigenous to Japan but including representative genera from adjacent areas, with keys for identification and classification of genera and species of each family. "Studies of the marine algae" appended. Name index.

Kokubo, Seiji 小久保清治 **S45**
Fuyū keisōrui 浮游硅藻類 Plankton diatomus. Nihon Gakujutsu Shinkōkai, 1955. 316p.

Covers general morphology, reproductive system, ecology and methods of collecting and processing specimens and shows about 350 species of float diatoms, with notes on gross morphology and distribution. Indexes. Many typographical errors.

Fungi

Hara, Kanesuke　原摂祐　　**S46**
Nihon kinrui mokuroku 日本菌類目録 A list of Japanese fungi, hitherto known.　Gifu, Nihon Kinrui Gakkai, 1954.　447p.

Alphabetical listing, with hosts and/or localities and references, of Eumycetes (excluding the Myxomycetes and Shizomycetes given in the 1927 edition) identified in the Japanese islands, Formosa, North China, Mongolia, Manchuria, Korea and the Kuriles. Host names indexed.

Itō, Seiya　伊藤誠哉　　**S47**
Nihon kinruishi 日本菌類誌 (Fungi of Japan) Yōkendō, 1936- .　6v.　In progress.

Treatise on Japanese fungi, citing sources and with key to class, genus, order, family and species. v.1, Eumycetes; v.2, Basidiomycetes, through no.5, Armillaria, have been published. Indexes of scientific and Japanese names of fungi and parasites. Sections issued through v.2, no.2 titled: *Dai Nihon kinruishi*.

Imazeki, Rokuya　今関六也 **and**　　**S48**
Hongō, Tsugio　本郷次雄
Genshoku Nihon kinrui zukan 原色日本菌類図鑑 Coloured illustrations of fungi of Japan. Osaka, Hoikusha, 1957.　181p.　68 plates. (Hoikusha no genshoku zukan, 23)

Covers Fungi in general but is especially strong in Agaricaceae, arranged by Singer's system (1951) with notes on morphology and sizes of spores and cystidia.　Indicates whether edible or poisonous. Name indexes.

Kawamura, Seiichi　川村清一　　**S49**
Genshoku Nihon kinrui zukan 原色日本菌類 図鑑 Icones of Japanese fungi.　Kazama Shobō, 1954-55.　8v.

Shows Basidomycetes and Ascomycetes, giving gross morphology, nature, how to identify poisonous types, and the symptoms and course of their poisoning, with Japanese common and scientific names and references. Indexes in v.8.

Ferns

Itō, Hiroshi　伊藤　洋　　**S50**
Nihon shidarui zukan 日本羊歯類図鑑 (Japa-

nese ferns illustrated)　Kōseisha Kōseikaku, 1944.　512, 14p.

Photographs of dry specimens of 512 selected species of 150 genera indigenous to Japan, Sakhalin, Formosa and Korea, arranged according to the classification in C. Christensen's *Manual of pteridology* (1938), with notes on critical characteristics and distribution. Name indexes.

Tagawa, Motoji　田川基二　　**S51**
Genshoku Nihon shida shokubutsu zukan 原色日本羊歯植物図鑑 Coloured illustrations of pteridophyta of Japan.　Osaka, Hoikusha, 1959.　270p.　72 plates. (Hoikusha no genshoku zukan, 24)

Shows about 400 indigenous ferns with Japanese common and scientific names and brief descriptions. Complete list of Japanese ferns, with name variants and references, appended.　Indexes.

Lichens

Asahina, Yasuhiko　朝比奈泰彦　　**S52**
Nihon no chii 日本の地衣 (Japanese lichens) Shigen Kagaku Shogakkai Renmei, 1950-56. 3v.

v.1, Cladoniaceae; v.2, Parmeliaceae; v.3, Usneaceae.　Gives ecological characteristics of each genus, followed by detailed descriptions of characters, reactions, components and specimens of various species of Japanese lichens. v.1 and 2 are written in Japanese with some notes in English; v.3 is entirely in English.　Index of scientific names and illustrations in each volume.

Flowering plants

Asahina, Yasuhiko　朝比奈泰彦　　**S53**
Nihon inka shokubutsu zukan 日本隠花植物 図鑑 (Japanese cryptogams illustrated) Sanseidō, 1939.　992p.

Monochrome plates show Myxomycetes, Algae, Fungi, Lichenes, Musci, Hepaticae, etc., with scientific names and notes on ecology and distribution.

Ōi, Jisaburō　大井次三郎　　**S54**
Nihon shokubutsushi 日本植物誌 Flora of Japan. Reprint ed. Shibundō, 1956.　1383p.

Lists all indigenous phanerogams, with keys of genera and species, Japanese common, scientific and alternate names and notes on ecology and distribution.　Gives list of Japanese discoverers. Name indexes.

Sequel, covering indigenous ferns, with 68 plates *Pteridophyta*, 1957.

Hara, Hiroshi 原 寛 **and** **S55**
Kanai, Hiroo 金井弘夫
Nihon shushi shokubutsu bunpu zushū 日本種子植物分布図集 Distribution maps of flowering plants in Japan. Inoue Shoten, 1958-59. 2v.

Each volume has dot map showing the distribution of 200 species of indigenous Angiospermae. Japanese phytogeography outlined in English. Name indexes.

Hara, Hiroshi 原 寛 **S56**
Nihon shushi shokubutsu shūran 日本種子植物集覧 Enumeratio spermatophytarum japonicarum. Iwanami Shoten, 1949-54. 3v.

Lists and gives notes on and references for some of the seed plants indigenous to Japan (from Pyrolaceae to Plantaginaceae in v.1, from Rubiaceae to Compositae in v.2 and from Geraniaceae to Cornaceae in v.3), arranged alphabetically by scientific names based on Dalla Torra et Harms' *Genera siphonogamarum*, with Japanese names and common alternates. Names indexed.

Trees

Sugimoto, Jun'ichi 杉本順一 **S57**
Nihon jumoku sōkensakushi 日本樹木総検索誌 Keys to Japanese trees and shrubs. Rev. ed. Rokugatsusha, 1961. 522p.

Useful for identification; brief descriptions and notes on geographical distribution and utilization.

Uehara, Keiji 上原敬二 **S58**
Jumoku daizusetsu 樹木大図説 (Illustrated guide to trees) Ariake Shobō, 1959-61. 4v.

Designed for use in landscape gardening, describes with photographs or drawings 10,000 species and varieties of 1,600 genera of 164 families of trees, mostly indigenous to Japan but including some of foreign origin. Index.

Kitamura, Shirō 北村四郎 **and** **S59**
Okamoto, Shōgo 岡本省吾
Genshoku Nihon jumoku zukan 原色日本樹木図鑑 Coloured illustrations of trees and shrubs of Japan. Osaka, Hoikusha, 1959. 306p. 68 plates. (Hoikusha no genshoku zukan, 19)

Identifies and gives geographical distribution of about 1,000 varieties of native Japanese trees, with 451 color plates. Index.

Nihon Ringyō Gijutsu Kyōkai **S60**
日本林業技術協会
Genshoku Nihon ringyō jumoku zukan 原色日本

林業樹木図鑑 Illustrated important forest trees of Japan. Chikyū Shuppan, 1964. 217p.

Shows in color, with English and Japanese explanations, about 100 wild trees important for timber, forest preservation and scenic beauty. Name index.

Kurata, Satoru 倉田悟 **S61**
Nihon shuyō jumokumei hōgenshū 日本主要樹木名方言集 (Dialect variants of the names for principal Japanese trees) Chikyū Shuppan, 1963. 291p.

Dialect terms, with the districts where used, for 275 trees, arranged by their Latin names.

Iwata, Toshiji 岩田利治 **and** **S62**
Kusaka, Masao 草下正男
Hōsan shōhakurui zusetsu 邦産松柏類図説 Coniferae japonicae illustratae. Rev. and enl. ed. Sangyō Tosho, 1954. 247p.

Gives the distribution, morphology and scientific names of conifers indigenous to Japan, a short history of studies of them and individual comments, with identification methods and Japanese and foreign references, on each family and genus. Indexes.

ZOOLOGY

DICTIONARIES

S63
Iwanami dōbutsugaku jiten 岩波動物学辞典 (Iwanami dictionary of zoology) Ed. by Naohide Yazu and Yaichirō Okada. Iwanami Shoten, 1935. 1333p.

Covers systematic and general zoology, including such branches as physiology, anatomy and ecology, and biographies of noted zoologists. Entry words in Western languages, followed by Japanese equivalents and brief explanations or identifications. Some illustrations. Appendix on preparation of slides and marine-animal specimens, and classification. Names indexed.

Ōshima, Masamitsu 大島正満 **et al.** **S64**
Ōyō dōbutsu jiten 応用動物事典 A cyclopedia of applied zoology. Hokuryūkan, 1961. 781, 158p.

Gives ecology, distribution and utilization of, or, if pests, extermination methods for, 9,000 species native to Japan, with scientific names from **S70**. Notes on feeding wild birds; lists of zoological gardens, aquariums, and animals reared in captivity. Indexes.

Taki, Isao 滝 庸 **et al.** **S65**
Dōbutsu no jiten 動物の事典 Encyclopedia

of animals. 5th ed. Tokyodo, 1958. 590p.

Defines technical terms and identifies animals, with notes on ecology, habitats and utilization, under 8,000 headings. Classification system, list of species, references and list of societies appended. General index.

Monbushō 文部省 **S66**
Gakujutsu yōgoshū: dōbutsugaku hen 学術用語集・動物学編 Japanese scientific terms: zoology. Dai Nihon Tosho, 1956. 128p.

Helps standardization of terms by equating them; listed in romanized Japanese, in Japanese-English, English-Japanese and Latin-Japanese sections.

Hyōjun Gakujutsu Yōgo Jiten Henshū **S67**
Iinkai 標準学術用語辞典編集委員会
Shinkyū Ei-Doku taishō ,hyōjun gakujutsu yōgo jiten 新旧英独対照標準学術用語辞典 動物学編 (Standard dictionary of new and old technical terms with English and German equivalents) Zoology. Seibundō Shinkōsha, 1963. 492p.

Helpful in determining relationships between old and new terms and their foreign equivalents and avoiding confusion in use by explaining each term briefly and giving synonyms. Table of geological periods, classification of animals and lists of fishes and birds appended. Subject, name indexes.

CLASSIFICATION

Imamura, Taiji 今村泰二 **S68**
Shin dōbutsu bunruihyō 新動物分類表 (New animal classification system) Hokuryūkan, 1961. 227p.

Divided into four subkingdoms and 27 phyla, with phylogenetic tree and references. Index.

Yazu, Naohide 谷津直秀 **S69**
Dōbutsu bunruihyō 動物分類表 (Animal classification table) 7th ed. Maruzen, 1952. 515 sheets.

Convenient taxonomy guide, giving the classes, orders, genera and species of all phyla, from Protozoa through Vertebrata, with common English, German and French names, major characteristics and references. Names indexed.

ILLUSTRATIONS

Uchida, Seinosuke 内田清之助 **et al.** **S70**
Genshoku dōbutsu daizukan 原色動物大図鑑 Encyclopaedia zoologica, illustrated in colours.

Hokuryūkan, 1957-60. 4v.

Gives Japanese and scientific names and information on distribution, morphology and ecology of animals arranged by classification. Index.

Uchida, Seinosuke 内田清之助 **et al.** **S71**
Nihon dōbutsu zukan 日本動物図鑑 New illustrated encyclopedia of the fauna of Japan. Rev. and enl. ed. Hokuryūkan, 1958. 28, 1899, 236p.

Covers the gross morphology, embryology, ecology, etc. of 4,895 species, excluding insects, indigenous to Japan, the Ryūkyū Islands, Formosa, Korea, Sakhalin, the Kuriles, China and the South Sea Islands, arranged by classification with Japanese and scientific names and namers. Gives separately fauna of foreign origin raised in Japan as pets or for industrial purposes. Index.

Ōyama, Katsura 大山桂 **et al.** **S72**
Illustrated handbook of Japanese paleogene mollusca. Kawasaki, Kōgyō Gijutsuin Chishitsu Chōsajo, 1960. 244p. 71 plates.

Shows 112 species of gastropods, 246 of bivalves and six of cephlapods of the early Tertiary period reported in Japan, Sakhalin, Taiwan and the Ogasawara Islands, with introductory study of the early Tertiary period in Japan and nearby areas, lists of genera and species and bibliography. Index. In English except for one-page Japanese summary and two tables.

Invertebrates

Satō, Hayao 佐藤隼夫 **and** **S73**
Itō, Takeo 伊藤猛夫
Musekitsui dōbutsu saishū 無脊椎動物採集 (Collecting invertebrata) Hokuryūkan, 1961. 446p.

Pt.1 outlines methods of collecting, rearing, specimen making, preservation and transportation of specimens. Pt.2 describes morphology, ecology, and methods of collecting, rearing, observation, and experimentation for each animal, classified by phylum, class and order. Classification table and indexes of Japanese and scientific names.

COASTAL WATER AND
SHORE ANIMALS

Uchinomi, Fujio 内海富士夫 **S74**
Genshoku Nihon kaigan dōbutsu zukan 原色日本海岸動物図鑑 Coloured illustrations of sea-side animals of Japan. Rev. ed. Osaka,

Hoikusha, 1964. 167p. 64 plates. (Hoikusha no genshoku zukan, 8)

Illustrates some 500 jellyfishes, sponges, corals, crabs, lobsters, shrimps, sea urchins, starfishes, etc. Guide to collecting specimens appended. Differs from first edition (1960) in classification and Latin and Japanese names.

Shikama, Tokio 鹿間時夫 **and** **S75**
Horikoshi, Masuoki 堀越増興
Genshoku zukan sekai no kai 原色図鑑世界の貝 Selected shells of the world, illustrated in colours. Hokuryūkan, 1963. 153p. 102 plates.

Covers 1,058 marine, fresh-water and land species of 60 familes of Japanese and exotic Gasteropoda. Many additional photographs in text. Japanese and Latin name indexes.

Kuroda, Tokubei 黒田徳兵衛 **and** **S76**
Habe, Tadashige 波部忠重
Check list and bibliography of the recent marine mollusca of Japan. Leo W. Stach, 1952. 210p.

Lists and gives distribution and references for 4,395 species of Japanese coastal Mollusca, arranged alphabetically by genera and species under Pelecypoda, Scaphopoda and Gasteropoda. Introduction surveys currents along Japan's coasts and distribution of Mollusca.

Kira, Tetsuaki 吉良哲明 **and** **S77**
Habe, Tadashige 波部忠重
Genshoku Nihon kairui zukan 原色日本貝類図鑑 Coloured illustrations of the shells of Japan. Rev. and enl. ed. Osaka, Hoikusha, 1959-61. 2v. (Hoikusha no genshoku zukan, 4, 25)

Shows about 1,200 of the some 6,000 known species, including Pulmonata and Opisthobranchia, with list of 1,465 common small shells, classified table of genera, technical glossary and notes on collecting and processing specimens. Name index.

Sakai, Wataru 酒井恒 **S78**
Nihon kanirui zusetsu 日本蟹類図説 (Illustrated survey of Japanese crabs) Sanseidō, 1945. 239p. 66 plates.

Explains names, classification and morphology of about 200 species of indigenous crabs, with some 120 line drawings and color photographs. Bibliography. Name index.

Spiders

Saitō, Saburō 斉藤三郎 **S79**
Genshoku kumorui zusetsu 原色蜘蛛類図説 The spider book, illustrated in colours. Hokuryūkan, 1959. 194p. 26 plates.

Gives taxonomy of Arachnida, with 226 illustrations of those indigenous to Japan; bibliography. Indexes.

Yaginuma, Takeo 八木沼健夫 **S80**
Genshoku Nihon kumorui daizukan 原色日本蜘蛛類大図鑑 Coloured illustrations of spiders of Japan. Osaka, Hoikusha, 1960. 186p. 56 plates. (Hoikusha no genshoku daizukan, 4)

Shows 355 species observed in Japan, with information on morphology, classification, breeding, etc. References. Index.

Insects

DICTIONARY

Shiraki, Tokuichi 素木得一 **S81**
Konchūgaku jiten 昆虫学辞典 A glossary of entomology. Kokuryūkan, 1962. 1098,114, 41p.

Defines entomological terms and identifies scientific and popular names of insects, giving for each its order. Illustrations. Indexes.

CLASSIFICATION

Asahina, Shōjirō 朝比奈正二郎 **et al.** **S82**
Nihon konchū bunrui zusetsu 日本昆虫分類図説 Insecta japonica. Hokuryūkan, 1961- . 2v. In progress.

Guide to the classification of Japanese insects, with color plates, English summary and name index. Divided into two series, each of four volumes, one on each of the following: Odonata, Libellulidae; Hemiptera, Cicadidae; Hemiptera, Gerridae; Lepidoptera, Geometridae; Lepidoptera, Drepanidae; Diptera, Doxidae; Coleoptera, Caribidae, and Hymenoptera, Siricidae.

Shiraki, Tokuichi 素木得一 **S83**
Konchū no bunrui 昆虫の分類 (Classification of insects) Reprint ed. Hokuryūkan, 1962. 961p.

Based on classification of insects in Europe and America, explains classification tables of

Arthropoda class and Insecta order. Also describes 628 species of 33 orders under 3 subclasses, Myrientomata, Oligoentoma and Euentoma of Insecta. Index.

Shiraki, Tokuichi　素木得一　**S84**
Konchū no kensaku　昆虫の検索 (Keys to insects) Hokuryūkan, 1956. 284, 70p.

Tables facilitate the identification and classification of 945 major insect families of the world, giving for each its subphylum, class, subclass, order, suborder and subfamilies. Lists under families and subfamilies, with common names, about 4,000 genera indigenous to Japan. Name Index.

ILLUSTRATIONS

Inoue, Hiroshi　井上寛　**S85**
Genshoku konchū daizukan　原色昆虫大図鑑 Iconographia insectorium japonicorum, colore naturali edita. Hokuryūkan, 1959- . 2v. In progerss.

Gives common and rare species of Lepidoptera (v.1) and Coleoptera (v.2), each with brief morphology, distribution, and scientific and common names. Indexes.

Kinki Kōchū Dōkōkai　近畿甲虫同好会 **S86**
Genshoku Nihon konchū zukan　原色日本昆虫図鑑　Coloured illustrations of the insects of Japan. Osaka, Hoikusha, 1959-62. 2v. (Hoikusha no genshoku zukan, 2-3)

v.1, revised by Takehiko Nakane, lists 1,588 species of Coleoptera; v.2, by Yoshizō Takeuchi, lists 1,134 species of Orthoptera, Odonata, Hemiptera, Neuroptera, Lepidoptera, Hymenoptera, and Diptera. Indexes of Japanese and scientific names in each volume.

Ishizawa, Jichō　石沢慈鳥　**S87**
Nihon konchū seitai zukan　日本昆虫生態図鑑 (Ecology of Japanese insects in pictures) Kōdansha, 1956. 260p.　34 plates.

Eight hundred photographs show the ecology and life cycles of 250 species, including 77 Rhopalocera, 86 Heterocera, some 20 parasitic Hymenoptera and Diptera and 16 Arachnida. Color illustrations of adult specimens of about 170 species of Lepidoptera.

Kawada, Akira　河田党　**S88**
Nihon yōchū zukan 日本幼虫図鑑 Illustrated insect larvae of Japan. Hokuryūkan, 1959. 712, 73, 50p.

Shows 1,304 species, with Japanese common and

scientific names. Index.

Chikuni, Yasunosuke　千国安之輔　**S89**
Konchū no seitai shashinshū　昆虫の生態写真集 (Photographs of insect ecology) Records of breeding and observation. 2d ed. Akatsuki Kyōiku Tosho, 1960. 288, 39p.

Shows Lepidoptera and miscellaneous other insects, with brief explanations in Japanese and English. Nine short articles on the life cycle and ecology of insects appended.

BUTTERFLIES · MOTHS

Inoue, Hiroshi　井上寛　**S90**
Nihon san chō ga sōmokuroku　日本産蝶蛾総目録　Checklist of the lepidoptera of Japan. Rikusuisha, 1954- . 6v. In progress.

Lists all known species and subspecies of butterflies and moths indigenous to Japan, arranged from lower to higher, with seasonal and unusual forms, original references and variant names. No index. To be completed in 7v.

Shirozu, Takashi　白水隆　**S91**
Nihon san chōrui bunpuhyō　日本産蝶類分布表 (Distribution tables of Japanese butterflies) Hokuryūkan, 1958. 283p.

Shows the distribution by prefectures of indigenous butterflies, with bibliography of distribution literature published before July, 1958, also arranged by prefectures.

Nakahara, Warō　中原和郎　**and**　**S92**
Kurosawa, Yoshihiko　黒沢良彦
Genshoku zukan sekai no chō　原色図鑑世界の蝶　Selected butterflies of the world, illustrated in colours. Hokuryūkan, 1958. 178p. 132 plates.

Shows about 500 species, with scientific and Japanese common names, gross morphology of both female and male, and distribution. Name index.

Okano, Masarō　岡野麿瑳郎 **and**　**S93**
Ōkura, Jōzaburō　大蔵丈三郎
Genshoku Taiwan san chōrui zufu　原色台湾産蝶類図譜 (Butterflies of Taiwan in color) Taniguchi Shoten, 1959. 93p. (Genshoku seibutsu zufu series, 1)

Shows and briefly describes about 500 of the 3,269 known species indigenous to Formosa and adjacent islands. Distribution map and notes on how to prepare and preserve specimens appended. Name index.

Shirozu, Takashi 白水隆 **S94**
Genshoku Taiwan chōrui daizukan 原色台湾
蝶類大図鑑 Butterflies of Formosa.
Osaka, Hoikusha, 1960. 481p. 76 plates.
(Hoikusha no genshoku daizukan, 1)

Color plates of about 330 species, with gross
morphology. All butterflies known in Taiwan listed
separately. Index.

Yokoyama, Mitsuo 横山光夫 **S95**
Genshoku Nihon chōrui zukan 原色日本
蝶類図鑑 Coloured illustrations of the
butterflies of Japan. Osaka, Hoikusha, 1954.
125p. 72 plates. (Hoikusha no genshoku
zukan, 1)

Shows about 200 species of eight families, with
notes on ovipositions, food habits of larvae,
developmental processes, habits of adults, hiber-
nation and winter states, distribution and food
plants. Japanese names indexed.

Shirozu, Takashi 白水隆 **and** **S96**
Hara, Akira 原章
Genshoku Nihon chōrui yōchū daizukan
原色日本蝶類幼虫大図鑑 The early
stages of Japanese butterflies. Osaka,
Hoikusha, 1960-62. 2v. (Hoikusha no genshoku
daizukan, 2-3)

Shows in color the development from eggs through
larvae to pupae of 197 species indigenous to Japan,
with glossary and ecological references. Index.
See also **S88**.

Ezaki, Teizō 江崎悌三 **et al.** **S97**
Genshoku Nihon garui zukan 原色日本蛾類
図鑑 Coloured illustrations of the moths of
Japan. Osaka, Hoikusha, 1957-58. 2v.
(Hoikusha no genshoku zukan, 21-22)

Illustrates and gives scientific names of over
2,200 of the 3,000 known species. Classified by
families in table of contents. Notes on collecting,
breeding, preparing specimens and research appended to v.2. Each volume indexed.

Vertebrates

Okada, Yaichirō 岡田弥一郎 **S98**
Nihon sekitsui dōbutsu mokuroku 日本脊椎
動物目録 (Catalogue of Japanese vertebrates) Maruzen, 1938. 412p.

Classifies indigenous vertebrates. Name index.

FISHES

Okada, Yaichirō 岡田弥一郎 **and** **S99**
Matsubara, Kiyomatsu 松原喜代松
Nihon san gyorui bunken mokuroku 日本産魚
類文献目録 (Bibliography of Japanese
fishes) 1612-1950. Tsu, Mie Daigaku Suisan
Gakubu, 1953. 228p.

Lists chronologically books, monographic works
in series and articles in Japanese and Western
languages. No index.

Shibusawa, Keizō 渋沢敬三 **S100**
Nihon gyomei shūran 日本魚名集覧 (Survey
of Japanese fish names) Kadokawa Shoten,
1958. 2v.

Gives 11,868 local common names, 3,822 found
in Japanese classics, and 2,795 local killifish
variants. Notes on etymology, ethnological meanings and misapplications of local common names
appended. Illustrations. Tables, indexes in v.2.

Aoyagi, Hyōji 青柳兵司 **S101**
Nihon rettō san tansui gyorui sōsetsu 日本
列島産淡水魚類総説 (Introduction to
fresh-water fishes of the Japanese archipelago)
Taishūkan Shoten, 1957. 272p.

Covers taxonomy, morphology, secondary sexual
characteristics, oviposition habits and distribution.
Illustrations. Bibliography. Name Index.

Miyaji, Denzaburō 宮地伝三郎 **et al.** **S102**
Genshoku Nihon tansui gyorui zukan 原色日本
淡水魚類図鑑 Coloured illustrations of the
fresh-water fishes of Japan. Osaka, Hoikusha,
1963. 259p. 44 plates. (Hoikusha no genshoku
zukan, 32)

Excluding cultivated fishes and those in lagoons,
describes adults, eggs, morphology of the young,
ecology and utilization. Annotated glossary,
keys, general summary and reference list. Name
index.

Nakamura, Morizumi 中村守純 **S103**
Genshoku tansui gyorui kensaku zukan 原色
淡水魚類検索図鑑 (Keys to the fresh-
water fishes of Japan, illustrated in color)
Hokuryūkan, 1963. 258p.

Outlines phylogeny of Japanese fresh-water
fishes, ecological and geographical distribution,
collecting and feeding, specimen making and preservation, and methods of identification. Also gives
tabular keys to 42 families, 102 genera, 175 species
and subspecies, including goldfish and red carp
with illustrations in color. Appended are a list of

references, and indexes of local Japanese names, scientific names, and a comparative list of English and Japanese names.

Matsubara, Kiyomatsu 松原喜代松 **S104**
Gyorui no keitai to kensaku 魚類の形態と 検索 (Fishes, morphology and keys) Ishizaki Shoten, 1955. 3v.

Gives common Japanese and scientific names, distribution and gross morphology, with selected references and glossary. Illustrations in v.3. Name indexes.

Abe, Tokiharu 阿部宗明 **S105**
Genshoku gyorui kensaku zukan 原色魚類 検索図鑑 (Fishes in color, with keys) Hokuryūkan, 1963. 36, 358p.

Shows 780 species, with Japanese common names, gross morphology and distribution. Keys for each systematic group. Name index.

Kamohara, Toshiji 蒲原稔治 **S106**
Genshoku Nihon gyorui zukan 原色日本魚類 図鑑 Coloured illustrations of the fishes of Japan. Osaka, Hoikusha, 1961. 2v. (Hoikusha no genshoku zukan, 5, 26)

Illustrates 645 species, including those designated for protection and some belonging to Cyclostomata, with common, scientific and local names and notes on distribution, habits, sizes and utilization. Local name index in v.2.

Hiyama, Yoshio 檜山義夫 **and** **S107**
Yasuda, Fujirō 安田富士郎
Nihon suisan gyofu 日本水産魚譜 (Japan fishery atlas) Uchida Rōkakuho, 1961. 650p.

Color pictures of about 400 species, each with common and local Japanese, scientific, and English names; brief notes on morphology, ecology, coloration, distribution, and utilization.

Okada, Yaichirō 岡田弥一郎 **et al.** **S108**
Nihon gyorui zusetsu 日本魚類図説 (Japanese fishes illustrated) Sanseidō, 1935. 425, 46p.

Pictures many in color, of about 500 species of edible indigenous coastal fishes and Asian gold-fishes, with notes on taxonomy, morphology, development, migration and distribution. Tables and selected references published before 1934 appended. Names indexed.

Tanaka, Shigeho 田中茂穂 **et al.** **S109**
Nihon san gyorui zusetsu 日本産魚類図説 Figures and descriptions of the fishes of Japan. Kazama Shobō, 1951-58. 59v.

Illustrates indigenous fishes, with Japanese

common and scientific names and notes in Japanese and English on distribution, morphology and habitat.

Makino, Shinji 牧野信司 **S110**
Genshoku nettaigyo zukan 原色熱帯魚図鑑 Coloured illustrations of exotic aquarium fishes. Rev. and enl. ed. Osaka, Hoikusha, 1960-61 2v. (Hoikusha no genshoku zukan, 20, 27)

Illustrations in color of about 290 species of tropical fishes propagated in Japan, each with notes on place of origin, habitat, variability of breeds, and breeding methods. Information on aquarium equipment, sex identification, etc., appended.

Tanaka, Shigeho 田中茂穂 **and** **S111**
Abe, Tokiharu 阿部宗明
Zusetsu yūyō gyorui senshu 図説有用魚類 千種 (One thousand useful fishes, illustrated) Morikita Shuppan, 1955-57. 2v.

Each described with common local names, habits, uses, fishing methods, annual yields, etc.

Tanaka, Shigeho 田中茂穂 **S112**
Jitsuyō gyokai hōgen zusetsu 実用魚介方言 図説 (Illustrations and local names of edible marine products) Kazama Shobō, 1954. 273, 50p.

Describes and gives distribution, morphology, of about 200 fish and shellfish commonly seen in the market. Index of local names.

AMPHIBIANS

Nakamura, Kenji 中村健児 **and** **S113**
Ueno, Shun'ichi 上野俊一
Genshoku Nihon ryōsei hachūrui zukan 原色 日本両生爬虫類図鑑 Coloured illustrations of the reptiles and amphibians of Japan. Osaka, Hoikusha, 1963. 214p. 42 plates. (Hoikusha no genshoku zukan, 30)

Describes 51 species of amphibians and 80 species of reptiles. Text contains classification table of family, genus and species. Glossary, bibliography, and name indexes.

Takahashi, Seiichi 高橋精一 **S114**
Nihon hebirui taikan 日本蛇類大観 (General survey of Japanese snakes) Shun'yōdō, 1930. 65 plates.

Color illustrations of 65 species of poisonous and non-poisonous snakes indigenous to Japan, Korea, Formosa and Sakhalin, each with common Japanese and scientific names, gross morphology, habitats and habits.

BIRDS

Udagawa, Tatsuo 宇田川竜男 **S115**
Genshoku yachō handobukku 原色野鳥ハンドブック (Handbook of wild birds in color)
Seibundō Shinkōsha, 1957. 93p. 84 plates.

Shows birds found near human communities, in open fields, on plateaus, in alpine regions, in low-land marshes, along the sea, on the ocean and on oceanic islands, each with Japanese common and dialect, English and scientific names, gross morphology, habits and distribution. Appendix treats of eggs, nests, organs and terminology. Name index.

Kiyosu, Yukiyasu 清棲幸保 **S116**
Genshoku Nihon yachō seitai zukan 原色日本野鳥生態図鑑 Bird's(sic) life in Japan.
Osaka, Hoikusha, 1959. 2v. (Hoikusha no genshoku daizukan, 6-7)

Color and monochrome pictures of land birds (v.1) and aquatic birds (v.2), with notes on habitats and seasonal appearances. List of literary essays and books on wild birds appended. Name index in each volume.

Kiyosu, Yukiyasu 清棲幸保 **S117**
Nihon chōrui daizukan 日本鳥類大図鑑
The birds of Japan. Kōdansha, 1952. 3v.

v.1, Passeres; v.2, Cypseli, Limicolae; v.3, Lari, Galli.

Describes habitats, habits, calls, propagation, food habits, migration routes and distribution of birds of Japan and nearby areas. Illustrated. Name index.

Kiyosu, Yukiyasu 清棲幸保 **S118**
Nihon chōrui seitai zukan 日本鳥類生態図鑑 (Ecology of Japanese birds in pictures) Kōdansha, 1954. 280p.

Arranged under place names, 637 photographs and drawings show birds in native habitats, with notes on conditions and temperature ranges during developmental stages. Japanese name index.

Kobayashi, Keisuke 小林桂助 **S119**
Genshoku Nihon chōrui zukan 原色日本鳥類図鑑 Birds of Japan in natural colours.
Osaka, Hoikusha, 1956. 204p. 64 plates. (Hoikusha no genshoku zukan, 6)

Morphology, ecology, distribution and subspecies

of 425 species of 59 families of 22 orders, constituting all birds recorded in Japan, with Japanese and English names taken from the 1942 revised edition of *Nihon chōrui mokuroku* (Catalogue of Japanese birds) compiled by the Ornithological Society of Japan. Table of nests and eggs of birds breeding in Japan. Name index.

Shimomura, Kenji 下村兼史 **S120**
Genshoku Nihon chōrui zukan 原色日本鳥類図鑑 (Japanese birds in color) Kazama Shobō, 1955. 167p.

Useful field guide, showing 382 species and subspecies, divided into land, shore-line, water, ocean and alpine birds, with notes for each on habitat, distribution, gross morphology, calls, ways of flight, food and nest. Appended notes on names of organs, measurement methods, common habits. Classified index of names under families.

MAMMALS

Imaizumi, Yoshinori 今泉吉典 **S121**
Genshoku Nihon honyūrui zukan 原色日本哺乳類図鑑 Coloured illustrations of the mammals of Japan. Osaka, Hoikusha, 1960. 196p. 68 plates. (Hoikusha no genshoku zukan, 7)

Sketches show all mammals, excluding whales, found in a wild state in Japan, with brief notes on classification, characteristics, measurements and distribution. Indexes of Latin and Japanese names.

Kuroda, Nagamichi 黒田長礼 **S122**
Genshoku Nihon honyūrui zusetsu 原色日本哺乳類図説 (Japanese mammals in color) Sanseidō, 1940. 311p.

Systematically arranged with Japanese and scientific (including family) names and notes on gross morphology, distribution and ecology. Bibliography. Index.

Kuroda, Nagamichi 黒田長礼 **S123**
Nihon jūrui zusetsu 日本獣類図説 (Japanese animals, illustrated) Sōgensha, 1953. 177p.

General introduction on gross morphological and anatomical characteristics of mammals, specimen techniques and taxonomy is followed by chapters on specific mammals under eight orders, with keys to genera, species and subspecies. Gives color illustration of Cetacea native to Japan. Bibliography on Japanese mammalian taxonomy. Name index.

AGRICULTURE

❧ Works pertaining to the agriculture, forestry and marine industries · are included in this section. As titles pertaining to agriculture often contain information on related fields, specialists working on forestry, for instance, should also look under agriculture. For other information related to agricultural problems see also basic studies in economics and management, the natural and applied sciences for information on surveying, engineering and the machine industry.

GENERAL WORKS

BIBLIOGRAPHY

Nōrinshō Toshokan 農林省図書館 **T1**
Nōrin bunken kaidai 農林文献解題 (Annotated bibliographies of agriculture and forestry) 1955- . 10v. Annual.

v. 1-2, comp. by Nōrinshō Tōkei Chōsabu.

Each volume consists of an introductory survey on a specific topic, followed by annotations of major works and a bibliography.

T2
Nihon nōgaku shinpo nenpō 日本農学進歩年報 (Annual report on agricultural progress in Japan) No. 1- . Comp. by Nihon Gakujutsu Kaigi and Nihon Nōgakkai. 1954- . 11v.

Continuation of *Nōgaku shinpo sōhō* (A survey of agricultural progress), 1952-53, 2v., summarizing research trends and listing publications in agronomy, agricultural chemistry, agricultural engineering, animal husbandry, sericulture, forestry, fisheries and agricultural economics.

Nōrinshō, Nōrin Suisan Gijutsu Kaigi **T3**
農林省農林水産技術会議
Nōgyō keizai kankei bunkenshū 農業経済関係文献集 (A bibliography of agricultural economics) 1948- . 16v. Semiannual since 1960.

Nōrinshō Nōrin Keizaikyoku **T4**
農林省農林経済局
Nōrinshō kankō tosho shiryō sōran 農林省刊行図書資料総覧 (Complete catalogue of books and materials published by the Ministry of Agriculture and Forestry) Sept. 1945 - Dec. 1952. Nōrin Kyōkai, 1954.

Arranged by issuing division, bureau, or agency.

Nōrinshō Toshokan 農林省図書館 **T5**
Nihon Nōgyō Bunko mokuroku 日本農業文庫目録 (Catalogue of the Japan Agriculture Library) 1957-59. 3v.

Lists prewar books published since 1868. Western language books in v. 3. Author index.

T6
Nōgyō Sōgō Kenkyūjo bunken sōsho 農業総合研究所文献叢書 (Bibliographic publications of the General Research Institute for Agriculture and Forestry) No. 1- . Nōgyō Sōgō Kenkyūjo, 1950- . 9v. In progress.

1. Bibliography on farm village finances. Tsutomu Ōuchi. 1950.
2. Bibliography on improvement and spread of agriculture. Masateru Uchiyama. 1950.
3. Bibliography on problems of farm women. Fusae Ide and Kazuko Nagahara. 1952.
4. Bibliography on agriculture in Hokkaido. Ryōshi Ishizeki. 1955.

5. Index to articles in central agricultural journals, the "Central agricultural review" and "Imperial Agricultural Society news". Tsutomu Takeda. 1956.
6. Index to articles to 1912 in the "Japan Agricultural Society news" and "Japan Agricultural Society report". Tsutomu Takeda. 1960.
7. Subject index to statistical compilations of Meiji period agriculture. Chieko Fujii. 1962.
8. Location list of directories of landowners. Ryūichi Shibuya. 1963.
9. Bibliography on industries and economy of the Tōhoku region. Shigeru Sugiyama. 1964.

DICTIONARIES

T7

Nōgyō shōjiten 農業小辞典 (Small dictionary of agriculture) Hakubunsha, 1954. 829, 145p.

Concise definitions of a wide range of terms.

T8

Nōgaku daijiten 農学大事典 (Comprehensive cyclopedia of agriculture) Yōkendō, 1961. 1716p.

Covers all aspects of agriculture under 50 broad headings, including the physiology and genetics of crops, livestock and silkworms, environmental factors, management, research and education. Statistics appended.

Ōuchi, Tsutomu 大内力 **T9**

Nōgyō keizai shōjiten 農業経済小辞典 (Small dictionary of agricultural economics) Gakuseisha, 1962. 261p.

Includes many agricultural, forestry and fishery terms not found in other economic and agricultural dictionaries, and brief biographies of outstanding persons.

T10

Nōgyō kindaika jiten 農業近代化事典 (A cyclopedia of agricultural modernization) Nōgyō Kindaika Kyōkai, 1964. 835p.

Discusses backgrounds and prospects of modernization, reforms in the structure of agriculture and pertinent laws. Glossary (89p.) of technical terms.

Nōson Hōsei Kenkyūkai **T11**
農村法制研究会
Nōrin suisan seido jiten 農林水産制度事典 (Cyclopedia of agricultural, forestry and fishery systems) Gakuyō Shobō, 1961. 1683p.

Detailed descriptions, statistics, graphs and tables classified under 130 categories, based on data as of Sept., 1960.

HANDBOOK

Nō-San-Gyoson Bunka Kyōkai **T12**
農山漁村文化協会
Nōgyō sōran 農業総覧 (Agricultural manual) 1962- . 6v. Loose-leaf.

Subjects range from fertilizers, chemicals, machines, installations, crops, flowers, vegetables, fruit, and feeding crops to welfare, cooperatives, distribution and agricultural trends.

YEARBOOKS

T13

Sekai nōgyō hakusho 世界農業白書 (White paper on world agriculture) 1956- . Comp. by the Food and Agricultural Organization. Tr. by Kokusai Shokuryō Nōgyō Kyōkai. 1957- . 8v.

Japanese translation of *The state of food and agriculture*, FAO annual survey, analyzing regional developments and problems.

T14

Nōrinshō nenpō 農林省年報 (Ministry of Agriculture and Forestry yearbook) 1953- . Nihon Nōson Chōsakai, 1954- . 10v.

Former titles: *Nōrin nenkan* (Agriculture and forestry yearbook), 1948-1949; *Nōrin Suisan nenkan* (Agriculture, forestry and fisheries yearbook), 1950-1953.

Reports general developments, trends and policies.

T15

Nihon nōgyō nenpō 日本農業年報 (Annual report on Japanese agriculture) No. 1- . Comp. by Tsutomu Ouchi and others. Ochanomizu Shobō, 1954- . 12v. Semiannual from no. 7.

Surveys current trends in a special subject with appended bibliography and chronology. Nos. 1-8 published by Chūō Kōronsha under supervision of Kōzō Uno and others. Titles follow:

1. Problems of postwar agriculture.
2. International aspects of fisheries and the food problem.
3. Agricultural administration in the second year of the trillion-yen budget.
4. The economics of a bumper crop.
5-6. Trends in postwar agricultural theories.
7. Japanese agriculture and agricultural cooperatives.
8. The new stage attained in agricultural techniques.
9. Fundamental problems of contemporary Japa-

nese agriculture.

10. Fundamental problems and policies of agriculture.

11. Structural reforms –– objectives and realities.

12. The farm village trembles before the onslaught of trade liberalization.

T16

Nihon nōgyō nenkan 日本農業年鑑 (Japan agricultural yearbook) 1948- . Ie no Hikari Kyōkai, 1948- . 16v.

Surveys farm developments, with brief sections on forestry and fisheries. Contains illustrations, bibliography, and directory of organizations and agencies. Compiled by Nōgyō Fukkō Kaigi (Agricultural Rehabilitation Congress) until 1953.

STATISTICS

Kokusai Shokuryō Nōgyō Kyōkai　　**T17**
国際食糧農業協会

Sekai nōgyō kiso tōkei 世界農業基礎統計 (Basic statistics of world agriculture) 1961. 416p.

A companion to **T24**, giving statistics for about 60 countries for four periods: prewar (usually 1934-38), 1948-52, 1953-57 and 1958- . Lists of members and specialized agencies of the United Nations, crop calendars and conversion tables for units of farm products appended.

U. S. S. R. Tsentral'noe Statisticheskoe　**T18**
Upravlenie

Tōkeishū: Soren no nōgyō 統計集：ソ連の農業 (Statistical compilation: Soviet agriculture) Tr. from the Russian by Masanobu Yamashita. Nōrin Tōkei Kyōkai, 1963. 336p.

Covers period 1940-59, with partial data for pre-1913.

Nōrinshō Nōrin Keizaikyoku　　**T19**
農林省農林経済局

Nihon no nōgyō: 1960 nen Sekai nōringyō sensasu 日本の農業： 1960年世界農林業センサス (Japanese agriculture: 1960 world census of agriculture and forestry) Nōrin Tōkei Kyōkai, 1961. 281p.

Statistical tables based on the census of Feb. 1, 1960, with some earlier statistics to indicate trends in agricultural production.

Nōrinshō Nōrin Keizaikyoku　　**T20**
農林省農林経済局

1960 nen Sekai nōringyō sensasu shi-chō-son

betsu tōkeisho 1960年世界農林業センサス市町村別統計書 (1960 world census of agriculture: statistics of Japanese cities and villages) Nōrin Tōkei Kyōkai, 1961-62. 46v. (No. 1-46, Hokkaido through Kagoshima)

Japanese decennial report to FAO. The first report was published in 1950.

T21

Nōrinshō ruinen tōkeihyō 農林省累年統計表 (Ministry of Agriculture and Forestry cumulative statistical tables) 1868-1953. Nōrin Tōkei Kyōkai, 1955. 236p.

Classified under 14 categories.

T22

Nōrinshō tōkeihyō 農林省統計表 (Ministry of Agriculture and Forestry statistical tables) No. 1, 1924- . Pub. 1924-43, 1946- . 39v. Annual.

Former title: *Nōshōmushō tōkeihyō*, no. 1-40, 1883-1923. Pub. 1886-1925. 40v.

Classified under 20 categories. The first ten numbers, 1883-1893, are being reprinted by Keiō Shobō.

T23

Poketto nōrin suisan tōkei ポケット農林水産統計 (Pocket statistics of agriculture, forestry and fisheries) 1952- . Comp. by Nōrinshō Nōrin Keizaikyoku. Nōrin Tōkei Kyōkai, 1951- . 13v. Annual.

Abridgement of **T22**, with statistical summaries of Japanese and world economies.

Nōrin Suisangyō Seisansei Kōjō Kaigi　**T24**
農林水産業生産性向上会議

Nihon nōgyō kiso tōkei 日本農業基礎統計 (Basic statistics of Japanese agriculture) 1958. 658p.

Mainly adjusted statistics, cumulative from 1868 to 1955 arranged under 20 categories.

HISTORY

Ono, Takeo 小野武夫　　**T25**

Nihon nōminshi goi 日本農民史語彙 (Glossary of Japanese farmers' history) Kaizōsha, 1926. 465, 8p.

Subtitled, "A popular explanation of terms concerning the socio-economic history of Japanese rural communities". Defines 1,200 terms. Yearly revenues of feudal *han* before 1868 appended.

**Kokuritsu Kokkai Toshokan Chōsa Rippō T26
Kōsakyoku**　国立国会図書館　調査立法
考査局
Nōmin undō kankei bunken mokuroku kō　農民
運動関係文献目録稿　(Draft bibliography of the farmers' movement) 1956. 117p.
(Kokuto Chōritsu shiryō, B140)

Lists chronologically, divided into monographs and articles, about 2,300 items published from 1868 to 1956, chiefly on the agricultural cooperative movement, with location of copies in Tokyo libraries. Catalogue of agricultural cooperative movement documents in the Ohara Social Problems Research Institute and list of references used in compilation of the bibliography appended.

Kawasaki, Hajime　川崎甫　**T27**
Nihon kindai nōgyōshi nenpyō　日本近代農業史年表　(Chronologies of modern Japanese agricultural history) Meibundō, 1957. 199p.

Gives rice yields and prices, and population with sources cited from 1868 to 1957. Bibliography. Index.

Nōgyō Hattatsushi Chōsakai　**T28**
農業発達史調査会
Nihon nōgyō hattatsushi　日本農業発達史
(A history of Japanese agricultural development)
Chūō Kōronsha, 1953-59. 12v.

Not only gives detailed attention to changing techniques from the Meiji period but also relates the growth of agriculture to socio-economic conditions, with extensive reproduction of source materials. Includes local agricultural histories and special studies. Chronology, bibliography and general index in v. 12.

Fujii, Chieko　藤井知江子　**T29**
Meijiki nōgyō kankei tōkeisho kōmoku sakuin mokuroku　明治期農業関係統計書項目
索引目録　(A subject index of agricultural statistics of the Meiji period) Ochanomizu Shobō, 1962. 259p. (Bunken sōsho, no. 7)

Indexes **J35** and **T22**. Lists references. Published also by Nōgyō Sōgō Kenkyūjo.

Land tenure

**Nōsei Chōsakai, Nōchi Kaikaku Kiroku T30
Iinkai**　農政調査会農地改革記録委員会
Nōchi kaikaku tenmatsu gaiyō　農地改革顛
末概要　(General outline of the results of agrarian reform) 3d ed. Nōsei Taimushusha, 1957. 1361p.

Basic source on the postwar agrarian reform, with

chapters on the historical background, progress in enforcement, financing and land reforms in other countries. Chronology appended. Statistics indexed.

Agricultural management

Isobe, Hidetoshi　磯辺秀俊　**T31**
Nōgyō keiei shinjiten　農業経営新事典
(New cyclopedia of agricultural management)
Hakuyūsha, 1958. 424p.

Covers theories and practices, with special attention to environment. Reference tables. Index.

T32
Nōgyō kyōdō kumiai nenkan　農業協同組合
年鑑　(Agricultural cooperative yearbook)
1950- . Comp. by Zenkoku Nōgyō Kyōdō Kumiai Chūōkai. 1949-53, 1959- . 11v.

Comp. by Zenkoku Shidō Nōgyō Kyōdō Kumiai Rengōkai. 1950-1954.

Surveys farm cooperatives in Japan and the cooperative movement in other countries.

Agricultural meteorology

Tsuboi, Yasoji　坪井八十二　**et al.**　**T33**
Nōgyō kishō handobukku　農業気象ハンド
ブック　(Handbook of agricultural meteorology) Yōkendō, 1961. 600p.

Covers weather and climate in relation to farming, including crop forecasting and control of insects, with bibliography and index.

Soils·Fertilizers

Mitsui, Shingo　三井進午　**and**　**T34**
Imaizumi, Yoshirō　今泉吉郎
Dojō hiryō shinjiten　土壌肥料新事典 (New dictionary of soils and fertilizers) Rev. and enl. ed. Hakuyūsha, 1961. 343p.

Explains technical terms under some 200 topics.

Okuda, Azuma　奥田東　**et al.**　**T35**
Dojō hiryō handobukku　土壌・肥料ハンド
ブック　(Handbook of soils and fertilizers)
Rev. ed. Yōkendō, 1960. 664p.

Covers soil physics, chemistry, formation, types, and fertilization of regular, special and perennial crops, including vegetables and flowers. References. Index.

Matsuki, Gorō 松木五楼 **T36**
Dojō handobukku 土壌ハンドブック (Soil handbook) Sangyō Tosho, 1955. 444p.

Discusses soil physics and chemistry in relation to utilization and fertilization. Index.

T37
Poketto hiryō yōran ポケット肥料要覧 (Pocket fertilizer handbook) 1953- . Comp. by Norinshō Norin Keizaikyoku. Nōrin Tōkei Kyōkai, 1952-55, 1957- . 11v. Annual.

Gives statistics, dictionary of terms, laws, chronology and lists of agencies concerned and chief producers.

AGRICULTURAL ENGINEERING

Tōkyō Daigaku Nōgakubu **T38**
東京大学農学部
Nōgyō kōgaku benran 農業工学便覧 (Handbook of agricultural engineering) Asakura Shoten, 1951. 785p.

Pocket-size compendium of mathematics, applied mechanics, hydrography and information about soils, construction materials, irrigation, machinery, etc. Index.

Nōgyō Doboku Gakkai 農業土木学会 **T39**
Nōgyō doboku handobukku 農業土木ハンドブック (Farm engineering handbook) Entirely rev. ed. Maruzen, 1957. 1112p.

Explains in simple language what farmers need to know about meteorology, hydrology, soil, geology, construction, irrigation, machinery, etc., with tables and formulas. Index.

Agricultural machinery

Kyūshū Daigaku Nōgakubu **T40**
九州大学農学部
Nōgyō kikai jiten 農業機械事典 (Dictionary of agricultural machinery) Shin Nōrinsha, 1962. 548p.

Illustrated with photographs, diagrams and graphs. Appended are lists of farm chemicals and fertilizers, tables of soil properties and conversion tables. Classified table of contents and index.

Tanaka, Akio 田中明夫 **T41**
Ei-Wa Wa-Ei nōgyō kikai yōgo jiten 英和和英農業機械用語辞典 English-Japanese, Japanese-English technical dictionary of farm machinery. Shin Nōrinsha, 1961. 266p.

Gives equivalents only.

Nōgyō Kikai Gakkai 農業機械学会 **T42**
Nōgyō kikai handobukku 農業機械ハンドブック (Handbook of farm machinery) Koronasha, 1957. 1185p.

Describes and explains how to use motors, windmills, water wheels, tractors and other prime movers, plows, measuring equipment, machinery and equipment for dairy and poultry farming and sericultrue, with guidance on cultivation, soils and fertilizers. Index.

T43
Nō-san-gyoson kindaika shisetsu benran 農産漁村近代化施設便覧 (Manual of equipment for modernization of farming and fishing communities) Taisei Shuppansha, 1962. 391p.

Describes machinery and equipment for more effective agricultural, livestock, forestry and fishing operations and better living conditions, with reference to official policies on farming and fishing villages. Index of machinery and equipment arranged by prefectures and names of makers.

T44
Nōgyō kikai nenkan 農業機械年鑑 (Farm machinery yearbook) 1962- Shin Nōrinsha, 1961- . 3v.

Former title: *Nōkigu nenkan* (Farm machines and implements yearbook) 1948-61. 7v.

Surveys developments in the engineering, production and distribution of farm machinery and activities of related organizations and financial agencies. Relevant laws and regulations appended. English table of contents.

T45
Nōgyō kikai zukan 農業機械図鑑 (Illustrated catalogue of farm machinery) No.1, 1950- . Shin Nōrinsha, 1950- . 9v. Annual.

Photographs and information on distinctive features and performances of new Japanese-made machinery and equipment. Makers and English names of machines indexed. Published irregularly until 1961, since then an annual supplement of the magazine *Kikaika nōgyō* (Mechanized agriculture).

FARM PRODUCTS

BIBLIOGRAPHY

Nōrinshō Toshokan 農林省図書館 **T46**
Beikoku Bunko mokuroku 米穀文庫目録
(Catalogue of the Rice Crop Library) Beikokuhō
Shikō Yonjusshūnen Kinenkai, 1963. 247p.

Lists about 2,000 books, chiefly on cereal crops,
published 1912-40, in the Rice Crop Library of the
Ministry of Agriculture and Forestry and the libraries of the Food Agency and other agricultural organizations.

Nihon Nōgyō Kishō Gakkai **T47**
日本農業気象学会
Suitō reigai no bunkenteki kenkyū 水稲冷害
の文献的研究 (A bibliographical study of
cold-weather damage to aquatic rice) Nōrinshō
Nōgyō Kairyōkyoku, 1955. 217p. (Nōgyō kai-
ryō gijutsu shiryō, 64)

Abstracts and annotates materials published to
1954, with discussion of conditions likely to bring
damage and how damage is done. No index.

DICTIONARIES

Saikin sakumotsu saibai jiten 最近作物栽培 **T48**
事典 (Up-to-date cyclopedia of crop cultivation) Hakuyūsha, 1958. 465p.

Morphology, physiology, heredity, breeding, environmental aspects and cultivation of crops is followed by detailed instructions on the growing of more
than 100 grains and vegetables. Many illustrations.
Index.

Abiko, Kōichi 安孫子孝一 **et al.** **T49**
Nōsakumotsu hinshu kaisetsu 農作物品種解
説 (Commentary on varieties of farm products) Nōgyō Gijutsu Kyōkai, 1955. 434p.

Gives the origin, characteristics, soil and cultivation requirements of varieties of 25 such major
crops as aquatic rice, rushes and sugar beets. Lists
varieties bred by the Ministry of Agriculture and
Forestry. Classified index.

Nōrin Suisan Gijutsu Kaigi Jimukyoku **T50**
農林水産技術会議事務局
Hatasakumotsu no shinhinshu 畑作物の新
品種 (New types of dry-field crops) 1955-
1963. 1963. 61, 381p.

Gives the history, properties and records of species
of soy beans, peanuts, corn, sweet potatoes, and

other important crops developed in 1955-63 by the
national and other experimental stations. Illustrations. Lists of plant breeds registered with the
Ministry of Agriculture and Forestry and of plant-
breeding stations appended.

DISEASES AND CONTROL

BIBLIOGRAPHY

Sakumotsu Bairasubyō ni kansuru Kenkyū **T51**
Kyōgikai 作物バイラス病に関する研究
協議会
Nihon ni okeru sakumotsu bairasubyō ni kansuru bunken mokuroku 日本における作物バイ
ラス病に関する文献目録 (A bibliogra-
phy of virus crop diseases in Japan) 1960. 127p.

Classifies by crops scientific and official reports,
lecture summaries and general articles published between 1890 and 1959.

HANDBOOKS

Hidaka, Jun 日高醇 **et al.** **T52**
Shokubutsu birusubyō 植物ウイルス病
(Virus diseases of plants) Experimental methods
and types. Asakura Shoten, 1960. 400p.

Covers identification, experimentation with and
eradication of diseases of a wide range of crops.
Many illustrations. Lists of references. Index.

Togashi, Kōgo 富樫浩吾 **T53**
Biological characters of plant pathogens temperature relation. Meibundō, 1949. 478p.

Useful as a manual of plant pathogens. Extensive
bibliography.

Nihon Shokubutsu Byōri Gakkai **T54**
日本植物病理学会
Nihon yūyō shokubutsu byōmei mokuroku 日本
有用植物病名目録 (List of diseases of
useful plants in Japan) v. 1. 1960. 154p.

Gives the standard names of diseases, their
English equivalents, synonyms, scientific names
and literature concerning them. Further volumes
planned.

Kawada, Akira 河田党 **et al.** **T55**
Sakumotsu byōchūgai handobukku 作物病虫
害ハンドブック (Handbook of crop dis-
eases and pests) 3d ed., rev. Yōkendō, 1955.
1286p.

Describes those affecting vegetables, fruit, flowers

and other crops and prescribes germicides, insecticides, herbicides, poisons and other agents for eliminating them, as well as explaining environmental and other factors contributing to their spread. Index.

ILLUSTRATIONS

Nōrinshō Nōgyō Kairyōkyoku　**T56**
農林省農業改良局
Nōsakumotsu byōgaichū genshoku zuhan　農作物病害虫原色図版 (Color plates of diseases and insects harmful to farm produce) Nōgyō Gijutsu Kyōkai, 1953-54.　2v.

Arranged by such staple crops as rice, wheat and potatoes, miscellaneous grains, special crops, vegetables and fruit. Useful for identification of diseases and insect damage in early stages.

Yoshii, Hajime　吉井甫　**et al.**　**T57**
Sakumotsu byōgai zuhen　作物病害図編 (Illustrated book of crop diseases) Rev. ed. Yōkendō, 1957.　644p.

Explains the appearance of diseases affecting grains, vegetables, fruit, etc., their causes and development, and control methods.

Kabe, Masaaki　加辺正明　**T58**
Nihonsan kikuimushirui shokkon zusetsu　日本産キクイムシ類食痕図説 (Illustrated study of traces of Japanese wood borers) Meibundō, 1959.　290p.　97 plates.

Shows the traces of and comments on 213 woodboring insect larva most harmful to Japanese forests. Index of Japanese and Latin names.

Chemicals

Katsuki, Shigetaka　香月繁孝 et al.　**T59**
Nōyaku benran　農薬便覧 (Handbook of agricultural chemicals) Nō-San-Gyoson-Bunka Kyōkai, 1959.　329p.

Classifies by composition and gives trade names of insecticides, germicides, rat poisons, herbicides, plant-growth regulators and other commercially available farm chemicals, with notes on precautions in using them, and pertinent laws. Trade names indexed.

T60
Nōyaku yōran　農薬要覧 (Manual of agricultural chemicals) 1963- . Nihon Shokubutsu Bōeki Kyōkai, 1963- . 2v. Annual.

Annual survey of the production, distribution, import and export and consumption. Includes list of registered agricultural chemicals, descriptions of new chemicals, and a table showing results of aerial spraying to prevent crop damages by diseases and pests.

Kawai, Ichirō　河合一郎 **and**　**T61**
Kariya, Shōjiro　苅谷正次郎
Nōyaku gaido　農薬ガイド (Guide to agricultural chemicals) Fumin Kyōkai, 1961.　434p.

Chemicals, classified by uses and listed by trade names, are described with effective uses and application methods for particular diseases and pests.

HORTICULTURE

Ishii, Yūgi　石井勇義　**T62**
Engei daijiten　園芸大辞典 (Comprehensive dictionary of horticulture) Seibundō Shinkōsha, 1952-56.　6v.

Covers fruit trees, vegetables, flowers, herbs, tropical and alpine plants, giving for each the place of origin, varieties, cultivation methods, diseases, and technical terms. Japanese, English and Latin names indexed.

Yamazaki, Morimasa　山崎守正 **and**　**T63**
Inoue, Yorikazu　井上頼数
Sakumotsu engei jiten　作物・園芸事典 (Dictionary of crops and gardening) Sangyō Tosho, 1957.　445p.

Concisely defines technical terms related to farm products, gardening and plant diseases. Foreign words indexed.

Sakurakai　桜会　**T64**
Engeika hikkei　園芸家必携 (Horticulturist's vade mecum) 3d ed., rev. and enl. Yōkendō, 1955.　621p.

Explains in detail cultivation methods of fruit trees and vegetables, based on the past 50 years research at experimental stations.

Fruit culture

Kobayashi, Akira　小林章　**T65**
Jikken katsuyō kaju engei handobukku　実験活用果樹園芸ハンドブック (Handbook of fruit-tree cultivation based on experimentation results) Yōkendō, 1955.　860p.

Covers fruit, nuts, olives, etc., with simple explanations, well illustrated, of their varieties, where they can be grown, trimming and pruning, soil supervision, fertilization, protection from diseases and pests, and handling of crops.

Kubo, Toshio 久保利夫 **T66**
Genshoku kajitsu zukan 原色果実図鑑
Coloured illustrations of the fruit. Osaka, Hoikusha, 1962. 178p. 56 plates. (Hoikusha no genshoku zukan, 29)

Shows 212 species of 22 major fruit trees cultivated in Japan, with histories, characteristics and cultivation methods.

Vegetable gardening

Hagiwara, Susumu 萩原十 **et al.** **T67**
Sosai saibai sōten 蔬菜栽培綜典 (Guide to vegetable growing) Asakura Shoten, 1953. 471p.

Gives for ordinary and fast-growing vegetables, edible roots, etc. information about varieties, where and when to plant, sowing, harvesting, packing, marketing, storage, and uses.

Matsubara, Shigeki 松原茂樹 **T68**
Sokusei sosai engei sōten 促成蔬菜園芸綜典 (Guide for cultivation of out-of-season vegetables) Asakura Shoten, 1955. 419p.

Helpful in the operation and management of hothouse and other forced cultivation of vegetables and fruit, with general introduction on forced cultivation, facilities and fertilizers, and the shipping and marketing of crops.

Floriculture

Asayama, Eiichi 浅山英一 **T69**
Kaki engei sōten 花卉園芸綜典 (Floricultural guide) Asakura Shoten, 1955. 546p.

Explains the classifications, varieties and breeding of floral plants, the cultivation of flower-bed, hothouse and potted plants, acceleration and retardation of growth, cutting and storage, soils and fertilizers. Many illustrations.

Ishii, Yūgi 石井勇義 **et al.** **T70**
Genshoku engei shokubutsu zufu 原色園芸植物図譜 Coloured illustrations of the ornamental plants. Seibundō Shinkōsha, 1954-59. 6v.

Identifies 945 seasonal flowering, greenhouse and foliage plants, trees, morning glories, insectivorous plants, cacti, roses and azaleas, with Japanese, English, German and Latin names and notes on their habitats, characteristics, varieties, uses, and cultivation requirements. Index.

Tsukamoto, Yōtarō 塚本洋太郎 **T71**
Genshoku engei shokubutsu zukan 原色園芸

植物図鑑 Coloured illustrations of the garden plants of the world. Osaka, Hoikusha, 1963- . 3v. (Hoikusha no genshoku zukan, 33-35) In progress.

Shows about 500 varieties of common perennial and bulbiferous plants and about 210 of annual and biennial plants, with notes on their classification, history and cultivation.

SERICULTURE

Ishikawa, Kintarō 石川金太郎 **T72**
Nihon sanshigaku bunkenshū 日本蚕糸学文献集 (Bibliography of Japanese sericulture) Meibundō, 1940. 1000p.

Limited to scientific papers published from 1670 through 1937, divided into Japanese and Western-language sections and listed chronologically under such headings as mulberry trees, silkworms, raw silk, spinning and wild silkworms. Subject and author indexes.

Zenkoku Sangyō Shikenjō Un'ei Kyōgikai **T73**
全国蚕業試験場運営協議会
Sanshigaku bunken mokuroku 蚕糸学文献目録 (A bibliography of sericultural science) 1938-57. 1958. 931p.

Classifies articles in Japanese and Western languages under mulberry trees, silkworms, raw silk, silk yarn and byproducts. Monographs are listed by authors. Author index.

Aoki, Kiyoshi 青木清 **et al.** **T74**
Sanshi gijutsu jiten 蚕糸技術事典 (Technical dictionary of sericulture) Azumi Shobō, 1962. 285p.

Explains all aspects from raising silkworms, diseases and cocoons to silk manufacture, with many illustrations.

T75
Sanshi nenkan 蚕糸年鑑 (Silk yarn yearbook) 1931- . Comp. by Nihon Sanshi Kōhō Kyōkai, 1931-39, 1948- . 25v.

Detailed coverage of domestic and international trends and policies, production and distribution, demand for silk fabrics, price stabilization measures, with statistical tables and directory. Compiled by different agencies until 1954.

ANIMAL HUSBANDRY
DICTIONARIES

T76
Chikusan daijiten 畜産大事典 (Cyclopedia of

animal husbandry) Yōkendō, 1964.   567p.

Up-to-date information on all aspects of livestock and poultry raising, with excerpts of registration regulations, judging criteria, laws and statistics appended. Indexes of Japanese and Western-language terms.

T77

Yōkei daijiten 養鶏大事典   (Cyclopedia of poultry raising) Nagoya, Yōkei no Nihon sha, 1963. 1098p.

Covers history, varieties, anatomy, physiology, raising, breeding, incubation, housing, equipment, feeding, diseases, management, etc., with many photographs, diagrams, statistics. No index.

HANDBOOKS

Iguchi, Kenzō 井口賢三   **et al.**   **T78**
Jikken katsuyō chikusan hōten 実験活用畜産宝典 (Livestock handbook based on experimentation results) 3d ed., rev. Yōkendō, 1959. 965p.

Gives practical information. Laws and regulations included.

Rakunō Gijutsu Fukyū Gakkai   **T79**
酪農技術普及学会
Nyūgyō gijutsu benran 乳業技術便覧 (Handbook of dairy techniques) Jitsugyō Tosho Shuppan, 1963-64. 3v.

Covers production and research. Lists of abbreviations, symbols, terms used in grading dairy products, etc. and pertinent laws and regulations appended. Index.

T80
Chikusan teiyō 畜産提要 (Livestock manual) 1930- . Comp. by Nōrinshō Chikusankyoku. 1930-39, 1951-53, 1962- . 14v. Irregular.

Management, production, distribution, feeding, sanitation, medicine, etc. of all animals and poultry.

Feed and feeding

Morimoto, Hiroshi 森本宏   **T81**
Shiryō yōgo handobukku 飼料用語ハンドブック (Handbook of feed terms) Rev. ed. Nihon Kagaku Shiryō Kyōkai, 1964. 220, 22, 21p.

Briefly explains Japanese terms giving English equivalents. List of abbreviations appended. Japanese and English indexes.

Sasaki, Rinjirō 佐々木林治郎   **T82**
Shiryō sōten 飼料綜典 (Feed manual) Asa-

kura Shoten, 1955.   511p.

Practical information on nutritional values of feed and fodder, feeding methods, cultivation of feed crops and feed economy.

Mitsui, Kazuo 三井計夫 **et al.**   **T83**
Shiryō sakumotsu kusachi handobukku 飼料作物・草地ハンドブック (Handbook for feed crops and grasslands) Yōkendō, 1964. 567p.

Explains technical aspects of feed crops, preparation and management of grasslands, harvesting, mixing and storage of feed, and feeding. Tables of yields of farm by-products, results of mixed seeding in various countries, etc. appended. Bibliography. Japanese and Western-language indexes.

FORESTRY

BIBLIOGRAPHY

Nōrinshō Ringyō Shikenjo   **T84**
農林省林業試験場
Ringyō ringaku ni kansuru ronbun oyobi chosho bunrui mokuroku 林業林学に関する論文及著書分類目録 (Classified list of articles and monographs on forestry) Dai Nihon Sanrinkai, 1925-30. 2v.

Cites books, serial and irregular research reports and scholarly periodicals published in Japan. v. 1 covers from 1868 to 1921, v. 2 from 1922 to 1925.

Kōrinkai 興林会   **T85**
Honpōsan shuyō jushu bunken mokuroku 本邦産主要樹種文献目録 (Catalogue of literature on major Japanese trees) Nihon Ringakkai, 1938-45. 4v.

Lists pre-1937 monographs and articles on growth, use, and economy.

DICTIONARIES

Nihon Ringyō Gijutsu Kyōkai   **T86**
日本林業技術協会
Ringyō hyakka jiten 林業百科事典   (Encyclopedia of forestry) Maruzen, 1961. 1086p.

Comprehensively covers management, environment, afforestation, protection, felling and transportation of timber, wood technology, chemistry, special products, botany, landscape architecture, etc.

T87
Jitsuyō Wa-Ei ringyō yōgoshū 実用和英林業用語集 (Practical Japanese-English glossa-

ry of forestry terms) Tōkei Shuppan, 1950. 10, 200p.

Rin'yachō 林野庁 **T88**
Kokuyū rin'ya kankei yōgo benran 国有林野関係用語便覧 (Handbook of terms related to nationally owned forests) Rev. ed. Rin'ya Kyōsaikai, 1961. 557p.

Defines 2,500 terms. Classified index.

HANDBOOKS

Honda, Seiroku 本多静六 **T89**
Shinrinka hikkei 森林家必携 (Handbook for foresters) Rev. and enl. ed. Rin'ya Kyōsaikai, 1961. 793p.

Gives basic information on important trees and shrubs, afforestation, landscape architecture, forest protection, management, utilization, water regulation, erosion control, products, soil, and legislation.

Rin'yachō 林野庁 **T90**
Ikurin sōten 育林綜典 (Forestry manual) Asakura Shoten, 1955. 670p.

Covers cultivation of useful and special trees, pertinent laws and regulations. Index.

San'emu Kenkyūkai 3 M 研究会 **T91**
Ringyō kikaika handobukku 林業機械化ハンドブック (Handbook of forestry mechanization) Ringyō Kikaika Kyōkai, 1964. 632p.

Covers the construction, performance and handling of forestry machinery, with directories of makers and distributors and laws and regulations appended. Machines, personal and company names indexed.

YEARBOOKS

T92
Nihon ringyō nenkan 日本林業年鑑 (Japan forestry yearbook) 1950- . Rin'ya Kyōsaikai, 1950, 1953, 1955- . 14v.

With 272 tables, reports developments in private and national forests and forest products, including chemicals, forestry and sawmill machinery, testing and research. Directory of agencies and companies.

T93
Ringyō tōkei yōran 林業統計要覧 (Survey of forestry statistics) 1948- . Comp. by Rin'yachō. Rin'ya Kyōsaikai, 1948, 1953- . 13v.

Basic source, preceded by *Sanrin yōran* (Forestry survey) published from 1929 to 1944 by the Forestry Bureau, Ministry of Agriculture and Forestry, and revived by the Forestry Agency in 1948.

Wood

Kyōto Daigaku, Mokuzai Kenkyūjo **T94**
京都大学木材研究所
Mokuzai jiten 木材辞典 (Wood dictionary) Osaka, Sōgensha, 1956. 417p.

Definitions with English and German equivalents of about 2,000 terms. Japanese common names and scientific names indexed.

Nōrinshō Ringyō Shikenjo **T95**
農林省林業試験場
Mokuzai kōgyō handobukku 木材工業ハンドブック (Lumber industry handbook) Maruzen, 1958. 1067p.

Gives technical data on the seasoning of wood, woodworking, veneers, plywood, pulp, preservation, insect control, treatment of wood, charcoal, etc., with references at the end of each section. Detailed index.

Nihon Mokuzai Kakō Gijutsu Kyōkai **T96**
日本木材加工技術協会
Mokuzai hozon handobukku 木材保存ハンドブック (Wood preservation handbook) Shōkōdō, 1961. 877p.

Covers preservation from decay, fire prevention, insect control, waterproofing and painting, with pertinent laws and regulations, standards, and references. Index.

Kobayashi, Yaichi 小林弥一 **and** **T97**
Sutō, Shōji 須藤彰司
Mokuzai shikibetsu kādo 木材識別カード (Lumber identification cards) Nihon Ringyō Gijutsu Kyōkai, 1960. 40p. 301 cards.

Punch cards for non-professional use in identifying by such characteristics as color, luster and cell structure 179 species of 119 genera of 53 families of deciduous trees native to Japan and 85 species of 27 genera of eight families of imported coniferous trees.

Kishima, Tsuneo 貴島恒夫 **et al.** **T98**
Genshoku mokuzai daizukan 原色木材大図鑑 Atlas of wood in colour. Osaka, Hoikusha, 1962. 204p. 64 plates. (Hoikusha no genshoku daizukan, 10)

Shows 256 kinds of useful woods, including 32 foreign. Tables of characteristics and guide to identification from appearance. Indexes of Latin, other Western-language, Chinese and Japanese names and technical terms.

Takeda, Shōzō 武田正三 **T99**
Seizai gijutsusha hikkei 製材技術者必携 (Manual for woodworking engineers) Morikita

Shuppan, 1954. 295p.

Covers saws, planers and other machinery, with lists of makers, references and standard specifications for saws.

FISHERIES

BIBLIOGRAPHY

Sakamoto, Takeo 坂本武雄   **T100**
Nihon suisan bunken shūsei 日本水産文献集成 (Bibliography on Japanese fisheries) 1868-1945. Hakodate, Hokkaidō Daigaku Suisan Gakubu, 1952. 10v. mimeo.

Monographs, reports, pamphlets and articles listed chronologically under such headings as general, economics, physics and chemistry, oceanography, foodstuffs and chemical products.

Asano, Nagamitsu 浅野長光   **T101**
Bunken mokuroku 文献目録 稿本 (Bibliography, preliminary draft) 1947-1962. Suisan Kenkyūkai, 1962. 101p. mimeo.

Lists about 300 monographs with important ones annotated. Appended list of publications of the Investigation and Documentation Section of the Fishery Agency and fishery organizations.

DICTIONARIES

    T102
Suisan jiten 水産辞典 (Fisheries dictionary) Tennensha, 1951. 478p.

Yanagida, Kunio 柳田国男 **and**   **T103**
Kurata, Ichirō 倉田一郎
Bunrui gyoson goi 分類漁村語彙 (Classified glossary of words used in fishing villages) Iwanami Shoten, 1938. 443p.

Classified under 33 headings, words for fishing vessels, implements, methods, ways of processing, beliefs, etc. not found in ordinary dictionaries are explained. Appended are special words used in inland fisheries. Index.

HANDBOOKS

Suehiro, Yasuo 末広恭雄 **et al.**   **T104**
Suisan handobukku 水産ハンドブック (Fisheries handbook) Tōyō Keizai Shinpōsha, 1962. 725p.

Has sections on environment, resources, hatcheries, fishing techniques and vessels, processing, refrigeration, laws and regulations, and economy. Statistics appended. Index.

Suisanchō 水産庁   **T105**
Suisan poketto bukku 水産ポケット・ブック (Marine products pocketbook) Isana Shobō, 1959. 460p.

Gives basic information on the sciences involved in fishing, fishing implements, transportation and navigation, marketing, etc., with tables, laws, and list of trade terms.

YEARBOOKS

    T106
Suisan nenkan 水産年鑑 (Fisheries yearbook) 1954- . Comp. by Suisan Kenkyūkai. Suisan Shuhōsha, 1954- . 11v.

Former titles: *Nihon suisan nenpō*, 1937-1942. 6v.; *Suisan nenpō*, 1948:

Includes revisions of laws and regulations, developments in international fishing, production and marketing, with statistics, tables and diagrams. Directory of agencies and companies.

    T107
Zusetsu gyōgyō nenji hōkoku 図説漁業年次報告 (Illustrated annual report on fisheries) 1963- . Comp. by Suisanchō. Nōrin Tōkei Kyōkai, 1964- . 1v.

Compiled for the Diet, it gives the full texts of "Annual report on fishery trends" and "Annual report on measures taken with regard to coastal fishing". v.1 covers 1957-62.

STATISTICS

    T108
Gyōgyō yōshokugyō gyokaku tōkeihyō 漁業養殖業漁獲統計表 Annual report of catch statistics on fishery and aquiculture. 1954- . Comp. by Nōrinshō Nōrin Keizaikyoku. Nōrin Tōkei Kyōkai, 1955- . 9v.

Covers all kinds of fishing, hatcheries, processing, market prices and total values of catches. catches) 1912-1958. Nōrin Tōkei Kyōkai, 1960. 87p.

Compiled from **T22** and **T108**.

Nōrinshō 農林省   **T109**
Gyokakuryō ruinen tōkeihyō 漁獲量累年統計表 (Cumulative statistical tables of fishery catches) 1912-1958. Nōrin Tōkei Kyōkai, 1960. 87p.

Compiled from **T22** and **T108**.

Implements

Suisanchō 水産庁   **T110**
Nihon gyosen gyogu zushū 日本漁船漁具図集 Illustrations of Japanese fishing boats and fishing gear. Nōrin Kyōkai, 1958. 208p.

Diagrammatic descriptions of modern fishing equipment and methods, with some notes in English.

MEDICAL SCIENCE

❧ Medicine and the allied subjects of public health, nutrition, dentistry, nursing and pharmacy are covered in this section. Abstracts and reviews limited to extremely specific subjects and popular materials are not included.

GENERAL WORKS

BIBLIOGRAPHY

Ika Daigaku Fuzoku Toshokan Kyōgikai　　**U1**
医科大学付属図書館協議会
Union catalogue of foreign books in the libraries of Japanese medical schools. 1949-56. 8v.

Arranges by author, with locations, holdings of 15 members of the Council of Libraries of Medical Colleges as of Mar., 1946.　The Association of Japanese Medical Libraries, successor to the Council, plans its continuation.

Ika Daigaku Fuzoku Toshokan Kyōgikai　　**U2**
医科大学付属図書館協議会
Ikadaigaku kyōdō gakujutsu zasshi mokuroku 医科大学協同学術雑誌目録 (Union catalogue of scientific journals in medical colleges) 3d ed.　1942.　305, 150, 67p.

Lists 2,822 European-language and 1,120 Japanese journals in the Niigata, Okayama, Chiba, Kanazawa, Nagasaki, Tōhoku, Osaka, Kyoto (Prefectural), Kumamoto, Nagoya, Tokyo, Keiō, Hokkaido, Keijo (Seoul) and Manshū medical schools as of 1938, with location marks within schools.　Title changes given under each title.　Classified index and index of foreign learned institutions and place names.

Nihon Igaku Toshokan Kyōkai　　**U3**
日本医学図書館協会
Igaku zasshi sōgō mokuroku　医学雑誌総合

目録　Union list of medical periodicals in the medical libraries of Japan. 1961-63. 2v.

Adds to **U2** holdings European-language journals in 46 institutions to Dec., 1959, and Japanese journals in 50 institutions to Dec., 1962, arranged by titles.

Nihon Igaku Toshokan Kyōgikai　　**U4**
日本医学図書館協議会
Gaikoku igaku zasshi sōgō mokuroku 外国医学雑誌総合目録　Union list of foreign medical periodicals, 1941-1952.　Kokusai Shobō, 1954. 124p.

Gives 1,734 titles in 77 institutions, including 46 medical schools, societies, research institutes, hospitals and government offices.　For later acquisitions, *Genkō igaku zasshi shozai mokuroku* (Location list of current medical journals), published annually since 1957, is useful.　132 institutions, including pharmacological organizations, participated in 1963.

Kondō, Jion　近藤慈恩　　**U5**
Nihon i-shi-yakugaku zasshi sōran　日本医歯薬学雑誌総覧　Union catalogue of medical, dental and pharmaceutical periodicals in Japan. Daigaku Shobō, 1958. 501p.

Alphabetical list of about 3,240 titles published from 1868 to Mar., 1958, with bibliographical details. Also arranged under 60 Nippon Decimal Classification numbers.　Indexed list of societies and institutions.

ABSTRACTS AND INDEXES

U6

Igaku chūō zasshi 医学中央雑誌
Japana centra revuo medicina. v.1, no.1, Mar., 1903- .　5 times a month (6 issues to a vol.,

total of 10v. a year)

Comprehensively abstracts articles in over 1,000 Japanese periodicals in medicine, dentistry, pharmacology and related fields, with index for each volume but no cumulative index. To compensate for lag of about year in abstracting, gives tables of contents of latest major journals in each issue. Abstracts on surgery, orthopedics and radiology extracted from the Central Medical Journal and compiled separately under the following title:

Gekagaku seikei gekagaku hōshasengaku chūō zasshi (Central journal of surgery, orthopedics and radiology) Igaku Chūō Zasshisha, 1959-65. **U6a.**

Japan science review: medical sciences. v.1- . **U7**
Comp. by Nihon Gakujutsu Kaigi. Gihōdō, 1953- . 11v. (30 issues) Quarterly.

Lists articles and abstracts important ones in English according to UNESCO abstracting rules (10,629 articles and 706 abstracts in v.10, 1962), classified by UDC. List of journals and author index in each volume. Quarterly since v.8, 1960.

Ōta, Tamesaburō 太田為三郎　**U8**
Nihon iji zasshi sakuin　日本医事雑誌索引 (Index of medical journals of Japan) 1892-1918. Nihon Iji Nenpōsha, 1903-21. 23v.

Classified index of medical and pharmacological journals. Titles abstracted in **U6.**

DICTIONARIES

Aoyagi, Yasumasa 青柳安誠　**et al.**　**U9**
Wa-Ra-Ei-Doku-Futsu taishō igaku daijiten 和羅英独仏対照医学大字典　Japanese-Latin-English-German-French medical terminology. Kanehara Shuppan, 1957. 1259p.

Gives Latin, English, German and French equivalents for and briefly explains, with some diagrams, about 80,000 Japanese terms, followed by glossaries of Latin, English, German, and French terms with their Japanese equivalents.

Igaku daijiten 医学大辞典　**U10**
Nanzandō's medical dictionary. 10th ed. Nanzandō, 1964. 1860p.

Explains, often with illustrations, about 15,000 medical, pharmaceutical and related terms, with emphasis on those in recent Japanese and foreign medical literature, giving synonyms and English, German, French and Latin equivalents. Index of foreign terms. Reduced-size edition available. ·

Ishikawa, Mitsuteru 石川光昭　**U11**
Ei-Wa igo daijiten 英和医語大辞典　English-Japanese medical dictionary. Bunkōdō, 1960. 1350p.

Based, with some modification, on Dorland's *The American illustrated medical dictionary,* 22nd ed., 1951, with brief translations of entries covering medicine, pharmacology, biochemistry, chemistry, dental surgery and veterinary science. Fewer illustrations than in the original.

Kagawa, Tetsuo 賀川哲夫　**U12**
Hyōjun igo jiten: Doku-Ra-Ei-Futsu-Wa 標準医語辞典　独羅英仏一和　Nanzandōs medizinische Terminologie deutsch-, latinisch-, englisch-, französisch-japanisch. 30th ed., rev. Nanzandō, 1963. 1092p.

German and Latin terms in medicine, pharmacology and related fields, including English and French terms used in Germany, with Japanese equivalents. Some entries explained. Reduced-size edition available.

Kaketa, Katsumi 懸田克躬　**et al.**　**U13**
Shin Ei-Wa igaku jiten 新英和医学辞典　New medical dictionary: English-Japanese. 2d ed. Igaku Shoin, 1962. 1045p.

Gives Japanese equivalents of about 30,000 terms in medicine, pharmacology, biochemistry, psychiatry, etc., with explanations, chemical structural formulas and illustrations when helpful. Anatomical chart, list of abbreviations, etc., appended.

Katō, Katsuji 加藤勝治　**U14**
Igaku Ei-Wa daijiten 医学英和大辞典　Katō's integrated English-Japanese medical dictionary. Nanzandō, 1960. 1718p.

Equates about 150,000 terms extending beyond medicine and pharmacology to nuclear physics, radiology, space science, etc. Includes international terms of German, French, Spanish, Italian and Latin origin, with synonyms, explanations and structural formulas and uses of chemical products and medicines.

Nichi Futsu Ikakai 日仏医科会　**U15**
Futsu-Wa igaku jiten 仏和医学辞典 Dictionnaire medicale français-japonais. Hakusuisha, 1956. 644p.

Explains briefly technical and popular terms in contemporary medical and allied literature. Gives formulas of chemical compounds.

Takemura, Bunshō 竹村文祥　**U16**
Katsuyō igo shinjiten 活用医語新字典　Medical terminology. Nankōdō, 1964. 776p.

Gives etymologies and related technical terms, without explanations, for about 14,000 entries in romanized Japanese with their Latin, English and German equivalents.

Okuda, Kunio 奥田邦夫 **et al.** **U17**
Igaku Eigo no kakikata 医学英語の書き方 Handbook of medical English. Igaku Shoin, 1963. 758p.

Instructions for writing articles, clinical reports, case studies, surgical views, reports on operations, lectures and correspondence, with examples and lists of standard phrases. The supplement, designed to help students going to the United States, explains qualifications, procedures and the American educational system, with lists of abbreviations, symbols and colloquial medical expressions.

TABLES

Hayashi, Kanae 林香苗 **U18**
Nihonjin narabini Nihon san igaku jikken dōbutsu kaibōgaku oyobi seirigaku keisū 日本人並に日本産医学実験動物解剖学及び生理学計数 (Anatomical and physiological measurements of the Japanese and of Japanese animals used in medical experiments) Okayama, Okayama Daigaku Kaibōgaku Seirigaku Keisūhyō Kankōkai, 1956. 700p.

Based on Japanese sources from 1868 to 1956 and arranged according to UDC classification. Includes monkeys, dogs, rabbits, beavers, white rats, mice, toads and frogs. Subject index.. For human measurements, see, **U19.**

Minoshima, Takashi 簑島高 **et al.** **U19**
Nihonjin jintai seijō sūchihyō 日本人人体正常数値表 (Normal physical measurements of the Japanese) Gihōdō, 1958. 457p.

Tables concerned with physiology, anatomy, medical chemistry and nutrition grouped by age, sex and occupation taken from about 300 Japanese journals. Index.

Yoshida, Akinobu 吉田章信 **U20**
Hitaijū hikyōi hizakō hayamihyō 比体重・比胸囲・比座高早見表 (Charts for finding proportionate weight, girth of chest, and sitting height) Reprint ed. Fukumura Shoten, 1959. 133p.

Applicable to heights from 100 to 162.9 cm. School health laws and regulations appended. First published in 1937.

Hasumi, Akijirō 荷見秋次郎 **U21**
Jidō seito taijū kyōi hyōjunhyō 児童・生徒・体重・胸囲標準表 (Standard tables of weights

and chest girths of school children) Daiichi Shuppan, 1963. 173p.

Gives nationwide measurements of boys and girls taken by the Ministry of Education in April, 1952, compiled in the same way as in **U20** to show postwar improvement.

DIRECTORIES

Igaku Kenkyūsha meibo 医学研究者名簿 **U22**
Japanese medical researchers directory. 1958-59- . Comp. by Takamichi Tsusaki and Hiromasa Kita. Igaku Shoin, 1959- . 3v.

Lists faculty members of medical, dental and pharmacy schools of universities, division chiefs of public and private research institutes and officers of the Japan Medical Society. Gives official English names of institutes and titles of their publications.

Nihon isekiroku 日本医籍録 **U23**
(Directory of Japanese physicians) No. 1, 1925- . Igaku Kōronsha, 1925- . 34v. Annual.

Gives the specialty, place of employment, home address, date of birth, schools, career, academic history, thesis, etc. of each clinical physician and medical practitioner on the basis of the register of the Bureau of Hygiene, Ministry of Health and Welfare. Index of names by regional blocs. Coverage alternates, East Japan in one year's volume and West Japan in the next.

Nihon igaku hakushiroku 日本医学博士録 **U24**
(Register of Japanese doctors of medicine) Chūō Igakusha, 1954. 1037, 350p.

Gives the specialty, place of employment, address, university, degree conferment date and thesis title of each of 27,808 doctors, from 1887 to 1953. Index of theses. Continued in **P35.**

INSTRUMENTS

Nihon Ika Kikai Gakkai 日本医科器械学会 **U25**
Ika kikai zuroku 医科器械図録 The illustrated issue of medical instruments. 34th issue. 1964. 440p. (Ika kikaigaku zasshi, supp.)

A catalogue with classified index by types of instruments and index of manufacturers.

Denshi Kikai Kōgyōkai 電子機械工業会 **U26**
Iyō denshi kiki sōran 医用電子機器総覧 Medical electronics instruments, with buyers' guide. 1962 ed. Denshi Keisoku Shuppan, 1961. 198p.

Shows and explains in detail the use of appliances for measuring and recording, observation, diagnosis and testing of materials, handling of medical data, measurement of radiation and medical use of television.

MEDICARE AND MEDICAL LAWS

Kōseishō Imukyoku 厚生省医務局 **U27**
Sekai kakkoku no iryō seido 世界各国の医療制度 (Systems of medical treatment in the countries of the world) I-shi-yaku Shuppan, 1960. 453p.

Surveys in the United States, England, West Germany, France, Italy, the Scandinavian countries and the Soviet Union, hospitals, clinics and other medical institutions, doctors, nurses and others concerned with treatment, agencies for administration of public health and medical security, and related organizations. References.

U28
Kōsei hakusho 厚生白書
(White paper on public welfare) 1956- . Comp. by Kōseishō. 1957- . 9v. Annual.

Gives general survey of developments and problems in medical care and welfare administration, with many statistics and diagrams.

Ogata, Tomio 緒方富雄 *et al.* **U29**
Igaku nenkan: igaku shigaku yakugaku hoken eisei no nenji sōran 医学年鑑：医学・歯学・薬学・保健衛生の年次総覧 (Medical yearbook: annual survey of medicine, dentistry, pharmacology, health and hygiene) 1963 ed. I-Shi-Yaku Shuppan, 1962. 648p.

Covers developments for the period, 1954-61, in all health fields, health administration and social security, with chronology. Appended are a guide to study abroad, tables, lists of periodicals and films, vital and therapeutical statistics and directories of government offices, health service centers, hospitals, schools, research institutes, related organizations and pharmaceutical companies. Preceded by *I-shi-yaku nenkan* (Medical, dental and pharmaceutical yearbook), 1954.

Kōseishō 厚生省 **U30**
Shippei shōgai oyobi shiin tōkei bunrui teiyō 疾病・傷害および死因統計分類提要 (Manual of statistical classification of diseases, injuries and causes of death) 1958 ed. 1958. 2v.

Based on the revised international statistical classification adopted by the 1956 World Health Assembly, v.1 gives a general survey, classification table, examples of its application, rules for determining cause of death, etc. v.2 is an index of symbols based mainly on the alphabetical index to the 1955 revision of the international classification of diseases. Reprinted in 1962.

Atsumi, Setsuo 渥美節夫 **U31**
Iryōhō ishihō kai 医療法・医師法解 (Laws on medical treatment, dental practitioners, annotated) Supplement: Medical Financing Corporation regulations, 1961 ed. Igaku Tsūshinsha, 1960. 655p.

Article-by-article commentary on current laws.

Suzuki, Kaichi 鈴木嘉一 **U32**
Hōshasei dōi genso tō ni yoru hōshasen shōgai... 放射性同位元素等による放射線障害の防止に関する法律施行令等の解説 (Commentaries on the ordinance for enforcement of the Law for Prevention of Harm by Rays of Radioisotopes, etc.) Teikoku Chihō Gyōsei Gakkai, 1959. 631p.

Tells how the law was enacted and explains its articles. Also covers related laws. The same author's 1958 book of the same title, a tentative draft, includes foreign laws on the subject.

Kōseishō 厚生省 **U33**
Kōsei hōki sōran 厚生法規総覧 (Manual of welfare laws) Chūō Hōki Shuppan, 1958- . 12v. Loose-leaf.

Pt.1, Index and general rules; pt.2, Public and environmental hygiene; pt.3, Medical affairs; pt.4, Pharmacological affairs; pt.5, Social welfare; pt.6, Social insurance; pt.7, National pensions.

U34
Sugawa, Yutaka 須川豊
Ishi hōrei handobukku 医師法令ハンドブック (Handbook of laws and regulations concerning physicians) Igaku Shoin, 1964. 153p.

Gives without comment laws and regulations in force in early 1964 classified by subjects, with those of direct bearing on the upper halves of pages and those of indirect bearing on the lower halves. Detailed table of contents.

HOSPITALS

Kōseishō Imukyoku 厚生省医務局 **U35**
Byōin yōran 病院要覧 Japanese hospital directory. 5th ed., rev. Igaku Shoin, 1964. 318p.
Statistical survey of hospital conditions, a di-

rectory of hospitals arranged by prefectures, with sponsoring organizations, addresses, clinical divisions, numbers of beds, names of directors, an outline of hospital classification and lists of medical institutions and organizations, universities and colleges of medicine, dentistry and pharmacology, institutes for training medical and clinical technicians and health service centers.

Nihon Byōin Setsubi Kyōkai　　　　**U36**
日本病院設備協会
Byōin setsubi yōran 病院設備要覧 (Survey of hospital equipment) 1962 ed. Rikō Tosho, 1962. 358p.

Collection of illustrated catalogues of accommodation for patients, therapeutic and building equipment, etc., with supplement giving standards for clinical appliances and directory of makers.

Medical history

Fujikawa, Yū 富士川游　　　　**U37**
Nihon igakushi 日本医学史 (History of Japanese medicine) Nisshin Shoin, 1941. 812, 122p.

From early times to about 1868, divided into periods, each with references. Chronology to about 1903 appended. Index of important subjects. Standard edition.

Tamura, Masao 田村正雄　　　　**U38**
Nihon igaku hyakunenshi 日本医学百年史 (History of a century of Japanese medicine) Rinshō Igakusha, 1957. 1046p.

Traces developments from the 1850s through the post-1945 reforms, including socialized medicine, health insurance, separation of medicine and pharmacy and progress in techniques. Brief biographical notes on medical pioneers. Chronology from 1854 to 1955 and important medical laws and regulations appended.

Nihon Gakushiin 日本学士院　　　　**U39**
Meiji zen Nihon igakushi 明治前日本医学史 (Pre-Meiji history of Japanese medicine) Nihon Gakujutsu Shinkokai, 1955-58. 4v.

A collection of separate histories of Japanese anatomy, diseases, physiology, pathology, internal medicine, care of wounds, Western medicine and surgery, therapeutics and legal medicine, with biographies of famous physicians and chronology. v.4 not published.

Nihon Ishi Gakkai 日本医史学会　　　　**U40**
Kindai Nihon igaku no akebono 資料でみる 近代日本医学のあけぼの Catalogue of the historical writings and materials in the early stage of the development of modern medicine in Japan. Kyoto, Benridō, 1959. 92p.

Illustrated catalogue of 108 items displayed at the 1959 general meeting of the Japan Medical Society, consisting of pre-1868 books on Western medicine, anatomical diagrams and models, achievements in experiments and medical instruments, with English and Japanese explanations. A companion volume, *Igaku ni kansuru ko-bijutsu shūei* (Selected classical art works related to medicine), was published by the Kyoto National Museum in 1955.

Fujii, Naohisa 藤井尚久　　　　**U41**
Igaku bunka nenpyō 医学文化年表 (Chronology of medical science) Nisshin Shoin, 1942. 424p.

Gives not only tabular comparison of medical developments in Japan and Europe and America but also lists chronologically principal pre-1868 Japanese medical men, including naturalized physicians, and genealogies of prominent medical families, with brief comparable Chinese and Western genealogies appended.

Nakano, Misao 中野操　　　　**U42**
Kōkoku iji dainenpyō 皇国医事大年表 (Comprehensive chronology of medical matters in the Japanese Empire) Nankōdō, 1942. 400p.

Records principal Japanese developments from mythological times to 1940, brief biographies of famous physicians, and book titles, with foreign developments and remarks in parallel columns. Era names, anniversaries of physicians, genealogies of schools of medicine and list of foreign physicians in Japan appended. Name and title indexes. Most detailed and useful of such chronologies.

Takeoka, Tomozō 竹岡友三　　　　**U43**
Ika jinmei jisho 医家人名辞書 (Biographical dictionary of medical men) Kyoto, Jigyokudō, 1931. 534p.

Covers about 1,860 physicians from ancient times to about 1912, with biographical sources given.

Shichiku, Heizan 柴竹屏山　　　　**U44**
Honchō ijinden 本朝医人伝 (Biographies of our country's physicians) Sūzandō, 1910. 244p.

Gives the lives and achievements of 166 famous physicians from mythological times to 1868, arranged chronologically.

BASIC MEDICINE
→ S10-S15

Nihon Kaibō Gakkai 日本解剖学会　　　　**U45**
Nihon kaibōgaku bunkenshū 日本解剖学文献集

(Bibliography of anatomy in Japan) 1936- .
3v. In progress.

Exhaustive classified list of Japanese literature on anatomy and related subjects from 1686 to 1935 in series 1, to 1943 in series 2 and to 1955, including omissions in series 2 and Japanese achievements published abroad, in series 3. Gives volume and issue numbers for journals but not pages. Name index.

Nihon Kaibō Gakkai 日本解剖学会 **U46**
Kaibōgaku yōgo 解剖学用語 Nomina anatomica japonica. 9th ed. Maruzen, 1963. 253, 71p.

Equates Japanese terms with Paris Nomina Anatomica terms as revised at the 1960 7th International Congress of Anatomists. Lists of terms in histology and embryology appended.

Nihon Kaibō Gakkai 日本解剖学会 **U47**
Shinkyū taishō kaibō gakumei shūran 新旧対照解剖学名集覧(Comparative glossary of anatomical terms, new and old) Nanzandō, 1961. 404p.

Compares Basle Nomina Anatomica and Jena Nomina Anatomica terms with Paris Nomina Anatomica terms as revised in 1960 and Japanese terms as revised in 1957. Japanese and Latin indexes.

Mori, Masaru 森 優 **U48**
Gakushū hikkei kaibōgaku yōran 学習必携解剖学要覧 (Students' manual of anatomy) Nanzandō, 1960. 553p.

Explains Paris Nomina Anatomica technical terms with diagrams, classified by subjects in the order commonly found in textbooks. Detailed indexes of Japanese and foreign terms.

Nihon seirigaku bunken 日本生理学文献 **U49**
(Bibliography of Japanese physiology) Tokyo Teikoku Daigaku Igakubu, 1932. 255p.

Lists by author books and articles from 1873 to 1930, with citation of those abstracted in **U6**. Classified index.

Nihon Seiri Gakkai 日本生理学会 **U50**
Ei-Doku-Wa taishō seirigaku yōgoshū 英独和対照生理学用語集 (English-German-Japanese glossary of physiology) Nanzandō, 1960. 239p.

Gives physiological and related terms in English-Japanese-German and German-Japanese-English sections. Index of Japanese terms.

Tamura, Kenzō 田村憲造 **U51**
Nihon yakurigaku bunkenshū 日本薬理学文献集 (Bibliography of Japanese pharmacology) 1887-1932. Tokyo Teikoku Daigaku Igakubu Yakurigaku Kyōshitsu Dōsōkai, 1935. 312p.

Articles on experimental pharmacology in 110 Japanese medical journals, arranged by authors' name. Subject indexes to medicines, poisons, organs, and functions.

Nihon byōri bōken shuhō 日本病理剖検輯報 **U52**
Annual of the pathological autopsy cases in Japan. No.1, 1958- . Comp. by Nihon Byōri Gakkai. 1960- . 5v. Annual.

Comprehensive list of autopsies in university and major public hospitals in Japan (13,276 in 105 institutions in 1962 edition), arranged by institutions, including for each case the autopsy number, age, sex, occupation and clinical and pathological diagnosis.

Mori, Shigeki 森 茂樹 **and** **U53**
Suzue, Kitasu 鈴江 懐
Nihon naibunpi bunkenshū 日本内分泌文献集 (Bibliography of Japanese endocrinology) Kumamoto, Kumamoto Ika Daigaku Naibunpi oyobi Jikken Chiryō Kenkyūkai, 1936. 474p.

Exhaustive list of articles on endocrinology and related aspects of the autonomic nervous system in Japanese medical journals from 1899 to 1936. Name index includes references to abstracts in **U6**. For later literature, see *Nihon naibunpi bunken tenbō* (Survey of endocrinological literature in Japan) 1954- . Igaku no Sekaisha, 1954- . 7v.

Komiya, Etsuzō 小宮悦造 **U54**
Nihonjin no seijō ketsuekizō 日本人の正常血液像 (Normal blood conditions of the Japanese) Nanzandō, 1962. 370p.

Reports the research results by 23 study groups of about 13,000 Japanese, including hemoglobin, red and white corpuscle and platelet figures for blood and marrow, with technical explanations and references.

General medicine

Watanabe, Yoshitaka 渡辺良孝 **U55**
Shōkōmei jiten 症候名辞典 (Dictionary of symptomatic terms) Urawa, Chūō Isho Shuppansha, 1955. 577p.

An English-Japanese dictionary of names of symptoms, reflexes, tests and operations in clinical medicine, with explanations and cross references to diseases. Index of Japanese terms.

Ōtsuka, Keisetsu 大塚敬節 **et al.** **U56**
Kanpō daiiten 漢方大医典 (Encyclopedia of Chinese medicine) Tōto Shobō, 1957. 542p.

Prefaced by an outline of Chinese medicine, it has sections on remedies for diseases, describing diseases and their symptoms according to modern medical classifications; on remedies for symptoms, covering pharmacological remedies, acupuncture, moxibustion and popular remedies; on pharmacology, describing all cited drugs and giving alternate names, production areas, cultivation methods, components and uses, and on prescriptions, with doses given in grams. Tables and diagrams appended.

Roentgenology

Takiuchi, Masajirō 滝内政治郎 **U57**
Hōshasen shōjiten 放射線小事典 (Small dictionary of radioactive rays) Kyoto, Kinpōdō, 1954. 474p.

Includes engineering and electrical terms. Unit conversion table, data on protection against radioactive substances and list of sensitive materials and X-ray films appended. Index of English, German and Latin terms and names.

Kimura, Kenjirō 木村健二郎 **U58**
Hōshasen dēta bukku 放射線データブック (Data book on radioactive rays) 1958 ed. Chijin Shokan, 1958. 243p. (Aisotōpu ōyō gijutsu kōza, v.5)

Useful information for engineers, research workers and users, including constants, units, radioisotopes, fission products, effects of radioactive rays on substances and human bodies, and mathematical tables.

CLINICAL MEDICINE
Internal medicine

Nihon Naika Gakkai 日本内科学会 **U59**
Nihon Naika Gakkai sōritsu gojusshūnen kinen sōsakuinshū 日本内科学会創立五十周年記念総索引集 (General indexes, commemorative of the fiftieth anniversary of the Japanese Society of Internal Medicine) 1903-1952. 1956. 1055p.

Subject index covers 21,500 articles in no.1-9 and v.1-41 of *Nihon Naika Gakkai zasshi* (Journal of the Japan Society of Internal Medicine), one of the oldest periodicals in the field. Author index has 21,000 entries. A history of the Society appended.

Nihon naika shōnika chūo zasshi **U60**
日本内科小児科中央雑誌
Abstracts of internal medicine and pediatrics from Japanese journals. Igaku Shoin, 1936-61. 27v.

Suspended publication between Mar.. 1944 and Apr., 1952.

Gives abstracts of research reports, case studies, etc. in 160 journals, divided into 24 sections. Subject index for each volume. There is a cumulative index of names and subjects for the first 9v.

Nihon Naika Gakkai 日本内科学会 **U61**
Naikagaku yōgoshū 内科学用語集 (Glossary of terms of internal medicine) 2d rev. ed. 1960. 191p.

Gives Japanese equivalents of foreign terms in internal medicine, anatomy, surgery, etc., with lists of tentative terms relating to kidney functions and lungs appended. No index.

Contagious diseases

Rai bunken mokuroku らい文献目録 (Bibliography of leprosy of Japan) Mokake-mura, Okayama Pref., Nagashima Aiseien, 1957. 2v. **U62**

Annotated list of scholarly works and articles from 1868 to 1956 in 20 sections, with author index. Includes survey of social aspects of leprosy, covering history, legislation, facilities, institutions, biographies and literary works.

Kekkaku bunken no shōroku sokuhō 結核文献 **U63**
の抄録速報 Abstracts of the current literature on tuberculosis. No.1, 1950- . Comp. by Kekkaku Yobōkai. Monthly.

Covers about 230 Japanese and 92 foreign journals under 12 headings. Name and subject indexes for each volume.

Surgery

Nihon geka seikei geka chūo zasshi 日本外科 **U64**
整形外科中央雑誌 (Central journal of surgery and orthopaedics in Japan) Comp. by Kyoto Daigaku Geka Seikei Geka Kyōshitsu. Osaka, Shinryōsha, 1956-63. Monthly.

Lists selected articles in about 200 Japanese journals under 19 headings. Subject index in each issue. Discontinued.

Menjō, Matsutoshi 毛受松寿 **U65**
Wa-Ei-Doku-Ra geka seikei geka yōgo jiten
和英独羅外科・整形外科用語字典
(Japanese-English-German-Latin dictionary of
terms of surgery and orthopaedics) Urawa,
Chūō Isho Shuppansha, 1957. 298p.

Entry words in Japanese followed by English and
German and/or Latin equivalents. Terms linked
with personal names appended with brief explanations.

Yokoyama, Katashi 横山砧 **U66**
Hifuka hi'nyōkika kanmei jiten 皮膚科・泌尿
器科冠名辞典 Medical terminology with per-
son's name in dermatology and urology. Igaku
Shoin, 1961. 181p.

Explains in detail names of diseases, symptoms,
tests, operations and instruments to which personal
names are attached.

Gynecology · Obstetrics

U67
Sekai sanfujinka sōran 世界産婦人科綜覧
Survey of world obstetrics and gynecology.
v.1, no.1, April, 1953- . Comp. by Igaku no
Sekaisha. Monthly.

Abstracts from 90 foreign and 100 Japanese
journals, divided into gynecology, obstetrics and
border areas. Subject and name indexes for each
volume.

PEDIATRICS

Hara, Hirotake 原弘毅 **U68**
Atarashii shōnika no shinryō jiten 新しい小児
科の診療事典 Concise encyclopedia paedi-
atrica. Bunkōdō, 1958. 775p.

Gives detailed descriptions of diseases and new
treatments.

OPHTHALMOLOGY

Yuge, Tsuneichi 弓削経一 **U69**
Nihon ganka bunkenshū 日本眼科文献集
(Bibliography of ophthalmology in Japan)
Kanehara Shuppan, 1959-61. 3v.

Chronological listing of articles, abstracts and
lectures in Japanese journals since 1868, covering
all aspects: anatomy, physiology, pathology, different systems, diseases, diagnoses, therapeutics

and glasses; conjunctiva, sclera, diaphragm, uvea,
retina, pupil, iris and vision, crystalline lens,
vitreous body, ocular chambers, eyesight, color
blindness and accessory organs.

Kanō, Shin'ichi 鹿野信一 **U70**
Ganka shinryō jiten 眼科診療事典 (Dictionary
of clinical ophthalmology) Chūgai Igakusha,
1961. 631p.

Explains and illustrates 2,121 items classified under anatomical terms, names of diseases,
diagnoses, tests, operation methods, drugs, etc.,
giving their Latin, German, English and/or French
equivalents. Index of foreign terms.

PUBLIC HEALTH

Saitō, Kiyoshi 斉藤潔 **and** **U71**
Fukuda, Kunizō 福田邦三
Hoken eisei jiten 保健衛生辞典 Dictionary of
health. Dōbun Shoin, 1962. 504, 215, 72p.

Fully explains terms concerning body and mental
health, with their English and German equivalents
and references. Measurement methods, first-aid
notes, laws and regulations, statistics and dietary
principles are appended.

U72
Kōshū eisei katsudō handobukku 公衆衛生活動
ハンドブック (Handbook of public health
services) Gihōdō, 1960. 1015p.

Surveys biological, medical, psychological and
sociological aspects of public health, school hygiene,
labor hygiene, medical and pharmaceutical administration and medical-care insurance. Subject index.
Similar work follows:

Kōshū eisei hikkei (Public helath manual) ed.
by Kōseishō Kōshū Eisei Konwakai. Igaku Shoin,
1961. 444p. **U72a.**

Motegi, Koki 茂手木皓喜 **and** **U73**
Suzuki, Hideo 鈴木秀郎
Eisei kensa handobukku 衛生検査ハンドブ
ック (Handbook of hygiene tests) Tōzai
Igakusha, 1961. 477p.

Explains for technicians the basic principles
involved in tests, lists with prices equipment and
appliances and gives normal blood and urine
measurements, chemical formulas of reagents and
pertinent laws and regulations.

Kōseishō Kōshū Eiseikyōku **U74**
厚生省公衆衛生局
Bōeki hikkei 防疫必携 The manual of communi-

cable disease control.   Igaku Shoin, 1955-59. 5v.

Series 1 outlines quarantine, examination of bacteria, disinfection, water hygiene and vaccination and gives statistics.   Series 2 explains the Epidemic Prevention Law article by article.   Series 3 and 4 give detailed technical descriptions of the pathology, diagnosis, therapy and prevention of legal and quasi-legal infectious diseases.   Series 5 gives standards for the building, equipment and management of isolation wards, with illustrations, in accordance with the regulations on their establishment.

Rōdō Kagaku Kenkyūjo 労働科学研究所 **U75**
Rōdō eisei handobukku   労働衛生ハンドブック (Labor health handbook)   1963.   1243p.

Explains how to survey industrial facilities and environments for unsanitary conditions and health hazards, with illustrations, diagrams and references. Lists of pertinent research institutes, associations and universities appended.   Index.

Rōdō Kagaku Kenkyūjo 労働科学研究所 **U76**
Tekisei kensa handobukku 適性検査ハンドブック (Handbook of aptitude tests)   1953. 722p.

Compares, explains and gives many examples of standard vocational aptitude tests, including measurements or evaluations of physical stature and strength, sensory and physiological qualities, intelligence, character and attitudes.   Indexes to names of tests and names and kinds of occupations.

Tōyama, Yūzō 遠山裕三 **et al.** **U77**
Shokuhin eisei handobukku   食品衛生 ハンドブック (Food hygiene handbook) Asakura Shoten, 1957.   642p.

Based on *Eisei kensa shishin III* (Guide to hygienic tests III), compiled by the Ministry of Health and Welfare and published by Kyōdō Isho Shuppan, 1950, it surveys relevant aspects of medicine, veterinary medicine, pharmacology, agriculture, agricultural chemistry, fisheries, housekeeping and dietetics and gives practical methods of testing foodstuffs.   Tables and Public Hygiene Law appended.   Useful for research workers and handlers of foodstuffs.   Index.

Kariyone, Tatsuo 刈米達夫 **et al.** **U78**
Shokuhin tenkabutsu kōteisho chūkai 食品添加物公定書注解 (Commentary on official book of food additives)   Kanehara Shuppan,   1961. 900p.

Gives the standards for the composition, use and labelling of 230 additives as required by regulations. Japanese and English names indexed.

Kanagawaken Eiseibu 神奈川縣衛生部 **U79**
Seisō jigyō handobukku   清掃事業ハンドブック (Waste disposal handbook)   Yokohama, Kanagawaken Kōshū Eisei Kyōkai, 1960.   2v.

Explains planning and operation of systems for the disposal of garbage, trash, sewage, etc. in towns, villages and housing areas by burning, purifying or converting into fertilizer.

Shiraki, Tokuichi 素木得一 **U80**
Eisei konchū 衛生昆虫 (Hygiene and insects) Hokuryūkan, 1958.   1566, 76p.

Illustrates and gives the morphology, ecology and relation to diseases of harmful and medically useful insects classified by families under 15 orders, with methods for exterminating those that are harmful. Exhaustive bibliography of Japanese and foreign monographs and articles published to 1950, listed by author.   Japanese and Western-language indexes.

Laws

Kōseishō 厚生省 **U81**
Eisei roppō 衛生六法 (Hygienic laws)   Ichiryūsha, 1958.   635p.

Gives selected laws on health and sanitation. The Local Autonomy Law, other related laws and ordinances, articles of medical associations, form of birth certificates, etc. appended.   Laws and regulations indexed by titles.

Nihon Yakugakkai   日本薬学会   **U82**
Eisei shikenhō   衛生試験法 (Hygiene test methods)   Nanzandō, 1962.   406p.

Explains standard tests and checks in enforcement of laws on food and environmental hygiene. Later additions and revisions are given in *Eisei kagaku* (Hygienic chemistry), compiled by the Japan Pharmaceutical Society.   Commentary of the laws follow:

Eisei shikenhō chūkai (Commentary on hygiene test methods)   Ed. by Nihon Yakugakkai. Kanehara Shuppan, 1961.   864p. **U82a.**

NUTRITION

DICTIONARIES

Arimoto, Kunitarō 有本邦太郎 **U83**
Eiyō sōten 栄養綜典   (Nutrition manual) Asakura Shoten, 1954.   369p.

Covers general dietetics, proteins,   sugars,   fats, mineral salts, vitamins, enzymes, hormones, digestion and absorption, calories, dietetic pathology, special nutrition, nutrition for invalids, etc., with tables.

Sakurai, Yoshito 桜井芳人　　**U84**
Sōgō shokuhin jiten 綜合食品事典 Dictionary of foods. Rev. ed. Dōbun Shoin, 1960. 748p.

　Defines and gives the foreign equivalents of 1,850 terms related to the preparation, nutritive value, taste, etc. of food, with tables and official standards. Index.

Hara, Minoru 原実 **et al.**　　**U85**
Byōki to shokuji no jiten 病気と食事の事典 (Cyclopedia of sickness and meals) I-Shi-Yaku Shuppan, 1963. 565p.

　Describes the causes, symptoms, developments and therapy of diseases in relation to food and gives sample menus, with notes on cooking. Indexes of diseases and foods.

HANDBOOKS

U86

Eiyōgaku handobukku 栄養学ハンドブック (Dietetics handbook) Gihōdō, 1961. 1259p.

　Discusses nutritional chemistry, digestion and absorption of food, metabolism, dietetic pathology, with references and appended tables of standard basic metabolism values, caloric intake, etc. Index.

Morikawa, Kiku 森川規矩　　**U87**
Eiyōshi benran 栄養士便覧 (Dieticians' manual) Rev. ed. Daiichi Shuppan, 1962. 212p.

　Covers nourishment requirements, standard portions, caloric intake, nutritive elements, enzymes, cooking, digestion, absorption and food for invalids.

Kokuritsu Eiyō Kenkyūjo 国立栄養研究所 **U88**
Shokuhin eiyōka yōran 食品栄養価要覧 Tables of food composition in Japan. Rev. and enl. ed. Daiichi Shuppan, 1960. 428p.

　Based on recent analyses by the National Institute of Nutrition, three tables give the nutritive values of 100 grams of 1,267 kinds of food, of single portions of 27 common dishes, and of food found in ordinary restaurants. Revised table of standard Japanese food components appended. Index.

Kagaku Gijutsuchō, Shigen Chōsakai **U89**
科学技術庁資源調査会
Nihon shokuhin hyōjun seibunhyō 日本食品標準成分表 (Standard table of components of Japanese food) 3d ed., rev. 1963. 118p.

　Gives the components and their calorie conversion coefficients, based on the FAO system (except for rice), of 878 kinds of food classified in 17 groups. Bibliography. Indexes of scientific terms and foods.

Nihon Eiyōshikai 日本栄養士会　　**U90**
Shokuhin hyōjun seibunhyō 食品標準成分表 Standard tables of food composition. Rev. new ed. Daiichi Shuppan, 1964. 120p.

　Gives the caloric values, water, protein, fat, carbohydrate and ash contents and other data on about 1,372 kinds of food grouped under cereals, potatoes and other starchy food, sugar and sweets, etc. Appended are figures for the nutritional requirements of Japanese by age groups for both sexes, standard statures and basic metabolism rates, etc., all projected for 1970, and recommended nutritional requirements as revised in U.S.A. in 1963.

DENTISTRY

Higaki, Rinzō 桧垣麟三 **et al.**　　**U91**
Shigaku jiten 歯学事典 Encyclopaedia dentalis. Kyoto, Nagasue Shoten, 1958. 1017p.

　Standard dictionary of about 8,600 terms taken mainly from lists of the Ministry of Education, Japan Medical Society and Odontological Society of Japan and the Japanese pharmacopoeia, with Latin, English, German and French equivalents. Many illustrations. Japanese and foreign-language indexes.

Satō, Kazuo 佐藤運雄　　**U92**
Igaku shigaku jiten 医学歯学辞典 Satō's medico-dental dictionary. Japanese-English-German-Latin. Nihon Daigaku Shigakubu, 1958. 1790p.

　Lists about 54,000 terms, each with English and German equivalents. Latin equivalents added for some botanical and zoological terms.

Igaku Kōronsha 医学公論社　　**U93**
Nihon shika isekiroku 日本歯科医籍録 (Register and record of Japanese dentists) 5th ed. 1958. 1600p.

　Names from the Ministry of Health and Welfare's register of dentists and the directory of the Dental Society, listed under six regions subdivided into prefectures, cities, etc., with addresses, birth dates, education, registration date and number, principal thesis, etc. Similar directory follows:

Nihon shika ishi meibo (Who's who of Japanese dentists) ed. by Shinjirō Yokota. Rinshō Tsūshinsha, 1961. 617p. **U93a.**

Yoshimi, Mitsufusa 能美光房　　**U94**
Shika gikōshi kankei hōki 歯科技工士関係法規 (Laws and regulations concerning dental technicians) I-Shi-Yaku Shuppan, 1962. 122p.

Includes regulations governing workshops, hygiene and welfare. Technicians' qualifying examination questions of 1959 and 1960 appended.

NURSING

Hara, Hirotake 原弘毅 **et al.** **U95**
Kango igaku jiten 看護・医学事典 Medical dictionary for nurses. Igaku Shoin, 1961. 844p.

Explains about 10,000 standard terms for nurses and nursing students. Similar dictionary follows:

Sutandādo kango jiten (Standard encyclopedia of nursing) ed.. by Keizō Ōta and others. Kanehara Shuppan, 1962. 570p. **U95a.**

Hinohara, Shigeaki 日野原重明 **et al.** **U96**
Kango hikkei 看護必携 Vade mecum for nurses. 3d ed., rev. Igaku Shoin, 1961. 682, 26p.

Covers all aspects of clinical medicine and principles of nursing. Anatomical charts and chronology of nursing appended.

Fujita, Gorō 藤田五郎 **U97**
Kyūkyū shochi handobukku 救急処置ハンドブック First aid handbook. Igaku Shoin, 1962. 189, 10p.

Ranging from simple treatments to blood transfusion, its illustrated explanations are intended for policemen, firemen, nurses and others faced with emergencies. Notes on human anatomy and body functions and accident statistics appended.

Nishikawa, Yoshikata 西川義方 **and** **U98**
Nishikawa, Ichirō 西川一郎
Kango no jissai 看護の実際 Practice of nursing in broad perspective. 17th ed., rev. Nanzandō, 1959. 1810p.

Illustrated question-and-answer introduction to various aspects of nursing, with Japanese-German-English glossary arranged by subjects.

Kokuritsu Tokyo Daiichi Byōin Kango **U99**
Kenkyūkai 国立東京第一病院看護研究会
Kango kijun 看護基準 Nursing manual. 2d ed. Igaku Shoin, 1962. 500p.

Practical guide describing in detail what is expected of nurses in giving medical tests and treatments and taking care of patients.

PHARMACOLOGY
DICTIONARIES

U100
Saishin yakugaku daijiten 最新薬学大事典

New and standard pharmaceutical lexicon. Seibundō Shinkōsha, 1958. 3v.

Gives extensive information about medicine, chemistry, new drugs, Chinese drugs, toxemia, tests, disease symptoms, prescriptions, equipment and implements, agricultural chemicals, plant hormones, cosmetics, etc. Abbreviations and alternate names of principal drugs, poisons, narcotics, dosage and incompatibility tables and list of manufacturers in v.3. General index and indexes of foreign terms and chemical terms.

Nihon Yakuzaishi Kyōkai 日本薬剤師協会 **U101**
Yakumei jiten 薬名辞典 Pharmaceutical index. Rev. ed. Wakō Shoin, 1960. 1165p.

Briefly explains the components, uses and ordinary and maximum doses of 45,000 Japanese and foreign drugs, with survey of drugs made by leading manufacturers appended. Indexed by official, common, chemical, alternate, abbreviated, trade and Western names.

Shimizu, Tōtarō 清水藤太郎 **U102**
Gendai iyakuhin jiten 現代医薬品辞典 (Dictionary of present-day drugs) Nanzandō, 1960. 1204p.

Though not so exhaustive as the *Dispensatory of the United States of America, British pharmaceutical codex and Hagers Handbuch der pharmazeutischen Praxis*, it covers the authorized medicines in **U116** and others that are in common use or new, giving for each the method of preparation, properties, components, place of production, incompatibility, application, dosage, trade and other names, etc. Terms indexed in Japanese and romanized Japanese.

Shimizu, Tōtarō 清水藤太郎 **U103**
Yakugaku Eigo jiten 薬学英語辞典 (Dictionary of pharmaceutical English) Nanzandō, 1955. 199p.

Explains in Japanese about 6,400 English terms. English translations of the names of drugs in the Japanese pharmacopoeia appended.

HANDBOOKS

Yokoyama, Mataji 横山復次 **U104**
Iyakuhin shūsei 医薬品集成 Modern drug encyclopedia; pharmacological action and application. Hirokawa Shoten, 1959. 1000p.

Gives chemical structures and relative efficacy of different prescriptions of all drugs on the market, including Chinese, omitting ordinary and maximum dosages and secondary effects. Uses authorized terms, including those of the Medical Vocabulary Unification Committee and the World Health Organization, with their English and German equivalents.

265

Ishihara, Heitarō 石原平太郎 **U105**
Shiyaku handobukku 試薬ハンドブック
(Reagents handbook) Nankōdō, 1957. 448p.

Guide to the handling and use of reagents. Index
of English names.

Mitsuhori, Shigemitsu 三堀重光 **et al.** **U106**
Shiyaku chūkai 試薬註解 (Commentary on reagents) Rev. and enl. ed. Nankōdō, 1963-65.
5v.

Outlines the history of reagents, their kinds,
tests to conform to JIS standards. Gives for each its
molecular formula, components, alternative names,
purity standard, properties, qualitative reaction,
methods of manufacture, testing and preservation,
and uses. General index.

Ichino, Kazuma 市野一磨 **and** **U107**
Muroya, Hiroshi 室屋博
Kōsei busshitsu benran 抗性物質便覧 (Anti-
biotics manual) Sangyō Tosho, 1961. 204p.

Gives the properties, chemical structure, manufacturing process, diseases against which use is
effective, dosage, secondary effects, concentration
in blood, absorption, excretion and dosage forms of
each antibiotic, including those imported into Japan
and on the American market.

Ozawa, Hikaru 小沢光 **U108**
Doku gekiyaku benran 毒劇薬便覧 (Manual of
poisonous and powerful drugs) Nanzandō, 1964.
330p.

Clarifies the distinction between poisons and
powerful drugs under the Pharmaceutical Law and
gives for each its nature, composition, official and
trade names, regulations, application and toxicity.
Indexes of Japanese and Western names of drugs.

Yamamura, Jun'ichi 山村醇一 **and** **U109**
Nojima, Sadae 野島貞栄
Doku gekibutsu toriatsukaisha hikkei 毒劇物取
扱者必携 (Vade mecum for handlers of
poisonous and powerful drugs) Sangyō Tosho,
1961. 314p.

Gives the properties, toxicities, uses, manufacturing methods, trade names and packaging of drugs
designated in the Law for Control of Poisonous and
Powerful Drugs. Questions and answers on the
handling of poisons and pertinent laws and regulations appended.

Ikeda, Yoshio 池田良雄 **U110**
Yakubutsu chishiryōshū 薬物致死量集(Compi-
lation of lethal doses of drugs) 6th ed.
Nanzandō, 1964. 256p.

Based on Abderhalden: *Handbuch der biolo-*

gischen Arbeitsmethoden and Sollmann, T. H. and
Hanzlik, F.J.: *Fundamentals of experimental
pharmacology* (1939), it tabulates information on
lethal doses for various animals of about 1,000
chemicals, with directions on how to administer
them, symptoms, and names of those who have done
research on them. Methods of determining lethal
doses appended. Index of chemical names.

YEARBOOK

U111
Yakuji nenkan 薬事年鑑 (Pharmaceutical
yearbook) 1961- . Comp. by Yakugyō Keizai
Kenkyūjo. Yakugyō Jihōsha, 1961- . 4v.

Surveys production, sales, management and other
aspects of the pharmaceutical industry, including
information about foreign companies, with statistics.
Directories of the Ministry of Health and Welfare,
institutions, organizations and dealers appended.

DIRECTORY

Nihon Yakuzaishi Kyōkai **U112**
日本薬剤師協会
Kaiin meibo 会員名簿 (Membership list of
pharmaceutical societies) 1961 ed. 1961. 331,
125p.

Lists by prefectures, subdivided into cities, etc.,
members of prefectural pharmaceutical societies as
of 1960, with addresses and places of employment.
Name index.

LAWS

Kōseishō 厚生省 **U113**
Yakuji roppō 薬事六法 (Pharmaceutical laws)
6th ed. Yakuji Nippōsha, 1964. 584p.

Yakuji Kenkyūkai 薬事研究会 **U114**
Yakujihō yakuzaishihō no tebiki 薬事法・薬
剤師法の手引 (Guide to the Pharmaceutical Law and Pharmacists' Law) Yakugyō
Jihōsha, 1961. 394p.

Explains the two laws with definitions of terms
and discussion of pharmaceutical administration.
Issued as a supplement to *Gekkan yakuji* (Monthly
pharmaceutics), published by Yakugyō Jihōsha.
Similar works follow:

Yakuzaishihō yakujihō no kaisetsu (Commentaries on the Pharmacists' Law and Pharmaceutical Law) by Hiroyuki Takada. Jiji Tsūshinsha, 1961. 430p. **U114a.**

Yakuji narabini eisei hōki (Laws and regulations on pharmaceutics and health) by Rakuya Kuma. Igaku Shoin, 1962. 293p. (Yakugaku sōsho) **U114b.**

PHARMACOPOEIA

World Health Organization   **U115**
Kokusai yakkyokuhō 国際薬局法 Pharmacopoeia internationalis. Tr. by Kiichirō Kakemi. Kyoto, Nihon Shin'yaku, 1955-61. 3v.

Tr. of the English edition, 1951-59. Comments on 334 basic chemicals and 195 prepared drugs entered by international Latin names. Eighty-six related laws appended. Indexes.

Kōseishō 厚生省   **U116**
Nihon yakkyokuhō 日本薬局方 Pharmacopoeia japonica. 7th ed., rev. Hirokawa Shoten, 1961-63. 4v. (with commentaries)

Covers 763 basic drugs and 464 compound preparations, with brief history of the pharmacopoeia, explanation of pertinent laws, testing methods, including a comparison of Japanese and foreign methods, manufacturing processes, a classified table of drugs, comparative table of old and new official and alternate names and list of poisons and powerful drugs.

Shimizu, Tōtarō 清水藤太郎   **U117**
Nihon yakkyokuhō handobukku 日本薬局方ハンドブック (Handbook of the Japanese pharmacopoeia) Nanzandō, 1962. 760p.

Rearranges the drugs in **U116** in the Japanese syllabic order and explains briefly their pharmacological effects, the diseases for the treatment of which they are appropriate, secondary effects and dosages. Similar work follows:

Nihon yakkyokuhō hyōkai (Tabular explanation of the Japanese pharmacopoeia) by Gen'ichirō Fukuchi and Tatsuo Emoto. Hirokawa Shoten, 1962. 353p. **U117a.**

Nihon Kōteisho Kyōkai 日本公定書協会 **U118**
Iyakuhin seizō shishin 医薬品製造指針 (Guide to the manufacture of drugs) Yakugyō Jihōsha, 1962. 301p.

Explains the requirements for permission to produce drugs, with cautions in applying for permission, production standards and the testing of new drugs.

     U119
Kōkinsei busshitsu seizai kijun 抗菌性物質 製剤基準 Minimum requirements of antibiotic products. 1953- . Comp. by Kōseishō.

1953- . 12v. Annual.

Gives the properties, standards for purity and packaging, preservation methods, duration of validity and tests of antibiotics. Issued in accordance with the Pharmaceutical Law, with revision each March.

     U120
Seibutsugakuteki seizai kijun 生物学的製剤 基準 Minimum requirements of biologic products. 1953- . Comp. by Kōseishō. 1953- . 12v. Annual.

Sets standards, as required by the Pharmaceutical Law, for vaccines, remedial serums, toxins, antitoxins and similar preparations used in diagnosis and therapy. Revised each March.

DRUGS

     U121
Saikin no shin'yaku 最近の新薬 New drugs in Japan. No.1, 1950- . Yakuji Nippōsha, 1950- . 15v. Annual.

Annual listing, with brief explanations, of drugs the manufacture or importation and sale of which have been newly authorized, classified by their efficacies. Excludes Chinese drugs, popular drugs and constituent chemicals. Cumulative indexes of about 8,000 drugs listed in Series 1-15. Directory of manufacturers.

Nihon Shin'yaku Kabushiki Kaisha   **U122**
日本新薬株式会社
Jōyō shin'yakushū 常用新薬集 (Compendium of new drugs in common use) 18th ed. Kyoto, 1963. 562p.

Useful guide for clinicians, pharmacists and pharmaceutical students, giving notes on the makers, prices, efficacies and uses of 2,800 drugs on the market in Oct., 1962. Tables of medicines with comparable efficacies appended. Index classified by efficacies.

Medicinal plants

     U123
Kokuritsu Kokkai Toshokan Shibu Ueno Toshokan shozō honzō kankei tosho mokuroku 国立 国会図書館支部上野図書館所蔵本草 関係図書目録 (Catalogue of books on herbal plants in the Ueno branch of the National Diet Library) Ueno Toshokan, 1951-53. 2v.

-Lists about 8,000 books and manuscripts mainly by 19th century herbalists. Author index.

Kimura, Kōichi 木村康一 **and**   **U124**
Kijima, Masao 木島正夫

Wa-Kan yakumeii 和漢薬名彙 (List of Japanese and Chinese drugs) Hirokawa Shoten, 1946. 316p.

Entered by medical names under plants, animals and minerals, with alternate and market names. Index.

Kariyone, Tatsuo 刈米達夫 **and**   **U125**
Kimura, Yūshirō 木村雄四郎
Saishin Wa-Kan yakuyō shokubutsu　最新和漢 薬用植物 (Up-to-date Japanese and Chinese medical herbs) Rev. and enl. ed. Hirokawa Shoten, 1961. 510p.

Arranged according to Engler's classification, it gives the botanical, common Japanese and Chinese, alternate and dialectical, and foreign (chiefly English and German) names, cultivation methods, habitats, chemical analyses, medical values, including directions for use and dosage, and literature published from 1939 to April, 1959. Many illustrations. Classification table of herbs. Indexed by names of plants, components, drugs and prescriptions.

Murakoshi, Michio　村越三千男　**U126**
Yakuyō shokubutsu jiten　薬用植物事典 (Dictionary of medicinal plants) Fukumura Shoten, 1961. 772p.

Gives the scientific, popular, Chinese and other names, habitats, properties, principal components and medical values of about 600 plants found in Japan, China, Korea and Formosa, with notes on their cultivation, gathering and processing. Illustrations. Index classified by diseases.

Kijima, Masao 木島正夫 **et al.**   **U127**
Hirokawa yakuyō shokubutsu daijiten 広川薬用 植物大事典 (Hirokawa's comprehensive dictionary of medicinal plants) Hirokawa Shoten, 1963. 468p.

Identifies about 2,000 species of medicinal, edible, poisonous, spice and dyestuff plants found in Japan and a few important ones in other countries, giving for each its habitat, distribution, form, uses, the name of the crude drug yielded by it, principal components, medicinal or other values and related plants, with 120 color and 56 monochrome plates. Indexes of Latin and Japanese names, components and crude drugs.

Tanaka, Fusatane　田中房種 **and**   **U128**
Kubota, Masao　久保田真雄
Zukan yakuyō shokubutsu jiten　図鑑薬用植 物事典　(Illustrated dictionary of medicinal plants) Takahashi Shoten, 1954. 608p.

Gives the habitats, properties, medical values, dosages, incompatibilities and applications of 300 herbs and detailed Chinese prescriptions under the names of diseases, with introduction to phytology and herbal medicine. Appendix covers dietetics, combinations of food, incompatibilities and antidotes.

Kariyone, Tatsuo　刈米達夫   **U129**
Yakuyō shokubutsu zufu 薬用植物図譜 (Medicinal plants illustrated) Kanehara Shuppan, 1961. 320p.

Comments briefly on about 600 medicinal, poisonous and spice plants divided into angiosperms, gymnosperms and cryptogams. Indexed by botanical names, crude drugs and components.

Kimura, Kōichi　木村康一   **U130**
Nihon no yakuyō shokubutsu 日本の薬用植物 (Dictionary of Japanese medicinal plants illustrated in colors) Hirokawa Shoten, 1958-60. 2v.

Each volume has 120 plates, with common names, original habitats, dates of introduction into Japan, descriptions and medical values. Index.

Ōkawa, Tokutarō　大川徳太郎   **U131**
Zusetsu doku shokubutsu　図説毒植物 (Illustrated poisonous plants) Toxicities and remedies. Sangyō Tosho, 1951. 241p.

Photographs of 104 major Japanese poisonous plants, with notes on their forms, distribution, allied plants, poisonous components, symptoms of toxemia and remedies.

Nihon Gakushiin　日本学士院   **U132**
Meiji zen Nihon yakubutsugakushi 明治前日本 薬物学史　(History of pre-1868 Japanese pharmacology)　Nihon Gakujutsu Shinkōkai, 1957-58. 2v.

v.1, Drugs in ancient times, drugs of early European and Dutch medicine, history of demand for and supply of drugs; v.2, Introduction of Chinese botany to Japan and its influence, Chinese pharmacological remedies and their influence.

INDEX

GYNECOLOGY, U67
Gyogyo yoshokugyo gyokaku to-
keihyo, T108
Gyokakuryo ruinen tokeihyo, T109
Gyorui no keitai to kensaku, S104
Gyoseiho jiten, L37
Gyosei Kanricho Tokei Kijun-
kyoku, J15, J23-J24, N31-
N32, R15
Gyunyu · nyuseihin handobukku,
R395

Habe, Tadashige, S76-S77
Hachiketa kansuhyo, Q45
Haga, Yaichi, D34, H18
Hagino, Kogo, Q47
Hagiwara Sakutaro shoshi, G187
Hagiwara, Susumu, T67
Hagiwara, Unrai, F124
Haguruma benran, R142
Haguruma sekkei handobukku,
R143
Haifu Yanagidaru, G182
Haikai daijiten, G111
Haikai jinmei jiten, G112
HAIKU, G107-G121
Haiku koza, G108
Haiku nenkan, G107, G107a
Hakko kogyo yogo jiten, R390
Hakko oyobi seibutsu kagaku bun-
kenshu, S10
Hakubutsu jiten, Q6
Hakumaku kogaku handobukku,
R260
Hakushisha Wa-Futsu jiten, F66
Halley, Henry H., D167
Hamamatsu chunagon monogatari
sosakuin, G161
Hampel, Clifford A., R286
Hanabusa, Nagamichi, K4
Hanabusa, Yoshitaro, P36
Hanashi no daijiten, C11
Hanayama, Shinsho, D92
Hanbai jiten, M160
Handbook of medical English, U17
A handbook of modern British and
American literature, G20
Handei Ei-Wa katsuyo jiten, F35a
Handotai handobukku, R256
A handy dictionary of etymology
and usage, F24
Haneda, Toru, F117
Hangari-go shojiten, F85
Hanrei taikei, L67
Hantaigo jiten, F182
Hanzai tokeisho, L54
Hara, Akira, S96
Hara, Hiroshi, S55-S56
Hara, Hirotake, U68, U95
Hara, Kanesuke, S46
Hara, Minoru, U85
Hara, Sanshichi, A77
Haraoka, Hideto, G178

Harada, Bizan, E50-E51
Harada, Minoru, F99
Haraoka, Hideto, G178
Harigaya, Shokichi, E57
Haruna, Yoshishige, E73
Hase, Akihisa, G77
Hasegawa, Masayoshi, R291
Hasegawa, Seiichi, G190
Hashiguchi, Ryukichi, R282
Hashikawa, Tadashi, D118
Hashikawa, Tokio, H8
Hashimoto, Hiroshi, H39
Hashimoto, Yoshio, R396
Hashimoto, Yoshiro, Q59, Q62, Q64
Hasumi, Akijiro, U21
Hatano, Kanji, D30
Hatano, Ken'ichi, A100
Hatasakumotsu no shinhinshu, T50
Hatsumei oyobi jitsuyo shinan no
bunruihyo, R18
Hatsumei oyobi jitsuyo shinan
bunrui no sakuin, R19
Hatta, Keizo, R145
Hattori, Shiro, F107
Hottori, Shiso, H138
Hattori, Unokichi, F164
Hayami, Keiji, D11
Hayashi, Hisakichi, M159
Hayashi, Ikkan, R61
Hayashi, Kanae, U18
Hayashi, Keiichi, Q39-Q40
Hayashi, Kentaro, H83
Hayashi, Shuzo, L39, M129
Hayashi, Taisuke, D18
HEAT ENGINES, R144-R146
Heibonsha ban haiku saijiki, G116
HERALDRY, H52
Hibino, Fumio, R296
Hidaka, Jun, T52
Hifuka hinyokika kanmei jiten,
U66
Hifuku daijiten, R408
Higa, Shuncho, A82
Higaki, Rinzo, U91
Higuchi, Hiroshi, R400
Higuchi, Yoshichiyo, G179
Hikaku tokei nenpo, R373
Himitsu jirin, D108
Hinohara, Shigeaki, U96
Hinonishi, Sukenori, N81
Hinshitsu kanri benran, R36
Hioki, Shoichi, C11-C12, H43
Hirabayashi, Harunori, G83
Hirabayashi, Hoji, G118
Hirai, Masao, F139
Hirai, Yasutaro, M89
Hirano, Ryuichi, L30
Hirano, Shizo, Q72
Hirao, Mitsuko, G170
Hirao, Nenokichi, S34
Hiraoka, Ryujo, F97

Hiraoka, Tomokazu, F140
Hirayama, Kenzo, Q84
Hirayama, Takashi, R84
Hirayama, Teruo, F145
Hirohama, Fumio, F151
Hirokawa yakuyo shokubutsu dai-
jiten, U127
Hirose, Hideo, Q88
Hirose, Toshi, A48
Hirota, Eitaro, F147, F176, F180
Hisamatsu, Ken'ichi, F186, G57,
G66
Hisamatsu Sen'ichi Hakushi Kan-
reki Kinenkai, G44
Hisatake, Masao, M21
HISTORICAL GEOGRAPHY, H180-
H189
HISTORY, WORLD, p.107-109
atlases, H80
bibliography, H69-H72
chronology, H76-H79
dictionaries, H73-H75
illustrations, H81-H82
Hitaiju · hikyoi · hizako hayami-
hyo, U20
Hitetsu kinzoku seihin tokei nen-
po, R289
Hitotsubashi Daigaku Keizai Ken-
kyujo, M68-M69
Hitotsubashi Daigaku Shinbunbu,
M22
Hitotsubashi Shobo's new diction-
ary of abbreviations and con-
tractions, F26
Hiyama, Yoshio, S107
Hobun horitsu zasshi kiji sakuin,
L8
Hobun jinko kankei bunken narabi-
ni shiryo kaidai, M81
Hobun rekishigaku kankei sho-
zasshi Toyoshi ronbun yo-
moku, H90
Hobun shinrigaku bunken moku-
roku ko, D26
Hobun zasshi somokuji sakuin
ichiran, A37a
Hoden handobukku, R227
Hogaku annai, L42
Hogaku jiten, L12
Hogaku kenkyu no shiori, L41
Hogaku yogo jiten, L17
Hogaku buyo jiten, E126
Hokan keisuhyo, Q42
Hoken eisei jiten, U71
Hoken jiten, M124-M125
Hoken nenkan, M126
Hoken taiikuka daijiten, E155
Hokkai Gakuen Daigaku Kaihatsu
Kenkyujo, M8
Homu nenkan, L50
Homusho, L53
—— Hosei chosashitsu, L55
Homu Toshokan, L7